Lecture Notes in Computer Science   10048

Commenced Publication in 1973
Founding and Former Series Editors:
Gerhard Goos, Juris Hartmanis, and Jan van Leeuwen

More information about this series at http://www.springer.com/series/7407

Jesus Carretero · Javier Garcia-Blas
Ryan K.L. Ko · Peter Mueller
Koji Nakano (Eds.)

Algorithms and Architectures for Parallel Processing

16th International Conference, ICA3PP 2016
Granada, Spain, December 14–16, 2016
Proceedings

 Springer

Editors
Jesus Carretero
University Carlos III of Madrid
Leganes
Spain

Javier Garcia-Blas
Carlos III University of Madrid
Leganes, Madrid
Spain

Ryan K.L. Ko
The University of Waikato
Hamilton
New Zealand

Peter Mueller
IBM Zurich Research Laboratory
Rüschlikon
Switzerland

Koji Nakano
Hiroshima University
Higashi-Hiroshima
Japan

ISSN 0302-9743   ISSN 1611-3349 (electronic)
Lecture Notes in Computer Science
ISBN 978-3-319-49582-8   ISBN 978-3-319-49583-5 (eBook)
DOI 10.1007/978-3-319-49583-5

Library of Congress Control Number: 2016959169

LNCS Sublibrary: SL1 – Theoretical Computer Science and General Issues

Printed on acid-free paper

This Springer imprint is published by Springer Nature
The registered company is Springer International Publishing AG
The registered company address is: Gewerbestrasse 11, 6330 Cham, Switzerland

Welcome Message from the ICA3PP 2016 General Chairs

Welcome to the proceedings of the 16th International Conference on Algorithms and Architectures for Parallel Processing (ICA3PP 2016), which was organized by the University of Madrid Carlos II and the University of Granada.

It was our great pleasure to organize the ICA3PP 2016 conference in Granada, Spain, during December 14–16, 2016. On behalf of the Organizing Committee of the conference, we would like to express our cordial gratitude to all participants who attended the conference.

ICA3PP 2016 was the 16th event in the series of conferences started in 1995 that is devoted to algorithms and architectures for parallel processing. ICA3PP is now recognized as the main regular international event that covers many dimensions of parallel algorithms and architectures, encompassing fundamental theoretical approaches, practical experimental projects, and commercial components and systems. The conference provides a forum for academics and practitioners from around the world to exchange ideas for improving the efficiency, performance, reliability, security, and interoperability of computing systems and applications.

ICA3PP 2016 attracted high-quality research papers highlighting the foundational work that strives to push beyond the limits of existing technologies, including experimental efforts, innovative systems, and investigations that identify weaknesses in existing parallel processing technology.

ICA3PP 2016 consisted of the main conference and five international symposia and workshops. Many individuals contributed to the success of the conference. We would like to express our special appreciation to Prof. Yang Xiang, Prof. Weijia Jia, Prof. Laurence T. Yang, Prof. Yi Pan, and Prof. Wanlei Zhou, the Steering Committee chairs, for giving us the opportunity to host this prestigious conference and for their guidance with the conference organization. Special thanks to the program chairs, Dr. Peter Muller, Dr. Ryan K.L. Ko, and Dr. Javier García Blas, for their outstanding work on the technical program. Thanks also to the workshop chairs, Dr. Atsushi Hori, Dr. Ryan K.L. Ko, and Dr. Florin Isaila, for their excellent work in organizing attractive symposia and workshops. Thanks also to the local arrangements chair, Prof. Julio Ortega. We would like to give our thanks to all the members of the Organizing Committee and Program Committee as well as the external reviewers for their efforts and support. We would also like to thank the keynote speakers, Prof. Vladimir Voevodin, Dr. Rafael Asenjo, and Prof. Pedro José Marrón, for offering insightful and enlightening talks. Last but not least, we would like to thank all the authors who submitted their papers to the conference.

December 2016

Jesús Carretero
Koji Nakano

Welcome Message from the ICA3PP 2016
Program Chairs

On behalf of the Program Committee of the 16th International Conference on Algorithms and Architectures for Parallel Processing (ICA3PP 2016), we would like to welcome you to the proceedings of conference, which was held in Granada, Spain, during December 14–16, 2016.

The ICA3PP conference aims at bringing together researchers and practitioners from both academia and industry who are working on algorithms and architectures for parallel processing. The conference features keynote speeches, technical presentations, symposiums, and workshops, where the technical presentations from both the research community and industry cover various aspects including fundamental theoretical approaches, practical experimental projects, and commercial components and systems. ICA3PP 2016 was the next event in a series of highly successful international conferences on algorithms and architectures for parallel processing, previously held as ICA3PP 2015 (Zhangjiajie, China, November 2015), ICA3PP 2014 (Dalian, China, August 2014), ICA3PP 2013 (Vietri sul Mare, Italy, December 2013), ICA3PP 2012 (Fukuoka, Japan, September 2012), ICA3PP 2011 (Melbourne, Australia, October 2011), ICA3PP 2010 (Busan, Korea, May 2010), ICA3PP 2009 (Taipei, Taiwan, June 2009), ICA3PP 2008 (Cyprus, June 2008), ICA3PP 2007 (Hangzhou, China, June 2007), ICA3PP 2005 (Melbourne, Australia, October 2005), ICA3PP 2002 (Beijing, China, October 2002), ICA3PP 2000 (Hong Kong, China, December 2000), ICA3PP 1997 (Melbourne, Australia, December 1997), ICA3PP 1996 (Singapore, June 1996), and ICA3PP 1995 (Brisbane, Australia, April 1995).

The ICA3PP 2016 conference collected research papers on related research issues from all around the world. This year we received 102 submissions for the main conference. All submissions received at least three reviews during a high-quality review process. The program provided a balanced and interesting view on current developments and trends in algorithms and parallel architectures. Two papers were selected as outstanding contributions to ICA3PP 2016. According to the review results, 30 papers were selected for oral presentation at the conference, giving an acceptance rate of 29.4%.

We would like to offer our gratitude to Prof. Yang Xiang, Prof. Weijia Jia, Prof. Laurence T. Yang, Prof. Yi Pan, and Prof. Wanlei Zhou, the Steering Committee chairs. Our thanks also go to the general chairs, Prof. Jesús Carretero and Prof. Koji Nakano, for their great support and good suggestions for a successful the final program. Special thanks to the workshop chairs, Dr. Atsushi Hori, Dr. Ryan K.L. Ko, and Dr. Florin Isaila. In particular, we would like to give our thanks to all researchers and practitioners who submitted their manuscripts, and to the Program Committee and the external reviewers, who contributed their valuable time and expertise to provide professional reviews working under a very tight schedule. Moreover, we are very grateful to our keynote speakers, who kindly accepted our invitation to give insightful and prospective talks.

December 2016

Peter Muller
Ryan K.L. Ko
Javier Garcia Blas

Organization

Program Committee

Habtamu Abie	Norwegian Computing Center, Norway
Marco Aldinucci	University of Turin, Italy
Giulio Aliberti	Università degli Studi Roma III, Italy
Pedro Alonso	Universitat Politècnica de València, Spain
Alba Amato	Seconda Università degli Studi di Napoli, Italy
Daniel Andresen	Kansas State University, USA
Cosimo Anglano	Universitá del Piemonte Orientale, Italy
Danilo Ardagna	Politecnico di Milano, Italy
Marcos Assuncao	Inria, LIP, ENS Lyon, France
David Del Rio Astorga	University Carlos III of Madrid, Spain
Hrachya Astsatryan	National Academy of Sciences of Armenia
Nikzad Babaii Rizvandi	University of Sydney, NICTA, Australia
Yan Bai	University of Washington Tacoma, USA
Muneer Masadeh Bani Yassein	Al al-Bayt University, Jordan
Saad Bani-Mohammad	Al al-Bayt University, Jordan
Jorge Barbosa	FEUP, Portugal
Novella Bartolini	University of Rome Sapienza, Italy
Ladjel Bellatreche	LIAS/ENSMA, France
Salima Benbernou	Université Paris Descartes, France
Siegfried Benkner	University of Vienna, Austria
Jorge Bernal Bernabe	University of Murcia, Spain
Md Zakirul Alam Bhuiyan	Temple University, USA
Javier Garcia Blas	University Carlos III of Madrid, Spain
Oana Boncalo	University Politehnica of Timisoara, Romania
Daniel Rubio Bonilla	HLRS – University of Stuttgart, Germany
George Bosilca	Innovative Computing Laboratory, University of Tennessee, USA
Pascal Bouvry	University of Luxembourg
Suren Byna	Lawrence Berkeley National Laboratory, USA
Massimo Cafaro	University of Salento, Italy
Silvina Caino Lores	University Carlos III of Madrid, Spain
Christian Callegari	University of Pisa, Italy
Aparicio Carranza	New York City College of Technology, USA
Jesus Carretero	University Carlos III of Madrid, Spain
Pedro A. Castillo Valdivieso	Universidad de Granada, Spain
Tania Cerquitelli	Politecnico di Torino, Italy

Sudip Chakraborty	Valdosta State University, USA
Jerry H. Chang	National Center for High-Performance Computing, China
Yue-Shan Chang	National Taipei University, Taiwan
Anupam Chattopadhyay	Nanyang Technological University, Singapore
Jing Chen	National Cheng Kung University, Taiwan
Tzung-Shi Chen	National University of Tainan, Taiwan
Yu Chen	State University of New York – Binghamton, USA
Zizhong Chen	University of California, Riverside, USA
John A. Clark	University of York, UK
Stefania Colonnese	Università di Roma La Sapienza, Italy
Massimo Coppola	Institute of Information Science and Technologies (ISTI/CNR), Italy
Ana Cortes	Universitat Autònoma de Barcelona, Spain
Raphaël Couturier	University of Franche Comte, France
Félix Cuadrado	Queen Mary University of London, UK
Alfredo Cuzzocrea	University of Trieste, Italy
Bogusław Cyganek	AGH University of Science and Technology, Poland
Georges Da Costa	IRIT/Toulouse III, France
Masoud Daneshtalab	KTH Royal Institute of Technology, Sweden
Gregoire Danoy	University of Luxembourg
Sabrina De Capitani di Vimercati	Università degli Studi di Milano, Italy
Saptarshi Debroy	City University of New York, USA
Casimer Decusatis	Marist College, USA
Eugen Dedu	University of Franche-Comté, France
Juan-Carlos Díaz-Martín	University of Extremadura, Spain
Yacine Djemaiel	Communication Networks and Security, Research Laboratory, Tunisia
Ciprian Dobre	University Politehnica of Bucharest, Romania
Manuel F. Dolz	University Carlos III of Madrid, Spain
Susan Donohue	University of Virginia, USA
Zhihui Du	Tsinghua University, Beijing, China
Yucong Duan	Hainan University, China
Christian Esposito	University of Salerno, Italy
Roberto R. Expósito	University of A Coruña, Spain
Jose Alfredo Ferreira Costa	UFRN – Universidade Federal do Rio Grande do Norte, Brazil
Ugo Fiore	Federico II University, Italy
Neki Frasheri	Polytechnic University of Tirana, Albania
Franco Frattolillo	University of Sannio, Italy
Marc Frincu	University of Southern California, USA
Jaafar Gaber	Université de Technologie de Belfort-Montbéliard, France
Jose Daniel Garcia	University Carlos III of Madrid, Spain
Luis Javier García Villalba	University Complutense of Madrid, Spain

Juan-L. García-Zapata	University of Extremadura, Spain
Saurabh Kumar Garg	University of Tasmania, Australia
Ester Martin Garzon	Almeria University, Spain
Paolo Gasti	New York Institute of Technology, USA
Victor Gergel	Nizhny Novgorod State University, Russia
Ansgar Gerlicher	Stuttgart Media University, Germany
Vladimir Getov	University of Westminster, UK
Harald Gjermundrod	University of Nicosia, Cyprus
Dieter Gollmann	Hamburg University of Technology, Germany
Jing Gong	KTH, Sweden
Arturo Gonzalez-Escribano	Universidad de Valladolid, Spain
Pilar Gonzalez-Ferez	ICS-FORTH, Greece
Jose-Luis Gonzalez-Sanchez	CINVESTAV, Mexico
José Gracia	High-Performance Computing Center Stuttgart, Germany
Christos Grecos	Independent Consultants, Greece
Daniel Grosu	Wayne State University, USA
Sheikh M. Habib	Technische Universität Darmstadt, Germany
Khalid Hasanov	IBM Research Ireland
Houcine Hassan	Universitat Politecnica de Valencia, Spain
Shi-Jinn Horng	National Taiwan University of Science and Technology, Taiwan
Atanas Hristov	University of Information Science and Technology, FYR Macedonia
Sun-Yuan Hsieh	National Cheng Kung University, Taiwan
Ching-Hsien Hsu	Chung Hua University, China
Jia Hu	Liverpool Hope University, UK
Xinyi Huang	Fujian Normal University, China
Yonggang Huang	Beijing Institute of Technology, China
Zhiyi Huang	University of Otago, New Zealand
Mauro Iacono	Seconda Università degli Studi di Napoli, Italy
Shadi Ibrahim	Inria, Rennes Bretagne Atlantique Research Center, France
Young-Sik Jeong	Dongguk University, South Korea
Hai Jiang	Arkansas State University, USA
Wenjun Jiang	Hunan University, China
Edward Jung	Southern Polytechnic State University
Vana Kalogeraki	Athens University of Economics and Business, Greece
Georgios Kambourakis	University of the Aegean, Greece
Panagiotis Karampelas	Hellenic American University, USA
Helen Karatza	Aristotle University of Thessaloniki, Greece
Christoph Kessler	Linköping University, Sweden
Muhammad Khurram Khan	King Saud University, Saudi Arabia
Peter Kilpatrick	Queen's University Belfast, UK
Sookyun Kim	Pai Chai University, South Korea

Ryan K.L. Ko	The University of Waikato, New Zealand
Peter Kropf	University of Neuchatel, Switzerland
Ruggero Donida Labati	Università degli Studi di Milano, Italy
Kuan-Chou Lai	National Taichung University, Taiwan
Algirdas Lančinskas	Vilnius University, Lithuania
Alexey Lastovetsky	University College Dublin, Ireland
Che-Rung Lee	National Tsing Hua University, Taiwan
Laurent Lefevre	Ecole Normal Lyon, France
Yingjiu Li	Singapore Management University, Singapore
Yusen Li	Nanyang Technological University, Singapore
Zengxiang Li	Institute of High Performance Computing Agency for Science, Technology and Research, Singapore
Xin Liao	Hunan University, China
Chunyu Lin	HTC Corp., Taiwan
Zhen Ling	Southeast University, China
Qin Liu	Hunan University, China
Haikun Liu	North China Electricity Power University
Xiao Liu	Software Engineering Institute, East China Normal University, China
Yongchao Liu	Georgia Institute of Technology, USA
Giovanni Livraga	Università degli Studi di Milano, Italy
Jaime Lloret	Universidad Politécnica de Valencia, Spain
George Loukas	University of Greenwich, UK
Haibing Lu	Santa Clara University, USA
Paul Lu	University of Alberta, Canada
Rongxing Lu	University of New Brunswick, Canada
Wei Lu	Keene State College, USA
Liang Luo	University of Washington, USA
Sidi Ahmed Mahmoudi	University of Mons, France
Amit Majumdar	University of California San Diego, San Diego Supercomputer Center, USA
Damian Alvarez Mallon	Forschungszentrum Jülich, Germany
Jose Miguel Mantas Ruiz	Universidad de Granada, Spain
Ravindranath Manumachu	University College Dublin, Ireland
Xinjun Mao	National University of Defense Technology, China
Tomas Margalef	Universitat Autonoma de Barcelona, Spain
Stefano Markidis	KTH, Sweden
Fabrizio Marozzo	DIMES, University of Calabria, Italy
Pedro J. Marron	University of Duisburg-Essen, Germany
Stefano Marrone	Second University of Naples, Italy
Alejandro Masrur	TU Chemnitz, Germany
Barbara Masucci	University of Salerno, Italy
Susumu Matsumae	Saga University, Japan
Rafael Mayo Gual	University Jaume I, Spain
Anatoly Melnyk	Lviv Polytechnic National University, Ukraine
Viktor Melnyk	John Paul II Catholic University of Lublin, Poland

Estefania Serrano	University Carlos III of Madrid, Spain
Jun Shen	University of Wollongong, Australia
Ali Shoker	INESC TEC and University of Minho, Portugal
Anna Sikora	University Autonoma of Barcelona, Spain
Dragan Simic	University of Novi Sad, Serbia
Dimitris E. Simos	SBA Research, Austria
David E. Singh	University Carlos III of Madrid, Spain
Genoveva Vargas Solar	CNRS-LIG-LAFMIA, France
Chao Song	University of Electronic Science and Technology of China
Andrey Sozykin	Ural Federal University, Russia
Giandomenico Spezzano	CNR-ICAR and University of Calabria, Italy
Patricia Stolf	IRIT, France
Peter Strazdins	The Australian National University, Australia
Chunhua Su	Japan Advanced Institute of Science and Technology
Chang-Ai Sun	University of Science and Technology Beijing, China
Magdalena Szmajduch	Cracow University of Technology, Poland
Daisuke Takahashi	University of Tsukuba, Japan
Domenico Talia	University of Calabria, Italy
Andrei Tchernykh	CICESE Research Center
Sabu M. Thampi	Indian Institute of Information Technology and Management, India
Hiroyuki Tomiyama	Ritsumeikan University, Japan
Massimo Torquati	University of Pisa, Italy
Paolo Trunfio	DEIS, University of Calabria, Italy
Tomoaki Tsumura	Nagoya Institute of Technology, Japan
Radu Tudoran	HUAWEI ERC, Germany
Didem Unat	Lawrence Berkeley National Laboratory, USA
Sebastien Varrette	University of Luxembourg, Luxembourg
Maria Barreda Vayá	Universitat Jaume I, Spain
Salvatore Venticinque	Seconda Università di Napoli, Italy
Vladimir Voevodin	Moscow University, Russia
Chen Wang	CSIRO ICT Center, Australia
Mingzhong Wang	University of the Sunshine Coast, Australia
Qian Wang	Wuhan University, China
You-Chiun Wang	National Sun Yat-sen University, China
Yunsheng Wang	Kettering University, USA
Zeke Wang	Nanyang Technological University, Singapore
Zhibo Wang	Wuhan University, China
Martine Wedlake	IBM, USA
Jin Wei	University of Akron, USA
Sheng Wen	Deakin University, Australia
Beat Wolf	HES-SO, University of Würzburg, Germany
Hejun Wu	Sun Yat-Sen University, China
Weigang Wu	Sun Yat-sen University, China

Yongdong Wu	Institute for Infocomm Research, Singapore
Roman Wyrzykowski	Czestochowa University of Technology, Poland
Liao Xiaofei	Huazhong University of Science and Technology, China
Xiaofei Xing	Guangzhou University, China
Quanqing Xu	Data Storage Institute, A*STAR, Singapore
Wei Xue	Tsinghua University, China
Ramin Yahyapour	GWDG – University of Göttingen, Germany
Chao-Tung Yang	Tunghai University, Taiwan
Baijian Yang	Purdue University, USA
Baoliu Ye	Nanjing University, China
Hua Yu	Huazhong University of Science and Technology, China
Shucheng Yu	University of Arkansas, USA
Mazdak Zamani	Kean University, USA
Sherali Zeadally	University of Kentucky, USA
Deze Zeng	University of Aizu, Japan
Peng Zhang	Stony Brook University, USA
Daqiang Zhang	Tongji University, China
Dongfang Zhao	Pacific Northwest National Laboratory
Yun-Wei Zhao	Nanyang Technological University, Singapore
Yunhui Zheng	IBM T.J. Watson Research Center, USA
Jianlong Zhong	GRAPHSQL INC, USA
Xingquan Zhu	Florida Atlantic University, USA
Sotirios Ziavras	New Jersey Institute of Technology, USA

Additional Reviewers

Andión, José M.
Bao, Tao
Bezemskij, Anatolij
Catuogno, Luigi
Cortez Mendoza,
    Jorge Mario
Crane, Paul
Dhoutaut, Dominique

Fernandez, Javier
García Zapata, Juan Luis
Heartfield, Ryan
Kieffer, Emmanuel
Mair, Jason
Niu, Zhaojie
Peng, Tao
Seo, Hwajeong

Soundararajan, Varun
Tao, Jinsong
Tygart, Adam
Veiga, Jorge
Zhang, Shaobo
Zhao, Jieyi

Contents

Big Data and Its Applications

Parallel and Distributed Algorithms

Applications of Parallel and Distributed Computing

Service Dependability and Security in Distributed and Parallel Systems

Performance Modeling and Evaluation

Parallel and Distributed Architectures

Intelligent SPARQL Endpoints: Optimizing Execution Performance by Automatic Query Relaxation and Queue Scheduling

Ana I. Torre-Bastida[1]([⊠]), Esther Villar-Rodriguez[1], Miren Nekane Bilbao[2], and Javier Del Ser[1,2,3]

[1] TECNALIA. OPTIMA Unit, 48160 Derio, Spain
{isabel.torre,esther.villar,javier.delser}@tecnalia.com
[2] University of the Basque Country UPV/EHU, 48013 Bilbao, Spain
{nekane.bilbao,javier.delser}@ehu.eus
[3] Basque Center for Applied Mathematics (BCAM), 48009 Bilbao, Spain

Abstract. The Web of Data is widely considered as one of the major global repositories populated with countless interconnected and structured data prompting these linked datasets to be continuously and sharply increasing. In this context the so-called SPARQL Protocol and RDF Query Language is commonly used to retrieve and manage stored data by means of SPARQL endpoints, a query processing service especially designed to get access to these databases. Nevertheless, due to the large amount of data tackled by such endpoints and their structural complexity, these services usually suffer from severe performance issues, including inadmissible processing times. This work aims at overcoming this noted inefficiency by designing a distributed parallel system architecture that improves the performance of SPARQL endpoints by incorporating two functionalities: (1) a queuing system to avoid bottlenecks during the execution of SPARQL queries; and (2) an intelligent relaxation of the queries submitted to the endpoint at hand whenever the relaxation itself and the consequently lowered complexity of the query are beneficial for the overall performance of the system. To this end the system relies on a two-fold optimization criterion: the minimization of the query running time, as predicted by a supervised learning model; and the maximization of the quality of the results of the query as quantified by a measure of similarity. These two conflicting optimization criteria are efficiently balanced by two bi-objective heuristic algorithms sequentially executed over groups of SPARQL queries. The approach is validated on a prototype and several experiments that evince the applicability of the proposed scheme.

Keywords: SPARQL · Query rewriting · Linked Open Data · Ontology management · Multiobjective optimization

1   Introduction and Motivation

It will be soon a decade since the so-called Linked Open Data (LOD) paradigm, along with several related projects and initiatives, became the main

© Springer International Publishing AG 2016
J. Carretero et al. (Eds.): ICA3PP 2016, LNCS 10048, pp. 3–17, 2016.
DOI: 10.1007/978-3-319-49583-5_1

technology enabler for the expansion of the Semantic Web, whose *raison d'être* was an intrinsic information technologies revolution centered on enriching the published data and coping with the inherent inability of machines to understand websites [1]. Over the last decade the increasing adoption of LOD led to the development of a distributed mesh of globally interlinked knowledge capable of providing a pioneering method to traverse the web and interpret its contents: the Web of Data. This huge, distributed, diverse database is deployed on manifold domains and a wide range of subjects such as government, libraries, life science and media, among many others. It allows for the execution of exploratory and selective queries over a enormous set of updated, comprehensive and pertinent data. The prevalent semantic query language for these repositories is SPARQL, which provides a full set of query operations and functionalities. Notwithstanding, in order to fully unleash the Semantic Web potential SPARQL users are forced to dominate the syntax of the SPARQL language. On this purpose the community has devoted considerable research effort towards deriving sophisticated yet friendly tools to help users properly exploit the vast amount of available data and achieve a satisfactory performance in terms of accuracy. Under this rationale, the systems and engines where SPARQL endpoints are deployed have become the primary target where to allocate specialized resources and intelligent software procedures to enhance the quality of service commonly jeopardized and called into question due to significant delays, specially when dealing with large datasets [2].

The contribution of this research work gravitates on three main axes to improve the performance of SPARQL systems: the performance prediction of SPARQL queries prior to their processing, their relaxation and the planning of run queues in processing engines. In the field of performance prediction there is a large number of works in the field of the SQL query language for relational databases, which have traditionally revolved around statistical or heuristics costs estimation. In regards to the prediction of the query execution time, supervised learning models have positioned themselves as the *off-the-shelf* estimators in recent years (see e.g. [3,4]). To the best of our knowledge there are very scarce studies that extrapolate this acquired knowledge with relational databases to the LOD repositories. The main difference between these two areas resides on the absence of an schematic structure in the RDF standard, as well as on the shortage of statistics of the datasets compounding the LOD environment. Justifiably, the current generation of SPARQL query cost estimation approaches that inspire from those derived for relational databases have been proven to be inadequate for the task of performance prediction. This is the rationale for the brand new direction started in [3] and subsequently followed in [4,5] that resorts to machine learning techniques to extract SPARQL performance metrics from already executed queries. Despite the good predictive scores reported in these references (with the latest work in [5] scoring an average R^2 of 0.94 with Support Vector Machines), we will show throughout this manuscript that there is still room for improvement in terms of the learning model and the set of features.

Concerning the second aspect that can be leveraged so as to improve the performance of endpoints, the optimization of SPARQL queries has hitherto mainly focused on rewriting the query at hand based on different objectives, such as the minimization of the execution time or the reduction of its structural complexity. We classify these studies into three categories depending on the utilized optimization technique: cost-based [6–8], heuristics-based [9–11] and machine learning techniques [12,13]. Cost-based schemes suffer from the aforementioned low availability of statistics in the LOD. Heuristic approaches assume that structurally simple queries are in general less expensive, but this is not the case in SPARQL due to the inference and variant extensional information contained in a SPARQL arrangement. The work by Bicer et al. in [12] introduce the concept of Relational Kernel Machines, which simplify the problem of extracting features from the complex structure of semantic data and hence improving naïve approximations based on Support Vector Machines. Likewise, in [13] long-running queries (detected by predicting its computational costs) are relaxed by applying a Genetic Algorithm (GA) based rewriting approach so as to yield a faster rewritten query. In our work we will take a step further so as to consider in the determination of the query relaxation policy the inherent Pareto trade-off between the quality of the results returned by the query and the relative running time with respect to its original version. This Pareto-optimal balance between both objectives will be shown to be tractable via evolutionary multi-objective heuristics.

Finally, the third axis refers to the scheduling of run queues to organize and coordinate query executions, around which our literature survey has identified a single, recent yet relevant contribution for SPARQL endpoints [14]. In this paper the authors explain that guaranteeing a consistently good quality of service in SPARQL endpoints is a difficult task to accomplish, for which the use of an scheduler is proposed to optimally manage the execution of queries in SPARQL endpoints. We go one step beyond the simple schedulers explored in this reference by proposing a novel approach in which we optimize the scheduling criterion based on the previously mentioned SPARQL relaxation policies.

Our software system blends together the three aspects commented above to improve the runtime performance of a SPARQL endpoint. The problem is that many of the queries processed by such systems can not be executed within a reasonable time for the user. To address this issue a bi-objective algorithm is designed to obtain the optimal set of relaxation rules on this dataset without disregarding the quality of the query result. By applying such a Pareto-optimal set of relaxation rules the execution time of the queries is reduced while keeping the quality degradation of their results to a minimum. Such rule sets can be further exploited by implementing a set of processing queues in the SPARQL endpoint, so that the optimization algorithm determines the adequate set of relaxation rules, the allocation of queries over the pool of processing queues and the execution order of the queries assigned to every queue. In summary, the main goal of this paper is the design of a software system capable of enhancing the performance of a SPARQL endpoint by combining optimized run queues, adequate query relaxation policies and SPARQL query run time predictions. Schematically the novel technical ingredients of this research work are as follows:

1. The derivation of new predictive features for the design of a runtime estimator for SPARQL queries, which can be divided in query language algebra and vocabulary features defining the terms of the query.
2. The design and implementation of a system based on run queues to improve the performance of SPARQL endpoints, which to our knowledge is the first one proposed in the literature.
3. A query relaxation optimization algorithm guided by two objectives: the maximization of the query quality (quantified in terms of similarity) and the minimization of the run time of the query.
4. The use of parallelizable evolutionary meta-heuristic solvers to the performance improvement of SPARQL endpoints in the particular aspects of query relaxation and run queue scheduling mentioned previously.

The rest of the manuscript is structured as follows: Sect. 2 overviews the general architecture of the proposed system and formulates the optimization problem that mathematically defines its operation. Subsects. 2.1 and 2.2 delve into the design of estimators for the query running time and quality on which the aforementioned optimization problem is based. Next, Sect. 3 elaborates on the meta-heuristic optimization algorithm designed to efficiently implement the proposed system, including relevant aspects such as the solution encoding and the design of the operators. Section 4 reports on the experimental evaluation of the proposed scheme and conclusions are drawn in Sect. 5.

2   Architecture Overview and Problem Formulation

In this section we briefly introduce key concepts and notation used throughout the rest of the paper. SPARQL is the standard query language for RDF. Let I be the set of all IRIs (Internationalized Resource Identifiers), L be the set of RDF *literals*, and B be the set of RDF *blank nodes*. These three infinite sets are pairwise disjoint. An RDF *triple* is a tuple $(s, p, o) \in (I \cup B) \times I \times (I \cup B \cup L)$; s is called the *subject*, p is the *predicate*, and o stands for the *object* of the triple, respectively. An RDF *graph* is a finite set of triples. For the purpose of this paper, a *dataset* D is an RDF graph. Given a dataset D, we refer to the set $voc(D) \subseteq (I \cup L)$ of IRIs and literals occurring in D as the *vocabulary* of D. We use the words *term* or *resource* to refer to elements in $I \cup L$.

The core of a SPARQL query is a *basic graph pattern*, which is used to match an RDF graph in order to search for the required answers. A *triple pattern* is a triple, without blank nodes, where a variable may occur in any place of the triple. A *graph pattern* is an expression recursively defined as follows: (1) a triple pattern is a graph pattern; (2) if P_1, P_2 are graph patterns, then (P_1 AND P_2), (P_1 UNION P_2), and (P_1 OPT P_2) are graph patterns; and (3) if P is a graph pattern and C is SPARQL constraint, then (P FILTER C) is a graph pattern. With these definitions in mind, a query is defined by $Q = (D, \delta)$ where D is the dataset to be used during the pattern matching and δ is the graph pattern of the query.

Figure 1 shows an overview of the proposed system, which is conceived as an intermediate manager between the users submitting their queries and the pool of parallel processing queues that compound the SPARQL endpoint. Several modules can be found in this diagram: first it is important to remark that the relaxation policies and the mapping to processing queues are optimized at the level of previously clustered query groups, so that queries within the same cluster undergo the same relaxation rules and are assigned to the same processing queue. This cluster analysis module is based on the methodology presented in [15] that follow these steps: data generation mimicking an input data source, query log mining, clustering and SPARQL feature analysis. As a result P query sets $\{\mathbf{Q}_p\}_{p=1}^P = \{\{Q_p^n\}_{n=1}^{N_p}\}_{p=1}^P$ (clusters) are produced with $Q_p^n = (D, \delta_p^n)$.

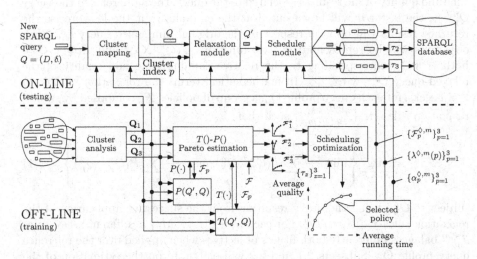

Fig. 1. Overview of the proposed architecture assuming $P = 3$ query profiles $\{\mathbf{Q}_p\}_{p=1}^3$ and $Z = 3$ processing queues at the endpoint. The lower part of the plot corresponds to the processing stages that are performed off-line based on a historic record of queries submitted to the endpoint, whereas the upper part illustrates the entire relaxation and scheduling procedure applied to a new incoming query submitted to the endpoint.

Prior to its online working regime the SPARQL endpoint must decide the set of relaxation policies, the queue and the priority within the queue for each of such clusters. Let $f_r(Q)$ be the generic definition for a relaxation rule, drawn from a R-sized vocabulary $\mathcal{F} = \{f_r(Q)\}_{r=1}^R$ of possible relaxation operators. It is important to note that $f_r(Q)$ may only impact on a certain triple (s, p, o) within Q or, instead, involve more terms within its expression. Three kind of rules have been considered in the setup:

1. Deletion rules, which consist of eliminating a triple (s, p, o), filter, terms, union and/or optional clauses from the query.

2. Addition rules, which add a restrictive clause to the query, e.g. a limit operator.
3. Hierarchical rules, by which a term of the query is substituted by its descendant or ascendant in the ontological hierarchy of the queried dataset.

The complete list of possible rules $\mathcal{F}$ is sorted by their estimated degree of degradation on the results of the relaxed query. Under this notation $\mathcal{F}_p \subseteq \mathcal{F}$ will denote the sequence of relaxation operators that will be applied to the queries belonging to cluster p, whereas $Q_p^{n,\prime}$ will denote the relaxed version of query Q_p^n after the application of the rules in $\mathcal{F}_p$.

The determination of $\{\mathcal{F}_p\}_{p=1}^P$ will be done under a twofold criteria: we seek to optimally balance the impact of the relaxation policy on the average running time and quality of the results associated to the query; the more relaxed the query $Q_p^{n,\prime}$ is, the faster it will be executed at the endpoint, but the less precise the returned results will be with respect to the original, unrelaxed query Q_p^n. Such objectives will be represented by two functions $T(Q_p^{n,\prime}, Q_p^n)$ and $P(Q_p^{n,\prime}, Q_p^n)$, both $\in [0,1]$, corresponding to the relative running time and quality of the relaxed query $Q_p^{n,\prime}$ w.r.t. Q_p^n. In mathematical terms the relaxation module in Fig. 1 seeks, for each query profile $\mathbf{Q}_p$, a group of policies $\mathcal{F}_p^*$ composed by several relaxation rule sets $\{\mathcal{F}_p^{*,m}\}_{m=1}^{M_r}$ such that

$$\mathcal{F}_p^{*,m} = \underset{\mathcal{F}_p \subseteq \mathcal{F}}{\arg} \left\{ \min \frac{1}{N_p} \sum_{n=1}^{N_p} T(Q_p^{n,\prime}, Q_p^n), \max \frac{1}{N_p} \sum_{n=1}^{N_p} P(Q_p^{n,\prime}, Q_p^n) \right\}, \quad (1)$$

subject to $Q_p^{n,\prime}$ being the query resulting from the successive application of the relaxation rules $f \in \mathcal{F}_p$ to Q_p^n. For each $m \in \{1, \ldots, M_r\}$ a different set of rules $\mathcal{F}_p^{*,m}$ balances differently both fitness objectives when applied over the reference query profile $\mathbf{Q}_p$. Subsects. 2.1 and 2.2 will elaborate on the estimation of the value for $T(Q_p^{n,\prime}, Q_p^n)$ and $P(Q_p^{n,\prime}, Q_p^n)$ prior to the execution of the query itself.

Once such Pareto estimations have been produced off-line for each query profile, the scheduler module exploits this information to determine (1) which processing queue should be assigned to an incoming query associated to a certain cluster $p \in \{1, \ldots, P\}$; (2) which relaxation policy should be applied to the query among those in $\mathcal{F}_p^*$; and (3) the execution order of the queries (i.e. their priority) in the case several of them are assigned to the same queue. Without loss of generality computing power differences between processing queues are assumed to yield factors $\{\tau_z\}_{z=1}^Z$ (with $\tau_z \in (0,1]$ and Z denoting the number of queues) such that the time taken by queue z to process Q_p^n is reduced by $100 \cdot \tau_z\%$. The queue allocation to be decided at this module will be denoted as a non-surjective, non-injective mapping function $\lambda : \{1, \ldots, P\} \mapsto \{1, \ldots, Z\}$, such that $\lambda(p)$ will stand for the queue to which the queries associated to profile $p \in \{1, \ldots, P\}$ will be forwarded. Priorities within queue $z \in \{1, \ldots, Z\}$ will be denoted as a real-valued variable $\alpha_p \in \mathbb{R}$ such that if $\lambda(p) = \lambda(p')$ (i.e. profiles p and p' are assigned the same processing queue), the queries in profile p will be executed first if $\alpha_p \leq \alpha_{p'}$. Conversely, if $\alpha_p > \alpha_{p'}$ queries belonging to cluster p' will be granted a higher execution priority level than those in p. The criterion to determine the optimal mapping $\lambda^\diamond(p)$, relaxation policies $\{\mathcal{F}_p^\diamond\}_{p=1}^P$ and priority factors $\boldsymbol{\alpha}^\diamond = \{\alpha_p^\diamond\}_{p=1}^P$ at the scheduler module will again rely on the aforementioned time-quality Pareto trade-off, but incorporating a subtle yet relevant aspect: queries within the same processing queue interact in terms of their completion time, i.e. both the relative order of queries within a given queue and the different processing capabilities of the queues themselves are meaningful for the overall evaluation of the average execution time taken by the endpoint to process incoming queries. In other words, a vector of mapping functions $\boldsymbol{\lambda}^\diamond(\cdot) \doteq \{\lambda^{\diamond,m}(\cdot)\}_{m=1}^{M_s}$, relaxation policies $\boldsymbol{\mathcal{F}}_p^\diamond \doteq \{\mathcal{F}_p^{\diamond,m}\}_{m=1}^{M_s}$ and priority levels $\boldsymbol{A}^\diamond(\cdot) \doteq \{\boldsymbol{\alpha}^{\diamond,m}\}_{m=1}^{M_s} = \{\{\alpha_p^{\diamond,m}\}_{p=1}^P\}_{m=1}^{M_s}$ will balance the following Pareto:

$$
\lambda^{\diamond,m}(\cdot),\ \boldsymbol{\alpha}^{\diamond,m}, \mathcal{F}_p^{\diamond,m} = \underset{\substack{\lambda\in\Lambda \\ \boldsymbol{\alpha}\in\mathbb{R}^P \\ \mathcal{F}_p\subseteq\mathcal{F}}}{\arg} \left\{ \min \frac{1}{P} \sum_{p=1}^P \frac{\tau_{\lambda(p)}}{N_p} \sum_{n=1}^{N_p} T(Q_p^{n,\prime}, Q_p^n) \right.
$$

$$
\sum_{\substack{\varrho=1 \\ \varrho\neq p}}^P \frac{1}{N_\varrho} \sum_{\eta=1}^{N_\varrho} \tau_{\lambda(\varrho)} T(Q_\varrho^{\eta,\prime}, Q_\varrho^\eta) \mathbb{I}(\alpha_\varrho \leq \alpha_p)\mathbb{I}(\lambda(\varrho)=\lambda(p)), \tag{2}
$$

$$
\left. \max \frac{1}{P} \sum_{p=1}^P \frac{1}{N_p} \sum_{n=1}^{N_p} P(Q_p^{n,\prime}, Q_p^n) \right\}, \tag{3}
$$

where $\mathbb{I}(\cdot)$ is an auxiliary indicator function taking value 1 if its argument is true and 0 otherwise; $\lambda(p) \in \{1,\ldots,Z\}$ denotes the index of the queue to which the queries in cluster p are assigned; and $Q_p^{n,\prime}$ is the result of relaxing query Q_p^n through policy $\mathcal{F}_p$. In words, Expression (2) denotes the time taken by the queries Q_p^n within cluster p, which depends not only on the assigned queue through $\tau_{\lambda(p)}$, but also on the average time taken by queries belonging to other clusters $\varrho \in \{1,\ldots,p-1,p+1,\ldots,P\}$ provided that they are assigned to the same processing queue and granted higher priority. Finally, Expression (3) poses the mean quality score averaged over all the considered query clusters.

Before proceeding with the algorithmic solution proposed to efficiently solve the above problems, it should be noted that in practice the relaxation and scheduling modules might be conceived and formulated as a single optimization problem driven by the objective functions in Expressions (2) and (3). However, by decoupling both modules a deeper understanding of the flexibility of the clusters with respect to the set of relaxation operators can be acquired, with further potential applications beyond the one addressed in this paper (e.g. optimizing a distributed deployment of the database at hand).

2.1 SPARQL Query Run-Time Prediction

As shown in Fig. 1 and argued above, an estimation of the running time required to complete a given relaxed query Q is needed when the proposed approach operates in both off-line and on-line modes. Such an estimation must be produced without executing the query itself. Therefore, a supervised learning model is included in order to predict execution times of generic SPARQL queries based on a historic set of already executed queries. The adopted approach is similar to the one presented by Hassan et al. in [5], but with novel ingredients: the learning model itself and the set of features extracted from the expression of the SPARQL queries to build the training dataset. As such, this dataset consist of a set of previously executed queries and the observed performance metric values (execution times) for those queries in their native, unrelaxed form. The goal is to extract proper features from the syntax of the queries to construct a prediction model that provide us with an accurate estimation of the execution time that can be generalized to new, possibly relaxed query sets. The proposed set of features are classified as:

1. Algebra features, which represent the syntax of the SPARQL query, its operators and structural information. First we transform a query into an algebra expression tree, from which we extract the following features: number of basic graph patterns, filter operator presence, type of filter, limit operator presence, optional operator presence, distinct operator presence, number of projected variables, group operator presence, number of union, number of joins and number of left joins.
2. Dataset vocabulary features, for which we use the dataset terms involved in the SPARQL query definition to extract intensional and semantic information about them. First we compute the overall set of terms, and with this *bag of words* we compute the TF-IDF frequency [16] as a quantitative score of the importance of the terms of the query (*words*) in the dataset (*document*) (Fig. 2).

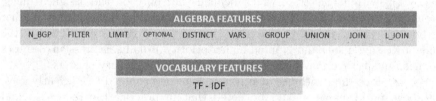

Fig. 2. SPARQL query features vector.

Regarding the supervised learning model we opt for a so-called Random Forest Classifier [17], a widely utilized ensemble model characterized by its good generalization properties and low tendency to overfit. In short Random Forests exploit the principle of bagging by randomly splitting the data into chunks, selecting a feature subset and training a weak learner (tree) on each of them, from where the predicted output is given by voting (classification) or averaging (prediction) the individual outputs of the aforementioned weak models.

2.2 SPARQL Quality Estimation

The estimation of the Pareto-optimal set of relaxation policies in the proposed system also requires an *a priori* estimation of the quality of the relaxed query with respect to its original version. This estimated function, heretofore denoted as $P(Q', Q)$, must be computed based exclusively on the query itself, i.e. without submitting any request to the endpoint. Within the scope of this paper it has been noted that a query can be defined by a pair $Q = (D, \delta)$. Based on this notation, the application of a relaxation policy to this query produces a relaxed query $Q' = (D, \delta')$, with δ defining the RDF graph pattern of the query. To this end, a similarity metric $S(Q', Q)$ has been designed to provide a quantitative estimation of the similarity between queries Q' and Q. This similarity metric is designed to replace the generic function $P(Q', Q)$. Basically, $S(Q', Q)$ maps two SPARQL queries to a real value in the closed interval $[0, 1]$, such that higher values indicate that queries are more similar to each other. Mathematically, $S : \mathcal{Q} \times \mathcal{Q} \mapsto [0, 1]$, with $\mathcal{Q}$ denoting the set of all possible SPARQL queries that can be defined over the dataset D.

To implement the similarity function, we follow the approach introduced in [18] by which similarity between Q' and Q depends on the similarity between their graph patterns δ' and δ. We can consider a graph pattern δ as composed by a number of triple patterns $\{P_1, \ldots, P_K\}$, each composed by three terms (s_k, p_k, o_k). In general a term t (either subject, predicate or object) can be assigned different *similarity factors* $\phi(t', t) \in \mathbb{R}[0, 1]$. These factors are meant to reflect a similarity measure between the term t of the original query pattern and its counterpart t' after the relaxation process.

Given a triple pattern $P = (s, p, o)$ and its relaxed counterpart $P' = (s', p', o')$, the vector $(\phi(s', s), \phi(p', p), \phi(o', o))$ can be conceived as a point in a three dimensional space, where the point $(1, 1, 1)$ represents the best (i.e. the triple P and its relaxed counterpart are equal to each other) and the point $(0, 0, 0)$ the worst. Therefore, the Euclidean distance between $(\phi(s', s), \phi(p', p), \phi(o', o))$ and $(1, 1, 1)$ can be deemed as a measure of pattern similarity $\sigma(P', P)$ given by

$$\sigma(P', P) = 1 - \sqrt{\frac{(1 - \phi(s', s))^2 + (1 - \phi(p', p))^2 + (1 - \phi(o', o))^2}{3}}. \qquad (4)$$

Given an original query Q compounded by graph patterns $\{P_1, \ldots, P_K)$ and its relaxed version Q', their pattern-wise similarity values $\{\sigma(P'_k, P_k)\}_{k=1}^K$ (computed as in the above expression) can be likewise regarded as coordinates in a K-dimensional space. Again, the Euclidean distance between the points $(\sigma(P'_1, P_1), \ldots, \sigma(P'_K, P_K))$ and $(1, \ldots, 1)$ yields the sought normalized similarity measure $S(Q', Q)$ expressed as

$$S(Q', Q) = 1 - \sqrt{\frac{\sum_{k=1}^K (1 - \sigma(P'_k, P_k))^2}{K}}, \qquad (5)$$

which serves as a predictive estimation of the quality of a given relaxed query Q' for the meta-heuristic optimization algorithm explained in what follows.

3   Proposed Meta-heuristic Solver

Following the mathematical formulation posed in Sect. 2 (Expressions (1) through (3)), it should be noticed that the two bi-objective optimization problems driving the relaxation and scheduling criteria of the proposed scheme are very similar to each other, the difference relying mainly on the alphabet of the variables involved. As such, the Pareto optimization of the relaxation policies $\mathcal{F}_p$ to be applied to a certain query profile $\mathbf{Q}_p$ can be encoded as a $|\mathcal{F}_p|$-sized vector of integers drawn from the set $\{1, \ldots, R\}$ (with R standing from the number of possible relaxation operators), each indexing a different rule within $\mathcal{F}$. On the other hand, the scheduling problem requires a mixed integer-real encoding strategy, as it implies optimizing not only – again – the relaxation policy to be applied for a given query profile, but also the relative ordering of queries along time when they belong to profiles assigned to the same processing queue. Such an encoding diversity imprints notable changes in the design of the solvers to face these problems.

In essence both optimization algorithms are based on approximate, self-learning approaches that allow evolving intermediate solutions towards areas of the solution space characterized by increasingly higher Pareto optimality. In this context there is a plethora of algorithmic alternatives in the literature to deal with multi-objective problems [19,20], among which we will focus on those inspiring from behavioral patterns observed in Nature and Social Sciences. Specifically the bi-objective solver utilized in this work stands on the so-called Harmony Search (HS) algorithm [21], which emulates the process of music improvisation and composition observed in practice so as to yield a population-based meta-heuristic solver quite similar to other schemes from Evolutionary computation[1], but outperforming them in many practical scenarios [22].

In its original definition, the HS algorithm breaks down in three stochastically-driven operators (HMCR, PAR and RSR) that are sequentially applied to every compounding variable (referred to as *instrument*) of a φ-sized population of potential solutions to the problem (correspondingly, *harmonies*) until a given stop condition is satisfied. The value taken by a variable is therefore a *note*, whose entire pitch range depends on the alphabet of the represented variable. This is the rationale why the design of the HS operators is closely linked to the encoding approach that allows numerically representing the produced solutions, specially those that do not permute elements among the population but rather impose perturbations on the variables based on their respective alphabets.

When particularized to the problem tackled in this work, the integer encoding approach used to deal with the first relaxation problem posed in Expression (1) permits to resort to the nominal HS operators for integer-variable problems first introduced in [21] (namely, HMCR, PAR and RSR), with the variable alphabet

---

[1] In fact there have been controversial discussions lately around the originality of the naïve HS algorithm in regards to its close resemblance to the more traditional $(\mu+1)$ Evolution Strategies. Having said this, foregoing algorithmic descriptions will use the HS terminology impartially with respect to the aforementioned controversy.

$\mathcal{F}$ sorted in terms of the estimated impact of its compounding relaxation rules in the fitness functions to be optimized. Likewise, each harmony produced by HS as a potential solution to the scheduling problem is divided in two parts, isolated from each other in regards to the application of the HS operators, but coupled together by its participation in both metric functions: (1) a P-sized vector of integer elements from the alphabet $\{1, \ldots, M_r\}$, with M_r denoting the number of Pareto-optimal relaxation rulesets previously produced for each query profile p by the relaxation module; and (2) a P-sized vector of real-valued variables from $\mathbb{R}[0, Z]$, with Z denoting the number of processing queues. Each of the variables within this second part represents both the profile-to-queue mapping $\lambda(p)$ and the relative ordering α_p by virtue of a Random Keys strategy [23]; if X_p denotes the p-th variable of this part, $\lambda(p) = \lfloor X_p \rfloor$ and $\alpha_p = X_p - \lfloor X_p \rfloor$. By sorting queues in terms of their processing capabilities $\{\tau_z\}_{z=1}^{Z}$ a more suitable relative queue ordering can be achieved for its processing through the vicinity-based PAR operator of HS.

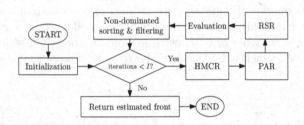

Fig. 3. Flow diagram of the proposed bi-objective optimization algorithm.

To end with, Fig. 3 schematically describes the 4 compounding steps of the utilized bi-objective HS solver:

1. Initialization: the harmonies (potential solutions) of the population are filled with notes (values) drawn uniformly at random from the alphabets of their compounding instruments (variables).
2. Application of the operators: a new population of harmonies is produced by sequentially applying, to each note of the prevailing population, the stochastic HMCR, PAR and RSR operators defined in [21] based on probabilistic parameters $Pr(\text{HMCR})$, $Pr(\text{PAR})$ and $Pr(\text{RSR})$. For real-valued variables the PAR operator requires an additional bandwidth parameter $BW \in \mathbb{R}(0, \infty)$, such that the new value X_p^{new} for X_p given by the PAR operator is $X_p^{new} = X_p + BW \cdot \text{Uniform}(-1, 1)$.
3. Evaluation and update: fitness values for every newly produced potential solution are computed, concatenated to those from the previous iterations, sorted and filtered based on the well-known non-dominated sorting criterion utilized in other solvers (e.g. NSGA-II). The application of this criterion yields a φ-sized set of harmonies that are kept for the next iteration due to their higher Pareto optimality and wider Pareto span (crowding distance).
4. Termination: steps 2 and 3 are repeated for I iterations.

4 Experimental Evaluation

In this section we assess the performance of the two novel technical aspects of our system: the prediction of SPARQL query run-times (Subsect. 2.1) and the bi-objective optimization algorithm (Sect. 3). To this end a distributed queue system based on Apache Kafka has been implemented. The SPARQL query and similarity computation module relies on the JENA framework, RDFLib, Wordnet Similarity (code.google.com/p/ws4j/) and SimMetrics (sourceforge.net/projects/simmetrics/), whereas the optimization and run-time prediction algorithms have been implemented in Python. The experiment discussed in what follows can be conceived as a SPARQL query rewriting scenario contextualized in the LOD semantic web. Specifically we select the so-called DBPSB benchmark, with DBpedia 3.5.1 as the RDF dataset. The training (70%), validation (25%), and test (5%) queries for the run-time prediction model are extracted from the 25 available DBPSB query templates in which RDF terms are assigned randomly from the DBpedia vocabulary, amounting to a total of 1260 queries. To measure its average execution time, each query is executed five times. This setup for the predictive model scores a 20-fold cross-validated average R^2 score of 0.977 with a Random Forest Classifier composed by 100 estimators, which is higher than the $R^2 = 0.94$ score reported in [5].

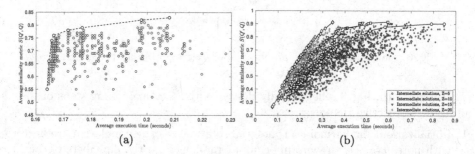

Fig. 4. (a) Pareto front estimated by the relaxation module for a query profile $\mathbf{Q}_p$; (b) Pareto front produced by the bi-objective scheduler for $P = 10$ query profiles and $Z \in \{5, 10, 15, 20\}$ queues with varying processing capabilities.

We begin our discussion by Fig. 4a, which depicts the estimated Pareto front (in bold black) of the relaxation module corresponding to a hypothesized query profile $\mathbf{Q}_p$ composed by the entire set of 1260 DBPSB queries previously generated for the predictive model. Such compounding queries can be processed through a maximum of 10 relaxation operators from an overall alphabet of $R = 18$ possible relaxation rules. Values for the parameters of the HS solvers are $\varphi = 25$, $Pr(\text{HMCR}) = 0.5$, $Pr(\text{PAR}) = 0.1$, $Pr(\text{RSR}) = 0.01$ and $I = 100$ iterations, which have been optimized via a off-line grid search. This figure also includes the Pareto fronts estimated during the execution of the bi-objective algorithm marked in increasing levels of gray. As seen in the plot the derived

HS-based algorithm succeeds at finding query relaxation policies that sacrifice the quality of the results returned by the queries for a lower execution time.

We finally proceed with the analysis of the results obtained by the proposed scheduler for $P = 10$ profiles as a function of the number of available processing queues $Z \in \{5, 10, 15, 20\}$. For simplicity profiles are generated by shuffling and splitting the set of DBPSB queries in 10 groups, but any other clustering scheme can be instead applied. For the sake of understandability of the results processing capabilities are forced to grow linearly with Z such that an increase of this parameter implies adding queues with lower τ_z to the simulation setup. Parameter values of the HS solver are as in the previous case, with $BW = 1$. As shown in Fig. 4b, as Z increases the Pareto fronts produced by the scheduler are better in the Pareto sense due to the availability of new queues with enhanced processing power. It is important to note that this trend also holds when $Z \leq P$, which evince that the proposed scheduler excels at relaxing profiles and allocating them to processing queues in scenarios with limited resources.

5   Concluding Remarks and Future Research Lines

This work has presented a novel approach to improve the performance of SPARQL endpoints by using an optimized run-queue system incorporating automatic query relaxation and intelligent queue scheduling functionalities. The proposed scheme hinges on a bi-objective optimization criterion, which permits the administrator of the endpoint to balance differently two conflicting objectives: the average run-time of queries incoming at the endpoint and the quality of such queries when relaxed with respect to their original versions. In order to efficiently solve this trade-off, a bi-objective solver based on the HS algorithm has been designed along with an encoding strategy aimed at handling mixed integer/real-valued variables. Besides this bi-objective formulation further novel aspects have been proposed in this manuscript: an improved feature set to predict the execution time of SPARQL queries and the use of semantic similarity to infer their quality. From a practical perspective the proposed system is useful in those cases when several users concurrently submit computationally expensive queries to SPARQL endpoints where other mechanism such as cost-based models are not effective due to the unavailability of data statistics.

There are several research directions to aim at from this study: to begin with the work can be extended to other benchmarks such as LUBM or BSBM, possibly incorporating real SPARQL endpoint logs in various domains such as UNIPROT (biological domain) or BNE (*Biblioteca Nacional de España*, bibliographic domain). There is also room for improvement in the optimization algorithm itself by leveraging other alternative bioinspired solvers. Other schemes for computing the semantic similarity can be explored such as the one proposed in [24].

References

1. Shadbolt, N., Hall, W., Berners-Lee, T.: The semantic web revisited. IEEE Intell. Syst. **21**(3), 96–101 (2006)
2. Schmidt, M., Meier, M., Lausen, G.: Foundations of SPARQL query optimization. In: ACM International Conference on Database Theory, pp. 4–33 (2010)
3. Ganapathi, A., Kuno, H., Dayal, U., Wiener, J.L., Fox, A., Jordan, M., Patterson, D.: Predicting multiple metrics for queries: better decisions enabled by machine learning. In: IEEE International Conference on Data Engineering, pp. 592–603 (2009)
4. Akdere, M., Çetintemel, U., Riondato, M., Upfal, E., Zdonik, S.B.: Learning-based query performance modeling and prediction. In: IEEE International Conference on Data Engineering, pp. 390–401 (2012)
5. Hasan, R., Gandon, F.: A machine learning approach to SPARQL query performance prediction. In: IEEE/WIC/ACM International Joint Conferences on Web Intelligence and Intelligent Agent Technologies, vol. 1, pp. 266–273 (2014)
6. Görlitz, O., Staab, S.: Splendid: SPARQL endpoint federation exploiting void descriptions. In: COLD, vol. 782 (2011)
7. Schwarte, A., Haase, P., Hose, K., Schenkel, R., Schmidt, M.: FedX: optimization techniques for federated query processing on linked data. In: Aroyo, L., Welty, C., Alani, H., Taylor, J., Bernstein, A., Kagal, L., Noy, N., Blomqvist, E. (eds.) ISWC 2011. LNCS, vol. 7031, pp. 601–616. Springer, Heidelberg (2011). doi:10.1007/978-3-642-25073-6_38
8. Bernstein, A., Kiefer, C., Stocker, M.: OptARQ: a SPARQL optimization approach based on triple pattern selectivity estimation. Technical report ifi-2007.03, University of Zurich (2007)
9. Tsialiamanis, P., Sidirourgos, L., Fundulaki, I., Christophides, V., Boncz, P.: Heuristics-based query optimisation for SPARQL. In: ACM International Conference on Extending Database Technology, pp. 324–335 (2012)
10. Gubichev, A., Neumann, T.: Exploiting the query structure for efficient join ordering in SPARQL queries. In: EDBT, pp. 439–450 (2014)
11. Stocker, M., Seaborne, A., Bernstein, A., Kiefer, C., Reynolds, D.: SPARQL basic graph pattern optimization using selectivity estimation. In: ACM International Conference on World Wide Web, pp. 595–604 (2008)
12. Bicer, V., Tran, T., Gossen, A.: Relational kernel machines for learning from graph-structured RDF data. In: Antoniou, G., Grobelnik, M., Simperl, E., Parsia, B., Plexousakis, D., Leenheer, P., Pan, J. (eds.) ESWC 2011. LNCS, vol. 6643, pp. 47–62. Springer, Heidelberg (2011). doi:10.1007/978-3-642-21034-1_4
13. Yamagata, Y., Fukuta, N.: An approach to dynamic query classification and approximation on an inference-enabled SPARQL endpoint. J. Inf. Process. **23**(6), 759–766 (2015)
14. Maali, F., Hassan, I.A., Decker, S.: Scheduling for SPARQL endpoints. In: International Semantic Web Conference, pp. 19–28 (2014)
15. Morsey, M., Lehmann, J., Auer, S., Ngonga Ngomo, A.-C.: DBpedia SPARQL benchmark – performance assessment with real queries on real data. In: Aroyo, L., Welty, C., Alani, H., Taylor, J., Bernstein, A., Kagal, L., Noy, N., Blomqvist, E. (eds.) ISWC 2011. LNCS, vol. 7031, pp. 454–469. Springer, Heidelberg (2011). doi:10.1007/978-3-642-25073-6_29
16. Robertson, S.: Understanding inverse document frequency: on theoretical arguments for IDF. J. Documentation **60**(5), 503–520 (2004)

17. Breiman, L.: Random forests. Mach. Learn. **45**(1), 5–32 (2001)
18. Trillo, R., Gracia, J., Espinoza, M., Mena, E.: Discovering the semantics of user keywords. J. Univ. Comput. Sci. **13**(12), 1908–1935 (2007)
19. Marler, R.T., Arora, J.S.: Survey of multi-objective optimization methods for engineering. Struct. Multi. Optim. **26**(6), 369–395 (2004)
20. Zitzler, E., Deb, K., Thiele, L.: Comparison of multiobjective evolutionary algorithms: empirical results. Evol. Comput. **8**(2), 173–195 (2000)
21. Geem, Z.W., Kim, J.H., Loganathan, G.: A new heuristic optimization algorithm: harmony search. Simulation **76**(2), 60–68 (2001)
22. Manjarres, D., Landa-Torres, I., Gil-Lopez, S., Del Ser, J., Bilbao, M.N., Salcedo-Sanz, S., Geem, Z.W.: A survey on applications of the harmony search algorithm. Eng. Appl. Artif. Intell. **26**(8), 1818–1831 (2013)
23. Bean, J.C.: Genetic algorithms and random keys for sequencing and optimization. ORSA J. Comput. **6**(2), 154–160 (1994)
24. Pirró, G., Euzenat, J.: A feature and information theoretic framework for semantic similarity and relatedness. In: Patel-Schneider, P.F., Pan, Y., Hitzler, P., Mika, P., Zhang, L., Pan, J.Z., Horrocks, I., Glimm, B. (eds.) ISWC 2010. LNCS, vol. 6496, pp. 615–630. Springer, Heidelberg (2010). doi:10.1007/978-3-642-17746-0_39

Hardware-Based Sequential Consistency Violation Detection Made Simpler

Mohammad Majharul Islam[✉], Riad Akram, and Abdullah Muzahid

University of Texas at San Antonio, San Antonio, USA
{mohammadmajharul.islam,riad.akram,abdullah.muzahid}@utsa.com

Abstract. Sequential Consistency (SC) is the most intuitive memory model for parallel programs. However, modern architectures aggressively reorder and overlap memory accesses, causing SC violations (SCVs). An SCV is practically always a bug. This paper proposes Dissector, a hardware software combined approach to detect SCVs in a conventional TSO machine. Dissector hardware works by piggybacking information about pending stores with cache coherence messages. Later, it detects if any of those pending stores can cause an SCV cycle. Dissector keeps hardware modifications minimal and simpler by sacrificing some degree of detection accuracy. Dissector recovers the loss in detection accuracy by using a postprocessing software which filters out false positives and extracts detail debugging information. Dissector hardware is lightweight, keeps the cache coherence protocol clean, does not generate any extra messages, and is unaffected by branch mispredictions. Moreover, due to the postprocessing phase, Dissector does not suffer from false positives. This paper presents a detailed design and implementation of Dissector in a conventional TSO machine. Our experiments with different concurrent algorithms, bug kernels, Splash2 and Parsec applications show that Dissector has a better SCV detection ability than a state-of-the-art hardware based approach with much less hardware. Dissector hardware induces a negligible execution overhead of 0.02%. Moreover, with more processors, the overhead remains virtually the same.

1 Introduction

Among various memory models, Sequential Consistency (SC) [15] is the most intuitive one. It guarantees a total global order among the memory operations where each thread maintains its program order. However, most commercial architectures sacrifice SC to improve performance. For example, x86 implements a memory model similar to TSO [30] which allows a later load operation to bypass an earlier store operation from the same processor. The overlapping and reordering of memory accesses can lead non SC behavior of a program, referred to as an *SC Violation* (SCV). Consider Dekker's algorithm in Fig. 1(a). Processor P0 first writes *flag1* (I1) and then reads *flag2* (I2) but P1 first writes *flag2* (J1) and then reads *flag1* (J2). Both flags are initially 0. In SC, either I2 or J2 will be the last one to complete. Therefore, either P0 finds *flag2* to be 1 or P1 finds *flag1* to

© Springer International Publishing AG 2016
J. Carretero et al. (Eds.): ICA3PP 2016, LNCS 10048, pp. 18–37, 2016.
DOI: 10.1007/978-3-319-49583-5_2

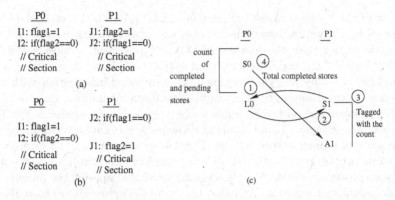

Fig. 1. (a) shows Dekker's algorithm and (b) shows how an SCV can occur there. (c) Steps in detecting an SCV.

be 1. It is even possible to have both flags to be 1 (e.g., if the completion order is I1, J1, I2, and J2). In any case, we can *never* have both flags to be 0. However, if the underlying memory model is TSO, it is possible for the load in J2 to bypass the store in J1 (Fig. 1(b)). As a result, the completion order becomes J2, I1, I2, J1 and both processors find the flags to be 0. The same problem can occur if I1 and I2 get reordered.

Detecting SCVs is crucial for the simplification of parallel programs. Maintaining SC is considered to be one of the major correctness criteria for parallel programs. Programmers can ensure SC semantics in any architecture by writing the programs in a data race free manner [2,19]. However, the programs can have occasional data races (intentional or unintentional) and hence, SCVs (Sect. 2.2 discusses how data races and SCVs are related). The situation gets complicated when the memory model specifications of commercial processors from Intel and AMD do not even match the actual behavior of the machines [27]. Therefore, programmers may not be able to reason about SC behavior with those specifications. To make things worse, many work on semantics and software checking [26] that can potentially make parallel programming easier, would not be useful in the presence of SCVs. Thus, it is necessary to have a technique that can detect SCVs.

Significant research has been done to detect SC violations. One line of work [5, 12,32] encode the program and memory model constraints as axioms and use a constraint solver to find violations of SC. There are some approaches [7,8] that detect data races and find SCV cycles among them. Software based approaches described so far cannot be used during production runs. A recent study [14] has shown that many real world applications like Apache, MySQL, Mozilla, Gcc, Java, Cilk [1], Splash2 etc. have SCV bugs. Only 20% of the bugs are detected by software testing tools. The rest are discovered by programmers during their analysis of source code. As a result, a lot of SCV bugs remain hidden for a long time. Such findings warrant always-on hardware based solutions that can detect these bugs as soon as they occur.

Most of the hardware based approaches [3,9,11,17,19,31] detect data races as proxies for SCVs. However, the number of data races can be two orders of magnitude higher than the number of SCVs [24]. Recent proposals like Volition [24], Vulcan [22], and Conflict Ordering (CO) [16] focus on detecting actual SCVs. They work by piggybacking memory reordering information with cache coherence protocol messages. They suffer from several limitations. *First,* they complicate coherence protocols significantly (e.g., Volition introduces *five* different network messages). *Second,* many of those proposals cannot work properly in the presence of branch mispredictions. *Third,* they require many hardware structures to be proportional to the number of processors and thus, are not suitable for higher processor count. *Finally,* existing hardware approaches provide very little debugging information. At most, they provide information about the last pair of memory accesses involved in an SCV. An SCV requires at least 4 memory accesses. Thus, the provided information is inadequate for a programmer.

This project aims to strike a balance between simplicity and effectiveness. We would like to propose a technique that can be used during production run without suffering from the previous shortcomings. Our proposed scheme, Dissector, works in two phases - an online phase to detect (potential) SCVs using a lightweight hardware and an offline post processing phase to filter out false alarms and extract detailed debugging information using a software. Dissector, targets TSO memory model for its widespread availability. In addition, it is streamlined for detecting 2 processor SCVs because of their sweeping majority [14,22]. Dissector exploits the fact that TSO allows only one type of memory reordering - a load bypassing an earlier store. Therefore, an SCV can occur when the earlier bypassed store communicates with some remote load or store. Whenever a write miss (due to a store, S1) invalidates (step 1 in Fig. 1(c)) a line accessed by a load L0, the processor P0 responds (step 2) with a count of stores. The count includes all completed stores as well as any pending store that is earlier (according to the program) than L0. In a sense, the count expresses after how many stores, L0 appears to be ordered. Upon receiving the response, the processor P1 keeps tagging (step 3) the lines accessed by subsequent memory instructions with the count. When P0 sends an invalidation (due to a store, S0) to P1 (step 4), P0 piggybacks a count of its total completed stores. If this count is smaller than the tag stored with the invalidated line, S0 must be one of P0's pending stores that initially got bypassed by L0. Hence, an SCV is reported by the Dissector hardware. The report consists of two instructions - S0 and the memory instruction, A1 that accessed the invalidated line in step 4. However, a 2-processor SCV requires 4 instructions - S0, L0, S1, and A1. In order to determine the other two instructions, Dissector keeps logging every communicating pair like L0 and S1, where L0 is a bypassing load that gets invalidated by S1 (before the prior stores of L0 are completed). Let us denote (L0, S1) as the First Pair (FP) and (S0, A1) as the Second Pair (SP). The post processing software takes the report of FPs and SPs and enumerates over their possible combinations. For each combination, it profiles some memory accesses and applies Shasha-Snir's SCV detection algorithm [28] to either confirm a true SCV or prune a false alarm. Since Dissector is a two-phased detection scheme, we envision its usage model to either (ii) reactive (default mode) where the report is processed only after a failure (crash, incorrect result etc.) occurs or (ii) proactive where the report of potential SCVs are processed immediately after the execution.

Dissector hardware relies solely on messages generated by cache coherence protocols. It does not introduce any new messages. It does not alter the behavior of coherence protocols either. It only piggybacks few extra bytes with existing coherence messages. Dissector requires a small amount of hardware structures per processor. The hardware requirement does not change with processor count. Dissector hardware works seamlessly with branch mispredictions. Dissector, with the help of its post processing phase, prunes false positives and provides detail information (i.e., all instruction and memory addresses) about true SCVs. Dissector is unconcerned about compiler induced SCVs. The paper presents a detail design of Dissector. We evaluated it in a multiprocessor system using a cycle accurate simulator [25] and Pin [18]. We experimented with different concurrent algorithms, bug kernels, SPLASH2, and PARSEC applications. Our results show that even with a simple non-intrusive design, Dissector has a better SCV detection ability than a prior state-of-the-art technique. For a 4-processor system, it incurs a negligible execution and network overhead of 0.02% and 2.78% respectively. It requires only 3.5 KB hardware per processor.

This paper is organized as follows. Section 2 gives a brief overview of background; Sect. 3 describes Dissector design; Sect. 4 explains implementation issues; Sect. 5 presents experimental results; Sect. 6 discusses related work; and finally, Sect. 7 concludes the work.

2   Background

2.1   TSO Memory Model

A TSO machine has a write buffer with each processor. When a store reaches the head of the Reorder Buffer (ROB), it retires into the write buffer. From there, the stores are performed in order. A store is *completed* when the local cache receives all invalidation acknowledgements for the write. When a store is completed, it is removed from the write buffer. Whenever a load reaches the head of the ROB and the data is returned from the local cache, it is allowed to retire even if the write buffer contains some earlier stores. This process essentially lets a load to bypass earlier stores in TSO. A load is said to *complete* when it retires from the ROB.

2.2   Patterns for an SCV

Shasha and Snir [28] show what leads to an SCV: overlapping data races that cause dependences to form a happened-before cycle at runtime. Recall that a data race occurs when two (or more) threads/processors access the same location without an intervening synchronization and at least one is writing. Figure 2(a)

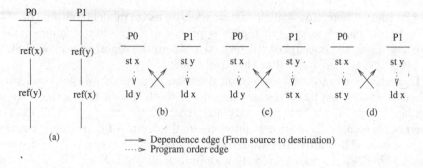

Fig. 2. Understanding SCVs in TSO.

shows the required program pattern for two processors (where each variable is written at least once) and Fig. 2(b)–(d) show the required order of the dependences for SCVs in TSO. The dependences are Write-After-Read or Write-After-Write dependences. Each arrow is shown from the earlier access to the later one. So, we refer to the earlier access as the *Source* and the later access as the *Destination* of the dependence.

If at least one of the dependences occur in the opposite direction or any other pattern appears at runtime, no cycle can form and hence, no SCV occurs. Note that for the pattern in Fig. 2(b), each dependence occurs between a store and a remote load whereas for the patterns in Fig. 2(c) and (d), the dependences occur between a store and a remote load/store. Thus, in TSO, an SCV can occur when a store depends on a remote load/store.

3   Dissector: A Hardware Software Co-designed Approach

Dissector consists of a lightweight hardware to detect SCVs and a post processing software to prune false alarms later. We will start by explaining the overall approach of Dissector hardware assuming a two processor system with a single word cache line in Sect. 3.2. Sections 3.4 and 3.5 extend the design to handle multiword cache line and more than two processors respectively. Section 3.6 handles all the subtleties of cache coherence protocol. Finally, Sect. 3.7 describes the post processing analysis. Keep in mind that Dissector is designed to detect two processor SCV cycles.

3.1   Definitions

We start by defining some terms that will be used throughout this section. (i) Completed Store Counter (CSC) is a per processor counter to keep track of the stores that the processor completed. (ii) If a processor completes a load while some earlier stores are pending, Violating Store Point (VSP) denotes the number of total completed stores (from the same processor) after which the load appears to be ordered. If the count of earlier pending stores is denoted by PS, then VSP is essentially the sum of CSC and PS i.e., $VSP = CSC + PS$. (iii) Each processor assigns a Serial Number (SN) to a memory reference instruction during the issue stage. SN is a scalar quantity that starts from 1 for the first memory reference instruction of a processor and keeps incrementing for subsequent memory reference instructions. SN is used to determine program order among memory reference instructions. (iv) For a multiword cache line, we keep 1 bit per word to indicate whether any access to that word can potentially cause an SCV. The bit is referred to as Unsafe (U) bit. (v) Finally, a two processor SCV cycle consists of two dependences (Sect. 2.2). The dependence that occurs first is referred to as the First Pair (FP) and the other one is referred to as the Second Pair (SP).

3.2   Basic Operation of Dissector Hardware

Let us assume that a processor, say P_0 completes a load L and the line accessed by the load gets invalidated by a remote store. P_0 responds with VSP. Recall that $VSP = CSC + PS$ where PS is the number of pending stores that are earlier than L. After P_0 completes a total of VSP stores, the load appears to be ordered and no longer causes any SCV. If the invalidated line of P_0 was last accessed by a store S (instead of the load L), the store should be already ordered in TSO i.e., $PS = 0$. So, P_0 responds with $VSP = CSC$.

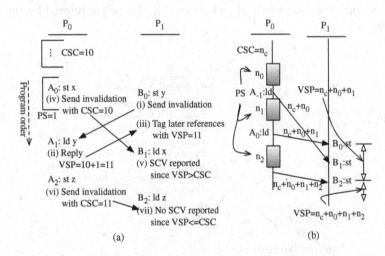

Fig. 3. (a) shows an overview of Dissector. (b) explains the assignment of VSP.

Let us consider the example in Fig. 3(a) where the load A_1 bypasses the pending store A_0 in processor P_0. Assume that P_0 has completed $CSC = 10$ stores so far. When P_0 receives an invalidation due to the store B_0, A_0 is still pending (i.e., $PS = 1$). So, P_0 replies with $VSP = CSC + PS = 11$. Thus, P_0 is letting P_1 know that the load A_1 will appear to be ordered when P_0 completes a total of 11 stores. P_1 starts tagging all later (issued) references (e.g., B_1 & B_2) with $VSP = 11$. When A_0 generates an invalidation request, P_0 sends CSC (which is still 10) along with the request. The load of the invalidated line, B_1, is tagged with $VSP = 11$. Since CSC has not reached VSP yet, P_0 has not completed all necessary stores to make A_1 appear to be ordered yet. This implies that the invalidation is coming from the pending store A_0 which was bypassed by A_1. Thus, the reordering of A_0 and A_1 gets exposed to P_1 and an SCV is detected. When A_0 completes, CSC of P_0 becomes 11. Now consider the store A_2 which is younger than A_1 and hence, is not reordered with A_1. When A_2 causes an invalidation request, P_0 sends CSC=11 with it. The load of the invalidated line, B_2 has VSP=11. Since CSC has reached VSP, P_0 has completed all the stores necessary to make A_1 appear to be ordered. So, no SCV is detected.

Note that the dependence $B_0 \rightarrow A_1$ starts the happened-before cycle. Therefore, FP is the instruction pair (B_0, A_1). The dependence $A_0 \rightarrow B_1$ finishes the happened-before cycle and therefore, SP is the instruction pair (A_0, B_1). When A_0 causes an invalidation and an SCV is detected with B_1, Dissector hardware logs the instruction address of A_0 and B_1 as SP in a memory mapped file. We assume that instruction address of A_0 is piggybacked with the invalidation message. To capture FP, Dissector hardware finds every instance where the line accessed by a bypassing load (e.g., A_1) is invalidated due to a store (e.g., B_0) and logs the instruction address of A_0 and B_1 as FP. This will cause dependences other than $B_0 \rightarrow A_1$ to be logged as FPs as well. Those are filtered by the post processing software.

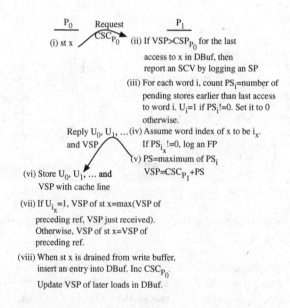

Fig. 4. SCV detection using CSC and VSP.

3.3   How VSP is Assigned?

Consider Fig. 3(b). Assume that P_0 has already completed a total of $CSC = n_c$ stores. Processor P_0 has some pending stores. The topmost box indicates a portion of execution where P_0 has n_0 pending stores. Subsequent boxes represent more execution portions where P_0 has n_1 and n_2 pending stores respectively. Processor P_1 sends a request to P_0 due to a store B_0. This creates a (write-after-read) dependence $A_0 \rightarrow B_0$, where A_0 is a load from P_0. As in Sect. 2.2, the dependence arrow is shown from the earlier access to the later access. P_0 responds with $n_c + n_0 + n_1$ as VSP. Any of the $n_0 + n_1$ pending stores from P_0 can cause an SCV with B_0 or later reference instructions. In other words, those pending stores can expose the reordering of A_0. Therefore, any memory reference instruction from B_0 to B_1 is tagged with $n_c + n_0 + n_1$ as VSP. For store B_1 in P_1, P_0 responds with $n_c + n_0$ as VSP (due to the dependence $A_{-1} \rightarrow B_1$). Note that even if some (say, $n_{0'}$) of the n_0 pending stores complete by the time B_1 causes an invalidation request, CSC will be increased to $n_c + n_{0'}$ while PS will be decreased to $n_0 - n_{0'}$. At the end, VSP returned by P_0 will still be $n_c + n_0$. Therefore, for the sake of simplicity, we can assume that P_0 does not complete any of its pending stores for the rest of the discussion. B_1 causes the receipt of $n_c + n_0$ as VSP. Thus, the dependence $A_{-1} \rightarrow B_1$ allows B_1 and later memory reference instructions of P_1 to have an SCV with any of the n_0 pending stores from P_0. On the other hand, the dependence $A_0 \rightarrow B_0$ allows B_1 and later reference instructions to have an SCV with any of the n_0 as well as n_1 pending stores from P_0. Therefore, B_1 and later reference instructions (up to B_2) are tagged with $n_c + n_0 + n_1$ as VSP. In other words, VSP of a memory reference instruction is set to the larger of the two - VSP of the preceding (in program order) memory reference instruction and the VSP received, if any, from another processor. Note that VSP is received only for a store. Therefore, a load simply inherits its VSP from the preceding reference instruction. Finally, store B_2 receives $n_c + n_0 + n_1 + n_2$ as VSP from P_0. This is larger than the VSP of the preceding reference instruction (which is $n_c + n_0 + n_1$). Hence, B_2 and later memory reference instructions have $n_c + n_0 + n_1 + n_2$ as VSP. A curious reader might wonder what happens if P_0 completes all of its pending stores before receiving the invalidation of B_0. In that case, B_0 and later reference instructions will have $n_c + n_0 + n_1 + n_2$ as VSP. Although this is an over-estimated value, invalidations of future stores from P_0 will have at least $n_c + n_0 + n_1 + n_2$ as CSC and hence, no false positives will occur.

Note that VSP of a memory reference instruction is used when a remote store has a dependence with it. A memory reference instruction has to complete before a remote store can depend on it. Therefore, a processor assigns VSP to a memory reference instruction when it completes. Thus, misspeculated loads are automatically discarded by Dissector hardware. When a memory reference instruction completes, the ROB (or, write buffer) no longer holds that reference. Therefore, each processor uses a buffer, called *DBuf*. DBuf keeps the reference instructions according to the order of issue (i.e., based on SN). When a memory reference instruction completes, SN and VSP are kept along with its memory and instruction address in DBuf. We only need to keep the last reference instruction to a particular address for SCV detection. Therefore, any new entry in DBuf can cause removal of earlier entries (i.e., the ones with smaller SN) with the same memory address. This buffer is checked in parallel with the local cache when an invalidation request arrives.

In TSO, when a store completes, some of the later loads from the same processor might already have completed. Therefore, when the store completes and VSP is assigned to it, a processor needs to check later loads (i.e., the ones with larger SN) and possibly update their VSPs. Recall that when a load completes, it inherits its VSP from the preceding memory reference instruction. The preceding reference instruction can be a pending store with no VSP assigned yet. In that case, the processor keeps inspecting the reference instructions in decreasing SN order until it finds one with an assigned VSP. The load simply inherits that VSP. Eventually, as the pending stores complete, the load gets its VSP updated.

3.4   Handling Multiword Cache Line

The algorithm described so far, works fine for a single word cache line system because any store that creates an interprocessor dependence causes a cache coherence message and the processors can piggyback CSC and VSP with those messages. For a multiword cache line system, not all stores that create interprocessor dependences cause cache coherence messages. Therefore, anytime a store generates a cache coherence message, the processors need to piggyback information not only for the requested word but also for other words in the same line. Assume that each cache line contains W words.

The straightforward way to extend the single word cache line algorithm is to send separate VSP for each word in the same cache line. Communication and storage of such VSPs would cause significant overhead. Therefore, a processor sends only 1 VSP for the entire cache line and associates 1 U bit with each word to indicate whether any access to that word can be potentially involved with an SCV. The algorithm is shown in Fig. 4. When processor P_0 sends a request due $st\ x$, it sends CSC_{P_0}. P_1 finds the last reference instruction to x in its DBuf and checks if the associated VSP is larger than CSC_{P_0}. If so, P_1 reports an SCV by logging the relevant instructions as an SP. After checking for an SCV, for each word i, for $0 \leq i < W$, P_1 counts the number of pending stores PS_i earlier than the last access to that word. If PS_i is not 0, there are some earlier pending stores that can cause an SCV with a remote access to the word. Thus, the remote access could be unsafe and so, unsafe bit U_i associated with the word is set. If there are some pending stores before the last access to word x (i.e., $PS_{i_x} \neq 0$), the dependence is logged as an FP. P_1 summarizes all PS_i by taking the maximum, denoted by PS. Thus, an access from P_1 to any word of the cache line bypasses at most PS pending stores. So, PS is a conservative estimate of pending stores and can lead to false positives. VSP is calculated by adding PS and CSC_{P_1}. P_1 sends all U_i bits and VSP with the reply message. After receiving these, P_0 stores U_i bits and VSP with the cache line so that they can be used in future. If the unsafe bit associated with word x (i.e., U_{i_x}) is set, P_0 sets VSP of $st\ x$ as the VSP of the preceding memory reference instruction or the VSP just received, whichever is the larger. If, however, U_{i_x} is cleared, there are no pending stores in P_1 (before its last access to x) that can cause an SCV. Hence, $st\ x$ copies its VSP from the preceding reference instruction. When the store is drained from P_0's write buffer, an entry is inserted into DBuf, CSC_{P_0} is incremented and VSPs of later loads are updated as usual.

3.5   Handling More Processors

Assume that the system has N processors for $N > 2$. Here, when a processor P_i, for $0 \leq i < N$, sends an invalidation due to a store, more than one processor can reply. The reply from processor P_j, for $0 \leq j < N$ and $j \neq i$, contains VSP_{P_j} and unsafe bits U_{jl}, for $0 \leq l < W$. P_i combines the replies. If a reply has all unsafe bits cleared, the corresponding processor has all of its last accesses to the line appear to be ordered. Hence, the reply is not considered during the combination process. From the remaining replies, unsafe bits are combined by taking the logical OR of the corresponding bits. So, if a word is marked unsafe at least in one reply, it is also marked unsafe after the combination. Thus, the resultant reply contains U_m bits, for $0 \leq m < W$, where $U_m = OR(U_{0m}, ..., U_{(N-1)m})$. VSPs are conservatively combined by taking the maximum from the remaining replies. Such merging can lead to false positives. Thus, the algorithm in Fig. 4 remains the same except that P_0 needs to combine the replies before applying steps (vi)–(viii).

3.6   Issues with Cache Coherence Protocol

Let us consider a bus based snoopy system. Section 4 explains a directory based scheme. Without loss of generality, let us assume an MSI protocol. We will discuss all cases – store miss/hit and load miss/hit. When a processor suffers a write miss due to a store, it broadcasts an invalidation. Every processor snoops on the bus and responds. All the steps mentioned in Fig. 4 are applied. When a store causes a write hit, the associated cache line contains unsafe bits and VSP which are used to calculate VSP of the store and possibly update VSPs of later loads in DBuf. However, a write hit can lead to both false positives and negatives. A write hit implies that the cache line is in modified state. Hence, no other processor has accessed it since the completion of the store that originally brought the line in modified state. Therefore, there is no new pending store from other processors that precedes those processors' last access to the line. Hence, the associated VSP still correctly specifies the stores (from those other processors) that can cause an SCV with an access to this line. So, VSP associated with the modified line is still accurate. The unsafe bits, however, may stay unsafe for longer. This is due to the fact that the pending stores might have completed. Moreover, instead of a write hit if the store could cause a write miss, other processors would have received an invalidation request, checked for an SCV with their last access to the requested word, and (sometimes) logged an FP. Such checking and logging cannot be done when a write hit occurs to a previously unaccessed word. Thus, when a write hit happens for a previously unaccessed word, the requested processor can end up using overestimated information (due to unsafe bits) which can cause false positives, other processors can lose a chance to detect an SCV resulting in false negatives, and some FPs may not be logged. False positives will be pruned by the post processing step. Missing SCVs (i.e., false negatives) will eventually be detected since we envision the hardware to be active in every execution even during the production run. Missing of some FPs are discussed in Sect. 3.7.

A load always inherits its VSP from the preceding (or even earlier) memory reference instruction. Therefore, a cache line that is brought due to a read miss has its unsafe bits and VSP assigned to the initialized values (i.e., all 0s). Any future write miss on the same line brings up-to-date VSP and unsafe bits. A read (hit/miss) simply causes the associated load to get its VSP from the preceding (or even earlier) instruction.

3.7 Postprocessing by Dissector Software

The goal of the postprocessing software is to filter out false SCVs and with the help of FPs and SPs, provide detail information for true SCVs. Recall that an FP is a dependence between a store and a load that bypasses some stores in another processor. An SP is a dependence between a store and a load/store in another processor where an SCV is detected. A 2-processor SCV consists of an FP and an SP. Consider the SCV in Fig. 3(a) where FP is the dependence between B_0 and A_1, and SP is the dependence between A_0 and B_1. Dissector hardware logs a set of FPs, SPs along with the id processors involved. An SP can be associated with any one of the FPs to cause an SCV. Therefore, Dissector software checks all possible combinations of FPs and SPs. Let us consider a combination where FP is between a store F_s and a load F_l, and SP is between a store S_s and a load/store S_{ls}. According to Shasha and Snir [28], this combination can cause an SCV if (i) there are data races between S_s and S_{ls} as well as F_s and F_l, (ii) S_s and S_{ls} access a location different than F_s and F_l, (iii) in the program, S_s is earlier than F_l in the same thread and F_s is earlier than S_{ls} in the same thread, and (iv) there is no fence between S_s and F_l (Fig. 5). One might wonder why we did not consider the case where there is a fence between S_s and F_l but no fence between F_s and S_{ls} (when S_{ls} is a load). Such a scenario can cause an SCV due to the reordering of S_{ls} and F_s. Therefore, (S_s, S_{ls}) would be logged as an FP instead of an SP and vice versa. Thus, without the loss of generality, we consider the absence of a fence only between S_s and F_l as the required constraint.

To check the constraints for a combination (S_s, S_{ls}, F_s, F_l), the program is run with a profiler using the same inputs as the original run. The profiler profiles $S_s, S_{ls}, F_s,$ and F_l instructions. It also profiles any other instruction that accesses the same locations as these instructions. For each of these instructions, it records the instruction and memory address and the id of the executing thread. The profiler captures the order of execution of different memory access instructions from the same thread. The profiler also captures any fence and synchronization

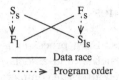

Data race
┈┈┈┈> Program order

Fig. 5. Required constraints for an SCV.

operation executed. The output of the profiler is a file that contains all these information. A happened-before race detection [23] algorithm is applied to the contents of the file. If a pair of memory accesses to the same location do not have any happened-before relation and at least one of them is a store, the pair is marked as a racing pair. Any instance of S_s, S_{ls}, F_s, or F_l that is not involved in a data race is discarded from further considerations. Algorithm 1 is then applied. It checks one thread at a time. It finds every instance of S_s and F_l in the same thread where S_s is earlier than F_l in the program and is not intervened by a fence or a local store to the same location as F_l. If such an instance exists, it finds every instance of F_s and S_{ls} that races with F_l and S_s respectively. If, at least once, F_s executes before S_{ls} by the same thread, then we identify a scenario where the combination (S_s, S_{ls}, F_s, F_l) can cause an SCV. If such a scenario is not found, the combination is filtered out as a false positive. In any case, the software then applies the same algorithm for other combinations of FPs and SPs.

Algorithm 1. Processing a combination (S_s, S_{ls}, F_s, F_l)

---

for each thread t **do**
  for each S_s in t **do**
    for each F_l that is later than S_s in t, accesses a location different than S_s, and is not intervened by a fence or a store to the same location as F_l in t **do**
      for each S_{ls} that (data) races with S_s **do**
        for each F_s that (data) races with F_l **do**
          Check if F_s and S_{ls} are from the same thread r such that $r \neq t$ and F_s is earlier than S_{ls}.
          If so, confirm an SCV and break.
        end for
      end for
    end for
  end for
end for

Note that our software phase relies on the presence of data races to confirm an SCV. It is possible that the required data races might not occur when we run the program with the profiler. To remedy this, we inject random delay during profiling and run the profiler several (e.g., 20) times. Since we are focusing mostly on 4 instructions at a time, it is even possible to consider tools like CHESS [21] to generate all possible interleavings. Finally, a write hit can cause the missing of an FP. To remedy this, we can record FPs found during different executions and use them all to generate different combinations with a set of SPs.

4   Implementation Issues

Additional Hardware Structures. Each processor is equipped with DBuf. DBuf holds a memory reference instruction and associated information after it completes. Since an entry is allocated after the completion of a reference instruction, the allocation process is outside the critical path of the pipeline. DBuf is implemented as a circular ordered list as shown in Fig. 6. The entries are ordered according to SN. The entry for the oldest reference is pointed to by *tail* and the newest reference is pointed to by *head*. The list grows up to a maximum size. When it reaches that size and a new memory reference instruction needs to be inserted, the oldest reference instruction is removed from the tail and the new reference instruction is added to the head. When a memory reference instruction is completed and the (word) address it accessed is already present with some older entry in the list, the older entry is removed and the newer one is inserted. DBuf might need to be accessed using a memory (word) address. To facilitate this process, a hash table is associated with the list (Fig. 6). Each entry in the hash table contains memory address and a pointer to an entry in the list that accessed the same address.

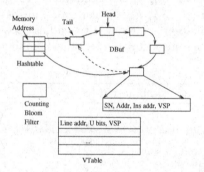

Fig. 6. Hardware structures required for Dissector.

So far we assumed that unsafe bits and VSP of a cache line is stored in the cache with the line itself. This can lead to significant overhead. Therefore, we keep unsafe bits and VSP in a per-processor small cache like structure, called VSP Table (VTable) as shown in Fig. 6. This is similar to Volition [24]. When a write miss brings unsafe bits and VSP, an entry containing them is inserted into VTable. The entry does not store actual data. When a line is invalidated or evicted from the processor's cache and VTable contains an associated entry, the entry is removed from VTable.

Handling Cache Line Evictions. When a line is evicted from the cache, some of the words of that line might still be present in the associated DBuf. We propose to use a Counting Bloom Filter (CBF) [4] that hashes (word) addresses of all entries of DBuf (similar to prior schemes [22, 24]). When there is an invalidation request in the bus, the CBF is checked to determine if the requested word may be present in DBuf. If so, the entry corresponding to the word is searched in DBuf and processed.

Handling a Directory Based Scheme. Dissector requires that a processor receives an invalidation request for any address in DBuf. If the corresponding line is present in the cache, the directory will send an invalidation request. However, if the line is not present, no invalidation will be sent. This issue is partially addressed if cache lines are evicted silently. Next store to the same line will cause the directory to send an invalidation request to processors whose cache previously contained that line. After this point, the directory will have updated information about the sharers and no more invalidations will be sent to those processors. However, those processors might still have some words of the evicted line in DBuf. Although it is possible to force the directory to send future invalidations to those processors with the help of some CBFs that keep track of the addresses in DBuf, such modifications will complicate the directory protocol. So, we choose not to change the directory protocol and accept few more false negatives.

Handing a Race Condition. Consider Fig. 3(a) where A_1 and B_1 are completed. Now, A_0 and B_0 try to complete simultaneously. As a result, before P_0's response arrives and changes VSP of B_1, P_1 checks for SCV at B_1 and detects no SCV. Similarly, before P_1's response has a chance to update VSP of A_1, P_0 checks for SCV at A_1 and detects no SCV. To prevent this race condition, whenever a processor handles an incoming invalidation request while one of its pending stores is in progress (i.e., already sent out invalidation request), the processor serializes the processing of requests according to some pre-defined order based on processor id. In the previous example, lets assume that the order is P_0 and then, P_1. In that case, P_0 will not process P_1's invalidation request until P_0 receives the response for its ongoing store A_0. The response will update VSP of A_1 and then P_0 handles P_1's request and detects an SCV. On the other side, P_1 does not wait for P_0's response due to B_0 and processes the incoming request due to A_0. P_1 does not detect any SCV and responds back to P_0. Eventually when P_0's response arrives, it updates VSP of B_1. The same principle can be applied to any number of processors.

Wrap-Around of VSPs, CSCs and SNs. When wrap-around occurs, two numbers that should be comparable become very far apart. Therefore, it is possible to detect this event by looking at few higher order bits. If they are completely opposite, Dissector hardware can realize that the smaller number is supposed to be higher than the other one.

5   Evaluation

Experimental Setup. We model Dissector hardware using a cycle accurate execution driven simulator [25]. We simulate a chip multiprocessor with private L1

Table 1. Multicore architecture evaluated.

Architecture	Chip multiprocessor with **4**, 8 or 16 cores.
Core pipeline	Out-of-order; 3.0GHz; 2-issue/2-retire.
ROB size	128 entries.
Write buffer size	16 entries.
Private L1 cache	32KB WB, 4-way associative, 6-cycle rt.
Shared L2 cache	1MB WB, 8-way associative, 12-cycle rt.
Cache line size	**32B** or 64B.
Coherence	Snoopy MSI protocol; 3.0GHz 32B-wide bus.
Consistency	TSO
Memory	300 cycle rt.
Dissector Parameters	DBuf: 32, **128** or 1024 entries. SN, VSP, CSC: 4B each. VTable: 32, 64 or **128** entries. CBF: 128B with 2 bit counters, H3 hash.

Table 2. Applications analyzed.

Set	Program	Description
Conc. Algo.	dekker	Algo. mutual exclusion.
	snark	Non-blocking double-end. queue.
	msn	Non-blocking queue.
	harris	Non-blocking set.
	lazylist	List-based concurrent set.
	peterson	Algo. for mutual exclusion.
Bug kernels	pthread_cancel from glibc	Unwind code after canceling thread needs a fence [22].
	crypt_util from glibc	Small table initialization code needs a fence [22].
	init from MySQL	Available charsets initialization code needs a fence [14].
	Cilk_unlock from cilk	Cilk_unlock needs full fence instead of store-store fence [8].
Full	SPLASH-2	8 programs form SPLASH-2.
Apps	Parsec	2 programs form Parsec.

caches and a shared L2 cache. Table 1 shows the architectural parameters. When there is a choice, the values in bold are the default ones. We use PIN [18] to write the profiler.

We use three sets of benchmarks for evaluation (Table 2). The first set has implementations of concurrent data structures and mutual exclusion algorithms that have potential SCVs [5,6]. The second set has some reported SCV bugs from open source programs and libraries (e.g., MySQL, Gcc, Cilk). Finally, we use eight applications from SPLASH-2 and two applications from Parsec.

SCV Detection. To measure Dissector's SCV detection ability, we run each application multiple times - the smaller ones 100 times and the larger ones (i.e. SPLASH2 & Parsec) 5 times. In each run, we force different interleavings by introducing some randomness. For each application, we collect, over all the runs, the number of unique SPs and FPs observed. The post processing software takes the report of FPs and SPs and enumerates over their all possible combinations. For each combination, it either confirms a true SCV or prunes a false alarm. We compare our scheme against an existing hardware based SCV detector, Vulcan [22]. The comparison remains the same even if we consider Volition [24] that is tuned to detect 2 processor cycle (*Volition**). Figure 7(a) shows the results and comparisons for different applications.

Figure 7(a) shows that Dissector hardware logs a total of 252 FPs and 86 SPs. The post processing software enumerates over 1780 combinations. For each combination, it collects a number of profiles (up to 20). It filters 1767 combinations as false alarms and reports detail information (i.e. instruction and memory addresses of all accesses) for the rest (i.e., 13) of the SCVs. Except for *pthread_cancel* and *peterson*, both Dissector and Vulcan/Volition* detect equal number of the SCVs. Dissector detects more SCVs in those programs. This is due to the fact that Vulcan/Volition* identifies an SCV only by the last pair of instructions (i.e., SP). Therefore, multiple different SCVs might be reported as a single one. Dissector, on the other hand, is able to distinguish and report

Codes	FP	SP	Total comb.	Filtered comb.	True SCV	Vulcan/Volition*
harris	2	1	2	2	0	0
lazylist	0	1	0	0	0	0
msn	3	1	3	3	0	0
snark	3	2	6	6	0	0
crypt_util	2	2	4	2	2	2
pthread_can.	4	4	16	13	3	2
dekker	2	1	2	2	0	0
peterson	3	3	9	5	4	3
init	2	4	8	7	1	1
Cilk_unlock	2	0	0	0	0	0
fft	5	1	5	5	0	0
radix	8	5	40	40	0	0
lu	2	0	0	0	0	0
ocean	121	5	605	605	0	0
water-ns	9	11	99	99	0	0
water-sp	9	7	63	63	0	0
barnes	29	15	435	435	0	0
fmm	35	13	455	452	3	3
swaptions	10	2	20	20	0	0
stream.	1	8	8	8	0	0
Total	252	86	1780	1767	13	11

(a) SCVs found in different applications

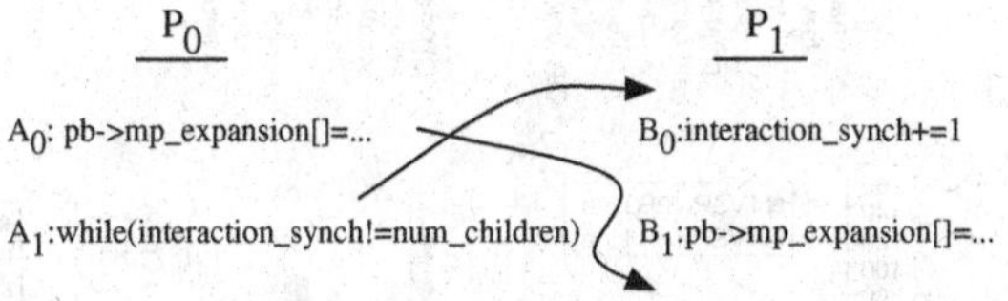

P_0 P_1

A_0: pb->mp_expansion[]=... B_0:interaction_synch+=1

A_1:while(interaction_synch!=num_children) B_1:pb->mp_expansion[]=...

(b) New SCV found in fmm

Fig. 7. Detected SCVs

them as separate SCVs. Note that even with a simpler and smaller hardware, Dissector does not have any false negatives.

We like to understand whether profiles of data races can be used in conjunction with a software based scheme such as Relaxer [7] to find out SCVs. We used *fmm* as an example. We found 15 data races using Intel Inspector [13]. The profile contained 24.3 million accesses. It was too much to be used with Relaxer. So, profile based software only schemes are not suitable especially for large applications.

We found a *previously unreported* SCV in *fmm*. It was detected by both Dissector and Vulcan/Volition*. In *fmm*, different threads can process *boxes* in opposite order. This can lead to an interleaving shown in Fig. 7(b). Here, processor P_0 reads *interaction_synch* in A_1 before modifying *mp_expansion* in A_0. Another processor P_1 modifies *interaction_synch* in B_0 and then modifies *mp_expansion* in B_1. Although no reordering is possible between B_0 and B_1 in TSO, the reordering of A_0 and A_1 causes an SCV. Note that *interaction_synch* is declared as *volatile* in code. However, its read in A_1 can still bypass A_0 and cause an SCV. To fix this bug, *interaction_synch* needs to be declared as *atomic* in C/C++.

Sensitivity Analysis. We evaluate three choices - 1VSP (default), 2VSP, and 4VSP per cache line. We compare each with Vulcan/Volition*. Dissector does not have any false negative in any case. We count the average number of false SCVs filtered by the postprocessing software (Fig. 8(a)). The average is calculated for each execution. On average, for each application, Dissector filters 17.29 combinations in the default version. However, 2VSP and 4VSP filter 6.55 and 1.24 combinations per application respectively. Recall that the filtering is done

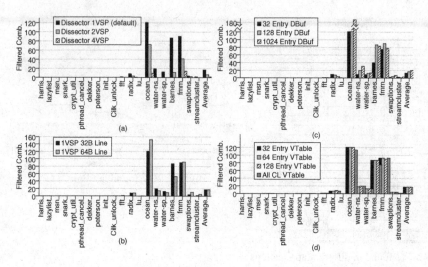

Fig. 8. Sensitivity to (a) number of VSP, (b) cache line size, (c) size of DBuf, and (d) size of VTable.

offline by the post processing software and the default choice is to do it only after a failure execution. We opt for 1VSP as our default design. We experiment with 2 cache line sizes - 32 and 64 Byte. Dissector does not have any false negative for 32 Byte line but 1 false negative in *peterson* program for 64 Byte line. Figure 8(b) shows the average number of combinations filtered for each execution. For 32 Byte line, the average is 17.29 per application whereas for 64 byte line, the number is 17.27. Dissector has two structure DBuf and VTable. In order to assess the impact of DBuf, we keep the size of VTable to be 128 and change the size of DBuf to be 32, 128, and 1024. For 32 entry DBuf, Dissector has 1 false negative in *init* program. For larger sizes, Dissector does not have any false negative. The filtered combinations are shown in Fig. 8(c). On average, for each application, the post processing software filters 13.59, 17.29, and 20.45 combinations per execution for 32, 64, and 128 entry DBuf respectively. We keep the size of DBuf to be 128 and change the size of VTable to be 32, 64, 128. We also simulate a case where VSP is stored with each cache line (*All CL*). There are no false negatives in any case. On average, for each application, the number of filtered combinations per application per execution are 17.25, 17.25, 17.29, and 16.41 for 32, 64, 128 entry VTable and All CL configuration respectively (Fig. 8(d)).

Network Traffic and Execution Overhead. We calculate execution and network traffic overhead. For overhead calculation, we use only large applications (i.e. SPLASH2 and Parsec). The overheads are calculated with respect to a baseline TSO machine. Figure 9(a) shows the network overhead due to the piggybacking of VSP and unsafe bits with write misses. On average, the overhead for a 4-core default system is ($\approx$) 2.8%. It increases by less than 1% for higher processor

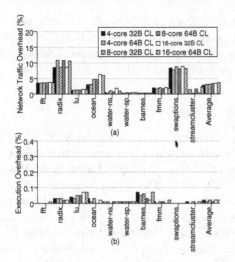

Criteria	Dissector	Vulcan	Volition
Add. message	None	1 type	5 type
Coh. protocol	Unmodified	Modified	Modified
Source of false positive	None	False sharing (bit level), branch mispred.	False sharing (bit level), branch mispred.
Source of false negative	Limited hw, some write hit	Limited hw	Limited hw
Per core hw for 4, 8, 16 core	3.5, 3.5, 3.5 KB	9, 17, 33 KB	6, 6, 6 KB
Scope	2 proc SCV	2 proc SCV	2+ proc SCV
Debugging info.	All inst. & mem. addr.	Last 2 inst addr.	Last 2 inst. addr.

(c) Comparison of Dissector, Vulcan and Volition.

Fig. 9. (a) shows network traffic overhead, (b) shows execution overhead, and (c) shows comparison.

count. The piggybacked traffic causes an average slowdown of ($\approx$) 0.02% for a 4-core system (Fig. 9(b)). This overhead remains virtually the same for more processors. The post processing phase requires 0.007 s, 0.005 s, 0.006 s, 0.007 s and 2456 s to confirm true SCVs in *crypt, init, peterson, pthread_cancel* and *fmm* respectively. To discard a false alarm, it takes 5 h in the worst case. This happens for *fmm*. Recall that post processing is done offline and the default choice is to do it only after a failure execution.

6 Related Work

The table in Fig. 9(c) shows a comparison between Dissector and the closest related work Vulcan & Volition. Besides them, majority of the existing work to detect SCVs focus on data races. Specifically, one line of work detects incoming coherence messages on data that has local outstanding loads or stores. This work started with Gharachorloo and Gibbons [9] and now includes many aggressive speculative designs (e.g., [3,11,31]). Another line of work detects a conflict between two concurrent synchronization-free regions. This includes DRFx [19] and Conflict Exceptions [17]. In general, all of these works look for a data race with two accesses that occur within a short time. Dissector, on the other hand, detects SCV cycles, not just data races. There are many proposals to implement SC. Most proposals to implement SC fall under two categories - in-window speculation [10] and post-retirement speculation [3,11,31]. At the high level, these proposals allow some accesses that would have been stalled in SC, to proceed speculatively. In case, there is a possibility of an SCV, the speculative accesses are squashed and retried. Some recent work [16,29] has been proposed that does not rely on speculation. Conflict Ordering [16] ensures SC by allowing an access to bypass a prior pending access unspeculatively. Singh et al. [29] proposed to implement SC by enforcing order only among shared accesses. Marino et al. [20] used the same principle to implement an SC preserving compiler. Dissector is different from this line of work in the sense that its goal is to detect SCVs.

7 Conclusion

This paper proposed Dissector, a hardware software co-designed SCV detector for a typical TSO machine. Dissector hardware works by piggybacking information about pending stores with cache coherence messages. Later, it detects if any of those pending stores cause an SCV cycle. The post processing software filters out false positives and extracts detail debugging information. Dissector hardware is very lightweight, does not generate any extra network message and seamlessly handles speculatively executed loads. Our results showed that Dissector has better SCV detection ability than a state-of-the-art hardware based SCV detector. Our experiments found a previously undiscovered SCV in *fmm*. Dissector induces a negligible execution overhead of 0.02% which remains the same for more processors. Finally, it requires 3.5 KB/core extra hardware.

References

1. Intel Cilk Plus. http://cilkplus.org/
2. Adve, S.V., Gharachorloo, K.: Shared memory consistency models: a tutorial. Western Reseach Laboratory-Compaq. Research report 95/7, September 1995
3. Blundell, C., Martin, M.M., Wenisch, T.F.: Invisifence: performance-transparent memory ordering in conventional multiprocessors. In: ISCA (2009)
4. Bonomi, F., et al.: An improved construction for counting Bloom filters. In: Annual European Symposium on Algorithms, September 2006
5. Burckhardt, S., Alur, R., Martin, M.M.K.: Checkfence: checking consistency of concurrent data types on relaxed memory models. In: PLDI (2007)
6. Burnim, J., Sen, K., Stergiou, C.: Sound and complete monitoring of sequential consistency for relaxed memory models. In: Abdulla, P.A., Leino, K.R.M. (eds.) TACAS 2011. LNCS, vol. 6605, pp. 11–25. Springer, Heidelberg (2011). doi:10.1007/978-3-642-19835-9_3
7. Burnim, J., Sen, K., Stergiou, C.: Testing concurrent programs on relaxed memory models. In: ISSTA (2011)
8. Duan, Y., Feng, X., Wang, L., Zhang, C., Yew, P.C.: Detecting and eliminating potential violations of sequential consistency for concurrent C/C++ programs. In: CGO (2009)
9. Gharachorloo, K., Gibbons, P.B.: Detecting violations of sequential consistency. In: SPAA (1991)
10. Gharachorloo, K., Gupta, A., Hennessy, J.: Two techniques to enhance the performance of memory consistency models. In: ICPP (1991)
11. Gniady, C., Falsafi, B., Vijaykumar, T.N.: Is sc + ilp = rc? In: ISCA (1999)
12. Gopalakrishnan, G., Yang, Y., Sivaraj, H.: QB or Not QB: an efficient execution verification tool for memory orderings. In: Alur, R., Peled, D.A. (eds.) CAV 2004. LNCS, vol. 3114, pp. 401–413. Springer, Heidelberg (2004). doi:10.1007/978-3-540-27813-9_31

13. Intel: Intel parallel studio. https://software.intel.com/en-us/intel-parallel-studio-xe
14. Islam, M., Muzahid, A.: Characterizing real world bugs causing sequential consistency violations. In: HotPar, June 2013
15. Lamport, L.: How to make a multiprocessor computer that correctly executes multiprocess programs. IEEE Trans. Comput. **28**(9), 690–691 (1979)
16. Lin, C., Nagarajan, V., Gupta, R., Rajaram, B.: Efficient sequential consistency via conflict ordering. In: ASPLOS (2012)
17. Lucia, B., Ceze, L., Strauss, K., Qadeer, S., Boehm, H.J.: Conflict exceptions: simplifying concurrent language semantics with precise hardware exceptions for data-races. In: ISCA (2010)
18. Luk, C.K., Cohn, R., Muth, R., Patil, H., Klauser, A., Lowney, G., Wallace, S., Reddi, V.J., Hazelwood, K.: Pin: building customized program analysis tools with dynamic instrumentation. In: PLDI (2005)
19. Marino, D., Singh, A., Millstein, T., Musuvathi, M., Narayanasamy, S.: DRFx: a simple and efficient memory model for concurrent programming languages. In: PLDI (2010)
20. Marino, D., Singh, A., Millstein, T., Musuvathi, M., Narayanasamy, S.: A case for an sc-preserving compiler. In: Proceedings of the 32th ACM SIGPLAN Conference on Programming Language and Implementation, PLDI 2011 (2011)
21. Musuvathi, M., Qadeer, S., Ball, T., Basler, G., Nainar, P.A., Neamtiu, I.: Finding and reproducing heisenbugs in concurrent programs. In: OSDI (2008)
22. Muzahid, A., Qi, S., Torrellas, J.: Vulcan: Hardware support for detecting sequential consistency violations dynamically. In: MICRO, December 2012
23. Muzahid, A., Suárez, D., Qi, S., Torrellas, J.: Sigrace: signature-based data race detection. In: ISCA (2009)
24. Qian, X., Sahelices, B., Torrellas, J., Qian, D.: Volition: precise and scalable sequential consistency violation detection. In: ASPLOS, March 2013
25. Renau, J., Fraguela, B., Tuck, J., Liu, W., Prvulovic, M., Ceze, L., Sarangi, S., Sack, P., Strauss, K., Montesinos, P.: SESC Simulator, January 2005. http://sesc.sourceforge.net
26. Sen, K.: Race directed random testing of concurrent programs. In: PLDI (2008)
27. Sewell, P., Sarkar, S., Owens, S., Nardelli, F.Z., Myreen, M.O.: X86-tso: A rigorous and usable programmer's model for x86 multiprocessors. Commun. ACM **53**(7), 89–97 (2010)
28. Shasha, D., Snir, M.: Efficient and correct execution of parallel programs that share memory. ACM Trans. Program. Lang. Syst. **10**(2), 282–312 (1988)
29. Singh, A., Narayanasamy, S., Marino, D., Millstein, T., Musuvathi, M.: End-to-end sequential consistency. In: ISCA (2012)
30. Weaver, D., Germond, T.: The SPARC Architecture Manual Version 9. Prentice Hall, Englewood Cliffs (1994)
31. Wenisch, T.F., Ailamaki, A., Falsafi, B., Moshovos, A.: Mechanisms for store-wait-free multiprocessors. In: ISCA (2007)
32. Yang, Y., Gopalakrishnan, G., Lindstrom, G., Slind, K.: Nemos: a framework for axiomatic and executable specifications of memory consistency models. In: IPDPS (2003)

Optimized Mapping Spiking Neural Networks onto Network-on-Chip

Yu Ji[1], Youhui Zhang[1,2,3(✉)], He Liu[1], and Weimin Zheng[1,2]

[1] Department of Computer Science and Technology,
Tsinghua University, Beijing, China
zyh02@tsinghua.edu.cn
[2] Technology Innovation Center at Yinzhou,
Yangtze Delta Region Institute of Tsinghua University, Jiaxing, Zhejiang, China
[3] Center for Brain-Inspired Computing Research,
Tsinghua University, Beijing, China

Abstract. Mapping spiking neural networks (SNNs) onto network-on-chips (NoCs) is pivotal to fully utilize the hardware resources of dedicated multi-core processors (CMPs) for SNNs' simulation. This paper presents such a mapping framework from the aspect of architecture evaluation. Under this framework, we present two strategies accordingly: The first tends to put highly communicating tasks together. The second is opposite, which aims at SNN features to achieve a balanced distribution of neurons according to their active degrees; for communication-intensive and unbalanced SNNs, this one can alleviate NoC congestion and improve the simulation speed more. This framework also contains a customized NoC simulator to evaluate mapping strategies. Results show that our strategies can achieve a higher simulation speed (up to 1.37 times), and energy consumptions can be reduced or rise very limited.

1 Introduction

The great potential of neural systems has aroused research enthusiasms [1]. Neural simulation is one of the important research methods. Typically, the neural network (NN) is expressed as a graph of neurons which take inputs from others and perform computation to produce an output which is, in turn, issued to other neurons. This model is known generally as an Artificial Neural Network (ANN). SNNs (Spiking Neural Networks) can be regarded as the third generation of ANNs [2]: in addition to neuronal and synaptic states, SNNs also incorporate the timing of the arrival of inputs (called spikes) into the operating model. It is believed that SNNs yield higher biological reality and have the potential of more computational power [3].

To speed up SNN simulation, very-large-scale integration (VLSI) systems have been widely used to mimic neuro-biological architectures. In addition, a multi-core

The work is supported by the Science and Technology Plan of Beijing under Grant No. Z161100000216126 and the Brain Inspired Computing Research of Tsinghua University under Grant No. 20141080934.

J. Carretero et al. (Eds.): ICA3PP 2016, LNCS 10048, pp. 38–52, 2016.
DOI: 10.1007/978-3-319-49583-5_3

processor (CMP) with a Network-on-Chip (NoC) has some characteristics similar to those of neural networks, which has emerged as a promising platform for neural network simulation, including [4–7], etc. On the other hand, a neural network usually includes a large number of neurons with a complex connectivity-scheme between them, which is fairly different from common NoC. Consequently, to design an optimized mapping method for distributing biology-analog networks onto hardware is an important topic, confronted with following challenges:

- Besides a large number of neurons, one issue is that each neuron is typically connected to many others; huge amounts of one-to-many communications may take place between the nodes simulating neurons. In contrast, common NoCs tend to feature one-to-one and one-to-a-few connections. Thus, much information about the neuron-connectivity has to be maintained and utilized efficiently.
- To meet timing constraint is another issue. SNNs have taken the arrival time of spikes into the operating model. But common NoCs usually employ the packet-switching technology so that shared resources can result in unwanted variation in transmission latencies, which may impact the accuracy of SNN operations [8].

Fortunately, neural networks also have some friendly characteristics: They show the locality property, i.e., a homogeneous collection of neurons (called a population) tends to connect a nearby population densely (the bundle of single connections between two populations is called a projection). Neurons also tend to fire at a relatively slow rate (measured in terms of hertz and the upper limit is 1000 Hz) while modern electronics operates at multiple gigahertz. Thus, time division multiplexing can be used to make a single processing node or communication channel handle many different neurons or connections at the same time.

This paper proposes a mapping methodology to cover the aforementioned issues, from the perspective of architecture evaluation: neural networks are regarded as parallel tasks and CMPs are the underlying execution substrate, while the mapping mechanism is a middle layer for optimized resource allocation. Furthermore, neuron populations can be regarded as sub-tasks while spikes are communications between them. We will formulate the mapping problem under the framework of application-mapping algorithms for NoCs; thus quite a few architecture-evaluation technologies can be used. In summary, the following contributions have been accomplished:

- We construct a mapping framework. Several existing SNN simulators are used to get golden models and running-traces of objective applications. Trace analyses illustrate that under different inputs, active degrees of one neuron-population are similar. It also contains a configurable NoC simulator for evaluation, which supports some proven effective features for SNN simulation.
- Through the framework, we analyze some existing mapping strategy and point out that transmission of any spike should be completed in one SNN cycle (regardless of the corresponding nominal delay-attribute) to avoid steep increase of the maximum transmission delay of spikes as the simulation speed is fairly high.
- Two mapping strategies are presented. The first is a relatively conventional approach that uses the Kernighan-Lin (KL) algorithm to put highly communicating tasks together. The second is optimized in the opposite direction, which aims at

SNN features to achieve a balanced distribution of neurons according to active degrees. Tests on the NoC simulator show that our strategies can achieve a higher simulation speed (up to 1.37 times) while energy consumptions can be reduced or rise very limited; for communication-intensive and unbalanced SNNs, the second can alleviate NoC congestion and improve the speed more.

2 Related Work

Neuromorphic VLSI systems usually consider neurons as the basic network components connected by directed edges (synapses) and describe the network in terms of neurons, their positions and projections (ignoring biological details). Moreover, communication through spikes is based on a dynamic event-driven scheme.

2.1 Neuromorphic Chips and Network-Mapping

Lots of works have been carried out to simulate SNNs using VLSI technologies. TrueNorth [4, 9] is a digital neuromorphic chip produced by IBM. It also proposed a programming paradigm, Corelet [10]. Moreover, TrueNorth has formulated the problem of mapping as a wire-length minimization problem in VLSI placement [11].

Neurogrid [6] is a brain-inspired analog/digital hybrid system. For mapping, three studies have been carried out: The first maps neuronal models onto neuromorphic hardware [12]; the second maps computations onto heterogeneous populations of spiking neurons based on a theoretical framework (Neural Engineering Framework [13], NEF); the last is to map a network to electronic circuits.

SpiNNaker [5]'s hardware is based on the CMPs of ARM cores. A sequential neuron-core mapping scheme was presented by [2]; [2] also disclaimed that the locality issues were not taken into account. In addition, SpiNNaker has provided technical details of NoC [14]; thus we use it as the reference design.

Dimitrios et al. [15] presented the optimal mapping of a biologically accurate neuron simulator on the Single-Chip Cloud Computer (SCC). But [15] is not a general solution; it is dedicated to inferior olive simulations and the SCC platform.

On the other side, there are quite a few studies [16, 17] on neuromorphic circuits to utilize emerging memory technologies to mimic synaptic behaviors, which are usually focused on prototype construction.

In addition, a few studies have designed customized NoCs to fix the transmission latency; the principle is resource-reservation. For example, EMBRACE [18] proposes such a ring topology for spike communications, which uses a time-stamped broadcast flow control scheme [19]. Philipp et al. [20] use isochronous connections to reserve network bandwidth, which relies on global synchronization of all nodes. Our work is complementary to them from the mapping aspect. Another related job is Vainbrand et al. [21], which performs the analytical evaluation and comparison of different interconnect architectures. It is shown that a multicast mesh NoC provides the highest performance/cost ratio. But no mapping strategy is proposed.

2.2 Application Mapping Algorithms for NoCs

Many studies have been done in application-to-NoC mapping algorithm. Their principles are usually similar: some algorithms have been used to map highly communicating tasks close to each other; and then some heuristic algorithms are used for optimization. For example, Zhu et al. [22] explored opportunities in optimizing application mapping for channel-based on-chip networks, based on the Kernighan-Lin (KL) algorithm. Others include Sahu et al. [23], KLMAP [24], Tosun et al. [25], etc.

As a summary, we compare our work with existing studies; the illuminations from them and our features are given as follows:

1. We adopt some NoC-architecture features that have been proved efficient for SNN simulation, including multicast-enabled routing and mesh topology.
2. From the methodology aspect, we try to carry out SNN studies from the computer architecture perspective and formulate the mapping problem under the application-mapping framework. Further, we have analyzed the limitation and application scope of existing mapping method, and then present our strategy accordingly. Especially, one strategy has extended the above-mentioned mapping framework. As far as we know, no existing study has done this way.

3 The Framework Design

In this section two essential factors of architecture evaluation have been presented first: (1) we introduce how to draw models and running-traces of quite a few objective applications (namely, SNNs), as well as the characteristic analysis; (2) we design and implement the corresponding simulator of NoC that is customized for SNN. In addition, we analyze the limitation of some existing mapping strategy.

3.1 Neural Networks from Software Simulators

Software simulation tools [26] have been widely used by the neuroscientists' community to obtain precise simulations of a given computational paradigm. Thus we can construct accurate neural networks and drive them on the simulators.

An SNN simulator (like NEST [27], Nengo [28], etc.) often provides programming interfaces for users to develop SNN models on the population/projection level; quite a few attributes of populations, connectivity and models can be set respectively.

The SNN model can be defined by user or set by the simulator under user's guidance. After construction, we extract the topological structure with information of nodes and edges. In addition, information of spikes can be obtained during the simulation phase; each record contains the ID of the source neuron and the issuing time. It means we can get the whole information of spikes, namely, running traces.

Then we analyze neurons' active degrees from the traces of some representative networks. Here the active degree for a neuron is defined as the average number of its spike-issues per unit time. For a population, the active degree is the sum of degrees of all its neurons. Each SNN model is extracted from one of the following two popular simulators: NEST (NEural Simulation Tool) [27] and Nengo [28].

The following 11 representative SNNs have been used; for all of them, the neuron model is the Leaky Integrate-and-Fire (LIF) model and all synaptic weights are fixed.

1. Basal Ganglia [29, 30] (abbreviated to *BG*), which models the basal ganglia. BG contains about 1200 neurons of 26 populations.
2. A Question Answering Network (*Question*). It simulates the question-answering function, which provides the answer by learning examples. This model includes about 8000 neurons and 80 populations, available at Nengo web site.
3. A Controlled Question Answering Network (*QAWC*), which performs question answering based on storing items in a working memory, under control of a basal ganglia. It contains 12000 neurons and 60 populations, available at Nengo web site.
4. RBM Digit Recognition (Digit). It is created by training an RBM Deep Belief Network on the MNIST database. It contains 6000 neurons and 5 populations.
5. Bandit Task [31] (4 NNs), a set of four models to exhibit how a simulated rat responds different environments. It contains four NNs (*arm, env, halflearn* and *quarterlearn*); each includes more than 1000 neurons and 15–20 populations.
6. Temporal Differentiation (*Diff*). It performs the computation of temporal differentiation [32], which contains 5000 neurons and 3 populations.
7. Spatiotemporal Processing and Coincidence Detection (*Spat*), which aims at simulating connections between the retina and the cochlea, and realizes a co-incidence detector. It has 8500 neurons and 63 populations.
8. Neural Path Integrator [33] (*Path*). It incorporates representations and updating of position into a single layer of neurons. It has 1600 neurons and 12 populations.

We simulate each network for many times with randomly-selected legal inputs, and record the spike-information of each neuron. Without loss of generality, active degrees of neurons of the Question model have been shown in Fig. 1 (others own the similar feature): for clarity, the degree is illustrated in terms of population. The x-axis is population IDs; the y-axis is the active degree of each population. Legends represent different test sequences. Analyses show that each neuron-population's active degrees are similar under different inputs.

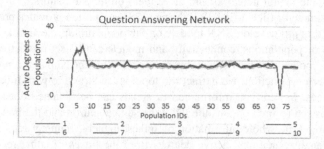

Fig. 1. Active degrees of populations

3.2   NoC of SNN Simulation

Metrics. From the aspect of NoCs' configuration, there is a very large design space. For simplification, we introduce one widely-used design option, multicast-enabled mesh, as the foundation, which has been proved highly efficient for simulation of neural networks [21]. In addition, the 2D-mesh NoC is widely used by CMP products, like SCC [34] and Tile [35]. Accordingly, the tree-based distributed routing is considered for multicast. Compared with the source routing mechanism, it has been proved that the distributed routing will introduce less storage overheads. Moreover, there are quite a few existing multicast routing strategies (Enright et al. [36], Fidalgo et al. [37], Rodrigo et al. [38] and so on) belonging to this category. Accordingly, the size of a multicast routing table will affect the ensuing energy and access time; thus the routing table size is considered a metric in evaluating mapping strategies.

The next metric is simulation speed. Usually, a real-time neuromorphic system means the simulated network is working as 'fast' as the real biological system. Considering a simulated neuron issues one spike per 1 ms (it is the upper bound for biological cells), from the aspect of the NoC electronics operating at hundreds of megahertz or gigahertz, 10^6 or 10^5 cycles will elapse between two issues. Therefore, the simulation speed can be denoted by its times as fast as the real-time speed (1000 Hz). Apparently, with the speed increase, more spikes per unit time will be inserted into the NoC and may cause traffic congestions, which inversely hinders the further speed improvement; otherwise some spike-packets with long latencies will violate timing constraints.

Multicast Routing. For the tree-based routing, a multicast continues along a common path and then branches the message when necessary to achieve a minimal route to each destination. At each hop, the router will complete corresponding operations based on the source ID of the incoming packet. By default, the X-Y routing strategy is used for each single message to avoid dead-lock. Specially, a two-level routing strategy is used as following:

As mentioned above, SNN models of software simulators usually represent projections between populations. Thus it looks beneficial to distribute all neurons of a population into one core as much as possible, or into several nearby cores if one cannot occupy all (it is just the principle of the existing sequential mapping strategy). Accordingly, we take the population ID as the look-up key of routing tables.

The second level is inside a core: on receipt of a spike, the target core will check which internal population should deal with it (if one node contains neurons from multiple populations). It is achieved by looking up a local table; the key is the source-population ID in the incoming packet.

Moreover, we propose that synaptic weights and other attributes are kept at the post-synaptic end (in the aforementioned local table). Hence, no synaptic information needs to be carried in a spike, which makes the multicast mechanism efficient.

Based on the above design, we can give the structure of entries of the routing table on a router, as well as the organization of a NoC-packet. The latter is simple, which just represents the arrival of a spike from some neuron. Correspondingly, a packet consists of only one flit (32-bit width): the first 8 bits represent the population ID; the second

14-bit is the neuron ID in the population and the subsequent 6-bit illustrates the issue time, so that the receiver can judge whether the incoming spike is in time or not. The remaining bits are reserved, which can be used to support inter-chip communication.

Moreover, the common scratchpad memory can be used as the routing table rather than expensive CAM (content addressable memory): population IDs are defined as a series of consecutive integers; thus they can be regarded as memory addresses to access the scratchpad. Accordingly, one entry of the routing table is represented in Table 1. We also use the turn-table routing: if population id is not found in the routing table, the default straight routing will be used. The same method can be applied to the local table, using the population & neuron ID as address.

Table 1. Entry of the routing table

Field	Up	Down	Left	Right	Core	Valid	Reserved
Description	To which directions the package should be transmitted					1/0	2 bits

Storage Consumptions of Routing. As mentioned previously, each router owns a routing table that can be regarded as common on-chip memory; population IDs are used as memory addresses. Therefore, the size of each table is not larger than the amount of populations (denoted as k) and the total consumption n cores is k × n. k is usually limited as shown before.

Implementation of the NoC Simulator. We greatly modify Noxim [39] to implement a detailed, cycle-accurate simulator for NoCs that provides not only the flexibility needed in a high-level simulator but also detailed modeling of all key components of a router. Our modification is focused on the tree-based multicast. We have referenced the micro-architecture design of the VCTM multicast router [36]. Moreover, as a NoC packet contains only one flit, the store-and-forwarding flow control is used, which simplifies the channel management and does not impair the transfer latency. Accordingly, the wire link latency is set to 1 cycle and the maximum routing latency is 2 cycles.

We use the Orion 3.0 tool to get the energy consumption of each pipeline stage. For routing tables, the CACTI tool [40] is used. Now the NoC simulator supports the 2D-mesh topology with different scales and the simulation speed can be configured.

3.3   Preliminary Tests

Owing the framework, we can map representative SNNs onto our NoC simulator and drive it with traces from SNN simulators. Specially, we use the strategy of SpiNNaker as the reference because it presented enough details. Currently SpiNNaker just uses a sequential mapping scheme: Neurons are numbered so that IDs of all neurons in one population are continuous. Then, they are uniformly distributed to NoC nodes in order. Thus, neurons in one population will be distributed into one core or nearby cores.

The NoC working frequency is set to 1 GHz while the SNN's is 1 kHz. The number of neurons that one processing node can occupy is set to 64, 128 and 256 respectively.

We study the effect of simulation speed on transmission delay. The distribution of transmission delays under different speeds has been presented. Without loss of generality, QAWC SNN is taken as the example (in Fig. 2) to show the cumulative distribution curve of spike-transmission delay. The y-axis stands for transmission delays and the x is the ratio of the spikes whose delays are less than the calibration value.

From Fig. 2(a), we can see that as the speed is relatively slow (600 times or less), the cumulative distributions are almost the same (in Fig. 2(a) all curves are overlapped with each other): The maximum transmission delay is 1660 NoC cycles while one simulated SNN contains 1667 NoC or more cycles, which means that all spikes can reach target nodes in one SNN cycle. Conversely, if not all spikes issued in one SNN cycle can reach their targets in the same cycle, the maximum transmission delay of spikes will be steeply raised: Fig. 2(b) shows that as the speed is 700 times or more, transmission delays of more than 3% of all spikes will reach 10^5 NoC cycles, far larger than several simulated SNN cycles. The reason lies in that during a short period, the number of issued spike from a population will remain relatively constant. Thus, when the previous case occurs, more and more delayed spikes will be accumulated to exacerbate the symptom.

More analyses can prove this situation: For the packets with long latencies, the ratio of the latency caused by channel-congestion to the total is over 90%. Thus, the effect of congestion on transmission will become vital as the speed is higher.

So far one preliminary conclusion can be drawn: the transmission of any spike should be completed in one SNN cycle to meet the timing constraint, regardless of its nominal delay-attribute that is usually one or several SNN cycles. The inference lies in that the decrease of the maximum transmission delay can improve simulation speed, which is one main target of optimized mapping.

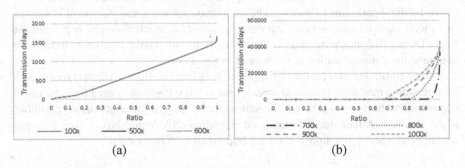

(a)   (b)

Fig. 2. Distribution of transmission delays under different speeds

4   Algorithm Design and Evaluations

Based on the aforementioned work, SNN mapping can be formulated under the application-mapping framework for NoCs.

Definition 1: Given an application characteristic graph, $G(V, E)$, it is a directed weighted graph in which $v_i \in V$ represents a task in the application; $e_{i,j} \in E$ represents the connection between v_i and v_j while $b_{i,j}$ is the traffic between v_i and v_j. From the SNN aspect, because we can get the activity degree of each population (as described in Sect. 3.1) that has shown similarity under different inputs, $b_{i,j}$ can be set to the degree of v_i.

Definition 2: Given a NoC topology graph, $P(R, P)$. $r_i \in R$ is a processing node of the NoC; $p_{i,j} \in P$ represents a link between r_i and r_j and $h_{i,j}$ is the Manhattan distance from r_i to r_j.

Accordingly, the mapping framework can be formulated as follows: Input $G(V, E)$ and $P(R, P)$ and output a mapping solution to distribute $G(V, E)$ onto $P(R, P)$, which will be evaluated based on the maximum transmission delay.

4.1   Strategy One

We propose a mapping algorithm that tends to put densely-communicating populations close together, and formulate it under the above-mentioned mapping framework.

Allocating highly-communicating populations onto nearby cores also accords with the principle of existing NoC mapping strategies [22–24] that map highly communicating tasks together. In addition, TrueNorth has formulated the problem of mapping neurons to cores as a wire-length minimization problem in VLSI placement [11], whose principle is similar with ours. Therefore, we outline this strategy here.

Without loss of generality, we use the Kernighan-Lin (KL) partitioning strategy[1] as the starting point. It bipartitions a set of modules, so that highly connected modules are kept in one partition. This procedure is applied (recursively and alternately along the two directions of 2D-mesh NoC, 'x' and 'y') till only the closest two nodes are left in any of the final partitions in a mesh. The motivation for using this algorithm is that the cores with more communication requirement should be attached nearby routers in the NoC. During the mapping phase, these partitions are taken into consideration to minimize the communication cost between mapped cores.

As the result depends on the initial partitioning, we run it for T (preset) times, each starting with a randomly generated initial partition. The best one is used for subsequent improvement; here the *best* means the sum of traffic ($b_{i,j}$) of the edges across partitions is the smallest. Afterward, the simulated annealing (SA) algorithm is used for optimization; its energy function is the total hop count of transmission.

---

[1] https://en.wikipedia.org/wiki/Kernighan%E2%80%93Lin_algorithm.

The whole workflow is given below:

Step 1: To draw the connection matrix of a SNN (we can get them from models on a SNN simulator, as mentioned in Sect. 3.1).

Step 2: To distribute neuron-populations to cores. It distributes all neurons in a population to a core as much as possible, or to nearby cores if one cannot occupy all.

Step 3: Placement of cores based on the previous algorithms.

Step 4: Based on Step 2 & 3, all table entries of each router can be filled: a multicast packet will follow the X-Y routing to complete common path before branch.

4.2 NoC Congestion

Now we carry out the evaluation of the first mapping strategy through our simulator. The simulation configuration is just the same as those of Sect. 3.3.

Results that for most models, the KL&SA algorithm improve the simulation speed. In other words, it can often decrease the maximum transmission delay because it tends to reduce the communication cost between mapped cores; results are presented in Table 2. The interesting point lies in that for Diff and Spat, the delay increases.

Detailed analyses show that as the KL&SA algorithm may aggravate the traffic congestion and lead to performance degradation: the default mapping principle tends to put neurons from the same population together and such neurons usually share the same set of destinations. In each simulated SNN cycle, those cores that contain active populations may produce a lot of packets, which often share the same destinations and may be blocked in the channel between the core and router or in some local queues.

Table 2. Maximum transmission delays (the number of neurons in one node is 64)

SNN model	SpiNNaker's sequential mapping	KL&SA
arm	128	80
env	123	115
halflearn	121	85
quarterlearn	136	110
bg	406	291
path	663	627
digit	165	125
diff	994	1034
spat	2035	2358
question	2460	1969
qawc	1648	1606

For example, Fig. 3 gives the average spike-processing time of each route for the two SNNs. We can see that after KL&SA, the maximum processing time is longer and the average delay on each router is more unbalanced. In addition, according to

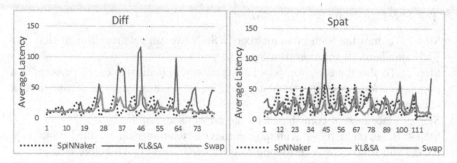

Fig. 3. Average transmission-delays of each router (the unit of the Y-axis is a NoC cycle; the X-axis is the router ID. Three strategies)

spike-traces, these two SNNs are the most active: their average active degrees per neuron are 398 and 57 respectively. In contrast, the maximum degree of others is only 16. Thus, it indicates that for communication-intensive SNNs, some local congestion has happened to impede the improvement of simulation. Therefore, we present a new mapping strategy in the next subsection.

4.3 Optimization in the Opposite Way

Under the existing application-mapping framework for NoCs, normally, any subtask is sequential and cannot be divided further. But SNN populations are different: they are divisible. Accordingly, we present a new strategy to reduce congestion. The principle is to swap neurons with each other in populations with different active degrees, to achieve a balanced distribution. As there is no connection among a single population, it will not introduce extra spikes.

However, the swap mechanism makes populations fragmented: neurons of a single population will be distributed into more cores, which causes more communications and longer paths (it is why we call it optimization in the opposite way). Thus, there is a tradeoff between the fragmentation and balance of active degrees: apparently, if the gap of two populations' degrees is limited, it is unnecessary to switch their neurons.

Accordingly, after the KL&SA mapping, we first sort all cores in a queue based on their active degrees. Second, the most active and most inactive cores will exchange half of neurons before removed from the queue, if the ratio of their degrees is larger than a threshold. This procedure will repeat till there is no exchange or all populations have been browsed. For the threshold, our test shows that 2 is a proper value. From the aspect of routing tables, the storage consumption is fixed, as we use the on-chip memory for storage and use population IDs as memory addresses.

After swap, the imbalance is weakened (in Fig. 3, too). Figure 4 gives the maximum delays under different mapping strategies: For cases of 64 neurons per node, the swap strategy decreases the maximum delay for 10 SNNs and 7 of them outperform the KL&SA; the latter decreases the maximum delay of 9 SNNs. For cases of 128, the three values are 11, 7 and 9 respectively. For cases of 256, they are 11, 8 and 11.

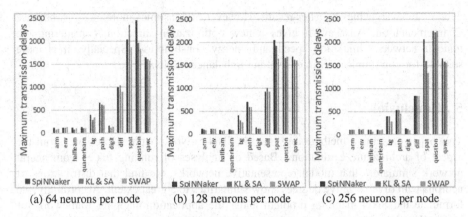

(a) 64 neurons per node   (b) 128 neurons per node   (c) 256 neurons per node

Fig. 4. Maximum delays of transmission

For KL&SA, the maximum improvement is 37% and the average improvement is 11%. For swap, the maximum is 36% and the average is 16%.

Statistics also show that compared with the sequential mapping, the KL&SA algorithm decreases the average transmission delay in all cases: For cases of 64 neurons per node, the average reduction is 4.3%; for 128 the reduction is 7.3%; for 256, it is 9.6%. For the swap strategy, because it makes populations fragmented, the average delay in cases of 128 increases a little, by 1.1%. In cases of 64 and 256, it decreases by 6.7% and 6.0% respectively.

Corresponding energy consumptions are presented in Fig. 5. The swap strategy causes more communications and more energy consumptions: compared with linear mapping, it increases the consumption by 1.7% averagely for cases of 64 neurons per node; for cases of 128, the average increase is 2.4%; for 256, the value is almost the same. KL&SA decreases the consumptions, by 14%, 16% and 14% respectively.

As a summary, two mapping optimizations are presented. The KL&SA tends to put highly communicating tasks close while the swap tries to achieve the balance in terms of populations' active degree. From the aspect of the simulation speed (the maximum

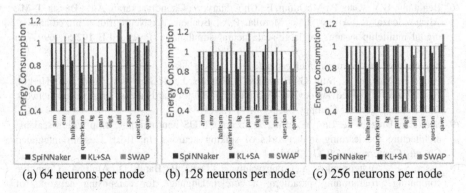

(a) 64 neurons per node   (b) 128 neurons per node   (c) 256 neurons per node

Fig. 5. Energy consumptions of a simulated second

delay), the swap achieves better results. However, it consumes more energies because of fragmentation. Anyway, it gives a new optimization direction, considering the tradeoff between simulation speed and energy consumption. Specially, it is more suitable for communication-intensive and unbalanced SNNs.

5 Conclusion

This paper presents a methodology for the SNN-to-NoC mapping problem, from the aspect of architecture evaluations. Based on analyses of running traces from neural network simulators that model representative networks, we find that distributions of neurons with diverse active degrees show similarities to a great extent. Accordingly, we formulate the SNN mapping problem under the application-mapping framework for NoCs. We also present strategies that are optimized in the opposite directions, which extend the existing mapping framework.

We believe it not only benefits the exploration of design space but also bridges the gap between applications and neuromorphic hardware.

References

1. National Academy of Engineering: Reverse-Engineer the Brain (2012). http://www.engineeringchallenges.org/cms/8996/9109.aspx
2. Jin, X.: Parallel simulation of neural networks on spinnaker universal neuromorphic hardware. Ph.D. thesis, University of Manchester (2010)
3. Paugam-Moisy, H., Bohte, S.: Computing with spiking neuron networks. In: Rozenberg, G., Bäck, T., Kok, J.N. (eds.) Handbook of Natural Computing, pp. 335–376. Springer, Heidelberg (2012)
4. Merolla, P.A., Arthur, J.V., Alvarez-Icaza, R., et al.: A million spiking-neuron integrated circuit with a scalable communication network and interface. Science 345(6197), 668–673 (2014)
5. Furber, S.B., Lester, D.R., Plana, L.A., Garside, J.D., Painkras, E., Temple, S., Brown, A.D.: Overview of the SpiNNaker system architecture. IEEE Trans. Comput. 62(12), 2454–2467 (2013)
6. Benjamin, B.V., Gao, P., McQuinn, E., Choudhary, S., Chandrasekaran, A.R., Bussat, J.-M., Alvarez-Icaza, R., Arthur, J.V., Merolla, P.A., Boahen, K.: Neurogrid: a mixed-analog-digital multichip system for large-scale neural simulations. Proc. IEEE 102(5), 699–716 (2014)
7. http://brainscales.kip.uni-heidelberg.de/
8. Pande, S., Morgan, F., Smit, G., Bruintjes, T., Rutgers, J., McGinley, B., Cawley, S., Harkin, J., McDaid, L.: Fixed latency on-chip interconnect for hardware spiking neural network architectures. Parallel Comput. 39, 357–371 (2013)
9. Seo, J.S., Brezzo, B., Liu, Y., et al.: A 45 nm CMOS neuromorphic chip with a scalable architecture for learning in networks of spiking neurons. In: IEEE Custom Integrated Circuits Conference (CICC) (2011)
10. Esser, S.K., Andreopoulos, A., Appuswamy, R., Datta, P., Barch, D., Amir, A.: Cognitive computing programming paradigm: a corelet language for composing networks of neurosynaptic cores. In: The International Joint Conference on Neural Networks (2013)

11. Akopyan, F., Sawada, J., Cassidy, A., et al.: TrueNorth design and tool flow of a 65 mW 1 million neuron programmable neurosynaptic chip. IEEE Trans. Comput. Aided Des. Integr. Circ. Syst. **34**(10), 1537–1557 (2015)
12. Gao, P., Benjamin, B.V., Boahen, K.: Dynamical system guided mapping of quantitative neuronal models onto neuromorphic hardware. IEEE Trans. Circ. Syst. **59**(11), 2383–2394 (2011)
13. Eliasmith, C., Anderson, C.H.: Neural Engineering: Computation, Representation, and Dynamics in Neurobiological Systems. A Bradford Book, Cambridge (2004)
14. Davies, S., Navaridas, J., Galluppi, F., Furber, S.: Population-based routing in the SpiNNaker neuromorphic architecture. In: International Joint Conference on Neural Networks (IJCNN 2012), Brisbane, Australia, 10–15 June 2012
15. Carrillo, S., Harkin, J., McDaid, L.J., Morgan, F., Pande, S., Cawley, S., McGinley, B.: Scalable hierarchical network-on-chip architecture for spiking neural network hardware implementations. IEEE Trans. Parallel Distrib. Syst. **24**(12), 2451–2461 (2013)
16. Rodopoulos, D., Chatzikonstantis, G., Pantelopoulos, A., Soudris, D., De Zeeuw, C.I., Strydis, C.: Optimal mapping of inferior olive neuron simulations on the single-chip cloud computer. In: 2014 International Conference on Embedded Computer Systems: Architectures, Modeling, and Simulation (2014)
17. Prezioso, M., Merrikh-Bayat, F., Hoskins, B.D., Adam, G.C., Likharev, K.K., Strukov, D.B.: Training and operation of an integrated neuromorphic network based on metal-oxide memristors. Nature **521**, 61–64 (2015)
18. Wendt, K., Ehrlich, M., Schüffny, R.: A graph theoretical approach for a multistep mapping software for the FACETS project. In: 2nd WSEAS International Conference on Computer Engineering and Applications (CEA 2008) (2008)
19. Pandea, S., Morgan, F., Smitb, G., Bruintjesb, T., Rutgersb, J., McGinleya, B., Cawleya, S., Harkin, J., McDaid, L.: Fixed latency on-chip interconnect for hardware spiking neural network architectures. Parallel Comput. J. (Elsevier) **39**, 357–371 (2013)
20. Philipp, S., Grübl, A., Meier, K., Schemmel, J.: Interconnecting VLSI spiking neural networks using isochronous connections. In: Sandoval, F., Prieto, A., Cabestany, J., Graña, M. (eds.) IWANN 2007. LNCS, vol. 4507, pp. 471–478. Springer, Heidelberg (2007). doi:10.1007/978-3-540-73007-1_58
21. Vainbrand, D., Ginosar, R.: Scalable network-on-chip architecture for configurable neural networks. Microprocess. Microsyst. **35**, 152–166 (2011)
22. Zhu, D., Chen, L., Yue, S., Pedram, M.: Application mapping for express channel-based networks-on-chip. In: Proceedings of Design, Automation and Test in Europe, DATE (2014)
23. Sahu, P.K., Manna, N.S., Chattopadhyay, S.: Extending Kernighan-Lin partitioning heuristic for application mapping onto Network-on-Chip. J. Syst. Archit. **60**(7), 562–578 (2014)
24. Nisarg, S., Kanchan, M., Santanu, C.: An application mapping technique for butterfly-fat-tree network-on-chip. In: Proceedings of 2nd International Conference on Emerging Applications of Information Technology, EAIT, pp. 383–386 (2011)
25. Tosun, S.: Cluster-based application mapping method for Network-on-Chip. Adv. Eng. Softw. **42**(10), 868–874 (2011)
26. Brette, R., Rudolph, M., Carnevale, T., et al.: Simulation of networks of spiking neurons: a review of tools and strategies. J. Comput. Neurosci. **23**(3), 349–398 (2007)
27. Plesser, H.E., Eppler, J.M., Morrison, A., Diesmann, M., Gewaltig, M.-O.: Efficient parallel simulation of large-scale neuronal networks on clusters of multiprocessor computers. In: Kermarrec, A.-M., Bougé, L., Priol, T. (eds.) Euro-Par 2007. LNCS, vol. 4641, pp. 672–681. Springer, Heidelberg (2007). doi:10.1007/978-3-540-74466-5_71
28. The Nengo Neural Simulator. http://www.nengo.ca/

29. Alexander, G.E., Crutcher, M.D.: Functional architecture of basal ganglia circuits: neural substrates of parallel processing. Trends Neurosci. **13**(7), 266–271 (1990)
30. Redgrave, P., Prescott, T.J., Gurney, K.: The basal ganglia: a vertebrate solution to the selection problem? Neuroscience **89**(4), 1009–1023 (1999)
31. Stewart, T.C., Bekolay, T., Eliasmith, C.: Learning to select actions with spiking neurons in the basal ganglia. Front. Neurosci. **6**, 2 (2012)
32. Tripp, B.P., Eliasmith, C.: Population models of temporal differentiation. Neural Comput. **22**(3), 621–659 (2010)
33. Conklin, J., Eliasmith, C.: A controlled attractor network model of path integration in the rat. J. Comput. Neurosci. **18**, 183–203 (2005)
34. Mattson, T.G., Van der Wijngaart, R.F., Lehnig, T., Brett, P., Haas, W., Kennedy, P.: The 48-core SCC processor: the programmer's view. In: Proceedings of 2010 International Conference for High Performance Computing, Networking, Storage and Analysis. New Orleans, LA (2010)
35. Wentzlaff, D., Griffin, P., Hoffmann, H., Bao, L., Edwards, B., Ramey, C., Mattina, M., Miao, C.-C., Brown III, J.F., Agarwal, A.: On-chip interconnection architecture of the tile processor. IEEE Comput. Soc. **27**, 15–31 (2007)
36. Jerger, N.E., Peh, L.-S., Lipasti, M.: Virtual circuit tree multicasting: a case for on-chip hardware multicast support. In: ISCA (2008)
37. Fidalgo, P.A., Puente, V., Gregorio, J.A.: MRR: enabling fully adaptive multicast routing for CMP interconnection networks. In: HPCA (2009)
38. Rodrigo, S., Flich, J., Duato, J., Hummel, M.: Efficient unicast and multicast support for CMPs. In: MICRO, pp. 364–375 (2008)
39. Noxim - the NoC Simulator. http://noxim.sourceforge.net/
40. CACTI - An integrated cache and memory access time, cycle time, area, leakage, and dynamic power model. http://www.hpl.hp.com/research/cacti/

Software Systems and Programming

A Portable Lock-Free Bounded Queue

Peter Pirkelbauer[1(✉)], Reed Milewicz[1], and Juan Felipe Gonzalez[2]

[1] University of Alabama at Birmingham, Birmingham, AL 35294, USA
{pirkelbauer,rmmilewi}@uab.edu
[2] Motorola Solutions, Birmingham, AL 35243, USA
juanfelipe.gonzalez-gomez@motorolasolutions.com

Abstract. Attaining efficient and portable lock-free containers is challenging as almost any CPU family implements slightly different memory models and atomic read-modify-write operations. C++11 offers a memory model and operation abstractions that enable portable implementations of non-blocking algorithms. In this paper, we present a first scalable and portable lock-free bounded queue supporting multiple readers and multiple writers. Our design uses unique empty values to decouple writing an element from incrementing the tail during enqueue. Dequeue employs a helping scheme that delays helping in the regular case, thereby reducing contention on shared memory. We evaluate our implementation on architectures featuring weak and strong memory consistency models. Our comparison with known blocking and lock-free designs shows that the presented implementation scales well on architectures that implement a weak memory consistency model.

1 Introduction

FIFO queues are a fundamental data structure for many software systems. Due to their importance in multi-core computing, bounded and unbounded lock-free queues have been extensively studied [3,9,12–14,27,29,31]. Unbounded queues use dynamic memory management to store an arbitrary number of elements. Bounded queues are often implemented as circular buffers with a maximum storage capacity. Circular buffers do not require dynamic memory management and are well suited for embedded devices, real-time systems, operating systems, and environments demanding low space and performance overhead.

Developing portable nonblocking data-structures is difficult, because the available read-modify-write operations and implemented memory models differ substantially across architectures. For example, the x86 processor family features a fairly strict memory model that only allows the reorderings of loads before independent store operations [17]. A read-modify-write operation with infinite consensus number [9] on the x86 are the atomic compare-and-swap (CAS) instructions. CAS takes an address, an old value, and a new value. If the address

P. Pirkelbauer—This work was partially funded by a Google Research Award, and by NSF grants CNS-0821497 and CNS-1229282. We thank the anonymous reviewers for their suggestions for improvements.

J. Carretero et al. (Eds.): ICA3PP 2016, LNCS 10048, pp. 55–73, 2016.
DOI: 10.1007/978-3-319-49583-5_4

contains the old value, the content is updated to the new value. CAS returns the content stored at the address. Modern x86 CPUs offer single-word and double-word CAS instructions. ARM and PowerPC implement a weak memory model that allow reorderings of non-dependent reads and writes. A read-modify-write operation with infinite consensus number on ARM and PowerPC is the instruction pair Load-linked/Store-conditional (LL/SC). LL reads a value from a memory location. SC writes a value to the same location under the condition that no one has modified that location meanwhile. Many hardware implementations of LL/SC can spuriously fail under certain conditions.

The 2011 revision of the ISO C++ programming language, C++11 [11,30], specifies a concurrent memory model. The memory model defines the behavior for data-race-free-0 (DRF0) programs [2]. Critical sections can be synchronized using mutual exclusion locks. The standard lock's semantics guarantees that any update to shared memory inside the critical section is visible to subsequent threads acquiring the same lock. Portable lock-free programming is supported by atomic types. They offer a unified interface to a system's read-modify-write operations and fine-grain control over when memory updates become visible to other threads. This paper presents a lock-free circular queue based on C++11's atomics. The choice of C++11 trades better portability for some performance (i.e., when an architecture makes stronger guarantees than C++11). Our implementation relies on unbounded counters, which are available for all practical purposes on any 64bit and many 32bit systems (double word atomic operations). A single enqueue operation relies on two acquire/release operations, a single dequeue operation uses two sequentially consistent operations and two acquire/release operations. An evaluation on three different architecture families (x86, Power8, and ARMv8) demonstrates the portability and scalability of our queue.

The contributions of these paper are: (1) a portable lock-free bounded queue using the relaxed memory model; (2) performance analysis of available bounded queues on a variety of architectures; (3) a descriptor that uses a short common path; (4) an ABA-free solution that does not require free-store management.

The paper is organized as follows: Sect. 2 offers background on lock-free programming and describes the C++11 concurrent memory model based on known lock-based bounded queue implementations. Section 3 discusses our implementation. Section 4 evaluates our approach in terms of correctness and performance. Section 5 presents related work and Sect. 6 provides a summary and outlook on future work.

2   Background

Many multi-threaded systems rely on mutual exclusion locks (mutex) to protect critical sections and shared resources. Deadlock, livelock, priority inversion, and termination safety pose serious challenges to the design, implementation, and lifetime of such systems [9].

Lock-Freedom, Linearizability, and History: Lock-free algorithms avoid those problems by not using locks. Instead they rely on a set of atomic read-modify-write operations such as CAS and LL/SC. Lock-free systems guarantee that one out of many contending threads will make progress in a finite number of steps. The principle correctness condition of nonblocking systems in a sequentially consistent memory model is linearizability [10]. An operation of a concurrent object is linearizable if it appears to execute instantaneously in some moment of time between the time point of its invocation and the time point of its response. This definition implies that for any concurrent execution there must exist an equivalent sequential execution of the same operations. The ordering of operations in the sequential history has to be consistent with the real-time order of invocation and response in the concurrent execution history. For relaxed memory models, Batty et al. [1] propose the notion of a *history* as a semantic correctness condition. A history records operations, call and return events from multiple partial orderings, and their interactions as defined by the memory model. An abstract data structure is stated in terms of a history. A data structure implements the abstraction if it can produce the same history.

The *ABA problem* [18] is fundamental to many lock-free algorithms and occurs when a thread T reads value a from a memory location m. Other threads set m to b and then back to a. Thread T is unaware of the intermediate change and its CAS operation to replace a with a value v will spuriously succeed.

C++11 Memory Model: C++11 distinguishes between data operations and synchronization operations. Memory locations subject to data races have to be of atomic type. A data race is defined as two or more concurrent memory accesses to the same memory location, where at least one of them is a write [25]. Atomic operations include load, store, and read-modify-write operations.

Programmers can exercise fine-grain control over memory ordering by tagging atomic operations Table 1. The default semantics on atomic memory operations is sequential consistency, `memory_order_seq_cst`, which establishes a total order among all sequential consistent atomic operations. Compiler and hardware are not allowed to perform any intra-thread reordering on sequentially consistent operations. All non-atomic operations are partially ordered with respect to the sequentially consistent atomic operations on the same thread. Maintaining sequentially consistency is expensive on many modern architectures. The tags `memory_order_release` and `memory_order_acquire` form pairs that establish a *synchronizes-with* relationship between a thread A that stores a value v to an atomic memory location l and a thread B that loads that value v from l. Release/acquire guarantee that any operation in thread A that happens before storing v to l can be observed in B after it has loaded v from l. The memory model allows reorderings with subsequent operations on the storing thread and preceding operations on the loading thread as long as the intra-thread dependencies allow the reordering. The C++11 locks use release and acquire semantics for `lock` and `unlock` operations [2]. On the PowerPC acquire/release can be implemented by a light-weight barrier [24]. Release/consume (`memory_order_consume`) consistency is similar to release/acquire except that it restricts memory

```
1   struct CircularBuffer {          bool enq(int elem) {      1   pair<int, bool> deq() {
        bool enq(int elem);      2     if (tail == head+N)             if (tail == head)
3       pair<int, bool> deq();             return false;      3         return make_pair(−1, false);
                                 4     buf[tail%N] = elem;           int res = buf[head%N];
5       size_t tail;                   ++tail;               5       ++head;
        size_t head;             6     return true;                  return make_pair(res, true);
7       int buf[N];                  }                       7   }
    };
```

Fig. 1. Sequential bounded queue

ordering to data dependent loads in a consuming thread. The consume tag does not require synchronization instructions on most architectures [17]. Relaxed consistency, memory_order_relaxed, does not guarantee any memory ordering and does not establish a synchronizes-with relationship. Memory operations can also be ordered by using atomic thread fences that can be tagged similarly.

Loads and stores tagged with relaxed or release/acquire may not become visible to all threads at the same time [33]. Consider two producers, A and B, that write to variables a and b respectively. A consumer Y could see the store to a but not b, while another consumer Z could see the store to b but not a. The ISO C++11 standard stipulates that an implementation must make an atomic store available to other threads in a finite amount of time and that all threads agree on a modification order of a memory location.

CAS and LL/SC are supported through compare_exchange_strong (CAS_S) and compare_exchange_weak (CAS_W). The two operations take a reference to an old value (old), a new value (val), and two memory ordering tags for success and failure respectively. If the atomic object equals the old-value, CAS sets it val and returns true. Otherwise the functions return false, and there semantics decay to a correspondingly tagged load operation that stores the value in old.

Descriptions of the C++11 memory model and more subtle details are described by the C++11 standard [11], Boehm and Adve [2], and Williams [33].

Circular Buffer and the C++11 Memory Model: The bounded queue in Fig. 1 stores integer values in an array buf. The maximum capacity of the data structure is given by the constant N. enq adds an element to the tail; deq reads an element from the head's position. Both operations enq and deq are nonblocking, as they return an error code when their preconditions not-full and not-empty are not met. The diagram in Fig. 2a sketches the data structure and shows a bounded queue of size 16 containing one element. The queue is empty when head equals tail and full when head+N equals tail. This implementation uses unbounded counters for head and tail, which are practically available on any 64bit architecture or any 32bit architecture supporting double-wide CAS.

A concurrent implementation can be derived by adding a mutex per bounded queue object. The use of a single lock for all operations avoids data races on shared data members (i.e., head, tail, buf) by serializing accesses. Although C++11 mutexes uses acquire/release semantics, the use of a single lock makes the queue quasi sequentially consistent.

Table 1. Memory order tags in C++11

Memory order	Relationship among/between operations
seq_cst	Atomic operations are totally ordered non-atomic operations are partially ordered with respect to sequentially consistent atomic operations on the same thread
Release/acquire	Form a pair on the stored/loaded value. This guarantees that the reading thread sees all memory updates in the storing thread that occurred before the store tagged with release
Release/consume	Form a pair on the stored/loaded value. This guarantees that the reading thread sees all memory updates in the storing thread that occurred before the store and where there is a dependency relationship to the loaded value
Relaxed	No synchronization relationship

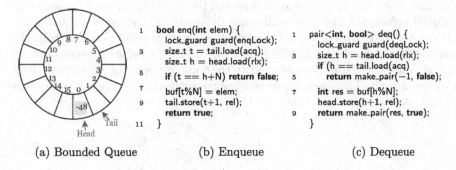

(a) Bounded Queue   (b) Enqueue   (c) Dequeue

Fig. 2. Concurrent bounded queue

To attain a higher degree of concurrency, the queue can be modified to support a single concurrent enqueuer and a single concurrent dequeuer. The key idea is that buf and tail are updated only in enq, and head in deq. enq stores the element before it increments the tail, thereby making the buffer element available to a concurrent deq operation. Likewise deq copies the buffer element to a local variable, before it makes the empty memory location available to a concurrent enq by incrementing the head. Figure 2b and c illustrate the additional changes for a two-lock implementation under the C++11 memory model. Both operations enq and deq use separate locks named enqLock and deqLock respectively. The locks order the execution of two enqueues and two dequeues, but there is no ordering between enqueue and dequeue. Consequently, head and tail have to be atomic. When enq updates tail in Line 9 to x, the use of release semantics makes all buffer stores up to location $x - 1$ observable to other threads that read x from tail. Note that deq's store operation incrementing head uses release semantics (Line 9) though there is no load of head tagged acquire. Release is necessary to prevent reordering with loading the value from the buffer (Line 8). buf is not atomic, because there exists no data race on buffer elements. Since enq and deq use two distinct locks, there is no more implicit order relationship between these operations. Hence, accessing `head` and `tail` may load "stale" values, where a dequeue (enqueue) could perceive the buffer to be spuriously empty (full).

3   Design and Implementation

The major challenges for the design of a lock-free bounded queue are: (1) an enqueue operation has to update the buffer location and the `tail` seemingly atomically. (2) Since the bounded queue's storage is reused, delayed threads are prone to the ABA problem. Software solutions exist in the form of multi compare and swap (MCAS) [5]. MCAS relies on a bit to distinguish a regular value from a descriptor identifier. In a first phase, MCAS replaces all affected memory locations with a descriptor identifier specifying old-values and new-values for all M memory locations. If this succeeds, MCAS exchanges the descriptor identifiers with the actual values in a second phase. If one memory location was updated before, the first phase fails, and the second phase restores the original values. Any interrupting thread that reads a descriptor identifier will help the original thread finish the MCAS (phase one and two) before it carries out its own operation. Helping threads execute the same sequence of operations along a common path. Thus, helping diminishes parallelism and increases contention on the same memory locations.

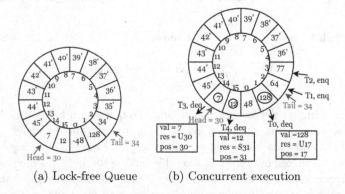

(a) Lock-free Queue   (b) Concurrent execution

Fig. 3. Lock-free bounded queue

3.1   Design

This section describes the high-level design of a lock-free bounded queue for integers. The bounded queue can be adapted for some type T, as long as atomic operations on T are available and we can distinguish a value of T from special entries, such as empty values and descriptors. The implementation on integers reserves a bit for marking special entries.

We address the identified problems the following way: In a first step, we decouple the two memory updates of the `enq` operation. This is achieved through storing unique empty values in empty queue locations [22,23]. Each empty value is a representation of the next `tail` position that will produce a successful enqueue operation. An empty value is marked using two bits (one to distinguish it from data and one to distinguish it from a dequeue descriptor.) An enqueue operation uses CAS_S to replace the expected empty value with the new value. This scheme prevents delayed threads from the ABA problem. A delayed enqueue can never succeed spuriously by overwriting a valid value or a later empty value because either the buffer location contains the expected empty value or other threads have enqueued (and possibly dequeued) at that location.

Figure 3a shows the class definition and Fig. 3b shows a graphical view of the data structure. The queue contains four elements stored between `tail` and `head`. The other entries are empty (indicated by the '). Each empty value represents the next `tail` position where an enqueue will be successful. A thread that attempts to enqueue a new value, reads the `tail` and attempts to store the new value there (using CAS_S). A thread that succeeded in storing the new element at position p will attempt to set the `tail` to the following position $p+1$ as long as `tail` contains a position that is less than $p+1$. If the CAS_S to store a new value is unsuccessful, another thread must have succeeded at that location. In this case, the enqueuing thread will retry at the next position $p+1$ as long as that position is less than `head` + *buffersize*.

The use of empty values shifts the burden of updating two memory locations atomically to dequeue. `deq` needs to update `head` and store the empty value associated with the next successful enqueue operation at that location. To this end, our dequeue operation utilizes descriptor identifiers. A descriptor identifier is marked using two bits (one to distinguish it from data and one to distinguish it from an empty value). A dequeue operation proceeds along the following steps:

1. Set up a descriptor and use CAS_S to store a descriptor identifier at the dequeue location. The descriptor contains information on the previous value, the position, and a result flag. The result flag stores three states (undecided, success, fail). If the CAS_S is successful, the dequeue operation is in progress and the descriptor can only be replaced by either a new empty value (success), or the previous value (failure).
2. Validate the operation by checking that the current `head` is at the location stored in the descriptor. This step updates the descriptor's flag.
3. If successful, move the `head` forward.
4. If successful, store the next empty value; otherwise restore the previous value.

The order of these steps prevents the ABA problem. At any given `head` location, a dequeue can only succeed once. In any successful dequeue, the descriptor is stored in the buffer when `head` < `loc` < `head` + N and it remains in the buffer until `head` has advanced beyond the descriptor position. Any validation of another dequeue at the same location will fail.

An Optimized Helping Scheme: If a thread gets delayed, other threads will read the descriptor identifier and help complete the delayed thread's operation to

```
// chkENTRY = 1, chkSTATE = 3           // dequeue descriptor
// stMAXBITS = 2, stVALID = 0           struct DeqDesc {
// stEMPTY = 1, stWIP = 3                 atomic<int> res;
// Circular Buffer                        atomic<int> pos;
struct CircularBuffer {                   atomic<int> val;
  bool enq(int elem);                   };
  pair<int, bool> deq();
                                        pair<int,bool> deq() {
  atomic<int> head;                       int descriptors[NUM_THREADS];
  atomic<int> tail;                       int threadid = this_thread_id();
  atomic<int> buf[N];                     int pos = head.load(rlx);
  DeqDesc ti[THREADS];
};                                        while (pos < tail.load(rlx)) {
// work in progress data                    atomic<int>& entry = buf[pos%N];
struct WipData { // local copy of descriptor   const int elem = entry.load(rlx);
  int desc; // identifier                   int pvel = elem;
  int res; // result flag
  int pos; // position                      if (is_val(elem)) {
  int val; // original entry                  const int descr = make_descr(pos, elem, threadid);
};                                            const bool succ = entry.CAS_S(pvel, descr, rel, rlx);

bool enq(int val) {                           if ( succ
  int pos = tail.load(rlx);                      && check_descr( descr, get_descriptor(threadid),
                                                     WipData(descr, descr, pos, elem), descriptors)))
  while (pos < head.load(acq) + N) {            return make_pair(elem, true);
    atomic<int>& entry = buf[pos%N];        }
    int elem = empty_val(pos);
                                            if (in_progress(pvel)) {
    if (entry.CAS_S(elem, val, rel, rlx)) {   atomic_thread_fence(cns);
      update_counter<rlx>(tail, pos+1);       if (eqpos_descr_counter(pvel, pos)) {
      return true;                              descriptors[pos % THRDS] = pvel;
    }                                           pos = pos + 1;
    atomic_thread_fence(cns);                 }
    if (is_val(elem))                         else if (this_was_delayed(pvel, pos))
      pos = pos+1;                              pos = head.load(rlx);
    else if (in_progress(elem)                else
             && !this_was_delayed(elem, pos))   check_descr(pvel);
      check_descr(elem);                    }
    else                                    else
      pos = tail.load(rlx);                   pos = head.load(rlx);
  }                                         }
  return false;                           return make_pair(-1, false);
}                                         }
```

Fig. 4. Lock-free bounded queue: enqueue and dequeue

guarantee progress. A straight-forward implementation of helping would lead to contention on the shared common path. We remedy this problem (a) by delaying helping until a thread has found a valid dequeue location and (b) by employing a helping scheme that minimizes the common path.

When a dequeuing thread t_0 reads another thread's descriptor whose location is the same as the thread's own dequeue position, then t_0 will attempt to dequeue from the next location (if elements are still available) before it helps the delayed thread. After a thread has successfully stored a descriptor it will validate all descriptors between the current head and the new head position. The validation step will *only* set the flag of each active descriptor. After these descriptors have been validated, the thread updates head and replaces its descriptor with the next empty value. This technique increases the chance that other threads finish their dequeue operation before they need help and reduces the contention on the buffer and head. Multiple dequeue operations can be in-flight concurrently.

A thread finding a descriptor that does not correspond to the expected head location helps the delayed thread finish all three steps (validation, head update, and descriptor replacement). This is needed in order to remove an invalid descriptor from the buffer and restore the existing value to be dequeued.

3.2   Implementation

In a lock-free bounded queue threads can concurrently attempt to read and write the head, tail, and the buffer elements (buf). All data members are modeled with atomic types. Each entry in the buf array is either a valid value (lowest bit is 0) or a special value (1). Special values can symbolize either an empty entry (lowest two bits 01) or a work descriptor (11) of an going dequeue operation.

Upon queue construction, each buffer element is initialized with a unique empty value. The empty values are a function of the tail position that will produce a successful enqueue operation at that location. Our implementation left-shifts the position by 2 and adds the tag for an empty value (Fig. 5 function empty_val). Unique empty values decouple the enqueue's write of the buffer element from advancing the tail. The empty values also help decide, when a enq operation is delayed and needs to resynchronize with tail. In addition, unique empty values prevent the ABA problem of delayed enqueue operations.

The Descriptor: deq employs a descriptor announcing the operations. Our implementation uses one reuseable descriptor for each thread and does not need lock-free memory reclamation. The descriptor consists of four entries desc, res, pos, and val store the original descriptor (used for validation), result of the head validation, the position, and the read value respectively.

Encoding of the Descriptor's Identifier: The task of the descriptor's identifier is to allow other threads find the descriptor. In addition, the identifier has to be sufficiently unique in order to guard against the ABA problem. Hence, we use an encoding similar to a technique described by Luchangco et al. [16]. In our implementation, the two lowest bits are reserved to encode the kind of entry (value, empty-value, or dequeue descriptor) and later the result of the started deq. The following n bits are reserved to encode the thread id. Our implementation uses eight bits for that. The remaining bits store the lowest bits of the corresponding buffer position. Assuming 256 threads, the descriptor prevents ABA if a helping thread is not delayed for more than 2^{54} and 2^{22} dequeue operations on 64bit and 32bit systems respectively. On 64bit systems, the number of supported threads can be easily increased without sacrificing ABA safety.

Validating the Descriptor: After the descriptor has been stored, thread will validate the descriptor. Descriptor validations query the current head. The dequeue is valid if the descriptor's position is equal or higher than head. Validation will update the descriptor's res field using a CAS_S with the result. The next step validates all other in-flight descriptors between head $\leq$ pos(desc$_{other}$) < pos(desc). In order to prevent an ABA problem introduced through reuse of descriptors, we encode the result field with the descriptor's position. The two lowest bits are reserved to store the result (undecided, success, fail), while the remaining

```
 1   template <memory_order mo>
 2   void update_counter(atomic<int>& ctr, int pos) {
       int curr = 0;
 3
 4     while ((curr < pos) && !ctr.CAS_S(curr, pos, mo, mo));
     }
 6
     int make_descr(int headpos, int entryval, int threadno) {
 8     DeqDesc& ti = get_descriptor(threadno);
       const int descr = encode_descr(headpos, threadno);
10     ti.res.store(descr, rlx);
12     ti.val.store(entryval, rlx);
       ti.pos.store(headpos, rlx);
14
16     return descr;
     }
18   void decide(DeqDesc& ti, WipData& wip, int descr) {
       if (ready(wip)) return;
20     int min = head.load(seq);
22     const int valid = (wip.pos >= min);
       const int result = (wip.desc & ~stWIP) | valid;
24     const bool succ = ti.res.CAS_S(wip.res, result, rlx, rlx);
26     if (succ) wip.res = result;
     }
28   bool check_descr(int descr) {
30     DeqDesc& ti = get_descriptor(descr);
32     return check_descr(descr, ti, load_threadinfo(ti, descr));
     }
34   bool check_descr(int descr, DeqDesc& ti,
36                    WipData wip, int* descriptors = nullptr) {
       if (inconsistent(wip)) return false;
38     decide(ti, wip, descr);
40     if (in_progress(wip)) return false;
42     return complete(descr, wip, descriptors);
     }
44   int validate_descr(int descr) {
46     return validate_descr(get_descriptor(descr), descr, true);
     }
48   bool in_progress(int v) {
50     return (v & chkSTATE) == stWIP;
     }

 1   void help_delayed(int pos, int* descriptors) {
       if (!descriptors) return;
 3     int p = pos - 1;
 5     int h = head.load(rlx);
 7     while (p >= h) {
         int entryval = descriptors[p % THRDS];
 9       validate_descr(entryval);
11       p = p - 1;
13       h = head.load(rlx);
       }
     }
15   int validate_descr(DeqDesc& ti, int descr, bool valid) {
17     const int result = (descr & ~stWIP) | valid;
19     const bool succ = ti.res.CAS_S(descr, result, rlx, rlx);
       return result;
     }
23   bool this_was_delayed(int descr, int thispos) {
       return thispos <= get_descriptor(descr).pos.load(rlx);
25   }
27   bool complete( int desc, const WipData& wip,
                    int* others) {
29     const bool succ = success(wip);
31     if (succ) {
         help_delayed(wip.pos, others);
33       update_counter<seq>(head, wip.pos+1);
       }
35     const int entryval =
37       (succ ? empty_val(wip.pos+1) : wip.val);
       atomic<int>& entry = buf[idx(wip.pos)];
39     entry.CAS_S(desc, entryval, rlx, rlx);
       return succ;
41   }
43   bool inconsistent(const WipData& wip) {
45     return ((wip.desc ^ wip.res) & ~stWIP) != 0
             || !eqpos_descr_counter(wip.res, wip.pos);
47   }
49   int empty_val(int pos) {
51     return ((pos << stMAXBITS) | stEMPTY);
     }
```

Fig. 5. Lock-free bounded queue: auxiliary functions

upper bits are tagged with the descriptors location. Any helping thread that gets delayed cannot erroneously update the res field, because any time the descriptor gets set up for a new location, the res tag changes. Consequently, any delayed thread that attempts to update that field will fail.

3.3 Detailed Description of Enqueue and Dequeue

The Enqueue Operation (Fig. 4): enq uses two loads to determine a range ($[tail, head + N)$) where new values could be stored. head is loaded using acquire (Line 26) which synchronizes with the sequentially consistent update of head in a dequeue operation. This guarantees that the oldest entry in a buffer that the CAS_S in Line 30 can see is a valid dequeue descriptor that was stored before head was advanced. The next step is to enqueue the new element by using CAS_S with an empty value ($tail+N'$) at the *first* available position. The CAS_S can be unsuccessful because the buffer may contain one of the following values:

- *a valid value*: in this case, the enqueue will be reattempted at the next buffer location. acquire on head's load guarantees that the enqueue cannot load a "stale" valid value that was stored at that location earlier. Only if loading head is delayed by more than $2N$ operations, enqueue could load a valid value. However, in this case either the enqueue fails earlier because the condition pos < head + N does not hold, or also tail's value is stale, in which case we could not enqueue at that location anyway. Thus, enqueue does not skip a valid location due to a "stale" value and stores the new element at the first available position.
- *descriptor*: in order to use a descriptor, we need to access its values. To this end, the thread fence consume is inserted before handling descriptors (Line 35). If the enqueuing operation was delayed, we load the new tail and reattempt the enqueue. Otherwise, the enqueue helps finish and remove the descriptor (Line 40) and retries at the same location.
- *an empty value*: in this case the empty value must be more recent than the enqueues expected empty value. Hence, we reload tail (Line 42) and retry the enqueue.

If no available buffer location was found, enqueue terminates. Otherwise, the tail location is advanced to one past the enqueued position.

The Dequeue Operation (Fig. 4) : deq declares a local circular buffer where it stores the descriptors of concurrent dequeue operations (Line 9). The local buffer avoids reading the buffer a second time during the helping phase of the descriptor validation. The thread_id of a thread is needed to encode the descriptor (Line 10). deq uses a local variable, pos, to iterate through the buffer elements until a valid element is found and a dequeue can be attempted. (while loop in Line 13). Lines 14–16 create an atomic reference of the buffer element and copy its current content into a mutable (pval - previous value) and non-mutable (elem) variable. The load is tagged with relaxed, because the content of the buffer will be confirmed through a successful CAS$_S$ operation later. If the loaded element is a dequeable value, deq sets up its own unique descriptor identifier and attempts to store it in the buffer (Lines 19, 20). If the CAS$_S$ fails, some other thread has modified the element at pos before (or another store to that location became visible). In this case CAS$_S$ falls back to a relaxed load. It can return one of the following values in pval:

- *descriptor identifier*: The atomic consume fence (Line 29) guarantees the memory ordering between reading the descriptor identifier and the descriptor data. If the descriptor indicates another dequeue at the same location, then deq stores the other descriptor identifier in its local buffer and attempts to dequeue from location pos+1. If the dequeue locations are different, then one of the two threads got delayed. If deq is delayed, it rereads head (Line 35), otherwise it helps the other thread finish the operation and remove the descriptor from the buffer (Line 39).
- *regular or empty value*: some other thread must have made progress at the same location and deq will resynchronize with head.

If the CAS$_S$ succeeds, deq invokes check_descr to complete the pending operation. If check_descr succeeds, deq returns the dequeued value (Line 25). The successful CAS$_S$ (Line 20) uses release to guarantee store ordering between the descriptor data and the buffer update.

Using Descriptors (Fig. 5 functions make_descr, check_descr, decide, complete): make_descr sets up a descriptor for the current dequeue operation and returns a unique identifier to the descriptor. The descriptor encodes the result field with the same unique identifier. Thus, the result field can be updated using CAS$_S$ to store whether the operation succeeded. This avoids the ABA problem when a helping thread gets delayed. The unique identifier encodes the current position and thread id. make_descr uses relaxed stores that will be *released* when the descriptor's identifier is stored to the buffer.

The check_descr functions' task is to validate the descriptor and complete the operation in progress. The unary version is called when a thread is helping another thread. In this case it decodes the descriptor's identifier to find a specific thread's descriptor (Line 30–32) and creates a local copy wip (work in progress). The main check_descr (Lines 37–42) makes sure that the local descriptor copy is consistent, calls decide to validate the dequeue at that location, and if successful calls complete to finish the operation.

inconsistent (Lines 42–45) validates that the loaded data is consistent. To this end, the descriptor identifier is compared with the identifier loaded from the descriptor, and the loaded position is compared with the encoded position in the identifier. If the thread that started the dequeue has already finished the operation associated with the loaded identifier and started another dequeue operation, this consistency check will fail and helping is no longer necessary.

decide validates the operation. It stores the outcome of the dequeue operation into the descriptor's res field and the local copy (wip). Line 19 returns immediately, if the outcome of the operation has already been decided. Line 20 loads the current head location. The read is sequentially consistent and synchronizes with the head update in complete. Using sequentially consistent memory ordering is necessary for two reasons: (1) storing the descriptor's identifier in the buffer and updating head are two independent operations that need to be ordered – we need to guarantee that the descriptor identifier was stored in the data structure before head was updated; (2) reads and writes to head need to be globally ordered; otherwise the read may return some "stale" value, which could lead to an erroneous validation. Lines 22 tests that head is smaller than the dequeue location. If head is larger some other thread has already dequeued an element from this position. This happens when some thread interleaves its deq between the time when deq read the head or when the dequeue's pos got out of sync with head. Line 30 attempts to store the result in the descriptor. If this fails, some other thread had modified the result in the meantime. If unsuccessful, wip.pos contains the result, otherwise we set it (Line 26).

complete finishes a started dequeue. If the operation is valid, complete helps other threads validate their descriptor and then advances head (Lines 30–32).

Updating head is a sequentially consistent operation that synchronizes with loading head's value in decide. Lines 35–38 either restore the old value, or store the next empty value corresponding to pos+N. If this operation fails, some other thread must have executed the same compare and exchange. Note it is also possible that a helping thread was delayed between check_descr's consistency check and the execution of decide's compare and exchange and therefore loaded a result corresponding to a later operation. In this case, executing complete will not modify the state of the bounded queue. The counter update will be unsuccessful, because some other thread must have succeeded on the current position and set head to a value greater than pos. Similar the compare and exchange in Line 46 will fail, because the descriptor's identifier must have been removed from the buffer before.

Example: Figure 3b shows the concurrent execution of five threads on the lock-free bounded queue. Two threads, T1 and T2, have successfully stored their values in the buffer. Since the tail is not yet updated, T2 must have attempted to store its value at location 35, but failed because T1 had succeeded before. T1 and T2 will attempt to set tail to 35 and 36 respectively. If T2 succeeds first, T1 will skip the tail update. Three threads (T0,T3,T4) are dequeuing. T0 was delayed between the time it read head and the time it placed the descriptor at location 17. Since head has been moved past 17, the validation against head will fail, and the original value (128) will be restored. T3 and T4 are dequeuing from a valid location. Since both threads are still active and tail has not been updated, T4 must have seen T3's descriptor at location 30 before placing its own descriptor at location 31. Then T4 will validate the descriptor against head. T4's res field is already set to success. Since T3's descriptor is undecided (res is U), T4 will help T3 validate its descriptor before updating head. After descriptor validation, T3 and T4 will attempt to update head, and then replace their descriptor identifier with the next unique empty values (46' and 47').

Local Descriptor Buffer: A dequeue uses a local circular queue to store descriptors that require validation. In our implementation, the local queues capacity equals the number of threads. Since a thread can have at most one valid descriptor in the queue, this size enables a deq to search for an element that can be dequeued without having to consider a full local queue. The local queue size could be reduced while retaining lock-free properties. In this case, a deq would need to help other threads when its local buffer becomes full, before it can continue searching for a valid queue element.

3.4 Alternative Implementations

We also experimented with other bounded queue designs. One of them is a *hybrid* implementation. They key observation for the hybrid design is that dequeue needs to update only head. This allows for a simple lock-free implementation displayed in Fig. 6. Reading tail uses acquire semantics in order to establish a happens before relationship with the previous store to tail. This guarantees that the buffer updates up to entry `tail-1` are visible. Line 5, stores the buffer entry in a local variable. If the CAS_S in Line 7 succeeds, this `deq` returns the dequeued element. Otherwise, dequeue is retried at the most recent `head` position. The implementation of enqueue continues using a lock and is the same as in Fig. 2b. Note, since there can be a data race between delayed dequeuing threads and an enqueue operation, the buffer elements have to be of atomic type.

4   Evaluation

This section discusses correctness tests, model checking, and performance evaluation of the circular queue implementation.

```
1   pair<int, bool> deq() {
        int pos = head.load(relaxed);
3       while (pos < tail.load(acq)) {
            int res = buf[idx(pos)].val.load(relaxed);
5           if (head.CAS_S(pos, pos+1, rel, rlx))
                return make_pair(res, true);
7       }
        return make_pair(-1, false);
9   }
```

Fig. 6. Lock-free dequeue in a hybrid implementation

Table 2. Description of test systems

System	Sockets	Cores/ socket	Threads/core	Total HW threads	Frequency (Ghz)	OS	Compiler
IBM power 8	2	10	8	160	3.4	Linux 3.10	xlc 13.1.3
Intel E5-2660	2	10	1 (HT disabled)	20	2.6	Linux 3.18	icc 15.0.3
AMD Opt. 6128	1	8	1	8	2	Linux 3.2	gcc 4.9
Snapdragon 410	1	4	1	4	1.2	Android 5.1 (32 bit)	clang 3.8

Correctness Tests: We performed multiple correctness tests on systems exhibiting weak and strong memory models and on single and dual socket configurations. We tested various load scenarios and used different buffer sizes (starting from a size of 2). We tested both with the same value across all enqueues (potentially prone to ABA) and with unique values for all enqueue operations. After reaching a quiescent state, we compared the history of each thread with the state of the queue to verify that the number of successful enqueues and dequeues agrees with the initial buffer size and state of the queue.

Model Checking: To test the validity of our implementation, we used Norris and Demsky's stateless model checker, CDSChecker [21]. CDSChecker provides its own implementation for atomics and threading. The CDSChecker exhaustively searches all possible interleavings and memory operation results (in particular for the relaxed memory model). The CDSChecker records an execution scenario

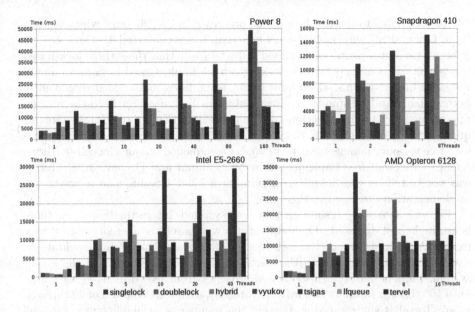

Fig. 7. Time of 40M successful operations on queues with a capacity of 1024 elements.

and prints an execution trace if a violation was detected. CDSChecker can report the presence or absence of data races, deadlocks, uninitialized atomic loads, and user-provided assertion failures. We modified our implementation slightly to make it compliant with the CDS framework. The most significant change was the replacement of `consume` with `acquire` tags, since CDS Checker does not yet support `consume` semantics. We devised scenarios where threads played the roles of enqueuers and/or dequeuers and attempted to modify the bounded queue concurrently. At the end of operations, we validated the state of the queue, and that the elements remaining in the data structure were consistent with the number of successful operations. An exhaustive examination of all combinations of two operations in two threads and some three thread cases revealed no bug.

Performance Evaluation: We used strong scaling to test the performance of each implementation. For each implementation, we varied the number of threads to complete a fixed 40 million operations and a buffer size of 1024 which was initialized with 512 elements. After spawning the threads waited until all were ready to operate on the queue. Each thread alternated enqueue and dequeue operations. Thus, in a sequentially consistent implementation any operation must succeed. In relaxed implementations a failed operation was not counted and immediately retried. We ran the results twelve times, removed one outlier on each end, and report the average of ten runs. Performance experiments were conducted on four systems described in Table 2. We tested seven different algorithms. Singlelock uses a single lock to synchronize access to the data structure. Since only a single lock is used, the result is a sequentially consistent implementation.

Doublelock refers to the two-lock queue presented in Fig. 2b and c which is similar to Linux SPSC implementation, where each role is protected by a lock; hybrid refers to the implementation outlined in Fig. 6 (note that these three lock-based implementations use a pthread mutex, which are implemented in terms of an OS Futex on Linux systems [4]. In most of our tests, futex locks scaled significantly better than standard spin-lock implementations.); Vyukov refers to the relaxed fine-grained lock implementation [32]; Zhang refers to Zhang and Tsigas' circular queue implementation (Note, to avoid the ABA problem and interference from a lock-free memory management technique, we enqueued unique elements); Tervel refers to the wait-free implementation by Feldman and Dechev [3, 28]. Tervel was not tested on the Snapdragon running a 32bit OS. Lfqueue refers to the implementation discussed in this paper.

Figure 7 shows the results on four test systems. Interestingly enough there is no single best approach. On architectures with a relaxed memory consistency model (ARM and Power), the lock-free and fine-grain locking implementations scale significantly better than the coarse-grain locking methods. On the Power system, Lfqueue outperforms other approaches from five threads ($\frac{1}{4}$ of cores) until 160 threads (number of hardware threads), with the exception of 40 threads, where Tervel is slightly faster. Beyond the number of available cores, Lfqueue and Tervel show significant better scalability than other approaches. On the ARM, the lock-free and fine-grain methods scale better than coarse-grain locking implementations. On x86 systems, the coarse-grain lock implementations scale slightly better than the Lfqueue, which in turn scales better than other lock-free and fine-grain locking approaches.

5   Related Work

The first non-blocking queue for a single enqueuer and single dequeuer was given by Lamport [14]. Other bounded queues also limit the number of concurrent enqueuers or dequeuers [7, 8, 15]. Stone [29] presents a lock-free bounded queue for multiple enqueuers and dequeuers using DCAS. DCAS atomically updates two independent memory location and is only available on older Motorola architectures. Shann et al. [27] present a lock-free bounded queue that relies on a double-word wide compare-and-swap (CAS2) instruction to prevent ABA problems. Tsigas and Zhang [31] present a scalable bounded queue that only uses single-wide compare-and-swap. Their implementation updates `head` and `tail` in steps of m, thereby reducing the contention on shared variables. To distinguish empty from full buffer entries, dequeue replaces a valid buffer element with a `null` value. In order to reduce the likelihood of ABA, their implementation reserves a bit of each buffer element, which is flipped after each enqueue/dequeue pair. This changes the ABA into an $AB\overline{AB}A$ problem. To avoid ABA on stored elements, their buffer utilizes pointers to objects and dynamic memory management. Shafiei [26] presents a lock-free bounded queue that use collect objects to represent `head` and `tail`. The implementation compresses a 32bit value, index, old and new counters into a 64bit field. Shafiei's queue can store up to 2^{14} elements. A wait-free technique is given by Feldman and Dechev [3]. The wait-free construction requires dynamic memory management.

A portable implementation relying on the C++11 memory consistency model supporting multi-producer and multi-consumer is given by Vyukov [32]. His implementation uses per-element locks. When an element is locked a thread moves on to the next element. Frechilla [6] presents another multi-producer and multi-consumer queue based on two tail pointers. A thread gets a slot in the data structure by atomically incrementing the first tail pointer. After an element has been written, the thread will spin until it can increment the second tail pointer. Consumers dequeue up to the second tail pointer. These and similar designs are not termination safe and remain prone to priority inversion.

When the use of dynamic memory is feasible, unbounded queues can be implemented as lists or similar data structures. Multiple implementations exist [9,12,13,19,34]. Back-off and enqueue/dequeue matching techniques [20] for unbounded queues can reduce the contention on shared data.

6   Conclusion and Future Work

In this paper, we have presented a portable lock-free queue implementation for the C++11 memory model. Our approach enhances the descriptor based *MCAS* design and allows for multiple concurrent descriptors without requiring lock-free memory management. We compared our implementation with other available lock-based and lock-free implementations on ARM, x86, and PowerPC architectures. Our approach scales particularly well on the Power8 architecture. On other systems, it scales as well as or better than other lock-free approaches. On systems where coarse grain locking implementations scale well, we posit that our queue is a better choice when predictability and fault-tolerance become critically important.

As a next step, we plan to experiment with different back-off schemes to improve the performance under high-contention.

References

1. Batty, M., Dodds, M., Gotsman, A.: Library abstraction for C/C++ concurrency. SIGPLAN Not. **48**(1), 235–248 (2013)
2. Boehm, H.-J., Adve, S.V.: Foundations of the C++ concurrency memory model. In: PLDI 2008, pp. 68–78. ACM (2008)
3. Feldman, S., Dechev, D.: A wait-free multi-producer multi-consumer ring buffer. SIGAPP Appl. Comput. Rev. **15**(3), 59–71 (2015)
4. Franke, H., Russell, R., Kirkwood, M.: Fuss, futexes, furwocks: fast user level locking in linux. In: Linux Symposium in Ottawa, pp. 479–491 (2002)
5. Fraser, K., Harris, T.: Concurrent programming without locks. ACM Trans. Comput. Syst. **25**(2), 5 (2007)
6. Frechilla, F.: Yet another implementation of a lock-free circular array queue, April 2011.   http://www.codeproject.com/Articles/153898/Yet-another-implementation-of-a-lock-free-circular. Accessed 3 Mar 2013

7. Greenebaum, K., Barzel, R.: Audio Anecdotes II: Tools, Tips, and Techniques for Digital Audio. A K Peters/CRC Press, Natick (2004)
8. Hedström, K.: Lock-free single-producer - single consumer circular queue, December 2012. http://www.codeproject.com/Articles/43510/Lock-Free-Single-Producer-Single-Consumer-Circular. Accessed 10 Jan 2013
9. Herlihy, M., Shavit, N.: The Art of Multiprocessor Programming, revised 1st edn. Morgan Kaufmann Publishers Inc., San Francisco (2012)
10. Herlihy, M.P., Wing, J.M.: Linearizability: a correctness condition for concurrent objects. ACM Trans. Program. Lang. Syst. **12**(3), 463–492 (1990)
11. ISO/IEC 14882 International Standard. Programming Language C++. JTC1/SC22/WG21 - The C++ Standards Committee (2011)
12. Kirsch, C., Lippautz, M., Payer, H.: Fast and scalable k-FIFO queues. Technical report TR2012-04, University of Salzburg (2012)
13. Kogan, A., Petrank, E.: Wait-free queues with multiple enqueuers and dequeuers. In: PPoPP 2011, pp. 223–234. ACM, New York (2011)
14. Lamport, L.: Specifying concurrent program modules. ACM Trans. Program. Lang. Syst. **5**(2), 190–222 (1983)
15. Lee, P.P.C., Bu, T., Chandranmenon, G.: A lock-free, cache-efficient shared ring buffer for multi-core architectures. In: ANCS 2009, pp. 78–79. ACM, New York (2009)
16. Luchangco, V., Moir, M., Shavit, N.: Nonblocking k-compare-single-swap. In: Proceedings of the Fifteenth Annual ACM Symposium on Parallel Algorithms and Architectures, SPAA 2003, pp. 314–323. ACM, New York (2003)
17. McKenney, P.: Memory ordering in modern microprocessors (draft), September 2007. http://www.rdrop.com/users/paulmck/scalability/paper/ordering.2007.09.19a.pdf. Accessed 20 Feb 2013
18. Michael, M.M.: Safe memory reclamation for dynamic lock-free objects using atomic reads and writes. In: PODC 2002, pp. 21–30. ACM, New York (2002)
19. Michael, M.M.: CAS-based lock-free algorithm for shared deques. In: Kosch, H., Böszörményi, L., Hellwagner, H. (eds.) Euro-Par 2003. LNCS, vol. 2790, pp. 651–660. Springer, Heidelberg (2003). doi:10.1007/978-3-540-45209-6_92
20. Moir, M., Nussbaum, D., Shalev, O., Shavit, N.: Using elimination to implement scalable and lock-free FIFO queues. In: SPAA 2005, pp. 253–262. ACM, New York (2005)
21. Norris, B., Demsky, B.: CDSchecker: checking concurrent data structures written with C/C++ atomics. In: OOPSLA 2013, pp. 131–150. ACM, New York (2013)
22. Pirkelbauer, P.: Non-blocking programming techniques. University of Innsbruck, Invited Talk (2013)
23. Pirkelbauer, P.: Portable non-blocking data structures. University of Alabama, Invited Talk (2013)
24. Sarkar, S., Memarian, K., Owens, S., Batty, M., Sewell, P., Maranget, L., Alglave, J., Williams, D.: Synchronising C/C++ and POWER. In: PLDI, PLDI 2012, pp. 311–322. ACM, New York (2012)
25. Savage, S., Burrows, M., Nelson, G., Sobalvarro, P., Anderson, T.: Eraser: a dynamic data race detector for multithreaded programs. ACM Trans. Comput. Syst. **15**(4), 391–411 (1997)
26. Shafiei, N.: Non-blocking array-based algorithms for stacks and queues. In: Garg, V., Wattenhofer, R., Kothapalli, K. (eds.) ICDCN 2009. LNCS, vol. 5408, pp. 55–66. Springer, Heidelberg (2008). doi:10.1007/978-3-540-92295-7_10

27. Shann, C.-H., Huang, T.L., Chen, C.: A practical nonblocking queue algorithm using compare-and-swap. In: 7th International Conference on Parallel and Distributed Systems, pp. 470–475 (2000)
28. Dechev, D., Feldman, S., LaBorde, P.: Tervel (2015). http://ucf-cs.github.io/Tervel/
29. Stone, J.M.: A nonblocking compare-and-swap algorithm for a shared circular queue. In: Parallel and Distributed Computing in Engineering Systems, pp. 147–152. Elsevier Science B.V. (1992)
30. Stroustrup, B.: The C++ Programming Language, 4th edn. Addison-Wesley Professional, Salt Lake City (2013)
31. Tsigas, P., Zhang, Y.: A simple, fast and scalable non-blocking concurrent FIFO queue for shared memory multiprocessor systems. In: SPAA 2001, pp. 134–143. ACM, New York (2001)
32. Vyukov, D.: Bounded MPMC queue (2013). http://www.1024cores.net/home/lock-free-algorithms/queues/bounded-mpmc-queue. Accessed 21 May 2016
33. Williams, A.: C++ Concurrency in Action: Practical Multithreading. Manning Publications, Shelter Island (2012)
34. Yang, C., Mellor-Crummey, J.: A wait-free queue as fast as fast as fetch-and-add. In: PPoPP 2016, pp. 16:1–16:13. ACM, New York (2016)

A C++ Generic Parallel Pattern Interface for Stream Processing

David del Rio Astorga$^{(\boxtimes)}$, Manuel F. Dolz, Luis Miguel Sanchez,
Javier García Blas, and J. Daniel García

Department of Computer Science, University Carlos III of Madrid,
28911 Leganés, Spain
drio@pa.uc3m.es, {mdolz,lmsanche,fjblas,jdgarcia}@inf.uc3m.es

Abstract. Current parallel programming frameworks aid to a great
extent developers to implement applications in order to exploit parallel
hardware resources. Nevertheless, developers require additional expertise
to properly use and tune them to operate on specific parallel platforms.
On the other hand, porting applications between different parallel programming models and platforms is not straightforward and requires, in
most of the cases, considerable efforts. Apart from that, the lack of high-
level parallel pattern abstractions in these frameworks increases even
more the complexity for developing parallel applications. To pave the
way in this direction, this paper proposes GRPPI, a generic and reusable
high-level parallel pattern interface for stream-based C++ applications.
Thanks to its high-level C++ API, this interface allows users to easily
expose parallelism in sequential applications using already existing parallel frameworks, such as C++ threads, OpenMP and Intel TBB. We
evaluate this approach using an image processing use case to demonstrate its benefits from the usability, flexibility, and performance points
of view.

Keywords: Parallel programming framework · Parallel pattern ·
Stream processing · High-level API

1 Introduction

Compared to sequential programming, designing and implementing parallel
applications for operating on modern hardware poses a number of new challenges to developers [3]. Communication overheads, load imbalance, poor data
locality, improper data layouts, contention in parallel I/O, deadlocks, starvation
or the appearance of data races in threaded environments are just examples of
these challenges. Besides, maintaining and migrating such applications to other

D. del Rio Astorga—This work was partially supported by the EU projects ICT
644235 "RePhrase" and FP7 609666 "REPARA" and the project TIN2013–41350-P
"Scalable Data Management Techniques for High-End Computing Systems" from
the *Ministerio de Economía y Competitividad*, Spain.

© Springer International Publishing AG 2016
J. Carretero et al. (Eds.): ICA3PP 2016, LNCS 10048, pp. 74–87, 2016.
DOI: 10.1007/978-3-319-49583-5_5

parallel platforms demands considerable efforts. Thus, it becomes clear that programmers require additional expertise and endeavor to implement parallel applications, apart from the knowledge necessary in the application domain.

Approaches to relieve this burden are pattern-based parallel programming frameworks, such as SkePU [5], FastFlow [2] or Intel TBB [17]. In this sense, patterns provide a way to encapsulate (using a building blocks approach) algorithmic aspects, allowing users to implement robust, readable and portable solutions with such high-level abstractions. Basically, these patterns instantiate parallelism while hide away the complexity of concurrency mechanisms, such as thread management, synchronizations or data sharing. Nevertheless, although all these skeletons aim to simplify the development of parallel applications, there is not a unified standard [7]. Therefore, users require understanding different libraries, and their capabilities, not only to decide which fits best for their purposes, but also to properly leverage them. Not to mention the migration of applications from one framework to another, which becomes as well an arduous task.

In the context of the C++ language, programmers are able to use a number of generic parallel algorithms from the standard library. However, all of them fall in the category of data parallel patterns, as for example `transform`, `reduce` and `inclusive_scan`. The contribution of this paper focuses on complementing this collection of patterns with novel stream parallel patterns. Different to other object-oriented implementations in the area, we use C++ template metaprogramming techniques to provide generic interfaces of these patterns without incurring in runtime overheads. An ultimate goal is to accommodate a layer on the top of existing execution environments (e.g. C++11 threads or OpenMP) and pattern-based parallel frameworks (e.g., Intel TBB), having as a result unified standard interface.

Overall, in this paper we contribute with the following:

- We present a generic, reusable set of parallel pattern for the C++ language that interface with different parallel programming frameworks such as C++ threads, OpenMP, and Intel TBB.
- We target the stream parallel processing patterns **Pipeline**, **Farm**, **Filter** and **Stream-Reduce**.
- We demonstrate the flexibility and composability of the pattern interface through diverse simple examples.
- We evaluate the overheads of the interface using a real-world image processing application with regard to other pattern-based parallel frameworks and runtime environments.

The remainder of this paper is organized as follows. Section 2 gives a brief overview of related works in the area. Section 3 states the formal definition of the stream parallel patterns supported by the interface. Section 4 describes the generic parallel pattern interface presented in this contribution. Section 5 evaluates the interface and compares it with other existing pattern-based parallel programming frameworks. Section 6 provides a few concluding remarks and future works.

2   Related Work

In the state-of-the-art, multiple works proposing patterns for developing applications to run on modern architectures can be found. Indeed, pattern programming has become one of the best codifying practices in software engineering [6]. The reason is clear: they simplify the application structure while achieve a good balance between maintainability and portability. In general, these methods started being widely adopted when parallel hardware started arising in desktop computers [11]. In this sense, one of the most common ways to express parallelism is through parallel skeletons or patterns [16]. These patterns can be divided in two main groups: data parallel, e.g., Map, Reduce or MapReduce; and stream parallel patterns, e.g., Pipeline, Farm or Filter [12].

Most of the existing pattern-based frameworks are data-parallel computing oriented. Focusing on implementations targeted to run on multi-core processors, we find solutions such as ArBB [14] and Kanga [10]. ArBB defines a collection of basic data classes and methods to define data-parallel skeletons, which are executed using an abstract machine. The Kanga framework also supports task-parallel skeletons, nevertheless, it lacks of stream-processing patterns. We can also find frameworks that implement data-parallel patterns tailored to accelerators. For example, open-source approaches, like SkePU [5], allow deploying applications to run on both multi-core CPUs and multi-GPU processors. Commercial solutions are also present in the market, such as Thrust [15] and SYCL [9] for CUDA and OpenCL devices, respectively. In both cases, these frameworks use a similar C++ Standard Template Library (STL) to ease the parallelization task. Simultaneously, standardized interfaces are being progressively developed. This is the case of C++ STL algorithms, available in the forthcoming C++17, that start defining parallel versions of already existing STL algorithms [8]. All these frameworks provide high-level interfaces, enabling performance portability between sequential code to multi-core CPUs and even GPUs. Although they support a well-established collection of data-parallel patterns, they still lack stream processing-oriented patterns.

Focusing on libraries that support stream-processing patterns, we encounter a set of well-known frameworks, such as Intel Thread Building Blocks (TBB), FastFlow, and RaftLib. TBB [17] is a C++ parallel framework based on the queue-based parallelism approach. However, it runs best on Intel-based architectures and has no support for GPUs. FastFlow [1,2] is a skeleton programming framework, using lock-free communication mechanisms to implement internally its parallel patterns. This approach has support for CUDA and OpenCL. Finally, RaftLib [4] is a C++ template library that aims to fully exploit the stream processing paradigm, supporting dynamic queue optimization, automatic parallelization, and real-time performance monitoring. In any case, all these parallel frameworks are not usable nor generic enough to be easily leveraged by users when developing parallel applications, making mandatory C++ inheritance techniques to enable stream-processing patterns.

3   Stream Parallel Patterns

Stream processing is a programming paradigm that allows applications to easily exploit computational resources available on systems, without explicitly managing allocation, synchronization or communicating among those units. In a similar way, pattern-based programming exploits parallelism in the processing of different items belonging to one or more input data streams. Therefore, an input data stream is characterized by containing and generating elements, one after the other, that will be processed. While in some cases these patterns might be seen as similar to other existing traditional data parallel algorithms, a key difference is that neither the full sequence nor the number of items in the sequence are known in advance.

In the following, we describe formally the stream parallel patterns Pipeline, Farm, Filter, and Stream-Reduce, implemented in the interface proposed in this paper.

Pipeline. The Pipeline parallel pattern computes in parallel several stages the items appearing on the input stream (see Fig. 1(a)). Each stage of this pattern processes data produced by the previous stage in the pipe and delivers results to the next stage in the pipe. Provided that the i-th stage in a n-staged Pipeline computes the function $f_i : \alpha \rightarrow \beta$, the Pipeline computes a function of type $\alpha \rightarrow \beta$ so that for each item x the input stream, an item $f_n(f_{n-1}(\ldots f_1(x)\ldots))$ is delivered in output stream of the Pipeline. The main requirement of this pattern is that the functions $f_1, \ldots, f_n$ related to the stages should be pure, i.e., they should be computed in parallel without side effects. The parallel implementation of this pattern can be performed using a set of concurrent activities, each of them taking care of a single stage. Therefore, assuming that the items appearing on the input stream are $\ldots, x_{i+1}, x_i, x_{i-1}, \ldots$ the computation of stage f_j over the partial result relative to x_i happens in parallel to the computation of f_{j+k} over the partial result relative to x_{i-k}.

Farm. The Farm parallel pattern computes in parallel the function $f : \alpha \rightarrow \beta$ over all the items appearing in the input stream (see Fig. 1(b)). Therefore, an item $f(x_i)$ is generated in the output for each x_i of the input stream. In this pattern, the computations performed by f for the items in the stream are completely independent to each other, so they can be processed in parallel. The parallel implementation of this pattern can be made by a set of entities $\{W_1, W_2, \ldots, W_N\}$, also known as worker threads, computing f in parallel for the different input items.

Filter. The Filter pattern computes in parallel a filter over the items appearing on the input stream, so that it only passes to the output stream those input data items that satisfy the boolean "filter" function (or predicate) $\mathcal{P} : \alpha \rightarrow \{true, false\}$ (see Fig. 1(c)). Basically, the pattern receives a sequence of input items $\ldots, x_{i+1}, x_i, x_{i-1}, \ldots$ and produces a sequence of output items of the same type with different cardinality. The results of the filtering function of any stream data item must be independent to each other, i.e., the predicate should be a pure function. In general, the Filter pattern can be processed in parallel using a Farm-like pattern structure.

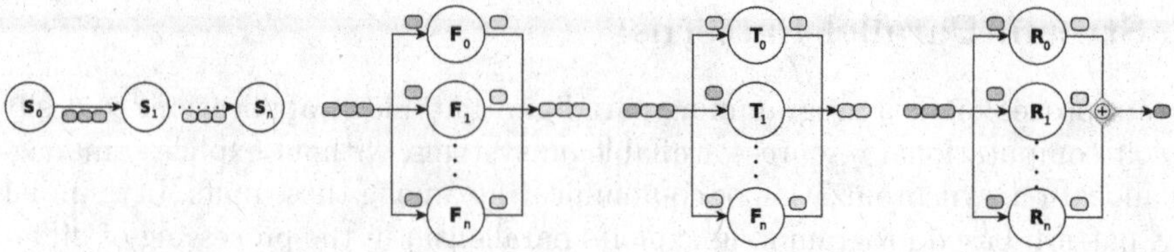

(a) Pipeline.   (b) Farm.   (c) Filter.   (d) Stream-Reduce.

Fig. 1. Stream parallel patterns.

Stream-Reduce. The Stream-Reduce pattern sums up all items appearing on the input stream and delivers results to the output stream (see Fig. 1(d)). The function used to sum up values $\oplus$ should be a pure binary function of type $\oplus : \alpha \times \alpha \rightarrow \alpha$, being usually associative and commutative. Basically, the pattern processes a sequence of input data items $\dots, x_{i+1}, x_i, x_{i-1}, \dots$ to produce a sequence of output items of the same type but with different cardinality. Each of these output items corresponds to the computation of the function $\oplus$ on a finite sequence of input items but collapsed into a single one. The number of elements to be accumulated depends on the window size set as parameter. The parallel implementation of the Stream-Reduce pattern, considering an associative and commutative function $\oplus$, can be performed by a set of worker threads, each of them computing the function on a subset of input items. Afterwards, their partial results are used to compute the final result of the accumulation. This computation can be performed serially, by a single worker thread, or in parallel, according to a tree-based structure.

4   A Generic and Reusable Parallel Pattern Interface

In this section we introduce our generic and reusable parallel pattern interface (GRPPI) for C++ applications. GRPPI takes full advantage of modern C++ features, metaprogramming concepts, and template-based programming to act as switch between already existing parallel programming models, such as OpenMP, C++ threads or Intel TBB. Its design allows users to simply leverage the aforementioned execution frameworks just in a single and compact interface, hiding away the complexity behind the use of concurrency mechanisms. Furthermore, the modularity of GRPPI permits to easily integrate new patterns, while combine them to arrange more complex ones. Thanks to this property, we believe that GRPPI can be used to implement wide range of existing stream processing-oriented applications with a relative small effort, having as a result portable applications that can be executed with multiple execution frameworks.

In the next sections, we describe in detail the interfaces for the stream parallel patterns offered by GRPPI and demonstrate its composability through different simple examples.

4.1   Description of the Interfaces

The interface proposed in GRPPI consists of a set of functions implementing the Pipeline, Farm, Filter, and Stream-Reduce stream parallel patterns that accommodate a layer between the user and execution frameworks supported.

Pipeline. The interface for the Pipeline pattern receives the execution model and the functions related to the stages of the Pipeline, in order to receive the items of the input stream, process, and send them to the next stage. As can be seen in Listing 1.1, its C++ interface uses generic programming, i.e., templates. This fact allows users to have a unique interface, so that, it can be reused for any data type. Note as well that is uses variadic templates, so the Pipeline can have an arbitrary number of stages by receiving a collection of functions passed as arguments. As for the first parameter, the execution model received as argument determines how the Pipeline should be executed. For instance, sequential or parallel executions can be performed by using different execution models; e.g. to operate with OpenMP, the structure that should be passed is `parallel_execution<OMP>`.

Listing 1.1. Pipeline interface.

```
template <typename ExecMod, typename InFunc, typename ... Arguments>
void Pipeline( ExecMod m, InFunc in, Arguments ... sts );
```

As an example, Listing 1.2 shows an instance of a Pipeline composed of 3 stages that is executed using the OpenMP programming model. These stages, passed as lambda functions, perform the following tasks: *(i)* to read the lines of an input file with space-separated values in order to pack them into a vector structure, *(ii)* to compute the maximum value in the vector and forward it to the next stage, and *(iii)* to print the maximum values onto an output stream. As this Pipeline receives the OpenMP parallel execution model (line 1), its stages are computed in parallel by the 3 worker threads involved in the execution. Note as well that `std::optional` variables from the experimental C++14 standard are used to mark the end of the streams.

Listing 1.2. Usage example of the Pipeline pattern.

```
Pipeline( parallel_execution<OMP>,
    // Stage 0: read values from a file
    [&]() {
        auto r = read_list(is);
        return ( r.size() == 0 ) ? optional<vector<int>>{} : make_optional(r);
    },
    // Stage 1: takes the maximum value of the vector
    [&]( optional<vector<int>> v ) {
        return ( v->size() > 0 ) ?
            make_optional( *max_element(begin(*v), end(*v)) ) :
            make_optional( numeric_limits<int>::min() );
    },
    // Stage 2: prints out the result
    [&os]( optional<int> x ) {
        if (x) os << *x << endl;
    }
);
```

Farm. In a similar way, the Farm pattern interface, shown Listing 1.3, receives the execution model and two functions that are in charge of *(i)* consuming the items from the input stream and *(ii)* processing and delivering them individually to the output stream. Note that the `farm` function will be executed in parallel by the different worker threads. In this case, the execution model structure can optionally receive, as parameter, the number of threads to be used for the parallel execution. Otherwise, if this parameter is not given, the interface takes the default number of threads set by the operating system. Here again, the implementation based on templates makes the interface more flexible and reusable for multiple data types.

Listing 1.3. Farm interface.

```
template <typename ExecMod, typename InFunc, typename TaskFunc>
void Farm( ExecMod m, InFunc const &in, TaskFunc const &farm );
```

Listing 1.4 presents an example of a Farm pattern in which the stream consumer function opens a file, whose name is received from the input stream, and returns consecutively its descriptor. Then, the 6 worker threads execute the lambda function to sum the values in the file and write, subsequently, the results into the same file.

Listing 1.4. Usage example of the Farm pattern.

```
Farm( parallel_execution<OMP>(6),
    // InFunc: stream consumer
    [&]() {
        auto r = read_line(is);
        return ( r ) ? optional<iostream>{ } : make_optional( open(r) );
    },
    // TaskFunc: farm compute function
    [&]( optional<iostream> file ) {
        auto v = read_list(file)
        for ( int j = 0; j < v.size(); j++ )
            acumm += v[j];
        file << acumm;
    }
);
```

Filter. The interface for the Filter pattern, described in Listing 1.5, receives the execution model, followed by a stream consumer, filter and producer functions, passed as lambda expressions. Specifically, the `in` function reads items from the input stream and forwards them to the next stage that is responsible to determine, via the `filter` function, whether an item should be accepted or not. Afterwards, those items that satisfy the `filter` routine, are received by the `out` function in order to deliver them to the output stream. Note that it is mandatory the `filter` to return a boolean expression.

Listing 1.5. Filter interface.

```
template <typename ExecMod, typename InFunc, typename FilterFunc, typename OutFunc>
void Filter( ExecMod m, InFunc const &in, FilterFunc const &filter, OutFunc const &out )
```

Listing 1.6 shows an example of a Filter pattern in which the stream consumer function reads lines of a file with space-separated values, then, for each line creates a vector containing its values. Next, the 6 worker threads executing the `filter` function discard the vectors received containing less than 10 items. The vectors that have not been filtered out are finally delivered to the output stream.

Listing 1.6. Usage example of the Filter pattern.

```
1  StreamFilter( parallel_execution<OMP>(6),
2      // InFunc: read values from a file
3      [&]() {
4          auto r = read_list(is);
5          return ( r.size() == 0 ) ? optional<vector<int>>{} : make_optional(r);
6      },
7      // Filter: discards vectors with less than 10 elements
8      [&]( optional<vector<int>> v ) {
9          return ( v->size() < 10 ) ? false : true;
10     },
11     // OutFunc: send vectors to the output stream
12     [&os]( optional<vector<int>> v ) {
13         os << *v << endl;
14     }
15 );
```

Stream-Reduce. The Stream-Reduce pattern aims at reducing, using a specific reduction functions, the items appearing on the input stream. Similar to the other interfaces, the Stream-Reduce interface, as shown in Listing 1.7, receives first the execution mode. Next, it receives the three following lambda expressions to perform its computations: *(i)* the in routine consumes elements from the input stream and forwards them, packed into a concrete structure capable of being reduced, to the next stage; *(ii)* the loc_red function computes the local reductions from the structures received as parameter; and finally *(iii)* the red function receives the local reductions to produce a global reduced result.

Listing 1.7. Stream-Reduce interface.

```
1  template <typename ExecMod, typename GenFunc, typename TaskFunc, typename RedFunc>
2  void StreamReduce(ExecMod m, GenFunc const &in, TaskFunc const &loc_red, RedFunc const &red)
```

As an example, Listing 1.6 shows an instance of a Stream-Reduce pattern summing up the values appearing in the input stream. In this case, the consumer function reads, from the input stream, a list of space-separated integer values, packs them into vectors, and forwards them to the local reduction stage. Then, the reduce function, executed in parallel by the 6 worker threads, picks consecutively these vectors and computes the local sum reduction of its entries. Finally, the local reductions are summed up to produce a total reduced result.

Listing 1.8. Usage example of the Stream-Reduce pattern.

```
1  StreamReduce( parallel_execution<OMP>(6),
2      // GenFunc: stream consumer
3      [&]() {
4          auto r = read_list(is);
5          return ( r.size() == 0 ) ? optional<vector<int>>{} : make_optional(r);
6      },
7      // TaskFunc: reduce kernel
8      [&]( vector<int> v ) {
9          int loc_red = 0;
10         for( int i = 0; i < v.size(); i++ )
11             loc_red += v[i];
12         return loc_red;
13     },
14     // RedFunc: final reduce
15     [&]( int loc_red ) {
16         reduce_var += loc_red;
17     }
18 );
```

4.2   Composing Patterns

As mentioned in the introduction, the patterns offered by GRPPI can be composed among them to produce more complex structures in order to match specific constructions, presented in stream parallel applications. As an example of composition, the code in Listing 1.9 implements a Pipeline, similar to that appearing in Listing 1.2, in which the second (and sequential) stage has now been replaced by a Farm pattern. Therefore, this stage is now computed in parallel by 6 different worker threads. The representation of this Pipeline is (s | f | s), being s and f sequential and Farm-based stages of the Pipeline, respectively. We use t and r to denote the Filter and Stream-Reduce patterns respectively. As can be seen, thanks to the use of metaprogramming techniques and templates, it is possible to compose parallel patterns and build more complex ones.

Listing 1.9. Usage example of the Pipeline pattern.

```
Pipeline( parallel_execution<OMP>,
    // Stage 0: read values from a file
    [&]() {
        auto r = read_list(is);
        return ( r.size() == 0 ) ? optional<vector<int>>{} : make_optional(r);
    },
    // Stage 1: takes the maximum value of the vector
    Farm(parallel_execution<OMP>(6) p,
        [&]( optional<vector<int>> v ) {
            return ( v->size() > 0 ) ?
                make_optional( *max_element(begin(*v), end(*v)) ) :
                make_optional( numeric_limits<int>::min() );
        }),
    //Stage 2: prints out the result
    [&os]( optional<int> x ) {
        if (x) os << *x << endl;
    }
);
```

5   Evaluation

In this section, we perform an experimental evaluation of GRPPI in order to analyze its usability, in terms of lines of code, and its performance, in comparison to the different parallel execution environments currently supported by the pattern interface. To do so, we use the following hardware and software components:

– *Target platform.* The evaluation has been carried out on a server platform comprised of 2× Intel Xeon Ivy Bridge E5–2695 v2 with a total of 24 cores running at 2.40 GHz, 30 MB of L3 cache and 128 GB of DDR3 RAM. The OS is a Linux Ubuntu 14.04.2 LTS with the kernel 3.13.0-57.
– *Software.* To develop the parallel versions and to implement the proposed interfaces, we leveraged the execution environments C++11 threads and OpenMP, and the pattern-based parallel framework Intel TBB. The C++ compiler used to assemble GRPPI is GCC v5.0.
– *Benchmark.* To evaluate the parallel patterns, we used a video stream-processing application composed by two filters, the Gaussian Blur and Sobel operators provided by the OpenCV library, which applied to the frames is capable of detecting edges in the video [2]. Specifically, this application

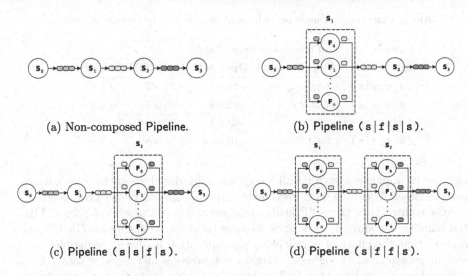

(a) Non-composed Pipeline.   (b) Pipeline (s | f | s | s).

(c) Pipeline (s | s | f | s).   (d) Pipeline (s | f | f | s).

Fig. 2. Pipeline and Farm compositions of the video application.

matches the parallel Pipeline pattern, in which the first stage reads the frames from a video file passed as input; the second and third stages apply the Gaussian Blur and Sobel filters, respectively; and the last stage dumps the processed frames to an output video file.

To carry out the experimental evaluation, we first parallelize this video application using the above-mentioned execution frameworks and the proposed interface. Afterwards, we compare both performance and lines of code required to implement such parallel versions with respect to the sequential one. Note that for the case of OpenMP, the implementation of the Pipeline pattern is not straightforward: it requires the use of queues to communication items between stages. In our particular case we leveraged a variant of the Michael and Scott lock-free queue in C++ [13]. To further experiment with our interface, we implement different versions of the video application using the execution frameworks and distinct compositions of patterns in its main pipeline. As depicted in Fig. 2, (a) we use a non-composed pipeline (s | s | s | s); (b) a pipeline composed of a farm in its second stage (s | f | s | s); (c) a pipeline composed of a farm in its third stage (s | s | f | s); and (d) a pipeline composed of two farms in the second and third stages (s | f | f | s).

5.1   Analysis of the Usability

In this section we analyze the usability and flexibility of the generic interface developed. To analyze this aspect, we compare the number of lines required to implement the parallel version of the application leveraging the interface, with respect to using directly the parallel execution frameworks. Table 1 summarizes the percentage of additional lines introduced into the sequential source code

Table 1. Percentage of increase of lines of code w.r.t. the sequential version.

Pipeline composition	% of increase of lines of code			
	C++ Threads	OpenMP	Intel TBB	GrPPI
(s|s|s|s)	+8.8%	+13.0%	+25.9%	+1.8%
(s|f|s|s)	+59.4%	+62.6%	+25.9%	+3.1%
(s|s|f|s)	+60.0%	+63.9%	+25.9%	+3.1%
(s|f|f|s)	+106.9%	+109.4%	+25.9%	+4.4%

in order to implement such parallel versions using the above-mentioned pattern compositions. As can be seen, implementing more complex pattern compositions via C++ threads or OpenMP leads to larger source codes, while for Intel TBB the number of required extra lines remains constant. Focusing on GrPPI, we observe that the effort of parallelizing an application is almost negligible: even the implementation of the most complex composition increases, at most, 4.4% the total number of lines of code. This behavior is contrary to the C++ threads or OpenMP frameworks, which require roughly twice of lines of code. Additionally, switching GrPPI to use a particular execution framework just needs changing a single parameter in the pattern function calls.

5.2 Performance Analysis of the **Pipeline** and **Farm** Patterns

Next, we analyze the performance with and without GrPPI along with the different execution frameworks and Pipeline compositions, as detailed in Fig. 2, for the video application. Concretely, we employ the frames per second (FPS) metric to analyze the behavior of the particular versions using a same input video with diverse resolutions. Also, we set the Farm stage(s) in all Pipeline compositions to be executed in parallel by 6 threads for all the execution models. A first observation is that the Pipeline combined with the Farm pattern for the filtering stages, in comparison to the non-composed Pipeline, improves substantially the FPS for all parallel frameworks. It is also remarkable that for the lowest video resolution, it is only needed to use a Farm pattern in one of the filtering stages in order to attain the maximum performance. However, as the video resolution increases, more complex pattern compositions deliver better FPS rates, given that the amount of computation also increases. We also observe that the usage of GrPPI does not lead to significant overheads: it is less than 2%, on average, for all the execution frameworks and compositions. An extra inspection into the plots reveals a corner case for the case of Intel TBB in all Pipeline combinations. This is due to the TBB implementation intensively relies on dynamic memory allocation primitives to communicate threads, while the GrPPI-TBB version employs implicitly C++11 data movement instructions (`std::move`). Finally, we find out that the OpenMP and C++ threads versions with and without GrPPI obtain a higher frame rate with respect to the TBB one. This is mainly because we leverage lock-free channels, while TBB internally uses blocking queues (Fig. 3).

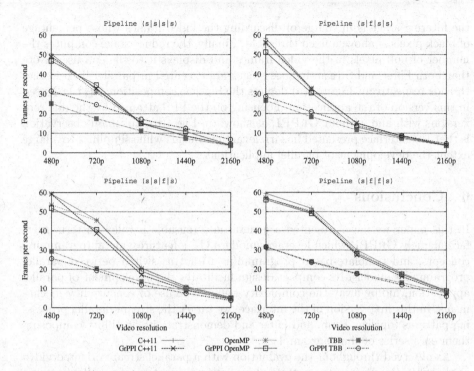

Fig. 3. FPS w/ and w/o using GRPPI along with the different frameworks and Pipeline compositions.

5.3 Performance Analysis of the **Filter** and **Stream-Reduce** Patterns

To evaluate the performance of the Filter and Stream-Reduce patterns, we implement a synthetic version of the video application in which we replace both filtering stages to incorporate a filter and a reduce patterns individually. Specifically,

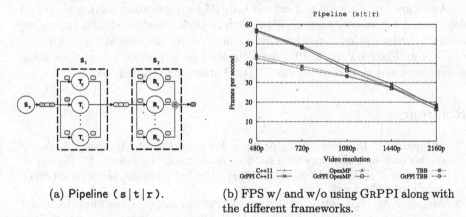

(a) Pipeline (s|t|r).   (b) FPS w/ and w/o using GRPPI along with the different frameworks.

Fig. 4. Synthetic version of the video application using the Filter and Stream-Reduce patterns.

the filtering stage is in charge of discarding the video frames whose percentage of black pixels is above a fixed threshold. Finally, the reduce stage computes the number of null pixels in the video frames and displays it to the end user. Note that both Filter and Stream-Reduce stages are executed in parallel by 6 worker threads respectively. Figure 4(a) depicts the Pipeline composition (s | t | r) used in this version of the application. Focusing on the FPS attained by the different versions with and without GRPPI, as shown in Fig. 4(b), our main observation is that the interface presented has irrelevant overheads while simplifies to a large extent the development of parallel applications.

6   Conclusions

In this paper we have presented a general and reusable parallel pattern interface, namely GRPPI, which leverages modern C++ features, metaprogramming concepts, and template-based programming to act as switch between parallel programming models. Its compact design facilitates the development of parallel application, hiding away the complexity behind the use of concurrency mechanisms. In this first version of the interface, we target the stream parallel processing patterns Pipeline, Farm, and Filter and demonstrate its flexibility composing them on a series of simple examples.

As observed throughout the evaluation with a parallel stream-oriented video application, the performance attained by each combination of parallel patterns using diverse parallel frameworks directly with respect to using GRPPI, is almost the same. We prove as well that our approach does not lead to considerable overheads while permits to easily parallelize applications by adding, on average, 4.4% of lines of codes. With GRPPI, we advocate for a usable, simple, generic, and high-level stream parallel pattern interface, allowing users to implement parallel applications without having a deep understanding of existing parallel programming frameworks or third-party interfaces.

As future work, we plan to extend GRPPI for supporting more stream and data parallel patterns, such as Map, Reduce or MapReduce. Furthermore, we intend to include other execution environments as for the offered parallel frameworks, e.g., FastFlow or SkePU. An ultimate goal is provide support for using accelerators and co-processors via CUDA Thrust and OpenCL SYCL.

References

1. Aldinucci, M., Danelutto, M., Kilpatrick, P., Meneghin, M., Torquati, M.: Accelerating code on multi-cores with fastflow. In: Jeannot, E., Namyst, R., Roman, J. (eds.) Euro-Par 2011. LNCS, vol. 6853, pp. 170–181. Springer, Heidelberg (2011). doi:10.1007/978-3-642-23397-5_17
2. Aldinucci, M., Danelutto, M., Kilpatrick, P., Torquati, M.: FastFlow: high-level and efficient streaming on multi-core. In: S. Pllana (ed.) Programming Multi-core and Many-core Computing Systems, Parallel and Distributed Computing, p. 13 (2012)

3. Amarasinghe, S., Hall, M., Lethin, R., Pingali, K., Quinlan, D., Sarkar, V., Shalf, J., Lucas, R., Yelick, K.: ASCR programming challenges for exascale computing. Technical report, U.S. DOE Office of Science (SC) (2011)
4. Beard, J.C., Li, P., Chamberlain, R.D.: RaftLib: a C++ template library for high performance stream parallel processing. In: Proceedings of the Sixth International Workshop on Programming Models and Applications for Multicores and Manycores, PMAM 2015, pp. 96–105. ACM, New York (2015)
5. Enmyren, J., Kessler, C.W.: SkePU: A multi-backend skeleton programming library for multi-GPU systems. In: Proceedings of the Fourth International Workshop on High-level Parallel Programming and Applications, HLPP 2010, pp. 5–14. ACM, New York (2010)
6. Gamma, E., Helm, R., Johnson, R., Vlissides, J.: Design Patterns: Elements of Reusable Object-Oriented Software. Addison-Wesley Longman Publishing Co. Inc., Boston (1995)
7. González-Vélez, H., Leyton, M.: A survey of algorithmic skeleton frameworks: high-level structured parallel programming enablers. Softw. Pract. Exp. **40**(12), 1135–1160 (2010)
8. Hoberock, J.: N4507: Programming Languages - Technical Specification for C++ Extensions for Parallelism. http://www.open-std.org/jtc1/sc22/wg21/docs/papers/2015/n4507.pdf
9. Khronos OpenCL Working Group: SYCL: C++ Single-source Heterogeneous Programming for OpenCL. https://www.khronos.org/sycl. Accessed May 2015
10. Kist, D., Pinto, B., Bazo, R., Bois, A.R.D., Cavalheiro, G.G.H.: Kanga: a skeleton-based generic interface for parallel programming. In: 2015 International Symposium on Computer Architecture and High Performance Computing Workshop (SBAC-PADW), pp. 68–72, October 2015
11. Mattson, T., Sanders, B., Massingill, B.: Patterns for Parallel Programming. Addison-Wesley Professional, Salt Lake (2004)
12. McCool, M., Reinders, J., Robison, A.: Structured Parallel Programming: Patterns for Efficient Computation, 1st edn. Morgan Kaufmann Publishers Inc., San Francisco (2012)
13. Michael, M.M., Scott, M.L.: Simple, fast, and practical non-blocking and blocking concurrent queue algorithms. In: Proceedings of the Fifteenth Annual ACM Symposium on Principles of Distributed Computing, PODC 1996, pp. 267–275. ACM, New York (1996)
14. Newburn, C.J., So, B., Liu, Z., McCool, M., Ghuloum, A., Toit, S.D., Wang, Z.G., Du, Z.H., Chen, Y., Wu, G., Guo, P., Liu, Z., Zhang, D.: Intel's array building blocks: a retargetable, dynamic compiler and embedded language. In: 2011 9th Annual IEEE/ACM International Symposium on Code Generation and Optimization (CGO), pp. 224–235, April 2011
15. NVIDIA Corporation: Thrust. https://thrust.github.io/
16. Rabhi, F.A., Gorlatch, S. (eds.): Patterns and Skeletons for Parallel and Distributed Computing. Springer, London (2003)
17. Reinders, J.: Intel Threading Building Blocks - Outfitting C++ for Multi-core Processor Parallelism. O'Reilly, Sebastopol (2007)

Creating Distributed Execution Plans with BobolangNG

David Bednárek[✉], Martin Kruliš, Jakub Yaghob, and Filip Zavoral

Parallel Architectures/Algorithms/Applications Research Group,
Faculty of Mathematics and Physics, Charles University,
Malostranské nám. 25, Prague, Czech Republic
{bednarek,krulis,yaghob,zavoral}@ksi.mff.cuni.cz

Abstract. Execution plans constitute the traditional interface between DBMS front-ends and back-ends; similar networks of interconnected operators are found also outside database systems. Tasks like adapting execution plans for distributed or heterogeneous runtime environments require a plan transformation mechanism which is simple enough to produce predictable results while general enough to express advanced communication schemes required for instance in skew-resistant partitioning. In this paper, we describe the BobolangNG language designed to express execution plans as well as their transformations, based on hierarchical models known from many environments but enhanced with a novel compile-time mechanism of component multiplication. Compared to approaches based on general graph rewriting, the plan transformation in BobolangNG is not iterative; therefore the consequences and limitations of the process are easier to understand and the development of distribution strategies and experimenting with distributed plans are easier and safer.

Keywords: Execution plan · Distributed computing · Partitioning · Distributed database · Datalog · Modeling language

1 Introduction

For several decades, *execution plans* (a.k.a. query plans or physical plans) have been one of the key ideas employed in database management systems, forming the interface between their front-ends and back-ends. While the first execution plans were just expressions in relational algebra, further development lead to various extensions covering object-oriented approaches, XML navigation, spatial and temporal queries, similarity measures, etc. Finally, many DBMSs became extensible using user-defined functions, indexes, and even join methods [6,10]. Thus, the execution plans now resemble a general programming environment

F. Zavoral—This paper was supported by the Czech Science Foundation (GAČR) project P103-14-14292P and by the Charles University Grant Agency (GAUK) project PRVOUK-P46.

J. Carretero et al. (Eds.): ICA3PP 2016, LNCS 10048, pp. 88–97, 2016.
DOI: 10.1007/978-3-319-49583-5_6

although still confined within the architecture of a DBMS. The original terminology inherited from relational algebra is also retained, using the term *operator* for the elements of an execution plan while the plan itself is now a directed acyclic graph of operators rather than a tree.

Furthermore, abstractions similar to an execution plan are also found outside classical DBMSs, serving for various purposes in streaming environments, Big Data processing, scientific computing, etc. In particular, the *pipeline* is an important design pattern in parallel programming which, in generalized form, becomes a directed acyclic graph of computing components similar to execution plan. These environments also brought new scenarios where the execution plan is not created by translation from a high-level query, but created explicitly – either direcly by a human designer or indirectly as the product of a program. The latter approach is, for instance, employed in the lazy evaluation in Apache Pig[1]; furthermore, many parallel programming environments create graphs of tasks or similar elements during run time.

Parallelism available in execution plans is traditionally divided into two categories: *Intra-operator* parallelism, implemented using some parallel programming technique inside an operator, and *inter-operator* parallelism, arising from the ability of the runtime environment to run different operators in parallel. Since the explicit intra-operator parallelism is error prone and more difficult to implement (and it often interferes with the scheduling strategy used by the runtime environment to achieve inter-operator parallelism), the parallelism logically available inside an operator is often converted to inter-operator parallelism by replacing the operator with a network of operators. This approach is the prevailing strategy in distributed databases [1], typically involving a partitioning scheme to divide the data among several copies of the original operator.

While replacing individual operators with sub-plans representing their distributed execution is easy, it is not sufficient because it does not remove the bottleneck associated with the communication between the operators. Therefore, the connections must be replaced as well, producing complex schemes involving distributed repartitioning operations, feedback communication, etc. Of course, expansion of connections and expansion of operators must be tightly coordinated in order to create a valid distributed plan.

Graph rewriting [4] is probably the most powerful tool available for this problem in theory; however, its iterative nature makes the consequences difficult to understand. A less powerful tool whose effects are easier to predict might be a reasonable choice, particularly when experimenting or performance tuning of the execution plans is involved.

In this paper we introduce a new declarative language named *BobolangNG*, used to define the execution plans both before and after their expansion to distributed form as well as to define the expansion strategy itself. BobolangNG is inspired by the principles of its predecessor *Bobolang* [2]; nevertheless, it was extended and completely reworked in a backward incompatible manner.

---

[1] https://pig.apache.org/.

Both versions of Bobolang were inspired by the hierarchical model approach which have had enormous success for instance in electronic design or software engineering. In addition, BobolangNG introduces two novel concepts:

- *Connection models* introduce bidirectional communication between connected operators in the execution plan, including compile-time communication to provide interaction between distribution strategies of the operators.
- *Model-part multiplication* is a mechanism used to generate the required number of operators (e.g., to represent partitioning) as well as to specify their connection topology and placement with respect to the computing nodes.

The two concepts together form a language powerful enough to express sophisticated distribution strategies like skew-resistant partitioning [1] while remaining predictable and understandable.

We will not show the concrete syntax of the BobolangNG language in this paper due to its limited space; instead, we will focus on the underlying logic and the effect of the associated model transformation. We will show examples in (simplified) graphical form instead of the concrete language (which would necessarily contain too many technical details). In reality, only the textual form of BobolangNG is currently used; however, a graphical form is contemplated as a natural future extension, similarly to the use of schematic capture tools in electronics design.

The paper is organized as follows. Section 2 reviews the related work. The principles of the BobolangNG language are presented in Sect. 3; the associated model transformation is explained in Sect. 4 and Sect. 5 concludes the paper.

2   Related Work

There are several systems and frameworks being currently developed. We present a brief overview of the ones which are probably the most similar to Bobox framework, which is our runtime for BobolangNG execution plans.

Summingbird [11] is a domain-specific language designed to integrate MapReduce computations in a single framework. Summingbird programs are written using dataflow abstractions such as sources, sinks, and stores, and can run on different execution platforms. Furthermore, Summingbird can operate in a hybrid processing mode that integrates batch and online results to efficiently generate up-to-date aggregations over long time spans.

Data streaming has become an important paradigm for the real-time processing of continuous data flows in domains such as finance, telecommunications, or networking. StreamCloud [12] is a data streaming system for processing large data volumes. It focuses on parallelization of continuous queries to obtain a highly scalable streaming infrastructure. StreamCloud goes beyond the state of the art by using a parallelization technique that splits queries into subqueries that are allocated to independent sets of nodes.

S4 [5] is a distributed, partially fault-tolerant platform for processing con-tinuous streams of data. Data events are routed to Processing Elements (PEs), which consume the events and emit other events.

Dryad [3] is a distributed execution engine for coarse-grained data-parallel applications. It combines computational *vertices* with communication *channels* to form a dataflow graph. The vertices are usually written as sequential programs with no thread creation or locking. Concurrency arises from Dryad scheduling vertices to run simultaneously on multiple computers or multiple CPU cores.

CIEL [8] is an execution engine for distributed data-flow programs. Sky-writing [9] is a language for expressing task-level parallelism that runs on top of CIEL. Skywriting can express data-dependent control flow using constructs such as while loops and recursive functions. The execution engine provides fault toler-ance and distribution to Skywriting scripts and high-performance code written in other programming languages.

Optimus [4] extends dynamic rewrite mechanisms present in Dryad and CIEL by integrating rewrite policy with a high-level data-parallel language DryadLINQ.

Naiad [7] is a distributed system for executing data parallel, cyclic dataflow programs. It offers the high throughput of batch processors, the low latency of stream processors, and the ability to perform iterative and incremental compu-tations. A new computational model, *timely dataflow*, enriches dataflow com-putation with timestamps that provide the basis for an efficient, lightweight coordination mechanism.

Our solution was inspired by the described systems, but we aim for a different domain. Bobox implementation is written in C++ as it is designed for high performance and computational efficiency. On the other hand, the system has no integrated support for fault tolerance, which would decrease the performance. Finally, the BobolangNG provides more elaborate ways how to fine-tune an execution plan for particular hardware configuration semiautomatically.

3   The Language

The BobolangNG language retained the following building blocks of the Bobolang language [2]:

- The language allows for hierarchical decomposition of the execution plan. The operators referenced in the *main* plan may either be *atomic* operators implemented in the associated procedural language or *compound* operators whose interior is defined by an *operator model* from a *model library*. All the models are again defined in Bobolang, allowing for nested decomposition into a tree-like hierarchy of models with atomic operators at leaves.
- *Connections* are used to pass data between operators; connections are attached to input and output *interfaces* of operators. For type safety, opera-tors declare *types* on all their interfaces and a connection may connect only interfaces of the same type.

- Library models as well as atomic operators may be generic – in this case, the types at their interfaces are determined from the context of their instantiation.

Above these foundations, two advanced concepts of BobolangNG support the steps necessary to expand execution plans into their distributed versions: *Connection models* and *model-part multiplication*.

3.1   Connection Models

In addition of operator models, connections (and, therefore, interfaces) may also have their models as a generalization of their types. The *connection models* enable the following features:

- Both operators and connections may be expanded into complex structures using their models.
- Connection models allow bidirectional communication at both compile time and run time.
- Compile-time communication via connection models allows adaptation of the model of an operator to the properties of the connected counterpart.

For instance, a distributed repartitioning operation may be needed between two join operators in an execution plan for a relational query. In BobolangNG, the repartitioning operation may be constructed using coordinated expansion of the two operators and their connection as shown in Fig. 1.

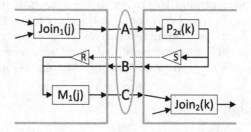

Fig. 1. Join-to-join interface with repartitioning

The bidirectionality of the connection model allows to interleave partitioning and merge operators of the two interconnected join models: The output of the first join operator $Join_1(j)$ is first connected (via the forward connection A) to the partitioning operator $P_2(k)$ of the second join model, the resulting doubly-partitioned data are then returned back (through the backward connection B) to the merge operator $M_1(j)$ of the first join model, and finally the repartitioned data are fed (through the forward connection C) to the second join operator. Some of the data channels between the partitioning and merge operators shall be transported remotely, which is marked by the presence of the S (send) and R (receive) operators.

3.2   Model-Part Multiplication

To allow description of execution plan transformations like partitioning which involve multiplication of model parts according to the number and topology of computing nodes, BobolangNG introduces the following features:

- Parts of models (operators and connections) may be multiplied to provide opportunities for parallel execution.
- Individual copies of operators and connections produced by the multiplication mechanism are identified using tuples of attributes. Thus, the set of copies of a model part is defined using a relation computed during model compilation. The relations assigned to operators and connections are called *multiplication relations*.
- Both the schema and the contents of multiplication relations are defined by the model creator. A part of the schema is recognized by the system and used to define the physical placement of the copies with respect to computing hardware. The rest of the schema may contain any attributes which the author of the model uses to distinguish the copies (e.g. partition indexes) and to properly connect them together.
- The number of the copies and their placement is usually derived from the computing hardware topology. The hardware and other configuration options are defined using relations, i.e. sets of tuples whose schema is partially recognized by the system and partially freely defined by the model author. These relations are called *configuration relations*.
- The author of the model uses relational operations like projections, selections, unions, and joins to derive the multiplication relations from the configuration relations. This process usually involves additional *intermediate relations* defined in the model.
- Intermediate relations may form a part of a connection model, i.e. they may be carried along connections between operator models. This is the way how operator models interact during compile time.

Figure 2 shows a result of multiplication applied to the repartitioning operation shown in Fig. 1. In this example, we assume that the first join operator $Join_1(j)$ is split into two partitions on the key j while the second join uses a different partitioning key k and four partitions.

The decision to use two partitions is done inside the first join model; however, it also results into twofold multiplication of the partitioning operator $P_2(k)$ inside the second join model. Thus, compile-time communication via the connection model is required to pass the partitioning decision between the models. Since the partitioning scheme involves not only the total number of partitions but also their distribution across computing nodes, the information passed through the connection model is a relation which maps the partition identifiers to the node identifiers.

The partition identifiers are used to distinguish individual $Join_1(j)$ operators as well as the connections forming the multiplied channel A; they are also part of the identification of the doubly-multiplied connections B. The partition

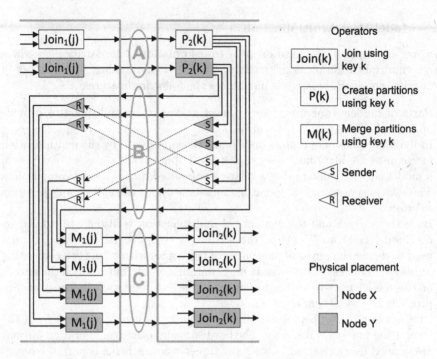

Fig. 2. Join-to-join interface with repartitioning (multiplied)

identifier must be a meaningful value related to the values of the key j because all the $P_1(j)$ operators (not shown in Fig. 2) must partition the data in the same way. On the other hand, for the second join model, this partition identifier is opaque as it serves only to properly identify the corresponding connections in the A and B channels.

The same compile-time information propagation is applied (in the opposite direction) to the partitioning decision done inside the second join model. Thus, two partitioning identifiers are involved in the connection model, both of them serving together as the identification of multiplied connections B.

Moreover, the B connections are implemented by two different mechanisms, as local and remote channels. The distinction is based on the computing node identifiers to which the partitioning identifiers are mapped by their respective partitioning-definition relations. In other words, the two kinds of B connections shown in Fig. 1 are multiplied using a complex relational formula involving selection (filtering).

4   Compilation

The generation of an execution plan from the BobolangNG sources consists of the following steps:

- *Instantiation phase* – All operators and connections are replaced by their respective models. The replacement is performed recursively until the plan is represented using atomic operators only. During instantiation, *multiplication relations* (as defined in Sect. 3.2) outside of compound models interact with the multiplication relations assigned to their parts; this interaction is reflected by forming more complex relations by Cartesian product and properly adjusting all relational operations which define them. The instantiation process generates both compile-time and runtime connections from the connection models; the compile-time connections become part of a network of relational variables bound together by relational operators. A part of the relational variables correspond to the *configuration relations* (Sect. 3.2), another part define the final multiplication relations for the atomic operators and their runtime connections.
- *Evaluation phase* – For given values of configurations relations, the system calculates the values of all relational variables in the system created during the instantiation phase, according to the equations produced during instantiation from the relation assignments in the models.
- *Multiplication phase* – Values of relational variables which correspond to atomic operators are used to generate the required number of copies of the operators in the execution plan. The operators are bound together as specified by the values of variables associated to the atomic connections. The matching between connections and operators is specified in the source model in a *match condition* similar to a join condition in relational algebra; thus, arbitrary user-defined attributes may be used in the match condition. Because such specification leaves a space for errors like unconnected or multiply connected interfaces, a sanity check is a part of the multiplication phase.

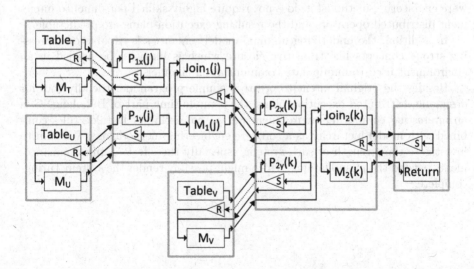

Fig. 3. Instantiated execution plan before multiplication

In sophisticated models, the bidirectional nature of compile-time communication may create cyclic dependencies between relational variables created during the instantiation phase. Fortunately, an equation system over relational variables may be assigned a well-defined solution using the minimal-model semantics [13], best known from Datalog. A sufficient condition for the existence of the minimal model is finiteness of the domains and monotonicity of the operations allowed in the equations. Therefore, we restricted the compile-time relational operations in BobolangNG to projections, selections, unions, and joins.

The choice of minimal-model semantics and operations known from Datalog also lead to the use of Datalog-like syntax in the corresponding parts of BobolangNG. Nevertheless, the same evaluation approach may be used with a different syntax for model-part multiplication clauses, for instance in the proposed graphical version of BobolangNG.

5   Conclusions

In this paper, we presented a novel language called BobolangNG designed to define execution plans and the distribution strategy of their operators. The environment is capable of combining the distribution-unaware execution plans with a library of distributed operators to create complex distributed execution plans like the one shown (in the phase before actual multiplication) in Fig. 3.

The advantage of this approach is that it confines the interaction between neighbor operators into connection models, involving both compile-time interaction and bidirectional runtime data channels. Implementing distributed plans then equals to creating operator models which adhere to given connection models. Since this approach acts along simple rules and resembles established software engineering methods, it does not require highly skilled personnel to implement distributed operators and the resulting execution plans are predictable.

In addition, the underlying minimal-model semantics is capable of expressing strong concepts like transitive closure which is likely to be needed in an environment used to manipulate communication channels.

Besides the original intent to create a simple programmer-friendly tool for designing distributed execution plans, the compile-time part of BobolangNG is an interesting computing environment per se, consisting of Datalog rules combined with model hierarchy as a software engineering methodology. We plan to investigate the strength of such system, especially the effect of minor enhancements beyond the plain Datalog, which might possibly render the system Turing-complete.

References

1. Bruno, N., Kwon, Y., Wu, M.C.: Advanced join strategies for large-scale distributed computation. Proc. VLDB Endow. **7**(13), 1484–1495 (2014). http://dx.doi.org/10.14778/2733004.2733020
2. Falt, Z., Bednárek, D., Kruliš, M., Yaghob, J., Zavoral, F.: Bobolang: a language for parallel streaming applications. In: Proceedings of the 23rd International Symposium on High-Performance Parallel and Distributed Computing, pp. 311–314. ACM (2014)
3. Isard, M., Budiu, M., Yu, Y., Birrell, A., Fetterly, D.: Dryad: distributed data-parallel programs from sequential building blocks. In: ACM SIGOPS Operating Systems Review, vol. 41, pp. 59–72. ACM (2007)
4. Ke, Q., Isard, M., Yu, Y.: Optimus: a dynamic rewriting framework for data-parallel execution plans. In: Proceedings of the 8th ACM European Conference on Computer Systems, pp. 15–28. ACM (2013)
5. Neumeyer, L., Robbins, B., Nair, A., Kesari, A.: S4: distributed stream computing platform. In: Proceedings of the IEEE International Conference on Data Mining Workshops (ICDMW), pp. 170–177. IEEE (2010)
6. Levandoski, J.J., Eldawy, A., Mokbel, M.F., Khalefa, M.E.: Flexible and extensible preference evaluation in database systems. ACM Trans. Database Syst. (TODS) **38**(3), 17 (2013)
7. Murray, D.G., McSherry, F., Isaacs, R., Isard, M., Barham, P., Abadi, M.: Naiad: a timely dataflow system. In: Proceedings of the Twenty-Fourth ACM Symposium on Operating Systems Principles, pp. 439–455. ACM (2013)
8. Murray, D.G., Schwarzkopf, M., Smowton, C., Smith, S., Madhavapeddy, A., Hand, S.: Ciel: a universal execution engine for distributed data-flow computing. In: Proceedings of 8th ACM/USENIX Symposium on Networked Systems Design and Implementation, pp. 113–126 (2011)
9. Murray, D.G., Hand, S.: Scripting the cloud with skywriting. HotCloud **10**, 12 (2010)
10. Nagendra, M., Candan, K.S.: Efficient processing of skyline-join queries over multiple data sources. ACM Trans. Database Syst. (TODS) **40**(2), 10 (2015)
11. Oscar, B., Sam, R., Ian, O., Jimmy, L.: Summingbird: a framework for integrating batch and online mapreduce computations. Proc. VLDB Endow. **7**(13), 1441–1451 (2014)
12. Gulisano, V., Jimenez-Peris, R., Patino-Martinez, M., Valduriez, P.: Streamcloud: a large scale data streaming system. In: Proceedings of the 30th International Conference on Distributed Computing Systems (ICDCS), pp. 126–137. IEEE (2010)
13. Van Emden, M.H., Kowalski, R.A.: The semantics of predicate logic as a programming language. J. ACM **23**(4), 733–742 (1976). http://doi.acm.org/10.1145/321978.321991

Deciding the Deadlock and Livelock in a Petri Net with a Target Marking Based on Its Basic Unfolding

Guanjun Liu[1,2(✉)], Kun Zhang[1], and Changjun Jiang[2]

[1] Department of Computer Science, Tongji University, Shanghai 201804, China
liuguanjun@tongji.edu.cn
[2] Key Lab of the Ministry of Education for Embedded Systems and Services Computing, Tongji University, Shanghai 201804, China

Abstract. Petri nets are widely used to model and analyse concurrent systems. It is an important study to check the deadlock and/or livelock in Petri nets. These checks are generally carried out by the reachability graph technique and thus the state explosion problem is a big obstacle to this technique. The unfolding technique can effectively avoid/alleviate the state explosion problem, especially for those Petri nets that have many concurrent actions. This paper considers the deadlock and livelock problem in a Petri net with a target state. We propose the notion of *basic unfolding*. Based on basic unfolding, we present a necessary and sufficient condition to decide whether a Petri net is both deadlock-free and livelock-free.

Keywords: Concurrent systems · Petri nets · Deadlock · Livelock · Partial order

1 Introduction

Petri nets are one kind of formal model of analysing concurrent systems [17]. Generally, deadlock and livelock are both bad phenomenons. A deadlock is a situation in which two or more processes are each waiting for the other one to execute (but neither does). A livelock is also a situation in which the states of some processes can be changed constantly but there is no chance to reach their final states. Therefore, it is necessary for designers to check deadlock and livelock when a system is designed.

There exist some methods to check deadlock and/or livelock in Petri nets. Net-structure-based methods are famous [5,6,12,13]. However, so far no one has presented a universal structure-based condition to decide deadlock and livelock

G. Liu—This paper was supported in part by the National Nature Science Foundation of China (Grant Nos. 61572360 and 91218301) and in part by the Shanghai Shuguang Program.

J. Carretero et al. (Eds.): ICA3PP 2016, LNCS 10048, pp. 98–105, 2016.
DOI: 10.1007/978-3-319-49583-5_7

for general Petri nets. Reachability-graph-based methods are often used, but the state explosion problem is a big obstacle to this method [3,18].

The unfolding method [4,15,16] is another efficient technique to alleviate the state explosion problem especially when a Petri net has concurrent transitions at many reachable states. This technique has been successfully used to verify many properties such as deadlock and liveness for safe Petri nets [8,10]. This paper considers more general cases including unbounded Petri nets. In [14] we propose *basic unfolding* that is used to decide the soundness for Workflow nets. In this paper we use basic unfolding to check whether a Petri net with a target marking is both deadlock-free and livelock-free.

The rest of this paper is organized as follows: Sect. 2 introduces Petri nets and branching processes. Section 3 reviews the notion of basic unfolding. Section 4 presents a necessary and sufficient condition to decide deadlock and livelock based on basic unfolding. Section 5 shows the tool of basic unfolding. Section 6 concludes this paper.

2   Basic Notions

For readability, this section introduces Petri nets and branching processes [8,17].

Denote $\mathbb{N} = \{0, 1, 2, \cdots\}$ as the set of all nonnegative integers. A *multiset* μ *over a set* X is a function from X to $\mathbb{N}$. To distinguish multisets from sets, all elements of a multiset are listed between brackets $[\![$ and $]\!]$ while all elements of a set are between brackets $\{$ and $\}$. For instance, $\mu = [\![x_1, x_4, x_4, x_4]\!] = [\![x_1, 3x_4]\!]$ is a multiset over the set $\{x_1, x_2, x_3, x_4\}$ such that $\mu(x_1) = 1$, $\mu(x_2) = \mu(x_3) = 0$, and $\mu(x_4) = 3$. Given two multisets μ_1 and μ_2 over X: $\mu_1 \geq \mu_2$ iff $\forall x \in X$: $\mu_1(x) \geq \mu_2(x)$; $\mu_1 \leq \mu_2$ iff $\forall x \in X$: $\mu_1(x) \leq \mu_2(x)$; and $\mu_1 = \mu_2$ iff $\forall x \in X$: $\mu_1(x) = \mu_2(x)$. $\mu_1 \leq \mu_2 \land \mu_1 \neq \mu_2$ is denoted as $\mu_1 \lneq \mu_2$ for short. A subset X' of a set X may be viewed as a special multiset over X such that $X'(x) = 1$ if $x \in X'$ and otherwise $X'(x) = 0$.

A *net* is a 3-tuple $N = (P, T, F)$ where P is a set of *places*, T is a set of *transitions*, $F \subseteq (P \times T) \cup (T \times P)$ is a *flow relation*, and $P \cap T = \emptyset$. A net may be thought of as a directed graph in which a circle represents a place, a box or bar represents a transition, and arcs between circles and boxes represent the flow relation. Figure 1(a) shows a net. In this paper, we assume that a net is strongly connected. Given a net $N = (P, T, F)$ and a node $x \in P \cup T$, ${}^\bullet x = \{y \in P \cup T \mid (y, x) \in F\}$ and $x^\bullet = \{y \in P \cup T \mid (x, y) \in F\}$ are called the *pre-set* and *post-set* of x, respectively.

A *marking* of $N = (P, T, F)$ is a multiset M over P. A net N with an *initial marking* M_0 is called a *Petri net* and denoted as (N, M_0). In a Petri net graph, a marking is usually represented by a distribution of tokens over places, i.e., place p has k tokens at current marking M if $M(p) = k$.

Transition t is *enabled* at M if $\forall p \in {}^\bullet t$: $M(p) > 0$. This is denoted as $M[t\rangle$. t is *disabled* at M if it is not enabled at M. This is denoted as $\neg M[t\rangle$. *Firing* an enabled transition t at M yields a new marking M', which is denoted as $M[t\rangle M'$, such that: $M'(p) = M(p) - 1$ if $p \in {}^\bullet t \setminus t^\bullet$; $M'(p) = M(p) + 1$

if $p \in t^\bullet \backslash {}^\bullet t$; and otherwise $M'(p) = M(p)$. A marking M_k is *reachable* from a marking M if there exists a firable sequence $\sigma = t_0 t_1 \cdots t_{k-1}$ such that $M[t_0\rangle M_1[t_1\rangle \cdots \rangle M_{k-1}[t_{k-1}\rangle M_k$, denoted by $M[\sigma\rangle M_k$ for short, which represents that M reaches M_k after firing σ. The set of all markings reachable from M in a net N is denoted as $R(N, M)$. A Petri net is *bounded* if $\forall p \in P, \exists k \in \mathbb{N},$ $\forall M \in R(N, M_0): M(p) < k$.

Definition 1 (Deadlock). *Let $N = (P, T, F, M_0)$ be a Petri net and M_f is a target marking. $M \in R(N, M_0)$ is a* deadlock *w.r.t. M_f (deadlock for short) if $\forall t \in T, \neg M[t\rangle \wedge M \neq M_f$.*

Definition 2 (Livelock). *Let $N = (P, T, F, M_0)$ be a Petri net and M_f is a target marking. $M \in R(N, M_0)$ is a* livelock *w.r.t. M_f (livelock for short) if $\forall M' \in R(N, M), \exists t \in T, M'[t\rangle \wedge M' \neq M_f$.*

When a Petri net with a target marking has neither deadlock not livelock, it is similar to a Workflow net that is weakly sound [1]. It is worth to note that a strongly connected Petri net is bounded if it has neither deadlock nor livelock w.r.t. a given target marking.

Two nodes x and y of a net $N = (P, T, F)$ are in *conflict*, denoted as $(x, y) \in \#$ (or, alternatively, $x \# y$), if there are two distinct transitions t_1 and t_2 such that $(t_1, x) \in F^+ \wedge (t_2, y) \in F^+ \wedge {}^\bullet t_1 \cap {}^\bullet t_2 \neq \emptyset$, where F^+ is the transitive closure of F. A node x is in *self-conflict* if $x \# x$.

A net $N = (P, T, F)$ is an *occurrence net* if $\forall x, y \in P \cup T: (x, y) \in F^+ \Rightarrow (y, x) \notin F^+; \forall p \in P: |{}^\bullet p| \leq 1$; and no transition is in self-conflict. For convenience, we use $O = (S, E, G)$ to denote an occurrence net where S, E, and G are the sets of places (also called *conditions*), transitions (also called *events*), and arcs, respectively. Let ${}^\circ O = \{c \in S \mid {}^\bullet c = \emptyset\}$ denote the set of all places that have no input transitions in the occurrent net $O = (S, E, G)$. Given a multiset μ_1 over X and a function $h: X \to Y$, the notation $[\![h(x)|x \in \mu_1]\!]$ (or, alternatively, $h[\![\mu_1]\!]$) denotes a multiset μ_2 over Y such that $\forall y \in Y$:

$$\mu_2(y) = \begin{cases} \sum_{\substack{x \in X \\ h(x) = y}} \mu_1(x) & \text{if } \exists x \in X, h(x) = y \\ 0 & \text{if } \forall x \in X, h(x) \neq y \end{cases}.$$

Let $(N, M_0) = (P, T, F, M_0)$ be a Petri net. (O, h) is a *branching process* of (N, M_0) if occurrence net $O = (S, E, G)$ and homomorphism $h: S \cup E \to P \cup T$ satisfy: $(S \cup E) \cap (P \cup T) = \emptyset \wedge h(S) \subseteq P \wedge h(E) \subseteq T; \forall t \in E:$ $h[\![{}^\bullet t]\!] = {}^\bullet h(t) \wedge h[\![t^\bullet]\!] = h(t)^\bullet; h[\![{}^\circ O]\!] = M_0$; and $\forall t_1, t_2 \in E: ({}^\bullet t_1 = {}^\bullet t_2 \wedge h(t_1) = h(t_2)) \Rightarrow t_1 = t_2$.

Infinitely many isomorphic occurrence nets may represent the same branching process. In order to represent all isomorphic branching processes in a uniform way, a canonical coding [7] is used to label all transitions and places of a branching process, i.e., $\forall x \in S \cup E: cod_O(x) = \langle h(x), \{cod_O(y)|\forall y \in {}^\bullet x\}\rangle$, where $(O, h) = (S, E, G, h)$ is a branching process of $(N, M_0) = (P, T, F, M_0)$.

Let $(O_j, h_j) = (S_j, E_j, G_j, h_j)$ be two branching processes of a net system where $j \in \{1, 2\}$. (O_1, h_1) is a *prefix* of (O_2, h_2) if $S_1 \subseteq S_2 \wedge E_1 \subseteq E_2$ [7]. In fact, the set of all branching processes of a net system is a *partially ordered set* w.r.t. the binary relation *prefix*, i.e., it is reflexive, antisymmetric, and transitive. Furthermore, it forms a *complete lattice* [7]. Therefore, it has a unique greatest element that is called the *unfolding* of the net system [7]. In theory, a branching process can interpret the concurrent semantics of a system. In application, it is an effective technique to analyze/verify the properties of a system since it can save space (after some events of the unfolding are cut off and thus the remainder is finite).

Let $(O, h) = (S, E, G, h)$ be a branching process of a net system and $X \subseteq S$. X is a *co-set* if $\forall c_1, c_2 \in X : (c_1, c_2) \notin \# \wedge (c_1, c_2) \notin G^+$. A *cut* is a maximal co-set (w.r.t. $\subseteq$). Each cut corresponds to a reachable marking of the original system, but a reachable marking of the original system possibly corresponds to multiple cuts since this marking can be reached by multiple firable sequences. We denote $\mathcal{C}(O)$ as the set of all cuts in a branching process (O, h). $\mathcal{C}_X(O)$ is denoted as the set of all cuts including a given co-set X in (O, h), i.e., $\mathcal{C}_X(O) = \{C \in \mathcal{C}(O) | X \subseteq C\}$. Therefore, for an event $\langle t, X \rangle$ of a branching process (O, h), $\mathcal{C}_X(O)$ represents all cuts at which the event is enabled.

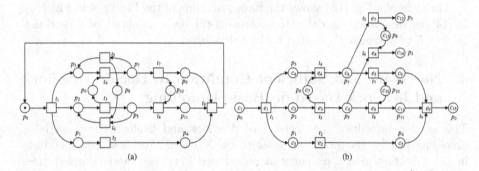

Fig. 1. (a) A Petri net and (b) its basic unfolding.

3   Basic Unfolding

For a Petri net with an infinite firable sequence, its unfolding is infinite. Therefore, one has to cut off some events from the unfolding and finally obtains a finite prefix of the unfolding which can be utilized to analyze/verify the related system [2,8,11]. In [14], we define such a finite prefix (called *basic unfolding*) and use it to decide the soundness of a Workflow net. This section introduces it again.

Let $(O, h) = (S, E, G, h)$ be a branching process of (N, M_0) and $C_1, C_2 \in \mathcal{C}(O)$. C_1 is a *predecessor* of C_2 (or, C_2 is a *successor* of C_1), denoted $C_1 \preceq C_2$, if $\forall c_1 \in C_1, \forall c_2 \in C_2: (c_2, c_1) \notin G^+ \wedge (c_2, c_1) \notin \#$. $C_1 \preceq C_2$ means that C_2 is not reached earlier than C_1 in (O, h). C_1 is a *proper predecessor* of C_2 if

$C_1 \preceq C_2 \wedge C_1 \neq C_2$, which is denoted as $C_1 \precnsim C_2$. Similarly, we can define the proper predecessor (resp., proper successor) of an event: e_1 is a *proper predecessor* of e_2 (resp., e_2 is a *proper successor* of e_1), denoted as $e_1 \precnsim e_2$, if $(e_1, e_2) \in G^+$.

Definition 3 (Possible extension [9]). *Let (O, h) be a branching process of a net system (N, M_0). $\langle t, X \rangle$ is a* possible extension *of (O, h) if X is a co-set of (O, h) and t is a transition of (N, M_0) such that: $h(X) = {}^\bullet t$ and $\langle t, X \rangle$ does not belong to (O, h).*

After a possible extension (with its output places) is added to a given branching process, the result is still a branching process [9].

Definition 4 (Basic unfolding). *Given a net system (N, M_0), the* basic unfolding *of (N, M_0) is a branching process $(O, h) = (S, E, G, h)$ such that:*

1. *Each event $\langle t, X \rangle$ of (O, h) satisfies that $\exists C \in \mathcal{C}_X(O)$, $\forall C' \in \mathcal{C}(O)$, $\forall C'' \in \mathcal{C}_X(O)$: $C' \precnsim C \preceq C'' \Rightarrow h[\![C']\!] \nleq h[\![C'']\!]$; and*
2. *Each possible extension $\langle t, X \rangle$ of (O, h) satisfies that $\forall C \in \mathcal{C}_X(O)$, $\exists C' \in \mathcal{C}(O)$, $\exists C'' \in \mathcal{C}_X(O)$: $C' \precnsim C \preceq C'' \wedge h[\![C']\!] \leq h[\![C'']\!]$.*

For example, Fig. 1(b) shows the basic unfolding of the Petri net in Fig. 1(a). In [14], we design an algorithm to generating the basic unfolding of a Petri net. In Sect. 5 we introduce a related tool we developed.

4   Necessary and Sufficient Condition to Decide Deadlock and Livelock Based on Basic Unfolding

This section introduce the decision of deadlock and livelock based on basic unfolding briefly. Its proof can refer to the work of Workflow net soundness in [14]. We first give a property of unbounded Petri nets and bounded ones, respectively. Notice that the set of places and transitions of a Petri net is finite by default.

Lemma 1. *Given an unbounded Petri net (N, M_0) and its basic unfolding (O, h), there exist $C \in \mathcal{C}(O)$ and $C' \in \mathcal{C}(O)$ such that $C' \precnsim C \wedge h[\![C']\!] \precnsim h[\![C]\!]$.*

Lemma 2. *Given a bounded Petri net (N, M_0) with a given target marking M_f such that $\exists M \in R(N, M_0)$, $\forall M' \in R(N, M)$: $M' \neq M_f$, its basic unfolding (O, h) has a cut C such that*

1. *$\forall C' \in \mathcal{C}(O)$: $C \preceq C' \Rightarrow h(C') \neq M_f$; and*
2. *$\forall C', C'' \in \mathcal{C}(O)$: $C' \precnsim C \preceq C'' \Rightarrow h[\![C']\!] \neq h[\![C'']\!]$.*

Based on the above conclusions, we can draw the follow one that describes a sufficient condition to decide deadlock and livelock.

Lemma 3. *Given a Petri net $N = (P, T, F, M_0)$ with a targe marking M_f and its basic unfolding $(O, h) = (S, E, G, h)$, (N, M_0) is deadlock-free and livelock-free if (O, h) satisfies:*

1. $\forall C, C' \in \mathcal{C}(O): C \npreceq C' \Rightarrow \neg(h[\![C]\!] \lneqq h[\![C']\!])$; and
2. $\forall C \in \mathcal{C}(O)$:
   2.1. $\exists C' \in \mathcal{C}(O): C \preceq C' \wedge h[\![C']\!] = M_f$; or
   2.2. $\exists C', C'' \in \mathcal{C}(O): C' \npreceq C \preceq C'' \wedge h[\![C']\!] = h[\![C'']\!]$.

Condition 1 in Lemma 3 means that the WF-net is bounded. Condition 2 is used to guarantee that for each marking reached from the initial one, it can reach the target one. More precisely, for an arbitrary cut C in the basic unfolding, either it can directly reach a cut C' such that $h[\![C']\!]$ is the target marking (Condition 2.1), or there are a proper predecessor C' and a successor C'' such that the two markings corresponding to the two cuts are the same (Condition 2.2). Due to the arbitrariness of C, we know that the marking corresponding to a cut in the basic unfolding can reach the target one. The converse of Lemma 3 also holds.

Lemma 4. *Given a Petri net $N = (P, T, F, M_0)$ with a target marking M_f and its basic unfolding $(O, h) = (S, E, G, h)$, if (N, M_0) is deadlock-free and livelock-free, then (O, h) satisfies:*

1. $\forall C, C' \in \mathcal{C}(O): C \npreceq C' \Rightarrow \neg(h[\![C]\!] \lneqq h[\![C']\!])$; and
2. $\forall C \in \mathcal{C}(O)$:
   2.1. $\exists C' \in \mathcal{C}(O): C \preceq C' \wedge h[\![C']\!] = M_f$; or
   2.2. $\exists C', C'' \in \mathcal{C}(O): C' \npreceq C \preceq C'' \wedge h[\![C']\!] = h[\![C'']\!]$.

Theorem 1. *Given a Petri net $N = (P, T, F, M_0)$ with a targe marking M_f and its basic unfolding $(O, h) = (S, E, G, h)$, (N, M_0) is deadlock-free and livelock-free iff (O, h) satisfies:*

1. $\forall C, C' \in \mathcal{C}(O): C \npreceq C' \Rightarrow \neg(h[\![C]\!] \lneqq h[\![C']\!])$; and
2. $\forall C \in \mathcal{C}(O)$:
   2.1. $\exists C' \in \mathcal{C}(O): C \preceq C' \wedge h[\![C']\!] = M_f$; or
   2.2. $\exists C', C'' \in \mathcal{C}(O): C' \npreceq C \preceq C'' \wedge h[\![C']\!] = h[\![C'']\!]$.

Figure 1(b) is the basic unfolding of the Petri net in (a). By Theorem 1 we know that this Petri net is deadlock-free and livelock-free.

5   Tool of Generating Basic Unfolding

We develop a tool of generating the basic unfolding of a Petri net on the basis of PIPE (Platform Independent Petri Net Editor that is an open source tool of Petri nets [19]). The related algorithm is in [14]. For example, Fig. 2(a) is a Petri net of 5 dining philosophers' problem and (b) is its basic unfolding. For this Petri net, its reachability graph has 1364 nodes and 6377 edges. Obviously, the basic unfolding is much smaller than the reachability graph.

In this basic unfolding, the cut $\{s20p3, s28p8, s22p13, s24p18, s26p22\}$ does not satisfy the second condition of Theorem 1. Actually, this cut corresponds to a deadlock.

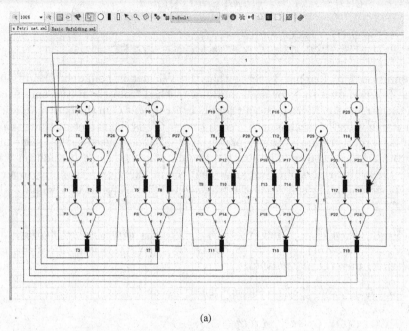

(a)

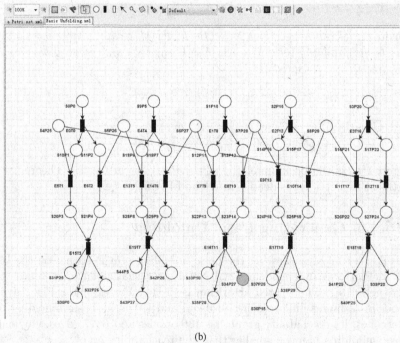

(b)

Fig. 2. (a) Petri net modeling 5 dining philosophers' problem and (b) its basic unfolding.

6   Conclusion

In [14] we present the notion of basic unfolding and give a condition of deciding soundness of Workflow nets based on it. In this paper we use it to decide the deadlock and livelock of Petri nets with a given target marking and develop a tool of generating basic unfolding. Future work is to implement this decision condition on the basis of this tool.

References

1. van der Aalst, W.M.P.: Workflow verification: finding control-flow errors using Petri-Net-Based techniques. In: Aalst, W.M.P., Desel, J., Oberweis, A. (eds.) Business Process Management. LNCS, vol. 1806, pp. 161–183. Springer, Heidelberg (2000). doi:10.1007/3-540-45594-9_11
2. Bonet, B., Haslum, P., Khomenko, V., Thiebaux, S., Vogler, W.: Recent advances in unfolding technique. Theoret. Comput. Sci. **551**, 84–101 (2014)
3. Clarke, E.M., Grumberg, O., Peled, D.: Modeling Chencking, 1st edn. The MIT Press, Cambridge (1999)
4. Couvreur, J.M., Poitrenaud, D., Weil, R.: Branching processes of general Petri nets. Fundamenta Informaticae **122**, 31–58 (2013)
5. Chu, F., Xie, X.L.: Deadlock analysis of Petri nets using siphons and mathematical programming. IEEE Trans. Robot Automat. **13**, 793–840 (1997)
6. Desel, J., Esparza, J.: Free Choice Petri Nets. Cambridge University Press, Cambridge (1995)
7. Engelfriet, J.: Branching processes of Petri nets. Acta Informatica **28**, 575–591 (1991)
8. Esparza, J., Heljanko, K.: Unfoldings: A Partial-Order Approach to Model Checking. Springer-Verlag, Berlin (2008)
9. Esparza, J., Romer, S., Vogler, W.: An improvement of McMillan's unfolding algorithm. Form. Methods Syst. Des. **20**(3), 285–310 (2002)
10. Khomenko, V.: Model checking based on prefixes of Petri net unfoldings. University of Newcastle upon Tyne (Ph.D. Dissertation) (2003)
11. Khomenko, V., Koutny, M., Vogler, W.: Canonical prefixes of Petri net unfoldings. Acta Informatica **40**, 95–118 (2003)
12. Liu, G.J., Liu, C.J., Chao, D.: A necessary and sufficient condition for the liveness of normal nets. Comput. J. **54**, 157–163 (2011)
13. Liu, G.J., Jiang, C.J., Zhou, M.C., Ohta, A.: The liveness of WS^{3}PR: complexity and decision. IEICE Trans. Fundam. **E96–A**, 1783–1793 (2013)
14. Liu, G.J., Reisig, W., Jiang, C.J., Zhou, M.C.: A branching-process-based method to check soundness of workflow systems. IEEE Access **4**, 4104–4118 (2016)
15. McMillan, K.L.: Symbolic Model Checking. Kluwer Academic Publishers, Berlin (1993)
16. McMillan, K.L.: A technique of state space search based on unfolding. Formal Meth. Syst. Des. **6**, 45–65 (1995)
17. Reisig, W.: Understanding Petri Nets: Modeling Techniques, Analysis Methods, Case Studies. Springer, Heidelberg (2013)
18. Valmari, A.: The state explosion problem. In: Reisig, W., Rozenberg, G. (eds.) ACPN 1996. LNCS, vol. 1491, pp. 429–528. Springer, Heidelberg (1998). doi:10.1007/3-540-65306-6_21
19. Dingle, N.J., Knottenbelt, W.J., Suto, T.: PIPE2: a tool for the performance evaluation of generalised stochastic Petri Nets. ACM SIGMETRICS Perform. Eval. Rev. **36**(4), 34–39 (2009)

A New Scalable Approach for Distributed Metadata in HPC

Cristina Rodríguez-Quintana[1,2], Antonio F. Díaz[1,2](✉), Julio Ortega[1,2],
Raúl H. Palacios[1,2], and Andrés Ortiz[1,2]

[1] Department of Computer Architecture and Technology,
University of Granada, Granada, Spain
{crodriguez,afdiaz,jortega,raulhp}@ugr.es, aortiz@ic.uma.es
[2] Communications Enginnering Department, University of Málaga, Málaga, Spain

Abstract. In the last years not only a growth of data-intensive storage
has been observed, but also compute-intensive workloads need a high
computing power and high parallelism with good performance and great
scalability. Many distributed filesystem have focused in how to distribute
data across multiple processing nodes, but one of the main problem to
solve is the management of the ever-greater number of metadata requests.
In fact, some studies have identified that an optimized metadata management is a key factor to achieve good performance. Applications in
high performance computing usually require filesystems able to provide
a huge amount of operations per second to achieve the required level of
performance. Although the metadata storage is smaller than data storage, metadata operations consume large CPU cycles, so a single metadata
server cannot be longer sufficient. In this paper we define a completely
distributed method that provides efficient metadata management and
seamlessly adapts to general purpose and scientific computing filesystem workloads. The throughput performance is measured by a metadata benchmark and compared with several distributed filesystems. The
results show great scalability in creating operations on a single directory
accessed by multiple clients.

Keywords: Distributed filesystems · HPC · Metadata management

1 Introduction

Data-intensive applications require high-performance computing to be able to
provide a huge amount of operations per second. The ever-growing amount of

A.F. Díaz—This work has been partially supported by European Union FEDER and
the Spanish Ministry of Economy and Competitiveness TIN2015-67020-P, FPA2015-
65150-C3-3-P, and PROMEP/103.5/13/6475 UAEH-146. The authors would like
to thank FCSCL (Fundación Centro de Supercomputación de Castilla y León) for
providing access to a cluster of its supercomputer Calendula.

© Springer International Publishing AG 2016
J. Carretero et al. (Eds.): ICA3PP 2016, LNCS 10048, pp. 106–117, 2016.
DOI: 10.1007/978-3-319-49583-5_8

data is expected to exceed billions of objects, making metadata scalability critical to overall performance. New efficient storage resources are used when system memory is not enough. Traditionally, data are often stored in file systems which are accessed remotely by a multiple number of nodes. Some penalty in the accessed data may cause to slow down the applications even these are not operational. For example, NFS, one of the most successful network filesystem, is an effective but not so efficient filesystem. NFS presents a drawback compiling Linux kernel that becames an insufferable process. In this way, we can wonder the following. Can the processing of data-intensive applications be runned efficiently in network filesystems? The answer is yes. But it depends on important factors in the design of a distributed filesystem.

Metadata store files and directory information. These can be directory trees, timestamps, attributes, and permissions. An optimized metadata management is able to distribute requests among different servers so it can improve its overall performance. Moreover, it has been shown that metadata transactions account for more than 50 percent of all filesystem operations [7]. Recently, different metadata management approaches have been developed to solve the partitioning problem of the namespace and inodes, but they lack redundancy at the metadata level.

In this paper, we propose an improved procedure to distribute metadata that has been implemented and evaluated on the filesystem AbFS [6]. This way, all metadata servers can actively be used to achieve an optimal distribution of the metadata management workload.

One of goals of AbFS is the scalability of metadata access, and thus the scalability of the entire filesystem. Experience with previous AbFS versions has helped us to reduce complexity while improving performance and reliability. To achieve this, our system offers an efficient metadata storage approach that combines hash/table and B+ trees, and provides excellent performance thanks to B+ tree speed. In the rest of the paper, Sect. 2 reviews related work and Sect. 3 describes the model. Finally, experimental results are presented in Sect. 4, and the conclusions in Sect. 5.

2   Related Work

The development of network filesystems has a high degree of current relevance. In fact, it has been researched for a long time. In the last years it has had an improvement of the network systems, CPU speed and reliability of systems, which has led to the develop more complex and optimised systems. For instance, the first versions of NFS were stateless due to crashes, system interruptions and network errors what it provided simplified and robust models. Nowadays, redundant systems or RAID have enabled more reliable resources. Network filesystems like NFS are a useful solution for multiple applications, but present several problems related to get high performance and scalability. Distributed filesystems are a good alternative because they are able to lead complex storage systems. They present some advantages and some limitations. Distributed filesystems are fundamental to high-performance computing for reducing the bottleneck, and providing scalability. Traditionally, metadata has always been studied in the background. Parallel filesystems have focused on scalable data distribution, but as supercomputers increased their computational power, it is necessary to improve the accesses to large amounts of metadata. In the last years, there has been a growing number of parallel filesystem that follow a distributional metadata approach. Metadata operations are very CPU consuming. A single metadata server is often no longer sufficient, even it might become a bottleneck of the system. HDFS [13] is one of the main distributed filesystems which was inspired by Google and invested by Yahoo!, whose namespace is maintained by a single metadata server architecture. The problem appeared when the store capacity grew up to Exabyte order, establishing practical limits of growth for this architecture. There are some filesystems based on multiples metadata servers like Ceph [18], OrangeFS [21], GIGA+ [11], PanFS [20] but this approach provides somewhat complexity and not all of them provide redundancy at metadata level. In anyway, Ceph is similar to PanFS, which store metadata and data on data servers, and replicated among groups of data servers. This approach can present some limitations.

Ceph [18] is one of the most recent object-based filesystems. It offers a dynamic management metadata based on current access patterns. Ceph stores both data and metadata on object servers using the same strategy, and these are replicated through on placement groups (PG). Ceph adaptively distributes the management of the filesystem directory hierarchy among the metadata servers using a pseudo-random data distribution random called CRUSH [19], which gets fast accesses. Initially, a hash function is applied to full pathname of a directory object and the obtained value is used as input to CRUSH. Any component of the system is able to calculate the location of any directory object. This approach maintains different issues associated to hashing such as symbolic links, permission changing and cluster changing.

The data cluster entirely carries out data migration, replication, failure detection, and failure recovery through a reliable autonomic distributed object store (RADOS) [17], an object storage service implemented by the OSDs themselves. A small cluster of monitors is in charge of maintaining a cluster map copy describing the cluster's members state.

Moreover, Metadata management in Ceph uses Dynamic Subtree Partitioning [10] which distributes responsibility for managing the filesystem directory hierarchy among metadata servers. On the one hand, such an approach has a drawback. Since the number of metadata servers can limit the sub-directory number, this method may not be enough to scale well when subdirectories grow excessively [8]. On the other hand, it provides an important advantage, since it preserves locality in the workload corresponding to each metadata server making possible efficient updates and prefetching to improve performance for common workloads.

Among the parallel filesystems, Lustre [3] has been one of the most successful. Its architecture has had a single metadata server for a long time. They presented some alternative solution based on an active-passive model, but in this model the second server was a copy of primary one and there was not any distribution of workload. Recently, the have developed some approach where not only distribute data but also metadata. The latest version includes an early implementation of the distributed namespace (DNE) that allows several MDTs. By default, each directory is created in the same node of its father, but the manager node can move subdirectories among different metadata servers. Some results of a pre-release [14] shows over 10,000 files per second. Furthermore, Lustre supports POSIX semantics.

Another popular filesystems is GPFS [12], developed by IBM. It supports efficient lookup and distributes hugedirs through extensible hashing [8]. Directory entries of a large directory are stored in multiple disk blocks. Given a directory, a hash function is applied to the entry name in order to locate the block containing the directory entry. GPFS guarantees POSIX semantics through a distributed locking mechanism to synchronize access to data and metadata at the same time. However, locking mechanisms limit parallelism and affect to creating operations. Because GPFS is a block-oriented filesystem, it may present several limitations related to the level of parallelism.

One of most typical problems in distributed systems is to guarantee the consistency of the information. From this point on, PVFS2 [21] is not POSIX-compliant. It abstracts from the block-level, seeing data and metadata as files, and assigning them unique handles. PVFS2 servers can act as metadata or data servers. Objects are statically distributed among servers. Furthermore, PVFS2 does not implement redundancy.

In [6,9,16] several approaches are analysed with more details. Existing techniques go from a coarse-grain approach like Static Subtree Partition (used by Lustre [3], Coda [6] etc.) to a fine-grain approach like File Hashing (e.g. table mapping, hash mapping).

A redundant decentralized model needs additional elements to detect operative servers, thus heartbeat systems [15] are usually used. Servers need metadata resiliency among them. Although this could imply some overhead due to the multiple messages to be sent, it can be reduced by using fast interfaces with low message latencies.

Finally, after evaluating different methods, and considering that complex solutions are not usually a good choice, we consider the alternative of an optimized design of our previously proposed AbFS filesystem. AbFS has distributed metadata implementing a hash/table-based model that takes advantage of communication between the servers to achieve a better performance. One of the goals of AbFS is the scalability of metadata access, and thus the scalability of the entire filesystem.

3   Design and Implementation

3.1   AbFS2 Components

One of the challenges in distributed filesystems is to provide a load balance of the workloads among servers. This is necessary to get high performance and an

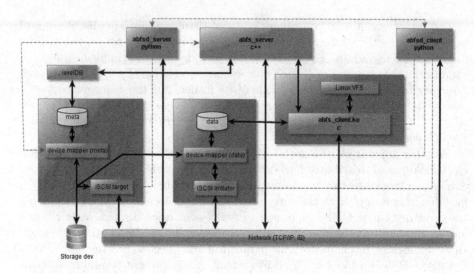

Fig. 1. AbFS2 general diagram.

optimal use of the resources. Scalability is one of the relevant topics to study, since is difficult to provide in distributed systems.

Moreover, distributed systems may present coherence problems so it is important that they use mechanisms which are able to distribute the information robustly. Distributed filesystems must guarantee the consistency using atomicity in metadata operations. In this way, POSIX semantic is guaranteed.

We have developed a new version of AbFS [6] called AbFS2, with an enhanced metadata management.

AbFS2 uses distributed servers and a symmetric model where each server node provides several resources. The main advantages of this system are:

- It distributes the workload among servers avoiding bottlenecks.
- It is based on a distributed configuration model with quorum to solve problems caused by failures in a master node or network errors (NSPOF: No Single Point of Failure).
- It uses the iSCSI layer data transfer whenever possible.

The client-server model also facilitates the division of each element and simplifies the possible states of operation. Figure 1 provides a general overview of the main elements of AbFS2.

AbFS2 is designed in a modular client-server model to simplify the development. Each node can act as client and server simultaneously, with different programs and files. On the server side:

- *abfsd_server*: Daemon that exchanges configuration information and manages all processes. (Python)
- *abfs_server*: Metadata server and cache coherence. (C ++).

- *abfsconfig*: It manages AbFS. It communicates with *abfsd* through events with tables in sqlite. (Python)
- *abfs_setup*: Resource Configuration Program. (Python)

  On the client side:

- *abfsd_client*: Daemon that receives configuration information and actions from the servers. (Python)
- *abfs_client.ko*: Kernel module that implements the client under Linux VFS.
- *abfs_setup_client*: Resource Configuration Program customers. (Python)

AbFS2 metadata uses a client-server model with different elements. In this paper, we evaluate metadata servers (MS) that manage the metadata information composed by three main components: directory structure (dentries), files and directory information (inodes) and files location (extents).

3.2   Distributed Metadata Model

Some of the most popular distributed filesystems and the previous version of AbFS use a hash on pathnames to locate metadata. This technique provides that clients can directly locate the metadata servers. Another advantage is that the load is evenly distributed. But this approach has several drawbacks such as low performance in large filesystems due to the required sequential search inside each sub-hash. To solve the problems with a hash approach, AbFS2 metadata model combines a hash/table and B+ trees. Hash/table distributes accesses among multiple groups assigned to metadata servers by using a hash function based on parent inode numbers and names. The previous version, AbFS, used this table to index the volumes where metadata were stored. Each group stores metadata into two B+ trees with ACID (Atomicity, Consistency, Isolation and Durability) properties that ensure reliable operations. It is indexed by LevelDB [2], that improve performance due to the $O(\log n)$ search complexity of metadata operations. These tables store lookup entries and inode information, respectively. This new approach simplifies data distribution among servers and takes advantage of B+ tree speed. We also prefer B+ trees rather than other binary trees, such as RB-trees, because B+ trees group their elements and they offer better performances as a disk access is done by using blocks of one or more sectors.

AbFS2 stores name entries and inodes into two different tables that provide better hard link support, independent inode delete operations when files are deleted and they are still in use, and directory related operations.

AbFS2 uses a delegation table with a fixed size (4096 entries, in the present implementation) in order to distribute the namespace, depending on the number of server. It stores the group id instead of the physical location. This approach reduces the migration penalty. It will be described later.

Information stored in the AbFS2 lookup table is indexed by the tuple {Parent inode number, name}. Each entry stores the inode number related to the name. Also, this table is used to obtain the entries in a directory to process *readdir* operations. The second table stores inodes and is indexed by inode number. Changes

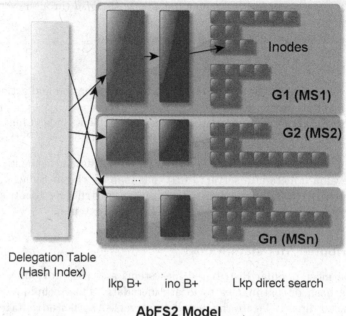

AbFS2 Model

Fig. 2. Hash/B+/B+ model in AbFS2.

in directories and files affect only to his table. Figure 2 shows relationship among Delegation Table, lookup B+ table and inode B+ table.

This decoupling allows the reduction of penalties due to directory renaming. In HBA [22], when an upper directory changes, it affects to hash values in all files and directories placed under this entry. This occurs because the hash is calculated based in the relative full pathname and requires complex solutions such as to store the names of files and subdirectories as part of the metadata of their parent directory, and to update the Bloom filters associated. On the other side, AbFS2 depends only on the inode number of the parent directory and, even when the parent directory is renamed, its inode number does not change.

When a client asks for a file within in a directory, the full pathname is processed and each name and i-node are solved. This approach presents some advantages: For example, rename operations are simplified. Since each file stored has as a key, its name and parent inode number, there is no need of storing the full pathname. Another advantage is that, the management of access privileges in the tree structure of the directory is simplified.

At implementation level, AbFS2 has metadata servers in the user space with good performance results. Metadata operations in the user space (e.g. create a file or a directory) are not penalized because each operation does not need an extra kernel call (as other filesystems need) in order to create another entry at lower level (ext3 or ext4). Most storage devices have a slow response time, so metadata operations in filesystem have to work asynchronously to achieve good performance.

A rendezvous mechanism is used to validate servers and to detect fails. Thus, when a server has a problem it is discarded and groups are out of sync. The Quorum model, based on Paxos [5], reduces inconsistent network failures and guarantees that the rest of the servers are operative. Clients also receive information about the state of the servers to decide the metadata server to be used. The rendezvous mechanism detects if a server has reestablished its functionality. In this case, the mechanism orders to resynchonize the metadata of this server with the valid metadata of another server.

On the other hand, client is maintained at kernel level to get good performance in metadata operations. It uses diverse Linux's Virtual File System (VFS) resources such as inode caches, dentry caches, or buffers to reduce network accesses and server workloads.

Migration is needed when the number of servers changes. In our model some of the entries have to change their locations, although it is not a penalty issue. In a hash model, the number of inode migrations depends on the number of servers. Thanks to the hash/table model, the number of the entries to migrate only depends on the new number of servers. Another advantage of the hash/table model is that the distribution is performed based on a probability assigned to each server, in order to assign more load to particular servers, avoiding hot spots. Message passing between servers are also optimized to send multiple migrations for the same request.

The topology of the servers can change by adding or deleting components. Thus, the Delegation Table is redefined and metadata entries migrate from old position to new ones.

The communication layer is also an important component to achieve good performance. An specific layer has been designed to support multiple requests that can be processed simultaneously to improve overall response time.

4 Performance Evaluation

This section describes the evaluations performed to analyse the system performance. In that, we evaluated the performance and scalability achieved on a single shared hugedir which are accessed by hundreds of processes to create, get the status and delete files (Fig. 3).

Since we have to evaluate metadata operations, it is necessary to use a specific and up-to-date metadata benchmark like mdtest. The mdtest benchmark [4] is a program that measures performance of various metadata operations with multiple clients concurrently using MPI to coordinate the operations and to collect the results. It is necessary to generate appropriate metadata workloads and include configurations with varying numbers of threads.

The performance of the scalable distributed system was evaluated on Fundación Centro de Supercomputación de Castilla y León [1] at the time of our experiments. The cluster was configured as follows. There were 13 nodes in total with 8 cores per node. Each compute node had two Intel Xeon E5472 Quad-core CPUs at 3.0 GHz, 16 GB of RAM, and GJ0120CAGSP disk. The network card

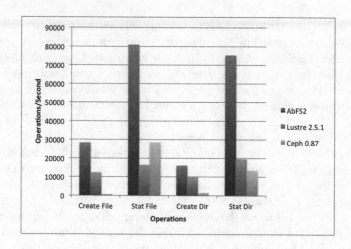

Fig. 3. Performance comparison by using of several distributed filesystems.

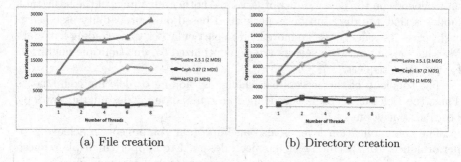

(a) File creation   (b) Directory creation

Fig. 4. Metadata performance of create operations in several filesystems.

was Infiniband DDR Mellanox MT25418. The nodes were running on Scientific Linux 6.3. High throughput storage is attached to all nodes.

The analysis of hugedirs includes different filesystems which were installed on cluster:

- **Lustre 2.5.1:** This version allows distributed Namespace (DNE).
- **Ceph 0.87:** This is the latest version at this moment. We had several problems when using more than one MDS, like very low performance (about 479 files creates per second, 149504 file stat per second and 1935 file removal per second), MDSs crashes, and memory leaks. When we used a single MDS and a single client, recommended in Ceph documentation, the stat operations were improved while creates and removals operations were slow.

The throughput results of three distributed filesystems are illustrated in Fig. 4. All of them were executed with the same configuration. They used two metadata servers and different number of clients varying the number of threads.

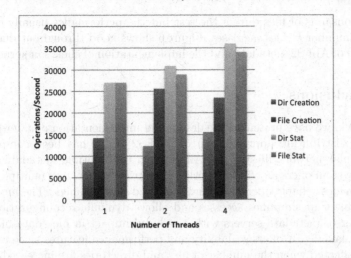

Fig. 5. Single client metadata performance in an unique directory.

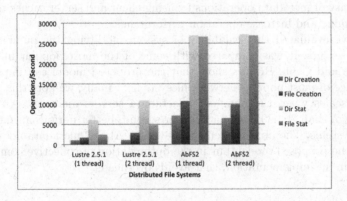

Fig. 6. Metadata performance with large number of files (400k files per directory).

The performance of AbFS2 can improve the results of the rest of distributed filesystems in the same environment. AbFS can reach more than 20,000 file creations in one second while Lustre reaches over 10,000 file creations. Figure 5 also shows that the metadata performance scales varying the number of threads. AbFS2 maintains the average file creation per second and the average directory creation per seconds that reach up to 16,000. AbFS offers better performance than other distributed Filesystem and, in fact, Ceph is not stable enough to take some measures.

Measures performance of multiple tasks creating and stating files and directories in an unique (per task) directory are show in Fig. 5 where AbFS2 scales with threads.

Next, we analysed the performance with the number of files in a filesystem to determine if it is sustained. Most metadata performance evaluations only check several thousands of files during the test but the performance usually decrease when the number of files increases. Figure 6 shows good throughput due to B+ tree model of AbFS2 metadata and the implementation of clients in kernel space.

5   Conclusions

In this work, we have presented the design and implementation of a new reliable metadata distribution approach run on AbFS2 which has been compared to other popular network filesystems. All of them use multiple metadata servers. The new system offers an efficient workload distribution accross multiple servers and it provides reliable operations and improved performances. The model uses a hash/table that simplifies accesses and allows dynamic reconfiguration when the number of metadata servers with a reduced impact in metadata migration for load balancing. It offers scalability and performance features since resources have not affected when the number of files and directories are increased. One of the aspect in order to provide good performance is that AbFS2 also guarantees the atomicity of metadata operations by using client and server caches to reduce network traffic and increase operation performance.

We have evaluated the scalability of system modifying the number of the metadata servers. It was compared with some of the most popular filesystems like Lustre and Ceph. Results show that the proposed model can improve the performance of most popular network filesystems. Finally, we note that the performance scales when the number of metadata servers increases. AbFS2 can achieve more than 20,000 file creations per second, better performance than the other filesystems. The improvements achieved by AbFS2 metadata not only are based on the proposed model, but in the optimization of collective communications and in an implementation, that avoids overheads.

References

1. Fundación centro de supercomputación de castilla y león. http://www.fcsc.es
2. Leveldb. http://www.leveldb.org
3. Official web page of lustre filesystem. http://www.lustre.org
4. Mdtest benchmark. http://www.nersc.gov. Accessed 29 Mar 2013
5. Chandra, T.D., Griesemer, R., Redstone, J.: Paxos made live: an engineering perspective. In: Proceedings of the Twenty-Sixth Annual ACM Symposium on Principles of Distributed Computing, pp. 398–407. ACM (2007)
6. Díaz, A.F., Anguita, M., Camacho, H.E., Nieto, E., Ortega, J.: Two-level hash/table approach for metadata management in distributed file systems. J. Supercomput. 64(1), 144–155 (2013)
7. Lorch, J.R., Anderson, T.E.: A comparison of file system workloads (2000)
8. Fagin, R., Nievergelt, J., Pippenger, N., Strong, H.R.: Extendible hashing-a fast access method for dynamic files. ACM Trans. Database Syst. 4(3), 315–344 (1979)
9. Hua, Y., Zhu, Y., Jiang, H., Feng, D., Tian, L.: Supporting scalable and adaptive metadata management in ultralarge-scale file systems. IEEE Trans. Parallel Distrib. Syst. 22(4), 580–593 (2011). ID: 1

10. Weil, S.A., Pollack, K.T., Brandt, S.A., Miller, E.L.: Dynamic metadata management for petabyte-scale file systems
11. Patil, S.V., Gibson, G.A., Lang, S., Polte, M.: Giga+: scalable directories for shared file systems. In: Proceedings of the 2nd International Workshop on Petascale Data Storage: Held in Conjunction with Supercomputing 2007, PDSW 2007, pp. 26–29. ACM, New York (2007)
12. Schmuck, F., Haskin, R.: GPFS: a shared-disk file system for large computing clusters. In: Proceedings of the 1st USENIX Conference on File and Storage Technologies, FAST 2002, pp. 19–23. USENIX Association, Berkeley (2002)
13. Shvachko, K.V.: HDFS scalability: the limits to growth. **35**(2), 6–16 (2010)
14. Studham, R.S., Subramaniyan, R.: Lustre: a future standard for parallel file systems. In: Invited Presentation at International Supercomputer Conference, Heidelberg, Germany (2005)
15. Tang, H., Gulbeden, A., Zhou, J., Strathearn, W., Yang, T., Chu, L.: A self-organizing storage cluster for parallel data-intensive applications. In: Proceedings of the 2004 ACM/IEEE Conference on Supercomputing, SC 2004, p. 52. IEEE Computer Society, Washington (2004)
16. Wang, F., Xin, Q., Hong, B., Brandt, S.A., Miller, E.L., Long, D.D., McLarty, T.T.: File system workload analysis for large scale scientific computing applications. In: Proceedings of the Twentieth IEEE/Eleventh NASA Goddard Conference on Mass Storage Systems and Technologies, College Park, MD. IEEE Computer Society Press, April 2004
17. Weil, S., Leung, A., Brandt, S., Maltzahn, C.: Rados. In: Proceedings of the 2nd International Workshop on Petascale Data Storage, pp. 35–44, 11 November 2007
18. Weil, S.A., Brandt, S.A., Miller, E.L., Long, D.D.E., Maltzahn, C.: Ceph: a scalable, high-performance distributed file system. In: Proceedings of the 7th Symposium on Operating Systems Design and Implementation, OSDI 2006, pp. 307–320. USENIX Association, Berkeley (2006)
19. Weil, S.A., Brandt, S.A., Miller, E.L., Maltzahn, C.: Crush: controlled, scalable, decentralized placement of replicated data. In: Proceedings of the 2006 ACM/IEEE Conference on Supercomputing, SC 2006, p. 122. ACM (2006)
20. Welch, B., Unangst, M., Abbasi, Z., Gibson, G.A., Mueller, B., Small, J., Zhou, B.: Scalable performance of the panasas parallel file system. In: FAST, vol. 8, pp. 1–17 (2008)
21. Yang, S., Walter, B.: Ligon III Parallel Architecture Research Laboratory Clemson University, Clemson, SC 29634, USA f, and g. Scalable distributed directory implementation on orange file system
22. Zhu, Y., Jiang, H., Wang, J., Xian, F.: HBA: distributed metadata management for large cluster-based storage systems. IEEE Trans. Parallel Distrib. Syst. **19**(6), 750–763 (2008)

Enabling Android-Based Devices
to High-End GPGPUs

Raffaele Montella[1,2], Carmine Ferraro[1], Sokol Kosta[3,4], Valentina Pelliccia[1],
and Giulio Giunta[1(✉)]

[1] Department of Science and Technologies, University of Napoli Parthenope,
Naples, Italy
{raffaele.montella,carmine.ferraro,valentina.pelliccia,
giulio.giunta}@uniparthenope.it
[2] Computation Institute, University of Chicago, Chicago, USA
montella@uchicago.edu
[3] Sapienza University of Rome, Rome, Italy
kosta@di.uniroma1.it
[4] CMI, Aalborg University Copenhagen, Copenhagen, Denmark
sok@cmi.aau.dk

Abstract. The success of Android is based on its unified Java programming model that allows to write platform-independent programs for a
variety of different target platforms. In this paper we describe the first,
to the best of our knowledge, offloading platform that enables Android
devices with no GPU support to run Nvidia CUDA kernels by migrating
their execution on high-end GPGPU servers. The framework is highly
modular and exposes a rich Application Programming Interface (API) to
the developers, making it highly transparent and hiding the complexity
of the network layer. We present the first preliminary results, showing
that not only GPGPU offloading is possible but it is also promising in
terms of performance.

Keywords: Virtualization · GPGPU · CUDA · Cloud · Android ·
Offloading

1   Introduction

Nowadays, we use mobile devices to write documents, browse the internet,
explore maps, watch and edit videos, play games, and perform all the tasks
we used to run on powerful computers, and many more. Users are so attached
to their smart mobile devices, that researchers have found that they would prefer to use their own devices even for working, a concept known as *Bring Your
Own Device (BYOD)*[1]. To keep up with users' demands and applications' needs
for ever increasing computational resources, devices are being equipped with
a myriad of additional hardware, sensors, and extra features. Nevertheless, to

---

[1] http://www.dell.com/en-uk/work/learn/mobility-byod.

© Springer International Publishing AG 2016
J. Carretero et al. (Eds.): ICA3PP 2016, LNCS 10048, pp. 118–125, 2016.
DOI: 10.1007/978-3-319-49583-5_9

always be updated, users are "forced" to replace their devices very frequently, which increases their costs. Furthermore, advances in battery technology have not been able to follow the fast smartphone developing race, making energy consumption a bottleneck for most users. To address these problems, developers and companies have developed solutions that offload the heavy operations from the low-powered mobile devices to more resourceful remote machines, usually residing on the cloud [4,6]. Recently, researchers have proposed the need for offloading not only the CPU tasks but also the operations performed by the GPU [2,8]. Unfortunately, the NVIDIA CUDA's GPGPU proprietary approach collides with Android's open source philosophy, limiting the CUDA availability only on a couple of brand-specific Android products, hindering this way the mass diffusion of GPU computation in the Android developers' community.

In this paper, we design and develop an offloading framework that supports transparent method offloading for Android applications, with focus on the GPU task offloading.

The rest of the paper is organized as follows: in Sect. 2 a short description of some related works; in Sect. 3 we describe the high-level architecture of the framework, identifying its main components; in Sect. 3.1 we give an overview of the GPU virtualization technique we designed and used in our system; in Sect. 4 we present the design and implementation details of the GPGPU task offloading component; in Sect. 5 we show the first preliminary results of and Android application exploiting GPU offloading; and finally, in Sect. 6 we conclude the paper with remarks on future directions.

2   Related Works

With the proliferation of mobile devices in the recent years, it was clear that the low computational capabilities and the limited battery capacity were obviously a bottleneck to the final users. To this end, researchers have proposed different solutions to alleviate the burden of the low-powered devices by migrating the heavy computations from low-powered devices to more powerful machines.

CloneCloud [3] uses an offline static analysis of the apps' binary to determine the pieces that are better to offload to the cloud. The developer should then use the output of the analysis to build a database of offloading decisions, which is later loaded on the device. On runtime, the framework looks up the database to decide where to execute the code. ThinkAir [6] is a method-based offloading framework for Android devices. The smartphone is associated with a virtual machine (VM) on a private or public cloud and the offloadable methods are sent to the VM for remote execution. ThinkAir also supports dynamic resource allocation, exploiting the power of the cloud whenever the offloaded method can be executed in parallel on multiple clones. Comet [4] is a platform that works on top of the Android's Dalvik Virtual Machine and performs task offloading at thread level. Comet uses the Distributed Shared Memory to achieve its light-weight synchronization and offloading procedure. All the above described works focus on offloading of CPU computations. Only recently researchers have started to propose the first ideas about GPU code offloading on mobile devices [2,8]. The rest of this section focuses on the available GPU virtualization technologies and frameworks, to better create the picture of our solution. JCUDA [10] is a Java framework which enables CUDA kernels invocation delegating the responsibility of generating the Java-CUDA bridge codes and host-device data transfer calls to the compiler. The JCUDA implementation handles data transfers of primitives and multidimensional arrays of primitives between the host and device. JCUDA works thanks to the Java Native method invocation, where C functions are declared as native external methods dealing with out-of-the-sandbox unmanaged memory. While JCUDA offers a remarkable solution to the problem of Java CUDA kernel development, it cannot be applied in the Android context because the CUDA compiler support is mandatory at runtime.

3   Offloading Service Architecture

The offloading framework is highly modular and is composed of two main entities: the Acceleration Client (AC) and the Acceleration Server (AS). The AC is an Android library that specifies the Application Programming Interface (API) that developers can use to implement method offloading without having to deal with the underlying networking solutions. The AS is a server application that runs on a remote machine and receives offloaded methods from the AC for remote execution. The AC defines two main sets of API, specialized to handle CPU and GPU instructions. The API dealing with CPU offloading is inspired by the ThinkAir framework [6], while the API dealing with GPU offloading is a totally novel implementation and Android-adapted of the GVirtuS system [7].

Figure 1 shows a device on the left with multiple applications, some of which make use of the AC to migrate the heavy tasks. We can notice the two different modules implemented by the AC that are used to handle the CPU and GPU tasks offloading. On the right side of the figure we can see the Acceleration

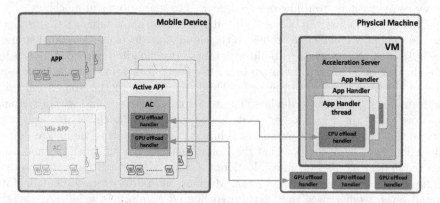

Fig. 1. The architecture of the offloading framework, showing the AC, AS, CPU offload handler, and GPU offload handler.

Server running on a Virtual Machine (VM) with the same operating system as the device (Android OS e.g.). When an AC connects with the AS, the AS starts a new thread (App Handler) to serve the respective application, making it possible to support multiple applications on one VM. The CPU offload handler on the AS receives the migrated code, executes it, and sends the result of the execution back to the AC. When the AC has to offload GPU operations, it connects to the GPU offload handler on the remote physical machine, which is part of the GPU virtualized framework. In the rest of the paper we describe in more details the architecture of the offloading framework, with emphasis on the GPU offloading component.

3.1 GPU Virtualization Architecture

The GPU virtualization architecture is inspired by our previous work GVirtuS, which is a generic virtualization framework for virtualization solutions based on a split-driver model [1]. GVirtuS is a framework that offers virtualization support for generic libraries on traditional x86 computers. In the current state, GVirtuS supports the main GPGPU accelerator libraries such as CUDA and OpenCL, with the advantage of being independent from all the underlying involved technologies: i.e. hypervisor, communicator, and target of virtualization. GVirtuS is composed of two main components: the *front-end* and the *back-end*, which are installed on the client device and on the GPU-capable remote device, respectively.

The front-end is transparent to the application developers, allowing applications to make CUDA or OPENCL calls without any adaption on the source code. If the client device is not able to execute the GPGPU calls, the front-end intercepts and transmits them to the back-end, which runs them on the remote machine and sends the result back to the front-end, which then forwards it to the caller application.

The interaction between the front-end and the back-end is performed through a *communicator* component, which is a pluggable module, meaning that it only presents a public API to the interested components without exposing the underlying communication technology. The communicator has an important role in the overall architecture, given that is responsible for the data transmission.

The back-end is the main component of the GVirtuS framework and runs on the GPU-capable host machine. The back-end daemon runs on the host operating system in the user or superuser space, depending on the specifics of applications and security policies waiting for an incoming connection from the front-end. The daemon implements the back-end functionality dealing with the physical device driver and performing the host-side virtualization.

4 Design and Implementation of Android GPU Offloading Framework

In this section we present the design of GVirtus4J, the Android GPU offloading framework, which is inspired by the architecture of GVirtuS described Sect. 3.1.

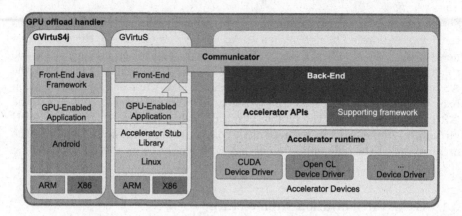

Fig. 2. The GVirtuS4J architecture.

A CUDA program is composed by two distinct elements: *(i)* the CUDA application programming interface functions[2], such as the memory management, and *(ii)* the kernel functions[3], which are written in CUDA language. As such, we implement GVirtuS4J along two axes: *(i)* Encapsulating the CUDA API functions and *(ii)* Handling the kernel functions.

To deal with the first problem, we build the front-end of GVirtuS4J as a Java/Android library that developers can include in their applications. We include the CUDA C++ methods with the same original signature, whenever possible. Following an approach similar to JCUDA [10], Android developers can write Java code that directly calls CUDA kernels by using our API. Differently from JCUDA, GVirtuS4J does not delegate the responsibility of generating the Java-CUDA bridge code and host-device data transfer calls to the compiler, but it behaves as local wrapper of the standard CUDA library. In the remote side, we use the original GVirtuS back-end.

The communication between the Android GVirtuS4J front-end and the back-end is implemented using a customized TCP/IP communication protocol (see Fig. 2). When a CUDA function is called in the Java/Android code, a socket connection with the back-end server is created and a buffer for the data to be sent is allocated. Then, the CUDA function name together with the data (the parameters passed to the function) are serialized and sent to the back-end. The latter assigns them to the appropriate variables and invokes the corresponding CUDA function. The processing result is returned to the Java/Android front-end, which forwards it to the caller object.

CUDA Kernels can be written using the CUDA instruction set architecture, called *Parallel Thread Execution* (PTX), or using a high-level programming language such as C. In both cases, kernels must be compiled into binary code by the *NVIDIA CUDA Compiler* (NVCC) to execute on the device. NVCC compiles

---

[2] http://docs.nvidia.com/cuda/cuda-runtime-api/.
[3] https://devblogs.nvidia.com/parallelforall/easy-introduction-cuda-c-and-c/.

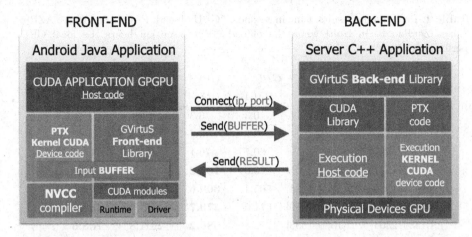

Fig. 3. Representation of a PTX source code offloaded by GVirtuS4J front-end to the back-end for remote execution.

applications written in C/C++ and CUDA by splitting the code in two parts: the pure C/C++ part, which will be compiled by traditional C/C++ compilers such as GCC, and the CUDA part, which will be compiled by the NVCC into a PTX file. To be able to include CUDA kernels in Java/Android and to execute them remotely, we send the PTX file containing the kernels to the backend, as shown in Fig. 3.

5 Preliminary Results

To evaluate our prototype, we performed some preliminary tests which proved that *(i)* GPU code offloading is feasible and *(ii)* convenient under the right circumstances. Choosing a performance testing suite accepted by the community was not possible, due to the lack of such suite, given that the GPU code offloading for Android devices is a novel approach. We chose one of the NVIDIA's CUDA SDK 6.5 samples, which are included with the CUDA distribution[4]. Precisely, in this paper we show the results of the *Matrix Multiplication*. The choice was motivated by its clarity of exposition on illustrating various CUDA programming principles, which makes it easy to clearly present the needed modifications for making it work with GVirtuS4J. Moreover, performing linear algebra operations is a common task assigned to GPGPUs [9]. The preliminary tests have been performed with a varying problem size as shown in Table 1, where the size of matrix A is given by 4*block_size, 6*block_size and the size of matrix B is given by 4*block_size, 4*block_size (bloc_size=32). The Accelerator server (Dual Xeon 6-core E5-2609v3 1.9 GHz - 8 GB DDR4) we used for this experiment is equipped by two NVIDIA Titan X CUDA enabled devices. We executed performance tests using a PineA64+ (Single Board Computer: Cortex A53 64bit quad) and

---

[4] http://docs.nvidia.com/cuda/cuda-samples/.

Table 1. Preliminary results: time in seconds, *GPU offload. PA64: PineA64+; AZP8: Ausus ZenPad 8. In **bold** when the offload GPU execution beats the local CPU performance.

$A \times B$	CPU (PA64, s)	GPU* (PA64, s)	CPU (AZP8, s)	GPU* (AZP8, s)
$A[128, 192] \times B[128, 128]$	0.3	6.3	0.6	6.3
$A[256, 384] \times B[256, 256]$	3.6	19.9	7.4	20.2
$A[512, 768] \times B[512, 512]$	60.7	79.1	81.0	**75.5**
$A[768, 1152] \times B[768, 768]$	223.6	**169.2**	288.5	**170.1**
$A[1024, 1536] \times B[1024, 1024]$	505.4	**309.6**	685.2	**302.5**
$A[1280, 1920] \times B[1280, 1280]$	1071.0	**479.7**	1531.3	**466.7**
$A[1536, 2304] \times B[1536, 1536]$	1772.3	**686.2**	2611.8	**708.6**

an Asus ZenPad 8 (Tablet: Qualcomm 64bit quad core, 1.2 GHz, 1 GB RAM). The connection between the front-end and the back-end was realized through a traditional WiFi infrastructure.

The experiment demonstrates the GPU offloading is convenient as the problem size increases. The break point of offloaded GPU beating the local CPU is related to the device (single board computer and tablet behaves differently), the algorithm used, and the network condition. These results have to be intended as very preliminary and a more extensive performance test and evaluation suite is needed in order to define the range of problem size reflecting on the feasibility of the proposed approach. Exploiting the result asset of this promising research is a keystone for the next level of distributed applications in which the scenario is not limited to mobile devices but to all embedded technologies.

6   Conclusions and Future Directions

In this paper we presented the design and implementation of GVirtuS4J, the first, to the best of our knowledge, GPGPU CUDA-based offloading framework for Android devices. We first presented the big picture of the generic offloading framework, describing its main components, with focus on the detailed description of the GPGPU related subsystem that deals with the GPU offloading process. We showed through preliminary experiments that the system is working correctly. Moreover, we showed that if the problem is complex enough, offloading to a GPU enabled machine reduces its execution time.

Currently, we are still working on the development of the proposed platform in three time-based future directions: *(i)* in a short term we will improve the efficiency and architectural design of the GPU offload handler, leveraging on a more extensive and robust test suite thanks to the availability of a more up-to-date hardware infrastructure; *(ii)* as medium term goal we will release the GVirtuS4J framework as open source software under Apache 2.0 license, offering to a selected group of early adopters the availability of cloud shared GPGPUs computing resources to test their applications, to explore framework's possible enhancements, and to contribute on improving the overall quality; *(iii)* as a long term goal we will leverage on a solid and stable GPGPU offloading infrastructure to implement real-world applications in the field of distributed computing and high-performance internet of things [5].

Acknowledgments. This research has been supported by the Grant Agreement number: 644312 - RAPID - H2020-ICT-2014/H2020-ICT-2014-1 "Heterogeneous Secure Multi-level Remote Acceleration Service for Low-Power Integrated Systems and Devices".

References

1. Armand, F., Gien, M., Maigné, G., Mardinian, G.: Shared device driver model for virtualized mobile handsets. In: Proceedings of the First Workshop on Virtualization in Mobile Computing, pp. 12–16. ACM (2008)
2. Choi, K., Lee, J., Kim, Y., Kang, S., Han, H.: Feasibility of the computation task offloading to GPGPU-enabled devices in mobile cloud. In: 2015 International Conference on Cloud and Autonomic Computing (ICCAC), pp. 244–251, September 2015
3. Chun, B.G., Ihm, S., Maniatis, P., Naik, M., Patti, A.: CloneCloud: elastic execution between mobile device and cloud. In: Proceedings of the Sixth Conference on Computer Systems, pp. 301–314. ACM (2011)
4. Gordon, M.S., Jamshidi, D.A., Mahlke, S., Mao, Z.M., Chen, X.: Comet: code offload by migrating execution transparently. In: Presented as Part of the 10th USENIX Symposium on Operating Systems Design and Implementation (OSDI 12), pp. 93–106. USENIX, Hollywood, CA (2012). https://www.usenix.org/conference/osdi12/technical-sessions/presentation/gordon
5. Kantarci, B., Mouftah, H.T.: Trustworthy sensing for public safety in cloud-centric internet of things. IEEE Internet Things J. **1**(4), 360–368 (2014)
6. Kosta, S., Aucinas, A., Hui, P., Mortier, R., Zhang, X.: Thinkair: dynamic resource allocation and parallel execution in the cloud for mobile code offloading. In: Proceedings of IEEE INFOCOM 2012, pp. 945–953, March 2012
7. Montella, R., Giunta, G., Laccetti, G., Lapegna, M., Palmieri, C., Ferraro, C., Pelliccia, V.: Virtualizing CUDA enabled GPGPUs on ARM clusters. In: Wyrzykowski, R., Deelman, E., Dongarra, J., Karczewski, K., Kitowski, J., Wiatr, K. (eds.) PPAM 2015. LNCS, vol. 9574, pp. 3–14. Springer, Heidelberg (2016). doi:10.1007/978-3-319-32152-3_1
8. Silva, F.A., Rodrigues, M., Maciel, P., Kosta, S., Mei, A.: Planning mobile cloud infrastructures using stochastic petri nets and graphic processing units. In: 2015 IEEE 7th International Conference on Cloud Computing Technology and Science (CloudCom), pp. 471–474, November 2015
9. Volkov, V., Demmel, J.W.: Benchmarking GPUs to tune dense linear algebra. In: International Conference for High Performance Computing, Networking, Storage and Analysis, SC 2008, pp. 1–11. IEEE (2008)
10. Yan, Y., Grossman, M., Sarkar, V.: JCUDA: a programmer-friendly interface for accelerating Java programs with CUDA. In: Sips, H., Epema, D., Lin, H.-X. (eds.) Euro-Par 2009. LNCS, vol. 5704, pp. 887–899. Springer, Heidelberg (2009). doi:10.1007/978-3-642-03869-3_82

Distributed and Network-Based Computing

3-Additive Approximation Algorithm
for Multicast Time in 2D Torus Networks

Hovhaness A. Harutyunyan and Meghrig Terzian$^{(\boxtimes)}$

Concordia University, Montreal, QC H3G 1M8, Canada
haruty@cs.concordia.ca, m_terzia@encs.concordia.ca

Abstract. In this paper, we propose 3-additive approximation algorithm for multicast time in wormhole-routed 2D torus networks. HMDIAG (Hybrid Modified DIAGonal) divides the 2D torus into four meshes and performs preprocessing at the source node to create the Diagonal Paths (DP), along which the message is sent in each mesh. At the source node and every intermediate node, another process is performed to send the message to a subset of destination nodes along a path branching from the DP. HMDIAG is a tree based multicast algorithm that uses two startup times. Simulation results show that the multicast time, latency, and coefficient variation of multicast time of HMDIAG is better than TASNEM and Multipath-HCM.

Keywords: Multicast · Wormhole-routing · Torus · Complexity

1 Introduction

Multicast is message propagation from a source node to a number of destination nodes in a network. It is used in collaborative applications and parallel computing. Collaborative applications include video conferencing and online games. Systems employing parallel computing include supercomputers. If multicast communication is not efficient, it degrades the performance of collaborative applications and deteriorates the capabilities of supercomputers.

The pattern in which nodes are connected in an interconnection network defines the network topology. Direct network topologies, like meshes and tori, are widely used in supercomputer systems [14].

A 2D mesh has $m \times n$ nodes where m is the number of nodes in the first dimension and n in the second. A node u in a 2D mesh has a 2-coordinate vector (x_u, y_u). Two nodes u and v are connected if $x_u = x_v$ and $y_u = y_v \pm 1$ or $y_u = y_v$ and $x_u = x_v \pm 1$ [12]. The distance between nodes u and v is $|x_v - x_u| + |y_v - y_u|$.

An $m \times n$ torus is an $m \times n$ mesh with wraparound links connecting end nodes $(x, 0)$ to $(x, n-1)$ for all x where $0 \le x \le m-1$ and $(0, y)$ to $(m-1, y)$ for all y where $0 \le y \le n-1$. The distance between nodes u and v is $\min(|x_v - x_u|, m - |x_v - x_u|) + \min(|y_v - y_u|, n - |y_v - y_u|)$ [12]. The properties resulting from the symmetric nature of a torus are low contention latency, high channel bandwidth, and balanced use of communication channels.

© Springer International Publishing AG 2016
J. Carretero et al. (Eds.): ICA3PP 2016, LNCS 10048, pp. 129–142, 2016.
DOI: 10.1007/978-3-319-49583-5_10

The symmetric nature of the torus has attracted many researchers. On the latest list of the TOP500, the third fastest supercomputer *Titan*, a Cray XK7 system, uses a 3D torus topology. The fourth entry on the list, IBM BlueGene/Q *Sequoia*, uses a 5D torus topology. In addition, the fifth entry on the list, Fujistu *K computer*, uses a 6D mesh/torus topology [16].

In wormhole-routing, a message is divided into flits, which is the smallest unit of message a queue and a channel can accept or reject. The header flit carrying the routing information, leads the route of flits holding data [12]. It is widely used in new-generation interconnection networks compared to packet switching, because of the low effect of path length on transmission latency and the need for a small buffer for a channel to store a flit. However, if the header flit is blocked due to resource contention, all trailing flits will be blocked, which in turn can further block other messages resulting in deadlock [14].

The main parameters for evaluating multicast are time and traffic, which are negatively correlated [11]. Traffic is the number of links and time is the number of time units needed to perform a multicast [11]. The communication latency consists of three parts: startup, network and blocking latency. Startup latency is the time required to start a message, including operating system overheads. Network latency is the latency caused by propagation and router delays, blocking latency is the latency caused by delays due to contention in the network. Network latency depends on the traffic generated by the routing algorithm. The startup latency is in microseconds (μs) and network latency is in nanoseconds (ns) [13]. Consequently, researchers have focused on minimizing the startup latency since it dominates the communication latency. The network latency has a slight effect on the communication latency, except when the maximum path length to reach all destination nodes is very long. In addition, when the network traffic increases, the blocking time, which is a function of path length, may become considerable.

Existing multicast algorithms for 2D torus networks fall into two categories: path based [3,17,18] and tree based [1,5,9]. Tree based multicast has high efficiency on time and traffic [10]. The message from the source node is sent to multiple neighbors, which in turn send the message to other nodes located at a further distance [12]. Time efficiency is due to high degree of parallelism in message distribution and traffic efficiency is due to destination nodes sharing as much common path as possible. Path based algorithms generate high traffic because of following a certain order along a single path. They also generate high latency, as the path lengths are generally long.

In our previous work we proposed MDIAG, a tree based multicast algorithm for store-and-forward routed 2D mesh and torus networks. We proved MDIAG generates optimal or optimal plus one time in 2D meshes [8]. In this paper, we propose a hybrid version of MDIAG, HMDIAG for wormhole-routed networks. We prove that HMDIAG gives 3-additive approximation for multicast time in 2D torus networks.

2   System Model

Multicast communication is modeled as a graph theoretical problem where $G(V, E)$ is a graph with a set of V nodes and E edges representing links between nodes. The source node, u_0 and $d_1, d_2, d_3, \ldots, d_k$ denoting k destination nodes form the multicast set, M. The symmetric structure of the torus makes all nodes identical. Thus, we assume multicast source is located at $(0, 0)$.

A d_i is a destination node where $1 \le i \le k$. D is the set of destination nodes. $D(a, b)$ is the distance between nodes a and b. d is the diagonal node $d = (X_{max}, Y_{max})$, where $X_{max} = \max\{x_1, \ldots, x_k\}$ and $Y_{max} = \max\{y_1, \ldots, y_k\}$. sd is the diagonal line from u_0 to d. DP is the diagonal path from u_0 to d, approximating the sd. $D_{max} = \max\{D(u_0, d_1), \ldots, D(u_0, d_k)\}$. Intermediate nodes are nodes between u_0 and leaf nodes. A zone Z of a 2D mesh is a submesh represented by its two diagonal nodes x and y as $\{x \leftrightarrow y\}$. A node z is in zone $\{x \leftrightarrow y\}$, if $x_x \le x_z \le x_y$ or $x_y \le x_z \le x_x$ and $y_x \le y_z \le y_y$ or $y_y \le y_z \le y_x$ [7].

The basic communication services required in wormhole-routed networks for multicast communication are Absorb (A), Forward (F) and Retransmit (R). The communication services we utilize are the following:

- *Permanent Absorb, Forward and Retransmit (PAFR)*: The message is absorbed while being forwarded to the node towards the next destination node. The node might also retransmit the message.
- *Forward and Retransmit (FR)*: The message is forwarded towards the next destination node. The node might also retransmit the message.
- *Permanent Absorb and Forward (PAF)*: The message is absorbed. The node might also forward the message.

We transform the problem of multicast in a 2D torus to multicast in four 2D meshes. An $m \times n$ torus is divided into four zones $\{(0, 0) \leftrightarrow (\lceil \frac{m}{2} \rceil - 1, \lceil \frac{n}{2} \rceil - 1)\}$, $\{(m - 1, 0) \leftrightarrow (\lceil \frac{m}{2} \rceil, \lceil \frac{n}{2} \rceil - 1)\}$, $\{(0, n - 1) \leftrightarrow (\lceil \frac{m}{2} \rceil - 1, \lceil \frac{n}{2} \rceil)\}$, $\{(m - 1, n - 1) \leftrightarrow (\lceil \frac{m}{2} \rceil, \lceil \frac{n}{2} \rceil)\}$ corresponding to $mesh_1$, $mesh_2$, $mesh_3$, and $mesh_4$. The source nodes of the meshes are $u_0(0, 0)$, $u_1(m - 1, 0)$, $u_2(0, n - 1)$ and $u_3(m - 1, n - 1)$ (Fig. 1). D is partitioned into four subsets D_1, D_2, D_3, and D_4 containing the destination nodes belonging to $mesh_1$, $mesh_2$, $mesh_3$, and $mesh_4$, respectively. Dividing a 2D torus into four equal meshes reduces the upper bound on multicast latency by almost half, enables destination nodes to receive the message in comparable time, and avoids traffic congestion by distributing the traffic load.

The Routing function $R(u, v) = w$ utilized for sending a message from a node u to a node v is:

$$R(u, v) = \begin{cases} (x_v, y_v) & \text{if } (x_u = y_u = y_v = 0 \wedge x_v = m - 1) \vee \\ & (x_u = y_u = x_v = 0 \wedge y_v = n - 1) \vee \\ & (x_u = x_v = m - 1 \wedge y_u = 0 \wedge y_v = n - 1) \\ (x_u, y_u + 1) & \text{if } x_u = x_v \wedge 1 \le y_v - y_u \le \lceil \frac{n}{2} \rceil - 1 \\ (x_u + 1, y_u) & \text{if } y_u = y_v \wedge 1 \le x_v - x_u \le \lceil \frac{m}{2} \rceil - 1 \\ (x_u, y_u - 1) & \text{if } x_u = x_v \wedge 1 \le y_u - y_v \le \lceil \frac{n}{2} \rceil - 1 \\ (x_u - 1, y_u) & \text{if } y_u = y_v \wedge 1 \le x_u - x_v \le \lceil \frac{m}{2} \rceil - 1 \ . \end{cases} \tag{1}$$

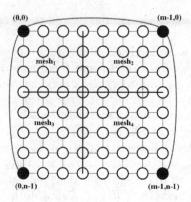

Fig. 1. 2D torus

3   Proposed Algorithm

HMDIAG divides the torus into four meshes and D into four subsets, creates at most four headers by Algorithm 2, encapsulates each header to a copy of the *message*, and transmits them (Algorithm 1).

In Algorithm 2, given a set of destination nodes $D' \in \{D_1, D_2, D_3, D_4\}$ and a source node $s \in \{u_0, u_1, u_2, u_3\}$, *header'* is created. *header'* includes nodes on the DP and destination nodes not on the DP with their corresponding flags.

When an intermediate node receives the header flit, if it is not the first node in the header, forwards it towards the first node in the header using R.

When an intermediate node is the first node in the header, it performs CommunicationServiceOperations (Algorithm 3). If flags P and A are set, the flit is absorbed. The current node is removed from the header. If flag R is set, the header is checked for nodes with flag "PAF" that represent destination nodes not on the DP. The goal is to check if there are destination nodes that can be reached through a horizontal or a vertical path branching from the current node, depending on the location of the previous and next nodes. If such nodes are found, the flit is copied, the header of the flit and the new flit are set, and the new flit is retransmitted. If flag F is set and there are destination nodes in the header, the current node forwards the flit towards the first node in the header using R. The remaining nodes with flag "FR" were added by CreateMessage-Header to make branchings possible. Data flits follow the header flit. The order of first forwarding then retransmitting is crucial to achieve optimal or optimal plus one time in a respective mesh (Proposition 1).

HMDIAG uses two startup times. At startup one, message transmission is performed along the DP-s. At startup two, retransmissions occur from nodes on the DP-s. HMDIAG is a deadlock free algorithm since the four meshes do not share links and the routing function R creates a channel dependency graph with no cycles.

Algorithm 1. HMDIAG

1: **procedure** HMDIAG($D, message$)
2:    partition the 2D torus into $mesh_1$, $mesh_2$, $mesh_3$, and $mesh_4$
3:    partition D into four subsets D_1, D_2, D_3, and D_4 containing destination nodes belonging to $mesh_1$, $mesh_2$, $mesh_3$, and $mesh_4$
4:    apply CreateMessageHeader on (D_1, u_0), (D_2, u_1), (D_3, u_2), and (D_4, u_3) to create $header_1$, $header_2$, $header_3$, and $header_4$
5:    encapsulate $header_i$ for all i where $1 \leq i \leq 4$ to $message$ to create $message_1$, $message_2$, $message_3$, and $message_4$
6:    send $message_1$, $message_2$, $message_3$, and $message_4$
7:    nodes in header of $message_i$ for all i where $1 \leq i \leq 4$ perform Communication-ServiceOperations
8: **end procedure**

Algorithm 2. CreateMessageHeader

1: **function** CREATEMESSAGEHEADER(D', s)
2:    Sort D' in increasing order of distances from u',$DP \leftarrow s$, $u \leftarrow s$
3:    **for** $i = 0 : k'$ **do** $dOnDP[i] \leftarrow 0$
4:    **if** ($x_s = 0$ and $y_s = 0$) **then** $x_d \leftarrow \text{Max}\{x_{d_i}\}$, $y_d \leftarrow \text{Max}\{y_{d_i}\}$
5:    **else if** ($x_s = m - 1$ and $y_s = 0$) **then** $x_d \leftarrow \text{Min}\{x_{d_i}\}$, $y_d \leftarrow \text{Max}\{y_{d_i}\}$
6:    **else if** ($x_s = 0$ and $y_s = n - 1$) **then** $x_d \leftarrow \text{Max}\{x_{d_i}\}$, $y_d \leftarrow \text{Min}\{y_{d_i}\}$
7:    **else if** ($x_s = m - 1$ and $y_s = n - 1$) **then** $x_d \leftarrow \text{Min}\{x_{d_i}\}$, $y_d \leftarrow \text{Min}\{y_{d_i}\}$
8:    **while** $u \neq d$ **do**
9:       **if** ($x_s = 0$ and $y_s = 0$) **then**
10:          $x'_u \leftarrow x_u + 1$, $y'_u \leftarrow y_u$, $x''_u \leftarrow x_u$, $y''_u \leftarrow y_u + 1$
11:       **else if** ($x_s = m - 1$ and $y_s = 0$) **then**
12:          $x'_u \leftarrow x_u - 1$, $y'_u \leftarrow y_u$, $x''_u \leftarrow x_u$, $y''_u \leftarrow y_u + 1$
13:       **else if** ($x_s = 0$ and $y_s = n - 1$) **then**
14:          $x'_u \leftarrow x_u + 1$, $y'_u \leftarrow y_u$, $x''_u \leftarrow x_u$, $y''_u \leftarrow y_u - 1$
15:       **else if** ($x_s = m - 1$ and $y_s = n - 1$) **then**
16:          $x'_u \leftarrow x_u - 1$, $y'_u \leftarrow y_u$, $x''_u \leftarrow x_u$, $y''_u \leftarrow y_u - 1$
17:       **if** $D(u', sd) \leq D(u'', sd)$ **then** $u \leftarrow u'$
18:       **else** $u \leftarrow u''$
19:       $index \leftarrow binarySearch(u, D')$
20:       **if** $index \neq -1$ **then** $u.flag \leftarrow$ "PAFR", $dOnDP[i] \leftarrow 1$
21:       **else** $u.flag \leftarrow$ "FR"
22:       $DP \leftarrow DP \cup u$
23:    $header' \leftarrow DP$
24:    **for** $i = 0 : k'$ **do**
25:       **if** $dOnDP[i] = 0$ **then**
26:          $u \leftarrow dOnDP[i]$, $u.flag \leftarrow$ "PAF", $header' \leftarrow header' \cup u$
27:    **return** $header'$
28: **end function**

Given $M = \{(0, 0), (1, 0), (1, 1), (2, 1), (2, 2), (1, 3)\}$ and message msg, Fig. 2 shows how HMDIAG performs multicast. Double lines represent the DP.

Algorithm 3. CommunicationServiceOperations

1: **procedure** COMMUNICATIONSERVICEOPERATIONS($flit$)
2:    **if** P and A flags are set **then**
3:        Absorb $flit$
4:    Remove $current$ from $flit.H$
5:    **if** R flag is set **then**
6:        $previous \leftarrow$ node from where $flit$ received
7:        $next \leftarrow$ first node in $flit.H$
8:        **for** all nodes d_i in $flit.H$ **do**
9:            **if** $d_i.flag =$ "PAF" **then**
10:                **if** $current = s$ and $x_{current} = x_{next}$ **then**
11:                    **if** $y_{d_i} = y_{current}$ **then**
12:                        $newheader \leftarrow newheader \cup d_i$
13:                **else if** $current = s$ and $y_{current} = y_{next}$ **then**
14:                    **if** $x_{d_i} = x_{current}$ **then**
15:                        $newheader \leftarrow newheader \cup d_i$
16:                **else if** $x_{previous} = x_{current}$ and $y_{current} = y_{next}$ **then**
17:                    **if** $x_{d_i} = x_{current}$ **then**
18:                        $newheader \leftarrow newheader \cup d_i$
19:                **else if** $y_{previous} = y_{current}$ and $x_{current} = x_{next}$ **then**
20:                    **if** $y_{d_i} = y_{current}$ **then**
21:                        $newheader \leftarrow newheader \cup d_i$
22:                **else if** $x_{previous} = x_{current} = x_{next}$ **then**
23:                    **if** $y_{d_i} = y_{current}$ **then**
24:                        $newheader \leftarrow newheader \cup d_i$
25:                **else if** $y_{previous} = y_{current} = y_{next}$ **then**
26:                    **if** $x_{d_i} = x_{current}$ **then**
27:                        $newheader \leftarrow newheader \cup d_i$
28:            **if** $d_i.flag =$ "PAF" or $d_i.flag =$ "$PAFR$" **then**
29:                $destinationNodesLeft \leftarrow destinationNodesLeft + 1$
30:        **if** $newheader \neq \emptyset$ **then**
31:            $newflit \leftarrow flit$
32:            $newflit.H \leftarrow newheader$
33:            $flit.H \leftarrow flit.H - newheader$
34:        **if** F flag is set and $destinationNodesLeft \neq 0$ **then**
35:            forward $flit$ to the node returned by R($current, next$)
36:        **if** newheader $\neq \emptyset$ **then**
37:            retransmit $newflit$ to the node returned by R($current$, first node in $newheader$)
38:    **if** F flag is set and R flag not set **then**
39:        **for** all nodes d_i in $flit.H$ **do**
40:            **if** $d_i.flag =$ "PAF" or $d_i.flag =$ "$PAFR$" **then**
41:                $destinationNodesLeft \leftarrow destinationNodesLeft + 1$
42:        **if** $destinationNodesLeft \neq 0$ **then**
43:            forward $flit$ to the node returned by R($current, next$)
44: **end procedure**

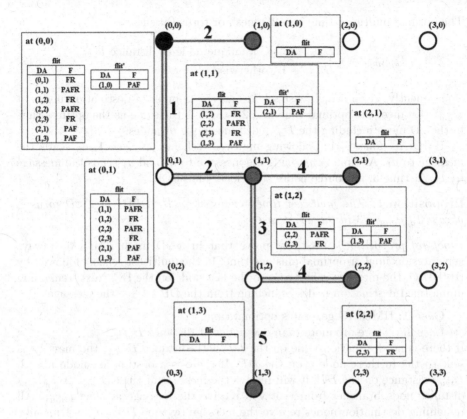

Fig. 2. HMDIAG multicast

3.1   Time Complexity of HMDIAG

Partitioning an $m \times n$ torus and a destination node set takes $O(k)$ time. Sorting k destination nodes takes $O(k \log k)$ time. Assume $n > m$. Creating the DP takes $O(n \log k + k \log k)$ time, since at most $2 \times (m + n - 2) + k$ nodes can be on the DP-s created for all four meshes and for each node a binary search takes $O(\log k)$ time. Adding destination nodes not on the DP to the header, takes $O(k)$ time. Thus, the time complexity of CreateMessageHeader is $O(n \log k + k \log k)$. The time complexity of CommunicationServiceOperations is $O(k + n)$, since at most $2 \times (m + n - 2) + k$ nodes can be in the headers of all four meshes.

Thus, the time complexity of the message preparation part of HMDIAG is $O(n \log k + k \log k)$ and at every node in the message header $O(k + n)$ time is spent.

3.2   3-Additive Approximation for Multicast Time

Dividing a 2D torus into four equal meshes forces every destination node to receive the message from the closest source node u_0, u_1, u_2, or u_3.

The optimal multicast time in a 2D mesh or torus satisfies:

$$T_{optimal} = \begin{cases} D_{max} & \exists \text{ a unique node at distance } D_{max} \\ D_{max} + 1 & \text{otherwise .} \end{cases} \tag{2}$$

Consequently, given a multicast set M and the number of destination nodes at D_{max} distance, the optimal time in a 2D torus is the same as the optimal time in the 2D mesh including the D_{max} distance node or nodes.

HMDIAG follows the following multicast scheme: at time 1, u_0 sends the message to u_1. At time 2, u_0 sends the message to u_2 and u_1 sends the message to u_3. At time 3, all source nodes start local multicast.

Proposition 1. *The multicast time generated by HMDIAG in a 2D torus is always $T_{optimal} + 3$ in the worst case.*

Proof (of proposition). First, we prove that in a 2D mesh HMDIAG always generates optimal or optimal plus one time. In the multicast scheme followed by HMDIAG, the message is first sent to the last node on the DP. Next, remaining uninformed destination nodes branching from the DP receive the message.

Case 1: HMDIAG generates optimal time.

Case 1a: There are more than one nodes at distance D_{max}.
If there is no destination node on the DP with distance D_{max}, the message is sent to the furthest node v on the DP. If there is a destination node u with D_{max} distance on the DP, it will receive the message at time D_{max}. If a D_{max} distance node branches from v, it will receive the message at time D_{max}. All remaining destination nodes receive the message by time $D(u_0, d_i) + 1$ for all i where $1 \leq i \leq k$. All these nodes branch from the path leading to v or u or are on the DP. A branching leads to a delay of one time unit. Since $D(u_0, d_i) \leq D_{max}$, $D(u_0, d_i) + 1 \leq D_{max} + 1$ for all i where $1 \leq i \leq k$. Thus, the multicast time is at most $D_{max} + 1$, which is optimal.

Case 1b: There is a unique node u at distance D_{max} on the DP.
If there is a unique node u at distance D_{max} on the DP, it receives the message at time D_{max}. All remaining destination nodes receive the message by time $D(u_0, d_i) + 1$ for all i where $1 \leq i \leq k$. The time unit of delay is the result of branching from the DP. Since $D(u_0, d_i) \leq D_{max} - 1$, $D(u_0, d_i) + 1 \leq D_{max}$ for all i where $1 \leq i \leq k$. Thus, the multicast time is at most D_{max}, which is optimal.

Case 1c: There is a unique node u at distance D_{max} branching from the last DP node.
The message is sent to the furthest node v on the DP. The D_{max} distance node branches from v, thus it receives the message at time D_{max}. All remaining destination nodes receive the message by time $D(u_0, d_i) + 1$ for all i where $1 \leq i \leq k$. All these nodes branch from the path leading to v. A branching leads to a delay of one time unit. Since $D(u_0, d_i) \leq D_{max} - 1$, $D(u_0, d_i) + 1 \leq D_{max}$ for all i where $1 \leq i \leq k$. Thus, the multicast time is at most D_{max}, which is optimal.

Case 2: HMDIAG does not generate optimal time when there is a unique node u at distance D_{max} not on the DP or branching from the last DP node.

The message is sent to the furthest node v on the DP, receiving it at time $D_{max} - 1$. All remaining destination nodes receive the message by time $D(u_0, d_i) + 1$ for all i where $1 \leq i \leq k$. All these nodes branch from the path leading to v. A branching leads to a delay of one time unit. Since $D(u_0, d_i) \leq D_{max}$, $D(u_0, d_i) + 1 \leq D_{max} + 1$ for all i where $1 \leq i \leq k$. Thus, the multicast time is at most $D_{max} + 1$ which is optimal plus one.

Thus, in the four meshes the time generated from their respective source nodes is $T_{optimal}$ or $T_{optimal} + 1$.

The four source nodes start local multicast at time 3. The time generated by HMDIAG depends on in which mesh the D_{max} distance node or nodes lie.

If the D_{max} distance node or nodes are in $mesh_4$, for any d_i in $mesh_4$, $D(u_0, d_i) = D(u_3, d_i) + 2$. Thus, the two time units of delay correspond to the two wraparound links connecting u_3 to u_0. Thus, the time is $T_{optimal}$ or $T_{optimal} + 1$.

If the D_{max} distance node or nodes are in $mesh_2$ or $mesh_3$, for any d_i in $mesh_2$, $D(u_0, d_i) = D(u_1, d_i) + 1$. Similarly, for any d_i in $mesh_3$, $D(u_0, d_i) = D(u_2, d_i) + 1$. Thus, there is one time unit of delay that makes the generated time equal to $T_{optimal} + 1$ or $T_{optimal} + 2$.

If the D_{max} distance node or nodes are in $mesh_1$, the two extra times are pure delays. Thus, the time is $T_{optimal} + 2$ or $T_{optimal} + 3$.

Consequently, HMDIAG is a 3-additive approximation algorithm for multicast time. □

4   Performance Evaluation

We compare the performance of HMDIAG with TASNEM [1] and Multipath-HCM [17] through a simulator written in C++ on a 40×40 torus.

TASNEM is a tree based multicast algorithm for 2D torus networks that divides the torus into two equal meshes. One mesh contains the nodes with y-coordinate value between that of the source node and source node $\pm \frac{m}{2}$. The other mesh contains the remaining nodes. In the meshes, the message is transmitted along a main path and several branching horizontal paths. The time complexity of both the message preparation part and time spent at every node participating in the multicast process in TASNEM is $O(k)$. TASNEM uses two startup times [1].

Multipath-HCM is a path based multicast algorithm based on the Hamiltonian cycle model. It divides the network into two subnetworks, after labeling nodes according to their position on a Hamiltonian cycle starting from the source. The high-channel network contains directional common links with nodes labeled from low to high and directional wraparound links with nodes labeled from high to low. The low-channel network contains directional common links with nodes labeled from high to low and directional wraparound links with nodes labeled from low to high. Destination nodes are partitioned into four subsets and two messages are sent to each subnetwork. The time complexity of the message preparation part of Multipath-HCM is $O(k \log k)$ and at every node participating in the multicast process constant time is spent. Multipath-HCM uses one startup time [17].

The routing performance under various multicast set sizes is examined starting from 40 destination nodes to 1560. Multicast sets are randomly generated and 100 runs are performed for the same cardinality of destination node set for each algorithm.

After generating a MT, the problem of multicast in the 2D mesh is transformed into broadcast in the MT. Thus, we calculate the broadcast time of the MT using the algorithm proposed by Slater et al. that reflects the time in hops needed to perform the broadcast communication [15].

The startup latency is set to $0.5\,\mu$s. $0.3\,\mu$s correspond to message sending latency and $0.2\,\mu$s correspond to message receiving latency. The network latency is set to $25\,$ns. $5\,$ns correspond to link propagation time and $20\,$ns correspond to router delays. These values reflect prevalent systems utilized values [1,18]. Blocking latency is ignored. Thus, multicast latency is $(500 \times NStartup) + (25 \times LPath)$, where $NStartup$ is the number of startups used by an algorithm and $LPath$ is the maximum path length to reach a destination node.

To reflect the parallelism achieved by the three algorithms, we compare the coefficient variation of multicast time they generate. It is calculated by $\frac{\sigma_{multicastTime}}{M_{nl}}$, where $\sigma_{multicastTime}$ is the standard deviation of the multicast time and M_{nl} is the mean multicast time [2]. A low variation indicates that destination nodes receive the multicast message in comparable arrival time.

We mark the traffic generated by the algorithms, which is the number of links in the MT and study the effect of torus size on multicast time and traffic.

Figure 3 shows that HMDIAG generates the least average time for all values of k. The maximum average time generated by HMDIAG is 40, TASNEM 243, and Multipath-HCM 800. Moreover, HMDIAG time increases with k until $k \leq 160$, after which it is constant. In TASNEM, as the multicast set size increases, the main path length decreases, resulting in a more parallel tree. This is displayed in Fig. 3, as the time decreases with increase in k. When $k \geq 800$, TASNEM generates on average approximately 61% more time than HMDIAG. In Multipath-HCM as the multicast set size increases, almost all nodes of the

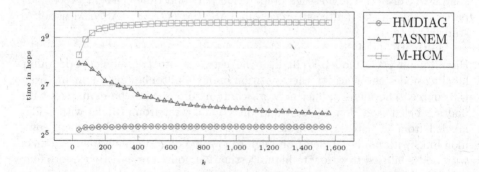

Fig. 3. Average time

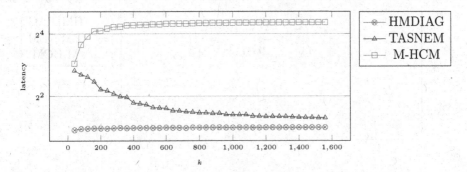

Fig. 4. Average latency

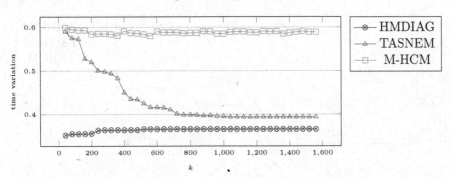

Fig. 5. Average coefficient variation of multicast time

torus are in the destination set, resulting in longer paths and higher multicast time.

Figure 4 shows that HMDIAG generates the least average latency for all values of k. The maximum average latency generated by HMDIAG is $2\,\mu s$, TAS-NEM $7.7\,\mu s$, and Multipath-HCM $20.5\,\mu s$. When $k \geq 800$, TASNEM generates on average approximately 31% more latency than HMDIAG.

Figure 5 shows that HMDIAG generates the least coefficient variation of multicast time for all values of k, proving that the MT-s generated by HMDIAG are the most parallel. The maximum coefficient variation of multicast time generated by HMDIAG is $0.36\,ns$, TASNEM $0.58\,ns$, and Multipath-HCM $0.60\,ns$. On average, the average coefficient variation of multicast time generated by TASNEM is approximately 19% more than that of HMDIAG.

Figure 6 shows that HMDIAG generates on average approximately 16% less traffic than TASNEM when $k \leq 160$, after which HMDIAG generates on average approximately 14% more traffic. Multipath-HCM generates the most traffic.

Figures 7 and 8 show the effect of network size on time and traffic generated by the three algorithms, respectively. The multicast set size is set to 20% of the maximum possible destination node set size.

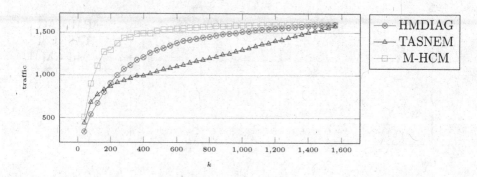

Fig. 6. Average traffic

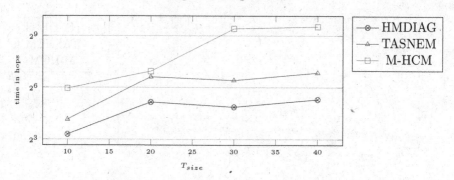

Fig. 7. Average time as a function of torus size

Figure 7 shows that increase in torus size increases the time generated by the three algorithms. The increase rate in time of HMDIAG is the least. The average increase in time of TASNEM is approximately three times the average increase of HMDIAG.

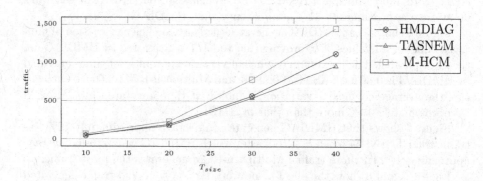

Fig. 8. Average traffic as a function of torus size

Figure 8 shows that increase in torus size increases the traffic generated by the three algorithms. The increase rate of HMDIAG and TASNEM is almost the same when $T_{size} \leq 30 \times 30$, after which the traffic increase rate of HMDIAG is more by approximately 11%.

5   Conclusion

In this paper, we propose HMDIAG algorithm for wormhole-routed 2D torus networks. HMDIAG is a hybrid algorithm that performs preprocessing at the source node. At the source and every intermediate node, another process is performed to retransmit the message to another subset of destination nodes. We prove that HMDIAG is 3-additive approximation algorithm for multicast time.

Simulation results show that HMDIAG generates less multicast time, latency and coefficient variation of multicast time than TASNEM and multipath-HCM. However, when the number of destination nodes is greater than 160, HMDIAG generates on average 14% more traffic than TASNEM. When studying the effect of network size on time and traffic generated by the three algorithms, the increase rate in time of HMDIAG is the least. The increase rate of HMDIAG and TAS-NEM is almost the same when $T_{size} \leq 30 \times 30$, after which the increase rate in traffic of HMDIAG is more by approximately 11%.

References

1. Abd El-Baky, M.A.: A tree-based algorithm for multicasting in 2D torus networks. Egypt. Inform. J. **16**, 45–53 (2015)
2. Al-Dubai, A., Ould-Khaoua, M., Romdhani, I.: On high performance multicast algorithms for interconnection networks. In: Gerndt, M., Kranzlmüller, D. (eds.) HPCC 2006. LNCS, vol. 4208, pp. 330–339. Springer, Heidelberg (2006). doi:10.1007/11847366_34
3. Darwish, M.G., Radwan, A.A., Abd El-Baky, M.A., Hamed, K.: TTPM - an efficient deadlock-free algorithm for multicast communication in 2D torus networks. J. Syst. Archit. **54**, 919–928 (2008)
4. Darwish, M.G., Radwan, A.A., Abd El-Baky, M.A., Hamed, K.: Ready groups: a path-based multicast algorithm for 2D torus networks. In: Proceedings of the 7th International Conference on Informatics and Systems, pp. 1–9. IEEE Press, New York (2010)
5. Francalanci, C., Giacomazzi, P.: A high-performance deadlock-free multicast routing algorithm for K-ary N-cubes. IEEE Trans. Comput. **59**(2), 174–187 (2010)
6. Fleury, E., Fraigniaud, P.: Strategies for path-based multicasting in wormhole-routed meshes. J. Parallel Distrib. Comput. **53**, 26–62 (1998)
7. Harutyunyan, H.A., Wang, S.: Efficient multicast algorithms for mesh-connected multicomputers. In: Tenth International Conference on Information Visualization, pp. 504–510. IEEE Press, New York (2006)
8. Harutyunyan, H.A., Terzian, M.: Two modified multicast algorithms for two dimensional mesh and torus networks. In: Proceedings of the 7th International Symposium on Parallel Architectures. Algorithms and Programming, pp. 122–128. IEEE Press, New York (2015)

9. Kumar, D.R., Najjar, W.A., Srimani, P.K.: A new adaptive hardware tree-based multicast routing in k-ary n-cubes. IEEE Trans. Comput. **50**(7), 647–659 (2001)
10. Lan, Y., Li, L.M., Esfahanian, A.-H.: Distributed multi-destination routing in hypercube multiprocessors. In: Proceedings of the Third Conference on Hypercube Concurrent Computers and Applications: Architecture. Software, Computer Systems, and General Issues, pp. 631–639. ACM, New York (1988)
11. Lin, X., Ni, L.M.: Multicast communication in multicomputer networks. IEEE Trans. Parallel Distrib. Comput. **4**, 1105–1117 (1993)
12. McKinley, P.K., Xu, H., Esfahanian, A.-H., Ni, L.M.: Unicast-based multicast communication in wormhole-routed networks. IEEE Trans. Parallel Distrib. Comput. **5**, 1252–1265 (1994)
13. Mohapatra, P., Varavithya, V.: A hardware multicast routing algorithm for two-dimensional meshes. In: Proceedings of the Eighth Symposium on Parallel and Distributed Processing, pp. 198–205. IEEE Press, New York (1996)
14. Ni, L.M., McKinley, P.K.: A survey of wormhole routing techniques in direct networks. Computer **26**, 62–76 (1993)
15. Slater, P.J., Cockayne, E.J., Hedetniemi, S.T.: Information dissemination in trees. SIAM J. Comput. **10**, 692–701 (1981)
16. Top500 Lists, June 2016. https://www.top500.org/lists/2016/06/
17. Wang, N.-C., Hung, Y.-P.: Multicast communication in wormhole-routed 2D torus networks with hamiltonian cycle model. J. Syst. Archit. **55**, 70–78 (2009)
18. Wang, N.-C., Hung, Y.-P., Chu, C.-P.: Multicast communication in wormhole-routed symmetric networks with hamiltonian cycle model. J. Syst. Archit. **51**, 165–183 (2005)

Online Resource Coalition Reorganization for Efficient Scheduling on the Intercloud

Adrian Spataru[1], Teodora Selea[1], and Marc Frincu[1,2($\boxtimes$)]

[1] e-Austria Research Institute, Timisoara, Romania
{adispataru,teodora.selea}@ieat.ro
[2] Department of Computer Science,
West University of Timisoara, Timisoara, Romania
marc.frincu@e-uvt.ro

Abstract. While users running applications on the intercloud can run their applications on configurations unavailable on single clouds they are faced with VM performance fluctuations among providers and even within the same provider as recent papers have indicated. These fluctuations can impact an application's objectives. A solution is to cluster intercloud resources into coalitions working together towards a common goal; i.e., ensuring that the deviation from the objectives is minimal. These coalitions are formed based on historical information on the performance of the underlying resources by assuming that patterns in the deployment of the applications are repeatable. However, static coalitions can lead to underutilized resources due to the fluctuating job flow leading to obsolete information. In this paper propose an online coalition formation metaheuristics which allows us to update existing and create new coalitions at run time based on the job flow. We test our AntClust online coalition formation method against a static coalition formation approach.

Keywords: Resource management · Cloud computing · Scheduling algorithms · Metaheuristics

1 Introduction

Cloud computing has become increasingly popular due to its on demand pay per use policy. Consequently, more public providers offer clients a wide range of choices regarding billing models, SLAs, and storage and processing infrastructure. In this context, the upcoming intercloud, a federation of clouds will allow customers to run their applications on configurations and requirements unavailable on single clouds. This complex environment adds two extra dimensions (i.e., multiple SLAs and billing models) to the already heterogeneous model existing in clouds.

This work was partially supported by the EU H2020 CloudLightning project under grant no. 643946 and the AMICAS grant (PN-II-ID-PCE-2011-3-0260) of the Romanian National Authority for Scientific Research.

© Springer International Publishing AG 2016
J. Carretero et al. (Eds.): ICA3PP 2016, LNCS 10048, pp. 143–161, 2016.
DOI: 10.1007/978-3-319-49583-5_11

Adding to the increased heterogeneity is the problem of efficiently processing the monitored data deluge from various providers. Hierarchical models where each provider independently models his resources either centralized or distributed and shares information with the others have been proposed. However, the occurrence of fog computing which brings intelligence near the edge of the network will increase the number of resources available for processing by several orders of magnitude. All these resources will be usable by the intercloud.

In this context, traditional scheduling techniques based on greedy methods, meta-heuristics, and linear programming may take too long to find suitable resources for certain classes of jobs such as time sensitive deadline constrained applications. In addition, these jobs may require multiple resources to successfully execute batch tasks (e.g., MapReduce jobs, workflows [12], or process variable data streams [17]). A solution is to cluster resources and to periodically reschedule jobs through VM migration [30]. Despite several existing clustering techniques (cf. Sect. 2), few algorithms consider the historical behavior of resources and the reliability of resource clusters. Furthermore, little work has been done towards online reclustering which is needed due to the variable arrival rate. Taking into account the historical behavior of resources and tasks can improve the chance that a specific job will meet its objectives (e.g., deadline, high availability, throughput) especially since clouds have been shown to exhibit VM performance fluctuations [11,21,29] due to VM interference. The rationale is to give more trust to intercloud resources that have exhibited predictable behavior during previous executions of *similar* jobs and to cluster them together into *resource coalitions*. Here we *focus on application containers* (e.g., Docker) running on bare bone machines rather than applications running on VMs.

Definition 1. *Resource coalitions are defined as resource clusters – possibly part of multiple clouds – successfully used by a particular job in the past to meet its objectives.*

We emphasize here the difference between resource clusters and resource coalitions. The latter behave more like an alliance of resources to achieve a common goal rather than being only a group (cluster) of resources.

In this work we address the previously mentioned challenges and propose a metaheuristics based on Ant Colony Clustering for online resource coalition formation and selection by mixing reorganization of unused coalitions with historical resource matchmaking for already used ones. We empirically analyze our method and compare it against a static coalition formation method (i.e., one in which the proposed algorithm is called only once at the start of the schedule). To the best of our knowledge this paper is the first one to deal with the reuse of intercloud resource coalitions and their online restructuring by matchmaking incoming jobs on existing coalitions. While our approach does not explicitly consider multi-tenancy interference it implicitly assumes it by placing new jobs on coalitions which have experienced stable performance on similar jobs in the past. Hence, it attempts to recreate the same environment (i.e., job schedule) as in the past on existing coalitions. However, as job configurations can change it also allows to dynamically update existing coalitions to maximize the chance of a new job – with no history – to successfully execute.

The rest of the paper is structured as follows: Sect. 2 describes the related work; Sect. 3 focuses on the envisioned architecture; Sect. 4 describes the proposed coalition formation algorithm; Sect. 5 describes the coalition selection algorithms; Sect. 6 tests and compares the proposed online algorithm with the static approach; finally Sect. 7 describes the main conclusions and future work.

2 Related Work

History Dependent Scheduling. Scheduling algorithms usually rely on the current state of the system to determine where to schedule incoming jobs [13, 26]. Recent work [8] has defined a history-dependent scheduling algorithm for scheduling workflow tasks. Given the fluctuations in cloud resource performance [11,21,29] focusing only on job run time by ignoring the historical performance of resources may not be the best approach, especially in the case of large scale dynamic systems. Our solution considers the historical behavior of the resource and of similar applications to determine where to place the incoming jobs. This approach enables us to reuse existing resource coalitions which proved successful in meeting past applications' objectives.

Historical data has also been used to determine the number of required resources in elastic clouds [2,17]. However, The proposed methods attempt only to predict the required throughput. Caglar et al. [3] have recently proposed a k-means clustering method for providing the lowest interference level on VMs based on their historic mean CPU and memory usage, and performance features. The method is designed to be applied for each client resource request. This approach can impact scheduling time if multiple requests arrive simultaneously. In contrast, our approach tries to match user requirements on existing "efficient" VM configurations by minimizing the coalition formation and trying to reuse as much as possible from the existing ones.

Cluster Based Scheduling. Clustering has been suggested as a way of improving schedules by grouping resources and tasks together based on various performance metrics [5]. Vasile et al. [28] propose a hierarchical clustering algorithm for heterogeneous clouds. The process consists of two phases, the clustering of resources and the job assignment on each cluster by using classical scheduling algorithms. In [4] a method to cluster resources in virtual datacenters for higher availability and scalability is proposed. These papers however do not consider historical data and job similarity when selecting clusters. In [10] a task clustering approach which focuses on client and provider side objectives is presented. The algorithm however does not consider resource performance history making it prone to constraints' violations such as overlapping tasks.

Latency Aware Clustering. In large scale distributed systems communication overhead is one of the main issues that require attention [9]. In these systems transferring data from clients to the resources running jobs or between jobs becomes a source of delay in completion time especially when Big Data is processed. Palmieri et al. [22] propose a GRASP based online reorganization of the communication networks to reduce this overhead. However, they do not look at historical performance of resources. Another approach for grouping resources based on latency is presented in [20]. In our work we propose a similar latency based organization of existing coalitions and favor clusters close to the client in terms of latency. From these we select coalitions with good historical record for similar jobs as candidates for executing the incoming jobs. Hence, instead of limiting to selecting clusters based solely on latency we add the historical component to ensure a higher reliability in meeting the clients' objectives.

A machine learning based clustering algorithm is presented in [27]. The paper proposes a random forest approach to calculate similarities and resource usage patterns among the services and feed them to the clustering algorithm. The similarity based matching is close to our own approach, however we focus also on resource history to cope with variations in resource behavior (usage pattern). The presented paper however ignores the resources where tasks were executed on.

Bin Packing. A common strategy to reduce the number of physical machines used on provider side is to bin pack VMs on them. This can reduce energy consumption and optimize resource usage. Recently [19], a consolidation technique based on machine learning has been proposed. In our work we prune the search space for resource selection, given that parallel jobs require similar resources. In the process of assigning jobs (each job task is running in a container) to resources several containers could end up running on the same resource depending on their aggregated load.

Summarizing, while there has been some work on resource clustering it has largely ignored the historical performance of resources and jobs. Furthermore, most work focuses on static clustering which effectively ignores the online arrival of jobs and the benefits of incrementally updating clusters instead of recomputing them from scratch for each job batch. Generic online clustering algorithms have been proposed [6,16]. We address these two problems by proposing a history aware resource coalition formation algorithm and by investigating online coalition reorganization.

3 Architecture Overview

To enable our online coalition formation and selection algorithms we are introducing the architecture on which they are designed. Figure 1 depicts the envisioned architecture which reduces communication overhead and allows for a hierarchical coalition management based on metainformation.

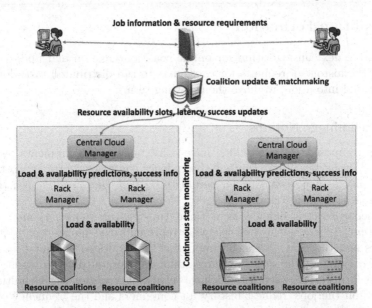

Fig. 1. Proposed architecture for large scale resource coalition handling.

Each cloud is governed by a *Central Cloud Manager* which receives resource load and availability predictions from distributed *Rack Managers*. These monitor each resource part of their racks. To reduce the communication overhead rack managers process real-time load and availability data locally and send to the central cloud manager (1) predictions on the future load and availability of each resource, (2) and information on the fulfillment of objectives by finished tasks. In this paper resources are assumed to be physical machines part of computing cell, each running one or more containers. The prediction window depends on the algorithm's accuracy. In this paper we do not deal with these algorithms.

Based on the predicted resource load and availability each central cloud manager sends to the *Central Coalition Matchmaking* module the available (idle) resource time slots, latency to each resource, and updated success rate of each resource that has executed a task since the last message. Updates are send only if they have changed since the last message.

The proposed architecture allows for the infrastructure to easily scale out by adding more central cloud managers. A criterion for adding new central cloud managers could be the throughput rate. If a deterioration below a specified threshold is observed, a new central cloud manager can be added. In turn, it can take over some of the newly added rack managers. The decision on which rack managers to join the newly added central manager could be taken based on the communication latency between them.

The matchmaking module creates or updates coalitions based on the request history and frequency of similar executed applications (cf. Sect. 4), and matches incoming jobs on coalitions based on their availability (cf. Sect. 5).

4   Coalition Formation

We describe next an algorithm for online coalition creation and update. Considering the history of requests for containers to run distributed tasks logically encapsulated into a job, we have the following terms:

4.1   Preliminary Notions

A *job* is composed of tasks which have constraints or requirements over the resources' properties. Tasks can have precedence constraints forming workflows, however, in this paper we consider *parallel tasks with hard deadline constraints*. Tasks are executed in containers.

A user *request* is defined as a tuple $\langle n, (cpu_1, mem_1), (cpu_2, mem_2), \ldots, (cpu_n, mem_n) \rangle$, where the first element represents the number of requested resources and the next n elements represent the requested cpu_i and $memory_i$ for each resource i. The set of resources that collaborate to accommodate such a request forms a logical entity which we refer to as *coalition* per Definition 1.

Based on the jobs' request history for containers and the frequency of *similar* requests our goal is to construct coalitions online, so that when a *similar* job request is submitted for execution at least one coalition will be ready to accommodate its tasks. Similarity is defined through a similarity function which is discussed in Sect. 4.2.

A task t is *schedulable* on resource r if each of the requested parameters is less than or equal to the parameters that the resource has to offer. We denote this relation as $t \rightarrow r$ and give the following definition:

Definition 2. *Let R be the set of available resources. Coalition creation means finding a partition C of R, for which, given the history H, and the relation $\rightarrow$, the following holds:*

$$\forall J \in H, \exists c \in C, \text{ s.t. } card(c) \geq size(J) \text{ and}$$
$$\forall t \in T_J, \exists r \in c, \text{ s.t. } t \rightarrow r.$$

where $size(J)$ yields the number of tasks in J, and T_J denotes the set of task requests for job J.

Definition 3. *A schedulable task can be scheduled iff there is an available slot that allows the task to be executed by its given deadline (cf. Sect. 5).*

The coalitions that execute distributed tasks reliably can accommodate future similar jobs eliminating the need to reconstruct them each time a job is submitted. The only exception is when either all coalitions are busy running jobs or when no similar jobs are found in any coalition's history.

The reliability of a coalition c for running a task i is defined in terms of its *confidence* τ_i^c. The confidence lets us assess the probability for a coalition to meet a client's objectives and the provider SLA.

We compute τ_i^c based on the run time and usage prediction accuracy. While several prediction algorithms have been proposed [1, 14, 15, 23, 24] in this paper we rely on a k-nearest neighbors method similar to [23]. We use a sliding window of size k taking the values of *the last k runs* of the job on coalitions having the same number of resources. For the load prediction we follow the same approach but look at the coalition usage history.

Each time the task's usage exceeds a certain threshold or its run time exceeds the predicted one we decrease the confidence value proportionally with the number of such violations. By default the confidence value is set to 1. At any time t, the confidence of a coalition c is defined as in Eq. 1:

$$\tau_i^c(t+1) = \tau_i^c(t) - w\tau_i^c(t)\frac{\#\text{violations}}{\#\text{tasks on coalition}} \tag{1}$$

where w is a dampening factor manually set. It allows us to set the impact of the total number of violations. To avoid relying on old estimates we use a sliding window and search for violations within a predefined time frame.

Algorithm 1. Clustering Strategy

1: **function** CREATECOALITIONS($R[1\ldots N]$)
2:     $learnThreshold(R)$
3:     $clusters = clusterResources(R)$
4:     $coalitions = processClusters(clusters)$
5:     **return** $coalitions$
6: **end function**

The method takes a local approach by considering only the history of a particular coalition. This may not be always the case as the particular global configuration of running/idle coalitions may play a role in the individual behavior. We plan on investigating this aspect in future work.

In order to adapt to recent requested features, unused coalitions will be dissolved and a reorganization step will take place, considering updated weights based on how recent the features were requested. Our approach considers that coalitions can be created by mirroring successful configurations by relying on meta-heuristics to estimate successful configuration.

4.2 Coalition Formation Strategy

The process of finding similarities between resources, grouping, and maintaining groups will further be referred as *coalition strategy*. As presented in Algorithm 1, a coalition strategy takes as input a set of resources with properties for which a *similarity function* can be applied. The similarity function computes a similarity threshold to decide if two resources should be part of the same coalition. Given the threshold (either predefined or computed through a metaheuristic), resources are grouped by the clustering heuristic. The clusters are then used as a guideline for creating coalitions. If resources remain outside the clusters, several coalitions of a single resource are created. Coalitions which do not accommodate jobs during any time window are dissolved and reorganized to increase the chances of upcoming tasks to get scheduled.

In this paper we consider two methods based on the ANTClust algorithm [18] to discover resource coalitions: one in which initial discovered clusters are used throughout the entire scheduling activity (static approach), and another in which unused coalitions are periodically dissolved and the underlying resources are creating new coalitions by updating the clusters identified by the algorithm (online approach). The modified AntClust algorithm is depicted next.

4.3   Ant Colony Clustering

This Ant Colony Clustering strategy uses ANTClust algorithm to identify clusters of resource collaboration. Algorithm 2 is an extension of Algorithm 1 and models resource information as ant entities. Ant based clustering is a metaheuristic inspired from the behavior of ants inside an ant colony. In general, metaheuristics have the advantage of exploring a wide set of possible solutions but can sometime converge to a local minimum. An ant contains information regarding the resource features useful to compute similarity (cf. Eq. 2), as well as information related to group membership: ⟨label, meeting counter, similarity threshold, perception of nest size (M), acceptance degree by other ants in nest $(M+)$⟩.

Algorithm 2. AntClust Clustering Strategy

1: **function** CREATECOALITIONS($R[1..N]$)
2:     $ants = []$
3:     **for all** $resource$ in R **do**
4:         $ant = createAnt(resource)$
5:         $ants.add(ant)$
6:     **end for**
7:     $learnThreshold(ants)$
8:     $clusters = randomMeetAnts(ants)$
9:     $coalitions = processClusters(clusters)$
10:     **return** $coalitions$
11: **end function**

The threshold learning procedure *learnThreshold* follows the one described in ANTClust algorithm and computes the maximum and average similarity for each ant which are then averaged to yield the acceptance threshold for the given ant. The threshold for an ant entity is computed by applying the similarity function to random sample from the data set, which we considered to have the size 10% of the data set. For the given problem, we would like to cluster together machines that had run similar number of tasks together, thus the similarity is computed using Eq. 2, where the *data* attribute refers to the maximum number of machines with which had collaborated to run a job. We notice in the equation that *ants* having equal *data* will have a similarity of 1, while *ants* with distant *data* will have a similarity close to 0.

$$Sim_{i,j} = 1 - \frac{abs(A_i.data - A_j.data)}{max(A_i.data, A_j.data)} \qquad (2)$$

After the two thresholds have been computed there follows a meeting step (cf. Algorithm 3) in which random ants are selected based on their similarity and acceptance thresholds. We apply meeting resolution rules described in the original ANTClust paper. The rules have the effect of creating new clusters and adding, removing, or exchanging ants from previously created clusters. Accept rules are applied if the similarity between two ants is larger than both their thresholds. Here we can distinguish four situations related to the ants' cluster membership:

1. No ant is member of a cluster: both ants form a new cluster;
2. One ant i is member of a cluster: the other ant is included in the cluster;
3. Both ants belong to the same cluster: their M parameters are increased;
4. Ants belong to different clusters: the ant with the smaller M is attracted in the other cluster and both M parameters are decreased.

If two ants belonging to the same cluster meet and reject each other (i.e., the similarity is smaller than the acceptance threshold) then the ant with the lowest $M+$ gets removed from the cluster and its parameters are reset, while for the other ant its M parameter gets increased and its $M+$ parameter is decreased. After the meeting procedure follows a cluster refining step, in which clusters will be removed if they do not reach a given ration between the desired size and the actual cluster size. In our experiments we found the best suited value for this ratio to be 0.5. All ants which do not belong to a cluster are considered to be *free ants* and they will be used to fill incomplete clusters in the next phase.

Algorithm 3. Random ant meeting procedure

```
 1: function RANDOMMEETANTS(ants[1..N])
 2:     meetingNo = N(N + 1)/2
 3:     clusters = {}
 4:     for i = 1 to meetingNo do
 5:         ant1 = selectRandom(ants)
 6:         ant2 = selectRandom(ants)
 7:         sim = getSimilarity(ant1, ant2)
 8:         if sim > ant1.threshold and sim > ant2.threshold then
 9:             applyAcceptRules(ant1, ant2, clusters)
10:         else
11:             applyRejectRules(ant1, ant2, clusters)
12:         end if
13:     end for
14:     return clusters
15: end function
```

In Algorithm 4 we process the clusters created by the ANTClust algorithm. The *label* of the cluster represents the desired coalition size by any resource belonging to that cluster. If the cluster contains the desired number of machines, then a coalition is created with the first *label* machines. Otherwise, similar machines from the *free ants* will be used to complete this coalition to the desired cluster size. If after all clusters have been processed there still exist *free ants* we create a new coalition for each of them.

For the online case the algorithm is executed periodically cf. Sect. 6.

5   Coalition Selection

The coalition selection matches the user requirements with a suitable coalition based on the desired run time, availability, coalition's confidence and the number of requested resources. It has two stages: (1) find a proper coalition, and (2) readjust the coalition's available time slots for future jobs.

5.1   Coalition Discovery

To enable coalition discovery we define the following entity:

$$e_k = \begin{cases} [t_{k1}, t_{k2}] & \text{time interval} \\ \{c_1, c_1, ..., c_n\} & \text{coalition list} \end{cases} \tag{3}$$

An entity corresponds to different time intervals. Each represents an available time interval in which a user job can be planned. An entity also contains a list of all the coalitions that are available in that time slot.

Algorithm 4. AntClust Clusters Processing

```
 1: function PROCESSCLUSTERS(clusters:dict)
 2:     coalitions = []
 3:     for all Label l in clusters do
 4:         while clusters[l].size > 0 do
 5:             if l < clusters[l].size then
 6:                 machines = remove(clusters[l], 0, l)
 7:                 c = createCoalition(machines)
 8:                 coalitions.add(c)
 9:             else
10:                 machines = removeAll(clusters[l])
11:                 c = createCoalition(machines)
12:                 addMachinesUntillFull(c, freeAnts)
13:                 coalitions.add(c)
14:             end if
15:         end while
16:     end for
17:     for all Machine m in freeAnts do
18:         c = createCoalition(m)
19:         coalitions.add(c)
20:     end for
21:     return coalitions
22: end function
```

The first criterion for coalition discovery is represented by the available time slot. Once an e_k is found we search its coalition list for a coalition c with a number of resources greater or equal to the requested user resources and with the highest confidence value (cf. Eq. 1). We propose two search algorithms: First-fit and Best-fit. Both search for a solution that matches a user request d_r:

$$d_r = \begin{cases} [t_{r1}, t_{r2}] & \text{requested free time interval slot} \\ m & \text{requested number of resources} \end{cases} \quad (4)$$

where t_{r2} represents the user given deadline, and t_{r1} the desired start time.

A matching entity's time interval must contain the requested slot and its coalition list has to contain a coalition whose resource number is equal or greater to the one requested by the job:

$$e_s \text{ is a solution if } \begin{cases} t_{s1} \leq t_{r1} \text{ and } t_{r2} \leq t_{s2} \\ c_s.numberOfResources \geq m \\ \max \tau_i^{c_s} \forall i \in T_J \end{cases} \quad (5)$$

Given the above, the proposed two search algorithms are described next.

First-fit holds a list of entities ordered by availability intervals and performs a linear search until it finds the first entity obeying Eq. 5.

Best-fit searches for an entity, noted e_{best} and defined as in Eq. 3, that minimizes: $t_{r1} - t_{best1}$ and $c_x.numberOfResources - m$ while obeying Eq. 5. The algorithm finds the closest available time slot to the requested one, minimizing the difference between the job's requested starting point (t_{r1}) and the entity's time interval starting point (t_{k1}). By searching the best match, we avoid defragmenting and leave more free interval slots for the jobs to come. Then, the algorithm chooses from the entity's coalitions list the coalition with the highest confidence and the closest (greater or equal) number of resources to the ones requested. To perform the search efficiently we have chosen a Red-Black Interval Tree structure [7, p. 348] as an underlying structure for our data. The algorithm is presented in Algorithm 5. We consider x as our current entity and $x.int$ its time interval. We define the *overlap(i,x.int)* function as the algorithm that checks if the intervals i and $x.int$ are in the overlapping situation II from Fig. 2. The entity (cf. Relation 3) maps on the nodes of the Red-Black Tree, with the available time slot as the interval and an extra fields or the coalition list. We have altered the search algorithm as follows. The original algorithm considers any type of the four cases of interval overlapping cf. Fig. 2 as possible solutions. However, in our case we only consider as valid the first type in order to satisfy (5). After we find a matching interval, we search for a coalition that covers the required resources. We keep a sorted list of the coalitions based on their number of resources, so we apply a

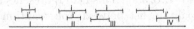

Fig. 2. Interval overlapping situations [7, p. 349].

Algorithm 5. Best-fit Searching Strategy.

```
1: function SEARCH(T, i, res)
2:     stackList = []
3:     x=T.root
4:     min=MAX_Value
5:     bestMatch=NULL
6:     while x ≠ T.nil and stackList not empty do
7:         if overlap(i, x.int) then
8:             if binarySearch(x.cList, res then
9:                 if min > (i.low − x.int.low) then
10:                    bestMatch=x
11:                    min=i.low − x.int.low
12:                end if
13:            end if
14:        end if
15:        if x.right ≠ T.nil and x.right.min ≤ i.low and x.right.max ≥ i.high and
               x.right.maxRes ≥ res then
16:            if x.left ≠ T.nil and x.left.min ≤ i.low() and x.left.max ≥ i.high
                   and x.left.maxRes ≥ res then
17:                stackList.push(x.left)
18:            end if
19:            x = x.right
20:        else
21:            if x.left ≠ T.nil and xleft.min ≤ i.low and x.left.max ≥ i.high and
                   x.left.maxRes ≥ res  then
22:                x = x.left
23:            else
24:                x = stackList.pop()
25:            end if
26:        end if
27:    end while
28:    return bestMatch
29: end function
```

Binary Search [7, p. 291] to find the coalition whose number of resources is the closest (equal or greater) to our requirement and has the highest confidence. In addition, we select the right branch, since its larger values suits our minimization goal. However, there are situations when we can not find a solution on the right branch (Step 2 cf. Fig. 3) and we must choose going left. In order to know if the left subtree may contain a viable solution we added an extra field to each node, $x.min$, representing the interval starting point of the left-most node in the sub-tree rooted by $x.tree$. This allows us to assess if there is a possible solution on the left part of the sub-tree.

Furthermore, we add another extra field to each node, computed in a similar way to the maximum field [7, p. 350]. This field represents the maximum number of resources from the coalition list between the coalition list from the current node and the ones in its sub-tree:

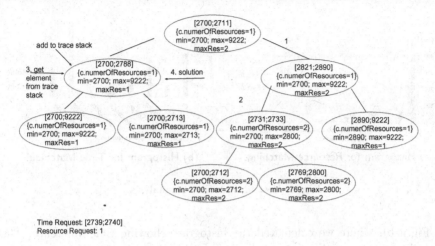

Fig. 3. Example of solution discovery process.

$$x.maxRes = max \begin{cases} x.list.maxResOnCoalition \\ x.left.maxRes \\ x.right.maxRes \end{cases} \quad (6)$$

Although a branch may have a solution for us, matching the time interval we desire, it might not have a coalition with enough resources to support our demand. So, we make use of this extra field ($x.maxRes$) to adjust our searching process in order to avoid going down on a branch that will not have enough resources to satisfy the demand.

Due to time and resource restrictions, there are situations where following the right branch of the tree leads to no solutions because neither the right nor the left sub-trees satisfy the user requirements. In this case we must backtrack and try to find a solution on higher levels of the tree, trying the left path where a decision to continue on the right branch was taken. So, at each step, if we choose to follow the right branch, we verify if the left branch is also an option and put the left child in a trace stack. When we hit a dead end and no solution was found, we return to the last node added to the stack (Step 3 cf. Fig. 3). The algorithm stops when no better match is found (Step 4 cf. Fig. 3).

The searching strategy has an $O(\log^2 n)$ complexity.

Algorithm Analysis. In Fig. 4(a) we present a histogram based on the difference between the number of resource of the chosen coalition and the requested number of resources. *Best-fit* makes an economy in the resource management process, by choosing the coalitions with the closest number of resources to the ones demanded by the job. As a result, *Best-fit* is able to plan more jobs then *First-fit*. In addition, *Best-fit* minimizes the difference between a job's requested starting point (t_{r1}) and the starting point of the matching entity's interval (t_{s1}),

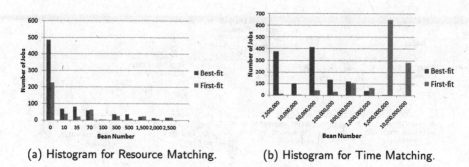

(a) Histogram for Resource Matching.   (b) Histogram for Time Matching.

Fig. 4. Best fit and First fit analysis.

cf. Fig. 4(b), where we calculated the histogram showing that difference. The analysis was done on the dataset depicted in Sect. 6.

5.2   Readjusting Available Time Slots

Let coalition c with the following list of available time intervals and let i be the index of the selected interval:

$$\{[t_{11}, t_{12}], [t_{21}, t_{22}], ...[t_{i1}, t_{i2}, ...[t_{1n}, t_{1n}]]\}$$

When a coalition is selected we have to adjust its available time slots cf. Fig. 5: the initial interval is removed and two intervals are created instead.

The selected entity can have either one coalition, which is the coalition we selected, or two or more coalitions. In the first case we have to remove the entire entity, while in the second case we only remove the matching coalition from the coalition list of the entity (cf. Eq. 5). In both of the cases, we insert two new entities. Each of them has the current coalition in their coalition list and one of the newly created intervals cf. Fig. 5.

The readjusting process is straightforward in *First-fit* because in either of the two cases we only have to remove the entity from the list. The *Best-fit* algorithm

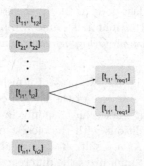

Fig. 5. A coalition's time interval after selection.

uses a tree as an underlying structure to reduce the searching space, but node deletions and insertions take $O(h)$ time, where h is the height of the tree.

6 Experiments

Dataset. We have tested the algorithm on real life traces from a Google compute cell [25]. A cell represents a set of machines usually belonging to a single compute cluster, sharing a high bandwidth network and a central management system which assigns work to machines. Despite experimenting on a single cell, due to the scalability and modularity of our architecture (cf. Sect. 3) we argue the dataset to be relevant for our analysis. In our scenario the Central Cloud Manager handles the cell. Work is defined to arrive at the cell in the form of jobs, which are composed of a number of tasks. Each task consists of a Linux program and defines its requirements for being scheduled onto a single machine. The trace contains jobs running on physical machines and each task is isolated within a container. Resource requirements and usage data for tasks are derived from information provided by the cell's management system and the individual machines in the cell. Resource units are normalized using a scaling relative to the largest capacity on any machine in the trace. The following resources are used in our experiments to define a job's requirements: (1) CPU (core count or core-second/second) - if a task is using two cores at all time, it will be reflected as 2 cores/s. We normalize this value in our experiments; (2) Memory (bytes) - a percentage of the kernel memory is accounted to the task and reported in the traces; and (3) Disk space (bytes) - represented by run time local capacity use. Measurements are reported at 5 min intervals. The trace subset we use contains of the following data: 12.5 K VMs, 150 K task usage records, and 50 jobs (totaling 2,000 tasks) every 300 s.

Experiment Setup. To demonstrate our approach we consider the above mentioned data set as describing a collection of resources on the intercloud. We have set up a simulated experiment in which 1/4 of the data was used to initialize the system as follows. The data collected within the window was used to predict job run time and to initialize the coalitions. For predicting run time, the run time of all previous jobs having a similar field logicJobName (which remains the same if a program is ran again by the same user), was aggregated, and the maximum run time was used as the prediction. Coalition formation was performed by the AntClust algorithm (cf. Algorithm 2) reorganizing unused coalitions every 300 s. Repeated experiments have provided the same results as depicted here.

The simulation is driven by the trace data, considering that jobs arrive in the same order as in the trace. The task usage values from the trace to compute the load of the system.

To quantify the efficiency of the algorithms we measured the following information every 300 s: (1) Number of successfully scheduled tasks; (2) Number of successfully scheduled jobs; and (3) Number of tasks using over-committed machines: computed as the number of tasks that were scheduled onto a machine with full capacity. We tested both Best Fit and First Fit with our algorithm in static and online cases.

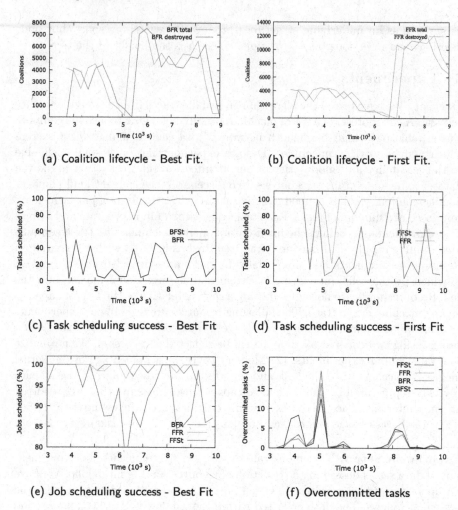

(a) Coalition lifecycle - Best Fit.

(b) Coalition lifecycle - First Fit.

(c) Task scheduling success - Best Fit

(d) Task scheduling success - First Fit

(e) Job scheduling success - Best Fit

(f) Overcommitted tasks

Fig. 6. Experiments.

Analysis. We show in Fig. 6c and d that using only the initially created coalitions – with AntClust – results in poor scheduling success in the immediate future. Best Fit Static (BFSt) falls drastically after two scheduling windows, while First Fit Static (FFSt) has few time windows where it can schedule jobs on coalitions with a larger size, improving its success rate. When the reorganization procedure is employed we see that the scheduling success rises significantly in both cases, showing greater improvement for Best Fit. In Fig. 6e we show the success in terms of percentage of scheduled jobs. The online reorganization algorithms present a maximum of 5% error, while the best static approach shows a maximum error of over 20%. A major cause for the improvement is the fact that during reorganization new large enough coalitions are created, while in the static case the matching algorithms must wait for the scheduled jobs to complete.

We also consider that several containers running on the same machine may over-commit to CPU and/or memory due to overloaded caused by wrong run time estimates – which cause confidence degradation in the coalition in future schedules – and depict in Fig. 6f the number of tasks using over-committed machines, as a percentage of the tasks scheduled in the previous tasks window. Here we notice few peaks due to the fact that run time was underestimated leading to more tasks to overlap. In future work we plan on addressing the run time accuracy confidence and to incorporate it into the coalition selection phase.

Figures 6a and b show the number of created and destroyed coalitions for each of the two scheduling algorithms. We notice that a large percentage of coalitions are destroyed immediately after their creation. This is in part due to not finding suitable tasks for them. Despite this behavior more than 95% of incoming jobs are matched on existing coalitions. This indicates that more coalitions than needed are being created. For future work we will consider an improved heuristics involving online merging of coalitions to accommodate jobs and a predictive approach for estimating coalition requirements for future jobs.

7   Conclusion

In this paper we presented a novel approach for clustering physical resources into logical coalitions having the goal of accommodating specific types of jobs by reusing as much as possible of already existing coalitions. We implemented and tested a scheduling platform consisting of coalition formation and coalition selection strategies and tested its behavior on a real resource management data set. Experiments show that our online method for coalition management mixing reorganization of unused coalitions and historical matchmaking can successfully match more than 95% of requested jobs. Considering that jobs which are not matched by our algorithm, can be scheduled in a traditional manner, we conclude that using a coalition based scheduling platform can reduce the search space for task-machine mapping.

Future Work. While several directions have been pointed out in the experiment analysis, another direction we plan on taking is to cluster resources which have similar attributes, weighting recent requested attributes as more important. We plan on implementing such formation and selection strategies and compare their behavior with the current approach. Our approach can also be extended to compute the similarity in terms of the distribution of previous ran tasks for each machine, and compare its behavior to the current one.

References

1. Chirkin, A.M., Kovalchuk, S.V.: Towards better workflow execution time estimation. IERI Procedia **10**, 216–223 (2014)
2. Antonescu, A.F., Oprescu, A.M., Demchenko, Y., de Laat, C., Braun, T.: Dynamic optimization of SLA-based services scaling rules. In: 2013 IEEE 5th International Conference on Cloud Computing Technology and Science (CloudCom), vol. 1, pp. 282–289 (2013)
3. Caglar, F., Shekhar, S., Gokhale, A.S.: Towards a performance interference-aware virtual machine placement strategy for supporting soft real-time applications in the cloud. In: Proceedings of 3rd IEEE International Workshop on Real-Time and Distributed Computing in Emerging Applications, REACTION 2014, Rome, Italy, 2 December 2014
4. Chavan, V., Kaveri, P.: Clustered virtual machines for higher availability of resources with improved scalability in cloud computing. In: 2014 First International Conference on Networks Soft Computing (ICNSC), pp. 221–225 (2014)
5. Chen, W., Da Silva, R., Deelman, E., Sakellariou, R.: Balanced task clustering in scientific workflows. In: 2013 IEEE 9th International Conference on eScience (eScience), pp. 188–195 (2013)
6. Choromanska, A., Monteleoni, C.: Online clustering with experts. In: Proceedings of the Fifteenth International Conference on Artificial Intelligence and Statistics, AISTATS 2012, La Palma, Canary Islands, 21–23 April 2012, pp. 227–235 (2012)
7. Cormen, T.H., Leiserson, C.E., Rivest, R.L., Stein, C.: Introduction to Algorithms, 3rd edn. MIT Press, Cambridge (2009)
8. Dayama, N.R., Krishnamoorthy, M., Ernst, A., Rangaraj, N., Narayanan, V.: History-dependent scheduling: models and algorithms for scheduling with general precedence and sequence dependence. Comput. Oper. Res. **64**, 245–261 (2015)
9. Deng, K., Kong, L., Song, J., Ren, K., Yuan, D.: A weighted k-means clustering based co-scheduling strategy towards efficient execution of scientific workflows in collaborative cloud environments. In: 2011 IEEE Ninth International Conference on Dependable, Autonomic and Secure Computing (DASC), pp. 547–554 (2011)
10. Doulamis, N., Kokkinos, P., Varvarigos, E.: Resource selection for tasks with time requirements using spectral clustering. IEEE Trans. Comput. **63**(2), 461–474 (2014)
11. Farley, B., Juels, A., Varadarajan, V., Ristenpart, T., Bowers, K.D., Swift, M.M.: More for your money: exploiting performance heterogeneity in public clouds. In: Proceedings of the Third ACM Symposium on Cloud Computing, pp. 20:1–20:14 (2012)
12. Frincu, M.E., Genaud, S., Gossa, J.: On the efficiency of several VM provisioning strategies for workflows with multi-threaded tasks on clouds. Computing **96**(11), 1059–1086 (2014)
13. Frincu, M.E., Genaud, S., Gossa, J.: Client-side resource management on the cloud: survey and future directions. Int. J. Cloud Comput. **4**(3), 234–257 (2015)
14. Iverson, M., Ozguner, F., Follen, G.: Run-time statistical estimation of task execution times for heterogeneous distributed computing. In: Proceedings of 5th IEEE International Symposium on High Performance Distributed Computing, pp. 263–270 (1996)
15. Iverson, M.A., Özgüner, F., Potter, L.: Statistical prediction of task execution times through analytic benchmarking for scheduling in a heterogeneous environment. IEEE Trans. Comput. **48**(12), 1374–1379 (1999)

16. King, A.: Online k-means clustering of non-stationary data. Technical report, MIT, May 2012
17. Kumbhare, A., Simmhan, Y., Prasanna, V.: Plasticc: predictive look-ahead scheduling for continuous dataflows on clouds. In: 2014 14th IEEE/ACM International Symposium on Cluster, Cloud and Grid Computing (CCGrid), pp. 344–353 (2014)
18. Labroche, N., Monmarche, N., Venturini, G.: A new clustering algorithm based on the chemical recognition system of ants. In: ECAI, pp. 345–349 (2002)
19. Lin, H., Qi, X., Yang, S., Midkiff, S.: Workload-driven VM consolidation in cloud data centers. In: 2015 IEEE International on Parallel and Distributed Processing Symposium (IPDPS), pp. 207–216 (2015)
20. Malik, S., Huet, F., Caromel, D.: Latency based dynamic grouping aware cloud scheduling. In: 2012 26th International Conference on Advanced Information Networking and Applications Workshops (WAINA), pp. 1190–1195 (2012)
21. Ou, Z., Zhuang, H., Lukyanenko, A., Nurminen, J.K., Hui, P., Mazalov, V., Yla-Jaaski, A.: Is the same instance type created equal? Exploiting heterogeneity of public clouds. IEEE Trans. Cloud Comput. **1**(2), 201–214 (2013)
22. Palmieri, F., Fiore, U., Ricciardi, S., Castiglione, A.: Grasp-based resource re-optimization for effective big data access in federated clouds. Future Gener. Comput. Syst. **54**, 168–179 (2016)
23. Phinjaroenphan, P., Bevinakoppa, S., Zeephongsekul, P.: A method for estimating the execution time of a parallel task on a grid node. In: Sloot, P.M.A., Hoekstra, A.G., Priol, T., Reinefeld, A., Bubak, M. (eds.) EGC 2005. LNCS, vol. 3470, pp. 226–236. Springer, Heidelberg (2005). doi:10.1007/11508380_24
24. Pietri, I., Juve, G., Deelman, E., Sakellariou, R.: A performance model to estimate execution time of scientific workflows on the cloud. In: Proceedings of the 9th Workshop on Workflows in Support of Large-Scale Science, pp. 11–19 (2014)
25. Reiss, C., Wilkes, J., Hellerstein, J.L.: Google cluster-usage traces: format + schema. Technical report, Google Inc., Mountain View, CA, USA (2011)
26. Smanchat, S., Viriyapant, K.: Taxonomies of workflow scheduling problem and techniques in the cloud. Future Gener. Comput. Syst. **52**, 1–12 (2015)
27. Uriarte, R., Tsaftaris, S., Tiezzi, F.: Service clustering for autonomic clouds using random forest. In: 2015 15th IEEE/ACM International Symposium on Cluster, Cloud and Grid Computing (CCGrid), pp. 515–524 (2015)
28. Vasile, M.A., Pop, F., Tutueanu, R.I., Cristea, V., Koodziej, J.: Resource-aware hybrid scheduling algorithm in heterogeneous distributed computing. Future Gener. Comput. Syst. **51**, 61–71 (2015)
29. Xu, F., Liu, F., Jin, H.: Heterogeneity and interference-aware virtual machine provisioning for predictable performance in the cloud. IEEE Trans. Comput. **PP**(99), 1 (2015)
30. Xu, Y.: Characterizing and mitigating virtual machine interference in public clouds. Ph.D. thesis, University of Michigan (2014)

Graphein: A Novel Optical High-Radix Switch Architecture for 3D Integration

Jie Jian, Mingche Lai, Liquan Xiao$^{(\boxtimes)}$, and Weixia Xu

College of Computer, National University of Defense Technology,
Changsha, Hunan, China
liquanxiao@nudt.edu.cn

Abstract. The demand from Exascale computing has made the design of high-radix switch chips an attractive and challenging research field in EHPC (Exascale High-Performance Computing). Recent development of silicon photonic and 3D integration technologies has inspired new methods of designing high-radix switch chips. In this paper, we propose Graphein—a novel optical high-radix switch architecture, which significantly reduces the radix of switch network by distributing a high-radix switch network into multiple layers via 3D integration, and which improves switch bandwidth while lowering switch chips power consumption by using silicon photonic technology. Our theoretical analysis shows that Graphein architecture can achieve 100% throughput. Our simulation shows that the average latencies under both random and hotspot patterns are less than 10 cycles, and the throughput under random pattern is almost 100%. Compared to hi-rise architecture, Graphein ensures the packets from different source ports receive fairer service, thereby yielding more concentrated latency distribution. The Graphein architecture also provides strong performance isolation under random traffic pattern. In addition, the power consumption of the Graphein chip is about 19.2 W, which totally satisfies the power constraint on a high-radix switch chip.

1 Introduction

As the core infrastructure of HPC (High-Performance Computing), interconnection network plays a key role to the realization of large-scale parallel computing, by determining the performance and scalability of the system. ITRS predicts that by 2022, the peak performance of HPC will reach exascale (10^{18}), with over 200,000 computational nodes [1]. Such large scale and high performance raises higher requirements to the bandwidth, power consumption, and latency of the EHPC interconnection network. High-radix switch chip, as the key component of the interconnection network, determines the power and cost of the network. In 2015, Mellenox proposed a 36 port IB router for the interconnection of supercomputing and large-scale datacenter [2]. Intel proposed a 48-port switch based on Omni-Path architecture [3], yielding performance 2.3 times higher than

J. Jian—This work was partially supported by 863 Program of China (2015AA 015302), NSFC (61572509).

J. Carretero et al. (Eds.): ICA3PP 2016, LNCS 10048, pp. 162–177, 2016.
DOI: 10.1007/978-3-319-49583-5_12

that of IB network switches. Despite these achievements, they cannot satisfy the demands from EHPC (Exascale High-Performance Computing) for the efficacy and density of interconnection network. Therefore high-radix switch chips with more ports and higher throughput (over tens of Tbps per port) are highly expected.

However, the design of high-radix switch chips raises following challenges to the conventional technologies: (1) **Power and area bottleneck of LR-Serdes.** Most existing high-radix switch chips connect with other chips through LR-Serdes, which have relatively high BTE (Bit Transport Energy), resulting in high port power. The high power of LR-Serdes makes it difficult to physically realize high-radix switch chips. (2) **Buffer layout bottleneck.** Typical YARC architectures usually contain multiple large buffers, in order to compensate for the negative effects of round-trip credit delay on persistent switch throughput. With the increase of I/O bandwidth and number of ports, the numerous buffers can cover over 60% of the chip's overall area. Besides, the large amount of row/column buses within the YARC architecture causes high density of lines on the chip, resulting in heavy RC and cross talk, which hinders effective chip layout.

In order to develop a realistic high-radix switch chip, we must first overcome the aforementioned two bottlenecks, which require innovative high-radix switch chip technologies. Most current switch chips support LR (Long Reach)-Serdes, which has signal transmission distance of about 100 cm. However, such long-distance signal transmission means higher driving and amplifying power. In 2015, OIF (Optical Connection Forum) defined SR-Serdes and USR (Ultra-Short Reach)-Serdes standards [4], which respectively support 20 cm and 5 cm signal transmission. The power of USR Serdes is only 4pj/bit, only 1/5–1/10 of LR Serdes, and the area is only 1/5 of LR Serdes. This means, with the development of silicon photonic, it is possible to solve the power bottleneck caused by LR Serdes, by directly applying the SR-Seders and USR Serdes in switch chips with the help of on-board E/O transmission and 2.5D/3D photonic integration. However, although using SR-Seders and USR Serdes enable more ports to be integrated to the chip, it also increase the demand for data switching, raising great challenge to the conventional YARC-based electric switch in architecture.

In this paper, we deal with the intra-chip data switching problem by applying on-chip photonic interconnection technology. As this technology advances, it is already possible to apply a complete on-chip photonic transmission component in an interconnection network of multi-core processors [5,6]. Compared to the conventional electric transmission network, silicon photonic networks have the advantage of high bandwidth density, low latency, low dynamic power and repeater-less communication, which makes it a viable choice for designing next-generation high-radix switch chips with up to 128–256 ports. In this work, we stack multiple layers of the 3D chip using silicon photonic on-chip network and TSV (Through Silicon Via)-based 3D integration technology [7], (1) to realize high-speed communication among multiple layers using inter-layer connections, and (2) to separate the optical data plane and the electric control plane. We can thus distribute the switch network and buffer of a high-radix switch chip into multiple layers, and realize 3D implementation of a high-radix switch network. Our approach is able to (1) decrease the length of waveguides on each layer, and (2) relieve the pressure of power, layout and bandwidth of the high-radix switch chip, thereby facilitating the design of high-radix switch chip.

In this paper, we propose Graphein − a novel Optical High-radix Switch Architecture for 3D Integration, which combines the advantages of silicon photonic and 3D integration. Graphein stacks 5 optical layers and 1 bottom port layer. Each optical layer is equipped with an optical switch network, which realizes intra- and inter- layer high-speed switching by using an intra-layer crossbar network and an inter-level TSV, The multi-layer network is able to lower the intra-layer crossbar radix, thereby (1) reducing the length of each optical waveguide, (2) reducing the count of micro-rings attached to each optical waveguide, and (3) lowering the overall power of the interconnection network. We have conducted a theoretical analysis on the throughput of the proposed 3D high-radix switch architecture under random balanced load, which shows that the proposed architecture is able to ensure 100% throughput. using a PhoenixSim simulator, we have empirically evaluated our architecture in terms of latency, throughput, power and fairness. Our main contributions in this paper are summarized as:

1. The design of a novel optical high-radix switch architecture that achieves 100% throughput and provides fair service to all ports with low power.
2. The theoretical throughput analysis of the Graphein architecture based on speed-up ratio shows the ideal throughput of this architecture is 100%.
3. The evaluation of latency, throughput and power of the proposed architecture relative to the Hi-Rise architecture using the random and hotspot traffic patterns.

2   Related Work

With the recent progress in silicon nanophotonics, many recent researches have turned their attention to optical on-chip interconnection network [8–10]. Silicon photonic components are CMOS-compatible and have lower production cost than electric components. As shown in Fig. 1(a), the main optical components stacked on chip include laser, modulator, waveguide, and demodulator. 3D integrated circuits (3D-ICs) with wafer-to-wafer bonding technology show promising capability in improving the scalability of chips. In wafer-to-wafer bonded 3D-ICs, active devices (processors, memories, peripherals) are placed on multiple active layers, while vertical Through Silicon Vias (TSVs) are used to connect modules across the stacked layers. The scale of a TSV is between $4\,\mu m$–$10\,\mu m$ and even can be further reduced to $1\,\mu m$. In addition, TSV can achieve very small communication delay (20 ps in a 20-layers 3D architecture). The appearance of 3D-ICs provides new opportunities for enabling higher performance and design efficiency of ICs [11]. Multiple active layers in 3D ICs can enable increased integration of chip within the same area footprint as traditional single layer 2D

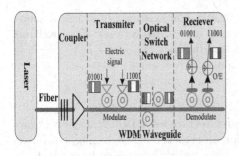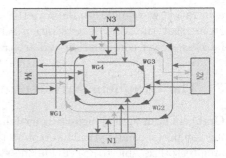

Fig. 1. (a) Architecture and components of ONoC (b) Ring based MWSR optical crossbar

ICs. In addition, long global interconnects between ports can be replaced by shorter inter-layer TSVs, improving performance and reducing on-chip power dissipation. Recent 3D IC test chips from Intel, IBM, and Tezzaron [12–14] have confirmed the benefits of 3D IC technology.

Jeloka [15] proposes a high-radix switch for 3D integration called Hi-Rise. The Hi-Rise architecture puts the 64 ports in 4 layers of the 3D architecture to improve the scalability of the chip, and the arbitration of the switch is also divided into intra-switch layer and inter-switch layers. This architecture guarantees the fairness and efficiency of the arbitration by CLRG scheme, however, the bandwidth of the TSV channels between layers is the bottleneck of the network, which also limits the throughput cannot reach 100%.

The flattened butterfly [16] and dragonfly [17] are also architectures used to build high-radix switches. When compared to the traditional architectures such as k-ary or n-cube, these architectures improve the IO bandwidth and scalability of the switch chip. However, these architectures cannot satisfy the demand of EHPC. Scott [18] proposes the YARC architecture with 64 port. The bandwidth of YARC achieves 2.4 Tb/s. In order to solve the HOL problem, the YARC divides the switch process into 2 steps by place a large amount of buffers and row/column buses. The demand of these resource makes it hard to scale to a higher radix. Binkert [19] rebuilds the YARC architecture by silicon photonic technology. The novel architecture replaces the buses by waveguides, and also decrease the buffer size. But it changes the arbitration process to only one step, and cannot guarantee the efficiency of the arbitration. The channel allocation strategies of photonic network can be divided into 3 models, SWMR (single-write-multiple-read), MWSR (multiple-write-single-read), MWMR (multiple-write-multiple-read). The MWSR model is the most popular one due to its high utilization of channels and low complexity of arbitration. MWSR crossbars provide each router with a dedicated receiving channel, and all the routers transmit data on the receivers' channels, forming a crossbar at the senders' end (Fig. 1(b)). Many MWSR arbitration schemes [20–22] have proposed in the last few years, most of them uses tokens to improve the efficiency of arbitration, and they also use broadcast waveguides or longer arbitration waveguides to improve the fairness. The existing literatures demonstrate that the MWSR arbitration schemes in optical network work well on fairness, power consumption and arbitration efficiency.

3   The Graphein Architecture

Graphein is an optical high-radix switch architecture for 3D integration, containing 256 ports. using optical interconnection and stacked 3D packaging, Graphein architecture is able to (1) divide the switch network into many layers and (2) provide efficient intra-chip routing according to the relative positions of source and destination ports.

3.1   Graphein Architecture and Optical Switch Layers

In the Graphein architecture, all the 256 switch ports are distributed on the bottom port layer of the 3D multi-layer chip, and the high-radix switch network is realized on the optical switch layers upon the port layer. In order to decrease the radix of switch network, we propose two kinds of switch layers, the intra-switch layer and the inter-switch layer. Different layers connect with each other by TSVs (see Fig. 2(a)). When the packets enter Graphein from the bottom port layer, they will be transmitted through the TSVs to the corresponding inter-/intra-switch optical switch layer according to the respective positions of source and destination ports. After completing the switching process in the optical switch network, they will return to the bottom port layer and leave the Graphein chip.

In order to allocate the flow rate of packets into the switch network, the Graphein divides its 256 ports into 4 layers with 64 ports per layer. Each layer is further divided into 4 sections. Figure 2(b) shows the overall layout of the ports and the way they are divided into layers and section.We use coordinate (L, S, P) to denote the position of ports, where (1) L represents the layer number of the port, (2) S represents the port's section number in its layer, and (3) P represents the port's position in its section. For example, given port coordinate (L, S, P), we can get its number N by using the following formula:

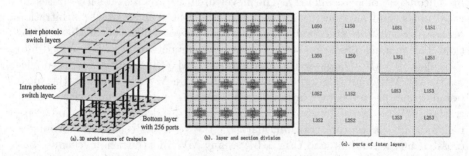

(a). 3D architecture of Grahpein   (b). layer and section division

(c). ports of inter layers

Fig. 2. Graphein architecture and its layers

$$N = L \cdot 64 + S \cdot 16 + P$$

and

$$0 \leq L \leq 3, 0 \leq S \leq 3, 0 \leq P \leq 15$$

Similarly, if we know a port's number is K, we can deduce its coordinate (L_k, S_k, P_k) by

$$L_k = K/64$$

$$S_k = (K/16)/4$$

$$P_k = K\%16$$

The switch network of the intra switch layer contains 4 crossbars − each of which consists of 64 ports from the corresponding layer (see Fig. 2(b)). Each inter-layer switch network chooses the crossbars which belong to 4 different layers but have the same intra-layer section number, and connects them into a fully connected switch network (see Fig. 2(c)). The entire Graphein architecture is thus composed of 4 inter-layer switch layers. For example, port 19 (with coordinate $(0, 1, 3)$), in the intra-switch layer, is connected with all the other ports in layer 0 into a crossbar network; while in the inter-switch layer, since its section number is 1, all the ports from Sect. 1 (i.e. 16−31, 80−96, 144−160, 208−224) form a 64-port crossbar network.

3.2   Switch

Packets that are injected into Graphein through input ports will leave from destination output port after going through the high-radix switching. The processes of switching can be classified as below according to the relative positions of the source and target ports. For the convenience of description, we abstract all 16 ports of the same section into one switch node, i.e., all the ports with layer number $L = i$ and section number $S = j$, are abstracted into one switch node $R(i, j)$, of which the port numbers(N) are within the following range:

$$i \cdot 64 + j \cdot 16 \quad \sim \quad i \cdot 64 + (j + 1) \cdot 16$$

Therefore, the optical switch network formed by multiple optical switch layers can be abstracted into the network shown in Fig. 3, where (1) the green lines denote the intra-switch network and the blue lines denote the inter-switch network, which are both realized by optical waveguides; and (2) the yellow lines denote the TSVs used to connect different switch layers.

The network is a two dimension unidirectional torus network. Here, we use the classic XY-dimension routing algorithm for transmitting packets in this network. The inter-switch network forms the X-dimension paths and intra-switch network forms the Y-dimension paths. The inter-layer TSVs (the yellow oblique lines) are used for data transmission during the shifting between local and global switching.

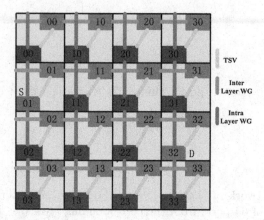

Fig. 3. Switch network of Graphein (Color figure online)

The flows can be classified into 4 types according to the relative positions of source and target ports: (1) If both the source port and the target port of the packet are in the same layer, but with different section numbers (i.e., $L_s = L_d; P_s \neq P_d$), then it only needs to be switched within the intra-switch layer, i.e., the Y-dimension switching in Fig. 3. In this case, the packet first enters the intra-switch network through TSV and then leaves the Graphein from the bottom port switch after being switched. (2) If the source port and the target port of the packet are in different layers, but with the same section numbers (i.e., $L_s \neq L_d; P_s = P_d$), then it only needs to be switched within the inter-switch layer. In this case, the packet first enters the inter-switch network through TSV, reaches the target port through inter-layer switching network, and then returns to the port layer through TSV. (3) If the source and target ports of the packet are in different layers, with different section numbers (i.e., $L_s \neq L_d; P_s \neq P_d$), then it requires following two steps of optical switching: (i) inter-layer switching on X-dimension, i.e., transmits the packet to the intermediate node in the inter-layer; (ii) intra-layer switching on Y-dimension, i.e., transmit the packet through the inter-switch network to the target port. (4) If the source and target ports of the packet share the same layer number and section number, apply the same switching process as case 1, i.e., the packet is only transmitted in the intra-switch layer. The pseudo code of the switch process is as follows:

4   Throughput Analysis of Graphein

In order to analyze the throughput of the Graphein architecture under the uniform random traffic pattern, this paper builds an throughput analysis model based on the speed-up ratio. The assumptions of the model are all independent to the topology, routing algorithm and arbitration scheme of the network.

```
         The switch process of Graphein architecture
1. When a packet pk inject to the switch:
2.          Ls ← Ps/64; Ss ← (Ps/64)/4;
3.          Ld ← Pd/64; Sd ← (Pd/64)/4;
4. if ( Ls == Ld)
5.     Transmit pk to intra-layer by TSV;
6.     Switch pk to Dest port;
7.     Transmit pk to port-layer by TSV;
8. endif
9. else if ( Ss == Sd)
10.     Transmit pk to inter-layer by TSV;
11.     Switch pk to dest port;
12.     Transmit pk to port-layer by TSV;
14. else
15.     Transmit pk to inter-layer by TSV;
16.     Switch pk to intermediate (Ld,Ss);
17.     Transmit pk to intra-layer by TSV;
18.     Switch pk to dest port;
19.     Transmit pk to port-layer by TSV;
20. endif
```

4.1   The Model of Throughput Based on Speed-Up Ratio

As shown in Fig. 4(a), in an interconnection network, the inject flow (i.e., flow from other routers) and the relay flow (i.e., flow from the inject port) will converge in the router, when there are multiple hops transmitted in the network. If both flows compete for the same output port of the router, according to the fair scheduling principle, the injection rate of the inject flow would be suppressed, which makes the inject port unable to inject packets to the network at full speed, reducing the effective throughput of the network.

As shown in Fig. 4(a), in the worst case, router A, B, C, D simultaneously send packets to the $X+$ direction, then the injection rates of router A, B, C, D are respectively 1/2, 1/4, 1/8, 1/16. The reason of this phenomenon is that when the four routers compete for the single output port simultaneously, each

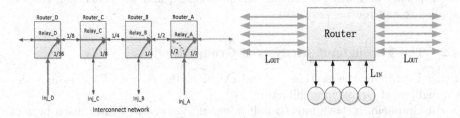

Fig. 4. (a) Flows in interconnection network (b) The model of a router

router can only achieve an inject rate of 1/4 under the fair condition. Thus, if the packets need to transmit many hops in the network, the superposition between the relay flows and the inject flows will influence the throughput of the interconnection network.

Figure 4(b) shows the model of a router. Assume (1) the number of inject port is L_{IN}, (2) the bandwidth of each inject port is B_{IN}, (3) the injection probability (utilization factor) of the inject port is R_{IN} (with $R_{IN} \leq 1$). We then assume the network size is N, the average hops of packets is H. Then the active packet numbers in the network is

$$P_{IN} = (L_{IN} \cdot B_{IN} \cdot R_{IN}) \cdot N \cdot H$$

that is: the sum of the active packets in the network equals to the sum of packets injected from the inject port multiplied by the average hops of all the packets. That means for each packet injected to the network, there are H active packets in the network simultaneously.

If the output port of each router is L_{OUT}, and the bandwidth of each port is B_{OUT}, the utilization factor of output port is R_{OUT}, (with $R_{OUT} \leq 1$, then the sum of the packets on all the network links is

$$P_{OUT} = (L_{OUT} \cdot B_{OUT} \cdot R_{OUT}) \cdot N$$

Obviously

$$P_{IN} = P_{OUT}$$
$$(L_{IN} \cdot B_{IN} \cdot R_{IN}) \cdot N \cdot H = (L_{OUT} \cdot B_{OUT} \cdot R_{OUT}) \cdot N$$
$$(L_{OUT} \cdot B_{OUT})/(L_{IN} \cdot B_{IN}) = (R_{IN} \cdot H)/R_{OUT}$$
$$S = (L_{OUT} \cdot B_{OUT})/(L_{IN} \cdot B_{IN}) \tag{1}$$

S is the speed up ratio of the output ports' bandwidth to the inject ports' bandwidth, and

$$S = (R_{IN} \cdot H)/R_{OUT} \tag{2}$$
$$R_{IN} = S \cdot R_{OUT}/H \tag{3}$$

From the analysis above, we can know that the utilization factor of the inject port depends on the speedup ratio of the router, the average hops of packets and the utilization factor of the output port. The deduction process does not involve the topology or routing algorithm of the network, and the conclusion can be applied to any routing networks.

4.2   The Throughput Analysis of Grahpein

Using Eq. (3), in this section, we will calculate the S and H values and the throughput of Graphein architecture.

In Graphein, in both inter-switch layer and intra-switch layer, each port is mapped to one switch node. The ports are interconnected by TSVs in bottom port layer, inter-switch layer, and intra-switch layer, respectively. Every port with its mapping nodes in the two kinds of switch network are connected by TSVs, and they are abstracted to a router in the torus-like network. As only the bottom port layer has packets injection and exportation, the TSV connections are inner links of each router (in Fig. 5). Every router contains one injection port and two output ports, the injection port is the port in the bottom port layer and the two output ports are used to connect with other routers in intra switch network and inter switch network respectively.

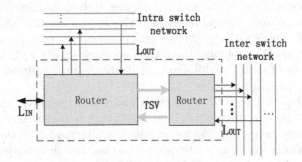

Fig. 5. Router architecture of Graphein

According to the architecture of Graphein in Fig. 2, let K denotes the count of layers in Graphein and M the count of sections in each layer. When under the uniform random traffic pattern, three of the four kinds packets divided in Sect. 3.2 only need transmit in the inter switch network, and their H value is 1, the ratio of these packets is:

$$\frac{K-1}{K \cdot M} + \frac{M-1}{K \cdot M} + \frac{1}{K \cdot M}$$

Only one of the four kinds packets need transmit 2 hops in the network, and the ratio of them is:

$$\frac{(K-1) \cdot (M-1)}{K \cdot M}$$

The average hop count of all the packets is:

$$H_{avg} = \frac{(K-1) \cdot (M-1)}{K \cdot M} \cdot 2 + \frac{K+M-1}{K \cdot M} \cdot 1 = 2 - \frac{K+M+1}{K \cdot M}$$

In our Graphein, $K = M = 4$, then the H is worked out to be 1.5, thus:

$$R_{IN} = \frac{L_{OUT} \cdot B_{OUT}}{L_{IN} \cdot B_{IN}} \cdot \frac{R_{OUT}}{H_{avg}}$$

and

$$L_{OUT} = 2; L_{IN} = 1; B_{OUT} = B_{IN};$$

$$R_{OUT} \leq 1; H_{avg} = 1.5$$

The value of R_{IN} would achieve 100% due to the above calculation, which predicts that the theoretical throughput of the Graphein architecture achieves 100%.

5   Evaluation

5.1   System Setup

The simulation is based on a cycle accurate simulator, the PhoenixSim [23] simulator. This simulator is based on the OMNeT++ environment, which is an object-oriented modular discrete event network simulation framework. This simulator can analyze and evaluate the key metrics such as delay, throughput and power consumption of the multi-processor systems connected by electric interconnection network, optical interconnection network or the hybrid interconnection network quantitatively. We use this simulator to model our high radix router architecture Graphein and the compared architectures Hi-Rise. We define the port number of switch architecture as P, the channel multiplicity between layers of hi-rise architecture as c.

The optical path length $T = 8$ cycles, and the frequency of the system is set to $8\,\text{GHz}$. The size of crossbar (N) is 256 with a packet size of 64 bytes. The depth of the queues is 8. We use synthetic traffic models to test these proposed architectures. For destination node selection, two distributions are used: (1) Normal Random (NR) and (2) Hotspot. When under the hotspot traffic, the hotspot is port 1.

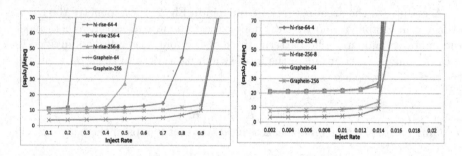

Fig. 6. Latency of hi-rise and Graphein under (a) random (b) hotspot patterns

5.2   Latency

We use the parameter P denotes the port count of the switch architecture, and the parameter c denotes the channel multiplicity of the hi-rise architecture. We build the simulation modes of hi-rise architecture [16] when $P = 64, c = 4; P = 256, c = 4; P = 256, c = 8$ and the simulation models of Graphein when $P = 64$ and $P = 256$, then statistics the average latency when the injection rate changes under the uniform random and hotspot traffic patterns. The results are in Fig. 6a and b.

When the injection rate is low, the Hi-Rise architectures with different parameters all have higher latencies than the Graphein architecture, this is because the arbitration latency of the optical network is lower than the electric network in the Hi-Rise. The more nodes in the network, the more write nodes to compete the write channel, which makes the arbitration latency is higher. This situation also occurs under the hotspot traffic patterns.

Meanwhile, under the random traffic pattern, the latency lines of the hi-rise architecture reach saturation faster than the Graphein, and the larger the ratio of P/c, the faster the line reaches saturation. As in the Hi-Rise architecture, the TSV channels between layers is the bottleneck of the network, and the larger of the value of P/c, the heavier of the congestion in the TSVs, which results in the average latency of packets increases rapidly. While in the Graphein architecture, there is no bottleneck in the network, and the latency line reaches saturation until the injection rate is almost 100%. When under the hotspot traffic pattern, all the nodes only send packets to the hotspot, the traffic in the TSVs is not so heavy that the TSV channels are not hotspot in the Hi-Rise architecture. Thus the saturation points of all the models are almost the same.

5.3   Throughput

We examine the performance with random and hotspot traffics and set the parameter $P = 256, c = 8$. Figure 7 shows the throughput of 16 ports choosing from all the 256 ports. The graphein architecture achieves almost ideal throughput under both traffic patterns, the simulation result agrees well with the analysis in Sect. 4. As the TSV channel is the bottleneck of the Hi-Rise architecture under the random traffic pattern, the throughput of nodes in Hi-Rise architecture is low. Generally, when the injection rate is r, the unidirectional flow between any layers is :

$$f = r \cdot P/L \cdot 1/L$$

L is the layer count of Hi-Rise, in this paper, is 4. When the utilization ratios of all the c TSV channels reach 100%, and the network is saturate, then, the flow between any layers is

$$f = r \cdot 256/(4 \cdot 4) = 8$$

That means only half of the flows can transmit through the TSVs timely. The throughput of the Hi-Rise architecture can only be 50%. The result is the same

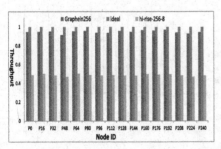 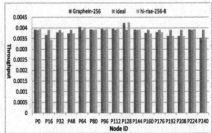

Fig. 7. Throughput of hi-rise and Graphein under (a) random (b) hotspot patterns

as Fig. 7 shows. While under the hotspot traffic pattern, there is no bottleneck in the Hi-Rise network and the throughput can approach to the ideal value.

5.4 Fairness

In order to evaluate the fairness of the Hi-Rise and the Graphein architecture, we draw the quartile diagram of the packets' latencies, the value of parameter P is 256 and c is 8. The result is shown in Fig. 8.

Under the random traffic, the 25% line, 50% line and 75% line of the Graphein architecture all concentrate on about 15 cycles. This shows that most of the packets in Graphein have similar latencies. The fairness of the Graphein is good. The 25% line and 50% line of the Hi-Rise architecture is concentrate on about 20 cycles, while the 75% line is scattered, most of the values are above 40 cycles, which demonstrates that under the saturate injection rate, the congestion between layers occurs. Though most of the packets can be transmitted timely, almost half of the packets cannot be serviced promptly and suffer a large latency.

Under the hotspot traffic, the unfairness of the Hi-Rise is more significant. As shown in Fig. 8c, the distribution of the 25% line, 50% line, 75% line of the Graphein is concentrated in a small range. Most of the packets have an similar latency in the architecture and they have a fair chance to gain the service. Meanwhile, we also notice that there is difference between nodes in the same layer: the nodes at the beginning of each layer have higher latencies and the nodes at the end of each layer have lower latencies. This is due to the unfairness of

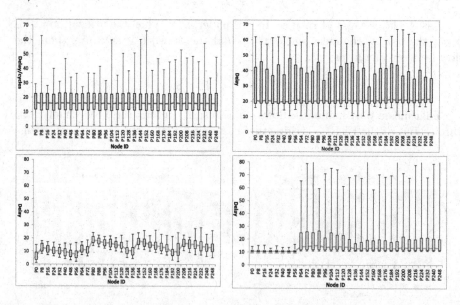

Fig. 8. The quartile diagram of the latencies (a) random & Graphein (b) random & Hi-Rise (c) hotspot & Graphein (d) hotspot & Hi-Rise

the 2-pass arbitration scheme in optical crossbar. The opportunity of nodes near to the downstream of the destination node is higher than that of the upstream ones, and the latencies of the nodes from the downstream are also lower.

However, when turn to Hi-Rise architecture, as can be seen in Fig. 8d, the latencies become various. Latencies of the packets from those nodes in the same layer with the hotspot node are small and their distribution is concentrate, while the latencies of packets from other layers are larger and their distribution is separate. This result shows that the TSV channels are the bottleneck of the Hi-Rise architecture, which make the architecture cannot be fair.

5.5 Power Consumption

Power consumption of an optical network consists of both static and dynamic components. The static component includes external laser power and ring heating power. The laser power includes distribution loss (laser coupling loss, beam splitter loss, laser E/O efficiency et. al) and ring resonance power. The ring heating power is generated by trimming the rings to the corresponding wavelengths. The dynamic power is expended by ring modulation and electrical back-end components including amplifier and detector. When to model the overall power consumption, we set the frequency of optical network as 8 GHz, The data channels are each a waveguide with 16 wavelengths. It is also important to choose the parameters of optical devices. However, as nano-photonic devices are an emerging technology, many of the parameters are subject to change as the technology progresses. From some sets of technology parameters, we adopt the optical model in [24]. We also list the parameters of photonic devices used in the simulation and the optical resource inventory in Table 1.

Table 1. Parameters and resource inventory

Parameters of photonic devices			
Photonic device	Loss	Photonic device	Loss
Waveguide loss	1 dB/cm	Coupling	1 dB
Insertion	0.017 dB	Ge RCEPD	3 dB
Scattering	0.001 dB	Trim	22 uW
Laser efficiency	5 dB	Biasing	91 uW
Detector sensitivity	0.15 fJ/b	Modulation	474 uW
Optical resource inventory			
Photonic network	Waveguides		Micro ring
Data network	Intra	256	256K
	Inter	256	256K
2-pass arbitration	Intra	4	8K
	Inter	4	8K

According to the parameters above, we can work out the bidirectional bandwidth of each port in the Graphein architecture:

$$B = 2 \cdot 16 \cdot 8G = 256\,Gbps$$

The assumption and parameters setting in this paper all satisfy the performance demand of EHPC. The ITRS predicts that, the demand of a single port in EHPC will not exceed 200 Gbps. The overall power consumption of the Graphein architecture is worked out to be no more than 19.2 W when following the parameters above, and this is within acceptable limits under the current industry process.

6   Conclusion

In this paper, we propose and explore Graphein − a novel optical high-radix switch architecture for 3D integration. The proposed 3D high-radix switch chip combines low cost photonic crossbars on multiple photonic layers with ports and switch logic modules in button electric port layers to reduce power dissipation and extend the scalability of the switch. The throughput analysis indicate the Graphein architecture has an ideal throughput of 100%. Experimental comparisons with the previously proposed Hi-Rise architecture indicate a strong motivation for considering Graphein for future high-radix switch ICs as it can provide high throughput for every port and fairness for all packets. Our future work will explore the adaptive switch in the interconnection network on chip.

References

1. 2015 International Technology Roadmap for Semiconductors, ITRS (2015)
2. SB7700: 36-port Non-blocking Managed EDR 100 Gb/s InfiniBand Switch, Mellanox Technologies (2015)
3. OIF Next Generation Interconnect Framework, April 2013. www.oiforum.com
4. Birrittella, M.S., Debbage, M.: Intel@ Omni-Path Architecture: Enabling Scalable, High Performance Fabrics. IEEE (2015)
5. Biberman, A., Bergman, K.: Optical interconnection networks for high-performance computing systems. IOP Sci. Rep. Prog. Phys. **75**, 046402 (15 p.) (2012)
6. Ophir, N., Mineo, C., Mountain, D., Bergman, K.: Silicon photonic microring links for high-bandwidth-density, low-power-chip I/O. IEEE MICRO **33**(1), 54–67 (2013)
7. Koonath, P., Jalali, B.: Multilayer 3-D photonics in silicon. Opt. Exp. **15**(20), 12686–12691 (2007)
8. Morris Jr., R.W.: The three-dimensional stacked nanophotonic network-on-chip architecture with minimal reconfiguration. IEEE Trans. Comput. **63**, 243–255 (2014)
9. Dang, D., Patra, B., Mahapatra, R.: A 2-layer laser multiplexed photonic network-on-chip. In: 16th International Symposium on Quality Electronic Design (2015)

10. Qi, X., Dou, Q., Feng, Q.: Modeling and evaluating the performance of the buffer-less optical interconnection network (BOIN). In: Proceedings of the 2009 International Conference on Information Technology and computer Science, vol. 2, pp. 81–85 (2009)
11. Pavlidis, V., Friedman, E.: Three-Dimensional Integrated Circuit Design. Morgan Kaufmann Publishers, San Francisco (2009)
12. Vangal, S., et al.: An 80-Tile 1.28 TFLOPS network-on-chip in 65 nm CMOS. In: IEEE International Solid State Circuits Conference, February 2007
13. Bernstein, K., et al.: Interconnects in the third dimension: design challenges for 3D ICs. In: DAC (2007)
14. Patti, R.S.: Three-dimensional integrated circuits and the future of system-on-chip design. Proc. IEEE **94**(6), 1214–1224 (2006)
15. Jeloka, S., Das, R.: Hi-Rise: a high-radix switch for 3D integration with single-cycle arbitration. In: MICRO (2014)
16. Kim, J., Balfour, J., Dally, W.: Flattened butterfly topology for on-chip networks. In: MICRO (2007)
17. Kim, J., Dally, W.J.: Technology-driven, highly-scalable dragonfly topology. In: ISCA (2008)
18. Scott, S., Abts, D., Kim, J.: The black widow high-radix clos network. In: ISCA (2006)
19. Binkert, N., Davis, A.: The role of optics in future high radix switch design. In: ISCA (2011)
20. Vantrease, D., et al.: Corona: system implications of emerging nanophotonic technology. In: ISCA (2008)
21. Pan, Y., et al.: Flexishare: channel sharing for an energy-efficient nanophotonic crossbar. In: HPCA (2010)
22. Vantrease, D., et al.: Light speed arbitration and flow control for nanophotonic interconnects. In: MICRO (2009)
23. Chan, J., Hendry, G., Bergman, K.: Phoenixsim: a simulator for physical-layer analysis of chip-scale photonic interconnection networks. In: DATE: Design, Automation and Test in Europe, March 2010
24. Joshi, A., Batten, C., Kwon, Y.: Silicon-photonic clos networks for global on-chip communication. In: IEEE International Symposium on Network-on-Chip (NOCS), San Diego, CA (2009)

Improving the Performance of Volunteer Computing with Data Volunteers: A Case Study with the ATLAS@home Project

Saúl Alonso-Monsalve[✉], Félix García-Carballeira, and Alejandro Calderón

Department of Computer Science and Engineering, Computer Architecture Group,
University Carlos III of Madrid, Leganés, Madrid, Spain
{saul.alonso,felix.garcia,alejandro.calderon}@uc3m.es

Abstract. Volunteer computing is a type of distributed computing in which ordinary people donate processing and storage resources to scientific projects. BOINC is the main middleware system for this type of computing. The aim of volunteer computing is that organizations be able to attain large computing power thanks to the participation of volunteer clients instead of a high investment in infrastructure. There are projects, like the ATLAS@home project, in which the number of running jobs has reached a plateau, due to a high load on data servers caused by file transfer. This is why we have designed an alternative, using the same BOINC infrastructure, in order to improve the performance of BOINC projects that have reached their physical limit. This alternative involves having a percentage of the volunteer clients running as data servers, called data volunteers, that improve the performance by reducing the load on data servers. This paper describes our alternative in detail and shows the performance of the solution using a simulator of our own, ComBoS.

Keywords: BOINC · Data volunteers · Throughput · Simulation · Volunteer computing

1 Introduction

Volunteer Computing (VC) is a type of distributed computing in which ordinary people donate processing and storage resources to one or more scientific projects. Most of the existing VC systems have the same basic structure: a client program runs on the volunteer's computer, periodically contacting project-operated servers over the Internet to request jobs and report the results of completed jobs. VC is important for several reasons [24]:

- Because of the huge number (> 1 billion) of computers in the world, VC can supply more computing power to science than any other type of computing. In addition, this advantage will increase over time, because the number of computers is in continuous growth.

S. Alonso-Monsalve—This work has been partially funded by the grant TIN2013-41350-P of the Spanish Ministry of Economics and Competitiveness.

© Springer International Publishing AG 2016
J. Carretero et al. (Eds.): ICA3PP 2016, LNCS 10048, pp. 178–191, 2016.
DOI: 10.1007/978-3-319-49583-5_13

– VC power cannot be bought; it must be earned. A research project that has limited funding but large public appeal can get remarkable computing power. In contrast, traditional supercomputers are extremely expensive, and are available only for applications or teams that can afford them.
– VC promotes public interest in science, and provides the public with a voice in determining the directions of scientific research.

BOINC (Berkeley Open Infrastructure for Network Computing) [3] is an open-source VC platform. It provides a complete middleware system for volunteer computing. In fact, BOINC is the most widely used middleware system. According to BOINCstats [11], currently there are 57 projects, with more than 13 million hosts participating in them. The number of active hosts is around 1 million, offering 190 PetaFLOPS of computation. One example of this is the Einstein@home project, in which users regularly contribute about 1,080 TeraFLOPS of computational power, which would rank Einstein@home among the top 100 on the TOP500 [23] list of the 500 fastest supercomputers of the world. From the data storage point of view, 13 million hosts with an average of 25 GB available per client can provide a total capacity of 310 PetaBytes.

The aim of Volunteer Computing (VC) is that organizations be able to attain large computing power thanks to the participation of volunteer clients instead of a high investment in infrastructure. This is why we have designed an alternative, using the same BOINC infrastructure, in order to improve the performance of BOINC projects that have reached their limit. This alternative involves having a percentage of the volunteer clients running as data servers, called data volunteers. We have evaluated the performance of our alternative using a simulator of our own, ComBoS [2].

The rest of the paper is organized as follows. Section 2 discusses related work; Sect. 3 presents our alternative to the current functioning of BOINC, using data volunteers; Sect. 4 presents and describes the simulator that we have developed; Sect. 5 analyzes the performance of our alternative, showing some case studies considering the ATLAS@home project; and finally, Sect. 6 concludes the paper and presents some future work.

2 Related Work

The computing resources that power Volunteer Computing (VC) are shared with the owners of the client machines. Because the resources are volunteered, utmost care is taken to ensure that the VC tasks do not obstruct the activities of each machine's owner; a VC task is suspended or terminated whenever the machine is in use by another person. As a result, VC resources are volatile in the sense that any number of factors can prevent the task of a VC application from being completed. These factors include mouse or keyboard activity, the execution of other user applications, machine reboots, or hardware failures. Moreover, VC resources are heterogeneous, in the sense that they differ in operating systems, CPU speeds, network bandwidth and memory and disk sizes. Consequently, the design of systems and applications that utilize this system is challenging.

BOINC [3] is the main middleware system for VC that makes it easy for scientists to create and operate public-resource computing projects. It supports diverse applications, including those with large storage or communication requirements. PC owners can participate in multiple BOINC projects, and can specify how their resources are allocated among these projects. BOINC is being used by several projects, including SETI@home, Climateprediction.net, LHC@home, Predictor@home, and Einstein@Home. Volunteers participate by running a BOINC client program on their computers.

The BOINC architecture is based on a strict master/worker model, with a central server responsible for dividing applications into thousands of small independent tasks and then distributing the tasks among the worker nodes as they request the workunits. To simplify network communication and bypass any NAT (Network Address Translation) problems that might arise from bidirectional communication, the centralized server never initiates communication with worker nodes: all communication is initiated by the worker when more work is needed or results are ready for submission.

The BOINC middleware uses a fixed set of data servers to provide input files to each client. Clients download input files from this set of data servers. Once the computation has been completed, they upload the output files to the same data servers. In projects with thousands of participants, the access to the data servers can form a bottleneck. The BOINC middleware is, therefore, appropriate for CPU-intensive jobs that process small files. Projects like ATLAS@home [1], in which each workunit requires large files (100 MB of input data and 50 MB of output data), a high number of volunteer participants can saturate the data servers. Some data-intensive projects use file replication to improve the performance; Einstein@home [21] uses large (40 MB) input files, and any given input file may be sent to a large number of hosts (in contrast with projects like SETI@home [5,22,25], in which each input file is different).

In the BOINC architecture [6] data servers can be located anywhere; they are simply web servers, and do not access the BOINC database. Current BOINC-based projects that use large files (Einstein@home [17] and Climateprediction.net [14]) use replicated and distributed data servers, located at partner institutions. The download and upload traffic is spread across the commodity Internet connections of those institutions. These components share data stored in disks, including relational databases and file storage. Data servers handle file uploads using a certificate-based mechanism to ensure that only legitimate files, with prescribed size limits, are uploaded. File downloads are handled by plain HTTP. BOINC provides a form of redundant computing in which each computation is performed on multiple clients [15], and the results are compared. Results are only validated when a 'consensus' is reached. In some cases new tasks must be created and sent to the clients to perform the computation again.

In [18], authors use the Attic File System (AtticFS), previously the Peer-to-Peer (P2P) Arhictecture for Data-Intensive Cycle Sharing (ADICS) [20], to decentralize data distribution in the BOINC achitecture. AtticFS is a decentralized P2P data sharing software for accessing distributed storage resources over the network in a similar way to BitTorrent. In this solution, when a BOINC client downloads input files to process, it caches them to be available to other clients, who can then process the same job. Although this solution can prevent the bottleneck in the BOINC data server, it requires the integration of AtticFS in the BOINC infrastructure, and a centralized data lookup service to obtain the list of BOINC clients that store the files to process. The use of VC systems for Big Data processing has been studied in [9]. In this article, the authors describe an architecture of intelligent agents to optimize Big Data processing. In [12], the authors present a VC solution called FreeCycles, which supports MapReduce jobs. FreeCycles improves data distribution (among mappers and reducers) by using the BitTorrent protocol to distribute data, and improves intermediate data availability by replicating files through volunteers in order to avoid losing intermediate data.

The main difference between our solution and the solutions described above, as described in the next section, is that our solution does not require that any external elements be added to the BOINC infrastructure. Besides, our solution uses the idea of edge computing [19], as it tries to decentralize VC servers.

3 Alternative with Data Volunteers Using BOINC

Even though the clients volunteer for free, the manpower required to set up and maintain a BOINC project is not negligible. Nevertheless, it is only a fraction of the power needed for a regular Grid site. On the other hand, there are projects in which the number of running jobs has reached a plateau. An example is the ATLAS@home project [1]. This project uses a single server host [7] that includes all the functionalities of the BOINC server side: upload/download server, scheduler, file deleter, etc. In this project, each workunit requires about 100 MB of input data, which are downloaded each time from the ATLAS@home server, and 50 MB of output data, which are uploaded to the ATLAS@home server when each task is computed. This is causing a problem in the server, as the current setup has reached its limit (mainly because I/O). The ATLAS@home project team are exploring to use multiple data servers, which makes it necessary to improve the infrastructure. Another problem is that there are not enough volunteers joining the project, but the one server is already saturated, so the team deliberately do not advertise too much. We have evaluated the performance of the ATLAS@home project using ComBoS [2], in terms of throughput (Fig. 1a) and the load of the server (Fig. 1b). As shown in Fig. 1b, data servers get saturated when there are about 1,200 Volunteer Nodes (VN), causing a severe deceleration in throughput (Fig. 1a). In this section, we will present a solution for this problem.

The aim of Volunteer Computing (VC) is that organizations be able to attain large computing power thanks to the participation of volunteer clients instead of a high investment in infrastructure. This is why we have designed an alternative, using the same infrastructure, in order to improve the performance of BOINC projects that have reached their limit. This alternative involves having

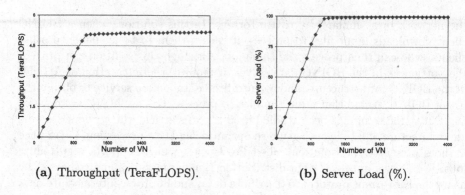

(a) Throughput (TeraFLOPS).   **(b)** Server Load (%).

Fig. 1. ATLAS@home current performance.

a percentage of the VN running as data servers, called data volunteers. Each file needed by a workunit must be replicated in N data volunteers (*dcreplication* attribute).

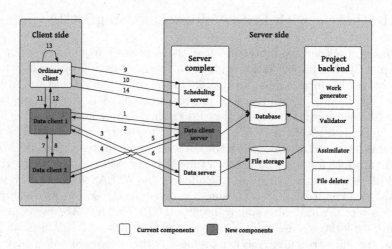

Fig. 2. Alternative with data volunteers.

Figure 2 shows the functioning of the system considering our alternative. It would only need another process on the server side (Data client server, Pseudocode 1) and the data client software (Data client, Pseudocode 2). Each data volunteers works as an ordinary VN (downloading input files) and as a server (sending input files) at the same time. Figure 2 contemplates an scenario with three volunteer nodes (Ordinary client, Data client 1, and Data client 2) and one project. First, Data client 1 requests and downloads some work from the Data client server (1 and 2). Then, Data client 1 downloads the corresponding input files from the Data server (3 and 4) and stores them in its file system. Data client 2 repeats the same process (5 and 6), but this time it downloads the corresponding input files from Data client 1 (7 and 8), which had downloaded them before. Note that in this case, Data client 2 does not access the Data server, thus reducing its load. Now, Ordinary client wants to execute tasks in the regular way, so it requests and downloads some work from the Scheduling server (9 and 10), but now it can download the corresponding input files from Data client 1, Data client 2, or the Data server, because the same input files are replicated in all of them. In our alternative, ordinary clients only download workunits that need files that are replicated *dcreplication* times in data clients. In the example of Fig. 2, the client downloads the input files from Data client 1 (11 and 12), executes the tasks (13) and returns the computation results to the Scheduling server (14). In some projects, it is necessary to upload the output files of the computation to the data server. In this case, each project should decide whether to upload the output files to the actual data servers or to the data clients.

Pseudocode 1. Data client server dispatcher

```
 1: function DATA_CLIENT_SERVER_DISPATCHER( )
 2:     while 1 do
 3:         POP message from received_messages_queue
 4:         switch message.type do
 5:             case Request
 6:                 CREATE_ANSWER ans
 7:                 for each workunit w in current_workunits do
 8:                     if w.status in progress and
 9:                         w.dataclients < dcreplication and
10:                         (w.dataclients == 0 or w.dataclients_confirmed > 0) then
11:                             w.ndata_clients+ = 1
12:                             ans.workunit = w
13:                     end if
14:                     break
15:                 end for
16:                 SEND ans to client
17:             case Confirmation
18:                 w = FIND_WORKUNIT(message.workunit)
19:                 PUSH(w.input_files_urls, message.client_address)
20:                 CREATE target_nresults instances of w
21:     end while
22: end function
```

Normally, a workunit has a list of associated input files [15], and each input file is defined as a list of addresses from where it can be downloaded, giving priority to the data volunteers (we do not want to collapse the data servers). For example, in the previous case, the definition of an input file that has been downloaded by Data client 1 and Data client 2 should be the list {Data client 1 address, Data client 2 address, Data server address}. Obviously, the fewer volunteer clients that access the data servers, the better this system works. In some projects, each input file is shared by multiple workunits, but each workunit describes a different computation using the same file. For these cases, locality scheduling can be used. The goal of locality scheduling [6,15] is to minimize the amount of data transfer to hosts by preferentially sending jobs to hosts that already have some or all of the input files required by those jobs. This would also be our ideal scenario, because each input file might be downloaded from a data server only once, and from data volunteers the rest of the time. For instance, consider a project where each input file is shared by five workunits and there is only one data server. With our alternative, only the first data client should download the file from the data server. In the current BOINC system, the same input file would have to be downloaded five times, one per workunit. With our alternative, the data server would have five times less load and allow for more VN in the system. In the next section we will show some examples of our alternative, considering real scenarios. An advantage of our alternative is that it can also be used when jobs do not share input files, unlike locality scheduling. For example, we can use our alternative to reduce the load on the data servers when the same job is sent to multiple VN in order to reach a consensus.

Pseudocode 2. Data client ask for files

```
 1: function DATA_CLIENT_ASK_FOR_FILES( )
 2:     while 1 do
 3:         if current_storage < max_storage then
 4:             SEND request to data client server
 5:             message = RECEIVE from to data client server
 6:             if message.workunit then
 7:                 for each url in message.workunit.input_files_urls do
 8:                     if url is active then
 9:                         SEND request to url
10:                         input_files = RECEIVE from url
11:                         STORE input_files
12:                         break
13:                     end if
14:                 end for
15:                 SEND confirmation to data client server
16:             else
17:                 EXPONENTIAL_BACKOFF
18:             end if
19:             SLEEP until current_storage < max_storage (files are deleted)
20:         end if
21:     end while
22: end function
```

---

4   Complete Simulator of BOINC Infrastructures

In order to study the alternative presented in the previous section, we have implemented the functionality in ComBoS. ComBoS [2] is a Complete simulator of BOINC Infrastructures developed by the authors. ComBoS has been implemented in C programming language, with the help of the tools provided by the MSG API of SimGrid [13]. In this section we describe the architecture of the simulator in the simplest possible way. We have divided all the components of the simulator into two groups: the server side and the client side. The specification of the networks that connect both groups is detailed in the client side. In the server side, jobs are created and distributed to the clients. A BOINC job has two parts [10]:

Table 1. ComBoS new parameters (necessary with our alternative).

Server parameter	Description
ndata_client_servers	Number of data client servers of the project.
dsreplication	Number of replicas of each file in the data servers.
dcreplication	Number of replicas of each file in the data clients.
output_file_storage	Where to upload output files [0 -> data servers, 1 -> data clients]. Default is 0.
Client parameter	Description
ndata_clients	Number of data volunteers of the group.
st_distri	Storage fit distribution of the data volunteers:
	Weibull, Gamma, Lognormal, Normal, Hyperexponential

- A *workunit* describing the computation to be performed.
- One or more *results*, each of which describes an instance of a computation, either unstarted, in progress, or completed. The BOINC client software refers to results as *tasks*. In this paper, we use both terms interchangeably.

4.1   Server Side

Servers are responsible for managing projects. The architecture of the server side is shown in Fig. 2. The server side of a project consist of two parts [15]:

- A *project back end* that supplies applications and workunits, and that handles the computational results. It includes: a *work generator*, which creates workunits and their corresponding input files; a *validator* that examines sets of results and selects canonical results; an *assimilator* that handles workunits that are completed; and a *file deleter*, which deletes input and output files that are no longer needed.
- A *BOINC server complex* that manages data distribution and collection. It includes: one or more *scheduling servers* (sometimes called *task servers*), that communicate with participant hosts; and *data servers*, that distribute input files and collect output files. For small projects, if there are no data servers, scheduling servers also operate as data servers.

ComBoS allows for the definition of multiple projects. For each project, users must define the parameters described in [2] and in Table 1. In addition, we have included the data client server functionality described in Sect. 3.

4.2   Client Side

In ComBoS [2], the client side is formed by groups of Volunteer Nodes (VN). VN are used by the participants who join a BOINC-based project. Each VN group in ComBoS can be attached to any set of projects, and the client performs CPU scheduling among all runnable jobs. A VN is responsible for asking a project for more work, and scheduling the jobs of the different projects.

The BOINC client implements two related scheduling policies:

- CPU scheduling: of the currently runnable jobs, which to run. Of the pre-empted jobs, which to keep in memory.
- Work fetch: when to ask a project for more work, which project to ask, and how much work to ask for.

The scheduling is based on a round-robin between projects, weighted according to their resource share. This scheduling is described in detail in [4]. In addition, we have relied on the client scheduler code implemented in [16]. In ComBoS, each client is implemented with at least three different threads: the client main thread, which updates the client parameters every scheduling interval; the work fetch thread, which selects the project to ask for work; and the execution threads, one per attached project, that execute the tasks. However, our simulator is complemented with the most important features of the real scheduler (deadline scheduling, long term debt, fair sharing and exponential back-off).

Apart from that, ComBoS allows for the definition of multiple VN groups. The power and the availability of each host of the group is obtained from a traces file. Alternatively, the power and the availability can be modelled with input statistical distributions. For each group, users must define the parameters described in [2] and in Table 1. To simulate VN groups using SimGrid, we have used the *cluster* entity. Like real clusters, each cluster contains many hosts interconnected by some dedicated network. SimGrid does not allow us to fix the power and availability of individual hosts within a cluster, so we have implemented the necessary functionality in order to solve the problem. Users can define the power and availability of the VN hosts via either a traces file or distribution functions. For example, in the case of the SETI@home project, we have analyzed the 3,900,000 hosts that participate in this project. In order to evaluate our alternative, we have included the data client functionality described in Sect. 3.

4.3   Validation of the Simulator

To validate the complete simulator, we have relied on data from the BOINCstats website [11], which provides official statistical results of BOINC projects. In this section, we analyze the behavior of ComBoS considering the simulation results of the SETI@home, Einstein@home and ATLAS@home projects.

We have used the CPU power traces of the client hosts that make up the VN of each project. We have not used any other traces. In order to model the availability and unavailability of the hosts, we used the results obtained in [8]. This research analyzed about 230,000 hosts' availability traces obtained from the SETI@home project. According to this paper, 21% of the hosts exhibit truly random availability intervals, and it also measured the goodness of fit of the resulting distributions using standard probability-probability (PP) plots. For availability, the authors saw that in most cases the Weibull distribution is a good fit. For unavailability, the distribution that offers the best fit is the log-normal. The parameters used for the Weibull distribution are $shape = 0.393$ and $scale = 2.964$. For the log-normal, the parameters obtained and used in ComBoS

Table 2. Validation of the whole simulator.

Project	Total hosts	Active hosts	*BOINCstats*		*ComBoS*	
			GigaFLOPS	*Credit/day*	*GigaFLOPS*	*Credit/day*
SETI@home	3,970,427	175,220	864,711	171,785,234	865,001	168,057,478
Einstein@home	1,496,566	68,338	1,044,515	208,902,921	1,028,172	205,634,486
ATLAS@home	13,144	3,206	5,293	1,052,649	5,172	968,370

are a distribution with mean $\mu = -0.586$ and standard deviation $\sigma = 2.844$. All these parameters were obtained from [8] too.

Table 2 compares the actual results of the SETI@home, Einstein@home and ATLAS@home projects with those obtained with ComBoS in terms of GigaFLOPS and credits. The error obtained is 2.2% for credit/day and 0.03% for GigaFLOPS compared to the SETI@home project; 1.6% for credit/day and for GigaFLOPS compared to the Einstein@home project; and 8.1% for credit/day and 2.3% for GigaFLOPS compared to the ATLAS@home project. We consider that these results allow us to validate the whole simulator.

5   Evaluation and Analysis Results

In this section we will present different test cases using ComBoS [2]. Our goal is to assess the performance of our alternative, which involves some volunteer clients working as data servers, and has been described in the previous sections. We are especially interested in analyzing bottlenecks and limits that this architecture presents compared to the current BOINC architecture. We will show some practical examples of the ATLAS@home project using ComBoS, with the subsequent analysis of the execution results. We have used the same host availability and unavailability parameters as those used in Sect. 4.3. Each simulation result presented in this section is based on the average of 20 runs. For a 95% confidence interval, the error is less than ± 3% for all values.

5.1   Files Replication

Input files can be replicated in one or more data volunteers, in addition to the main server. In this case study we analyzed the throughput (in TeraFLOPS) and the load of the server of the ATLAS@home project using five different values for the replication parameter: from 1 to 5 (number of data volunteers that must store a copy of each input file). We also compared these results with the results of the original system (without our alternative). The storage capacity of the data volunteers of the experiment follows a normal distribution with a mean of 20 GB of storage per host. All simulations were performed with 3,200 hosts, which is the current number of active hosts of the ATLAS@home project. Figure 3 shows these results.

Figure 3a shows that for a certain percentage of data volunteers, the performance of our alternative considerably surpasses the performance of the original system. For example, with a replication factor of 3 and an amount of data

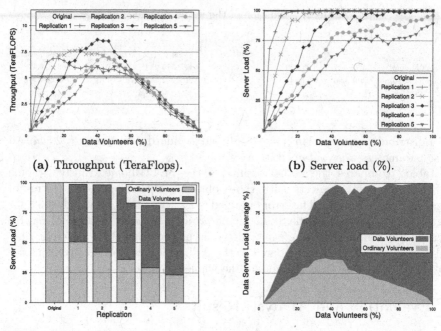

(a) Throughput (TeraFlops).

(b) Server load (%).

(c) Server load (% caused by ordinary volunteers and by data volunteers) at the peek of throughput.

(d) Server load (% caused by ordinary volunteers and by data volunteers) with replication 3.

Fig. 3. ATLAS@home performance using our alternative and varying the input files replication in data volunteers (3,200 active hosts).

volunteers that ranges between 20% to 60% of the total number of VN, our alternative outperforms the original system in terms of throughput. Figure 3b shows the server load in each simulation. The results obtained show that the load of the server with our alternative is greatly reduced compared to the original server load. Note that the higher the percentage of data volunteers, the larger the load on the server is, because more data volunteers request input files from the server. This shows that in order to implement this model, designers must carefully choose the number of data volunteers. Figure 3c shows the server load at the throughput peak of each replication factor. This figure shows the server load caused by the ordinary volunteers and by the data volunteers. The lower the replication factor, the greater the load that ordinary volunteers cause on the main server, because when an ordinary client tries to download a file from a data volunteer that turns out to be unavailable, the client then tries to download the file from the next host on the input file address list, in which the last address is always that of the main server. With a high replication factor (e.g. 5), there are more options to download the same input file, so the load that ordinary volunteers cause on the data server is solely due to the upload of output files. Finally, Fig. 3d shows in detail the server load for a replication factor of 3.

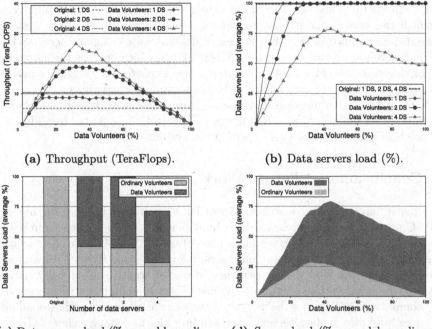

(a) Throughput (TeraFlops).

(b) Data servers load (%).

(c) Data servers load (% caused by ordinary volunteers and by data volunteers) at the peek of throughput.

(d) Server load (% caused by ordinary volunteers and by data volunteers) with 4 data servers.

Fig. 4. ATLAS@home performance using our alternative and varying the number of data servers (10,000 active hosts).

On the other hand, some projects, such as the ATLAS@home project, validate each result just by checking that the corresponding output file exists, without checking the file content. Therefore, for future work, it would be interesting to analyze the performance of the project if ordinary volunteers upload output files to data volunteers instead of uploading them to data servers.

5.2 Data Servers

In this experiment, we have tested our alternative using different numbers of data servers. In these tests we have combined our alternative (usage of data volunteers) with an improvement of the infrastructure (increasing the number of data servers). We have set the replication parameter to 3 and increased the number of volunteer nodes to 10,000. The other simulation parameters were the same as in the previous experiment. Figure 4 shows the results of this experiment for 1, 2, and 4 data servers. Like in the previous experiment, we have focused our work on showing the throughput and the average load of the data servers of the system.

Like in the previous case, there is a range in the percentage of data volunteers in which the system throughput considerably outperforms that of the system without data volunteers (Fig. 4a). For example, with twice as many servers, our alternative renders a throughput of 18 GigaFLOPS, which doubles the throughput of the same system without our alternative. Furthermore, Fig. 4b, c and d show the average server load analogously to the previous experiment.

It is interesting to mention how a small improvement in the infrastructure, combined with our solution, can enhance the project throughput. In addition, our solution allows for more volunteers in the system.

6   Conclusion and Future Work

This paper has presented a solution in order to improve the performance of BOINC projects that have reached their limit due to the I/O bottleneck in data servers. This solution involves having a percentage of the volunteer clients running as data servers, called data volunteers, using the same BOINC infrastructure. We have evaluated the performance of our alternative using a simulator of our own, ComBoS. Our solution combines volunteer computing with peer-to-peer computing (P2P), since the data volunteers run as clients when downloading data files, and also as data servers when sending files to ordinary clients. To be implemented, our alternative needs to include the security protocols (for example, to traverse firewalls) that the P2P communications use. For future work, we want to analyze more case studies and use the simulator in order to analyze the energy consumption of the machines involved in a volunteer computing project.

References

1. Adam-Boundarios, C., Cameron, D., Filipcic, A., Lancon, E., Wu, W.: ATLAS@Home: harnessing volunteer computing for HEP. In: 21st International Conference on Computing in High Energy and Nuclear Physics, CHEP2015, Okinawa, Japan (2015)
2. Alonso-Monsalve, S., García-Carballeira, F., Calderón, A.: Analyzing the performance of volunteer computing for data intensive applications. In: 14th International Conference on High Performance Computing & Simulation, HPCS 2016, Innsbruck, Austria (2016)
3. Anderson, D.P.: BOINC: a system for public-resource computing and storage. In: 5th IEEE/ACM International Workshop on Grid Computing, pp. 4–10 (2004)
4. Anderson, D.P.: Local scheduling for volunteer computing. In: IEEE International Parallel and Distributed Processing Symposium, IPDPS 2007, pp. 1–8. IEEE (2007)
5. Anderson, D.P., Cobb, J., Korpela, E., Lebofsky, M., Werthimer, D.: SETI@home: an experiment in public-resource computing. Commun. ACM 45(11), 56–61 (2002)
6. Anderson, D., Korpela, E., Walton, R.: High-performance task distribution for volunteer computing. In: 2005 First International Conference on e-Science and Grid Computing, pp. 8–203 (2005)
7. ATLAS@home Project Status. http://atlasathome.cern.ch/server_status.php

8. Javadi, B., Kondo, D., Vincent, J.-M., Anderson, D.P.: Discovering statistical models of availability in large distributed systems: an empirical study of SETI@home. IEEE Trans. Parallel Distrib. Syst. **22**, 1896–1903 (2011)
9. Balicki, J., Korłub, W., Paluszak, J.: Big data processing by volunteer computing supported by intelligent agents. In: Kryszkiewicz, M., Bandyopadhyay, S., Rybinski, H., Pal, S.K. (eds.) PReMI 2015. LNCS, vol. 9124, pp. 268–278. Springer, Heidelberg (2015). doi:10.1007/978-3-319-19941-2_26
10. BOINC Jobs. https://boinc.berkeley.edu/trac/wiki/JobIn
11. BOINCstats. http://boincstats.com/en/stats
12. Bruno, R., Ferreira, P.: FreeCycles: efficient data distribution for volunteer computing. In: CloudDP 2014 Proceedings of the Fourth International Workshop on Cloud Data and Platforms (2014)
13. Casanova, H., Giersch, A., Legrand, A., Quinson, M., Suter, F.: Versatile, scalable, and accurate simulation of distributed applications and platforms. J. Parallel Distrib. Comput. **74**(10), 2899–2917 (2014)
14. Climateprediction.net. http://climateprediction.net
15. Creating BOINC Projects. https://boinc.berkeley.edu/boinc.pdf
16. Donassolo, B., Casanova, H., Legrand, A., Velho, P.: Fast and scalable simulation of volunteer computing systems using SimGrid. In: Proceedings of the 19th ACM International Symposium on High Performance Distributed Computing, HPDC 2010, pp. 605–612. ACM, New York (2010)
17. Einstein@home. http://www.einsteinathome.org
18. Elwaer, A., Taylor, I.J., Rana, O.: Optimizing data distribution in volunteer computing systems using resources of participants. Scalable Comput.: Pract. Exp. **12**, 193–208 (2011)
19. García-López, P., Datta, A., Barcellos, M., Montresor, A., Higashino, T., Felber, P., Epema, D., Iamnitchi, A., Riviere, E.: Edge-centric computing: vision and challenges. ACM SIGCOMM Comput. Commun. **45**, 37–42 (2015)
20. Kelly, I., Taulor, I.: Bridging the data management gap between service and desktop grids. In: Kacsuk, P., Lovas, R., Nemeth, Z. (eds.) Distributed and Parallel Systems In Focus: Desktop Grid Computing. Springer, Heidelberg (2008)
21. LIGO Scientific Collaboration, Anderson, D.P.: Einstein@Home search for periodic gravitational waves in early S5 LIGO data. Phys. Rev. D, 80, 042003 (2009)
22. Paul, P.: SETI@home project and its website. Crossroads **8**(3), 3–5 (2002)
23. Top. 500 Supercomputer list. http://www.top500.org/
24. Volunteer Computing. http://boinc.berkeley.edu/trac/wiki/VolunteerComputing
25. Werthimer, D., Cobb, J., Lebofsky, M., Anderson, D., Korpela, E.: SETI@HOME–massively distributed computing for SETI. Comput. Sci. Eng. **3**(1), 78–83 (2001)

Microcities: A Platform Based on Microclouds for Neighborhood Services

Ismael Cuadrado-Cordero[1][(✉)], Felix Cuadrado[2], Chris Phillips[2], Anne-Cécile Orgerie[3], and Christine Morin[1]

[1] Inria, Rennes, France
{ismael.cuadrado-cordero,christine.morin}@inria.fr
[2] Queen Mary University of London, London, UK
{felix.cuadrado,chris.i.phillips}@qmul.ac.uk
[3] CNRS, IRISA, Rennes, France
anne-cecile.orgerie@irisa.fr

Abstract. The current datacenter-centralized architecture limits the cloud to the location of the datacenters, generally far from the user. This architecture collides with the latest trend of ubiquity of Cloud computing. Distance leads to increased utilization of the broadband Wide Area Network and poor user experience, especially for interactive applications. A semi-decentralized approach can provide a better Quality of Experience (QoE) in large urban populations in mobile cloud networks, by confining local traffic near the user while maintaining centralized characteristics, running on the users and network devices. In this paper, we propose a novel semi-decentralized cloud architecture based on microclouds. Microclouds are dynamically created and allow users to contribute resources from their computers, mobile and network devices to the cloud. Microclouds provide a dynamic and scalable system without an extra investment in infrastructure. We also provide a description of a realistic mobile cloud use case, and its adaptation to microclouds.

1 Introduction

The wide uptake of Cloud architectures have caused global IP traffic to increase five fold [1], catalyzed by the ubiquity of mobile devices. According to Cisco, global IP traffic is envisioned to increase threefold over the next five years, with mobile wireless traffic exceeding wired traffic by 2016 [1]. This adds to the limitations of mobile devices in terms of resources and connectivity [2], bringing new challenges to the Cloud. In order to address these issues, a new paradigm is emerging: Mobile Cloud computing. This paradigm improves resource-hungry mobile services such as Internet data sharing [3], wearables [4] or augmented reality [5], by offloading data and computation into the Cloud [2].

This offloading of computation requires high-speed connectivity between the clients and the Cloud. However, highly geographically-centralized Cloud architectures cannot properly handle it. Fernando et al. argue that considering access fees, latency, bandwidth and energy consumption of wireless connectivity, a

© Springer International Publishing AG 2016
J. Carretero et al. (Eds.): ICA3PP 2016, LNCS 10048, pp. 192–202, 2016.
DOI: 10.1007/978-3-319-49583-5_14

Mobile local Cloud - constrained to the location of the user - is a better alternative than a remote one [2]. Local Clouds also provide locality-awareness and support for latency-critical interactions, thus a better Quality of Experience (QoE).

In this paper, we go a step further into Mobile Cloud computing by integrating the mobile devices themselves into the Cloud. Our proposed architecture introduces a flexible, semi-decentralized and yet efficient solution for locality-related applications. We build a local cloud on top of static private (i.e. computers) and public infrastructures (i.e. networking equipment); and the users' mobile devices spread across a defined area. This local cloud is managed by lightweight mechanisms which handle the dynamism of users who can appear/disappear and move. We eliminate the need for dedicated infrastructures, i.e. datacenters, and provide a dynamic environment where multiple services coexist.

Our contributions are: (1) a semi-decentralized mobile cloud architecture based on microclouds and (2) a realistic mobile cloud use case for smart cities.

The remainder of this paper is structured as follows. Section 2 provides the context and motivation and establishes the case study. In Sect. 3 we describe our design and implementation. Finally, Sect. 4 highlights our conclusions and draws directions to future work.

2 Motivation and Scenario

2.1 Context and Motivation

The use of centralized datacenters is, nowadays, the most realistic approach regarding the deployment of heavy computation services. This architecture relies on a robust communication infrastructure between distant clients, obtaining a computing power otherwise unattainable. However, centralized architectures suffer downsides such as traffic delays and scalability issues related with the physical constraints of datacenter resources. Moreover, it forces other actors involved in the communication (such as Internet Service Providers) to oversize their infrastructure in consequence [6].

As studied in [7–9], information propagation in real-life is usually not distant. This is because interactions in the Internet are conditioned by our interactions as a society. Groups of interest are generally geographically constrained. This is the case with sports teams (whose fans are generally located in the same area), departments in a company (whose users are located in the same building) or Geographic Information Systems [10].

This situation is, by design, approached by Cloud computing, as it is described as a versatile and ubiquitous system. However, in reality, Cloud platforms run on large centralized datacenters, which provide the needed infrastructure. Yet, since existing infrastructures cannot effectively host ever increasing demands, datacenters need to be expanded, which is costly and requires advanced planning. In fact, this situation has already been anticipated by Cloud providers, which started to balance the connection between datacenters around the globe.

The use of centralized systems in users' inclusive - citizens are both providers and consumers of information - and non-heavy computation services with low propagation is, thus, inappropriate. A distributed approach, where the flow of information is not only produced and consumed, but also processed in the same area is, in this case, desirable. The main advantages of distributed approaches in this scenario are low latency, scalability, and adaptability. This kind of approach fits the mobile clouds created in smart cities initiatives all around the world (Santa Cruz, Amsterdam, Barcelona, etc.) where local authorities deploy wireless platforms to manage traffic or emergency situations.

Even if the proportion of geographically constrained traffic is difficult to estimate, traffic characterization in different areas can be found in literature. For example, in [11] the authors evaluate the consumed and generated traffic in a rural African village. In this scenario, the authors show that most of the generated and consumed traffic is of a local scope, with web and social networking services being the most utilized ones. In addition, in [12] the authors characterize usage of a freely available outdoor wireless Internet in California (USA). Their results show a peak of smartphone connections in transit areas, while in residential areas the connections are more balanced between static and mobile. Commercial areas show a higher activity than either transit or residential areas.

In this paper, we propose a semi-decentralized Cloud architecture for localized communities such as neighborhoods. We propose a mobile Cloud case study based on smart cities initiatives combining mobile and static devices - other existing Cloud infrastructures provide either a mobile peer-to-peer network [3] or local clouds with connectivity to remote cloud servers [13]. We expect that, through the use of microclouds, latency is reduced - compared to centralized systems - while providing a robust, elastic and adaptive platform of services. We also expect that traffic in datacenters, and network providers' broadband utilization and transit costs are reduced.

2.2 Related Work

Two main approaches in the literature are of interest to the case study.

Centralized Clouds are based on a specific infrastructure to which all clients connect. An issue commonly attributed to these architectures is the excessive distance between clients and the computation infrastructure. Adaptability is also a problem, because once the infrastructure has been allocated, it is expensive and complicated to extend. To provide a service "closer to the user", which is handles better the increase in demand of computation, Cloud providers - such as Google [14] or Amazon [15] - disperse their datacenters around the globe.

Centralized local clouds reduce the distance between the user and the infrastructure. In [16], the authors describe an environment where mobile devices outsource their computation to a CloudLet - domestic servers which provide cloud services to a relatively small set of users. It reduces the computational load of the devices, the replication of data, and the delay, and provides a service adapted to users' needs. However, CloudLets require a, sometimes, prohibitive investment (which rockets if its computational resources need to be scaled), they are rigid and the dependence on the infrastructure ties the user to the system. Since CloudLets are motivated by the need of domestic solutions in relatively dynamic environments, they are not easily integrated with external infrastructures. Moreover, when a users connect to a CloudLet from the outside - for instance from a workplaces - the communication is done through the Internet. This situation causes the same problems than datacenter centralized solutions.

Distributed Clouds are not deployed on a single infrastructure but among several independent nodes, providing a more robust and adaptable system compared to a lone infrastructure that offers a single point of failure. Representative examples of distributed cloud systems are Content Distribution Networks (CDNs) [17] and Peer-To-Peer (P2P) Clouds [18,19] - systems where individual computers are distributed across the globe and connected through the Internet hosting VMs for parallel computation, content distribution or storage. A thorough review of distributed technologies is shown in [20]. One of the more praised benefits of distributed approaches is the low latency experienced by users.

Distributed approaches also have disadvantages, such as network restrictions (they are rather network demanding) and excessive replication of content. As a solution, the union of distributed and centralized architectures (semi-decentralized) is also covered in literature. In [21], authors propose the replication of data in the Internet Provider's datacenter in order to reduce latency and energy consumption. However, this system still suffers from higher delay than a totally centralized approach, in addition to an excessive replication (for example, in between users connecting to different providers).

2.3   Scenario: Neighborhood Services

Neighborhood-related applications are a good example of geographically localized services. In a neighborhood, many services are only of interest to the community, like street works, water or electricity cuts or local store information (stocks, opening hours, etc.). These networks are heterogeneous - comprising both mobile and fixed nodes provided by both citizens and city infrastructures that serve up and consume information [22]. Social networks such as [23,24] - where users share information of interest only with their neighbors - are examples of neighborhood-oriented applications. A system appropriate for this environment should adjust to the following characteristics:

Consistency: Data can be classified in *Announcements*, which are immutable and distributed through the network to inform of an event; and *collaborative/interactive information* (shared documents, forums, etc.), which have several contributors and are prone to version conflicts and extensive replication in non-centralized systems (broadband utilization in multipurpose networks is very dynamic, and information may flood the network if not handled correctly). Therefore, no replication of data and/or management is allowed, as it saturates the network and provides poor consistency in very dynamic situations. This characteristic automatically discards distributed Clouds defined in Sect. 2.2 from the possible solutions, given that those require replication of data as a design principle.

Adaptability and Virtualization: The workload inside a neighborhood is very dynamic, specially when many clients are connected through mobile devices. Also, different neighborhoods show differences in communication patterns and infrastructural support (for example, in residential neighborhoods the number of active users would boost out of working hours, on the contrary to business ones). A suitable platform should dynamically adapt its topology to the characteristics of the neighborhood. Furthermore, adaptability is linked with virtualization. Virtualization allows migration and robustness and enhances the *isolation* and *coexistence* of different services in different neighborhoods.

Versatility: The main characteristic of the proposed use case is the heterogeneity of its components. They are either private (laptops, smartphones, domestic servers and routers, etc.) or public (ISP's routers, smart-city infrastructure, etc.). The common characteristic of all these components is that they share an application layer, and thus services can be run on them [25].

Network Orientation, Locality Awareness and Asynchronous Communication: Since a neighborhood exists within a relatively small geographical area, the system should take into account the physical location of the nodes to obtain the best possible utilization of the network. Knowing the location of the nodes, the platform is able to manage *information dissemination*, adapting to the *available bandwidth*. Due to the interactive nature of *real-time information*, disruptive behavior (asynchronous communication) is not desirable.

3   Our Solution: Microcities

We propose a semi-decentralized platform oriented to the use of shared services in Mobile Clouds. Our platform extends the concept of microcloud proposed in [26] in order to support interactivity of multiple services with no replication in very dynamic environments. A microcloud is an overlay topology that connects independent users employing the same service. For each service a microcloud is created. As a consequence, multiple microclouds coexists (and may overlap) on the same network. For each microcloud, a Light Virtual Machine or LVM - a type of operating-system-level virtualization which runs the service is hosted in one of the involved devices. Using the LVM only one copy of each service is kept, avoiding conflicts. On the other hand, while microclouds distribute the computation across the network. Our solution makes use of existing resources and does not require extra infrastructure or investment, such as a datacenter.

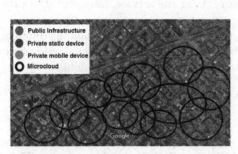 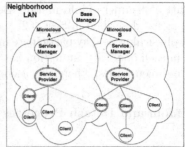

(a) Microclouds operating within a neigh-borhood (Google Maps)

(b) Logical distribution of micro-clouds

Fig. 1. Neighborhood overlay services (microclouds)

3.1   Architecture Design

Figure 1 describes our use case. In Fig. 1a, all devices participating in the platform are represented. A public infrastructure device is any device belonging either to the city council or a private company which offers public access. It includes network devices - such as datacenter routers or domestic routers rented to its users - and specific purpose hardware - such as smart-cities infrastructures. Private devices may be static - such as laptops or personal computers - or mobile - such as smartphones or tablets. In Fig. 1b, Microcloud A and B represent different services, overlapping on the same network and, sometimes, on the same devices. We distinguish the following roles, all transparent to the end user.

Base Manager (BM): This role is taken by a resilient and trustworthy device, to manage all microclouds in a given neighborhood (including the creation/deletion of microclouds and failure management). It can request microclouds to change their topologies, if it determines that one or more microclouds can be better arranged (or they can be merged/split). It is also used as a service repository. In each neighborhood, the BM is a unique global service.

Service Manager (SM): Controls the topology, distributes other roles and manages failures in one microcloud. This role is assigned by the base manager depending on the nodes' computing capacity and robustness. Only one service manager exists per microcloud, and it is assigned to a stable, static node.

Service Provider (SP): Hosts the LVM in a microcloud. This role is assigned by the SM based on the minimum delay between the service provider and every client, reliability in time and hardware capabilities, and it is unique in the microcloud. It is also preferably assigned to a stable, static node. When the SM detects a more efficient position for LVM, both LVM and SP role are migrated.

Client: Consumer of information. Before using the service, the client starts the join process described in Sect. 3.2.

A physical node may participate in two or more microclouds, holding different roles in each one. No assumption has been made about the communication links used between nodes. Therefore, a node may be either static or mobile.

3.2 Join and Detach Processes

Join/rejoin process is depicted in Fig. 2a. When a user launches the client service, it contacts the BM and an API lists all the available services. Then, the user selects the service to be joined and the process starts. When the client needs to rejoin, due to detachment, reconfigurations triggered by the *BM* or the mobility of the client, the same process occurs. The process is the same, but is initiated without a user request. This process uses the DEEPACC protocol presented in [26] to find the fastest path between the client and the *SP*.

1. The client obtains the address of the *SM* through a request to the base manager. After that, a join request is sent towards the *SM*, which answers with the address of the *SP*. Then, the client runs the DEEPACC protocol.
2. Best route: In DEEPACC protocol, a discovery message is sent through every possible path. In every node, the message is captured, processed and updated with the current Round-Trip Time (RTT); and forwarded.
3. Once the *SP* obtains all the possible paths, those are sent to the service manager. The *SM* uses a Branch and Bound algorithm [26] to plan the microcloud's topology and communicates this topology to the *SP* and the *BM*. It also keeps updated information about possible routes in the microcloud.
4. The *SP* sends an acceptance message to the client with its address and a list of the nodes in the route through the chosen route. Before forwarding the message, every node that intercepts it, updates its routing table and extracts itself from the list until the client receives the message.

Detachment process follows the process depicted in Fig. 2b. This is launched once a user detaches from the service (properly or due to a failure in communications). This detachment is either processed or discovered and communicated to the *SM*, which restructures the network without the failing client.

3.3 Migration of LVMs

The system shall ensure the QoE for all clients. When the topology of the network changes, the configuration of the microclouds dynamically adapts. Topology changes may be caused by new clients joining the network, existing clients leaving it or changes in the connections between clients (due to mobility of nodes or either BM or SM started reconfiguration). The dynamic nature of the use case makes unrealistic an approach where all clients always find the best route to the SP. Such an approach would introduce an exponential computation time when

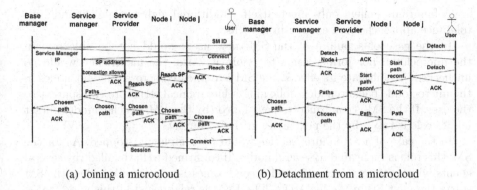

(a) Joining a microcloud   (b) Detachment from a microcloud

Fig. 2. Protocol description

the network grows, affecting the QoE. The best solution is using efficiency heuristics. Thus, reconfigurations would be launched to keep efficiency over a minimum threshold, set experimentally. There exist two heuristics:

Global Optimization Heuristic: Since every microcloud is independent, their best configuration may result in a global inefficiency. On the other hand, the BM has information about every possible route in the system, as it is transmitted to it during the join process. The BM accepts every configuration which provides, at least, a minimum efficiency. This efficiency is calculated by the number of nodes connecting clients and SP which are not clients of the microcloud, for example, network infrastructure nodes; and the size of the microclouds. If the BM detects a configuration under the minimum efficiency threshold, it requests a redistribution to one or more microclouds. This redistribution may imply changing routes between clients and SP, split/merge between microclouds.

Local Optimization Heuristic: Inside a microcloud, the SM accepts every configuration providing a minimum efficiency (in terms of clients' QoE), to reduce the number of redistributions needed. If this threshold is surpassed, then a redistribution - new routes or SP migration - is requested inside the microcloud.

3.4   Failure Management

Four different roles may fail in our system: BM, SM, SP and client. In the case of the BM, a failure would not stop the services already running, but it would the system would not be checked for inefficiency. Furthermore, no new service or node would be able to join while the BM is unavailable. Traditional high availability and fault tolerance approaches can be used in this case. Also, the rejoin process would be affected, as the BM is unavailable. In this case, the clients would launch DEEPACC targeting their last known SM. If responsive, the process would proceed. If not, the rejoin is impossible until the BM is available.

A failure in a client only affects itself. Traditional high availability and fault tolerance approaches are enough in this case.

In the case of a failure of the SM, new users would not be able to join the microcloud, nor former users to rejoin it. Also, the inefficiency would go unchecked. To mitigate its effects, the SM is replicated across different nodes in the microcloud (backup nodes) following a hierarchical structure transparent to the user. If the SM is confirmed to have failed (by the *BM*, which cannot contact it), its role is taken by the next node in the hierarchy.

In the case of a SP failure, service would be completely stopped. As for the SM, this role is replicated in several nodes. If confirmed to have failed (by several clients which cannot contact it, which send a message to the SM), then the SM starts the next SP in the hierarchy. The LVM is relaunched in this node (to do so, the nodes selected as backups periodically retrieve a snapshot of the LVM).

To determine connectivity and/or physical failures a keepalive protocol is used. That way, every client in a microcloud is responsible for the state of its connection with its main neighbor (the first hop between the node and the *SP*), running a periodic check. If a link fails, a new join process is launched by the client or clients which detected the failure. Finally, the split of microclouds offers higher resilience - as a node crash would affect a smaller number of nodes if a large microcloud is split in several smaller ones.

4   Conclusions and Future Work

In this paper we proposed a microcloud-based platform, a semi-decentralized approach for managing services used in a limited geographical area - such as neighborhoods - in the context of Mobile Clouds. Our design is semi-decentralized and network-oriented, that is, it considers the network as a participating entity and profits from it. Our approach exploits network resources to reduce unnecessary data transportation over long distance networks, running computation on the nodes participating from the communication (personal devices, network equipment and/or specific purpose hardware such as smart-cities networks). We described the expected benefits of using our architecture over the dominant datacenter-centralized approach in terms of QoE.

Our next step is testing our design, and evaluate its performance in terms of QoS. We are working on evaluating the latency, overhead time and robustness of our approach compared to a totally centralized approach. Second, we understand that one main concern for the adoption of our system is the unfair distribution of computation. Some devices run computation while other are free riders. We plan to design a pricing model, as an extra incentive to adopt a microclouds-based system. Service creators would benefit from the open market and the increase in competition, while clients would receive a faster and more personalized service, together with financial benefits from making their computational resources available for hosting or relaying service information. Together with this, we plan to work on mobile congestion issues to refine our protocol and address security.

References

1. Cisco: The zettabyte era: trends and analysis. White paper (2015)
2. Fernando, N., Loke, S.W., Rahayu, W.: Mobile cloud computing: a survey. Future Gener. Comput. Syst. **29**(1), 84–106 (2013)
3. Marinelli, E.: Hyrax: cloud computing on mobile devices using MapReduce. Master's thesis, Carnegie Mellon University (2009)
4. Amft, O., Lukowicz, P.: From backpacks to smartphones: past, present, and future of wearable computers. IEEE Pervasive Comput. **8**(3), 8–13 (2009)
5. Luo, X.: From augmented reality to augmented computing: a look at cloud-mobile convergence. In: IEEE International Symposium on Ubiquitous Virtual Reality (ISURV), pp. 29–32, July 2009
6. Bertier, M., et al.: Beyond the clouds: how should next generation utility computing infrastructures be designed? In: Mahmood, Z. (ed.) Cloud Computing. CCN, pp. 325–345. Springer, Heidelberg (2014)
7. Scellato, S., Mascolo, C., Musolesi, M., Crowcroft, J.: Track globally, deliver locally: improving content delivery networks by tracking geographic social cascades. In: International Conference on World Wide Web (WWW), pp. 457–466 (2011)
8. Hristova, D., Musolesi, M., Mascolo, C.: Keep your friends close, your Facebook friends closer: a multiplex network approach to the analysis of offline and online social ties. CoRR, abs/1403.8034 (2014)
9. Cha, M., Mislove, A., Gummadi, K.P.: A measurement-driven analysis of information propagation in the Flickr social network. In: International Conference on World Wide Web (WWW), pp. 721–730 (2009)
10. Longley, P.A., Goodchild, M.F., Maguire, D.J., Rhind, D.W.: Geographic Information Science and Systems. Wiley, Hoboken (2015)
11. Johnson, D.L., Belding, E.M., van Stam, G.: Network traffic locality in a rural African village. In: International Conference on Information and Communication Technologies and Development (ICTD), pp. 268–277 (2012)
12. Afanasyev, M., Chen, T., Voelker, G., Snoeren, A.: Usage patterns in an urban WiFi network. IEEE/ACM Trans. Netw. **18**, 1359–1372 (2010)
13. Kristensen, M.: Scavenger: transparent development of efficient cyber foraging applications. In: IEEE International Conference on Pervasive Computing and Communications (PerCom), pp. 217–226, March 2010
14. GoogleTM: Google cloud. https://cloud.google.com/
15. AmazonTM: Amazon cloud infrastructure. http://aws.amazon.com/about-aws/global-infrastructure/
16. Satyanarayanan, M., Bahl, P., Caceres, R., Davies, N.: The case for VM-based cloudlets in mobile computing. IEEE Pervasive Comput. **8**(4), 14–23 (2009)
17. Bakiras, S., Loukopoulos, T.: Combining replica placement and caching techniques in content distribution networks. Comput. Commun. **28**(9), 1062–1073 (2005)
18. Zhao, P., Huang, T.L., Liu, C.X., Wang, X.: Research of P2P architecture based on cloud computing. In: International Conference on Intelligent Computing and Integrated Systems (ICISS), pp. 652–655, October 2010
19. Xu, K., Song, M., Zhang, X., Song, J.: A cloud computing platform based on P2P. In: International Symposium on IT in Medicine Education (ITIME), pp. 427–432 (2009)
20. Babaoglu, O., Marzolla, M.: The people's cloud. IEEE Spectr. **51**(10), 50–55 (2014)
21. Valancius, V., Laoutaris, N., Massoulié, L., Diot, C., Rodriguez, P.: Greening the internet with nano data centers. In: International Conference on Emerging Networking Experiments and Technologies (CoNEXT), pp. 37–48 (2009)

22. IEC: Orchestrating infrastructure for sustainable Smart Cities. Technical report, International Electrotechnical Commission (2015)
23. Nextdoor. https://nextdoor.com/
24. Goneighbour. http://www.goneighbour.org/
25. Kim, C.G., Kim, K.J.: Implementation of a cost-effective home lighting control system on embedded linux with openwrt. Pers. Ubiquit. Comput. **18**(3), 535–542 (2014)
26. Cuadrado Cordero, I., Orgerie, A.-C., Morin, C.A.: GRaNADA: a network-aware and energy-efficient PaaS cloud architecture. In: IEEE International Conference on Green Computing and Communications (GreenCom), December 2015

Impact of Shutdown Techniques
for Energy-Efficient Cloud Data Centers

Issam Raïs[1]([⊠]), Anne-Cécile Orgerie[2], and Martin Quinson[3]

[1] Inria, LIP, Lyon, France
issam.rais@inria.fr
[2] CNRS, IRISA, Rennes, France
anne-cecile.orgerie@irisa.fr
[3] ENS Rennes, IRISA, Rennes, France
martin.quinson@ens-rennes.fr

Abstract. Electricity consumption is a worrying concern in current large-scale systems like datacenters and supercomputers. The consumption of a computing unit is not power-proportional: when the workload is low, the consumption is still high. Shutdown techniques have been developed to adapt the number of switched-on servers to the actual workload. However, datacenter operators are reluctant to adopt such approaches because of their potential impact on reactivity and hardware failures. In this article, we evaluate the potential gain of shutdown techniques by taking into account shutdown and boot up costs in time and energy. This evaluation is made on recent server architectures. We also determine if the knowledge of future is required for saving energy with such techniques. We present simulation results exploiting real traces collected on different infrastructures under various machine configurations with several shutdown policies, with and without workload prediction.

1 Introduction

In order to make data centers more energy-efficient, a wide variety of approaches have been proposed in the recent years, ranging from free cooling to low-power processors, and tackling wasted watts at each level of the data center [3]. While such an on/off approach has been extensively studied in literature, most infrastructure administrators still dare not use it in their datacenters. This situation is due to two factors: firstly, until very recently, servers were not designed to be switched off; secondly, switching off takes time and energy. So it is difficult for administrators to estimate their potential energy gains versus their potential

Experiments presented in this paper were carried out using the Grid'5000 experimental testbed, being developed under the INRIA ALADDIN development action with support from CNRS, RENATER and several Universities as well as other funding bodies (see https://www.grid5000.fr).

This work is integrated and supported by the ELCI project, a French FSN ("Fond pour la Société Numérique") project that associates academic and industrial partners to design and provide software environment for very high performance computing.

J. Carretero et al. (Eds.): ICA3PP 2016, LNCS 10048, pp. 203–210, 2016.
DOI: 10.1007/978-3-319-49583-5_15

loss of reactivity due to a too long booting time. Several solutions have been proposed to limit this possible performance impact, like keeping few nodes idle or using hibernation or standby modes to fasten the boot.

In this paper, we study different shutdown techniques for computing resources in data centers, like actual switching off and hibernation modes. Moreover, we estimate the impact of such techniques on the energy consumption, the reactivity of the platform and on the lifetime of the servers. Our validations combines real power measurements and real datacenter traces with simulation tools.

The main contributions of this paper consists in:

1. evaluating the impact of shutdown techniques (i.e. switching off unused servers) on the energy consumption;
2. showing the impact of such shutdown techniques on disk lifetime and energy consumption with and without workload prediction algorithm;

The reminder of this paper is structured as follows. Section 2 presents the related work. The on/off energy model and the shutdown policies are introduced in Sect. 3. The experimental setup is provided in Sect. 4. The experimental validation is shown in Sect. 5. Finally, Sect. 6 concludes this work and presents the future directions.

2   Related Work

Shutdown techniques require (1) the hardware ability to remotely switch on and off servers, and (2) energy-aware algorithms to timely employ such an ability. This section describes the state-of-the-art approaches for both features.

2.1   Suspend Modes on Linux Kernel

We focus on the Linux implementation of ACPI specification system power management. The available sleep states on the Linux kernel are:

- S0 or "Suspend to Idle": freezing user space and putting all I/O devices into low-power states
- S1 or "Standby/Power-On Suspend": same as S0 adding the fact that non boot CPUs are put in offline mode and all low-level systems functions are suspended during transitions into this state. The CPU retains power meaning operating state is lost, so the system easily starts up again where it left off
- S3 or "Suspend-to-RAM": Everything in the system is put into low power state mode. System and device state is saved and kept in memory (RAM).
- S4 or "Suspend-to-disk": Like S3, adding a final step of writing memory contents to disk.
- S5 or "System shutdown state": Similar to S4, except that the OS doesn't save any context.

On the top of our knowledge, many datacenters servers do not implement or allow S3 (Suspend-to-RAM) sleep state, because of numerous errors when resuming (especially errors due to network connections with Myrinet or Ethernet protocols). Typically, only S0, S5 (regular shutdown) are available for operational use.

2.2   Shutdown Policies

The resource manager is responsible for deciding when to suspend and resume nodes. It takes decisions either based on pre-determined policy [8] or on workload predictions [4]. In this paper, we study simple shutdown techniques, without combining them to scheduling algorithms in order to evaluate the impacts of such techniques without interfering with the workload of real platforms and with the users' expected performances.

The main disadvantage of shutdown policies resides in the energy and time losses that may occur when switching off and on takes longer the actual idle period. The various suspend modes offer different performances concerning the time they need to switch between the On and Off states and the energy they consume while in Off state. The next section provides formalism for evaluating the impact of parameters for shutdown techniques.

3   Models

In this section, we describe the different models used by the shutdown policies we want to evaluate in order to determine when a node has to be switched off.

3.1   Energy Efficiency Time Threshold

Switching on and off a server consumes time and energy, it is thus required to take these costs into account when deciding whether to switch off an idle server or not. In [5], the authors introduce T_s a time threshold such that if the server is idle for less than T_s, it should remain idle to save energy. Moreover, T_s needs to be greater than the time requited to switch off and on again a server in order for this threshold to be physically acceptable.

In order to compute T_s, all parameters described in it's definition [5] have to be known for each concerned server. These parameters can be acquired through a calibration measurement campaign. Then a shutdown policy is required to know when to switch off nodes. Indeed, as future is not known in the general case, it is difficult to determine for a given idle data center server if it will stay idle for more than T_s or not.

3.2   Studied Shutdown Policies

As the goal of this paper is to evaluate the impacts of on/off strategies rather than proposing new shutdown policies, we chose to lean on two ideal policies which will provide theoretical values about energy consumption.

Policy P1: Knowing the Future. In this first policy, we consider that the future is completely known. Thus, dates and lengths of idle period are known for each server. This policy will give a theoretical lower bound for energy consumption with a perfect prediction algorithm.

Policy P2: Aggressive Shutdown. The second policy does not consider the future and tries to switch off a server as soon as it is in idle state without any prediction attempt. Such an aggressive approach is expected to result in a higher energy consumption than Policy 1 because some idle periods may be lower than T_s. In such cases, switching off increases the energy consumption compared to staying idle. This policy provides a simplified version of actual algorithms that wait for a given amount of time (usually greater than T_s) before switching off idle nodes.

These two policies depict a representative sample of typical shutdown policies deployed on real data centers. They will be compared in order to provide an evaluation of the potential impacts of such policies on energy consumption and nodes lifetime.

4   Experiment Setup

In order to provide a fair comparison among policies P1 and P2, we simulate their behavior on real workload traces. The simulation tool is using real diversified calibration measurements. Simulations combine the workload traces and the energy calibration values to compare the two policies according to relevant metrics presented at the end of this section.

4.1   Workload Traces

The utilized workload traces come from two kinds of data centers providing two different utilization scenarios which exhibit different workload patterns and utilization levels.

Operational Cloud Platform: E-Biothon. The E-Biothon platform is an experimental Cloud platform to help speed up and advance research in biology, health and environment [2]. It is based on four Blue Gene/P racks and a web portal that allow members of the bioinformatics community to easily launch their scientific applications. Overall, the platform offers 4096 4-cores nodes, reaching a peak power of 56 TeraFlop [2]. We obtained a workload trace for this platform covering from the 1st of January 2015 to the 1st of April 2016, so roughly 15 months of resource utilization.

Experimental Testbed: Grid'5000. Grid'5000 is a large-scale and versatile testbed for experiment-driven research in all areas of computer science, with a focus on parallel and distributed computing including Cloud, HPC and Big Data [1]. For our evaluation, we took the workload trace of the Rennes site from the 1st of April 2010 to the 1st of April 2016, thus representing 6 years of resource utilization on this site. During this period, the weighted arithmetic mean of the number of nodes is 149.

4.2   Energy Calibration

Grid'5000 provides management tools like kapower3, a utility that allows a user to have control on the power status of a reserved node[1], and, on some sites, it gives access to external wattmeters monitoring entire servers with a 0.125 Watts accuracy. This infrastructure is used for obtaining the energy calibration measurements required to compute T_s as described in Sect. 3.1.

Table 1. Calibration nodes' characteristics and energy parameters for On-Off and Off-On sequences (average on 100 experimental measurements)

Features	Orion	Taurus	Paravance
Server model	Dell PowerEdge R720	Dell PowerEdge R720	Dell PowerEdge R630
CPU model	Intel Xeon E5-2630	Intel Xeon E5-2630	Intel Xeon E5-2630v3
Number of CPU	2	2	2
Cores per CPU	6	6	8
Memory (GB)	32	32	128
Storage (GB)	2×300 (HDD)	2×300 (HDD)	2×600 (HDD)
GPU	Nvidia Tesla M2075	-	-
Parameters	Orion	Taurus	Paravance
E_{OffOn} (Joules)	23,386	19,000	19,893
E_{OnOff} (Joules)	2,300	2,000	2,000
T_{OffOn} (seconds)	150	150	167.5
T_{OnOff} (seconds)	10	10	7.5
P_{idle} (Watts)	135	95	150
P_{off} (Watts)	18.5	8.5	4.5
T_s (seconds)	195	227	172

The results presented on the bottom part of Table 1 show values for regular shutdown, S5 mode (average of 100 run).

4.3   Evaluation Metrics

In order to fairly compare the shutdown policies in the determined use cases, we define several evaluation metrics. In particular, for evaluating their energy impact, we compare the energy consumed with each policy against the energy used without any shutdown policy (i.e. policy where the nodes stays idle and consumes P_{idle} Watts during periods without any work). This metric will indicate the potential energy savings with each policy.

We also provide the theoretical maximum energy savings if switching operations had a null cost (i.e. zero energy, zero time for switching between on and off states). This provides an idea on how far the policies are from the theoretical ideal

---

[1] https://www.grid5000.fr/mediawiki/index.php/Power_State_Manipulation_commands.

case and how much the costs related to switching operations are impacting the energy savings. The ideal case does not provide 100% energy gains compared to the idle case as switched off nodes consume energy ($P_{off} \neq 0$).

Finally, the results include the number of On-Off cycles per node for each workload in order to evaluate the impact of shutdown policies on the servers' lifetime. Indeed, one obstacle to the adoption of shutdown policies lies in the number of On-Off cycles imposed to the servers. In case of a too high number of cycles, it could damage the hardware parts like the hard disk drives (HDD). Typically, it is considered that hard drives can support a given amount of switching on and off during their lifetime. This parameter, known as *Contact Start/Stop Cycles* or *load/unload cycles* depending on the physical configuration of the hard drive head, is typically around 50,000 and 300,000 respectively for desktop HDD [6], and around 600,000 for NAS HDD (Network-Attached Storage) which use only load/unload technology [7]. So, the number of On-Off cycles per node will be compared with these figures to determine whether the policy may alter or not the servers' lifetime.

5   Experiments: Simulation Results Based on Actual Hardware Calibration

This section explores the simulation results of the shutdown policies with the various hardware calibrations and the workload traces described in Sect. 4. For every trace replay, the nodes are assumed to be homogeneous. Thus, every node of the trace is respecting the configuration of one of the calibrated nodes for each run.

5.1   Impacts of Shutdown Policies and Prediction Influence on Energy Consumption

We examine the case of current architectures based on the calibration made on the Grid'5000 nodes and described in Table 1.

Table 2 shows the percentage of energy that could be saved during idle periods with each policy compared to the energy consumed if nodes are never switched off. The last two columns present the average number of On-off cycles per node for the entire duration of the workload.

The results show that by turning off nodes, even when considering On-Off and Off-On costs, consequent energy gains can be made on real platforms. In the most unfavorable configuration (i.e. Orion configuration), we can theoretically save up to 86% of the energy consumed while being in idle state. In the case of Grid'5000 trace, this percentage represents around 706,000 kWh for the 6 years. For the E-Biothon trace, we can also save up to 86% of the energy consumed in the idle case, this represents 109,000 kWh for 15 months of loss to keep servers idle.

Table 2. Energy gains on idle periods and number of on-off cycles per node for current servers

Calibration	% energy saved on idle periods			# On-Off cycles per node	
	P1	P2	Ideal	P1	P2
Grid'5000 trace, 6 years, 149 nodes on average					
Orion	85.87%	85.59%	86.29%	3,080	5,690
Taurus	90.56%	90.22%	91.05%	2,980	5,690
Paravance	96.66%	96.46%	97.00%	3,333	5,690
E-Biothon trace, 15 months, 4096 nodes					
Orion	85.18%	84.56%	86.29%	33	70
Taurus	89.83%	89.07%	91.05%	33	70
Paravance	96.03%	95.61%	97.00%	38	70

The number of On-Off cycles per node reaches at the maximum 5,690 for the 6-year Grid'5000 traces, far less than the 50,000 start/stop cycles typically allowed by HDD manufacturers [6,7]. This clearly states that even aggressive shutdown policies have no impact on disk lifetime.

It is worth noticing that significant energy gains can be performed for both traces even though they present completely different use cases. In particular, the E-Biothon trace comes from an operational bioinformatics supercomputer and although energy savings are smaller than for the Grid'5000 trace in comparison with the infrastructure size, they are still not negligible, representing around 73,680 kWh per year for the Orion case (most unfavorable case) with a basic shutdown policy like P2 (without prediction algorithm).

The energy saved with policies P1 and P2 are very close to the ideal case (around 2% difference in the worst case). Even without knowledge about the future (policy P2), energy gains are quite similar. This means that even simple shutdown policies – not including workload predictions – can save consequent amounts of energy, close to the optimal bound. These results show that the energy gains of P1 and P2 is too close (for Orion 0.28% of difference between the policies, roughly 2,000 kWh over 6 years) to justify the elaboration of a prediction algorithm: such a complex algorithm to design would only bring negligible benefits.

6   Conclusion and Future Work

Energy consumption is more and more a worrying concern for Cloud data centers. Although shutdown techniques are available to reduce the overall energy consumption during idle periods, they are rarely employed because of their supposed impact on hardware.

Simulation results combining real workload traces and energy calibration measurements conducted in this paper allow us to draw several conclusions:

– Shutdown techniques can save important amounts of energy otherwise wasted during idle periods
– Even aggressive shutdown policies have no negative impact on disk lifetime.
– Reducing the consumption while in Off state has a greater impact on energy savings than reducing the switching energy and time costs between On and Off states. For this reason, S3 (Suspend-to-RAM) and S4 (Suspend-to-Disk) states are currently not beneficial in terms of energy consumption.
– Workload prediction is not worth the few energy it can save.

Our future work includes an integration of failure models when resuming from Off state in order to study the impact of bad resuming behavior. We also plan to evaluate other shutdown policies which are applied in current data centers like switching nodes by portions of the total number to control the impact on data center cooling system. We would like to explore heterogeneous architectures such as ARM big.LITTLE for instance to see whether future architectures closer to energy-proportionality could still benefit from shutdown techniques.

References

1. Balouek, D., et al.: Adding virtualization capabilities to the Grid'5000 testbed. In: Ivanov, I.I., Sinderen, M., Leymann, F., Shan, T. (eds.) CLOSER 2012. CCIS, vol. 367, pp. 3–20. Springer, Heidelberg (2013). doi:10.1007/978-3-319-04519-1_1
2. Daydé, M., Depardon, B., Franc, A., Gibrat, J.-F., Guilllier, R., Karami, Y., Suter, F., Taddese, B., Chabbert, M., Thérond, S.: E-Biothon: an experimental platform for BioInformatics. In: International Conference on Computer Science and Information Technologies (CSIT), pp. 1–4 (2015)
3. Orgerie, A.-C., Dias de Assunção, M., Lefèvre, L.: A survey on techniques for improving the energy efficiency of large-scale distributed systems. ACM Comput. Surv. **46**(4), 47:1–47:31 (2014)
4. Orgerie, A.-C., Lefèvre, L.: ERIDIS: energy-efficient reservation infrastructure for large-scale distributed systems. Parallel Process. Lett. **21**(02), 133–154 (2011)
5. Orgerie, A.-C., Lefèvre, L., Gelas, J.-P.: Save Watts in your grid: green strategies for energy-aware framework in large scale distributed systems. In: IEEE International Conference on Parallel and Distributed Systems (ICPADS), pp. 171–178, December 2008
6. Seagate: Desktop HDD specification sheet (2012). http://www.seagate.com/staticfiles/docs/pdf/datasheet/disc/desktop-hdd-data-sheet-ds1770-1-1212us.pdf
7. Seagate: NAS HDD specification sheet (2015). http://www.seagate.com/www-content/product-content/nas-fam/nas-hdd/_shared/docs/nas-hdd-8tb-ds1789-5-1 510DS1789-5-1510US-en_US.pdf
8. Yoo, A.B., Jette, M.A., Grondona, M.: SLURM: simple linux utility for resource management. In: Feitelson, D., Rudolph, L., Schwiegelshohn, U. (eds.) JSSPP 2003. LNCS, vol. 2862, pp. 44–60. Springer, Heidelberg (2003). doi:10.1007/10968987_3

Processing Partially Ordered Requests in Distributed Stream Processing Systems

Rijun Cai[1], Weigang Wu[1,2(✉)], Ning Huang[1], and Lihui Wu[1]

[1] School of Data and Computer Science, Sun Yat-sen University, Guangzhou, China
wuweig@mail.sysu.edu.cn
[2] Guangdong Province Key Laboratory of Big Data Analysis and Processing,
Guangzhou, China

Abstract. In many application scenarios of distributed stream processing, there might be partial order relations among the requests. However, existing stream processing systems can not directly handle partially ordered requests, while indirect mechanisms are usually strongly coupled with business logic, which lack flexibility and have limited performance. We propose Pork, a novel distributed stream processing system targeting at partially ordered requests. In the experiments, the new system has achieved a parallelism and request throughput larger than the traditional mechanism in the presented example, and the performance overhead due to parallelism is considerably small. Then the scalability characteristic of the new system is discussed. What's more, the experiment results also show that the new system has a more flexible load balancing ability.

1 Introduction

Distributed stream processing systems, exemplified by Storm [9] from Twitter, offers a paradigm for processing large scale continuous data streams. However, existing distributed stream processing systems cannot deal with the order among requests in natural and efficient ways. They have to sacrifice performance to ensure a strict processing order, or enforce the business logic code to take over the order maintenance work. When it comes to some more general scenarios, say, partially ordered requests, they normally do not have an elegant solution.

In this paper, a novel distributed stream processing system targeting at partially ordered requests, Pork (Partially Ordered Request Queue), is proposed. This system maintains a message queue on a few extra nodes, in which requests are dispatched efficiently while their partial order relations are guaranteed. Such a mechanism can easily maximize the parallelism of request processing and fully utilize the computing resources of the clusters.

W. Wu—This research is partially supported by National Natural Science Foundation of China (No. 61379157), Program of Science and Technology of Guangdong (No. 2015A010103007), Program of Science and Technology of Guangzhou (No. 201510010068), and Guangdong Frontier and Key Technology Innovation Fund (No. 2015B010111001).

J. Carretero et al. (Eds.): ICA3PP 2016, LNCS 10048, pp. 211–219, 2016.
DOI: 10.1007/978-3-319-49583-5_16

In Sect. 2 we describe a typical partially ordered request processing problem, with which we design our experiment scenario later. Two simple solutions to this problem are presented in Sect. 3. Some relevant research on processing with order requirements in stream processing systems are presented in Sect. 4. Section 5 gives a detailed discussion on our new system. The experiments and results are presented in Sect. 6.

2 Background

To better discuss the architecture and algorithms of Pork, we are going to describe a typical scenario involving partially ordered request processing as follows. This example is also adopted in our experiments presented in Sect. 6.

Consider an automatic stock tracking and trading system, which is comprised of three step. First receive real-time stock price data, then analyse the data *in parallel*, and finally generate *ordered* trading operations based on the previous results. This system can be implemented as a distributed stream processing system according to the data flowing relations among these three step, each of which is considered as a "stage" of the system. For a given stock t, the involved requests in the system are as follows.

1. The *ordered* requests generated by some external data source, as in (1),
2. The requests sent from stage 1 to stage 2, supposing that there are k different kinds of analyses to be conducted in stage 2, as in (2),
3. The analysis results sent from stage 2 to stage 3, as in (3).

$$S^{(t)} = [s_1^{(t)}, s_2^{(t)}, s_3^{(t)}, \ldots] \tag{1}$$
$$P^{(t)} = \{p_{1,1}^{(t)}, p_{1,2}^{(t)}, \ldots, p_{1,k}^{(t)}, p_{2,1}^{(t)}, p_{2,2}^{(t)}, \ldots, p_{2,k}^{(t)}, \ldots\} \tag{2}$$
$$R^{(t)} = \{r_{1,1}^{(t)}, r_{1,2}^{(t)}, \ldots, r_{1,k}^{(t)}, r_{2,1}^{(t)}, r_{2,2}^{(t)}, \ldots, r_{2,k}^{(t)}, \ldots\}. \tag{3}$$

For clarity, we use some notations to describe the relations among requests. Let $a \to b$ denote that request b is *derived from* request a, and $a \prec b$ denote that request a is *processed before*[1] request b. Following that, we have

$$a \to b \implies a \prec b \tag{4}$$
$$i < j \implies s_i^{(t)} \prec s_j^{(t)} \tag{5}$$
$$s_i^{(t)} \to p_{i,1}^{(t)}, p_{i,2}^{(t)}, \ldots, p_{i,k}^{(t)} \tag{6}$$
$$p_{i,j}^{(t)} \to r_{i,j}^{(t)}. \tag{7}$$

As stage 3 needs to produce *ordered* trading operations, we hope to ensure that the input of stage 3, $R^{(t)}$, is ordered as well — that is to say, the processing

---

[1] This is a transitive, irreflexive and asymmetric relation, i.e. a strict partial order.

results derived from $s_i^{(t)}$ should arrive at stage 3 prior to those from $s_{i+1}^{(t)}$. In other words, we want to guarantee the following partial order relations over $\mathcal{R}^{(t)}$:

$$\mathbb{R}^{(t)} = \{r_{i,x}^{(t)} \prec r_{i+1,y}^{(t)} \mid r^{(t)} \in \mathcal{R}^{(t)}, x \le k, y \le k\}. \tag{8}$$

3   Simple Solutions

3.1   Key-Based Parallelism

Many stream processing systems allow distributing requests based on some specific attribute of the requests, and that attribute is usually called the "key". Requests with the same key are dispatched to the same processing node *in order*. Formally speaking, given four requests a_i, a_j, $b_i^{(t)}$ and $b_j^{(t)}$, if $a_i \to b_i^{(t)}, a_j \to b_j^{(t)}$, and $b_i^{(t)}, b_j^{(t)}$ have the same key t, then we have

$$a_i \prec a_j \implies b_i^{(t)} \prec b_j^{(t)}. \tag{9}$$

When it comes to the scenario described in Sect. 2, if the order requirement (8) is guaranteed to affect only the requests with the same key, then requests with different keys can be processed in parallel without worrying about the order. For example, we can choose the stock name t as the key attribute. Derived from (5) to (7) and (9), we have

$$p_{i,x}^{(t)} \prec p_{i+1,y}^{(t)}, r_{i,x}^{(t)} \prec r_{i+1,y}^{(t)}. \tag{10}$$

Thus our desired order (8) is ensured.

However, it is not always easy to find an attribute strongly related to order requirement that can be used as the key attribute. Second, it is difficult to add more processing nodes to the system on the fly without breaking the order requirement, as the key-node mapping must be fixed to ensure requests with the same key will go through the same node, while the system is running.

3.2   Intra-node Parallelism

If a single second stage node has sufficient computing resources, we can process $p_{i,1}^{(t)}, p_{i,2}^{(t)}, \ldots, p_{i,k}^{(t)}$ in parallel in that node. We just need to pack $p_{i,1}^{(t)}, p_{i,2}^{(t)}, \ldots, p_{i,k}^{(t)}$ into a single request $P_i^{(t)}$ in the first stage and send it to the second stage node in order. However, the degree of parallelism is limited by k in this paradigm. Besides, the total processing time of $P_i^{(t)}$ is at least that of the slowest one among $p_{i,1}^{(t)}, p_{i,2}^{(t)}, \ldots, p_{i,k}^{(t)}$, which may affect the performance of the system.

4   Related Work

There exist many distributed stream processing systems, exemplified by Storm [9], which operates on streams of tuples flowing in a predefined "topology" and only guarantees tuples with the same keys will be delivered to the same nodes in order. Spark Streaming [10] operates on streams of small batches of data and makes no guarantee of order when there are multiple nodes. Apache Samza [1] is similar to Storm but operates with an external message queue service. Apache Flink [2] allows requests arrive out of order by reordering them according to their timestamps, but does not support partial order. Most of these systems can implement the solutions in Sects. 3.1 and 3.2. But they do not directly deal with the order requirements among requests. Rather, they fulfill the requirements by introducing some stronger order requirements.

There are some other research targeting at the ordering problem in stream processing systems. AQ-K-slack by Ji et al. [3] manages to reorder requests efficiently in a buffer, but it does not guarantee the order can be fully restored and has to make a trade-off between latency and accuracy. An out-of-order execution mechanism proposed by Li et al. [7] inserts "punctuations" into the original ordered input streams at some regular interval, in order to track out-of-order requests and reorder them when needed. This mechanism handles total order only and supports only several operations at present such as Join, Union and Window Aggregation. S-Store proposed by Meehan et al. [8] supports partial order, but requires it to exist within a finite, continuous and disjoint "atomic batch" of requests.

5   Partially Ordered Request Queue

In this section, we propose a distributed stream processing system that can efficiently handle partially ordered requests called Pork (Partially Ordered Request Queue).

Inspired by Kafka [5] and Samza [1], Pork exploits one to several nodes to implement a high-performance and fault-tolerant message queue, which is responsible for order maintenance and request dispatch. This architecture relieves processing nodes of the burden of maintaining request order and greatly simplifies the implementation of processing nodes. And the sender of a request just needs to specify the "dependencies"[2] of the request.

5.1   Dependency Representation

As the dependencies of requests need to be stored and transferred over networks, an efficient dependency representation is vital. Take (8) as an example, directly storing every pair of relation requires $O(k^2)$ space complexity for $r_{i,1}^{(t)}, \ldots, r_{i,k}^{(t)}$. Pork relieves this problem by introducing *dependency groups* as follows.

---

[2]   Requests that should be processed directly prior to the current request.

A request in Pork is represented by tuple $(id, payload, deps, resolve)$, where id is the ID of the request, $payload$ is the content, $deps$ are arbitrary number of dependency groups on which this request depends, and $resolve$ is the dependency group to be resolved by this request.

A dependency group is represented by tuple (id, n), where id is the group ID, and n is the size of the group, which is defined as the number requests that have to be processed in order to resolve this dependency group. Unlike a request, a dependency group does not need to be created explicitly, as it will be created automatically at the first time it appears in some request.

With this representation, multiple order relations are packed into one dependency group, resulting in a reduction of space complexity. The designation of dependency groups is usually relevant to business logic. For instance, order relation (8) can be represented as Table 1, and the space complexity is $O(k)$ now.

Table 1. Representation of (8) in Pork

Requests	deps	resolve
...	...	...
$r_{i,1}^{(t)}, \ldots, r_{i,k}^{(t)}$	$\{(i-1, k)\}$	(i, k)
$r_{i+1,1}^{(t)}, \ldots, r_{i+1,k}^{(t)}$	$\{(i, k)\}$	$(i+1, k)$
$r_{i+2,1}^{(t)}, \ldots, r_{i+2,k}^{(t)}$	$\{(i+1, k)\}$	$(i+2, k)$
...	...	...

Another advantage of dependency groups is that the IDs of depended requests need not to be known when the dependent request specifies its dependencies. As a result, the depended requests can be sent by other processing nodes, and even after the dependent request. Since it is difficult to have determined numbering for requests in distributed systems [6], such a characteristic enables more flexible and efficient dispatching strategies of requests in Pork.

5.2   Message Queue Operations

With dependency groups, requests along with the relations among them can be represented as a directed acyclic graph. Pork uses a set of operations based on topological sorting [4] to maintain the required order relations as follows. F denotes the set of requests without unresolved dependency, and D denotes the set of all dependency groups, and both of them are initialized to empty sets.

Add a New Request. To add a new request with d dependency groups to the message queue, there are two cases for each dependency group. If the group does not exist, or exists but has not been fully resolved, the new request will be appended to the dependant list of the group, and the in-degree of the request will be increased. But if the group has been resolved, it will be ignored as it can be seen as a deleted vertex in the graph. The group existence checking is done using hashmaps. This operation has a time complexity of $O(d)$.

Acknowledge a Request. Request acknowledgment may happen when a request is successfully processed or arrives at the processing node, according to business logic. If the request being acknowledged claims to resolve a dependency group with w dependent requests, the size of the group will be decreased by one, indicating the resolution of a depended request. And if the request is the last one in that group, the group will be resolved as well, and all the dependent requests will be notified, which results in a $O(w)$ worst case time complexity. However, since the group resolution happens only when all requests have been acknowledged, the average time complexity is $O(w/n)$, where n is the original size of the group.

Dispatch a Request. To dispatch a request, the message queue just needs to pop one request from F and sends it to an available processing node, as other operations have guaranteed that requests pushed to F do not have any unresolved dependency. The time complexity is $O(1)$.

5.3 State Pruning

The state of the message queue can be represented by (F, D). F will stay in a reasonable size as the requests are dispatched to the processing nodes, but D will grow without limit because resolved dependency groups need to be kept to be distinguishable from non-existing groups. The inflation of state causes performance pressure on the queue, and increases time cost of snapshot generation and fault recovery. Therefore, it is vital to prune the state occasionally to keep it in a reasonable size. Pork adopts a watermark-based strategy. First, let I denotes the maximum ID of dependency groups used [3] may only use dependency groups whose IDs I' fall in a left-bounded range around I, i.e. $I - I' < c, c > 0$. Then at any moment, the node knows the minimum group ID i that it may use in the future, and it will report i to the message queue at regular interval. If the message queue receives the minimum possible dependency group IDs $i_1, i_2, \ldots, i_n$, from all processing nodes, then it is safe to drop $\forall d \in D, d.id < \min_{1 \le j \le n} i_j$ without breaking subsequent dependency requirements. The pruning procedure is trigger at regular intervals and will not increase the average complexity of queue operations.

6 Experiments

Several experiments were conducted in order to analyse the performance characteristics of Pork. These experiments are based on the example described in Sect. 2. In the second stage, there are $k = 4$ different jobs to be done, each of which costs about 1 ms. Performance is measured by the request throughput of the third stage. Pork was written in C++ and compiled using GCC 5.0 with

---

[3] Either in *deps* or *resolve* of requests.

default optimization level. The Pork and Kafka servers run on a machine with four 2.6 GHz cores and 8 GB memory, while the processing nodes run within VMs on several machines. The softwares we used are Kafka 0.9.0 and Samza 0.10. The results are presented as follows.

6.1   Comparison with Samza/Kafka

Samza [1], running on top of a message queue service such as Kafka [5], is chosen for comparison because it uses a node-queue architecture similar to that used by Pork. The intra-node parallelism paradigm in Sect. 3.2 is implemented for the Samza/Kafka scheme. As shown in Table 2, Pork performs slightly worse than Samza/Kafka when the DoP is low, which is a result of the overhead of order maintenance. But Pork outperforms Samza/Kafka as the DoP grows, and the performance gains from the increase of DoP are much larger and more stable. This is because Samza needs to wait for the slowest sub-requests in the second stage, but Pork can find and dispatch the next available request without violating the order requirement. Furthermore, Pork can achieve a higher DoP, while the DoP of Samza/Kafka is limited by k.

Table 2. Request throughput comparison (#reqs/s)

DoP[a]	Samze/Kafka	Pork
1	754.76	657.89
2	1477.31	1338.69
4	2339.26	2706.36
8	N/A	5899.71

[a]Degree of Parallelism. For Samza/Kafka, it is the number of threads in a second stage node. For Pork, it is the number of second stage nodes

6.2   Scalability

In this experiment, we analyse the relation between Pork's performance and DoP. The results are shown in Fig. 1. The dashed line in the graph represents the multiples of the performance with only one node. Surprisingly, Pork fails to fully utilize the resources of processing nodes when the DoP is low, which leads to a "hump" on the curve as the DoP grows. We suppose this is because low activity affects the cache hit rates of some critical data structures, which is more like an implementation issue. The performance will decrease when the DoP grows above 10. The bottleneck is that the previous stage is not able to generate enough requests. And the race conditions caused by plenty of simultaneous operations bring pressure on the message queue.

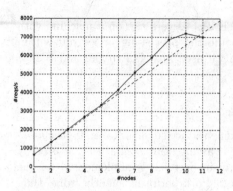

Fig. 1. Scalability of Pork   **Fig. 2.** Load balancing of Pork

6.3   Load Balancing

The third experiment tests the load balancing ability of Pork. We monitor the real time throughput of the system, then add more processing nodes to the system and observe the performance changes. The results are shown in Fig. 2. The system starts with 4 s stage nodes, and one more node is started at the time indicated by a vertical dashed line in the graph. As can be seen in the graph, after an extra node being started, the overall performance increases rapidly and stabilizes in a short time, and the performance improvement is roughly equal to the processing ability of a single node.

7   Summary

Pork reduces the complexity of partial order representation by dependency group, and adopts a set of algorithms and strategies to efficiently maintain the processing order of requests in a message queue with fault-tolerance. Pork provides an effective mechanism to process partially ordered requests in stream processing.

References

1. Apache Software Foundation: Apache Samza (2013). http://samza.apache.org/
2. Apache Software Foundation: Apache Flink (2015). http://flink.apache.org/
3. Ji, Y., Zhou, H., Jerzak, Z., Nica, A., Hackenbroich, G., Fetzer, C.: Quality-driven continuous query execution over out-of-order data streams. In: Proceedings of the 2015 ACM SIGMOD International Conference on Management of Data, pp. 889–894. ACM (2015)
4. Kahn, A.B.: Topological sorting of large networks. Commun. ACM 5(11), 558–562 (1962)
5. Kreps, J., Narkhede, N., Rao, J.: Kafka: a distributed messaging system for log processing. In: NetDB (2011)

6. Lamport, L.: Time, clocks, and the ordering of events in a distributed system. Commun. ACM **21**(7), 558–565 (1978)
7. Li, J., Tufte, K., Shkapenyuk, V., Papadimos, V., Johnson, T., Maier, D.: Out-of-order processing: a new architecture for high-performance stream systems. Proc. VLDB Endowment **1**(1), 274–288 (2008)
8. Meehan, J., Tatbul, N., Zdonik, S., Aslantas, C., Cetintemel, U., Du, J., Kraska, T., Madden, S., Maier, D., Pavlo, A., et al.: S-Store: streaming meets transaction processing. Proc. VLDB Endowment **8**(13), 2134–2145 (2015)
9. Toshniwal, A., Taneja, S., Shukla, A., Ramasamy, K., Patel, J.M., Kulkarni, S., Jackson, J., Gade, K., Fu, M., Donham, J., et al.: Storm@ Twitter. In: Proceedings of the 2014 ACM SIGMOD International Conference on Management of Data, pp. 147–156. ACM (2014)
10. Zaharia, M., Das, T., Li, H., Hunter, T., Shenker, S., Stoica, I.: Discretized streams: fault-tolerant streaming computation at scale. In: Proceedings of the Twenty-Fourth ACM Symposium on Operating Systems Principles, pp. 423–438. ACM (2013)

Implement and Optimization of Indoor Positioning System Based on Wi-Fi Signal

Chongsheng Yu[1], Xin Li[1(⊠)], Lei Dou[2], Jianwei Li[1], Yu Zhang[1],
Jian Qin[1], Yuqing Sun[1], and Zhiyue Cao[3]

[1] School of Computer Science and Technology,
Shandong University, Jinan 250101, China
lx@sdu.edu.cn
[2] College of Business, Shandong Normal University,
Jinan 250014, China
[3] Information Engineering Department,
Weichai Power Company, Weifang, China

Abstract. As wireless routers are used widely, indoor positioning technology based on Wi-Fi signal has drawn more attentions. The positioning process in our solution is divided into two phases: collection phase and positioning phase. In the collection phase, according to the fingerprint algorithm, data collectors (e.g. mobile phones) submit received Wi-Fi strength data at location-known points to the server. The collected locations and strength data will be saved in database. In the positioning phase, the server calculates positioning result according to the differences between Wi-Fi strength data stored in database and Wi-Fi strength data uploaded by mobile terminals request to be located. All the data are clustered using K-Means algorithm for increasing the positioning efficiency. K-Nearest-Neighbor (KNN) algorithm is performed in positioning phase. The result of experiment shows that the proposed approach can achieve high positioning accuracy with the use of filtered data and the weighted KNN algorithm.

Keywords: Indoor positioning · Wi-Fi signal · KNN

1 Introduction

With the increasing demand for indoor positioning, related researches and applications in this field are rapidly developed. According to the different types of sensors used in positioning technology, indoor positioning systems can be divided into Radio Frequency Identification (RFID)-based approach, infrared-based approach [1], Ultra-wideband (UWB)-based approach [2], ZigBee-based approach and Wi-Fi based approach. There are several types of measuring methods, such as angle of arrival signal [3], time difference of arrival signal [4], or received signal strength [5, 6].

The Wi-Fi based approach is more feasible in practice and draws many attentions of researchers. Most of researchers in this field use Received Signal Strength (RSS)-based approach after the RADAR localization system [7] had been released, developed by Microsoft Corporation. RSS-based positioning system has very practical significances. We calculate the distances between target and several signal sources according

© Springer International Publishing AG 2016
J. Carretero et al. (Eds.): ICA3PP 2016, LNCS 10048, pp. 220–228, 2016.
DOI: 10.1007/978-3-319-49583-5_17

to the received signal strength values and implement positioning. However, the RSS values received by mobile devices may not always be stable enough to implement indoor positioning exactly due to the impact of surrounding environment.

This paper presents an optimization approach to reduce the random error, in which the Kalman filter algorithm is introduced to improve the precision of position and K-Means algorithm is performed to increase positioning efficiency. We developed an indoor localization system to calculate these methods. Experiments show that our system realizes indoor positioning efficiently.

The reminder of this paper is organized as follows. In Sect. 2, we survey related work in Wi-Fi indoor localization techniques. Section 3 presents the framework of our system and discuss our implement. Section 4 discusses the results of experiments. Finally, we conclude our research work and its perspective in the last section.

2 Related Work and Motivation

In the past years, many indoor positioning systems have been developed by the researchers. Most of these systems are based on exist infrastructures (e.g. 802.11-compliant). RADAR is the first Wi-Fi based positioning system that performs positioning based on the RSS values received from many APs. Placelab [8] is a system that depends on information about the AP's coordinates in a database in order to predict location. Both systems use the mean RSS vector on a grid to represent the fingerprint. Some research works study the signal strength distributions from APs and use probabilistic algorithms to estimate the location.

Currently, the most popular solution for RSS-based positioning is the fingerprint scheme [9, 10]. There are mainly two phases in the fingerprint algorithm: the off-line phase and the on-line phase. In the off-line phase, a two-dimensional rectangular coordinate system is established. The points P_n represent each intersection of the grid in the coordinate system. P_n can also be expressed as (x_p, y_p). Then RSS data samples are collected at each node, which contain the received signal strength sequences $\{value_1, value_2, ..., value_n\}$ corresponding to the signal source sequence $\{AP_1, AP_2, ..., AP_n\}$. In the on-line phase, the received signal strength data collected by user terminals are submitted to server. The server will calculate user's current position and then response the result to the user.

Although the fingerprint scheme has been investigated in many studies, the positioning results still have big errors during experiments. The error is mainly derived from the instability of Wi-Fi signal strength. The strength is affected by many factors, such as the distances between mobile terminals and Wi-Fi access points, with/without obstacles (walls, usually) between them.

In this paper, we propose an optimization approach to improve the positioning accuracy, and prove the feasibility and practicability of our solution.

3   System Framework

The system framework is shown in Fig. 1. According to the fingerprint algorithm, in the off-line collection phase, data collectors (e.g. mobile phones) submit received Wi-Fi strength data to the server. After processed, the collected data will be saved in database. In the on-line positioning phase, the server calculates positioning result according to the differences between RSS data stored in database and those uploaded by mobile terminals request to be located.

The organization chart of the system is shown in Fig. 2.

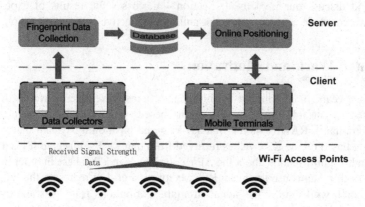

Fig. 1. Indoor positioning system based on RSS.

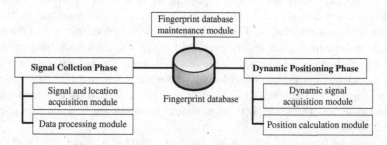

Fig. 2. Internal structure of indoor localization system.

It can be seen from the figure that the indoor localization system is divided into a signal and location collection phase, a dynamic positioning phase and a fingerprint database maintenance module.

3.1   Signal Collection Phase

The signal collection phase is divided into a signal and location acquisition module and a data processing module.

The signal and location acquisition module has a signal acquisition function and a communication function. The signal acquisition function realizes the procedure of collecting the signal strength values of the mobile phone network from the location-known sample points. This function regularly collects Wi-Fi signals around one mobile terminal including the names and MAC addresses of Wi-Fi Routers, their signal strength, and the location information, such as building name and room number. Signal acquisition function filters unstable signals. Multiple acquisitions will be executed at one point, and the maximal and minimal values will be removed, then the average of remain values will be submitted to server. The communication function implements the communication between mobile terminals and the server. After the collection module is initialized, it will connect to the background server and collect fingerprint data to server. The authorized mobile terminals can send the fingerprint information to server through wireless network. The server refuses to connect the devices without authorization and returns a connection error.

The data processing module comprises of a signal filter function and a fingerprint database pre-processing function. The filter function cleans the collected fingerprint data, removing the noise points in the data, extracting valuable information from the system and reducing the interference of the invalid information for positioning. The function of preprocessing fingerprint data realizes the function of data preprocessing. After the data collection is completed, the data preprocessing will be performed on the fingerprint data. A K-Means algorithm is used to cluster all the fingerprint data so that all the data is divided into k clusters. Then the fingerprint values recorded in the system are marked to indicate which cluster the values belong to.

3.2   Dynamic Positioning Phase

The dynamic positioning phase also has two modules: a dynamic signal acquisition module and a position calculation module.

The dynamic signal acquisition module is similar to the signal acquisition module in mobile terminal. The complexity of signal acquisition in the positioning stage is relatively low. A mobile terminal will upload the data directly with the average of multiple acquisitions.

After receiving the positioning request, the position calculation module in the server will call a KNN algorithm to match the received data with the fingerprint data in database and response the positioning result to the mobile terminal. The module will determine which cluster the RSS value belongs to, and determine the cluster nearest to the request point in the KNN algorithm. If receiving several location requests from one terminal continuously, the localization server will combine the last three signal strength values to calculate the location result.

3.3   Fingerprint Database Maintenance Module

The fingerprint database maintenance module includes two sub modules, access control sub-model and operation sub-model.

Database access control sub-model realizes access management to other modules need to access database. Some modules can only read the database; some modules can read and update the records in the database. Database access control can deploy the databases and import or export data.

Database operation sub-module realizes the functions of records creating, retrieving, updating and deleting. This feature isolates the database from illegal accesses. The database server can be accessed only through the server proxy interface.

4   System Testing and Result Analysis

The experiments in the rest of the paper were performed at Shandong University. The layout of the building is presented in Fig. 3. Each grid presents approximately the sampling area of 2×2 m. We limited our work to floor 2 of the building. Positions of collection points are illustrated in the Fig. 3 with star symbols. The black circle symbols represent the positions where the localization techniques were performed.

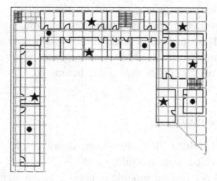

Fig. 3. The layout of the floor plan where we performed the experiment.

After installing the localization software on mobile terminal, we can enter the location selection interface, as shown in Fig. 4. The thumbtack on map presents the location of acquisition point. By clicking the map, new location can be set. After selecting the collection point, we can click the OK button to enter data acquisition interface. In data acquisition interface, the collected signal strength values are submitted to the database server after the submit button was clicked. The strength value can be repeatedly collected and submitted at the same location to provide sufficient data for Kalman filter.

The calculation and position displaying of the real location are performed in the online phrase. Current location and the floor plan can be viewed on mobile terminals.

We collected the signal strength value of the same Wi-Fi access point in different distances for several times to verify the relationship between Wi-Fi signal attenuation and distance. Analysis results are shown in Figs. 5 and 6.

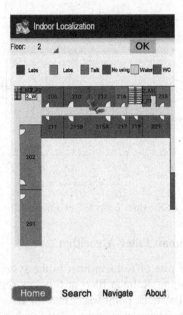

Fig. 4. Data acquisition interface in mobile terminal.

During the experiment, we collected the signal strength values of one access point in six different positions. Obviously, the received signal strength is inversely proportional to the distance between AP and mobile terminal.

In order to test the optimization effect of the system, we designed the following two groups of experiments.

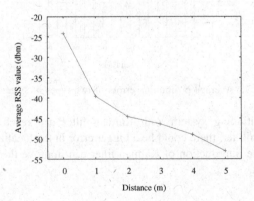

Fig. 5. The mean value of RSS_values collected in different distances to the same AP.

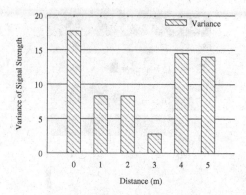

Fig. 6. The variance of RSS values collected in different distances to the same AP.

4.1 Performance of Kalman Filter Algorithm

In order to demonstrate the role of Kalman filter in the system, we tested the systems with Kalman filter and without Kalman filter at 6 points separately, and ensured the consistency of other variables. Each point was tested for 10 times. Average range error is used as the measure of localization accuracy. The result is shown in Fig. 7.

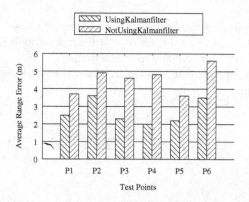

Fig. 7. Average positioning errors of two types of systems.

Obviously, positioning system with Kalman filter can reach higher accuracy. Without the Kalman filter, there could be a bigger error in the localization system. The result shows that the introduction of Kalman filter can improve the positioning accuracy to some extent.

4.2 Performance of K-Means Algorithm

Similarly, we designed an experiment for K-Means clustering algorithm. The time consuming of the positioning process is used as a measure of efficiency. The result of the experiment is shown in Fig. 8.

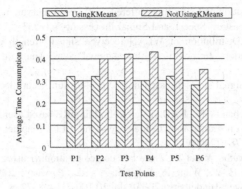

Fig. 8. Average time consumption of two types of systems.

In this experiment environment, the K-Means algorithm shortens the time consumption of the localization process.

5   Conclusion

We use the thin client design ideas to design and implement the positioning system. All calculations are carried out on the server. Web services provide users location-based services. The sampling and processing of the system and the key modules such as positioning information analysis and comparison are described in detail. Kalman filter algorithm, K-Means algorithm and the weighted k-Nearest-Neighbor (KNN) algorithm used in online positioning stage are introduced. Through the actual test, our system is able to quickly response the positioning result. The error rate is within the acceptable range. The system realizes RSS-based positioning effectively.

Acknowledgements. This work is supported by NSF China (61173140), SAICT Experts Program, Independent Innovation & Achievements Transformation Program (2014ZZCX03301), the Science & Technology Development Program of Shandong Province (2014GGX101046), the Natural Science Foundation of Shandong Province (ZR2014FM014) and the Key R&D Program of Shandong Province (2015GGX106002).

References

1. Ning, J.: Indoor object location technology using infrared weaving. Laser Infrared **41**(7), 774–778 (2011)
2. Yang, D., Tang, X., Li, B., Wang, F.: A review of ultra-wideband indoor localization technology. GNSS World Chin. **40**(5), 34–40 (2015)
3. Rong, P., Sichitiu, M.: Angle of arrival localization for wireless sensor networks. In: The 3rd Annual IEEE Communications Society on Sensor and Ad Hoc Communications and Networks, pp. 374–382 (2006)

4. Gustafsson, F.: Positioning using time-difference of arrival measurements. In: International Conference on Acoustics, Speech and Signal Processing, pp. 553–559 (2003)
5. Kaemarungsi, K.: Distribution of WLAN received signal strength indication for indoor location determination. In: 2006 1st International Symposium on Wireless Pervasive Computing (2006)
6. Chen, Y., Li, X.: Signal strength based indoor geolocation. Acta Electronica Sinica **32**(9), 1456–1458 (2004)
7. Bahl, P., Padmanabhan, V.N.: RADAR: an in-building RF-based user location and tracking system. In: Nineteenth Annual Joint Conference of the IEEE Computer and Communications Societies, pp. 775–784 (2000)
8. LaMarca, A., Chawathe, Y., et al.: Place lab: device positioning using radio beacons in the wild. In: Gellersen, H.-W., Want, R., Schmidt, A. (eds.) Pervasive 2005. LNCS, vol. 3468, pp. 116–133. Springer, Heidelberg (2005). doi:10.1007/11428572_8
9. Yu, Z., Jiang, Y., Jiang, J., Zhu, M.: Indoor positioning technology and its application in hospital. Chin. Med. Equip. J. **36**(6), 124–126 (2015)
10. Wang, Q.: Indoor fingerprint localization technology based on WiFi signal. Comput. Netw. **41**(21), 65–67 (2015)

Big Data and Its Applications

Optimizing Inter-server Communications by Exploiting Overlapping Communities in Online Social Networks

Jingya Zhou[1,2(✉)], Jianxi Fan[1,2], Baolei Cheng[1,2], and Juncheng Jia[1,2]

[1] School of Computer Science and Technology,
Soochow University, Suzhou 215006, China
{jy_zhou,jxfan,chengbaolei,jiajuncheng}@suda.edu.cn
[2] Collaborative Innovation Center of Novel Software Technology
and Industrialization, Nanjing 210046, China

Abstract. As the rapid growth of online social networks (OSNs), inter-server communications are becoming an obstacle to scaling the storage systems of OSNs. To address the problem, network partitioning and data replication are two commonly used approaches. In this paper, we exploit the combination of both approaches simultaneously and propose a data placement scheme based on overlapping communities detection. The principle behind the proposed scheme is to co-locate frequently inter-active users together as long as it brings positive traffic reduction and satisfies load constraint. We conduct trace-driven experiments and the results show that our scheme significantly reduces the inter-server communications as well as preserving good load balancing.

Keywords: Inter-server communications · Online social networks · Data placement · Network partitioning · Data replication

1 Introduction

Due to the convenient communications with no time and geographical restrictions, an increasing number of people have begun to join online social networks (OSNs). For example, Facebook's MAUs during the 2nd quarter 2015 have reached up to 1.5 billion, which implies more than twenty percent of people around the world use Facebook for communication. The popularity of OSNs has driven a dramatic surge in the amount of user data. Different from traditional web applications, OSNs need to deal with highly interactive operations. Usually the data of both users and their friends are distributed across multiple servers, and inter-server communications are inevitable. Frequent inter-server communications consume a high amount of network bandwidth and hurts the scalability

J. Zhou—This work is supported by National Natural Science Foundation of China (No. 61502328, No. 61572337), Natural Science Foundation of the Higher Education Institutions of Jiangsu Province (No. 15KJB520032, No. 14KJB520034), Joint Innovation Funding of Jiangsu Province (No. BY2014059-02).

J. Carretero et al. (Eds.): ICA3PP 2016, LNCS 10048, pp. 231–244, 2016.
DOI: 10.1007/978-3-319-49583-5_18

of OSNs. As a result, how to store user data efficiently in a distributed scalable manner has become a challenging issue.

Nowadays, key-value store as a defacto standard for big data storage, has been widely used to construct storage systems for OSNs (e.g., HDFS [1] and Cassandra [2]). Most of key-value store systems assign user data across servers randomly by using hashing which could help the system to achieve good load balancing. However, the random nature of hashing fails to preserve *social locality* well and produce high inter-server communication traffic. Existing studies suggest to apply network partitioning [3,4] and data replication [5–7] to address the problem. However, both optimizing approaches are conducted in a separated manner, which hurts the optimization results.

Our design philosophy departs from the existing work in such a way that we explore to optimize partitioning and replication simultaneously. To realize the integrated optimization, we model data placement problem as an overlapping communities detection problem. Users inside the overlap area belong to multiple partitions, and naturally corresponds to multiple replicas on different servers. Finally the inter-server communications are further reduced by determining the optimal locations of master replicas.

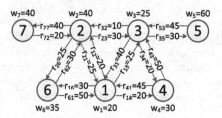

Fig. 1. An example of social graph.

2   Preliminaries

2.1   System Model

Social Graph. Many previous work modeled an online social network as a social graph, where each edge corresponds to a social link between a pair of users (e.g., the friendship between Facebook users). Figure 1 shows an example of social graph $G = (V, E)$, where V corresponds to user set and E corresponds to the set of social links between every pair of users. To represent the interaction behaviors, each social link e_{ij} has a direction and is associated with a nonzero weight which represents the read rate r_{ij} from users i to j. Users are mutual friends if there are bi-directional social links between them. Besides read operation, a user may often update her data, and each vertex in Fig. 1 is associated with a value of write rate w_i. Note that users often make updates on her friends' data as well, for example, a Facebook user comments on her friends' status and photos. For simplicity, we do not explicitly consider the write updates made by a user on her friends' data, while this kind of interactions can be divided into two operations:

a read operation to a friend's data and the friend updating her own data. Since the social link has directions, each user has two sets of friends denoted by

$$\begin{cases} F_i^+ = \{j \in V | e_{ij} \in E\}, \\ F_i^- = \{j \in V | e_{ji} \in E\}. \end{cases} \tag{1}$$

Therefore, the social graph defined here can account for both types of interactions including read and write operations, and its nature is equivalent to the interaction graph proposed in [8].

Single master multi-slave paradigm is widely used in OSN's backend storage systems, which requires that each user i has only one replica of her data as the master replica stored on one server and the server is called her master server, denoted by m_i. The other replicas work as slave ones stored on a set of slave servers, denoted by s_i. We define a binary function $\phi(i, x)$ to decide whether server x is i's slave server,

$$\phi(i, x) = \begin{cases} 1, & if\ x\ is\ i's\ slave\ server, \\ 0, & otherwise. \end{cases} \tag{2}$$

Then the set of slave servers can be defined by $s_i = \{x \in S | \phi(i, x) = 1\}$, where S denotes the set of servers.

Inter-server Communications. The inter-server communications consist of both read traffic and write traffic, and become the main metric we try to optimize. For a pair of neighboring users i and j, the inter-server read traffic is incurred if and only if i's master server does not host j's replica including master replica and slave replica, and then i's master server m_i acts as a relay node and fetches the required data from one of j's replicas. We define a binary function $g(i, j)$ to decide whether an operation of cross-server read is issued, i.e.,

$$g(i, j) = \begin{cases} 1, & m_i \notin s_j \cup m_j, \\ 0, & otherwise. \end{cases} \tag{3}$$

The inter-server write traffic is incurred by synchronizing all slave replicas, denoted by $\sum_{i \in V} (w_i |s_i|)$, where w_i represents user i's write rate and $|s_i|$ represents the number of i's slave servers. As a result, the total inter-server traffic can be calculated by

$$T = \sum_{i \in V} \sum_{j \in F_i^+} r_{ij} g(i, j) + \sum_{i \in V} (w_i |s_i|). \tag{4}$$

Load Balancing. The workload a server x need to handle mainly depends on the set D_x of users whose data stored on it,

$$D_x = \{i \in V | m_i = x \lor x \in s_i\}. \tag{5}$$

Thus, we use the set size $|D_x|$ as the indicator of server x's load, i.e., $l_x = |D_x|$. Load balancing across servers is another metric we try to preserve. For the purpose of illustration, we use Gini coefficient to measure the degree of load balancing across servers, due to its independence of system size. Generally Gini coefficient is defined as a ratio between the sum of value differences and the sum of values, and we give its definition as below:

$$L = \frac{\sum\limits_{x \in S} \sum\limits_{y \in S} |l_x - l_y|}{2n \sum\limits_{x \in S} l_x}, \tag{6}$$

where n is the size of server set, i.e., $n = |S|$. Gini coefficient naturally captures the fairness of load distribution, with a value of 0 expressing perfect balance and a value of 1 worst imbalance.

2.2 Data Placement Problem

Having the system model and metrics, we are interested in the problem that given an existing social graph G including the set of all users' read rates r_{ij} and write rates w_i, a set of available servers S, finding out the optimal placement solution $\bigcup\limits_{x \in S} D_x$ that produces the minimum inter-server traffic denoted by Eq. (4) subject to a pre-defined load balancing constraint L^*. Thus, we formulate the problem as follows:

$$\min \quad T$$
$$s.t. \ \text{(i)} \ |m_i| + |s_i| \geq 1,$$
$$\text{(ii)} \ m_i \cap s_i = \emptyset,$$
$$\text{(iii)} \ L \leq L^*.$$

Constraint (i) ensures that each user has at least one replica (i.e., master replica) stored in the system. Constraint (ii) ensures that each user does not have more than one replica stored in the same server. Constraint (iii) ensures that load balancing must be guaranteed.

3 Design of Our Scheme

3.1 Motivation

Before starting to present our scheme, we first give a simple example of comparison among varied schemes as a motivation to illustrate the basic idea of our scheme. Given a social graph with 7 users as shown in Fig. 1, and those users should be assigned to two servers. Figure 2(a) illustrates the partitioning results by using Hashing scheme. Since Hashing scheme does not perform replication, there is no write traffic generated by synchronization. It preserves a very good load balancing (0.036). However, the read traffic between servers is very high due to its random operations without any optimization.

The inter-server communication traffic can be optimized by applying METIS [3] to our problem, and the results are illustrated in Fig. 2(b). It tries to improve

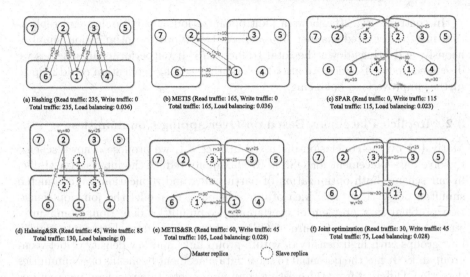

(a) Hashing (Read traffic: 235, Write traffic: 0
Total traffic: 235, Load balancing: 0.036)

(b) METIS (Read traffic: 165, Write traffic: 0
Total traffic: 165, Load balancing: 0.036)

(c) SPAR (Read traffic: 0, Write traffic: 115
Total traffic: 115, Load balancing: 0.023)

(d) Hahsing&SR (Read traffic: 45, Write traffic: 85
Total traffic: 130, Load balancing: 0)

(e) METIS&SR (Read traffic: 60, Write traffic: 45
Total traffic: 105, Load balancing: 0.028)

(f) Joint optimization (Read traffic: 30, Write traffic: 45
Total traffic: 75, Load balancing: 0.028)

◯ Master replica   ⬭ Slave replica

Fig. 2. Comparison of different schemes.

the traffic performance through finding out the minimal cut weight under the premise of meeting load balancing. Since METIS is a type of partitioning optimization, no additional write traffic be generated.

From analysis on the results of METIS, we conclude that the effect of single partitioning optimization is limited. By using replication SPAR [5] can achieve zero inter-server read traffic. However, SPAR preserves perfect *social locality* by co-locating the data of users every friend in the same server by replication. It does not optimize replication. More replicas inevitably lead to the higher inter-server write traffic for synchronization. As shown in Fig. 2(c), SPAR produces a lower traffic than METIS, but the write traffic is high and should be decreased.

Each user's data are associated with both read rate and write rate. Considering the difference between them, selective replication (SR) [6] creates replicas if and only if they can save the total inter-server traffic. We apply SR to optimize Hashing scheme, denoted by Hashing&SR, and Fig. 2(d) shows the results. The total inter-server traffic brings down obviously compared with Hashing (from 235 to 130). Interesting, Hashing&SR achieves perfect load balancing. However, the effect of single replication optimization is still limited. Then we combine SR with METIS, denoted by METIS&SR. METIS&SR firstly applies METIS to achieve a minimal cut weight without replicas, and then applies SR to conduct replication optimization. Figure 2(e) shows that METIS&SR can achieve the lowest traffic compared with anyone of the previous schemes. It largely verifies the effectiveness of joint optimization of both partitioning and replication. Nevertheless, METIS&SR optimizes partitioning and replication independently. The optimization effect of replication primarily depends on the partitioning result, and this manner cannot optimize the results maximally.

In contrast, Fig. 2(f) shows a joint optimization of partitioning and replication in an integrated manner. It conducts two types of optimization simultaneously, and brings down the total traffic to 75. It outperforms all schemes we discussed above. Besides, we also conclude that adding replication could help to further improve load balancing.

3.2   Replica Placement Based on Overlapping Communities

Motivated by the conclusion discussed in Sect. 3.1, we propose a novel scheme to solve data placement for OSNs. To maximally reduce the inter-server traffic, in our scheme both optimization of partitioning and replication are conducted simultaneously. The basic idea of our scheme is to model the joint optimization problem as a problem of overlapping communities detection. Community structure is a common feature of OSNs, where users often cluster into tightly knit groups with high density of within-group links and low density of between-group links. It has the potential to solve data placement by means of communities detection. Different from the existing community detection problem that requires each user belonging to only one community, we allow users being attributed to multiple communities. Hence there exists overlaps among communities, and overlap can be naturally used here to represent data replication. For example, user i is attributed to two communities after partitioning, and then two replicas are created on two servers.

Overlapping Community. A community c consists of a group of frequently interacted users and the corresponding links between them, and is denoted by a set of users for simplicity. Since a user can join more than one communities, two or more communities may overlap each other, i.e., $c_a \cap c_b \neq \emptyset$.

User Value. We use user value to depict a user's activity in a social network. The user value v_i of user i is defined as the sum of its correlated link weights, i.e.,

$$v_i = \sum_{j \in F_i^+ \cup F_i^-} (r_{ij} + r_{ji}). \tag{7}$$

Membership Degree. To reflect how tight a user i is with community c, we define membership degree as follows:

$$M(i,c) = \frac{\sum\limits_{j \in c \cap (F_i^+ \cup F_i^-)} (r_{ij} + r_{ji})}{v_i}. \tag{8}$$

Generally, we have $0 < M(i,c) < 1$, except that all friends of user i belong to community c, i.e., $M(i,c) = 1$. For example, if community c includes users 7, 2 and 6 in Fig. 1, user 1's membership degree to c is $125/255 = 0.49$. In other case, when community c includes users 7, 2, 6, 3 and 4, the membership degree of user 1 becomes 1.

Traffic Reduction. We start by assuming that there exists several communities in a social network, and we are interested in the traffic reduction when a user joins a community. According to the fact whether the user has been included in one or more communities, we discuss the following two scenarios.

First, user i has never been allocated to any community. Let us assume that all unallocated users including i belong to a virtual community vc. For a user i and a community c, i's c-relevant traffic is the sum of read traffic between i and her friends in c, i.e., $\sum\limits_{j \in c \cap (F_i^+ \cup F_i^-)} (r_{ij} + r_{ji})$. After i joins c, i's c-relevant traffic becomes zero, and its vc-relevant traffic becomes the sum of read traffic between i and her friends in vc, i.e., $\sum\limits_{u \in vc \cap (F_i^+ \cup F_i^-)} (r_{iu} + r_{ui})$. Thus, the traffic reduction can be calculated by

$$T_{reduction}(i, c) = \sum_{j \in c \cap (F_i^+ \cup F_i^-)} (r_{ij} + r_{ji}) - \sum_{u \in vc \cap (F_i^+ \cup F_i^-)} (r_{iu} + r_{ui}). \quad (9)$$

Second, user i has been included in at least one community. User i joins community c by means of creating a replica in c. On the one hand, replication brings additional write traffic due to synchronization, i.e., w_i. On the other hand, it can save the read traffic from j to i, i.e., $\sum\limits_{j \in c \cap (F_i^+ \cup F_i^-)} r_{ji}$. Thus, the traffic reduction is

$$T_{reduction}(i, c) = \sum_{j \in c \cap (F_i^+ \cup F_i^-)} r_{ji} - w_i. \quad (10)$$

Initial Communities Detection. Our scheme consists of two phases: initial communities detection and expansion of communities. In order to support overlapping communities detection, each user i is associated with a set of communities C_i that i belongs to. During the first phase, our goal is to find out n initial communities where n is the number of servers available, i.e., $n = |V|$, and the pseudo code is described by Algorithm 1. Before detection, there is no community exists, so $C_i = \emptyset$ for every user i (lines 1–2). Then we select the top-n users with the highest values, and let these users as the start points to form n initial communities separately (lines 3–10). Furthermore, we set up a threshold M^* of membership degree, and use it to refine initial communities by means of filtering out users whose membership degree is below M^* (lines 11–18). The threshold value M^* determines how tight the formed community is. Since the communities produced by Algorithm 1 act as the cores of potential larger communities and would be expanded, their tightness should be preserved, and M^* should be high.

Expansion of Communities. After obtaining the initial communities, we still have to expand them to cover the entire network. Algorithm 2 describes how

Algorithm 1. $detInitialCommunities(G, n)$

1: **for** each user $i, i \in V$ **do**
2:     $C_i \leftarrow \emptyset$;
3:     Calculate user value v_i based on Eq (7);
4: **end for**
5: Find out the top-n users based on their values;
6: **for** each user $i, i \in$ top-n users **do**
7:     Add i's friends into community $c_a, a \in [1, n]$;
8:     $C_i \leftarrow C_i \cup c_a$;
9:     Update community C_j for i's every friend $j, j \in F_i^+ \cup F_i^-$;
10: **end for**
11: **for** each community $c_a, a \in [1, n]$ **do**
12:     **for** each user $j, j \in c_a$ **do**
13:         **if** $M(j, c_a) < M^*$ **then**
14:             Remove user j from c_a;
15:             $C_j \leftarrow C_j - c_a$;
16:         **end if**
17:     **end for**
18: **end for**
19: **return** $\{c_a | \forall a \in [1, n]\}$;

---

to expand these initial communities, and it consists of two segments. In segment one, we find out the set $F(c_a)$ of friends for each community c_a, similarly select friends with higher membership degree than M^*, and add them into the corresponding communities (lines 2–11). In segment two, besides membership degree, we continue to expand the communities based on the traffic reduction. To preserve load balancing, we add a checkpoint before expanding (lines 15–16). It requires to update the current average size l_c of expanded communities at every iteration (l_c corresponds to the average server load)(line 23), and the initial value of l_c is calculated by $\frac{|V|\rho}{n}$, where ρ is the maximal replication degree (line 1). If the current size of c_a does not exceed $l_c(1 + L^*)$, we continue to decide whether adding a user i into community c_a brings a reduction in traffic. If traffic reduction $T_{reduction}(i, c_a) > 0$, user i should be included in community c_a no matter whether j has been included in other communities (lines 18–19). To avoid unnecessary computations, we set up a lower threshold M^{**}, and filter out users whose membership degree is lower than M^{**} (line 17). Finally, Algorithm 2 stops as soon as all communities can never be expanded, and it divides a social graph into n communities with overlaps. Each community corresponds to a cluster of frequently interacted users, and is co-located in one server.

4   Performance Evaluation

4.1   Experimental Settings

We crawled Facebook during November and December 2015 by the way of Metropolis-Hasting random walk [9] and created a social graph with 947,276

Algorithm 2. $expCommunities(\{c_a | \forall a \in [1, n]\})$

1: $l_c \leftarrow \frac{|V|\rho}{n}$;
2: **for** each community $c_a, a \in [1, n]$ **do**
3:     **do**
4:         Find out all friends $F(c_a)$ of c_a;
5:         **for** each user $i \in F(c_a)$
6:             **if** $M(i, c_a) \geq M^*$
7:                 Add user i into community c_a;
8:                 $C_i \leftarrow C_i \cup c_a$;
9:             **endif**
10:         **endfor**
11:     **while** c_a is expanded
12:     **do**
13:         Find out all friends $F(c_a)$ of c_a;
14:         **for** each user $i \in F(c_a)$
15:             **if** $|c_a| \geq l_c(1 + L^*)$
16:                 **break**;
17:             **else if** $M(i, c_a) \geq M^{**} \wedge T_{reduction}(i, c_a) > 0$
18:                 Add user i into community c_a;
19:                 $C_i \leftarrow C_i \cup c_a$;
20:             **endif**
21:         **endfor**
22:     **while** c_a is expanded
23:     Update l_c with the expanded community c_a;
24: **end for**
25: **return** $\{c_a | \forall a \in [1, n]\}$;

---

users and 626,767 directed edges. The edge weight was assigned with the value of read rate from one user to another. To simulate a more practical environment, we generate profile browsing events based on the findings reported in [10]. Each user's profile browsing rate, i.e., read rate, is generated according to a Zipf distribution,

$$r_i = \beta \lambda_i^{-\alpha}, \tag{11}$$

where r_i is user i's read rate, and corresponds to how often user i is viewed, i.e., $r_i = \sum_{j \in F_i^-} r_{ji}$, and λ_i refers to the rank number of user i sorted by read rate. The total interaction rates include status update rates (visible interactions) collected, and profile browsing rates (silent interactions) generated.

In this evaluation, we primarily focus on two types of metrics: inter-server traffic and load balancing. We implement several state-of-the-art schemes including Hashing, METIS, SPAR, Hashing&SR and METIS&SR, and compare them with our proposed scheme.

Table 1 lists the default parameter settings, where R/W refers to the ratio between read rate and write rate, and its value is set according to the statistics reported in [11]. $L^* = 0.1$ indicates a good load balancing. Based on the fitting result reported in [10], α and β are set as 0.72 and 697 respectively.

Table 1. Default parameter settings

Parameter	n	L^*	R/W	α	β	M^*	M^{**}	ρ
Value	128	0.1	11	0.72	697	0.5	0.2	5

The thresholds of membership degree are set as 0.5 and 0.2 respectively. The maximal replication degree ρ is set as 5, which means the average number of replicas for all users is 5 at most.

4.2 Comparison Under Different Numbers of Servers

Figure 3 illustrates how the number of servers impacts the inter-server traffic. As the number of servers increases from 64 to 512, more and more social links have to be cut off, and the inter-server traffic increases accordingly. SPAR tries to use replication to preserve *social locality* and reduces inter-server read traffic, but its aggressive replication manner incurs higher inter-server write traffic with the increase of number of servers. Selective replication can help Hashing and MEITS to significantly save inter-server read traffic without incurring more inter-server write traffic. But Hashing&SR and METIS&SR conduct partitioning and replication separately. Our scheme conducts a joint optimization and always performs best under different numbers of servers.

4.3 Comparison Under Different Replication Degrees

The replication degree reflects how many replicas could be created in the system, the optimization effect of many schemes except Hashing and METIS are restricted by the number of replicas that is often used to measure the storage cost. In this group of experiments, we explore the influence of replication degree upon inter-server traffic, and the results are depicted in Fig. 4. When $\rho = 1$, all schemes degenerate into partitioning algorithms with no replication, so METIS&SR (Hashing&SR) achieves the same traffic performance as that of METIS (Hashing), where METIS performs even better than our scheme. However, the traffic begin to decline along with the increase of ρ, and our scheme outperforms the others when $\rho \geq 3$. It is because a lower ρ may impose a tighter constraint that weakens the optimization effects of replication. But it does not always hold with the continuous increase in ρ, since higher value has a less effect on optimization. SPAR is not reported in the figure, since the replication degree is one of the metrics rather than constraint need to be optimized by SPAR.

4.4 Tradeoff Between Traffic and Load Balancing

Figure 5 illustrates how load balancing constraints may influence inter-server traffic. Note that a lower value of load balancing implies a more even distribution of users, and it will become a tighter constraint for schemes. Hence, the increase

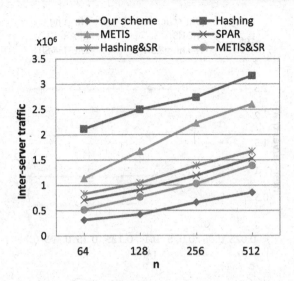

Fig. 3. Inter-server traffic under different n.

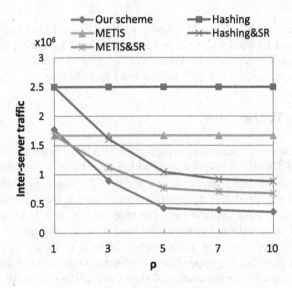

Fig. 4. Inter-server traffic under different ρ.

of threshold is helpful to improve the traffic performance, which is evaluated by results described in Fig. 5. The improvement does not tend to getting better as the threshold increases continuously. Since a larger constraint value has a less effect on partitioning. The traffic improvement decreases along with the increase of threshold. The results depicted in Fig. 5 illustrate that most of schemes except Hashing can obtain a stable traffic performance as the threshold of load balancing increases. There is no optimization design for Hashing, it always generates the

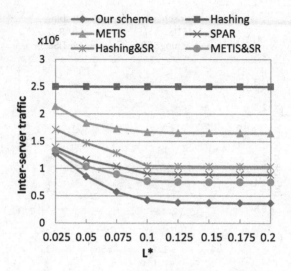

Fig. 5. Inter-server traffic vs. load balancing.

highest traffic meanwhile it could achieve a relative good load balancing, and is almost unaffected by load balancing constraint. Compared with other schemes, our scheme always generates the lowest traffic. It is because two phases design of our scheme can achieve a relative even load distribution.

5   Related Work

In order to preserve *social locality* perfectly, SPAR [5] ensures the co-location of every pair of friends by replication, which inevitably results in the increase in consistency maintaining traffic across servers. To avoid excessive replication, Tran et al. [12] explored the data replication under a fixed storage space and update cost required for replication, and proposed a socially-aware replication scheme. The scheme attempts to reduce visit cost by placing replicas of each user i to the servers that host most friends of user i. Yu et al. [13] employed the hypergraph partitioning approach to optimize the associated data placement under the scenario without replicas, and then proposed an iterative method ADP to solve the problem of routing and replica placement. Although it is interesting to model multi-participant interactions for OSNs based on hypergraph, the separated execution manner of partitioning and replication loses the opportunity to optimize result maximally.

Liu et al. [6] focused on data replication for different OSN users, and suggested creating various numbers of replicas according to the heterogeneous requesting rates. They jointly considered both read rate and update rate. However, the main goal of [6] is to reduce inter-data center communication traffic as well as response latency, while our work primarily focuses on the minimization of inter-server traffic inside one data center. Tran et al. [14] investigated the socially aware data partitioning by modeling it as a multi-objective optimization problem, and proposed to utilize evolutionary algorithms to minimize server load and keep a good load balancing. Like SPAR, they did not differentiate read rate from write rate, which is apt to incur more write traffic than the reduced read traffic.

6   Conclusions

The optimization of inter-server communication has become one of the most important issues for so many OSN providers. In this paper, we investigate the inter-server traffic optimization problem under load balancing constraint, and propose to solve the problem based on overlapping communities detection. Compared with other work, the most dramatic feature of our scheme is that it conducts optimization of both partitioning and replication in an integrated manner. Through extensive experiments with trace collected from Facebook, we verify that our scheme significantly reduces inter-server traffic as well as guarantee load balancing, and its performance is superior to state-of-the-art schemes.

References

1. Shvachko, K., Kuang, H., Radia, S., Chansler, R.: The hadoop distributed file system. In: MSST, pp. 1–10 (2010)
2. Lakshman, A., Malik, P.: Cassandra: a decentralized structured storage system. Oper. Syst. Rev. **44**(2), 35–40 (2010)
3. Karypis, G., Kumar, V.: A fast and high quality multilevel scheme for partitioning irregular graphs. SIAM J. Sci. Comput. **20**, 359–392 (1998)
4. Chen, H., Jin, H., Jin, N., Gu, T.: Minimizing inter-server communications by exploiting self-similarity in online social networks. In: ICNP, pp. 1–10 (2012)
5. Pujol, J.M., Erramilli, V., Siganos, G., Yang, X., Laoutaris, N., Chhabra, P., Rodriguez, P.: The little engine(s) that could: scaling online social networks. IEEE/ACM Trans. Netw. **20**(4), 1162–1175 (2012)
6. Liu, G., Shen, H., Chandler, H.: Selective data replication for online social networks with distributed datacenters. In: ICNP, pp. 1–10 (2013)
7. Zhou, J., Fan, J., Wang, J., Cheng, B., Jia, J.: Towards traffic minimization for data placement in online social networks. Concurrency and Computation: Practice and Experience, May 2016
8. Wilson, C., Sala, A., Puttaswamy, K.P.N., Zhao, B.Y.: Beyond social graphs: user interactions in online social networks and their implications. ACM Trans. Web **6**, 17:1–17:31 (2012)
9. Gjoka, M., Kurant, M., Butts, C.T., Markopoulou, A.: Walking in facebook: a case study of unbiased sampling of OSNs. In: INFOCOM, pp. 2498–2506 (2010)
10. Jiang, J., Wilson, C., Wang, X., Sha, W., Huang, P., Dai, Y., Zhao, B.Y.: Understanding latent interactions in online social networks. ACM Trans. Web **7**, 18 (2013)
11. Benevenuto, F., Rodrigues, T., Cha, M., Almeida, V.A.F.: Characterizing user behavior in online social networks. In: IMC, pp. 49–62 (2009)

12. Tran, D.A., Nguyen, K., Pham, C.: S-clone: socially-aware data replication for social networks. Comput. Netw. **56**, 2001–2013 (2012)
13. Yu, B., Pan, J.: Location-aware associated data placement for geo-distributed data-intensive applications. In: INFOCOM, pp. 603–611 (2015)
14. Tran, D.A., Zhang, T.: S-PUT: an EA-based framework for socially aware data partitioning. Comput. Netw. **75**, 504–518 (2014)

Road Segment Information Based Named Data Networking for Vehicular Environments

Junlan Xiao[1,2], Jian Deng[1,2], Hui Cao[1,2], and Weigang Wu[1,2(✉)]

[1] School of Data and Computer Science, Sun Yat-sen University,
Guangzhou, China
easylovexjl@foxmail.com, a_408085345@126.com,
1003932334@qq.com, wuweig@mail.sysu.edn.cn
[2] Guangdong Province Key Laboratory of Big Data Analysis and Processing,
Guangzhou, China

Abstract. Vehicular Ad Hoc Network (VANET) can provide strong support for intelligent transportation systems and Internet services. How to disseminate data to vehicular nodes has been always at the core of VANET technologies. In this paper, we consider data dissemination via Named Data Networking (NDN), which is a new and promising Internet technology to realize content centric networking. NDN can route and forward data according to data content (or ID) rather than the address/location of the data, so that it can disseminate and share data more efficiently. Our work focuses on how to cope with the mobility of vehicular nodes, which is not considered in original NDN. Different from existing NDN for vehicular environments, we propose to establish data dissemination route using road segment information rather than node information. Such a new approach can avoid the effect of topology changes on data routes so as to keep data routes stable. A road segment route is instantiated as routes of nodes upon data forwarding demands. The mechanism to realize such an instantiation is the major challenge addressed in our design. Simulations via ndnSIM clearly show that our design performs much better than existing ones.

Keywords: Named Data Networking · Vehicular Ad Hoc Networks · Data dissemination · Data forwarding · Road segment

1 Introduction

Vehicular Ad Hoc Network (VANET) is part of the Internet of Things (IoT) and plays an important role in Intelligent Traffic Systems and other vehicular applications [1–5]. Data communication, especially data dissemination, is always the core task of VANETs. Due to high mobility of vehicular nodes, topology changes make data dissemination in VANET quite challenging [6].

W. Wu—This research is partially supported by National Natural Science Foundation of China (No. 61379157), Program of Science and Technology of Guangdong (No. 2015A010103007), and Program of Science and Technology of Guangzhou (No. 201510010068).

© Springer International Publishing AG 2016
J. Carretero et al. (Eds.): ICA3PP 2016, LNCS 10048, pp. 245–259, 2016.
DOI: 10.1007/978-3-319-49583-5_19

Named Data Networking (NDN) [7] is a new and promising technology for data centric networks. Different from traditional network based on IP addresses or node IDs, NDN routes and forwards data packets according to data content or data ID. That is, NDN concerns about "what the packet is" rather than "where the packet is". Such a data-centric approach can improve data communication efficiency by sharing data routes and data packets.

Recently, NDN has been applied in VANETs [8] to achieve low data dissemination cost. NDN mechanisms and data structures have been modified and changed to adapt to vehicular environments, especially the dynamic network topology due to vehicle movements.

In this paper, we propose to construct data routes in NDN using road segment information rather than node information. That is, the data hops in a route are represented by road segments rather than vehicular nodes. Since the road network is static and stable, road segment based data routes are much more stable than node routes. Therefore, NDN data structure and mechanisms are realized using road segment information and keep stable, so that data communication cost can be reduced. Of course, a road segment must be instantiated as nodes in the data forwarding operations. Such instantiations are done upon data forwarding demands. We design sophisticated mechanisms for route instantiations.

The main contributions of this paper are outlined as follows:

(1) We propose road segment information based NDN mechanisms to construct data forwarding Tables.
(2) We design new route discovery and maintenance mechanism for our road segment based NDN. New packet types and operations are proposed.
(3) We conduct simulations using a simulator combining ns3, SUMO and ndnSIM, to evaluate the performance of our proposed design and compare it with similar works.

The rest of this paper is organized as follows. Related works are reviewed in Sect. 2. Section 3 describes system model and assumptions involved in our design. The segment information based NDN technology is described in Sect. 4, which is followed by performance evaluation in Sect. 5. Finally, Sect. 6 concludes the paper with future directions.

2 Related Works

Data dissemination has been always a major concern of VANET. Various algorithms and approaches have been proposed, including flooding-based algorithm [9], position-based algorithm [10], clustering-based algorithm [11], dominating-set-based algorithm [12].

As aforementioned, NDN is a promising networking technology for data dissemination and has attracted a lot of attention. Most NDN studies focus on optimization of data structure design and route mechanisms in the environment of Internet [13–16].

A few efforts have also been put on applying NDN into VANETs [8, 17–20]. The major challenge issue in such works is how to handle topology/link changes due to vehicle movements. Grassi et al. [8] considered disconnections among vehicular nodes and proposed a data mule based mechanism to realize data dissemination in a store-forward way.

Amadeo et al. [17] proposed a distance based data source node selection mechanism in NDN for VANETs. This work proposes two types of interest packet: B-Int and A-Int. Consumers broadcast B-Int packets firstly to discover data source nodes. Upon replies from producers, the consumer chooses a producer based on distance and send an A-Int packet to request data.

Lucas et al. [18] proposed a collision minimization traffic information dissemination algorithm based on NDN. The algorithm classifies traffic information into different types to set different timer and takes a different broadcast way, achieving high efficiency with low cost.

Giulio et al. [19] introduced a producer location based NDN algorithm for data dissemination. The algorithm encodes geo locations into data names, so that interest packets can be forwarded towards the geo location where the desired data is produced. If an interest packet meets a car with the requested data before approaching the named location, it will reply at once so that efficiency is improved.

TalebiFard et al. [20] leveraged the expansion properties of interacting nodes in a cluster to be interpreted in terms of social connections among nodes and performed a selective random network coding approach.

All these NDN algorithms for VANETs construct data forwarding routes using vehicular nodes directly, and consequently suffer from frequent route changes due to node mobility. Our road segments based NDN can eliminate such effect significantly.

3   System Model and Assumptions

3.1   Network and Application Scenario

The vehicles are assumed to be equipped with navigation system. The navigation system can provide location of the vehicle and plan favorite path for movement. The movement path of a vehicle consists of a series of road segments. A segment refers to a road segment between two intersections.

We also assume that vehicles are equipped with wireless communication device, with which vehicles can communicate with each other via inter-vehicle wireless links in an ad hoc way. Due to broadcasting feature of wireless links, all nodes within the transmission range of a sender will receive the packets sent. Neighborhood among vehicle nodes are maintained using heartbeat packets. We assume signal decay is the same and neighbor information is symmetric.

For convenience, we assume the link quality among vehicles is reliable and there is no packet loss. We also assume the network is connected and vehicle node have enough energy and never fail due to crash or other reasons.

The data considered in this paper can be large files, like movie files, music files or others. Such large files are usually split into packets and transferred to vehicle nodes. We assume the owner or producer of such data are static nodes, e.g. road side unit nodes, which act as data servers.

Vehicle node generate data requests as they want, and try to get data via wireless links, based on the operation of data dissemination algorithms. We do not consider road side units during data dissemination.

4   The Proposed Algorithm/Mechanism

Our algorithm establishes routing information using segment information instead of vehicle ID, and designs a routing updating mechanism in order to solve the problem of routing information failure caused by vehicles movement in VANET. Same as NDN, we use three typical setting roles to present the nodes in network and interest packet and data packet to transfer data. We design two new message packet types to solve the condition of losing routing information resulted from vehicles movement. This algorithm includes four phases, which respectively are routing establishment, resource detection, data request and table maintenance. It should be noticed that the four phases are not sequentially processed but at the same time without a certain order.

4.1   Node Roles and Message Types

Roles of the System. We follow NDN designs and use three typical setting roles to present the nodes in network, which are consumer, producer and forwarder.

- *Consumer.* The vehicle who requests data. During the vehicle moves, it will require a certain type of data, such as road traffic information, at any time.
- *Producer.* The vehicle who offers data resources. When a vehicle has data resources, it needs to broadcast a resource packet to inform other vehicles.
- *Forwarder.* The vehicle who forwards data. As an intermediate node, it not only forwards data but also caches the data contents.

In this paper, we assume the producer is fixed nodes, the consumer is common vehicles which move depending on its route. In addition, all nodes play a forwarder role.

Message Types. Same as NDN, we use interest packets and data packets to transfer data between the producer and the consumers. Besides, the producer informs other nodes itself owning resource by broadcasting packets. We follow this design and named it as resource packet. For the sake of adapting to characteristics of VANET, we design two other types of packet, detect packet and confirm packet, to find the resource while the vehicle moves. Without loss of generality, we use heartbeat package to detect the neighbors. Each message type format is shown in Table 1.

Resource Packet. The producer broadcasts a resource packet to inform the position of the resource to other nodes, while other nodes establish routing information based on resource packets. In our algorithm, the maximum of hops is limited to 15.

Table 1. Message types

Resource packet	Interest packet	Data packet	Detect packet	Confirm packet
Name	Name	Name	Name	Name
Signature	Nonce	Signature	Nonce	Signature
Time stamp	Time stamp	Time stamp	Time stamp	Time stamp
Hop count tag	Hop count tag	Hop count tag	Hop count tag	Hop count tag
Current segment	Current segment	Next segment	Current segment	Current segment
	Next segment	Data	Segment list	Segment list
				TTL

Name is the name of resource data, distinguishing the data content. Signature is for checking duplication. Time Stamp records the time when the packet is sent. Hop Count Tag saves the number of hops that the packet has been forwarded. Current Segment records the packet from which segment, and is used to establish routing information.

Interest Packet. The consumer sends an interest packet to request data. An interest packet will inform the producer what contents the consumer requires, and also be used to establish routing relationship.

The usage of Name, Time Stamp, Hop Count Tag and Current Segment is the same as previously described. Nonce is for checking duplication. Next Segment indicates next segment the packet should go, which will be obtained after inquiring routing information.

Data Packet. Once the interest packet reaches a node that has the requested data, the node will return a data packet that contains name, content and other necessary information.

The usage of Name, Signature, Time Stamp, Hop Count Tag and Next Segment is the same as described before. Data is generated by the producer in accordance with the interest of consumer.

Detect Packet. When a consumer want a data but its routing information has no records on how to achieve the related producer, the consumer will broadcast a detect packet to find the data resource it needs.

The usage of the first five entries is the same interest packet. Segment List lists all the segments the detect packet has gone, and is saved in order for routing corresponding confirm packet (introduced below). The maximum hop of detect packet is limited to 3.

Confirm Packet. When a node receives a detect packet, and it has relevant data or relevant routing records, the node replies a confirm packet to inform the consumer. The intermediate nodes supplement their routing information based on confirm packet.

The usage of the first six entries is the same as detect packet. TTL records the distance between the current segment and data resource, which means the hops from consumer to the producer.

Heartbeat Packet. Every nodes will broadcast heartbeat packet periodically, to establish the neighbor relationship with vehicles around, and save coordinate, speed and direction of neighbors to facilitate decision-making.

Data Structure. Same as NDN, we use Pending Interest Table (PIT) to record all the interest packets that a node has forwarded but not satisfied yet and route relevant data packet. We use forwarding information base (FIB) to save the routing information which maps source name to segment. Content Store (CS) is used to cache received data, in order to share data, improve the efficiency and stabilize data dissemination. Tables 2, 3 and 4 show their format respectively.

Table 2. PIT format

Source name 1	Interest packet 1: next segment time stamp nonce	Interest packet 2: next segment time stamp nonce	...
Source name 2	Interest packet 1: next segment time stamp nonce	Interest packet 2: next segment time stamp nonce	...
......	......	......	...

Table 3. FIB format

Source name 1	Data 1: next segment TTL	Data 2: next segment TTL	...
Source name 2	Data 1: next segment TTL	Data 2: next segment TTL	...
......	......	......	...

Table 4. CS format

Source name 1	Data
Source name 2	Data
......	......

4.2 Route Establishment Phase

In route establishment phase, the producer broadcasts resource packet to inform other vehicles the resources position. Other vehicles establish route, which is FIB table entry, based on resource packet to satisfy subsequent data request. In this paper, we use farthest distance priority approach to broadcast ensuring that resource packets broadcast as soon as possible, that is the vehicle farthest from last hop forwards firstly. To make sure of the hit rate of resource packet, we broadcast the resource packet to each direction in the intersection, unless the segment has received the same resource packet.

As shown in Fig. 1, a resource packet is forwarded from segment A to the inter-section. Segment B, C and D will forward the packet. Every vehicle received the resource packet in every segment will set the timer based on the distance away from the last hop vehicle, and the farthest vehicle will forward the packet. For an example, in segment D all vehicles in the big ellipse have received the packet, and the vehicle in a small circle is farthest distance, so it forwards the packet preferentially. Other vehicles in the box will not forward the packet. Its pseudo code is shown in Algorithm 1.

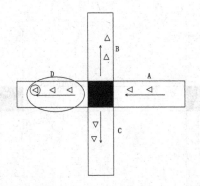

Fig. 1. Resource packet forwarding diagram

Algorithm. 1. Resource Packet Forwarding algorithm

```
Function ForwardResourcePacket (ResourcePacket )
  if repeated or TTL > 15  return
  if (!FIB.find(ResourcePacket.GetName()) )
    FIB.add(ResourcePacket)
  else
    FIB.update(ResourcePacket)
  start waiting timer
  if no same package forwarded on this segment
    forward( ResourcePacket) return
end function
```

4.3   Resource Detection Phase

In routing establishment phase, the vehicle has built FIB which stores information on how to achieve the right segment and right producer to obtain the resources. However, the resource packet may not reach all the vehicles due to high-frequency movement of vehicles in VANET. When a vehicle requests a resource, it probably cannot find any relevant routing records in FIB. At this time, the vehicle need to enter the resource detection phase to find the resources needed.

In resource detection phase, firstly, consumer broadcast the detect packet, if a node receives the detect packet having corresponding entry in FIB or data in CS, the node replies confirm packet. The confirm packet will follow in reverse route taken by the detect packet back to the node. If not, the node continue to forward the detect packet. If a detect packet hops is over 3, the packet will stop being forwarded. As shown in Fig. 2, vehicle 1 in segment A broadcasts a detect packet, and vehicle 2 in segment B has received it and replies a confirm packet. The confirm packet will follow in reverse route taken by the detect packet to vehicle 1. Vehicle 2 and its neighbors will not continue to broadcast the detect packet. At the same time, the detect packet is forwarded to segment C, D and E, and reaches the third hop, the packet will not to be forwarded again.

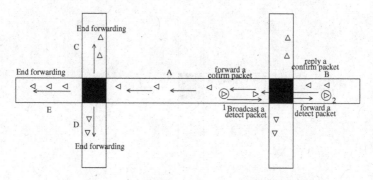

Fig. 2. Resource detection phase forwarding process

Algorithm. 2. Detect Packet Forwarding algorithm

```
Function ForwardDetectingPacket ( DetectingPacket )
   if (repeated or TTL>3) return
   if (FIB.find(DetectingPacket.GetName()) or
       CS.find(DetectingPacket.GetName()))
     send(ConfirmingPacket)
   else
     add this->segment into packet
     start a waiting timer
     if no forwarded package received in this segment
       forward (DetectingPacket)
   return
end function
```

Detect Packet Forwarding Algorithm. When a consumer requests a resource and itself has no relevant entry in FIB, the consumer will send a detect packet to find the resource. In our algorithm, most vehicles' FIB has stored current resources entries after resource packet has broadcast. So detect packet does not need to be forwarded many times, and its maximum hops is limited to 3. To ensure confirm packet will follow in reverse route taken by detect packet to get back to the consumer, we need to be recorded current segment. The pseudo code is shown in Algorithm 2.

Algorithm. 3. Confirm Packet Forwarding algorithm

```
Function ForwardConfirmingPacket ( ConfirmingPacket )
  if !(FIB.find(ConfirmingPacket.GetName()))
    FIB.add(ConfirmingPacket)
    if this->segment == next segment
      start a waiting timer
      if no forward package received
        forward( ConfirmingPacket)
  return
end function
```

Confirm Packet Forwarding Algorithm. When a node has received a detect packet, and has the relevant resource in CS or routing record in FIB, the node needs to reply a confirm packet to inform the consumer. The confirm packet will follow in reverse route taken by the detect packet to get back to the consumer. The pseudo code is shown in Algorithm 3.

4.4 Data Request Phase

We divide data request phase into two parts. First part is the consumer checks its FIB and sends the interest packet depending on the FIB entry, and intermediate nodes forward the interest packet to the producer. Second part is the producer replies data packet. The following will introduce these two parts separately.

Interest Packet Forwarding Algorithm. When a consumer requests a data and has no record in FIB, the consumer will send an interest packet to request the data. The intermediate nodes forward the interest packet based on FIB records, and create PIT entry to forward the relevant data in the following. As shown in Fig. 3, vehicle 1 in segment A checks its FIB and forwards the interest packet, appoints the next hop segment is segment B. Because it can't reach segment B in one hop, the vehicles in segment A need to continue to forward the interest packet until some vehicles in segment B receive the packet. Meanwhile, all vehicles in segment A should create the relevant PIT entry to store the forwarding record. The same, the vehicles in segment B check FIB and forward the interest packet to segment C, and create PIT entry. The pseudo code is shown in Algorithm 4.

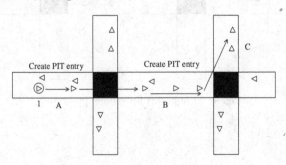

Fig. 3. Interest packet forwarding process

Algorithm. 4. Interest Packet Forwarding algorithm

```
Function ForwardInterestPacket (InterestPacket )
    If (repeated or TTL>15) return
    if CS.Find(InterestPacket.GetName())
        send(DataPacket)
    else if this->segment == next segment
        if PIT.Find(InterestPacket.GetName())
            PIT.update()
        else
            if FIB.Find(InterestPacket.GetName())
                PIT.Add(InterestPacket)
                start a waiting timer
                if no forward package received
                    forward( InterestPacket)
    return
end function
```

Data Packet Forwarding Algorithm. When a consumer receives an interest packet and has the corresponding resource, the consumer will reply the data packet. The intermediate node forwards the data packet based on its PIT to make sure that the data packet can follow in reverse route taken by the interest packet to get back to the destination. After forwarding, the node should delete the relevant PIT entry. As shown in Fig. 4, vehicle 1 in segment A has sent an interest which is forwarded to the producer, vehicle 2 in segment C, at the end. Then, vehicle 2 replies the data packet, the intermediate nodes check their PITs and forward the data packet hop by hop through segment C, B and A, back to the consumer (vehicle 1). The intermediate nodes will delete their relevant PIT entries after forwarded. The pseudo code is shown in Algorithm 5.

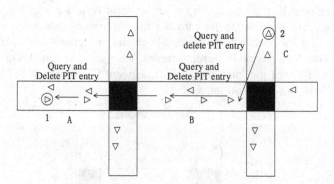

Fig. 4. Data packet forwarding process

Algorithm. 5. Data Packet Forwarding algorithm

```
Function ForwardDataPacket (DataPacket )
  if (repeated of TTL > 15) return
  else if PIT.Find(DataPacket.GetName())
    CS.Add(DataPacket)
    PIT.delete(DataPacket.GetName())
    start a waiting timer
    forward(DataPacket)
  return
end function
```

4.5   Table Maintenance

In this paper, the algorithm establishes the routing information based on the road segments, so when a vehicle moves to a new segment, its table information is invalid. The vehicle will arrive at a new road segment every several tens of seconds caused by high mobility of the vehicles in the network. Because of this, we need to design a table maintenance mechanism to make sure the table validity stored by the vehicle.

The maintenance mechanism of the algorithm consists of two parts. First part is about the consumer. When a consumer moves to a new segment, it should inform the vehicles at the last segment its current segment and querying data. The vehicle who receives the message should create a new PIT entry to forward the data packet to the current segment of the consumer when receiving the data packet.

Second part is about all vehicles. When a vehicle moves to a new segment, the original table is invalid and need to be deleted. Meanwhile, the vehicle requests the tables from the neighbor vehicle in new segment.

As shown in Fig. 5, when a vehicle in a small circle moves from segment A to B, it need to delete the table of segment A and requests the new table from the vehicle in segment B. If vehicle 1 is a consumer and has sent an interest packet but not received the data packet, it should broadcast a message to inform the vehicles in segment A its current segment and request before. The vehicles in segment A will create a PIT entry based on the message. Once the vehicles in segment A receive the data packet for vehicle 1, they can forward the packet to the segment B.

5   Simulation and Performance Evaluation

To evaluate the performance of our algorithm, we conduct simulation using ns3, SUMO and ndnSIM. The mobility of vehicles is simulated via SUMO, which is a tool to model vehicles mobility and can be integrated with ns3, and ndnSIM which is as a framework to complete the simulation. Besides our proposed Segment Information-based Vehicular Named Data Networking (SI-VNDN) algorithm, we also simulate a current Vehicular Named Data Networking (V-NDN) algorithm.

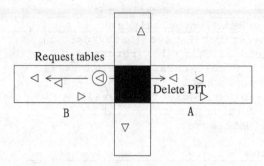

Fig. 5. Table maintenance mechanism diagram

5.1 Simulation Setup and Performance Metrics

We set a road network of a grid topology, with 10 horizontal roads and 10 vertical roads. Each road has eight lanes, four for each direction. A segment is the road part between two intersections. Each segment is set to be 500 m and has a unique name. In our algorithm, the producer is in a fixed position, so we appoint 10 vehicles fixed as producers. Each producer generate 20 types of resources, and all the other vehicles are set as consumers, and all vehicles will play forwarder roles. We will randomize 300 request events in our simulation. Major parameters of vehicle mobility are listed as Table 5.

Table 5. Key parameters of vehicle mobility

Parameters	Values
Simulation time	1000 s
Number of vehicles	1000
MAC protocol	802.11p
Transmission range	336 m
Mobility model	Waypoint model from SUMO

With reference to existing works and characteristics of our algorithm, we use four different metrics to measure the performance of our proposed algorithm.

- *Average Hit Rate (AHR):* it plots the proportion of number of vehicles that receives the data packet to the total number vehicles that requests data by sending an interest packet. It is used to measure the stability. The larger the rate value is, the more stable the algorithm is.
- *Average Delay (AD):* it plots the average time from sending an interest packet to receiving the data packet by the producer. It is used to measure the message transfer speed. The smaller the value is, the smaller the delay used to receive data is, and the faster the message transfer speed is.

- *Cost of Routing Updating (CRU):* it plots the cost used for route maintenance, which consists of resource packet forwarding times, querying and replying table times after the vehicle arriving in the new segment.
- *Average Forward Times (AFT):* it plots the times of node forwarding packets including interest packet, data packet, confirm packet and detect packet during a process of requesting a data.

5.2 Simulation Results

Average Hit Rate. Figure 6(a) is the result of the average hit rate of SI-VNDN and V-NDN. As shown in the result, the AHR of SI-VNDN is about 75% instead of 20% of V-NDN. Since our proposed SI-VNDN establishes route based on segment information, even if the vehicles move frequently, we appoint the next segment and make sure that messages can reach the destination. However, V-NDN algorithm appoints the next hop vehicle directly, once the vehicle moves, it is hard to maintain the routing information and cannot guarantee the data dissemination stability. With vehicles speed getting faster, the AHR of V-NDN declines obviously.

Average Delay. Figure 6(b) is the result of the average delay of SI-VNDN and V-NDN. As shown in the result, the AD of SI-VNDN is about 1.4 s instead of 0.4 s of V-NDN. This is because we set several forwarding timer in algorithm, which leads to higher delay. But V-NDN forwards the packet by appointment node without timer, which results in low delay.

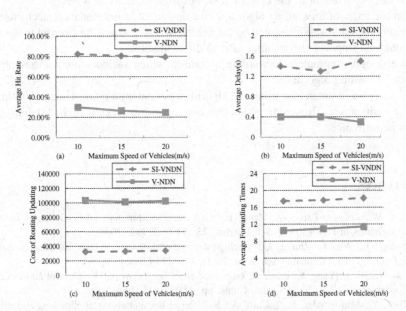

Fig. 6. (a) The result of AHR (b) The result of AD (c) The result of CRU (d) The result of AFT

Cost of Routing Updating. Figure 6(c) is the result of the cost of routing updating of SI-VNDN and V-NDN. In our proposed algorithm, the cost includes the cost of forwarding the resource packets and the cost of maintaining tables. As shown in the result, the CRU of SI-VNDN is about 32000 which the resource packets forwarding cost about 10000 and tables maintaining cost about 22000, much less than the cost of the V-NDN that is about 110000. This is because SI-VNDN broadcasts resource packet just one time instead of periodical in V-NDN.

Average Forwarding Times. Figure 6(d) is the result of the average forwarding times of SI-VNDN and V-NDN. As shown in the result, the AFT of SI-VNDN is about 18 times instead of about 11 times of V-NDN. This is because in SI-VNDN the consumer can get the further producer data which need more hops, and V-NDN algorithm directly appoints the node to reply the data packet which leads to a less forwarding times.

6 Conclusions

In this paper, we propose a method that applies NDN in VANET, and a novel data dissemination mechanism based on segment information for Vehicular Named Data Networking. Our main works are as follows.

Our proposed algorithm follows the three roles of consumer, producer and forwarder, the two message types of interest packet and data packet, the table design of PIT, FIB and CS of NDN, and adds detect packet and confirm packet for VANET, designs corresponding forwarding algorithm.

We adopt static segment information to establish route rather than a particular node, which can better adapt to the characteristics of high mobility in VANET.

On the basis of forwarding algorithm, we design table maintenance mechanism to make sure the table validity stored by the vehicle when a vehicle has moved to the new segment, and improve the stability of data dissemination.

We design a complete forwarding algorithm which include four various phases packet forwarding algorithm.

Finally, we simulate our proposed algorithm and adopt a comparison algorithm in [8] for verification. The results show that our algorithm reaches higher stability and better performance.

References

1. Qin, W., Jia, L., Pang, Q., Zang, L.: Genetic algorithm and artificial neural network applications in ITS. Chin. J. Sci. Instrum. **25**(z1), 990–992 (2004)
2. Yang, D., Wu, J., Zhang, Q.: Intelligent transport system and its informatics model. J. Beijing Univ. Aeronaut. Astronaut. **26**(3), 270–273 (2000)
3. Liu, Y., Bi, J., Yang, J.: Research on vehicular ad hoc networks. In: Control and Decision Conference, CCDC 2009, Guilin, China, pp. 4430–4435, June 2009
4. Toor, Y., Muhlethaler, P., Laouiti, A.: Vehicle ad hoc networks: applications and related technical issues. IEEE Commun. Surv. Tutor. **10**(3), 74–88 (2008)

5. Hartenstein, H., Laberteaux, K.P.: A tutorial survey on vehicular ad hoc networks. IEEE Commun. Mag. **46**(6), 164–171 (2008)

6. Li, F., Wang, Y.: Routing in vehicular ad hoc networks: a survey. IEEE Veh. Technol. Mag. **2**(2), 12–22 (2007)

7. Zhang, L., Afanasyev, A., Burke, J., et al.: Named data networking. ACM SIGCOMM Comput. Commun. Rev. **44**(3), 66–73 (2014)

8. Grassi, G., Pesavento, D., Pau, G., et al.: VANET via named data networking. In: 2014 IEEE Conference on Computer Communications Workshops (INFOCOM WKSHPS), Philadelphia, USA, pp. 410–415. IEEE, November 2014

9. Tseng, Y.C., Ni, S.Y., Chen, Y.S., et al.: The broadcast storm problem in a mobile ad hoc network. In: Proceedings of the 5th Annual ACM/IEEE International Conference on Mobile Computing and Networking, MOBICOM 2099, Washington, USA, pp. 151–162, August 1999

10. FuBler, H., Mauve, M., Hartenstein, H., et al.: A comparison of routing strategies for vehicular ad hoc networks. In: Proceedings of MOBICOM (2002)

11. Lin, C.R., Gerla, M.: Adaptive clustering for mobile wireless networks. IEEE J. Sel. Areas Commun. **15**(7), 1265–1275 (1997)

12. Wu, J., Li, H.: A dominating-set-based routing scheme in ad hoc wireless networks. Telecommun. Syst. **18**(1), 13–36 (2001)

13. Yi, C., Afanasyev, A., Wang, L., et al.: Adaptive forwarding in named data networking. ACM SIGCOMM Comput. Commun. Rev. **42**(3), 62–67 (2012)

14. Yuan, H., Crowley, P.: Scalable pending interest table design: from principles to practice. In: INFOCOM 2014 Proceedings IEEE, Toronto, Canada, pp. 2049–2057. IEEE, April 2014

15. So, W., Narayanan, A., Oran, D., et al.: Toward fast NDN software forwarding lookup engine based on hash tables. In: Proceedings of the Eighth ACM/IEEE Symposium on Architectures for Networking and Communications Systems, Austin, USA, pp. 85–86. ACM, October 2012

16. Wang, J., Peng, C., Li, C., et al.: Implementing instant messaging using named data. In: Proceedings of the Sixth Asian Internet Engineering Conference, Bangkok, Thailand, pp. 40–47. ACM, November 2010

17. Amadeo, M., Campolo, C., Molinaro, A.: Enhancing content-centric networking for vehicular environments. Comput. Netw. **57**(16), 3222–3234 (2013)

18. Lucas, W., Alexander, A., Romain, K., et al.: Rapid traffic information dissemination using named data. In: Proceedings of the 1st ACM workshop on Emerging Name-Oriented Mobile Networking Design, pp. 7–12. ACM, New York (2012)

19. Giulio, G., Davide, P., Lucas, W., et al.: ACM HotMobile 2013 poster: vehicular inter-networking via named data. ACM SIGMOBILE Mob. Comput. Commun. Rev. **17**(3), 23–24 (2013). ACM, New York

20. TalebiFard, P., Leung, V.: A content centric approach to dissemination of information in vehicular networks. In: Proceedings of the Second ACM International Symposium on Design and Analysis of Intelligent Vehicular Networks and Applications, Paphos, Cyprus, pp. 17–24. ACM, October 2012

Energy-Aware Query Processing on a Parallel Database Cluster Node

Amine Roukh[1(✉)], Ladjel Bellatreche[2], Nikos Tziritas[3], and Carlos Ordonez[4]

[1] University of Mostaganem, Mostaganem, Algeria
roukh.amine@univ-mosta.dz
[2] LIAS/ISAE-ENSMA, Poitiers University, Poitiers, France
bellatreche@ensma.fr
[3] Chinese Academy of Sciences, Shenzhen, China
nikolaos@siat.ac.cn
[4] Houston University, Houston, USA
ordonez@cs.uh.edu

Abstract. In the last few years, we have been seeing a significant increase in research about the energy efficiency of hardware and software components in both centralized and parallel platforms. In data centers, DBMSs are one of the major energy consumers, in which, a large amount of data is queried by complex queries running daily. Having green nodes is a pre-condition to design an energy-aware parallel database cluster. Generally, the most existing DBMSs focus on high-performance during query optimization phase, while usually ignoring the energy consumption of the queries. In this paper, we propose a methodology, supported by a tool called *EnerQuery*, that makes nodes of parallel database clusters saving energy when optimizing queries. To show its effectiveness, we implement our proposal on the top of PostgreSQL DBMS query optimizer. A mathematical cost model based on a machine learning technique is defined and used to estimate the energy consumption of SQL queries.

1 Introduction

The COP21[1] event shows the willingness of countries (Over 145 foreign Heads of State and Government attended the conference at Le Bourget, Paris), companies, individuals, government and non-governmental associations, etc. to save the planet. The continued expansion of the industry means that the energy used by data centers, and the associated emissions of greenhouse gases and other air pollutants will continue to grow. Industry experts, such as the *SMARTer 2020*, reports that global data center emissions will grow 7 percent year-on-year through 2020 [1]. In a typical data center, DBMS is one of the most important consumers of computational resources among other software deployed, which turn DBMS to be a considerable energy consumer [2]. Traditionally, the design process of a database considers one non-functional requirement, which represents the query response time. Note that in the *Beckman report* on databases published

---

[1] http://www.gouvernement.fr/en/cop21.

© Springer International Publishing AG 2016
J. Carretero et al. (Eds.): ICA3PP 2016, LNCS 10048, pp. 260–269, 2016.
DOI: 10.1007/978-3-319-49583-5_20

in last February, energy constrained processing and scientific data management are considered as challenging issues [3]. Face to the strong requirement of saving energy, database community did not stand idly, but from last decade, it continuously proposes initiatives covering centralized and parallel and distributed databases [4,5]. In this paper, we concentrate on parallel database clusters storing and managing data warehouses [6]. To ensure a high performance of parallel database clusters, the DBMS of each node has to save energy. Advanced query optimizers perform two main tasks: (i) enumeration of execution plans for a given query and (ii) the selection of the best plan. The existing studies on energy-aware query optimizers consider mainly the second task, by reforming the cost models to integrate energy. In this paper, we focus on the query optimization component of the PostgreSQL DBMS. We propose a design methodology, supported by a tool called *EnerQuery*[2], that tries to integrate energy in the query generation phase. This is done by revisiting all the query optimizer steps and studying their effect on energy consumption. The new query optimizer will have to deal with two objective functions, namely: improving performance and minimizing energy. In our design, the end users can specify preferences in their profiles by setting weights on different objectives, representing relative importance. The role of the *EnerQuery* is to minimize the weighted sum over different cost metrics. Our paper is organized as follows. Section 2 presents the related work. Section 3 describes our green query optimizers. Section 4 shows and interprets our experimental results while our conclusion is given in Sect. 5.

2   Related Work

Recently, there has been a plethora of work by the research community in the field of energy-efficiency optimizations in database systems covering hardware and software levels. This section reviews only the research efforts related to software aspects that mainly concern the definition of cost models estimating the energy consumption and their usage in proposing optimization techniques. In [7,8], the authors discussed the opportunities for energy-based query optimization, and a power cost model is developed in the conjunction of PostgreSQL's cost model to predict the query power consumption. A static power profile for each basic database operation in query processing is defined. The authors adapt their static model to dynamic workloads using a feedback control mechanism to periodically update model parameters using real-time energy measurements. In [9], a technique for modeling the peak power of database operations is given. A pipeline-based model of query execution plans was developed to identify the sources of the peak power consumption for a query and to recommend plans with low peak power. In the same direction, the work of [10] proposes a framework for energy-aware database query processing. It augments query plans produced by traditional query optimizer with an energy consumption prediction for some specific database operators. [11] attempts to model energy and peak power of

---

[2] http://www.lias-lab.fr/forge/projects/ecoprod.

simple selection queries on single relations using linear regression. In our previous works [12], we proposed cost models to predict the power consumption of single and concurrent queries. Our model is based on pipeline segmenting of the query and predicting their power based on its Inputs-outputs (IO) and CPU costs, using polynomial regression techniques. The presence of energy consumption cost models motivates the research community to propose cost-driven techniques. The work in [13] proposed an Improved Query Energy-Efficiency by Introducing Explicit Delays mechanism, which uses query aggregation to leverage common components of queries in a workload. The work of [10] showed that processing a query as fast as possible does not always turn out to be the most energy-efficient way to operate a DBMS. Based on their proposed framework, they choose query plans that reduce energy consumption. In [9], a cost-based driven approach is proposed to generate query plans minimizing the peak power. In [14], an evolutionary algorithm with a fitness function based on an energy consumption cost model, is given to select materialized views reducing energy and optimizing queries.

3   Energy-Aware Query Processing

In order to build energy-aware query optimizers, we first propose an audit of each component to understand whether it is energy-sensitive or not.

3.1   An Audit of Query Optimizers

Recall that a query optimizer is responsible for executing queries respecting one or several non-functional requirements such as response time. The process of executing a given query passes through four main steps: (i) parsing, (ii) rewriting, (iii) planning and optimizing and (iv) executing. To illustrate these steps, we consider PostgreSQL DBMS as a case study.

The *parser* checks the query string for valid syntax using a set of grammar rules, then translates the query into an equivalent relational algebra expression. The output is the *query tree*. The cost of this phase is *generally ignored*. The *rewriter* processes and rewrites the tree using a set of rules. In our study, the energy cost of query parser and rewrite is negligible. The *planner* creates an optimal execution plan. A given SQL query can be executed in different ways while producing the same results. The planner examines different possible execution plans to find the cheapest one. If the query uses less than a certain defined threshold, a near-exhaustive search is conducted to find the best join sequences; otherwise, a heuristics based genetic algorithm is used. To study the effects of such searching strategies, let us consider the query *Q8* of the TPC-H benchmark[3]. This is a complex query which involves the join of 7 tables. We modify the planner of PostgreSQL in three manners: (i) searching for a plan by employing actual DBMS strategy (ii) using the genetic algorithm, and (iii) manually

---

[3] http://www.tpc.org/tpch/.

by forcing the planner to choose a certain plan. For each strategy, we calculate its execution time, and the total energy consumption during query execution against 10GB datasets. Results are presented in Table 1.

Table 1. Planning step for TPC-H *Q8* with different searching strategies.

Search strategies	Planning time (s)	Energy (j)
Default	0.110006	5200.362
GA	0.977013	5387.648
Manual	0.092054	5160.036

From the table, we can see that setting the query plan manually gives the betters results, in both time and energy. While the default searching algorithms lead to a slightly more execution time and energy consumption. The genetic algorithm gives the worst results in this example, perhaps due to the small number of tables in the query, since this strategy is used by the DBMS where there are more than 12 tables. The *optimizer's* task is to estimate the cost of executing each plan using a mathematical cost model and to find out the fast one. The general formula to estimate the cost of operator *op* can be expressed as: $Cost_{op} = \alpha \times I/O \oplus \beta \times CPU \oplus \gamma \times Net$. Where I/O, CPU, and Net are the estimated pages numbers, tuples numbers, communication messages, respectively, required to execute *op*. They are usually calculated using database statistics and selectivity formulas. The coefficients α, β and γ are used to convert estimations to the desired unit (e.g., time, energy). $\oplus$ represents the relationship between the parameters (linear, non-linear). The coefficient parameters and their relationship can be obtained using various techniques such as calibration, regression, and statistics. Thus, an energy cost model must be defined at this stage with the relevant parameters.

The *executor.* takes the plan created by the planner/optimizer and recursively processes it to extract the required set of rows. This is essentially a demand-pull *pipeline* mechanism. Each time a plan node is called, it must deliver one more row, or report that it is done delivering rows.

In [12], we showed that the power consumption is directly influenced by execution model of the DBMS. The execution plan can be divided into a set of segments, we refer to these segments as *pipelines*, where the pipelines are the concurrent execution of a contiguous sequence of operators. A partial order of the execution of these pipelines is enforced by their terminal *blocking* operators. We showed that *when a query switches from one pipeline to another, its power consumption also changes.*

3.2 Our Methodology

In this section, we describe the design and the implementation of our proposal into PostgreSQL database. We extended the cost model and the query optimizer

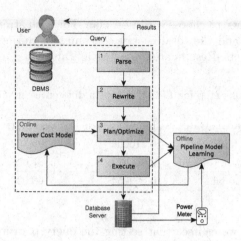

Fig. 1. The design methodology

of PostgreSQL to include the energy dimension. The work-flow of our method-ology is described in Fig. 1.

3.3   Power Cost Model

In this section, we present our methodology for estimating energy consumption. The characteristics of our model include: (i) the segmentation of an execution plan into a set of pipelines, (ii) the utilization of the pipeline parameters to build the model by employing machine learning techniques (*off-line*), and (iii) the estimation of the power of future pipeline based on pipeline parameters and the final model (*on-line*).

Pipeline Segmentation. A physical operator of an execution plan can be either *blocking* or *nonblocking*. An operator is blocking if it cannot produce any output tuple without reading at least one of its inputs (e.g., sort operator). Based on the notion of blocking/nonblocking operators, we decompose a plan in a set of pipelines delimited by blocking operators. Thus, a pipeline consists of a set of concurrently running operators [15]. As in previous work [15], the pipelines are created in an inductive manner, starting from the leaf operators of the plan. Whenever we encounter a blocking operator, the current pipeline ends, and a new pipeline starts.

Model Parameters. Our strategy for pipeline modeling is to extend the cost models that are built into the PostgreSQL database systems for query opti-mization. For a given query Q composed of p pipelines $\{PL_1, PL_2, \ldots, PL_p\}$. The power cost $Power(Q)$ of the query Q is given by the following equation:

$$Power(Q) = \frac{\sum_{i=1}^{p} Power(PL_i) * Time(PL_i)}{Time(Q)} \tag{1}$$

The *time* function represents the pipelines and the query estimated time to finish the execution. The DBMS statistics module provide us with this information.

Let a pipeline PL_i composed of n algebraic operations $\{OP_1, OP_2, \ldots, OP_n\}$. The power cost $Power(PL_i)$ of the pipeline PL_i is the sum of CPU and I/O costs of all its operators:

$$Power(PL_i) = \beta_{cpu} \times \sum_{j=1}^{n_i} CPU\_COST_j + \beta_{io} \times \sum_{j=1}^{n_i} IO\_COST_j \qquad (2)$$

where β_{cpu} and β_{io} are the model parameters (i.e., unit power costs) for the pipelines. The IO_COST is the predicted number of I/O it will require for DBMS to run the specified operator. The CPU_COST is the predicted number of *CPU Tuples* it will require for DBMS to run the specified operator.

Parameters Calibration. To find the model parameters β_{cpu} and β_{io} in Eq. (2), we employed multiple polynomial regression techniques. This method is suitable when there is a *nonlinear* relationship between the independents variables and the corresponding dependent variable. To compute the power of pipelines we use the same formulas elaborated in our earlier work [12].

3.4   Plans Evaluation

The query optimizer evaluates each possible execution path and takes the fastest. Adding the energy criterion, we must adjust the comparison functions to reflect the trade-offs between energy cost and processing time. In order to give the database administrator a solution with the desired trade-off, we propose to use the weighted sum of the cost functions method:

$$\text{minimize } y = f(x) = \sum_{i=1}^{k} \omega_i \cdot f_i(\overrightarrow{x}) \quad \text{such that } \sum_{i=1}^{k} \omega_i = 1 \qquad (3)$$

where ω_i are the weighting coefficients representing the relative importance of the k cost functions. $f_i(x)$ represents power cost and performance cost functions respectively.

Figure 2 shows the optimal query plan returned by the modified query planner/optimizer for TPC-H query $Q3$ and how it changes when user preferences vary. Initially, we used a performance only optimization goal, the total estimated processing cost is 371080 and the total estimated power is 153. Changing the goal to be only power, the processing cost increased to 626035 but the power falls down to 120. In the trade-off configuration, the processing cost is 377426 and the power is 134. In Fig. 2a, the nested loop operator draws the high amount of power in the query (33 watts) but the plan is chosen by the optimizer because it is very fast. In Fig. 2b, we realize that the merge join operator is the slowest in the query, its processing cost is 539200, with its power being minimal. The two hash join operators used in Fig. 2c give a good trade-off, for a 1.7 % of performance degradation, we get 12.4 % of power saving.

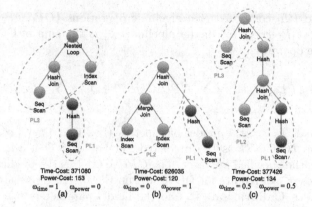

Fig. 2. The optimal plan for TPC-H query *Q3* when changing user preferences.

4   Experiments and Results

To evaluate the effectiveness of our proposal, we conduct several experiments. Next, we present our experimental machine to compute the energy and the used datasets.

Experiment Setup. We use a similar setup used in the state-of-the-arts [7,9,10] to measure power consumption. We used a Dell PowerEdge R310 workstation having a Xeon X3430 2.40 GHz processor and 32 GB of DDR3 memory. We installed our modified version of PostgreSQL 9.4.5 DBMS under Ubuntu 14.04 LTS with kernel 3.13. We use TPC-H datasets and queries with 10 GB and 100 GB scale factor. In our experiments, we consider three types of PostgreSQL configuration: (1) Power-PG, which is the configuration that gives the minimal power cost, (2) Time-PG, is the configuration with minimal time cost, (3) Tradeoff-PG, using weighted sum method with $\omega_1 = 0.5$, $\omega_2 = 0.5$.

Query Characterization. To study the characterization of the TPC-H 22 query, we conduct a series of tests using the modified PostgreSQL. In such tests and for each configuration (Time-PG, Power-PG, Tradeoff-PG) we run all the TPC-H queries and collect the estimated performance cost and power cost returned by the query optimizer. From Fig. 3 (values are plotted on a logarithmic scale) we can see that 16 of 22 queries have the potential for power saving in the Power-PG configuration. Normally, the benefit of power saving for these queries has a negative impact on the processing time cost as shown in the same figure. However, choosing the trade-off configuration can lead to good power saving values with less performance degradation. These queries are characterized by an important number of SQL operators and various I/O and CPU operations, which gives the query optimizer a variety of plans to choose from. Therefore, we can achieve good power saving queries from those plans. On the other hand, the rest of queries that do not show opportunities for power saving, are simple queries with a few tables and SQL operators. This leads the query

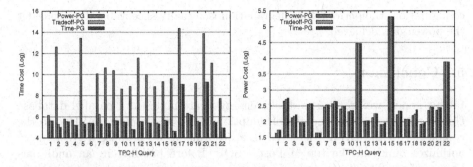

Fig. 3. Performance and power for queries using different PostgreSQL configurations.

optimizer to choose the same plan in every PostgreSQL configuration, due to the small search space of the plans.

Power Saving. The purpose of this set of experiments is to investigate the benefit of our approach in terms of energy efficiency. We configured the DBMS to evaluate the performance and power consumption cost models for the three configurations (Time-PG, Power-PG, Tradeoff-PG) under two different database sizes: 10 GB, and 100 GB. In Fig. 4 we present the results of the experiments. We can clearly see that workloads consume significantly lower power when choosing a query optimizer configuration that favors low-power plans. When comparing the power-only (Power-PG) with the performance-only (Time-PG) results, we observe a large margin in power savings, the benefit is remarkably considerable in small database size, perhaps this is due to the large amount of I/O operations and data processing required by queries of big database size which translate in more power consumption regardless of the chosen plan by query optimizer. As expected, the savings of the Tradeoff-PG configuration are smaller than those obtained by the power-only experiment, but it is still acceptable, especially, in 100 GB datasets they are approximate. On the other hand, the power-only configuration takes more time to finish executing all the queries, which translate in a noticeable performance degradation. The above is not surprising, since if we gain in power we automatically lose in performance. In the Tradeoff-PG

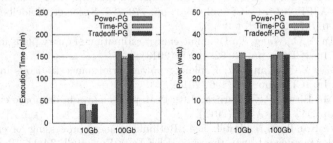

Fig. 4. Performance and power saving with different PostgreSQL configurations.

configuration, the performance degradation is actually acceptable if we consider the power gain achieved.

5   Conclusion

In this paper, we propose to design energy-aware nodes of a parallel database cluster to ensure a low energy consumption of the whole platform. Due to the complexity of the DBMS deployed in a given node, we propose a green-query optimizer build on the top of PostgreSQL. Before building it, an audit has been performed to identify energy-sensitive components of the query optimizers. Based on this audit, a methodology of building such a query optimizer is given. It is supported by an open source tool available at the forge of our laboratory to allow researchers, industrials, and students to get benefit from it. Intensive experiments were conducted to demonstrate the efficiency and usage of our proposal. The obtained results are encouraging. Currently, we are integrating the communication cost in our cost models.

References

1. e Sustainability Initiative, G., the Boston Consulting Group, I: Gesi smarter 2020: The role of ict in driving a sustainable future. Press Release, December 2012
2. Poess, M., Nambiar, R.O.: Energy cost, the key challenge of today's data centers: a power consumption analysis of TPC-C results. PVLDB 1(2), 1229–1240 (2008)
3. Abadi, D., Agrawal, R., Ailamaki, A., Balazinska, M., Bernstein, P.A., Carey, M.J., Chaudhuri, S., Dean, J., Doan, A., Franklin, M.J., et al.: The beckman report on database research. Commun. ACM 59(2), 92–99 (2016)
4. Lang, W., Harizopoulos, S., Patel, J.M., Shah, M.A., Tsirogiannis, D.: Towards energy-efficient database cluster design. PVLDB 5(11), 1684–1695 (2012)
5. Li, X., Zhao, Y., Li, Y., Ju, L., Jia, Z.: An improved energy-efficient scheduling for precedence constrained tasks in multiprocessor clusters. In: Sun, X., Qu, W., Stojmenovic, I., Zhou, W., Li, Z., Guo, H., Min, G., Yang, T., Wu, Y., Liu, L. (eds.) ICA3PP 2014. LNCS, vol. 8630, pp. 323–337. Springer, Heidelberg (2014). doi:10.1007/978-3-319-11197-1_25
6. Boukorca, A., Bellatreche, L., Benkrid, S.: HYPAD: hyper-graph-driven approach for parallel data warehouse design. In: Wang, G., Zomaya, A., Perez, G.M., Li, K. (eds.) ICA3PP 2015. LNCS, vol. 9531, pp. 770–783. Springer, Heidelberg (2015). doi:10.1007/978-3-319-27140-8_53
7. Xu, Z., Tu, Y.C., Wang, X.: Dynamic energy estimation of query plans in database systems. In: ICDCS, pp. 83–92. IEEE (2013)
8. Xu, Z., Tu, Y.C., Wang, X.: Exploring power-performance tradeoffs in database systems. In: ICDE, pp. 485–496 (2010)
9. Kunjir, M., Birwa, P.K., Haritsa, J.R.: Peak power plays in database engines. In: EDBT, pp. 444–455. ACM (2012)
10. Lang, W., Kandhan, R., Patel, J.M.: Rethinking query processing for energy efficiency: slowing down to win the race. IEEE Data Eng. Bull. 34(1), 12–23 (2011)
11. Rodriguez-Martinez, M., Valdivia, H., et al.: Estimating power/energy consumption in database servers. Procedia Comput. Sci. 6, 112–117 (2011)

12. Roukh, A., Bellatreche, L.: Eco-processing of OLAP complex queries. In: Madria, S., Hara, T. (eds.) DaWaK 2015. LNCS, vol. 9263, pp. 229–242. Springer, Heidelberg (2015). doi:10.1007/978-3-319-22729-0_18

13. Lang, W., Patel, J.: Towards eco-friendly database management systems. arXiv preprint arXiv:0909.1767 (2009)

14. Roukh, A., Bellatreche, L., Boukorca, A., Bouarar, S.: Eco-dmw: eco-design methodology for data warehouses. In: DOLAP, pp. 1–10. ACM (2015)

15. Chaudhuri, S., Narasayya, V., Ramamurthy, R.: Estimating progress of execution for SQL queries. In: ACM SIGMOD, pp. 803–814. ACM (2004)

Current Flow Betweenness Centrality
with Apache Spark

Massimiliano Bertolucci[1]([✉]), Alessandro Lulli[1,2], and Laura Ricci[1,2]

[1] Dipartimento di Informatica, Università di Pisa, Pisa, Italy
{massimiliano.bertolucci,lulli,ricci}@di.unipi.it
[2] Istituto di Scienza e Tecnologie dell'Informazione (ISTI, CNR), Pisa, Italy
{alessandro.lulli,laura.ricci}@isti.cnr.it

Abstract. The identification of the most central nodes of a graph is a fundamental task of data analysis. The current flow betweenness is a centrality index which considers how the information flows along all the paths of a graph, not only on the shortest ones. Finding the exact value of the current flow betweenness is computationally expensive for large graphs, so the definition of algorithms returning an approximation of this measure is mandatory. In this paper we propose a solution, based on the Gather Apply Scatter model, that estimates the current flow betweenness in a distributed setting using the Apache Spark framework. The experimental evaluation shows that the algorithm achieves high correlation with the exact value of the index and outperforms other algorithms.

Keywords: Centrality measure · Thinking like a vertex · Apache Spark

1 Introduction

In the last years, with the proliferation of mobile devices and internet usage, we are experiencing an increasing amounts of data being produced and collected. For instance, the users of a social network, when publishing content like posts and photos, are contributing to increase the amount of data. Data often represent relations among entities, so graphs provide a natural way to represent them.

Several analysis may be performed on graphs, such as searching for connected components [12,17], clustering [14,15] and many others. One of the most important indexes is the centrality which identifies the most important nodes and/or edges of the graph. The Betweenness Centrality [9] measures the importance of a node by evaluating the number of times that it is present on the shortest-paths between any pair of other nodes of the graph and is used in several contexts [23]. The goal is to obtain a ranking of the nodes. Alternative to this, the Flow Betweenness considers also information flowing through non-geodesic paths. Also, Newman and Brandes [5,21] suggest to model the flow of information through the network as a current flowing through an electric circuit. The approach of DUCKWEED [16] is to provide an approximation for the current flow betweenness centrality targeting the analysis of large graphs.

© Springer International Publishing AG 2016
J. Carretero et al. (Eds.): ICA3PP 2016, LNCS 10048, pp. 270–278, 2016.
DOI: 10.1007/978-3-319-49583-5_21

This algorithm exploits a vertex-centric approach where each node performs the same computation and relies only on the information exchanged with its neighbours to reach the solution. This computational model is suitable for a distributed execution of the algorithm because the computation is described from the point of view of the node and requires only its local knowledge. A prototype of DUCKWEED has been originally developed through PeerSim [20], a popular and scalable simulator targeted at a fast development and evaluation of distributed algorithms. However, the use of a simulator may hinder the identification of important characteristics or issues that arise in real environments. For instance, it is not easy to evaluate real communication costs, memory issues, data partitioning and workload balancing strategies. In this paper we present an implementation of DUCKWEED which exploits the Gather, Apply, Scatter computational model on Apache Spark [26]. The main contributions of the paper are the following ones: the definition of DUCKWEED on a real distributed environment which requires some optimizations to adapt the algorithm to the Apache Spark framework using the Gather-Apply-Scatter model (GAS); the comparison of two versions of DUCKWEED, DUCKWEED_X and DUCKWEED_MP, on GraphX and MAPREDUCE, both exploiting a GAS decomposition; an experimental analysis comparing our approach against two competitors.

2   Related Works

In this section we provide an overview of some works related to ours and distributed computation frameworks.

Centrality Measures and Algorithms. The original definition of betweenness centrality of a node n of a graph is based on the computation of the number of all shortest paths from all vertices to all others that pass through n. Several generalization of this basic measure have been proposed [1]. For instance, k-betweenness centrality [11] includes paths whose length exceeds or is lesser than the length of the shortest path at most of a configurable value k. The computation of these measures is intrinsically expensive because of their combinatorial nature. The naive centralized algorithm requires $O(n^3)$ time and $O(n^2)$ space, where n is the number of vertices [9]. An improvement to the basic solution, is proposed in [4], which obtains, for undirected graphs, $O(n + m)$ space and $O(nm)$ time bounds. Newman [21] and Brandes et al. [5] provided an alternative measure, the current flow betweenness, derived from Kirchoff's law of current conservation, in which edges are resistors with a given conductance, and the nodes are junctions between resistors. Madduri and Bader [2] developed a parallel betweenness centrality algorithm based on Brandes' approach. An extension of this work for k-betweenness centrality is presented in [11].

Distributed Computation Frameworks. In the last years, a plethora of different frameworks for distributed data analytics have been proposed. Among these frameworks, MapReduce [8] has been the first to exploit distributed computation on commodity hardware. Its first evolution for graph processing has been Pregel [18], where the computation follows the Bulk Synchronous Parallel model. Spark [26] is a distributed framework recently proposed which provides in memory computation making use of Resilient Distribute Dataset (RDD), immutable, partitioned data structures that can be manipulated through multiple operators like Map, Reduce, and Join. Spark provides also an API for graph processing, borrowing the idea of Pregel, called GraphX [25]. In GraphX each graph is mapped into different RDDs. The majority of these frameworks, share the "think like a vertex" model [19] to define the computation on a graph. According to this model, the computation is organized as a sequence of iterations, and can be described from the point of view of a vertex, that manages its state and sends messages only to its neighbours. These frameworks [7,13] can be characterized by four pillars [19]: timing, communication, execution model and partitioning [3,6,22].

3   Distributed Current Flow Betweeness on Apache Spark

DUCKWEED [16] is a distributed algorithm for computing an approximation of the Current Flow Betweenness (CFBTW). The main idea of DUCKWEED is that each vertex can calculate iteratively, locally and autonomously, its own electric potential exploiting the Kirchhoff's law [5]. The CFBTW is computed by considering the graph as an electric network whose edges are resistance and whose nodes are points of junction between the resistances. A current flow $F^{(s,t)}$ over the graph G from s, the source node, to t, the target node, is the current flowing in the graph when a unit of current is injected at s and extracted at t. To compute the current flow betweenness of a vertex i, $i \neq s, t$, it is required to compute the current flowing through i. Given a flow $F^{(s,t)}$, this value may be computed by the Kirchhoff's laws, as half of the sum of the absolute values of the currents flowing along the edges incident on that vertex. The betweenness is then calculated averaging the current flowing in i for all the possible flows (i.e. each couple of (s, t) in the graph). DUCKWEED approximate the CFBTW by generating a subset of flows. Additional details can be found in the original paper [16].

In this section we describe how the computation of CFBTW has been defined according to the *GAS (Gather-Apply-Scatter)* model, an iterative graph-parallel paradigm [10], which can be easily implemented on distributed frameworks like Spark and GraphX. In the following, we present the algorithm, GAS-Duckweed, and the optimizations which exploit the characteristics of the GAS model.

Algorithm 1, shows the high level structure of GAS-Duckweed. The algorithm is splitted into three data-parallel phases:

- *Gather* combines two incoming messages (M1 and M2). It optimizes communications by aggregating the potentials relative to the same flow.
- *Apply* consumes the aggregated message, in particular it updates all potentials of the flows, and eventually updates the CFBTW.
- *Scatter* defines the messages that are dispatched to the neighbours.

Let us detail now some characteristics and optimizations of the algorithm.

Algorithm 1. The GAS Duckweed Algorithm

```
1  def Gather (M1,M2 ← receive messages from neighbours)
2  |   Map ← old collected message;
3  |   for ∀F^{(s,t)} ∈ M1 ∪ M2 do
4  |   |   F_old ← Map.get (F^{(s,t)});
5  |   |   if F^{(s,t)} isConverged then
6  |   |   |   F_old.PutList (F^{(s,t)})
7  |   |   else
8  |   |   |   F_old.PutSum(F^{(s,t)})
9  def Apply (F ← aggregated message)
10 |   forall f ∈ F do
11 |   |   p_f ← Update () ;
12 |   |   Δf ← difference between p_f and p_f of the previous iteration ;
13 |   |   if Terminate( Δf) then
14 |   |   |   mark f as terminate
15 |   UpdateCentrality (f) ;
16 def Scatter ()
17 |   F ← new message with all flows p_f updated;
18 |   Send(F) to neigthbours ;
```

Reducing the Number of Messages. The algorithm is characterized by a neighbour-to-neighbour communication pattern. In each iteration all vertices receive and send messages through their edges. The value of a generic message exchanged between neighbours is a map consisting of key-value pairs, where the keys uniquely identify the flows by s and t, respectively the source and the target of the flow, and the value is the current potential for that flow. The gather function is exploited to combine all messages towards to the same vertex, which refer to the same flow, into one single message.

Reducing the Size of Messages. All the messages include information of a set of flows. If all the flows are sent at all the iterations, many duplicate data may be sent in consecutive iterations. We can reduce the number of messages by the *avoid re-sending* and their size by the *combine message* techniques.

Avoid Re-sending. Each vertex has a local view of the flows that have been injected and that are flowing through the graph and each vertex characterizes its flows by their state, which can be *Active, Converged*, or *Terminated*. The *Active* state identifies flows currently processed by a vertex. A flow is considered *Converged* when the difference of the values of its potential, in two consecutive iterations, is less than a system-wide parameter D_ϵ. A flow is considered *Terminated* by vertex i, if its state is *Converged* in i and in all its neighbours, in this case it can be exploited to update the current flow betweenness of i. When a flow $F^{(s,t)}$ is *Converged* on i but still *Active* on some neighbours, such neighbours still requires the value of the flow on i to continue the computation in the next iterations. If this is the case, i sends one last time its converged flow tagged with a flag notifying to all the neighbours that this is the last time that they will receive the potential for that flow from i.

Combine Message. At each iteration, each vertex receives the messages generated in the previous iteration. GAS-Duckweed, during the gather phase, consider each flow separately and sums its values before sending the message, so reducing the size of all messages even more. Not all the values of the flows can be aggregated.

The converged flows have to be saved in local memory and they must not be considered in the gather phase. Algorithm 1 shows the pseudo code of the Gather function. This is applied to all messages and reduces both the number of messages and the size of each message.

Flow Generation. We assume that the vertices are labelled from 0 to $n - 1$, where n is the number of vertices in the graph. In order to create the flow $F^{(s,t)}$, the source and the target are selected by generating a random value $\in [0, n-1]$. We define a system-wide parameter φ equal to the maximum number of flows in status *Active* on each node. At each iteration t, DUCKWEED monitors the average number A_t of flows in status *Active* on each node. At each iteration, k flows are generated by DUCKWEED where k is equal to $\varphi - A_t$.

Termination. In each iteration DUCKWEED removes the completed flows from the computation and generates new ones. Due to this, in each iteration, DUCK-WEED can provide an approximation of the CFBTW. Clearly, when more flows are completed the approximation will be closer to the exact value. We define the parameter θ equals to the percentage of all possible flows that need to be calculated before stopping. At each iteration t, DUCKWEED sets the value of the variable F_t equal to the average number of completed flows on each node. Given F_{all} equal to the amount of all the possible flows that can be generated for the graph G, DUCKWEED stops the computation when $F_t = \theta F_{all}$. The algorithm exploits also a parameter *iter* to avoid too long executions so that, in any case, DUCKWEED stops the execution when *iter* iterations have been completed.

4   Experimental Evaluation

In this section, we evaluate the performance of the DUCKWEED_X and DUCK-WEED_MP algorithms which are the implementations of the Algorithm 1 which make use, respectively, of GraphX and Spark. Evaluations were performed on a cluster of 4 nodes, each having 4 cores and 16 GB of memory. We compare our approach with two competitors, Betweenness Centrality [9][1] and K-betweenness [11], both implemented by their proposers in Spark:[2].

Evaluation of the Approximation. We measure the correlation between the results obtained by our approach and those obtained by NetworkX [24] which provides an implementation of the algorithm proposed by Brandes et. al. [5] to compute the CFBTW and returns an exact result. We generate a preferential attachment graph by means of the Snap library[3]. The size of the graph is restricted to 10 000 nodes, because in NetworkX it is not possible to obtain the exact value of CFBTW for larger graphs.

Figure 1a shows the result returned when using a different number of concurrent flows with DUCKWEED_MP (we obtain analogous result with DUCKWEED_X). The Y axis reports the Kendall Tau correlation of the top 50 nodes, while the X axis the computational time. We fix the iteration number to 25. We run the

---

[1] http://neo4j.com/developer/apache-spark/.
[2] https://github.com/kbastani/neo4j-mazerunner.
[3] http://snap.stanford.edu/.

algorithm 4 times for each configuration. We can observe that the correlation increases very quickly until it reaches the 0,9 %. We obtain the best result with $\varphi = 350$. Greater values requires more time to complete and do not bring benefits in terms of quality. Figure 1b shows the results when varying the number of iterations. We fix the number of concurrent flows to 25 and we increase the number of iterations. Similarly as before, a high number of iterations does not bring to a large increase of the correlation value.

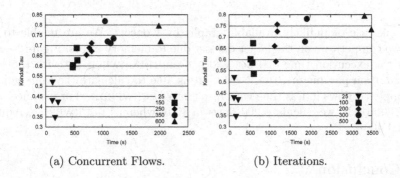

(a) Concurrent Flows.   (b) Iterations.

Fig. 1. Evaluation of the approximation. Kendall tau correlation with NetworkX.

Performance Evaluation. We compare the computational time of our algorithm against the two competitors. Figure 2a shows the execution time of the different algorithms when the size of the graph varies in the set $\{250, 500, 750, 1000, 2000, 3000, 5000\}$ for a preferential attachment graph. We omit results for random graphs that show similar outcome. DUCKWEED_MP yields better completion times in all cases. In addition, the two competitors are unable to provide a result for the larger graphs due to memory errors. DUCKWEED_MP is able to provide a result 10 times faster with respect to the best competitor. Next, we perform an evaluation using real graphs, results are presented in Table 1.

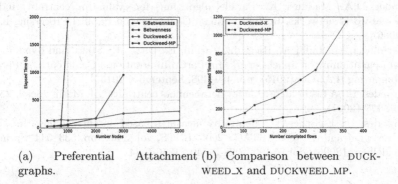

(a) Preferential Attachment (b) Comparison between DUCK-
graphs.   WEED_X and DUCKWEED_MP.

Fig. 2. Comparison with competitors and DUCKWEED_X, DUCKWEED_MP.

Table 1. Execution time on real world graphs.

Algorithm	Netscience (379)	Email (1133)	Brightike (56739)	WordNet (145145)
Betweenness	62	160	-	-
K-Betweenness	30	49	-	-
DUCKWEED_X	410	110	-	-
DUCKWEED_MP	33	51	4232	4636

We make use of publicly available graphs by Konect[4]. We are unable to run the two competitors on the larger dataset due to memory errors. Figure 2b compares the execution time of DUCKWEED_X and DUCKWEED_MP with the same configuration parameters. DUCKWEED_MP is able to calculate the same number of completed flows in less time with respect to DUCKWEED_X. For instance, with DUCKWEED_MP we calculate 200 flows in 150 s whereas DUCKWEED_X requires around 400 s.

5 Conclusion

In this paper, we presented a distributed algorithm for the computation of the current flow betweenness centrality. The algorithm makes use of the GAS (Gather-Apply-Scatter) decomposition which is suitable for the implementation on Apache Spark and on GraphX. Our algorithm is faster than two well known competitors and is able to return approximate results for larger graphs.

References

1. Avrachenkov, K., Litvak, N., Medyanikov, V., Sokol, M.: Alpha current flow betweenness centrality. In: Bonato, A., Mitzenmacher, M., Prałat, P. (eds.) WAW 2013. LNCS, vol. 8305, pp. 106–117. Springer, Heidelberg (2013). doi:10.1007/978-3-319-03536-9_9
2. Bader, D.A., Madduri, K.: Parallel algorithms for evaluating centrality indices in real-world networks. In: International Conference on Parallel Processing ICCP (2006)
3. Bertolucci, M., Lulli, A., Ricci, L., Carlini, E., Dazzi, P.: Static and dynamic big data partitioning on apache spark. In: ParCo International Conference on Parallel Computing, PARCO (2015), pp. 489–498, September 2015
4. Brandes, U.: A faster algorithm for betweenness centrality*. J. Math. Sociol. **25**(2), 163–177 (2001)
5. Brandes, U., Fleischer, D.: Centrality measures based on current flow. In: Diekert, V., Durand, B. (eds.) STACS 2005. LNCS, vol. 3404, pp. 533–544. Springer, Heidelberg (2005). doi:10.1007/978-3-540-31856-9_44

---

[4] http://konect.uni-koblenz.de/networks/.

6. Carlini, E., Dazzi, P., Esposito, A., Lulli, A., Ricci, L.: Balanced graph partitioning with apache spark. In: Lopes, L., Žilinskas, J., Costan, A., Cascella, R.G., Kecskemeti, G., Jeannot, E., Cannataro, M., Ricci, L., Benkner, S., Petit, S., Scarano, V., Gracia, J., Hunold, S., Scott, S.L., Lankes, S., Lengauer, C., Carretero, J., Breitbart, J., Alexander, M. (eds.) Euro-Par 2014. LNCS, vol. 8805, pp. 129–140. Springer, Heidelberg (2014). doi:10.1007/978-3-319-14325-5_12

7. Carlini, E., Dazzi, P., Lulli, A., Ricci, L.: Distributed graph processing: an approach based on overlay composition. In: Proceedings of the 31st Annual ACM Symposium on Applied Computing, pp. 1912–1917. ACM (2016)

8. Dean, J., Ghemawat, S.: Mapreduce: simplified data processing on large clusters. Commun. ACM 51(1), 107–113 (2008)

9. Freeman, L.C.: A set of measures of centrality based on betweenness. Sociometry 40, 35–41 (1977)

10. Gonzalez, J.E., et al.: Graphx: graph processing in a distributed dataflow framework. In: OSDI 14, pp. 599–613 (2014)

11. Jiang, K.A.: Generalizing k-betweenness centrality using short paths and a parallel multithreaded implementation. In: ICPP 2009, pp. 542–549. IEEE (2009)

12. Lulli, A., Carlini, E., Dazzi, P., Lucchese, C., Ricci, L.: Fast connected components computation in large graphs by vertex pruning. IEEE Trans. Parallel Distrib. Syst. (2016). doi:10.1109/TPDS.2016.2591038

13. Lulli, A., Dazzi, P., Ricci, L., Carlini, E.: A multi-layer framework for graph processing via overlay composition. In: Hunold, S., Costan, A., Giménez, D., Iosup, A., Ricci, L., Gómez Requena, M.E., Scarano, V., Varbanescu, A.L., Scott, S.L., Lankes, S., Weidendorfer, J., Alexander, M. (eds.) Euro-Par 2015. LNCS, vol. 9523, pp. 515–527. Springer, Heidelberg (2015). doi:10.1007/978-3-319-27308-2_42

14. Lulli, A., Debatty, T., Dell'Amico, M., Michiardi, P., Ricci, L.: Scalable K-NN based text clustering. In: 2015 IEEE International Conference on Big Data (Big Data), pp. 958–963. IEEE (2015)

15. Lulli, A., Gabrielli, L., Dazzi, P., Dell'Amico, M., Michiardi, P., Nanni, M., Ricci, L.: Improving population estimation from mobile calls: a clustering approach. In: 2016 IEEE Symposium on Computers and Communication (ISCC), pp. 1097–1102. IEEE (2016)

16. Lulli, A., Ricci, L., Carlini, E., Dazzi, P.: Distributed current flow betweenness centrality. In: 2015 IEEE 9th International Conference on Self-adaptive and Self-organizing Systems (SASO), pp. 71–80. IEEE (2015)

17. Lulli, A., Ricci, L., Carlini, E., Dazzi, P., Lucchese, C.: Cracker: crumbling large graphs into connected components. In: 2015 IEEE Symposium on Computers and Communication (ISCC), pp. 574–581. IEEE (2015)

18. Malewicz, G., et al.: Pregel: a system for large-scale graph processing. In: SIGMOD, pp. 135–146. ACM (2010)

19. McCune, R.R., et al.: Thinking like a vertex: a survey of vertex-centric frameworks for large-scale distributed graph processing. ACM Comput. Surv. 48, 25 (2015)

20. Montresor, A., Jelasity, M.: Peersim: a scalable P2P simulator. In: IEEE Ninth Conference on Peer-to-Peer Computing, P2P 2009, pp. 99–100. IEEE (2009)

21. Newman, M.E.: A measure of betweenness centrality based on random walks. Soc. Netw. 27(1), 39–54 (2005)

22. Rahimian, F., Payberah, A.H., Girdzijauskas, S., Jelasity, M., Haridi, S.: Ja-be-ja: A distributed algorithm for balanced graph partitioning (2013)

23. Ricci, L., Carlini, E.: Distributed virtual environments: from client server to P2P architectures. In: Proceedings of the International Conference on High Performance Computing and Simulation, HPCS 2012 (2012)

24. Schult, D.A., et al.: Exploring network structure, dynamics, and function using networkx. In: SciPy 2008, vol. 2008, pp. 11–16 (2008)
25. Xin, R., et al.: Graphx: a resilient distributed graph system on spark. In: Graph Data Management Experiences and Systems, p. 2. ACM (2013)
26. Zaharia, M., et al.: Resilient distributed datasets: a fault-tolerant abstraction for in-memory cluster computing. In: Proceedings of the 9th USENIX Conference on Networked Systems Design and Implementation, p. 2 (2012)

Parallel and Distributed Algorithms

Light Loss-Less Data Compression, with GPU Implementation

Shunji Funasaka, Koji Nakano[✉], and Yasuaki Ito

Department of Information Engineering, Hiroshima University, Kagamiyama 1-4-1,
Higashihiroshima 739-8527, Japan
{funasaka,nakano,yasuaki}@cs.hiroshima-u.ac.jp

Abstract. There is no doubt that data compression is very important in computer engineering. However, most lossless data compression and decompression algorithms are very hard to parallelize, because they use dictionaries updated sequentially. The main contribution of this paper is to present a new lossless data compression method that we call Light Loss-Less (LLL) compression. It is designed so that decompression can be highly parallelized and run very efficiently on the GPU. This makes sense for many applications in which compressed data is read and decompressed many times and decompression performed more frequently than compression. We show optimal sequential and parallel algorithms for LLL decompression and implement them to run on Core i7-4790 CPU and GeForce GTX 1080 GPU, respectively. To show the potentiality of LLL compression method, we have evaluated the running time using five images and compared with well-known compression methods LZW and LZSS. Our GPU implementation of LLL decompression runs 91.1–176 times faster than the CPU implementation. Also, the running time on the GPU of our experiments show that LLL decompression is 2.49–9.13 times faster than LZW decompression and 4.30–14.1 times faster that LZSS decompression, although their compression ratios are comparable.

Keywords: Data compression · Parallel algorithms · GPGPU

1 Introduction

A GPU (Graphics Processing Unit) is a specialized circuit designed to accelerate computation for building and manipulating images [6]. Latest GPUs are designed for general purpose computing and can perform computation in applications traditionally handled by the CPU. Hence, GPUs have recently attracted the attention of many application developers [7,11]. NVIDIA provides a parallel computing architecture called *CUDA* (Compute Unified Device Architecture) [12], the computing engine for NVIDIA GPUs. CUDA gives developers access to the virtual instruction set and memory of the parallel computational elements in NVIDIA GPUs. In many cases, GPUs are more efficient than multi-core processors [10], since they have thousands of processor cores and very high memory bandwidth.

© Springer International Publishing AG 2016
J. Carretero et al. (Eds.): ICA3PP 2016, LNCS 10048, pp. 281–294, 2016.
DOI: 10.1007/978-3-319-49583-5_22

There is no doubt that data compression is one of the most important tasks in the area of computer engineering. In particular, almost all image data are stored in files as compressed data formats. There are basically two types of image compression methods: *lossy* and *lossless* [15]. Lossy compression can generate smaller files, but some information in original files are discarded. On the other hand, lossless compression creates compressed files, from which we can obtain the exactly same original files by decompression. The main contribution of this paper is to present a novel lossless data compression method, in which decompression can be done very fast using the GPU.

Usually, data to be compressed is a sequence of 8-bit numbers (or a string of characters). LZSS (Lempel-Ziv-Storer-Szymanski) [16] is a well-known dictionary-based lossless compression method, which replaces a substring appearing before by a pair of offset and length. For example, ABCDEBCDEF is encoded into ABCDE(1,4)F, where (1,4) is a code representing a substring of length 4 from offset 1. LZSS decompression is performed using a buffer storing recently decoded substring. We can think that the buffer is a dictionary and an offset/length pair is decoded by retrieving the corresponding substring in the dictionary. For example, the dictionary stores ABCDE when (1,4) is decoded and BCDE in a dictionary is read and output. Since the dictionary is updated every time after a code is decoded and output, it is very hard to parallelize LZSS compression. To parallelize LZSS compression, the input string is partitioned into equal-sized strips, each of which is encoded sequentially using one thread. The LZSS decompression is also performed using one thread for each encoded strip. Since every strip is encoded/decoded sequentially, we call this low parallelism *strip-wise*. Strip-wise parallel LZSS compression/decompression have been implemented in a GPU [13], but it achieves very small acceleration ratio over the sequential implementation on the CPU.

LZW (Lempel-Ziv-Welch) is a patented lossless compression method [17] used in Unix file compression utility "compress" and in GIF image format. Also, LZW compression option is included in TIFF file format standard [1], which is commonly used in the area of commercial digital printing. In LZW compression/decompression, a newly appeared substring is added to the dictionary. Hence, it is very hard to parallelize them. Parallel algorithms for LZW compression and decompression have been presented [2,8]. However, processors perform compression and decompression with strip-wise low parallelism. Quite recently, we have presented GPU implementation of LZW decompression with high parallelism [3]. This parallel algorithm is *code-wise* in the sense that a thread is arranged in each code of a compressed string. Hence, it has very high parallelism and a lot of threads work in parallel. Since memory access latency of the GPU is quite large, higher parallelism can hide large memory access latency and can attain better performance. The experimental results in [3] show that it achieves a speedup factor up to 69.4 over sequential CPU decompression. This code-wise LZW decompression on the GPU is much faster than the strip-wise LZSS decompression, although it performs complicated pointer traversing operations.

We present a simple lossless compression method called *LLL (Light Loss-Less)* data compression that can be implemented in the GPU as code-wise. Basically, it combines run-length and LZSS encoding. In the LLL compression, each strip is partitioned into several segments, say 16 segments of size 4096 bytes. The previous segment is used as a dictionary when a segment is encoded/decoded. We focus on LLL decompression in this paper, because decompression is performed more frequently than compression in many applications. For example, an image compressed and stored in a storage may be read and decompressed every time when it is necessary. Thus, compression is performed once for this image, but decompression may be performed many times. We first show a sequential LLL decompression algorithm that computes and outputs characters corresponding to every code one by one. This algorithm runs $O(n)$ time, where n is the number of output characters. Since $\Omega(n)$ time is necessary, this sequential algorithm is optimal.

Our parallel LLL decompression algorithm has 2 stages. Stage 1 computes some prefix-sums twice, to determine, for each code, reading offsets of the previous segment, writing offsets of the current segment, and the lengths of substrings to be copied. Stage 2 performs, for each code, copy operations from the previous segment to the current segment. We have evaluated the performance of this parallel algorithm using the CREW-PRAM (Concurrent Read and Exclusive Write Parallel Random Access Machine), which is a standard theoretical parallel computing model with a number of processors and the shared memory [4]. Our parallel LLL decompression algorithm runs $O(k \log m)$ time and $O(n)$ total work using $\frac{m}{\log m}$ processors on the CREW-PRAM, where m and k are the number of codes and the maximum length of all codes, respectively, and the total work is the total number of instructions executed by all processors. Since at least $\Omega(n)$ work is necessary, this parallel algorithm is work optimal.

We have implemented our parallel LLL decompression algorithm in the GPU. Since the GPU can compute the prefix-sums very efficiently, our GPU implementation for LLL decompression run much faster than those for LZSS decompression and LZW decompression. The experimental results using five images show that LLL decompression on the GPU runs 91.1–176 times faster than that on the CPU. Also, the LLL compression method achieves comparable compression ratio to the LZW and LZSS compression methods. Despite good compression ratio, LLL decompression is 2.49–9.13 times faster than LZW decompression and 4.30–14.1 times faster than LZSS decompression on the GPU.

As far as we know, there is few published work which aims to design a data compression method to be implemented in the GPU. In [9], a compression method for a sequence of sensing data has been presented. The idea is so simple that it finds the maximum value of a segment and removes unnecessary significant bits from sensing data. Hence, it does not work well for data with high dynamic range and cannot attain good compression ratio. In [14], a bzip2-like lossless data compression scheme and the GPU implementation have been presented, but it did not succeed in GPU acceleration of compression.

This paper is organized as follows. Section 2 introduces LLL encoding and shows sequential algorithm for LLL decompression. We then go on to show that LLL decompression can be done in parallel by computing prefix-sums twice and by copy operations in Sect. 3. We show the details of GPU implementation of LLL decompression in Sect. 4. Section 5 offers various experimental results including compression ratio, running time on the CPU and the GPU, the SSD-GPU loading time. Section 6 concludes our work.

2   LLL: Light Loss-Less Data Compression

The main purpose of this section is to present *LLL (Light Loss-Less)* data compression method and efficient sequential algorithms for it.

Non-dictionary Encoding

Non-dictionary has two codes, single character code and run-length code as follows:

Single Character (SC) code: A 1-byte SC code simply represents an 8-bit character.

Run-Length (RL) code: A 2-byte RC code has two fields: an 8-bit character field c and an 8-bit length field l. This code represents a run (or a sequence of the same character) with $l + 2$ characters c.

Dictionary Encoding

Dictionary encoding has five codes: single character code (1-byte word), short run-length code (2-byte word), long run-length code (2-byte word plus 1-byte word), short interval code (2-byte word), and long interval code (2-byte word plus 1-byte word). A 2-byte word has two fields: 12-bit offset field t and 4-bit length field l. Also, let c denote the value of a 1-byte word. The string corresponding a code can be determined by the following five encoding rules:

Single Character (SC) code: If a 1-byte code is not that of a long run-length or long interval code defined next, then it is an SC code, which represents an 8-bit character.

Short Run-Length (SRL) code: If the offset t of the 2-byte word is 4095 ($= 111111111111$ in binary) and the length l is NOT 15 ($= 1111$ in binary) then the 2-byte word is *short run-length code* and represents a run of length $l + 2$ with the previous character.

Long Run-Length (LRL) code: If the offset t of the 2-byte word is 4095 and the length l is 15 then a 1-byte word follows, and these two words constitute a *long run-length code*, which represents a run of length $c + 18$ with the previous character.

Short Interval (SI) code: If offset t of a 2-byte word is NOT 4095 and length l
is NOT 15 then the 2-byte word is *short interval code* and represents reading
offset t and length $l + 2$. The decoded string of this code is a substring of
length $l + 2$ in the previous segment from offset t.

Long Interval (LI) code: If offset t of a 2-byte word is NOT 4095 and the
length l is 15 then a 1-byte word must follow, and these two words constitute
a *long interval code*, which represents reading offset t and length $c + 18$. The
decoded string of this code is a substring of length $c + 18$ in the previous
segment from offset t.

Additional Rule: Two run-length codes should not be consecutive.

The reader should refer to Table 1 that summarizes five codes. Note that,
one SI/SRL code and one SC code combined in 3 bytes can represent up to
17 characters. Thus, it is not necessary for a 3-byte LI/LRL code to support
length 17.

Table 1. Rules of codes: p is the previous character and $x(0)x(1)\cdots x(4095)$ is the
previous segment

Codes	words			length	encoded string
	Non-dictionary encoding				
SC Single Character	c			1	c
RL Run-Length	c	l		$l + 2$	$cc \cdots c$
	Dictionary encoding				
SC Single Character	c			1	c
SRL Short Run-Length	111111111111	l		$l + 2$	$pp \cdots p$
LRL Long Run-Length	111111111111	1111	c	$c + 18$	$pp \cdots p$
SI Short Interval	t	l		$l + 2$	$x(t) \cdots x(t + l + 1)$
LI Long Interval	t	1111	c	$c + 18$	$x(t) \cdots x(t + c + 17)$

Figure 1 shows examples of LLL-compressed data for two segments. We
assume that each segment has 64 characters each although it is defined to be
4096 characters. The first segment is compressed by non-dictionary encoding.
The encoded data has four RL codes and four SC codes. For example, the first
RL code with character A and length 30 corresponds to run of $30 + 2 = 32$ A's.
Next SC code with character B corresponds to one B.

The second segment in Fig. 1 is encoded using the first segment as a dictionary. The compressed data has six 2-byte words and two 1-byte words. The
first 26 characters appear from offset 16 of the first segment. Hence, they are
encoded using one LI code with length $8 + 18 = 26$. After that, six E's follow.
Since the previous character is also E, they can be encoded using one SRL code

with length $2 + 4 = 6$. The following string of 16 characters appears in the first segment. It is encoded using one SI code with length $2 + 14 = 16$ and one SC code. Remaining characters can be partitioned into three strings appearing in the first string. Hence, they are encoded using three SI codes.

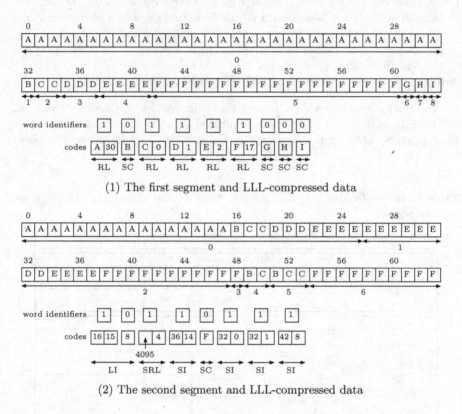

(1) The first segment and LLL-compressed data

(2) The second segment and LLL-compressed data

Fig. 1. Examples of LLL-compressed data for two segments with 64 characters each

2.1   LLL with Segment Halving

Recall that the first segment with 4096 characters is encoded using non-dictionary encoding, by which we cannot expect good compression ratio. We introduce *the segment halving technique*, that reduces the length of a segment compressed by non-dictionary encoding.

In the segment halving technique, the first segment is partitioned into subsegments such that subsegment 0 and subsegment 1 have 512 characters, subsegment 2 has 1024 characters, and segment 3 has 2048 characters. Subsegment 0 is compressed using non-dictionary encoding. The remaining subsegments are compressed using dictionary encoding.

2.2   LLL File Format

We will show how a large data are encoded and compressed using LLL data compression. An input sequence is partitioned into segments of 4096 characters. Several, say, 8 consecutive segments constitute *a strip*. Each strip with 32 K characters is encoded independently by the LLL compression method. Figure 2 illustrates an example of LLL-compressed file format. It has *a header*, which contains tags storing several setting data such as the number of segments per strip and the number of strips. It also has *a directory*, which stores an array of addresses pointing the heads of encoded strips. The encoded strip has two blocks: the word identifier block and the word array block. The word identifier block stores all word identifiers in a strip. All word identifiers of all segments are concatenated and stored in the word identifier block. Similarly, the word arrays of all segments are concatenated and stored in the word array block. Using this file format, decompression of each strip can be done independently.

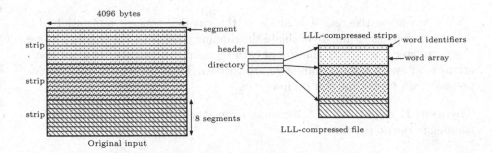

Fig. 2. LLL-compressed file format

2.3   Sequential LLL Decompression Algorithm

We show a sequential LLL decompression algorithm for dictionary encoding. Since those for non-dictionary encoding can be performed easier, we omit to describe it.

Let $x(0)x(1) \cdots x(4095)$ be a sequence of characters in the previous segment. Let $w(0)w(1) \cdots w(m-1)$ be m bits of the word identifiers and $b(0)b(1) \cdots b(m_1 + 2m_2 - 1)$ be bytes in the word array, where m, m_1, and m_2 be the numbers of words, 1-byte words, and 2-byte words, respectively. Sequential LLL decompression can be done by reading the word identifiers as follows:

[Sequential LLL decompression algorithm]
$j \leftarrow 0$; $p \leftarrow$ NULL;
for $i \leftarrow 0$ to $m - 1$ do
    if($w(i) = 0$) write($b(j)$);$p \leftarrow b(j)$; $j \leftarrow j + 1$;// SC code
    else

$(t, l) \leftarrow$ the offset and the length fields of 2-byte word $b(j)b(j + 1)$;
if($l = 15$)
   $c \leftarrow b(j + 2)$;
   if($t = 4095$) write(p) is executed $c + 18$ times; // LRL code
   else
      write($x(t)x(t + 1) \cdots x(t + c + 17)$); // LI code
      $p = x(t + c + 17)$;
   $j \leftarrow j + 3$;
   $i \leftarrow i + 1$;
else
   if($t = 4095$) write(p) is executed $l + 2$ times; // SRL code
   else
      write($x(t)x(t + 1) \cdots x(t + l + 1)$); // SI code
      $p = x(t + l + 1)$;
   $j \leftarrow j + 2$;
if($t = 4095$) $p \leftarrow$ NULL;// run-length codes should not be consecutive

We will show theoretical analysis of the running time of sequential LLL decompression algorithm. To evaluate the running time using big-O notation, we use parameter n to denote the size of each segment. The number of write operations is m and totally n characters are written. Thus, sequential LLL decompression runs $O(n)$ time and we have,

Theorem 1. *Sequential LLL decompression algorithm for a segment with n characters runs $O(n)$ time.*

Since at least n characters are output, this sequential algorithm is time optimal.

3   Parallel LLL Decompression Algorithm

This section shows a parallel LLL decompression algorithm. We focus on how a segment compressed by dictionary encoding can be decoded. Decoding for non-dictionary encoding can be done in a similar way. Parallel prefix-sums computation is a key ingredient of LLL decompression. For later reference, we use "^" to denote the prefix-sums of a sequence of numbers. For example, the prefix-sums of a sequence $a(0), a(1), \ldots$ are $\hat{a}(0), \hat{a}(1), \ldots$, where $\hat{a}(i) = a(0) + a(1) + \cdots + a(i)$ for all i (≥ 0). For simplicity, let $\hat{a}(-1) = 0$.

We assume that m-bit word identifiers $w(0)w(1) \cdots w(m - 1)$, word array $b(0)b(1) \cdots b(m_1 + m_2 - 1)$, and the previous segment $x(0)x(1) \cdots x(4095)$ are given. Our goal is to compute the decoded string $y(0)y(1) \cdots y(4095)$ from these given data.

Let code-type(i) $(0 \leq i \leq m - 1)$ be a function returning *the code type* of the i-th word, SC, SI, LI, SRL, or LRL. It also returns NULL if the i-th word is the 1-byte word of a LI/LRL code. Also, let code-length(i) be a function returning *the code length*, or the number of characters corresponding to the code. Let $w'(i) = w(i) + 1$ denote the number of bytes in word i. Since the i-th word $(0 \leq i \leq m - 1)$ is $b(\hat{w'}(i - 1))$ if 1-byte and $b(\hat{w'}(i - 1))b(\hat{w'}(i - 1) + 1)$ if 2-byte, these functions can be computed in $O(1)$ time after the prefix-sums $\hat{w}'$ of w' are computed. Our parallel LLL decompression can be done in two stages using these functions. Let $c(i) = \text{code} - \text{length}(i)$ be the code length of the i-th word. Clearly, $c(i)$ characters must be written from $y(\hat{c}(i{-}1))$. If it is a run-length code, a run with $c(i)$ characters is written. If it is an interval code, $c(i)$ characters from $x(t(i))$ are read and written. Stage 1 computes the values of $t(i)$ (*read offset*), $\hat{c}(i-1)$ (*write offset*), and $c(i)$ (*code length*) for all i ($0 \le i \le m-1$). Stage 2 performs reading/writing operations using the values to decode all codes. The details are spelled out as follows:

[Parallel LLL decompression algorithm]
// Stage 1: Compute $t(i)$, $c(i)$, and $\hat{c}(i)$.
Compute the prefix-sums $\hat{w}'(0)\hat{w}'(1)\cdots\hat{w}'(m-2)$ in parallel;
for $i \leftarrow 0$ to $m-1$ do in parallel
   if($w(i) = 1$) // 2-byte word
      ($t(i), l(i)$) $\leftarrow$ the offset and the length fields of $b(\hat{w}'(i-1))b(\hat{w}'(i-1)+1)$
   $c(i) \leftarrow$ code-length(i);
Compute the prefix-sums $\hat{c}(0)\hat{c}(1)\cdots\hat{c}(m-2)$ in parallel;
// Stage 2: Write the decoded string using the values of $t(i)$, $c(i)$, and $\hat{c}(i)$.
for $i \leftarrow 0$ to $m-1$ do in parallel
   if(code-type(i)=SC) $y(\hat{c}(i-1)) \leftarrow b(\hat{w}'(i-1))$;
   else if(code-type(i)=LI or SI)
      for $j \leftarrow 0$ to $c(i) - 1$ do $y(\hat{c}(i-1) + j) \leftarrow x(t(i) + j)$;
for $i \leftarrow 0$ to $m-1$ do in parallel
   if(code-type(i)=LRL or SRL)
      for $j \leftarrow 0$ to $c(i) - 1$ do $y(\hat{c}(i-1) + j) \leftarrow y(\hat{c}(i-1) - 1)$;

We will show theoretical analysis of parallel LLL decompression algorithm. We use the CREW-PRAM (Concurrent Read and Exclusive Write-Parallel Random Access Machine), a standard theoretical model of a parallel machine with a number of processors and the shared memory [4]. Let n and k be the size of a segment and the maximum length of codes, respectively. The prefix-sums of $m-1$ numbers can be computed in $O(\log m)$ time using $\frac{m}{\log m}$ processors on the CREW-PRAM [4]. Also both code-type(i) and code-length(i) for any i can be computed in $O(1)$ time using a single processor. Thus, Stage 1 can be completed in $O(\log m)$ time using $\frac{m}{\log m}$ processors. Suppose that we use m processor and each processor i ($0 \le i \le m-1$) is used to decode a code for the i-th word in Stage 2. Clearly, each processor runs at most $O(k)$ time. Also, since n characters are output, the total work of Stage 2 is $O(n)$. If we use $\frac{m}{\log m}$ processors each of which simulates $\log m$ processors, Stage 2 runs $O(k \log m)$ time and $O(n)$ work. Thus, we have,

Theorem 2. *Parallel LLL decompression algorithm runs in $O(k \log m)$ time and $O(n)$ work using $\frac{m}{\log m}$ processors on the CREW-PRAM.*

At least $\Omega(n)$ work is necessary, this parallel LLL decompression algorithm is work optimal.

4   GPU Implementation of LLL Decompression

This section shows an efficient GPU implementation of parallel LLL decompression algorithm. We assume that a compressed file is stored in the global memory of the GPU. Our goal is to write decompressed data in the global memory. Each CUDA block is assigned to a compressed strip to decode it.

4.1   LLL Decompression on the GPU

We assume that a compressed file is stored in the global memory of the GPU. Our GPU implementation decompresses it and the resulting decoded string of characters is written in the global memory. We use CUDA blocks with 128 threads each. Each CUDA block is assigned a compressed strip to decode it. Thus, the number of CUDA blocks is equal to the number of strip. We will show how a CUDA block decodes an assigned compressed strip.

A CUDA block repeats decompression of 256 words of the compressed segment. It uses the shared memory in a streaming multiprocessor as follows:

Read offsets (512 bytes): an array to store the values of 256 $t(i)$'s
Write offsets (514 bytes): an array to store the values of 257 $\hat{c}(i)$'s
Work space (6 bytes): three short integers used for prefix-sums computation
Current segment (4096 bytes): an array to store decoded characters of a
   segment with 4096 characters
Previous segment (4096 bytes): an array to store decoded characters of the
   previous segment with 4096 characters

Basically, the parallel LLL decompression algorithm is used for this decompression. Stage 1 computes read offsets and write offsets, and write them in the shared memory. Since the length can be computed from write offsets by formula $c(i) = \hat{c}(i) - \hat{c}(i-1)$, it is not necessary to write the code lengths in the shared memory. Note that, 257 values of $\hat{c}(i)$'s are necessary for computing 256 $c(i)$'s and thus we use 514 bytes for the write offsets. Stage 2 writes out decoded characters to the current segment using read and write offsets and the previous segment. If the computation of the current segment is completed, they are written out in the global memory.

We will show the details of Stage 1. We focus on the k-th $(k \geq 1)$ iteration of 256-word decompression and assume the previous segment have been already computed. A CUDA block reads 256 word identifiers $w(256k), w(256k + 1), \ldots, w(256k + 255)$ in the global memory and computes the prefix-sums $w'(256k), \hat{w}'(256k+1), \ldots, \hat{w}'(256k+255)$ by the prefix-sums computation [5] on the shared memory. By the values of the prefix-sums, it reads words in the word array and determine code-type(i), code-length(i)($= c(i)$), and read offset $t(i)$ for all i $(256k \leq i \leq 256k + 255)$. The prefix-sums $\hat{c}$ of c are computed on the shared memory, and write offsets $\hat{c}(256k - 1), \hat{c}(256k), \ldots \hat{c}(256k + 255)$ are written in the shared memory. Also, read offsets $t(256k), t(256k + 1), \ldots, t(256k + 255)$ are written in the shared memory.

We should note that we have optimized the prefix-sums computation for w's and c's using the fact that these numbers are 16-bit unsigned short integers. The idea is to store two 16-bit unsigned short integers in one unsigned 32-bit integer and compute the sum of two pairs of 16-bit integers by one addition for 32-bit integers.

Since read offsets and write offsets are stored in the shared memory, we can execute Stage 2, which writes out decoded characters in the global memory. We use one thread assigned to a word writes out decoded characters if the code is SC, SRL, or SI. If the code is LRL or LI, then the code consists of two words and two threads are assigned. Thus, two threads are used to writes out decoded characters for LRL and LI codes in the current segment of the shared memory. Each of them writes out a half of decoded characters of the LRL/LI codes. If all 256 words are in the same segment, a CUDA block writes out all decoded characters for the 256 words. If they are separated into two or more segments, we need to perform this writing operation for each segment in turn. If all words of a segment are obtained in the current segment of the shared memory, they are written in the global memory. The pointers for the heads of the current segment and the previous segment are swapped to avoid copy operation between the current segment and the previous segment.

Let us evaluate the occupancy of a streaming multiprocessor in GeForce GTX 1080, which has 96K-byte shared memory, 64K 32-bit registers, 2048 resident threads, and 32 resident CUDA blocks. Since a CUDA block uses 9224 bytes in the shared memory, it can have up to $\lfloor \frac{98304}{9224} \rfloor = 10$ CUDA blocks from the shared memory capacity. From the compiler report, each thread uses 41 32-bit registers. Hence, $41 \times 128 \times 10 = 52480$ 32-bit registers are sufficient to arrange 10 CUDA blocks in a streaming multiprocessor at the same time, and the occupancy is $\frac{1280}{2048} = 62.5\%$, which is reasonably high to maximize the memory access throughput.

5   Experimental Results

We have used GeForce GTX 1080 GPU and Core i7-4790(3.6GHz) CPU to evaluate the performance. GeForce GTX 1080 has 20 streaming multiprocessor with 128 cores each. We have used five gray scale images to evaluate the performance. Three of them shown in Fig. 3 are converted from JIS X 9204-2004 standard color image data of size 4096×3072. We also use two gray scale images, Random and Black with the same size. Each pixel value of Random is selected from the range $[0, 255]$ independently at random. Every pixel in Black takes value 0.

Each strip has 64k pixels for LLL and LZW compressions. Thus, each image has 192 strips and 192 CUDA blocks are invoked for decompression. LLL and LZW compression uses CUDA blocks with 128 and 1024 threads each, respectively. To maximize the performance of LZSS, the number of strips must be larger. Hence, we partition each image into 3072 strips for LZSS. Also, 48 CUDA blocks with 64 threads are invoked for LZSS decompression. Further, we use 7-bit offset and 7-bit length for LZSS, because CULZSS [13] also uses these parameters.

Crafts   Flowers   Graph

Fig. 3. Gray scale images with 4096×3072 pixels used for experiments

Table 2 shows the compression ratios for the five images. The size of compressed image of Random is larger than the original, and that of Black is very small. We can see that the compression ratios obtained by LZW and LLL are almost the same. Those by LZSS are slightly worse than the others.

Table 2. Compression ratios for five images using three compression methods

Images	Crafts	Flowers	Graph	Random	Black
LZSS	84.7%	80.3%	6.78%	111%	1.81%
LZW	78.3%	63.9%	3.22%	137%	0.643%
LLL	77.5%	65.9%	4.54%	112%	1.21%

Table 3 shows the running time of three decompression methods on the CPU and the GPU. The running time on the CPU are not so different. On the other hand, the LLL decompression on the GPU attains higher acceleration ratio and runs faster than the other decompression methods. Actually, LLL decompression is 2.49–9.13 times faster than LZW decompression and 4.30–14.1 times faster that LZSS decompression.

Table 4 shows the SSD-GPU loading time, which is the time necessary to load uncompressed data in the global memory of the GPU from the SSD. We have evaluated the SSD-GPU loading time for the following three scenarios:

Scenario A: Uncompressed data in the SSD is transferred to the global memory of the GPU through the CPU.

Scenario B: LLL-compressed data is transferred to the CPU, it is decompressed using the CPU, and then the resulting decompressed data is copied to the global memory of the GPU.

Scenario C: LLL-compressed data is transferred to the GPU, and decompression is performed by the GPU.

Since all images have the same size, the SSD-GPU loading times for Scenario A are almost the same. In Scenario B, the time for CPU decompression dominates

Table 3. The running time for decompression on the CPU and on the GPU in milliseconds and the speed-up ratios

Images		Crafts	Flowers	Graph	Random	Black
LZSS	CPU	53.0	35.9	22.2	61.5	19.1
	GPU	3.00	2.98	1.67	3.19	1.90
Speed-up	GPU/CPU	17.6	12.1	13.3	19.3	10.1
LZW	CPU	63.1	52.1	26.0	76.9	27.1
	GPU	1.81	0.912	1.09	2.00	1.23
Speed-up	GPU/CPU	34.8	57.1	23.9	38.5	22
LLL	CPU	56.7	40.6	28.3	67.6	23.8
	GPU	0.521	0.366	0.284	0.741	0.135
Speed-up	GPU/CPU	109	111	99.8	91.1	176
Speed-up	LLL/LZSS	5.76	8.14	5.88	4.30	14.1
	LLL/LZW	3.48	2.49	3.84	2.70	9.13

Table 4. The SSD-GPU loading time in milliseconds using LLL decompression for three scenarios

Images		Crafts	Flowers	Graph	Random	Black
Scenario A	SSD→CPU	6.38	6.39	6.38	6.39	6.39
	CPU→GPU	3.84	3.85	3.84	3.85	3.91
	Total	10.2	10.2	10.2	10.2	10.3
Scenario B	SSD→CPU	4.92	4.19	0.290	7.06	0.152
	CPU decompression	56.8	40.7	28.1	67.2	23.6
	CPU→GPU	3.83	3.87	3.81	3.82	3.93
	Total	65.5	48.7	32.2	78.1	27.7
Scenario C	SSD→CPU	4.92	4.18	0.289	6.99	0.150
	CPU→GPU	2.95	2.53	0.174	4.25	0.149
	GPU decompression	0.520	0.366	0.284	0.741	0.135
	Total	8.40	7.08	0.748	12.0	0.434

data transfer time. Hence, it makes no sense to use CPU decompression to load data in the GPU. The total time of Scenario C is smaller than that of Scenario A except Random image, in which the compressed data is larger than the original image. Hence, it makes sense to use GPU decompression to load data, even if the storage capacity is so large that all uncompressed data can be stored.

6   Conclusion

In this paper, we have presented a new data compression method called LLL (Light Loss-Less) compression. Although the compression ratio is comparable, the LLL decompression on the GPU is much faster than previously published LZW decompression and LZSS decompression. We also provided the SSD-GPU loading time using LLL decompression, which shows that our GPU LLL decompression can be useful for many applications.

References

1. Adobe Developers Association: TIFF Revision 6.0, http://partners.adobe.com/public/developer/en/tiff/TIFF6.pdf
2. Funasaka, S., Nakano, K., Ito, Y.: Fast LZW compression using a GPU. In: Proceedings of International Symposium on Computing and Networking, pp. 303–308, December 2015
3. Funasaka, S., Nakano, K., Ito, Y.: A parallel algorithm for LZW decompression, with GPU implementation. In: Wyrzykowski, R., Deelman, E., Dongarra, J., Karczewski, K., Kitowski, J., Wiatr, K. (eds.) PPAM 2015. LNCS, vol. 9573, pp. 228–237. Springer, Heidelberg (2016). doi:10.1007/978-3-319-32149-3_22
4. Gibbons, A., Rytter, W.: Efficient Parallel Algorithms. Cambridge University Press, Cambridge (1988)
5. Harris, M., Sengupta, S., Owens, J.D.: Chapter 39. Parallel prefix sum (scan) with CUDA. In: GPU Gems 3. Addison-Wesley (2007)
6. Hwu, W.W.: GPU Computing Gems Emerald Edition. Morgan Kaufmann (2011)
7. Kasagi, A., Nakano, K., Ito, Y.: Parallel algorithms for the summed area table on the asynchronous hierarchical memory machine, with GPU implementations. In: Proceedings of International Conference on Parallel Processing (ICPP), pp. 251–250, September 2014
8. Klein, S.T., Wiseman, Y.: Parallel lempel ziv coding. Discrete Appl. Math. **146**, 180–191 (2005)
9. Lok, U.W., Fan, G.W., Li, P.C.: Lossless compression with parallel decoder for improving performance of a GPU-based beamformer. In: Proceedings of International Ultrasonics Symposium, pp. 561–564, July 2014
10. Man, D., Uda, K., Ueyama, H., Ito, Y., Nakano, K.: Implementations of a parallel algorithm for computing Euclidean distance map in multicore processors and GPUs. Int. J. Netw. Comput. **1**(2), 260–276 (2011)
11. Nishida, K., Ito, Y., Nakano, K.: Accelerating the dynamic programming for the matrix chain product on the GPU. In: Proceedings of International Conference on Networking and Computing, pp. 320–326, December 2011
12. Corporation, N.: NVIDIA CUDA C programming guide version 7.0., March 2015
13. Ozsoy, A., Swany, M.: Culzss: Lzss lossless data compression on cuda. In: Proceedings of International Conference on Cluster Computing, pp. 403–41, September 2011
14. Patel, R.A., Zhang, Y., Mak, J., Davidson, A.: Parallel lossless data compression on the GPU. In: Proceedings of Innovative Parallel Computing (InPar), pp. 1–9, May 2012
15. Sayood, K.: Introduction to Data Compression, 4th edn. Morgan Kaufmann (2012)
16. Storer, J.A., Szymanski, T.G.: Data compression via textual substitution. J. ACM **29**(4), 928–951 (1982)
17. Welch, T.: High speed data compression and decompression apparatus and method. US patent 4558302, December 1985

Deterministic Construction of Regular Geometric Graphs with Short Average Distance and Limited Edge Length

Satoshi Fujita[1](✉), Koji Nakano[1], Michihiro Koibuchi[2], and Ikki Fujiwara[2]

[1] Department of Information Engineering, Hiroshima University,
Higashi-Hiroshima 739-8527, Japan
`fujita@se.hiroshima-u.ac.jp, nakano@cs.hiroshima-u.ac.jp`
[2] National Institute of Informatics, Tokyo 101-8430, Japan
`{koibuchi,ikki}@nii.ac.jp`

Abstract. This paper proposes a deterministic method to construct 5-regular geometric graphs with short average distance under the constraint such that the set of vertices is a subset of $\mathbb{N} \times \mathbb{N}$ and the length of each edge is at most 4. This problem is motivated by the design of efficient floor plan of parallel computers consisting of a number of computing nodes arranged on a two-dimensional array. In such systems, the degree of vertices is determined by the number of ports of the routers and the edge length is limited by a certain value determined by the cycle time. The goodness of the resulting geometric graph is evaluated by the average shortest path length (ASPL) between vertices which reflects the average communication delay between computing nodes. The idea of the proposed method is to arrange the basic component derived from $(3, g)$-cage in a two-dimensional manner and to connect adjacent components by parallel edges of length 4 each. The result of numerical calculations shows that the average distance in the resulting graph is close to the lower bound so that the gap to the lower bound is less than 0.98 when the number of vertices is 432000.

Keywords: Regular geometric graphs · Average shortest path length · Cage theory

1 Introduction

Graphs with geometric information are widely used in many fields, such as the layout of digital circuits [2], structural analysis of proteins [9], medical image analysis [17] and so on. In such **geometric graphs**, each vertex is associated with a point in an appropriate coordinate space and several designated pairs of vertices are connected by edges of a certain length. In this paper we assume that

This work was partially supported by MIC/SCOPE (152103004), JSPS KAKENHI (15K00144, 16H02807) and JST CREST.

the set of vertices is a subset of $\mathbb{N} \times \mathbb{N}$ and the **length** of each edge is the Manhattan distance between two end vertices. The other terms such as "distance" and "diameter" are used to represent the topological property of graphs; e.g., we say that the distance between two vertices is d if they are connected by a path consisting of d edges and it is the smallest among all such paths.

Consider a class of geometric graphs to have $\{(i,j) \mid 0 \leq i \leq N - 1 \text{ and } 0 \leq j \leq M - 1\}$ as the set of vertices and a set of edges of length at most L each. The diameter of such graphs is at least $\lceil (M + N - 2)/L \rceil$ since the sum of edge lengths on any path connecting upper left and lower right corners is at least $(N - 1) + (M - 1)$ and the length of each edge is at most L. Among such geometric graphs, we are interested in graphs such that the average shortest path length (ASPL, for short) in terms of the distance over all pairs of the vertices is as small as possible. The problem of constructing a geometric graph with small ASPL is motivated by the layout of modern parallel computing systems such as super-computers and network on chip. In such systems, each vertex can have a limited number of incident edges such as 8 and 16, and the transmission delay through edges significantly increases as the edge length increases. Since such a transmission delay dominates the clock time of the overall system, it is common to *bound* the length of each edge by a constant; e.g., it is bounded by 5 m in off-chip networks. See Appendix for the details about the restriction of the maximum degree and the maximum edge length in actual parallel computing systems. The performance of those systems is dominated by the ASPL of the underlying geometric graph since the message delay due to switching overhead is proportional to the number of vertices traversed by the message and the traffic pattern can generally be assumed to be random [8,12].

The above optimization problem is related to the order/degree problem which is the problem of finding a graph with minimum diameter for given number of vertices n and maximum degree r [15]. It is also related with the theory of cages since (r, g)-cage with diameter $\lfloor g/2 \rfloor$ attains the lower bound on the ASPL provided that the value of L is large enough (see Sect. 2 for the details). A graph is called r-**regular** if each vertex in the graph has exactly r neighbors. This paper proposes a deterministic method to construct a 5-regular graph with small ASPL for $L = 4$. The reader might wonder that why the authors consider a specific combination of parameters r and L in the current paper. Intuitively speaking, "five" is the smallest degree which allows a significant improvement of the ASPL compared with a two-dimensional mesh of maximum degree four. Similarly "four" is the shortest maximum edge length which allows a significant improvement of the ASPL compared with a regular mesh of edge length one. On the other hand, although the ASPL does not grow as r and/or L increase, it is known that for any given L, there exists a degree d_L such that the increase of the degree exceeding d_L does not improve the ASPL; namely there is a non-trivial relationship between r and L concerned with the improvement of the ASPL. Readers who are interested in this issue should refer to [16] for the details.

The basic idea of the proposed method is to arrange the basic component derived from $(3, g)$-cage in a two-dimensional manner and to connect adjacent components by parallel edges of length L each. As will be formally described in Sect. 2, $(3, g)$-cage is a graph with the smallest number of vertices among all 3-regular graphs with girth g. Thus, each vertex in the resulting geometric graph has (at least) three neighbors in the same component and has (at most) two neighbors in the adjacent components, so that the degree of every vertex is exactly 5. Such a deterministic construction of hierarchical geometric graphs has the following advantages compared with the randomized construction of geometric graphs with small ASPL [16]:

- The size of routing tables can be small due to the regularity of the resulting geometric graphs. In fact, a variant of XY routing does work. This issue will be discussed in Sect. 5 in more detail.
- Several important communication patterns such as broadcast and local communication with neighborhood in a two-dimensional array can be efficiently realized. Such patterns frequently occur in many parallel algorithms.
- Due to the periodical structure, the cabling between computing nodes associated to the resulting geometric graph is easy to maintain compared with random graphs, where the task of maintenance includes the repair and the replacement of faulty nodes and cables.

The performance of the proposed method is numerically evaluated by comparing the ASPL of the resulting geometric graphs with a lower bound. The result of evaluations shows that the ASPL of the resulting graphs is larger than the lower bound by less than 0.98 even if the number of vertices in the graph is 432000. Although it is worse than random 5-regular graphs with $L = 4$ [16], the resulting ASPL is much smaller than trivial extensions of two-dimensional meshes in which pairs of vertices are connected by shortcut edges of length at most 4.

The remainder of the paper is organized as follows. Section 2 overviews related works. Section 3 describes the proposed method. Section 4 summarizes the result of numerical calculations of the ASPL and the lower bound. Section 5 describes the routing algorithm in the resulting geometric graphs. Finally Sect. 6 concludes the paper with future work.

2   Related Work

There are many works concerned with the graphs with small ASPL for $L \to \infty$. Let G be an r-regular graph consisting of n vertices and $\frac{n \times r}{2}$ edges, where in the following the number of vertices in G is called the **order** of G. For any vertex u in G, there are at most $r(r-1)^{i-1}$ vertices at distance $i \geq 1$ from u. Thus, an upper bound on the number of vertices within distance k from u is given as

$$n_{r,k} \stackrel{\text{def}}{=} 1 + r \sum_{i=0}^{k-1} (r-1)^i. \tag{1}$$

In other words, there is no r-regular graph with diameter k consisting of more than $n_{r,k}$ vertices. An r-regular graph is called a **Moore graph** if it has diameter k and with exactly $n_{r,k}$ vertices. It is known that there are at most three

Table 1. The order of known (r, g)-cages.

degree r	girth g									
	3	4	5	6	7	8	9	10	11	12
3	4	6	10	14	24	30	58	70	112	126
4	5	8	19	26	67	80				728
5	6	10	30	42		170				2730
6	7	12	40	62		312				7812
7	8	14	50	90						

Moore graphs with diameter $k \geq 2$ and degree $r \geq 3$ [6,10]; the first one is Peterson graph with diameter two and degree three; the second is Hoffman-Singleton graph with diameter two and degree seven; and the third is a graph with diameter two and degree 57, where the existence of the last graph is just conjectured but not yet explicitly constructed.

In this paper, we will focus on a special class of r-regular graphs to have small ASPL. An r-regular graph G is called an (r, g)-**cage** if it has as few vertices as possible among all r-regular graphs with girth g, where the **girth** of G is the size of shortest cycle in G. It is known that an (r, g)-graph exists for any combination of $r \geq 2$ and $g \geq 3$ [7] and that any Moore graph with degree r and girth g is an (r, g)-cage. Table 1 summarizes the order of known (r, g)-cages, where the column of "$g = 3$" corresponds to complete graph K_{r+1} and the column of "$g = 4$" corresponds to complete bipartite graph $K_{r,r}$. Two known Moore graphs are also listed in the table; i.e., Peterson graph is a $(3, 5)$-cage and Hoffman-Singleton graph is a $(7, 5)$-cage.

Let $k_{n,r}$ be the smallest k' such that $n \leq n_{r,k'}$. Note that $k_{n,r}$ denotes a lower bound on the diameter of r-regular graphs of order n. In the following, we say that an r-regular graph G of order n is **Moore-like** if

- the diameter of G is $k_{n,r}$ and
- the number of vertices at distance i from vertex u is exactly $r(r - 1)^{i-1}$ for any u in G and for any $1 \leq i < k_{n,r}$.

Any Moore-like graph tightly attains the lower bound on the ASPL [4]. (r, g)-cage with diameter $\lfloor g/2 \rfloor$ is a representative of such graphs. Here the reader should notice that *not every (r, g)-cage has diameter $\lfloor g/2 \rfloor$*; in fact, the order of $(3, 9)$-cage is 58 (see Table 1 again) which exceeds the upper bound on the number of vertices of 3-regular graphs with diameter 4. It is known that the girth of such special (r, g)-cages to have diameter $\lfloor g/2 \rfloor$ must be either 5, 6, 8 or 12 except for trivial graphs such as K_{r+1}, $K_{r,r}$ and cycles [15]. Concrete examples of such cages include Heawood graph and Tutte-Coxeter graph, where the former is a $(3, 6)$-cage with diameter 3 consisting of $14 (= 1 + 3 + 6 + 4)$ vertices and the latter is a $(3, 8)$-cage with diameter 4 consisting of 30 $(= 1 + 3 + 6 + 12 + 8)$ vertices. Note that those two graphs are Moore-like and tightly attain the lower bound on the ASPL.

The problem of minimizing the ASPL of r-regular graphs for designated L has recently attracted considerable attention [3, 11, 18, 19, 22]. For example, Nakano *et al.* proposed a heuristic scheme based on the randomization and local search, which proceeds as follows [16]: (1) Generate an initial r-regular grid graph $G^{(0)}$ consisting of $N \times M$ vertices; (2) Repeatedly apply random 2-toggle operation to $G^{(0)}$ to generate a random r-regular graph $G^{(1)}$; and (3) Repeatedly apply random 2-opt operation to $G^{(1)}$ to reduce the ASPL of the resulting graph as much as possible, where all graphs generated during the execution of the scheme satisfy the constraint on the edge length L. Numerical calculations indicate that the ASPL of the resulting geometric graph is very close to the lower bound for a wide range of parameters r and L, while it is difficult to converge to a quasi-optimal solution within a reasonable computing time for large N and M. In addition, as an interconnection network of parallel computers, it has a flaw such that the size of routing tables becomes large since the topology of the resulting geometric graph is highly irregular. Such flaws of the Nakano's scheme is overcome by the proposed method with a slight degradation of the ASPL, as will be described later.

3   Proposed Method

3.1   Overview

In this paper we propose a deterministic method to construct a collection of geometric graphs for parameters $r = 5$ and $L = 4$. Each geometric graph constructed by the method is a two-dimensional array of basic components connected by parallel edges. As will be described later, we will use a geometric graph associated with a variant of $(3, g)$-cages as the basic component.

Let A be the collection of basic components in the resulting geometric graph and let $A[x, y]$ denote the component located at the xth column and the yth row. Each component has two local variables V and E which represent the set of vertices and the set of edges within the component, respectively. Variable V takes the same value for all components, but variable E takes different values depending on the number of neighboring components which is either two, three or four. More specifically, a component is called **standard** if it has four neighbors (i.e., top, bottom, left and right), called **border** if it has three neighbors (e.g., top, bottom and left) and called **corner** if it has two neighbors (e.g., top and left). The value of variable E for border and corner components is obtained by adding several edges to the variable E of standard component. Thus in the following explanation, we first describe the set of edges E for standard components and then explain how to modify it for border and corner components.

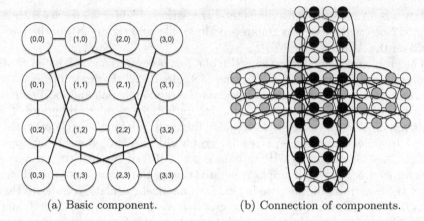

(a) Basic component.   (b) Connection of components.

Fig. 1. Basic component in the first method, where in (b), green vertices with even parity have horizontal connections and yellow vertices with odd parity have vertical connections. (Color figure online)

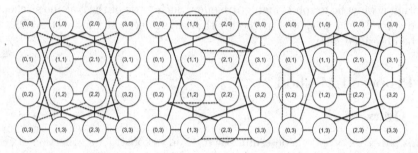

Fig. 2. Corner and border components used in the first method (dashed lines indicate edges augmented to the standard component).

3.2   First Method

In the first method, we adopt a variant of the Heawood graph as the topology of the basic component which is known as the Möbius-Kantor graph in the literature. At first, the set of vertices V is determined as

$$V := \{v_{i,j} \mid 0 \le i \le 3 \text{ and } 0 \le j \le 3\},$$

where for each i and j, vertex $v_{i,j}$ is located at point (i, j) in the Cartesian coordinate plane. Recall that the length of shortest edge connecting vertices $v_{i,j}$ and $v_{i',j'}$ is $|i - i'| + |j - j'|$. Next, in each standard component, vertices in V are connected by the set of edges E in the following manner:

$$E := E_{chord} \cup E_{cycle}$$

where $E_{chord} := \{\{v_{j,0}, v_{j,1}\}, \{v_{j,2}, v_{j,3}\} \mid 0 \le j \le 3\}$ and

$$E_{cycle} := \{\{v_{0,0}, v_{1,2}\}, \{v_{1,2}, v_{2,2}\}, \{v_{2,2}, v_{3,0}\}, \{v_{3,0}, v_{2,0}\},$$
$$\{v_{2,0}, v_{0,1}\}, \{v_{0,1}, v_{0,2}\}, \{v_{0,2}, v_{2,3}\}, \{v_{2,3}, v_{3,3}\},$$
$$\{v_{3,3}, v_{2,1}\}, \{v_{2,1}, v_{1,1}\}, \{v_{1,1}, v_{0,3}\}, \{v_{0,3}, v_{1,3}\},$$
$$\{v_{1,3}, v_{3,2}\}, \{v_{3,2}, v_{3,1}\}, \{v_{3,1}, v_{1,0}\}, \{v_{1,0}, v_{0,0}\}\}.$$

See Fig. 1(a) for illustration, where edges connecting two vertices are illustrated as line segments to simplify the exposition. Recall that in actual layout of parallel computers including super-computers and NoC, each edge connecting two vertices is realized by a *sequence of line segments* parallel to horizontal or vertical axis and this is why we measure the length of each edge by the Manhattan distance between two end vertices. In the resulting geometric graph, the length of each edge is at most three (e.g., the length of edge connecting $(0,0)$ and $(1,2)$ is $3 = 1 + 2$) and any two vertices in V are connected by a path consisting of at most four edges; i.e., it has diameter four (note that this is greater than the diameter of the Heawood graph by one). In addition, the girth of the component is six which is the same as the girth of the Heawood graph.

Consider a two-dimensional array of such basic components. We denote vertex $v_{i,j}$ in component $A[x, y]$ as $A[x, y].v_{i,j}$, and locate it at point $(4x+i, 4y+j)$ in the coordinate plane. In the proposed method, each vertex in a component is connected with a vertex in an adjacent component by an edge of length $L (= 4)$ in the following manner:

– If the parity of $i + j$ is even, then vertex $A[x, y].v_{i,j}$ is connected with vertices $A[x - 1, y].v_{i,j}$ and $A[x + 1, y].v_{i,j}$, and
– If the parity of $i + j$ is odd, then vertex $A[x, y].v_{i,j}$ is connected with vertices $A[x, y - 1].v_{i,j}$ and $A[x, y + 1].v_{i,j}$,

where some adjacent vertices might not exist for boarder and corner components. See Fig. 1(b) for illustration.

The goodness of the above construction in terms of ASPL can be verified as follows. For simplicity, assume that there are infinitely many basic components arranged in the coordinate plane. Let u be a vertex in the (infinite) geometric graph and let $f(i)$ denote the number of vertices at distance i from u. Then, by a simple counting, we can show that $f(i + 1) - f(i) = 64$ holds for any $i \ge 5$. On the other hand, in the same coordinate plane, the number of vertices which can be reached through i edges of length $L = 4$ is 40 $(= 4 \times (1 + 2 + 3 + 4))$ for $i = 1$ and $64i - 24$ for any $i \ge 2$. In other words, even in an ideal graph, the number of vertices at distance $i + 1$ is larger than the number of vertices at distance i in the constructed graph by exactly 64. This observation implies that in the resulting graph, the number of vertices within a designated distance from u increases almost ideally except for the neighborhood of vertex u at distance 5 or less. A more detailed numerical evaluation will be given in Sect. 4.

In the above construction, each vertex in a corner component has only four neighbors. Similarly a half of vertices in a border component have four neighbors.

To reduce the ASPL of the graph as much as possible, for example, we can define the local variable E of corner and border components as in Fig. 2.

3.3 Second Method

In the second method, we adopt the Tutte-Coxeter graph as the topology of the basic component. At first, the set of vertices V is determined as

$$V := \{v_{i,j} \mid 0 \leq i \leq 4 \text{ and } 0 \leq j \leq 5\},$$

where for each i and j, vertex $v_{i,j}$ is located at point (i,j) in the Cartesian coordinate plane. Next, in each standard component, vertices in V are connected by the set of edges E in the following manner:

$$E := E_{chord} \cup E_{cycle}$$

where

$$
\begin{aligned}
E_{chord} := \{&\{v_{0,0}, v_{3,0}\}, \{v_{1,0}, v_{3,1}\}, \{v_{2,0}, v_{0,1}\}, \{v_{4,0}, v_{2,1}\}, \{v_{1,1}, v_{1,2}\},\\
&\{v_{4,1}, v_{4,4}\}, \{v_{0,2}, v_{0,3}\}, \{v_{2,2}, v_{4,3}\}, \{v_{3,2}, v_{3,3}\}, \{v_{4,2}, v_{2,3}\},\\
&\{v_{1,3}, v_{1,4}\}, \{v_{0,4}, v_{2,5}\}, \{v_{2,4}, v_{4,5}\}, \{v_{3,4}, v_{1,5}\}, \{v_{0,5}, v_{3,5}\}\}, \text{ and}
\end{aligned}
$$

$$
\begin{aligned}
E_{cycle} := \{&\{v_{0,0}, v_{0,3}\}, \{v_{0,3}, v_{1,5}\}, \{v_{1,5}, v_{2,5}\}, \{v_{2,5}, v_{4,4}\}, \{v_{4,4}, v_{4,5}\},\\
&\{v_{4,5}, v_{3,5}\}, \{v_{3,5}, v_{4,3}\}, \{v_{4,3}, v_{4,2}\}, \{v_{4,2}, v_{3,0}\}, \{v_{3,0}, v_{4,0}\},\\
&\{v_{4,0}, v_{4,1}\}, \{v_{4,1}, v_{2,0}\}, \{v_{2,0}, v_{1,0}\}, \{v_{1,0}, v_{0,2}\}, \{v_{0,2}, v_{0,5}\},\\
&\{v_{0,5}, v_{1,3}\}, \{v_{1,3}, v_{2,1}\}, \{v_{2,1}, v_{3,3}\}, \{v_{3,3}, v_{3,4}\}, \{v_{3,4}, v_{2,2}\},\\
&\{v_{2,2}, v_{0,1}\}, \{v_{0,1}, v_{1,1}\}, \{v_{1,1}, v_{1,4}\}, \{v_{1,4}, v_{0,4}\}, \{v_{0,4}, v_{2,3}\},\\
&\{v_{2,3}, v_{3,1}\}, \{v_{3,1}, v_{3,2}\}, \{v_{3,2}, v_{2,4}\}, \{v_{2,4}, v_{1,2}\}, \{v_{1,2}, v_{0,0}\}\}.
\end{aligned}
$$

See Fig. 3 for illustration. In the resulting geometric graph, the length of each edge is at most three ($\leq L$). In addition, it has diameter four and girth eight since it has the same topology with the Tutte-Coxeter graph.

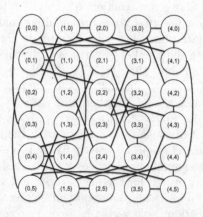

Fig. 3. Basic component used in the second method.

Table 2. Lower bound on the ASPL within designated distance i^*.

i^*	1	2	3	4	5	6	7	8	9	10
α ($L = 4$)	1.000	1.717	2.406	3.084	3.759	4.430	5.101	5.770	6.439	7.108
γ ($L = 4$ & $r = 5$)	1.000	1.769	2.698	3.676	4.329	4.830	5.396	5.998	6.620	7.254
γ ($L = 4$ & $r = 4$)	1.000	1.706	2.585	3.534	4.513	5.400	5.817	6.321	6.876	7.463
γ ($L = 4$ & $r = 3$)	1.000	1.600	2.364	3.217	4.128	5.074	6.042	7.023	8.013	9.007
α ($L = 5$)	1.000	1.724	2.414	3.093	3.767	4.439	5.109	5.779	6.448	7.116
γ ($L = 5$ & $r = 5$)	1.000	1.769	2.698	3.676	4.566	4.998	5.522	6.096	6.699	7.320
γ ($L = 5$ & $r = 4$)	1.000	1.706	2.585	3.534	4.513	5.505	6.136	6.568	7.073	7.624

Copies of such basic component are arranged in the two-dimensional plane and are connected by parallel edges similar to the first method; i.e., vertex located at (i, j) is connected with vertices located at $(i - 4, j)$ and $(i + 4, j)$ if the parity of $i + j$ is even and is connected with vertices located at $(i, j - 4)$ and $(i, j + 4)$ if the parity of $i + j$ is odd.

3.4   Lower Bound

Let u be a vertex located at a point in a coordinate plane. This subsection derives a sharp lower bound on the average distance from u through edges of length L in r-regular graphs. If we omit the constraint on the degree of the vertices, the number of vertices within distance i from u is at most

$$\alpha(i) \stackrel{\text{def}}{=} 2(L^2 \times i^2 + L \times i) + 1 \tag{2}$$

since it coincides with the number of vertices within Manhattan distance $L \times i$ from u. On the other hand, if we omit the constraint on the edge length, the number of such vertices in r-regular graphs is at most

$$\beta(i) \stackrel{\text{def}}{=} 1 + r \sum_{j=0}^{i-1} (r - 1)^j \; = \; 1 + r \frac{(r - 1)^i - 1}{r - 2}. \tag{3}$$

Let $\gamma(i) \stackrel{\text{def}}{=} \min\{\alpha(i), \beta(i)\}$. Note that $\gamma(i)$ equals to $\beta(i)$ for small i's while $\gamma(i)$ equals to $\alpha(i)$ for large i's. Let i^* be a positive integer. If we use γ as an upper bound on the number of vertices, the average number of vertices within distance i^* from u (including u) is at least

$$\frac{\sum_{j=1}^{i^*} j(\gamma(j) - \gamma(j - 1))}{\gamma(i^*)}$$

which is sharper than the lower bound derived from α particularly when i^* is large. Table 2 compares lower bounds derived from α and γ, respectively, for several combinations of L and r. We can find that by using γ instead of α, we have a sharper lower bound on the ASPL than the bound derived by using α.

4   Numerical Analysis

We conducted numerical calculation to evaluate the ASPL of the resulting graphs. Figure 4 compares the ASPL of the first method with the lower bound derived in Sect. 3.4. The horizontal axis is the number of basic components per side (e.g., the order of the resulting graph is 20×20 when the number of components per side is five), and green, blue and red lines indicate diameter, lower bound and ASPL of the first method, respectively. We can observe that ASPL of the first method increases almost linearly and is slightly larger than the lower bound. In fact, the gap to the lower bound is less than 1.85 when the number of vertices is 16384, which gradually increases to 1.87 when the number of vertices becomes 230400. A similar phenomenon can be found for the second method in a stronger sense. Figure 5 illustrates ASPL of the second method, where we can find that the gap to the lower bound reduces to less than 0.98 when the number of vertices is 432000 (note that the basic component used in the second method is larger than the component used in the first method). Although we cannot directly compare the first and the second methods since the number of vertices takes different values for each method, the above results indicate that we can reduce the ASPL of the overall graph by using a graph with larger girth as the basic component.

The superiority of the second method can be verified by counting the number of vertices at distance i from a designated vertex and by comparing the resulting distance distributions with an ideal distribution. Figure 6 illustrates such a distribution for $1 \leq i \leq 15$, where two proposed methods are indicated by

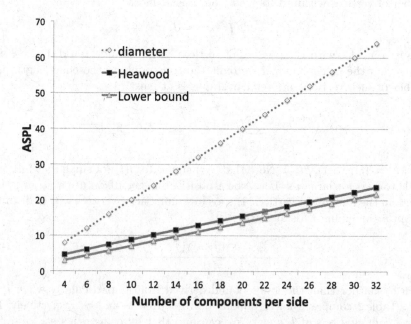

Fig. 4. ASPL of the first method. (Color figure online)

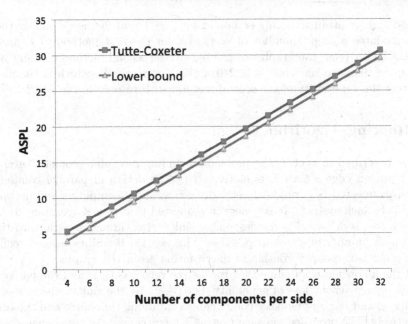

Fig. 5. ASPL of the second method.

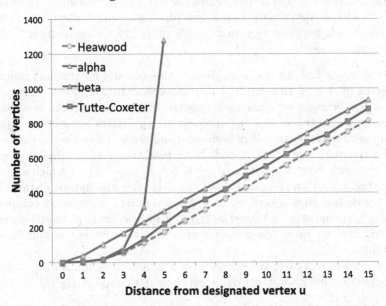

Fig. 6. The number of vertices from a designated vertex. (Color figure online)

dashed and solid orange lines, respectively. An ideal distribution is the minimum of functions α and β introduced in Sect. 3.4, which are indicated by blue and green lines, respectively. The result of counting indicates that although the first method tightly attains the upper bound for $i = 1$ and 2, the second method accommodates a larger number of vertices than the first method at distance three or larger (e.g., the graph constructed by the second method contains 308 vertices at distance six while it is 240 in the first method), which is the main reason of the superiority of the second method with respect to the ASPL.

5   Routing Algorithm

As was described in Sect. 1, the problem of finding r-regular geometric graphs with bounded edge length L is motivated by the design of parallel computer systems connected by a physical network such as super-computers and network on chip. In such systems, it is generally requested that a message given to the source vertex is delivered to the designated sink vertex through a path consisting of as small number of edges as possible. This section describes how to realize such an efficient message routing in the resulting geometric graphs.

In the following, we assume that the source vertex is (i, j) and the parity of $i + j$ is even, without loss of generality. Let (i', j') be the sink of the message. Let $A[x, y]$ and $A[x', y']$ be basic components containing the source and the sink, respectively. The proposed message routing scheme consists of three phases; i.e., (1) routing within $A[x, y]$; (2) routing from $A[x, y]$ to $A[x', y']$; and (3) routing to sink (i', j') within $A[x', y']$, where the first phase is skipped when $x \neq x'$. More concretely, a message given to vertex (i, j) is routed to the destination (i', j') in the following manner:

When $x \neq x'$: At first, the message given to the source is *horizontally* routed to a vertex in $A[x', y]$ through $|x - x'|$ edges connecting adjacent components, *turns left or right* by traversing an edge within $A[x', y]$, and is *vertically* routed to a vertex in $A[x', y']$ through $|y - y'|$ edges connecting adjacent components, where the role of horizontal and vertical directions is exchanged when the parity of $i + j$ is odd. Note that the number of edges on the delivery path from $A[x, y]$ to $A[x', y']$ is $|x - x'| + |y - y'| + 1$ which is greater than the trivial lower bound determined by the Manhattan distance and the maximum edge length by one. After reaching destination component $A[x', y']$, the message is routed to the sink by traversing at most four edges within $A[x', y']$ since the diameter of a basic component is four in both methods.

When $x = x'$: In this case, we may spend one more step within $A[x, y]$ to change the direction before starting the delivery to $A[x', y'](= A[x, y'])$.

In summary we have the following remark concerned with the performance of the proposed routing scheme.

Remark 1. Let $q(s, t)$ be the number of edges on the resulting path from s to t. Then, $q(s, t)$ is greater than the lower bound derived from L and the Manhattan distance between s and t by at most five.

6   Concluding Remarks

This paper proposes a scheme to construct 5-regular geometric graphs with small ASPL and with a limited edge length four. The idea of the proposed scheme is to arrange the basic component derived from $(3, g)$-cage in a two-dimensional manner and to connect those components by parallel edges of length four each. The result of numerical calculations indicates that the proposed method attains small ASPL for a large number of vertices. For example, the gap to the lower bound on the ASPL is less than 0.98 for graphs consisting of 432000 vertices.

The result graph is applicable to the design of on-chip and off-chip low-latency interconnection networks of parallel computing systems which usually have a severe constraints on the edge length in the floor plan, as well described in Appendix. Our future work is to illustrate such an application that includes the performance evaluation by using an event-driven parallel program simulator [5, 21]. Another future work is to find the tight bound on the ASPL for given r, L and N by refining the argument and the construction given in Sect. 3.

A   Application of the Result Graph to Off- and On-chip Interconnection Networks

Recent interconnection networks potentially have tight constraints on link length especially when conventional electric media is used. Short-cable design is still preferred in various interconnection networks, such as supercomputers [1, 20]. This constraint efficiently reduces power consumption of links, thus giving a significant impact on the design of interconnection networks. For example, when 40 Gbps passive electric cables whose length can be up to 7 m are used, the Mellanox IS5024 36-port InfiniBand switch saves the power consumption to 111.54 W, while active optical cables impose the same switch for 200.4 W [13, 14]. Since a supercomputer has a large number of cables (remind that the K computer has 200,000 cables reaching 1,000 km), the network design under cable geometric constraints becomes important for low-power interconnection network design.

The link length limitation is also a severe issue in on-chip interconnection network designs, especially with an advanced CMOS process technology. In general, a wire delay increases with the square of the wire length. Inserting repeater buffers on the wire can mitigate the wire delay, while it increases the energy consumption on the wire. Thus the longest wire length between on-chip routers should be carefully tuned under given design constraints, such as operating frequency, dimensions of cores, wire delay, and wire energy. However, it is most likely to be automatically determined by underlying regular topologies (e.g., 2-D mesh and torus). As an alternative to such regular topologies, a low-latency topology optimized for a given longest wire length parameter would become an attractive design option when the design constraints severely affect the cost and the performance.

The above fact motivates us to explore the use of short links in the off- and on-chip network topology design. This is just the application of the result graph in this study to such interconnection networks.

References

1. Ajima, Y., Sumimoto, S., Shimizu, T.: Tofu: a 6D Mesh/Torus interconnect for exascale computers. IEEE Comput. **42**(11), 36–40 (2009)
2. Battista, G.D., Eades, P., Tamassia, R., Tollis, I.G.: Algorithms for drawing graphs: an annotated bibliography. Comput. Geom. Theor. Appl. **4**(5), 235–282 (1994)
3. Besta, M., Hoefler, T.: Slim fly: a cost effective low-diameter network topology. In: SC 2014, pp. 348–359 (2014)
4. Cerf, V.G., Cowan, D.D., Mullin, R.C., Stanton, R.G.: A lower bound on the average shortest path length in regular graphs. Netw. **4**(4), 335–342 (1974)
5. Chaix, F., Koibuchi, M., Fujiwara, I.: Suitability of the random topology for HPC applications. In: Proceedings 24th Euromicro Int'l Conference on Parallel, Distributed, and Network-Based Processing (PDP 2016), pp. 301–304 (2016)
6. Damerell, R.M.: On Moore graphs. Proc. Cambridge Phil. Soc. **74**, 227–236 (1973)
7. Erdös, P., Sachs, H.: Reguläre graphen gegebener taillenweite mitminimaler knotenzahl. Wiss. Z. Uni. Halle (Math. Nat.) **12**, 251–257 (1963)
8. Fujiwara, I., Koibuchi, M., Matsutani, H., Casanova, H.: Swap-and-randomize: a method for building low-latency HPC interconnects. IEEE Trans. Parallel Distrib. Syst. **26**(7), 2051–2060 (2015)
9. Higham, D.J., Rasajski, M., Przulj, N.: Fitting a geometric graph to a protein-protein interaction network. Bioinform. **24**(8), 1093–1099 (2008)
10. Hoffman, A.J., Singleton, R.R.: On Moore graphs with diameter 2 and 3. IBM J. Res. Develop. **4**, 497–504 (1960)
11. Kim, J., Dally, W.J., Scott, S., Abts, D.: Technology-driven, highly-scalable Dragonfly topology. In: Proceedings of the 35th International Symposium on Computer Architecture (ISCA), pp. 77–88 (2008)
12. Koibuchi, M., Matsutani, H., Amano, H., Hsu, D.F., Casanova, H.: A case for random shortcut topologies for HPC interconnects. In: Proceedings of the 39th International Symposium on Computer Architecture (ISCA), pp. 177–188 (2012)
13. Mellanox Technologies. IS5024, Mellanox Technologies. http://www.mellanox.com/related-docs/user_manuals/IS5024_User_Manual.pdf
14. Mellanox Technologies. http://www.mellanox.com/page/cables
15. Miller, M., Širáň, J.: Moore graphs and beyond: a survey of the degree/diameter problem. Electron. J. Comb., No. DS14 (2005)
16. Nakano, K., Takafuji, D., Fujita, S., Matsutani, H., Fujiwara, I., Koibuchi, M.: Randomly optimized grid graph for low-latency interconnection networks. In: Proceedings International Conference on Parallel Processing (ICPP) (2016, to appear)
17. Pinheiro, M.A., Kybic, J.: Path descriptors for geometric graph matching and registration. In: Campilho, A., Kamel, M. (eds.) ICIAR 2014. LNCS, vol. 8814, pp. 3–11. Springer, Heidelberg (2014). doi:10.1007/978-3-319-11758-4_1
18. Hemmert, K.S., Vetter, J.S., Bergman, K., Das, C., Emami, A., Janssen, C., Panda, D.K., Stunkel, C., Underwood, K., Yalamanchili, S.: Report on institute for advanced architectures and algorithms. In: Proceedings Interconnection Networks Workshop (2008)
19. Tomkins, J.: Interconnects: a buyers point of view. In: Proceedings ACS Workshop (2007)
20. Towles, B., Grossman, J.P., Greskamp, B., Shaw, D.E.: Unifying on-chip and inter-node switching within the Anton 2 network. In: Proceedings of the 41st International Symposium on Computer Architecture (ISCA), pp. 1–12 (2014)

21. SimGrid: Versatile simulation of distributed systems. http://simgrid.gforge.inria.fr/
22. Yang, H., Tripathi, J., Jerger, N.E., Gibson, D.: Dodec: random-link, low-radix on-chip networks. In: MICRO, pp. 496–508 (2014)

A GPU-Based Backtracking Algorithm for Permutation Combinatorial Problems

Tiago Carneiro Pessoa[1]([✉]), Jan Gmys[2,3], Nouredine Melab[3],
Francisco Heron de Carvalho Junior[1], and Daniel Tuyttens[2]

[1] ParGO Research Group (Parallelism, Optimization and Graphs),
Mestrado e Doutorado em Ciência da Computação,
Universidade Federal do Ceará, Fortaleza, Brazil
{carneiro,heron}@lia.ufc.br
[2] Mathematics and Operational Research Department (MARO),
University of Mons, Mons, Belgium
{jan.gmys,daniel.tuyttens}@umons.ac.be
[3] INRIA Lille Nord Europe, Université Lille 1, CNRS/CRIStAL,
Cité scientifique, 59655 Villeneuve D'Ascq, France
Nouredine.Melab@univ-lille1.fr

Abstract. This work presents a GPU-based backtracking algorithm for permutation combinatorial problems based on the Integer-Vector-Matrix (IVM) data structure. IVM is a data structure dedicated to permutation combinatorial optimization problems. In this algorithm, the load balancing is performed without intervention of the CPU, inside a work stealing phase invoked after each node expansion phase. The proposed work stealing approach uses a virtual n-dimensional hypercube topology and a triggering mechanism to reduce the overhead incurred by dynamic load balancing. We have implemented this new algorithm for solving instances of the Asymmetric Travelling Salesman Problem by implicit enumeration, a scenario where the cost of node evaluation is low, compared to the overall search procedure. Experimental results show that the dynamically load balanced IVM-algorithm reaches speed-ups up to $17\times$ over a serial implementation using a bitset-data structure and up to $2\times$ over its GPU counterpart.

Keywords: GPU computing · Backtracking · Depth-first search · Load balancing · Work stealing

1 Introduction

Graphics Processing Units (GPUs) have been used to substantially accelerate many regular applications. In such applications, the threads, organized in 1D, 2D or 3D blocks, perform identical operations on contiguous portions of data in

---

T.C. Pessoa was partially supported by the Institutional Program of Overseas Sandwich Doctorate (PDSE-CAPES) grant 3376/2015-00.

© Springer International Publishing AG 2016
J. Carretero et al. (Eds.): ICA3PP 2016, LNCS 10048, pp. 310–324, 2016.
DOI: 10.1007/978-3-319-49583-5_24

a statically predictable manner [1]. However, there are applications where the degree of parallelism, control flow, memory access and communication patterns are irregular and unpredictable. They are known as irregular or unstructured applications [11,18]. Backtracking, a search strategy that dynamically generates and explores a tree in a depth-first order, falls into this class of applications.

Backtracking algorithms are highly parallelizable, because many processes can explore different regions of the search space in parallel [10]. Due to the pruning of branches, the shape of the explored tree is irregular and unpredictable, resulting in load imbalance, diverging control flow and scattered memory accesses. These irregularities can be highly detrimental to the overall performance of GPU-based backtracking algorithms [6]. Thus, load balancing is one of the most critical components of parallel backtracking algorithms [11].

Some efficient strategies for load balancing inside the GPU were proposed for depth-first Branch-and-Bound (B&B) algorithms applied to permutation problems [8]. B&B is a systematic tree search strategy that uses a bounding operator which computes bounds on the optimal cost of subproblems to decide whether to continue their exploration. These bounds are often obtained by solving a relaxation of the problem at hand. In B&B algorithms the bounding operator is often very time-consuming. In this situation, the overhead induced by dynamic load balancing is easily compensated by the performance gains that result from a more regular workload. In such coarse-grained cases GPUs can provide speedup factors of 100 and more over sequential single-core CPU implementations. However, GPU-based backtracking performs poorly in cases where the evaluation cost of a node is low. It is reported that, in such irregular and fine-grained scenarios, GPU-based algorithms may be outperformed by single-core CPU implementations, or, attain much lower speed-ups than the ones obtained in situations where the node evaluation is computationally intensive [3,7–9].

In this paper we consider the case where the cost of evaluating a node is very low, meaning that the focus is put on the implementation of the parallel search process. For fine-grained problems, the implementations of such mechanisms is even more challenging and it has been loosely addressed in the literature [9,11,13]. This work proposes a new load balance strategy for GPU-based backtracking, based on the Integer-Vector-Matrix (IVM) data structure. In this algorithm, load balancing is performed without intervention of the CPU, inside a work stealing phase, which is invoked after each node expansion phase. The proposed approach uses a virtual n-dimensional hypercube topology and a triggering mechanism to reduce the overhead incurred by dynamic load balancing.

As a test-case, we solve instances of the Asymmetric Travelling Salesman Problem (ATSP) by implicit enumeration, a scenario where the evaluation of a node requires almost no arithmetic operations (two integer additions and one comparison). We compare the proposed IVM-based algorithm with a bitset-based GPU-backtracking algorithm for fine-grained problems and its serial version. Experimental results show that the dynamically load balanced IVM-algorithm outperforms the static bitset-based GPU algorithm on 60% of the test-cases that show speedup. The proposed GPU-based backtracking algorithm reaches speedups up to 17× over the serial algorithm using a bitset-data structure and up to 2× over the bitset GPU algorithm with no load balancing.

The remainder of this paper is organized as follows. Section 2 presents the background and related works. Section 3 describes the proposed algorithm. Section 4 presents details about methodology of evaluation and analysis of results. Conclusions are presented in Sect. 5.

2 Context

2.1 Test Case: Asymmetric Travelling Salesman Problem

The Asymmetric Travelling Salesman Problem (ATSP) is a well-known permutation-based combinatorial optimization problem with many real-world applications [5]. It consists in finding the shortest Hamiltonian cycle(s) through a given number of cities in such a way that each city is visited exactly once. For each pair of cities i, j a cost c_{ij} is given and stored in a cost matrix $C_{N \times N}$. The TSP is called *symmetric* if the cost matrix is symmetric ($\forall i, j : c_{ij} = c_{ji}$), and *asymmetric* otherwise.

The ATSP instances used in this case-study come from the instance generator proposed by [4], which creates instances using properties found in real-world situations. Three classes of instances were selected: *coin*, modeling a person collecting money from pay phones in a grid-like city; *crane*, modeling stacker crane operations and *tsmat*, consisting of asymmetric instances where the triangle inequality holds. We use instances from size 10 to 20.

2.2 Parallel Backtracking

Backtracking is a search strategy that consists in exploring the nodes of a tree, which is dynamically generated in depth-first fashion [10]. Internal nodes of this tree are incomplete solutions and leaves are solutions. The search begins at the root of the tree. Each step of the algorithm generates and evaluates a new node, more restricted than its father node. These newly generated nodes are kept inside a data structure, usually a stack. At each iteration, a node is removed from the data structure. The search strategy continues to generate and evaluate nodes until the data structure is empty. During the search procedure, an undesirable node may be reached, so the algorithm backtracks to an unexplored (frontier) node. This action prunes some regions of the solution space, keeping the algorithm from unnecessary computation.

Backtracking search strategies are well suited candidates for parallelization. One parallel model consists in evaluating/expanding nodes in parallel. Another approach, used in this work, consists in splitting the tree among processes, such that each process independently explores a different part of the search space in parallel [10,11].

2.3   GPU-Based Backtracking Strategies

GPU backtracking strategies for fine-grained combinatorial problems usually consist in two steps: initial CPU backtracking and parallel backtracking on GPU [2,3,7,13,15,16]. The initial CPU search performs a depth-first search (DFS) until a cutoff depth d_{cpu} is reached. All objective nodes (frontier nodes at d_{cpu}) are stored in the Active Set A_{cpu}, which keeps all nodes evaluated but not yet branched. The cutoff depth is problem-dependent and ad-hoc defined parameter. For a puzzle problem, the depth d_{cpu} may, for instance, express the configuration of the puzzle after d_{cpu} modifications. For ATSP, it means a permutation represented by an incomplete Hamiltonian cycle with d_{cpu} cities.

After the initial CPU search, A_{cpu} is sent to the GPU, and the backtracking kernel is configured and launched by the CPU. In the kernel, each node belonging to A_{cpu} is a concurrent backtracking root R_i. Each thread Th_i is responsible for evaluating a subset S_i of the solutions space concurrently, as one can see in Fig. 1. The GPU search ends when all threads Th_i have finished the exploration of S_i.

This kind of parallel backtracking strategy performs well in regular scenarios [3,9,13], but faces strong performance degradations in more irregular ones [7]. The main reason is that it suffers from load imbalance and instruction flow divergences. In order to achieve a good utilization of the multiprocessors, this kind of parallel backtracking strategy needs to launch a huge amount of threads [9].

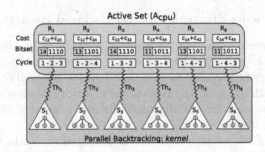

Fig. 1. Each thread Th_i evaluates a subset S_i of the solutions space.

2.4   Data Structures for GPU-Based Backtracking

Backtracking algorithms usually use a stack to store the frontier nodes. However, dynamic memory allocations on GPUs are slow. So, the use of dynamically allocated stacks may be harmful for the performance of GPU-based algorithms [15].

Other data structures may be used, such as bitsets [17]. Instead of performing operations on each position of a vector, set operations can be done in constant time using instruction-level parallelism. Backtracking algorithms may use bitsets to accelerate set operations and reduce the amount of memory used per thread [7,15]. Algorithms that apply this kind of instruction level parallelism are often called bit-parallel algorithms (BP).

The GPU-based backtracking algorithms mentioned in Sect. 2.3 use very similar data structures, thus, we describe the one used by [2,3] for solving ATSP by implicit enumeration. It is illustrated in Fig. 1.

The search strategy applied is a non recursive version of backtracking that uses no dynamic data structures. On the CPU, for representing a node that keeps the current state of the search the algorithm uses a char vector of size d_{cpu} and two integer variables. The vector of char keeps the incomplete solution and the first integer contains the cost of this sub-cycle. The second integer is seen as a bitset that keeps track of the cities already visited by the salesman. The bit k of this integer is set if the city k has already been visited.

When the initial CPU search finds an objective node at depth d_{cpu}, it stores this node and its properties in the so-called *active set* A_{cpu}. The active set A_{cpu} contains three vectors: $A_{cpu}.cycles$, $A_{cpu}.bitsets$, $A_{cpu}.costs$. In order to avoid dynamic memory allocations, the memory required for storing A_{cpu} is pre-allocated, based on the upper bound of nodes expected at depth d_{cpu}, i.e. $max_{cpu} = \frac{(N-1)!}{(N-d_{cpu})!}$ nodes. So, the vector $A_{cpu}.cycles$ requires $max_{cpu} \times d_{cpu}$ bytes. The vectors $A_{cpu}.bitsets$ and $A_{cpu}.costs$ require $max_{cpu} \times sizeof(int)$ bytes each. Once the active set A_{cpu} is filled, it is sent to the GPU.

On the GPU, each thread Th_i uses its own vector of char of size N, bitset and integer variables. Before beginning the search, each explorer thread initializes its local data structure with the values of the root node represented by A_{cpu}^i.

2.5 Load Balancing Strategies for GPU-Based Backtracking

Load balancing mechanisms are critical components of parallel backtracking algorithms [11]. The employed load balancing approach is intimately linked to the data structure which is used to store and manage the pool of frontier nodes. For instance, if each explorer has its own stack, a work stealing approach using stack splits may be used. In this approach idle explorers steal a fixed portion of another explorer's stack.

A CPU-GPU stack-splitting strategy is proposed in [9]. In this algorithm, each warp has its own stack and the load-balancing is done by the CPU after each iteration of the algorithm. However, due to the irregular and fine-grained nature of the problem solved, this strategy could not obtain high speedups compared to the serial version of the same algorithm, reaching speedups up to 2.25×. In the node-based approach described on Sect. 2.3, the node representation makes difficult to share work among processes. On this scope, a trigger mechanism to halt the kernel and redistribute the load among the processors was proposed for SIMD architectures by [11].

In order to tackle the workload imbalance in GPU DFS-B&B algorithms for permutation problems, a work stealing approach has been proposed by [8]. This approach uses an Integer-Vector-Matrix (IVM) [14] data structure, dedicated to permutation COPs, that will shortly be discussed in detail. The load balancing is performed without intervention of the CPU, inside a work stealing phase, which is invoked after each node expansion phase.

3 A GPU-Based Backtracking Algorithm for Permutation Problems

IVM-based work stealing approaches are proposed for multi-core and, respectively, GPU-based B&B algorithms in [8,14]. In B&B algorithms the cost of evaluating a node is usually high and the overhead induced by work stealing is easily compensated by the performance gains that result from a more regular workload. Furthermore, the high cost of the node evaluation function may justify the use of a second level of parallelism, in which the generated children nodes are evaluated in parallel. Using such a two-level parallelization, as in [8], means that fewer explorers are needed to yield good device occupancy.

In this paper, we consider the opposite case, where the cost of evaluating a node is very low. As a consequence, only parallel tree exploration but no further parallelization of the node evaluation is used. In this section, we present a GPU backtracking algorithm based on the IVM data structure. In this algorithm, load balancing is performed without intervention of the CPU, inside a work stealing phase, which is invoked as soon as the workload decreases below a certain level. The new algorithm has been implemented for solving ATSP by implicit enumeration.

The evaluation of a node consists in updating the current cost of the sub-cycle and comparing this partial cost with the best solution found so far. Nodes whose partial cost is greater than the best solution found so far are eliminated. Using such a naive bounding operator, the considered workload is extremely fine-grained, providing a good test-case for the proposed load-balancing mechanism. The concepts herein applied can be used to solve other permutation based problems, such as N-Queens, flow shop scheduling problem and quadratic assignment problem.

In what follows, we detail the IVM data structure, the work stealing phase and the trigger mechanism used by the proposed algorithm.

3.1 IVM Data Structure

Integer-Vector-Matrix (IVM) [14] is a data structure dedicated to permutation problems. It is illustrated in Fig. 2, using a permutation problem of size four. The left-hand side (Fig. 2a) shows a tree-based representation in which the horizontal and vertical solid lines represent the state of the corresponding stack. In the tree-based representation, each node designates an incomplete solution (partial permutation) or a full solution (permutation). For the ATSP, the cities before the "/" symbol are visited while the following ones remain to be visited. On the right-hand side (Fig. 2b) the corresponding IVM data structure is represented.

At each moment, IVM indicates the next node (subproblem) to be processed. The integer I of IVM indicates the level of the next subproblem and at each level $k \leq I$ the components $V[k]$ of the vector point to the selected cities. In this example, cities 2 and 3 are visited at levels 0 and 1, respectively. The triangular matrix M contains the cities that remain to be visited at each level. A subproblem is decomposed by increasing the level, i.e. the value of I, and copying all cities except the selected one to the next row in M. In this example, cities 1, 3 and 4 are copied to row 1, as city 2 is selected at level 0.

Using the matrix M, the vector V indicates the position of a subproblem among its sibling nodes in the tree. Therefore, throughout the depth-first exploration process, the vector V behaves like a factoradic counter. In the example of Fig. 2b, the vector successively takes the values *0000, 0010, 0100, ..., 3200, 3210*. These 24 values correspond to the numbering of the 4! solutions using the *factorial number system* [12] in which the weight of the ith position is equal to $i!$ and the digits allowed for the ith position are $0, 1, ..., i$.

In the example of Fig. 2b, the serial backtracking algorithm explores the interval $[0000, 3210[$. It is possible to have two IVM-based workers, R_1 and R_2, such that R_1 explores $[0000, X[$ and R_2 explores $[X, 3210[$. If R_2 ends exploring its interval before R_1 does, then R_2 steals a portion of R_1's interval. Therefore, R_1 and R_2 can exchange their interval portions until the exploration of all $[0, N![$. In the IVM-based approach intervals of factoradics are used as work units.

Each cell of the triangular $N \times N$ matrix corresponds to a subproblem which, in the tree-based representation, is kept in memory as a permutation of N integers. Thus, the worst-case memory footprint of IVM is N times lower than the worst-case memory requirements for stack-based DFS. Moreover (as for bitset representations), the memory requirements of IVM are known in advance, making the IVM data structure particularly suitable for a GPU implementation of DFS.

However, because of the matrix M IVM has a larger memory footprint than the bitset representation introduced in Sect. 2.3. This larger memory footprint can be seen as a tradeoff for having work units that can be efficiently split among workers.

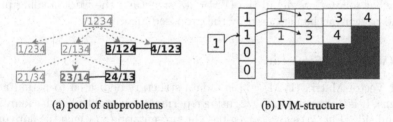

(a) pool of subproblems   (b) IVM-structure

Fig. 2. Example of a pool of subproblems and an IVM-structure obtained when solving a permutation problem of size four.

3.2   Work Stealing for GPU-based Parallel Backtracking

In this section we present the work stealing mechanism for the IVM-based backtracking algorithm. The pseudo-code of this algorithm is shown in Algorithm 1. Before starting the exploration, the interval $[O, N![$ is partitioned into T parts, where T is the number of IVM structures used (*line 2*). These intervals are copied to the device (*line 3*).

Algorithm 1. IVM-Backtracking

```
 1: procedure IVM-BACKTRACK
 2:     intervals←divide-interval([0,N!])
 3:     copyH2D(intervals)
 4:     repeat
 5:         count←0 ; copyHostToDevice(count) ;
 6:         call kernel TreeExplore(count)
 7:         call WorkStealing-phase                          ▷ shown in Algorithm 2
 8:         call kernel determine-end(end-all,states)
 9:         copy DeviceToHost(end-all)
10:     until (end-all)
11: end procedure
12: procedure KERNEL : TREEEXPLORE(count)
13:     Th_i ← blockIdx.x*blockDim.x+threadIdx.x
14:     repeat
15:         if (not-interval-empty(Th_i)) then
16:             go to next node using IVM(Th_i)
17:             state[Th_i] ← 1
18:         else
19:             state[Th_i] ← 0
20:             atomicIncrement(count);
21:             break;
22:         end if
23:     until (count<TRIGGER)
24: end procedure
```

The algorithm starts by initializing a global device variable count at 0 (*line 6*). Its purpose will be explained shortly. Then, the kernel TreeExplore is launched with T threads (*line 6*). The body of this kernel is shown in lines 11 to 24 of Algorithm 1. In this kernel each thread $Th_i \in \{0, ..., T-1\}$ uses its IVM structure to explore a distinct interval (*line 16*).

When a thread finds its interval empty, then its state flag is set to *empty* and the variable count is atomically incremented in global memory (*lines 19–21*). As mentioned, this global counter is reset to 0 before the launching of the TreeExplore kernel and it is only incremented by threads that have run out of work. Before exploring a new node, each thread checks the value of this counter and compares it to a fixed value trigger (*line 23*). If the value of the counter is greater than trigger, the thread stops the exploration process. In other words, the kernel TreeExplore kernel terminates only if at least trigger explorers have finished exploring their local interval.

A trigger value equal to 1 corresponds to the situation where the work stealing phase is invoked as soon as a single explorer finds it interval empty. If trigger is set to a value $\geq T$ no load balancing is used, since the work stealing phase is only triggered if all intervals have been explored.

After the termination of the TreeExplore kernel, the algorithm enters a work stealing phase where workers with empty intervals try to acquire work from workers with non-empty intervals (*line 7*). The pseudo-code for the work stealing phase, which is explained shortly, is shown in Algorithm 2. Following each work stealing phase a parallel reduction is performed on the vector of states in order to determine whether all IVMs are in the *empty* state (Algorithm 1, *line 8*). Until this condition is true (*line 10*), the algorithm continues to alternate exploration and work stealing phases.

In the work stealing phase, an empty IVM becomes a *thief* that tries to steal a portion of an exploring IVM's (a *victim*'s) interval. These work stealing operations must be performed in parallel and without using synchronization primitives. The work stealing phase, described in Algorithm 2, is composed of several kernels. First, the length of all intervals and the mean interval-length are computed (*lines 2–3*). This information is used in the victim selection phase where a mapping of *empty* onto *exploring* IVMs is build. As the stealing operations are carried out in parallel, the parallel victim selection must avoid the double selection of victims.

In the victim selection phase (*lines 4–8*), IVMs are seen as vertices of a n-dimensional p-ary hypercube. Each IVM is labeled with a unique ID R that can be written as $R = (a_{n-1}, a_{n-2}, ..., a_0)$ in base p. We assume that the number of IVMs, say T, is a power of p, i.e. $T = p^n$. Two IVMs whose base-p label differs in one single digit are connected to each other. Thus, in this topology, each IVM has $n(p-1)$ neighbors and the diameter of the graph connecting IVMs is n.

The victim selection phase is an iterative procedure which consists in launching a kernel $(n-1)(p-1)$ times (*line 6*). The pseudo-code of this kernel is given in lines 11–17. At iteration $i \cdot p + j$ ($i = 0, ..., n-1; j = 1, ..., p-1$), an attempt is made for all empty IVMs to select the IVM of ID $R_v = (a_{n-1}, a_{n-2}, \cdots, (a_i + j)\%p, ..., a_0)$ as a victim.

The matching succeeds if the IVM R_v has not yet been selected, and IVM R_v has a non-empty interval whose length is greater than the mean interval-length. The ID of an IVM R_v that is selected as a victim by IVM R is stored at the Rth position of a vector **victim**, i.e. $victim[R] = R_v$ (*lines 14, 15*). This mapping of empty onto exploring IVMs is used in the kernel **stealWork**, where IVM R steals the right half of IVM R's interval.

Algorithm 2. Work stealing phase

```
 1: procedure WORKSTEALING-PHASE
 2:     call kernel computeLengths
 3:     call kernel computeMeanLength
 4:     for (i:1→n) do
 5:         for (j:1→p) do
 6:             call kernel trySelect(i, j, victim, ...)
 7:         end for
 8:     end for
 9:     call kernel stealWork(victim, ...)
10: end procedure
11: procedure KERNEL TRYSELECT(i, j, victim, ...)
12:     /*NB: the operations in this kernel can be performed in base 10 - for clarity this
        pseudo-code describes them in base p*/
13:     (a_{n-1}, a_{n-2}, ..., a_0)←blockIdx.x*blockDim.x+threadIdx.x;
14:     if   (has-work(a_{n-1}, ..., (a_i + j)%p, ..., a_0)  AND  length(a_{n-1}, ..., (a_i +
        j)%p, ..., a_0)>mean-length) then
15:         victim[(a_{n-1}, a_{n-2}, ..., a_0)]← (a_{n-1}, ..., (a_i + j)%p, ..., a_0)
16:     end if
17: end procedure
18: procedure KERNEL STEALWORK(victim,...)
19:     ivm←blockIdx.x*blockDim.x+threadIdx.x
20:     v←victim[ivm]
21:     interval[ivm]←steal-half(interval[v])
22: end procedure
```

4   Performance Evaluation

In this section, we evaluate the parallel backtracking algorithm proposed in Sect. 3. In Sect. 4.1, we describe the experimental protocol. In Sect. 4.2, we provide additional parameter settings. Finally, we report and discuss the results in Sect. 4.3.

4.1   Experimental Protocol

We compare the algorithm proposed in Sect. 3 to the bit-parallel version of the GPU-based backtracking algorithm described in Sect. 2.3 (BP-DFS) and its serial version.

To compare the performance of two backtracking algorithms, both should explore the same search space. When an instance is solved twice using a parallel tree search algorithm, the number of explored nodes varies between two resolutions. Therefore, for all instances, the initial upper bound (cost of the best found solution) is set to the optimal value, and the search proves the optimality of this solution. This initialization ensures that exactly the critical subtree is explored, i.e. the nodes visited are exactly those nodes who have a partial cost lower than the optimal solution. For each of the ATSP instances *coin*10–20, *crane*10–20, *tsmat*10–19, the number of nodes (in millions) that are decomposed for proving the optimality of the initial upper bound is shown in Table 1. For *tsmat*20, the time limit of 6 h of parallel processing was exceeded.

As one can see from Table 1 the size of the explored tree increases rapidly with the instance size, ranging from a few thousand to millions of millions of nodes. On each experiment, execution times and resulting backtracking tree have been collected.

Table 1. Number of nodes decomposed during the resolution of ATSP instances *coin*10–20, *crane*10–20, *tsmat*10–19 (in 10^6 nodes), initialized at the optimal solution

Instance-#	10	11	12	13	14	15	16	17	18	19	20
crane	0.04	0.11	0.67	3.81	43.6	218.8	1,088	6,954	37,916	245,204	1,055,804
coin	0.11	0.43	1.87	10.7	107.8	500.4	1,379	3,710	15,089	116,840	674,308
tsmat	0.03	1.01	0.71	26.4	89.8	6,578	3,979	240,292	2,903,808	6,866,667	–

4.2   Parameters Settings

According to preliminary experiments the number of used IVM-structures is set to $T = 8^5 = 32,768$. Moreover, preliminary experiments were conducted to find a suitable value for the work stealing trigger. Figure 3 shows the node processing speed (in *decomposed nodes/second*) for different values of the trigger when solving instance coin15.

As explained in Subsect. 3.2, if the value of the trigger is too low, too much time is spend in the work stealing phase. On the other hand, if the trigger-value

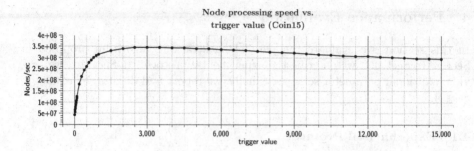

Fig. 3. Experimental calibration of the trigger value: node processing speed for different trigger-values, solving instance `coin15` using 32,768 IVM structures.

is too high, load balance degrades too much as the work stealing mechanism becomes inefficient. As one can see in Fig. 3, the best performance is reached for a value of about $3,000$, i.e., about 10% of the used $32,768$ IVM structures.

BP-DFS is a revisited version of the backtracking algorithm proposed by [2] for solving ATSP. This implementation is different from the original version as it uses a bitset-based data structure, as described in Sect. 2.3. The values chosen for block size and depth d_{cpu} are 128 and 7, respectively. The setting of parameters, such as block size, d_{cpu} and number of explorers was determined experimentally, since these parameters are influenced by instance's properties and system's characteristics [2,8,13,15].

Both GPU-implementations are based on CUDA C 7.5 and compiler versions NVCC 7.5 and GCC 4.8.2 are used. The kernel execution time is measured through CUDA's `cudaEventRecord` function, whereas the `clock` function of C is used to measure the overall application time. The testbed environment, operating under Linux Ubuntu 14.04.3 LTS 64 bits, is composed of an Intel Xeon E5-2630 v3 @ 2.40 GHz with eight cores and 32 GB RAM. It is equipped with a GeForce NVIDIA GTX 980 (GM204 chipset, 4 GB RAM, 2048 CUDA cores @ 1126 MHz).

4.3   Experimental Results and Discussion

Figure 4 shows the achieved node processing speed (in 10^6 nodes/sec) for both GPU-based implementations, considering only the kernel time and the tree processed on GPU. For the BP-DFS implementation, the node processing rate grows for instances from size 10 to 14, where it reaches a peak. This behavior is strongly related to the occupancy achieved, as mentioned in Sect. 2.3.

For instance, the initial CPU search is able to generate more threads for the instance *tsmat15*. Thus, *tsmat15* reached occupancy of 75% (the same for *tsmat11*), resulting in a bigger *nodes/sec* rate. Instances *coin15* and *crane15* reached occupancy of 64% and 57%, respectively. For problems of size 14, *coin14* could reach occupancy of 66%, while *tsmat14* and *crane14* could reach 61% and 56% respectively. For the IVM-based implementation, the occupancy value is almost constant for instances of size bigger than 13 cities, reaching on average

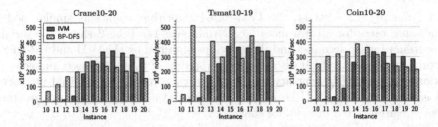

Fig. 4. Node processing speed (in 10^6 Nodes/sec) for ATSP instances *crane*10–20, *tsmat*10–19 and *coin*10–20 initialized at the optimal solution.

65% of occupancy. Due to shared memory utilization, the occupancy of the IVM-kernel was limited to 75%.

The IVM implementation reaches low *nodes/seconds* rates for instances of size 10 to 13, being much slower than the BP-DFS implementation. The resolution time for those instances is in the order of a few milliseconds. There are two reasons for this poor performance on small instances. On the one hand, for instances 10–13 the overhead induced by work stealing amounts on average for 60% of the execution time. One can see this in Fig. 5, which shows the percentage of time the IVM-based algorithm spends in both phases. For instances of size 14–16 the IVM-algorithm spends 10–20% of time in the load balancing phase and work stealing amounts for less than 2% for instances of sizes 17–20. The time spent in the work stealing phase is also a good indicator for the irregularity of an instance. For example, comparing the instances of size 15 one can see that relatively few time is spent in work stealing for the *tsmat* class. At the same time Fig. 4 shows that BP-DFS perform particularly well for *tsmat*15. On the other hand, the IVM-based exploration process is more costly than the bitset-based approach. In other words, for small and/or regular workloads the IVM-based approach is clearly outperformed by its bitset-based counterpart.

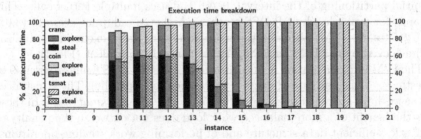

Fig. 5. Percentage of execution time spent in work stealing and exploration phases for ATSP instances *crane*10–20, *tsmat*10–19 and *coin*10–20.

Figure 4 also shows that node processing rate achieved by BP-DFS varies strongly according to the instance being solved (comparing, for example *tsmat*15 and *tsmat*16). In contrast, the IVM-based algorithm maintains similar node processing rates for all instances larger than size 14. Table 2 shows the serial execution time (in seconds) and the speedups obtained by the IVM and BP-DFS algorithms, respectively. It also shows the speedup of the IVM-based implementation over BP-DFS. Contrary to Fig. 4, the time required for initial memory allocations, copies and CUDA API calls is included in Table 2. Speedups greater than one are printed in boldface characters.

Both parallel implementations are unable to obtain speedups on instances of sizes smaller than 13 cities. Instances of size 10–12 have the serial execution time of a fraction of second. For these instances, the cost of memory allocation on GPU, data transfer and CUDA calls exceeds the time required to processing the tree sequentially on the CPU.

Table 2. Serial execution time (in seconds) and speedups for the IVM and BP-DFS algorithms.

Inst-#	crane				coin				tsmat			
	t_{serial} (sec)	$\frac{t_{serial}}{t_{IVM}}$	$\frac{t_{serial}}{t_{BP-DFS}}$	$\frac{t_{IVM}}{t_{BP-DFS}}$	t_{serial} (sec)	$\frac{t_{serial}}{t_{IVM}}$	$\frac{t_{serial}}{t_{BP-DFS}}$	$\frac{t_{IVM}}{t_{BP-DFS}}$	t_{serial} (sec)	$\frac{t_{serial}}{t_{IVM}}$	$\frac{t_{serial}}{t_{BP-DFS}}$	$\frac{t_{IVM}}{t_{BP-DFS}}$
10	0.004	0.007	0.01	0.70	0.01	0.02	0.03	0.67	0.002	0.004	0.006	0.67
11	0.012	0.02	0.04	0.50	0.04	0.06	0.11	0.55	0.06	0.1	0.17	0.59
12	0.066	0.1	0.2	0.50	0.16	0.25	0.44	0.57	0.06	0.09	0.16	0.56
13	0.265	0.4	0.7	0.57	0.66	0.6	**1.6**	0.38	1.2	**1.1**	**2.8**	0.39
14	2.2	**1.9**	**4.0**	0.48	4.7	**3.7**	**6.9**	0.54	3.6	**1.3**	**5.0**	0.26
15	10.2	**5.9**	**8.0**	0.74	22.2	**8.8**	**12.2**	0.72	220	**11.6**	**16.2**	0.72
16	53.0	**13.4**	**10.6**	**1.26**	63.8	**13.1**	**13.0**	**1.01**	171	**14.7**	**12.0**	**1.23**
17	350	**16.6**	**11.4**	**1.46**	183	**15.3**	**12.0**	**1.28**	8,952	**13.3**	**16.3**	0.92
18	1,946	**16.6**	**10.4**	**1.60**	830	**17.1**	**12.9**	**1.33**	110,282	**13.8**	**12.7**	**1.09**
19	12,839	**16.4**	**8.3**	**1.98**	6,662	**17.4**	**13.1**	**1.33**	325,744	**16.1**	**13.7**	**1.18**
20	56,900	**15.7**	**8.2**	**1.91**	37,191	**15.8**	**11.7**	**1.35**	–	–	–	–

Compared to the IVM-based version, the BP-DFS implementation has low overhead of CUDA API calls. It has only one kernel call and low memory requirements per thread. The IVM-based algorithm requires more memory, performs an initial partitioning of the interval $[0, N![$ and uses multiple kernel calls. This explains, for example why BP-DFS reaches a higher speedup for *crane*15 (8.0× against 5.9× for IVM) although the node processing rate (excluding initialization) achieved by the IVM-based algorithm is nearly equivalent (Fig. 4).

The IVM implementation is outperformed by its BP-DFS counterpart in 9 of 22 test cases that reach speedups over the sequential algorithm. These instances are the medium-sized instances *crane*14–15, *coin*13–15 and *tsmat*13–15. In these cases the benefit of a more balanced work load does not outweigh the penalty of using a less efficient data structure and of performing work stealing operations. In *tsmat*17, BP-DFS could reach high *nodes/sec* rate and outperform the IVM-based implementation as well.

However, as shown in Table 2, the dynamically load-balanced IVM implementation outperforms BP-DFS in 13 of 22 test cases that reach speedups over the sequential algorithm. The IVM-based algorithm reaches speedups up to 17× over a serial algorithm using a bitset-data structure, and is up to 2 times faster then the BP-DFS version for instances *crane*19–20. Based on the results, BP-DFS may be preferable to solve small instances or to perform a complete enumeration of the search space in a depth-first manner, a quite regular application [2,9,13]. However, this is not an usual backtracking application. For larger instances, the experimental results reveal the superiority of the IVM-based algorithm over BP-DFS, an optimized version of a well-known lightweight backtracking strategy. Aside from being faster than BP-DFS for most instances that last at least one minute, the IVM-based approach is less subject to performance variations according to different tree shapes.

5   Conclusions and Future Works

We have presented a GPU-based backtracking algorithm for permutation combinatorial problems. The presented algorithm is based on the IVM data structure. In this algorithm, the load balancing is performed without intervention of the CPU, inside work stealing phases which are triggered as soon as the workload decreases below a predefined level.

The experimental results show that algorithm benefits from a more regular load even in extremely fine-grained irregular scenarios. The performance of the load-balanced IVM-based algorithm has been compared to a bitset-based backtracking (BP-DFS) implementation. Although the bitset-based data structure is less costly to maintain than IVM, the IVM-based algorithm outperforms BP-DFS in 60% of the test-cases that show speedup over the sequential implementation and is up to 2 times faster.

For some smaller instances, the cost of work-stealing strategy is high compared to the cost of exploring the whole tree. In such cases, the BP-DFS algorithm outperforms its IVM-based counterpart. For medium and large-sized instances the overhead induced by work stealing is largely compensated by the benefits of a more regular workload.

As a future work, a dynamic trigger mechanism could be considered to overcome the limitations of the proposed algorithm while solving smaller instances. Also, we plan to investigate whether the use of CUDA Dynamic Parallelism (CDP) can help to better address recursive patterns of computation on GPUs, like the ones considered in this work.

References

1. Burtscher, M., Nasre, R., Pingali, K.: A quantitative study of irregular programs on GPUs. In: 2012 IEEE International Symposium on Workload Characterization (IISWC), pp. 141–151. IEEE (2012)
2. Carneiro, T., Muritiba, A., Negreiros, M., de Campos, G.: A new parallel schema for branch-and-bound algorithms using GPGPU. In: 23rd International Symposium on Computer Architecture and High Performance Computing (SBAC-PAD), pp. 41–47 (2011)

3. Carneiro, T., Nobre, R.H., Negreiros, M., de Campos, G.A.L.: Depth-first search versus jurema search on GPU branch-and-bound algorithms: a case study. In: NVIDIA's GCDF - GPU Computing Developer Forum on XXXII Congresso da Sociedade Brasileira de Computação (CSBC) (2012)

4. Cirasella, J., Johnson, D.S., McGeoch, L.A., Zhang, W.: The asymmetric traveling salesman problem: algorithms, instance generators, and tests. In: Buchsbaum, A.L., Snoeyink, J. (eds.) ALENEX 2001. LNCS, vol. 2153, pp. 32–59. Springer, Heidelberg (2001). doi:10.1007/3-540-44808-X_3

5. Cook, W.: In Pursuit of the Traveling Salesman: Mathematics at the Limits of Computation. Princeton University Press, Princeton (2012)

6. Defour, D., Marin, M.: Regularity versus load-balancing on GPU for treefix computations. Procedia Comput. Sci. 18, 309–318 (2013)

7. Feinbube, F., Rabe, B., von Lowis, M., Polze, A.: NQueens on CUDA: optimization issues. In: 2010 Ninth International Symposium on Parallel and Distributed Computing (ISPDC), pp. 63–70. IEEE (2010)

8. Gmys, J., Mezmaz, M., Melab, N., Tuyttens, D.: A GPU-based Branch-and-Bound algorithm using Integer–Vector–Matrix data structure. Parallel Comput. (2016). http://www.sciencedirect.com/science/article/pii/S0167819116000387

9. Jenkins, J., Arkatkar, I., Owens, J.D., Choudhary, A., Samatova, N.F.: Lessons learned from exploring the backtracking paradigm on the GPU. In: Jeannot, E., Namyst, R., Roman, J. (eds.) Euro-Par 2011. LNCS, vol. 6853, pp. 425–437. Springer, Heidelberg (2011). doi:10.1007/978-3-642-23397-5_42

10. Karp, R.M., Zhang, Y.: Randomized parallel algorithms for backtrack search and branch-and-bound computation. J. ACM (JACM) 40(3), 765–789 (1993)

11. Karypis, G., Kumar, V.: Unstructured tree search on SIMD parallel computers. IEEE Trans. Parallel Distrib. Syst. 5(10), 1057–1072 (1994)

12. Knuth, D.: The Art of Computer Programming. Seminumerical Algorithms, vol. 2, p. 192. Addison-Wesley, Reading (1997). iSBN=9780201896848

13. Li, L., Liu, H., Wang, H., Liu, T., Li, W.: A parallel algorithm for game tree search using GPGPU. IEEE Trans. Parallel Distrib. Syst. 26(8), 2114–2127 (2015)

14. Mezmaz, M., Leroy, R., Melab, N., Tuyttens, D.: A multi-core parallel branch-and-bound algorithm using factorial number system. In: 28th IEEE International Parallel & Distributed Processing Symposium (IPDPS), Phoenix, AZ, pp. 1203–1212, May 2014

15. Plauth, M., Feinbube, F., Schlegel, F., Polze, A.: Using dynamic parallelism for fine-grained, irregular workloads: a case study of the n-queens problem. In: 2015 Third International Symposium on Computing and Networking (CANDAR), pp. 404–407. IEEE (2015)

16. Rocki, K., Suda, R.: Parallel minimax tree searching on GPU. In: Wyrzykowski, R., Dongarra, J., Karczewski, K., Wasniewski, J. (eds.) PPAM 2009. LNCS, vol. 6067, pp. 449–456. Springer, Heidelberg (2010). doi:10.1007/978-3-642-14390-8_47

17. San Segundo, P., Rossi, C., Rodriguez-Losada, D.: Recent Developments in Bit-Parallel Algorithms. INTECH Open Access Publisher (2008)

18. Yelick, K.A.: Programming models for irregular applications. ACM SIGPLAN Not. 28(1), 28–31 (1993)

Buffer Minimization for Rate-Optimal Scheduling of Synchronous Dataflow Graphs on Multicore Systems

Mingze Ma[✉] and Rizos Sakellariou

School of Computer Science, University of Manchester, Manchester, UK
{mingze.ma,rizos}@manchester.ac.uk

Abstract. Streaming applications are generally modelled by dataflow graphs, among which Synchronous Dataflow Graphs (SDFGs) are one of the most popular models. Self-timed Execution (STE) based methods are proved to be very powerful for analyzing and scheduling SDFGs. In this paper, an extension of STE is presented based on which, an exact algorithm is proposed to find the minimal memory usage for buffering to guarantee execution under maximal throughput (rate-optimal execution) of an SDFG on a multicore system. Experimental results show that the proposed exact algorithm obtains less buffer usage than a widely used state-of-art heuristic in a number of cases and equal buffer usage in the rest. In addition, a heuristic is proposed as an efficient approximate method, which gives equal or less buffer usage than a state-of-art heuristic.

1 Introduction

Many multimedia applications (e.g. audio/video encoders/decoders) or digital signal processing applications (e.g. digital filters) share the same property, namely that the applications need to be executed iteratively to process a continuously received data stream; these applications are known as streaming applications. Dataflow graphs are extensively adopted to model these applications [3], with a widely used model being the *Synchronous Dataflow Graph* (SDFG) [13]. Different from conventional dataflow graph models, an SDFG can describe the cyclic and multi-rate nature of streaming applications by allowing cycles and different execution rates of the nodes in the graph. A schedule of an SDFG gives a periodic execution pattern for the graph; in one iteration during the execution all nodes of the graph are executed according to their execution rates. The average computation time per iteration is called the *iteration period* [25]. The reciprocal of the iteration period is *throughput*. Different objectives may be considered when scheduling SDFGs, such as throughput [7,8,14], energy consumption [6,11], latency [12], memory use [22,25], task remapping/rescheduling overhead for fault-tolerant scheduling [6,12], number of cores [24], etc. Among the different scheduling objectives, throughput, which indicates data processing speed, is one of the key objectives; a *rate-optimal* schedule is a schedule that can achieve the maximal throughput for a given SDFG.

© Springer International Publishing AG 2016
J. Carretero et al. (Eds.): ICA3PP 2016, LNCS 10048, pp. 325–340, 2016.
DOI: 10.1007/978-3-319-49583-5_25

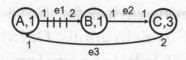

Fig. 1. An example SDFG.

A simple SDFG example is given in Fig. 1. The SDFG consists of nodes and edges. The nodes are submodules of an application (e.g. motion estimation function or discrete cosine transform function in a H.263 encoder), which are referred to as *actors*, and the edges represent data dependencies between nodes, which are referred to as *channels*. The execution of actors is called *firing*. The numbers within actors are the execution time of the actors. Communication data is modelled as *tokens*, where each token represents an application-specific set of data. The numbers on the two ends of a channel are the token producing and consuming rates of the corresponding actors. The bars on channels are called as *initial tokens* (or *delays* [13]). Since the applications represented by SDFGs are always executed iteratively, the edges with initial tokens are used to indicate data dependencies between the actors in different iterations. For instance, in Fig. 1, there are 4 initial tokens on the edge $A \rightarrow B$, the token producing rate of actor A is 1 and the token consuming rate of actor B is 2, therefore the $(i+2)$-th execution of actor B depends on the output data of the $(2i-1)$-th and $2i$-th execution of actor A, $i > 0$. The memory used to store the tokens exchanged between actors is referred to as *buffers*. The buffer size is represented by the number of tokens it can hold.

On a single-core system, throughput is not affected by scheduling. On a multicore system, which allows actors to fire in parallel on different cores, throughput and buffer usage are both decided by the scheduling process. For example, for the SDFG shown in Fig. 1, actor A fires twice and actor B and C fire once within one iteration of the execution. If all actors are scheduled onto one core, the iteration of the graph (*iteration period*) should be the sum of the execution time of these firings, which is 6. However, by firing actor B 2 times on 2 cores, actor C 2 times on 2 cores and actor A 4 times on 4 cores sequentially, two iterations can be completed during a period of 5, which means the period of one iteration is only 2.5. Therefore, different schedules decide the throughput of a system. Besides, the scheduling process is also constrained by the buffer sizes on channels. The firings of actors can be blocked by insufficient buffer space and further decrease the throughput. Therefore, minimizing buffer usage while guaranteeing certain throughput is a problem for multicore systems. Minimization of buffer usage is extremely desirable in embedded systems, where on-chip resources are expensive.

This paper addresses the problem of minimizing the buffer size for rate-optimal SDFG schedules on multicore systems. Existing algorithms all have their limitations: either they aim at a subset of SDFGs [15] or they cannot guarantee an optimal solution [4,16,17,20,25]. One of the best heuristics is proposed by

Zhu et al. in [25], which can get near-optimal buffer usage for most SDFGs. However, as shown in Sect. 5, their solutions may still require as much as 50% more buffer usage than the optimal solutions for some extreme cases. This gives scope for an exact algorithm and/or a more effective heuristic.

The contributions of this paper are the following:

- An exact algorithm to find a rate-optimal schedule with minimal buffer requirements for an SDFG based on the search algorithm in [20]. The execution time of the search is decreased significantly by using more accurate bounds for the search than the bounds used in [25].
- A fast and efficient heuristic, which can be used when time limits are applied to the scheduling process and our exact algorithm cannot finish within these time limits, based on the exact algorithm improving the idea of the quantization factor in [20].
- An extended self-timed execution method to eliminate the extra buffer requirements caused by initial tokens.

The remainder of the paper is organized as follows. Section 2 presents related work. Section 3 explains the concepts used in this paper. The proposed algorithms, including the exact algorithm and the heuristic are introduced in Sect. 4. Then, experimental results are presented in Sect. 5. Finally, Sect. 6 concludes the paper.

2   Related Work

Decreasing buffer requirements for systems modelled by SDFGs is a well-studied topic. Most of the existing work only aims at single-core systems. However, as the complexity of modern systems is getting higher, multicore architectures are more and more widely used and there is a lot of research on buffer minimization and/or throughput increase [4,9,15–17,19,20,24,25]. Some research only pursues the minimization of the buffer requirements giving an executable schedule without considering the optimization of the throughput, e.g. the work in [3,9]. Since throughput is always one of the most significant metrics of a streaming application, these papers may not be applicable for the design of throughput-intense systems. There is recently also some work that only considers throughput but no memory constraints in terms of buffer usage [7,8,14].

In [15], an algorithm is proposed to solve the buffer minimization problem for homogeneous SDFGs (HSDFGs), a subset of SDFGs. Since SDFGs can be converted to their equivalent HSDFGs, this algorithm can also be applied to SDFGs. However, the minimal buffer sizes obtained from the HSDFGs are not always minimal for their equivalent SDFGs [20]. Throughput-constrained buffer minimization algorithms are also proposed in [4,16,17]. However, these techniques leave space for improvement, particularly as graph transformation techniques like retiming and unfolding are not considered. At this point it is useful to explain the importance of *retiming* and *unfolding*. *Retiming* adjusts the distribution of initial tokens in the original graph. *Unfolding* is used to unfold the original graph and makes more iterations to be explicitly revealed in one iteration of the unfolded graph, so that the parallelism between different iterations can be presented in the unfolded graph and utilized in the scheduling process that follows. Both retiming and unfolding are widely used in the literature [14, 23–25].

By using retiming and unfolding, the original graph can be transformed to an equivalent graph which has the potential to get better scheduling results. For example, for the SDFG in Fig. 1, the minimal buffer usage for rate-optimal scheduling is 10. However, after retiming the 4 initial tokens on channel $e1$ to 1 token on channel $e2$ and 2 tokens on channel $e3$, and then unfolding the graph using an unfolding factor of 2, the minimal buffer usage for rate-optimal scheduling is decreased to 8. Although retiming and unfolding are both useful techniques, extra steps have to be taken to get the retiming operations and unfolding factors. As shown in [24, 25], state-space exploration based scheduling can perform retiming and unfolding automatically during the exploration process. State-space exploration is widely used to solve SDFG scheduling problems [2, 9, 10, 19, 20, 24, 25].

Solutions for buffer usage minimization for rate-optimal schedules are given in [20, 25]. Memory-constrained state-space exploration was firstly adopted in [20] to explore trade-offs in buffer usage and throughput constraints for SDFGs. However, initial tokens are viewed as real data and affect the lower bound of the buffer usage, and therefore minimal buffer usage is usually unable to obtain. In addition, the work in [20] is not specific for buffer size minimization for rate-optimal scheduling: Although the minimal buffer usage for rate-optimal schedules is included in the output of the algorithm, the algorithm has to spend a large amount of time to find the buffer sizes for non-maximal throughput schedules. Thus, the speed of this algorithm is comparatively slow. The work in [25] develops a heuristic to solve the problem, where the effect of the initial tokens is eliminated. However, as mentioned in [25], their heuristic cannot guarantee the achievement of the minimal buffer sizes.

3   Background

3.1   Synchronous Dataflow Graphs

A graph theory based definition for an SDFG is given in Definition 1, following by a definition for HSDFGs, a subset of SDFGs. Any legal SDFG can be converted to its equivalent HSDFG. A conversion algorithm is introduced in [18].

Definition 1. *An SDFG G is a tuple (V, E), where V is a finite set of actors and E is a set of directed channels which connect the actors in set V. An actor α in V is a tuple $(input, output)$, where input is the set of input channels to the actor and output is the set of output channels from the actor. A channel $e \in E$ is a tuple (src, snk, p, c, it), where actor snk depends on actor src (i.e. $src \rightarrow snk$), p is the token producing rate of actor src, c is the token consuming rate of actor snk, and it is the number of initial tokens on the channel.*

Definition 2. *For an SDFG $G = (V, E)$, if $\forall e \in E$, we can get $e(p) = e(c) = 1$, then this SDFG is referred to as an HSDFG.*

The execution time of actor α is denoted by $\tau(\alpha)$. For a channel $e = (src, snk, p, c, it)$, actor src is a *predecessor* of actor snk, and actor snk is a *successor* of actor src. Buffer space on a channel is occupied when the firing of a predecessor actor begins and released when the firing of its successor actor ends. Then, a useful concept proposed by Lee in [13] is the *repetition vector*, which is given in Definition 3.

Definition 3. *The repetition vector q of an SDFG has N entries, which specifies the smallest execution times of actors to perform one cycle of a periodic schedule, where N is the number of actors.*

Because of the existence of cycles and multiple token producing/consuming rates in SDFGs, to ensure an SDFG has at least one feasible schedule, the *sample rate consistency* of the graph has to be verified before scheduling. If an SDFG has a legal (i.e. all elements are positive integers) repetition vector q in which all elements meet the *balance equation* shown in Eq. 1, it is sample rate consistent.

$$e(p)q(e(snk)) = e(c)q(e(src)) \tag{1}$$

As a streaming application is used to process a continuous data stream, the application needs to run iteratively. Therefore, the criterion for the timing performance of a schedule is usually the *iteration period* (IP) or the *throughput* of the schedule. As the scheduling process is always conducted after the sample rate consistency checking, we assume the SDFGs discussed in this paper are all sample rate consistent. Based on the assumption, we define the IP and the throughput of SDFGs in Definition 4.

Definition 4. *For a periodic schedule of an SDFG $G = (V, E)$, its iteration period IP is the time consumed to execute all actors $\alpha \in A$ by $q(\alpha)$ times, where q is the repetition vector of the SDFG. Then, $\mathcal{T} = 1/IP$ is the throughput of the schedule.*

The IP of an SDFG can always be obtained from its equivalent HSDFG. For an HSDFG, the lower bound of its iteration period is its maximum cycle mean (MCM) as defined in Eq. 2 [18]. The definition of cycles in HSDFGs are given in Definition 5.

$$MCM(G) = \max_{cycle\ C \in G} \frac{\sum_{\alpha \in C} \tau(\alpha)}{\sum_{e \in C} e(it)} \tag{2}$$

Definition 5. *A cycle C in an HSDFG consists of a directed sequence of actors and edges starting and ending at the same actor, while all elements in the sequence but the starting and ending ones are unique.*

As the MCM of a graph is only decided by the graph itself, the greatest lower *iteration bound* (IB) of IP can be obtained without considering the hardware resources. Effective algorithms to get the throughput and IB of an SDFG are introduced in [10, 24], respectively. If the IP of a schedule is equal to the IB of the graph, this schedule is a *rate-optimal* schedule.

3.2   Self-Timed Execution

Most analysis and scheduling methods are based on HSDFGs, so an SDFG-to-HSDFG conversion has to be used [19]. However, this conversion may cause an exponential increase in the number of actors of the converted HSDFG. To avoid this conversion, simulation of the execution of SDFGs is used as an analysis or a scheduling method [10,19,20,24,25]. The simulation is based on a state-space exploration technique [20,24]. *States* represent execution stages of an SDFG. Analysis and scheduling for an SDFG are conducted by analyzing and constraining the transition of the states. The definition of a state is given in Definition 6.

Definition 6. *A state in an execution is represented by three vectors* $(\boldsymbol{T}, \boldsymbol{S}, \boldsymbol{R})$. *$\boldsymbol{T}$ and $\boldsymbol{S}$ are both M-dimensional vectors, where M is the number of channels in the graph. Each element in $\boldsymbol{T}$ represents the amount of the tokens on a channel, and each element in $\boldsymbol{S}$ represents the remaining buffer space on a channel. The initial value of $\boldsymbol{T}(e)$ equals to $e(it)$. The initial value of $\boldsymbol{S}(e)$ is obtained by $d(e) - e(it)$. $\boldsymbol{R}$ is a N-dimensional vector, where N is the number of actors. The elements in $\boldsymbol{R}$ denote the remaining time of the firing of actors. Since an actor may keep firing on different processing cores at the same time, the elements of R are multisets. Since no actors are firing at the beginning of the execution, the initial values of all elements in R are all empty multisets denoted by* {}.

The simulation based scheduling is an earliest start time scheduling, which means the actors fire as soon as possible during the execution process. This form of execution is referred to as *self-timed execution* (STE) in [24,25]. If the number of cores is unlimited, the rate-optimal scheduling is guaranteed by the STE. This conclusion is confirmed by Chretienne in [5] for HSDFGs and Ghamarian et al. in [10] for SDFGs. STE usually consists of a *transient phase* and a *periodic phase* [24]. Retiming is completed by the transient phase, and the periodic scheduling pattern is given by the periodic phase. No transient phase in the STE of an SDFG means no retiming has been applied to the original SDFG.

Two different buffer-constrained STE models are proposed in [20,24], respectively. In [20], the buffer constraints are modelled as extra edges on the original graphs, while in [24] the buffer constraints are mapped on real buffers and checked during the execution process. Our extended STE is based on the execution model in [24], since our proposed algorithms are implemented using SDF3 [21], same as in [24].

As an example, Fig. 2 gives the STE of the SDFG in Fig. 1 according to the technique in [24]. The execution of an SDFG is represented by the transformation of the states. In Fig. 2, the rectangles represent the states of the execution of the SDFG in Fig. 1. The rectangle on the top left corner is the initial state. The states are transformed by the actions shown between two states. *CLK* is the clock count, which is used to label the happening time of each action. There is a cycle which consists of states and directed arrows, forming the periodic phase of the STE. A state in Fig. 2 consists of three elements: the first row is the vector of the token number on channels ($\boldsymbol{T}$), the second row is the vector of the unused buffer space on channels ($\boldsymbol{S}$), and the third row is the vector of the remaining

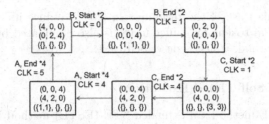

Fig. 2. The STE of the example SDFG.

execution time of the firing actors (R). No transient phase exists in this STE. The IP of this STE is 5.

3.3 Problem Formulation

The objective of this paper is to minimize buffer requirements for rate-optimal schedules on multicore systems. The data buffering in a multicore system can be realized on a shared memory space or on separate (distributed) memory spaces. In this paper, we aim at platforms where the memory cannot be shared by different cores. Thus, we assume that buffers on different channels cannot be shared with each other; and unoccupied buffer space on a channel cannot be used by other channels. The definition of the concepts of *buffer distribution* and *distribution size* are given in Definition 7.

Definition 7. *A buffer distribution d is a mapping set for the channel set E of an SDFG(V, E), where a element d(e) corresponds to the buffer size on the channel e, e ∈ E. The distribution size is denoted by* $|d| = \sum_{e \in E} d(e)$.

Then, the objective of this paper can be stated as: minimize $|d|$ of schedules which satisfy the condition $IP = IB$.

4 Proposed Algorithms

By using an effective retiming method, a state-of-art algorithm in [25] is the first work which can eliminate the extra buffer usage introduced by the initial tokens. We denote this algorithm by ZHU and use it as a comparison algorithm in this paper. The results of ZHU are affected by the higher bounds of the buffers and the sequences of the channels during the binary search of the algorithm and, as a result, only sub-optimal results can be obtained by the algorithm in many cases. To improve this, we propose an exact search algorithm and a heuristic, which outperforms ZHU.

Our exact algorithm first narrows down the range of the search. Then, a solution space searching algorithm is applied to find a buffer distribution d_{min} with the minimal distribution size. The storage dependencies proposed in [20] are used to accelerate the searching process. Based on the exact algorithm, our heuristic also makes use of the technique in [20] to reduce its execution time. The effect of initial tokens for buffer usage is also eliminated by proposing an extended STE method, which is described next.

4.1 Extended Self-Timed Execution

Based on the STE method, an extended STE (ESTE) method is developed to get the IP of an SDFG under the constraint of different buffer distributions. The effect of initial tokens can be eliminated by the proposed ESTE. Except for the three vectors used in STE, the states of the ESTE have an additional vector IT to represent the number of the initial tokens on channels. In this way, the number of initial tokens does not have to be the initial value of T as mentioned in Definition 6, and therefore, does not affect the lower bound of the buffer requirements on channels. Then, the initial value of T is set to a zero vector, and the initial value of an element $IT(e)$ is set to be $e(it)$.

During the extended execution, initial tokens are consumed first. Tokens in T cannot be consumed until all initial tokens are consumed. Initial tokens can only be consumed and cannot be produced. By using the ESTE, the nature of the initial tokens is reverted, since they are just used to represent the delays between actors in the SDFGs but not realistic data, and therefore should not occupy any memory space. Similar with the STE in [24,25], ESTE also performs retiming and unfolding during the execution process. The retiming can be obtained from the transient phase and the unfolding factor can be obtained from the periodic phase by using Algorithm $conSTE(G, P)$ in [24]. The effect of the initial tokens can be eliminated after retiming and unfolding are applied to the original graph.

Figure 3 is the ESTE of the SDFG in Fig. 1. In Fig. 3, an extra element IT is introduced between the vector S and R in states, which presents the remaining initial tokens in channels. We can view a transient phase in Fig. 3, following by

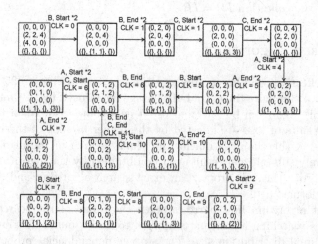

Fig. 3. The ESTE of the example SDFG.

Algorithm 1. Obtaining the Initial Point

Input:
  An SDFG $G = (V, E)$
Output:
  The initial point of the searching d_{st}
Iteration:
1: Get the IB and d_{UB} from $STE(G)$, get d_{LB}
2: **for all** $e \in E$ **do**
3:     Perform a binary search over $[d_{LB}(e), d_{UB}(e)]$; assuming x is the value considered, let vector MC be set as $MC(e) = x$ and $MC(e') = \infty$ if $e' \neq e$; use ESTE to get IP and check whether MC is feasible for a rate-optimal schedule and let $d_{st}(e) = MC(e)$ if so.
4: **end for**
5: **return** d_{st}

---

a periodic phase. Since the transient phase only needs to be obeyed once while the periodic phase runs iteratively, the time consumed by the transient phase is negligible. Therefore, the IP of the periodic phase is also 5, which is the same as the IP of the STE in Fig. 2. Since IT is not used in Fig. 2, the number of initial tokens on channel $e1$ has to be used as the initial value of the token number on that channel. Therefore to store these tokens, the buffer size on channel $e1$ cannot be less than 4. Instead, in Fig. 3, initial tokens are represented by IT; the number of initial tokens no longer affects the buffer size on channels. Therefore, the buffer size on $e1$ can be reduced from 4 in Fig. 2 to 2 in Fig. 3, while the IP of the execution remains the same.

4.2   Obtaining the Initial Point

The proposed exact algorithm is a solution-space searching algorithm. The *initial point* of the searching should be set first. Since the search is limited to rate-optimal schedules, a good initial point should avoid searching on undesirable solutions, and should be much closer to rate-optimal solutions, rather than $[0, 0, ..., 0]$ in [20] or $max(E(src), E(snk))$ in [25].

Algorithm 1 is used to get the initial point of the search. In line 1, we get the IB of the graph to check if a schedule is rate-optimal. If the IP of a schedule is equal to IB, then it is rate-optimal. The variables d_{LB} and d_{UB} are the lower bound and the upper bound of the buffer distributions on channels. $STE(G)$ is an algorithm proposed in [24] and also used in [25] to get IB and d_{UB}. The variable d_{LB} can be obtained according to Sect. 5 of [25]. The variable MC is a temporary vector. The variable d_{st} is the initial point to be solved. A conclusion for d_{st} is given: each element in d_{st} is the exact lower bound of the buffer size on that channel for rate-optimal schedules. This conclusion can be proved as follows. A theorem is given first.

Theorem 1. *The maximum throughput of an SDFG with a certain buffer distribution does not decrease because of the increase of the buffer size on one or more channels.*

Proof. For an SDFG with a buffer distribution $[d_0, d_1, ..., d_n]$, if there exists a schedule S that makes the maximum throughput $\mathcal{T}_{max}$, increasing the buffer

---

Algorithm 2. Obtaining Minimal Storage Distribution For Rate-Optimal Schedules

---

Input:
    An SDFG $G = (V, E)$, iteration bound IB, initial point d_{st} obtained by Algorithm 1, and the buffer distribution of the upper bound d_{TUB}
Output:
    The minimal buffer distribution d_{min}
Iteration:
1: **if** $|d_{st}| \equiv |d_{TUB}|$ **then**
2:    **return** $d_{min} = d_{TUB}$
3: **end if**
4: Insert initial point d_{st} to a buffer distribution set $dSet$
5: **while** $dSet$ not empty **do**
6:    Set the first distribution in $dSet$ to be the current distribution d
7:    If $|d|$ is greater than or equal to $|d_{TUB}|$, break out of the while loop
8:    Use ESTE to compute current IP and dependency graph $\triangle$ of the graph under the constraint of current buffer distribution d
9:    **if** $IP > IB$ **then**
10:       Let SD be the set of storage dependencies in $\triangle$
11:       **for all** channel $e \in SD$ **do**
12:          $d' = d$
13:          $d'(e) = d'(e) + step(e)$
14:          insert d' to $dSet$ in ascending order of distribution size
15:       **end for**
16:       Delete d from $dSet$
17:    **else**
18:       **return** $d_{min} = d$
19:    **end if**
20: **end while**
21: **return** $d_{min} = d_{TUB}$

---

size of one or more channels does not affect the constraints of the schedule. Then, the schedule S is still applicable to the graph, and therefore the maximum throughput of the graph is at least to be $\mathcal{T}_{max}$. □

Then, the conclusion for d_{st} can be derived by the following analysis. Assume there exists a storage distribution d_{lst} with a less buffer requirement on channel e than d_{st} which can still have a rate-optimal schedule. If we increase the buffer size on other channels except for e to ∞, the obtained storage distribution should also have at least one rate-optimal schedule according to Theorem 1. Then the distribution d_{lst} must be reached by the binary search in Algorithm 1. This is a contradiction, hence the assumption is false and it is not possible to have a buffer size on that channel smaller than d_{st}.

4.3   Exact Algorithm for Buffer Size Minimization

The exact search algorithm is shown in Algorithm 2. The initial point of the searching is obtained by Algorithm 1. We use the buffer distribution d_{TUB} obtained by ZHU as a tighter upper bound. This tighter upper bound and a better initial point aim to reduce the search range of our algorithm. Since the algorithms used to obtain the upper bound and the initial point are relatively fast, this search range reducing process is quite time efficient. Its effectiveness is illustrated in Sect. 5.2.

The storage dependency graph introduced in [20] is used to accelerate the search. Only the channels included in the dependency graph need to be increased

Procedure 3. Modifications for the Heuristic
_____
1: **for all** channel $e \in SD$ **do**
2:      $d' = d$
3:      **if** the time limit is exceeded **then**
4:          $QF = \lceil (|d_{TUB}| - |d_{st}|) * 0.1 * ef \rceil$
5:          $ef ++$
6:      **end if**
7:      $d'(e) = d'(e) + step(e) * QF$
8:      insert d' to $dSet$ in ascending order of distribution size
9: **end for**
_____

within the for loop, or we have to traverse all channels in the SDFG. The effectiveness of this technique is illustrated in [20]. The while loop is used to do the search and only stops when the upper bound $|d_{TUB}|$ is reached or a minimal buffer distribution is found. If $|d_{TUB}|$ is reached, the algorithm returns d_{TUB} as the minimal buffer distribution, since all distributions which have distribution sizes less than d_{TUB} cannot produce a rate-optimal schedule.

4.4 Heuristic for Buffer Size Minimization

If the execution time of the scheduling algorithm is limited and the exact algorithm cannot finish within some time constraints, the heuristic technique in [20] can be used. According to [20], the execution time can be exponentially decreased by enlarging the $step(e)$ in Algorithm 2. Therefore, a quantization factor QF can be used to multiply the $step(e)$ if a time limit is exceeded for a graph. Then, a heuristic algorithm can be obtained by simply replacing lines 11 to 15 in Algorithm 2 by Procedure 3. The initial values for QF and ef are both set to 1. Large values of QF can significantly reduce the execution time since they enlarge the steps of the search and ignore some solutions between two steps. However, if QF is too large, which means too many solutions are ignored, then the quality of the results will be decreased. Line 4 of Procedure 3 proposes an approach to compute large values of QF which is used in this paper. Finding an efficient approach is an interesting problem for further research.

5 Evaluation

5.1 Preliminaries

In our evaluation, ZHU is used as the comparison algorithm. The algorithm in [20] is not used since it is too time-consuming and generally performs worse than ZHU according to the experimental results given in [25]. Our proposed algorithms and ZHU are implemented within SDF3 [21] and tested on a virtual machine with the Ubuntu system on a PC running Windows 7 with an Intel i7-2670QM CPU and 8 GB RAM. Four cores and 2.6 GB RAM are allocated to the virtual machine. We set a 30-min time limit for all algorithms, since the same time limit is also applied in the work we compare against [25].

Using the SDFGs of the eight applications in the "Explore throughput/storage-space trade-offs" benchmark of [1] and the SDFGs of an H.263 encoder,

Table 1. The graph generation parameters.

	Actor (nr)	Degree (avg/var/min/max)	Rate (avg/var/min/max/rVS)	initialTokens (prop)	execTime (avg/var/min/max)
Benchmark15	15	3/1/1/5	3/1/1/5/100	0	50/250/10/100
Benchmark30	30	3/1/1/5	12/144/1/24/400	0	50/250/10/100
Benchmark60	60	3/1/1/5	48/2304/1/96/800	0	50/250/10/100

an H.263 decoder, a granule-level MP3 decoder, a block-level MP3 decoder and an MP3 playback application also from [1] (Download/Examples section), we compared our exact algorithm and our heuristic with ZHU. The exact algorithm cannot finish within the 30-min time limit for fig8 and the block-level MP3 decoder. For all other SDFGs our exact algorithm produces equal results for buffer size with ZHU. The same is also true for our heuristic, which, however, results in a buffer size of 1 less than ZHU for fig8 (53 versus 54) and 10 less for the block-level MP3 decoder (1858 versus 1868). Thus, to compare and analyze our proposed algorithms in more detail, we used three groups of randomly-generated SDFGs using SDF3. The three groups are denoted by Benchmark15, Benchmark30 and Benchmark60. Each group contains 1000 SDFGs with 15, 30, or 60 actors, respectively. The graph generation parameters used are shown in Table 1, where the parameter repetitionVectorSum is abbreviated to rVS. The explanation of the parameters is given in the website of SDF3 [1].

5.2 Results

The Exact Algorithm. The result improvement and runtime increase of our exact algorithm compared with ZHU is shown in Table 2. In the table, the column *equal cases* shows the percentage of cases for which the two algorithms produce the same results, the column *improved cases* shows the percentage of cases for which our algorithm produces better results than ZHU, the columns *runtime* next to *equal cases* and *improved cases* give the average/median multiple of the runtime increase of our algorithm compared with ZHU. The column *improvement* shows the average/maximum/minimum percentages of reduction for the buffer requirements produced by our algorithm for the improved cases compared with ZHU. The column *completion rate* shows the percentage of the cases that can finish within the time limit. According to the table, most cases can finish within the time limit. For Benchmark15, 95.60% of the cases have finished within the time limit, in which our algorithm achieves better results for 11.80% of the cases and for other cases gets the same buffer requirements compared with ZHU. On average, the runtime of our algorithm increases 15.40 times for the equal cases and 182.39 times for the improved cases compared with ZHU. However, the median values of the two categories of the cases are both close to 2, which means the runtime increase for most cases is not that high.

According to the results for Benchmark30 and Benchmark60, it appears that the completion rate decreases with the size of the graphs, while the percentage

Table 2. Result improvement and runtime increase for the exact algorithm.

	Equal cases	Runtime increase (AVG/MED)	Improved cases	Runtime increase (AVG/MED)	Improvement (AVG/MAX/MIN)	Completion rate
Benchmark15	83.80%	15.40/1.80	11.80%	182.39/1.94	4.84%/51.26%/0.04‰	95.60%
Benchmark30	72.60%	6.54/1.93	16.00%	37.99/2.00	5.83%/56.50%/0.05‰	88.60%
Benchmark60	66.50%	2.55/1.92	18.90%	7.39/2.00	5.58%/54.28%/0.01‰	85.40%

Table 3. Result improvement and runtime increase for our heuristic.

	Equal cases	Runtime increase (AVG/MED)	Improved cases	Runtime increase (AVG/MED)	Improvement (AVG/MAX/MIN)	Completion rate
$QF = 1$						
Benchmark15	83.80%	15.40/1.80	11.80%	182.39/1.94	4.84%/51.26%/0.04%	95.60%
Benchmark30	72.60%	6.54/1.93	16.00%	37.99/2.00	5.83%/56.50%/0.05‰	88.60%
Benchmark60	66.50%	2.55/1.92	18.90%	7.39/2.00	5.58%/54.28%/0.01‰	85.40%
$QF = \lceil(|d_{TUB}| - |d_{st}|) \times 0.1\rceil$						
Benchmark15	1.60%	249.31/59.27	2.60%	113.28/7.81	10.44%/24.92%/0.55%	4.20%
Benchmark30	4.00%	35.01/11.00	7.10%	16.86/3.93	10.33%/49.86%/0.04‰	11.10%
Benchmark60	3.70%	15.04/4.43	9.10%	6.82/2.71	9.96%/54.07%/0.02‰	12.80%
$QF = \lceil(|d_{TUB}| - |d_{st}|) \times 0.2\rceil$						
Benchmark15	0.20%	33.71/33.71	0	—	—	0.20%
Benchmark30	0.30%	7.47/6.55	0	—	—	0.30%
Benchmark60	1.80%	5.31/4.53	0	—	—	1.80%
$TOTAL$						
Benchmark15	85.60%	19.81/1.81	14.40%	169.92/2.05	5.85%/51.26%/0.04%	100.00%
Benchmark30	76.90%	8.02/1.94	23.10%	31.49/2.23	7.21%/56.50%/0.04‰	100.00%
Benchmark60	72.00%	3.26/1.94	28.00%	7.21/2.04	7.00%/54.28%/0.01‰	100.00%

of improved cases increases. This may be because the solution space gets more complicated as the scale of the graphs increases. Therefore, the performance of heuristic algorithms like ZHU is degraded, while the performance of the proposed exact algorithm is not affected by the size of the solution space, even though its runtime becomes longer. According to Table 2, the runtime increase is still limited for most cases in Benchmark30 and Benchmark60.

The Heuristic Algorithm. To balance execution time with the quality of scheduling, a heuristic algorithm was proposed in Sect. 4.4. The heuristic keeps increasing the value of QF when the time limit is exceeded during the execution of the heuristic. This makes it possible to find solutions for all cases when QF has increased to the value $\lceil(|d_{TUB}| - |d_{st}|) \times 0.2\rceil$. Compared with ZHU, the result improvement and runtime increase of the heuristic are shown in Table 3. There are four parts in the Table 3. The first three parts give the outcome when QF equals to 1, $\lceil(|d_{TUB}| - |d_{st}|)*0.1\rceil$ and $\lceil(|d_{TUB}| - |d_{st}|)*0.2\rceil$, respectively. The last part, $TOTAL$, combines the data of the above parts and gives the total results

Table 4. Search range reduction.

	Benchmark15	Benchmark30	Benchmark60
Average reduction	97.02%	95.52%	94.24%
Equal rate	69.20%	53.30%	37.50%

of the heuristic. The values of *equal cases, improved cases* and *completion rate* in the second and third parts of Table 3 are much lower than the corresponding values in the first part of Table 3, as most cases can finish when the quantization factor is 1 and are not counted in part 2 and 3 in Table 3.

We define cases that cannot finish by our exact algorithm within time limit as *overtime cases*. These cases are solved in the heuristic when QF has increased to $\lceil (|d_{TUB}| - |d_{st}|) * 0.1 \rceil$ or $\lceil (|d_{TUB}| - |d_{st}|) * 0.2 \rceil$. From part 2 and 3 of Table 3, we notice that more than half of the overtime cases can be improved by our heuristic compared with ZHU, and the average improvement of the buffer requirements is higher than the data in Table 2. This means most overtime cases are cases which have the potential to be optimized, and therefore they demand more runtime to do the search in their solution spaces.

The Effectiveness of the Search Range Reducing Process. This paper has proposed Algorithm 1 as a better initial point for the search in Algorithm 2 and has used the approach of ZHU as a tighter upper bound of the search, so that the solution space (search range) is reduced. In this experiment, the effectiveness of this method is evaluated. As shown in Table 4, the *reduction* of the solution space is calculated by the equation $\frac{|d_{UB}| - |d_{TUB}| + |d_{st}| - |d_{LB}|}{|d_{UB}| - |d_{LB}|}$. We can see that the solution space is greatly reduced by our search range reducing process.

The *equal rate* is the proportion of the cases which satisfy the condition $|d_{TUB}| = |d_{st}|$. This means that the condition in line 1 of Algorithm 2 is met and the algorithm terminates. Then, the runtime of the exact algorithm only contains the time consumed by Algorithm 1 and ZHU which is used to get the d_{TUB}. For Benchmark15, the equal rate is close to 70% but this value decreases as the size of the graphs increases. This suggests that the search range reducing process works better on small scale graphs, and the effectiveness of this process decreases as the scale of the graphs increases.

6   Conclusion

This paper has presented an exact algorithm and a heuristic to solve the buffer minimization problem for rate-optimal schedules of SDFGs. By traversing the solution space, our exact algorithm can produce minimal buffer requirements. Efficient accelerating methods are introduced to decrease the runtime of the algorithm. Compared with a state-of-art algorithm in [25], the proposed exact algorithm and heuristic achieve the same or less buffer use for a small set of realistic applications. A detailed experimental analysis using randomly generated SDFGs demonstrated the improvements achieved by our proposed exact algorithm and heuristic. Future work can include the consideration of communication costs and limitations in the number of available cores as this paper assumes an unlimited number of cores. Another assumption in this paper is that the buffer of one channel cannot be shared with other channels. By removing this assumption and allowing buffer sharing between different channels, our work can be extended to shared memory systems.

References

1. http://www.es.ele.tue.nl/sdf3/
2. Amnell, T., Fersman, E., Mokrushin, L., Pettersson, P., Yi, W.: TIMES: a tool for schedulability analysis and code generation of real-time systems. In: Larsen, K.G., Niebert, P. (eds.) FORMATS 2003. LNCS, vol. 2791, pp. 60–72. Springer, Heidelberg (2004). doi:10.1007/978-3-540-40903-8_6
3. Bhattacharyya, S.S., Murthy, P.K., Lee, E.A.: Software Synthesis from Dataflow Graphs. Springer Science & Business Media, Heidelberg (2012)
4. Chen, Y., Zhou, H.: Buffer minimization in pipelined SDF scheduling on multi-core platforms. In: ASP-DAC (2012)
5. Chretienne, P.: The basic cyclic scheduling problem with deadlines. Discret. Appl. Math. 30(2), 109–123 (1991)
6. Das, A., Kumar, A., Veeravalli, B.: Energy-aware task mapping and scheduling for reliable embedded computing systems. ACM Trans. Embed. Comput. Syst. (TECS) 13(2s), 72 (2014)
7. Dkhil, A., Do, X.K., Louise, S., Rochange, C.: A hybrid scheduling algorithm based on self-timed and periodic scheduling for embedded streaming applications. In: PDP (2015)
8. Do, X.K., Dkhil, A., Louise, S.: Self-timed periodic scheduling of data-dependent tasks in embedded streaming applications. In: Wang, G., Zomaya, A., Perez, G.M., Li, K. (eds.) ICA3PP 2015. LNCS, vol. 9529, pp. 458–478. Springer, Heidelberg (2015). doi:10.1007/978-3-319-27122-4_32
9. Geilen, M., Basten, T., Stuijk, S.: Minimising buffer requirements of synchronous dataflow graphs with model checking. In: DAC (2005)
10. Ghamarian, A.H., Geilen, M., Stuijk, S., Basten, T., Moonen, A., Bekooij, M.J., Theelen, B.D., Mousavi, M.: Throughput analysis of synchronous data flow graphs. In: ACSD (2006)
11. Jung, H., Lee, C., Kang, S.-H., Kim, S., Oh, H., Ha, S.: Dynamic behavior specification and dynamic mapping for real-time embedded systems: hopes approach. ACM Trans. Embed. Comput. Syst. (TECS) 13(4s), 135 (2014)
12. Lee, C., Kim, S., Oh, H., Ha, S.: Failure-aware task scheduling of synchronous data flow graphs under real-time constraints. J. Signal Process. Syst. 73(2), 201–212 (2013)
13. Lee, E.A., Messerschmitt, D.G.: Static scheduling of synchronous data flow programs for digital signal processing. IEEE Trans. Comput. 100(1), 24–35 (1987)
14. Liu, W., Gu, Z., Yaoyao, Y.: Efficient SAT-based application mapping and scheduling on multiprocessor systems for throughput maximization. In: CASES (2015)
15. Moreira, O., Basten, T., Geilen, M., Stuijk, S.: Buffer sizing for rate-optimal single-rate data-flow scheduling revisited. IEEE Trans. Comput. 59(2), 188–201 (2010)

16. Rosvall, K., Sander, I.: A constraint-based design space exploration framework for real-time applications on MPSoCs. In: DATE (2014)

17. Shin, T.-H., Oh, H., Ha, S.: Minimizing buffer requirements for throughput constrained parallel execution of synchronous dataflow graph. In: ASP-DAC (2011)

18. Sriram, S., Bhattacharyya, S.S.: Embedded Multiprocessors: Scheduling and Synchronization. CRC Press, Boca Raton (2009)

19. Stuijk, S., Basten, T., Geilen, M., Corporaal, H.: Multiprocessor resource allocation for throughput-constrained synchronous dataflow graphs. In: DAC (2007)

20. Stuijk, S., Geilen, M., Basten, T.: Exploring trade-offs in buffer requirements and throughput constraints for synchronous dataflow graphs. In: DAC (2006)

21. Stuijk, S., Geilen, M., Basten, T.: SDF^3: SDF for free. In: ACSD (2006)

22. Wang, G., Allen, R., Andrade, H.A., Sangiovanni-Vincentelli, A.: Communication storage optimization for static dataflow with access patterns under periodic scheduling and throughput constraint. Comput. Electr. Eng. **40**(6), 1858–1873 (2014)

23. Wang, Y., Shao, Z., Chan, H., Liu, D., Guan, Y.: Memory-aware task scheduling with communication overhead minimization for streaming applications on bus-based multiprocessor system-on-chips. IEEE Trans. Parallel Distrib. Syst. **25**(7), 1797–1807 (2014)

24. Zhu, X.-Y., Geilen, M., Basten, T., Stuijk, S.: Static rate-optimal scheduling of multirate DSP algorithms via retiming and unfolding. In: RTAS (2012)

25. Zhu, X.-Y., Geilen, M., Basten, T., Stuijk, S.: Memory-constrained static rate-optimal scheduling of synchronous dataflow graphs via retiming. In: DATE (2014)

Implementing Snapshot Objects on Top of Crash-Prone Asynchronous Message-Passing Systems

Carole Delporte-Gallet[1], Hugues Fauconnier[1], Sergio Rajsbaum[2], and Michel Raynal[3(✉)]

[1] IRIF, Université Paris Diderot, Paris, France
[2] Instituto de Matemáticas, UNAM, 04510 México D.F, Mexico
[3] IUF and IRISA, Université de Rennes, Rennes, France
raynal@irisa.fr

Abstract. Distributed snapshots, as introduced by Chandy and Lamport in the context of asynchronous failure-free message-passing distributed systems, are consistent global states in which the observed distributed application might have passed through. It appears that two such distributed snapshots cannot necessarily be compared (in the sense of determining which one of them is the "first"). Differently, snapshots introduced in asynchronous crash-prone read/write distributed systems are totally ordered, which greatly simplify their use by upper layer applications.

In order to benefit from shared memory snapshot objects, it is possible to simulate a read/write shared memory on top of an asynchronous crash-prone message-passing system, and build then snapshot objects on top of it. This algorithm stacking is costly in both time and messages. To circumvent this drawback, this paper presents algorithms building snapshot objects *directly* on top of asynchronous crash-prone message-passing system. "Directly" means here "without building an intermediate layer such as a read/write shared memory". To the authors knowledge, the proposed algorithms are the first providing such constructions. Interestingly enough, these algorithms are efficient and relatively simple.

Keywords: Asynchronous message-passing system · Atomic read/write register · Linearizability · Process crash failure · Snapshot object

1 Introduction

Snapshots in Message-Passing Systems. Being able to compute global states of message-passing distributed applications is a central issue of distributed computing. This is because many problems can be stated as properties on global states.

M. Raynal—The French authors were partially supported by the French ANR project DESCARTES devoted to abstraction layers in distributed computing. The third author was supported in part by UNAM PAPIIT-DGAPA project IN107714.

© Springer International Publishing AG 2016
J. Carretero et al. (Eds.): ICA3PP 2016, LNCS 10048, pp. 341–355, 2016.
DOI: 10.1007/978-3-319-49583-5_26

One of the most famous example is the detection of stable properties of distributed computations, such as termination detection or deadlock detection (once true, a stable property remains true forever).

One of the very first algorithms computing consistent global states of a distributed computation is due to Chandy and Lamport [5]. This simple and elegant algorithm introduced the term *snapshot* to denote a computed global state. It assumes FIFO channels, and uses additional control messages called *markers*. Later, snapshot algorithms, which require neither FIFO channels nor additional control messages, have been introduced (e.g., [9,14]).

It was shown in [5] that, while the snapshot returned by a snapshot algorithm is consistent, it is impossible to prove that the computation passed through it. It is only possible to claim a very weak property, namely that the computation could have passed through it. This has sometimes been called the relativistic nature of distributed computing. More generally, it was shown in [6] that the set of consistent global states that can be computed has a lattice structure. This means that if two processes launch concurrently two independent snapshot computations, each process obtain a consistent snapshot, but the snapshots they obtain, not only can be different, but can be incomparable in the sense that it is impossible to show that one of them occurred before the other one (the interested reader will find a pedagogical presentation of these issues in Chap. 6 of [18]). As far as fault-tolerance is concerned, the message-passing snapshot algorithms described in [5,9,14] assume failure-free systems (no process crash).

Snapshots in Shared Memory Read/Write Systems. Considering crash-prone asynchronous systems where the processes communicate by accessing atomic Single-Writer/Multi-Reader (SWMR) registers, the notion of a *snapshot object* was introduced in [1]. *Crash-prone* means here that any number of processes may unexpectedly stop progressing. *Atomic registers* means that each read or write operation appears as if it has been executed instantaneously at some point between its start and its end, and each read of a register returns the value written by the closest preceding write on this register. The term *Linearizability* introduced in [11] is synonym of atomicity. A correct sequence of read and write operations is called a *linearization* of these operations, and the time at which an operation appear to be instantaneously executed (linearized) is called its *linearization point*.

In this context a snapshot object is composed of n SWMR atomic registers, where n is the number of processes, which means that, while each process can read all registers, it can write only "its" register. The snapshot object offers to the processes a higher abstraction level, defined by two operations, denoted write() and snapshot(). A process invokes write() to define the value of its atomic register. When it invokes snapshot(), a process obtains the whole array of registers as if it read them simultaneously. Said differently, a snapshot object is atomic (linearizable): the operations write() and snapshot() appear as if they have been executed one after the other.

In a very interesting way, it is possible to build a snapshot object on top of SWMR atomic registers in a system of n asynchronous processes where up to

$t = n - 1$ of them may crash [1]. This progress condition, which tolerates any number of process crashes, is called the *wait-freedom* [10]. More precisely, any process that executes an operation and does not crash, terminates it whatever the behavior of the other processes.

Snapshot objects have a lot of applications in crash-prone asynchronous systems where processes communicate through a read/write shared memory (examples of algorithms based on snapshot objects can be found in several following textbooks such as [4,19,20]. This comes from the fact that a snapshot object allows processes to define and use consistent global states of a read/write-based computation: each process deposits the relevant part of its local state in the snapshot object, and can then obtain consistent global states by invoking the operation snapshot().

The previous snapshot object considers that each process has its "own" underlying atomic register. Hence, they are called SWMR snapshot objects. Snapshot objects, where the underlying atomic registers are Multi-Writer/Multi-Reader (MWMR) registers, have also been studied (e.g., [12,13]).

Construction of Read/Write Registers in Message-Passing Systems. Read/write registers are the most basic objects of computing science, and consequently, a fundamental problem of asynchronous message-passing distributed systems consists in building an SWMR or MWMR atomic register providing the processes with a higher abstraction level than message-passing. This allows to use read/write-based algorithms on top of message-passing systems. Moreover, as in distributed systems "failures are not on option but are blunded with software", such constructions must tolerate as many process failures as possible.

One of the most celebrated algorithm implementing an atomic read/write register on top of an asynchronous message-passing system is the algorithm due to Attiya et al. [3], called ABD in the literature. This construction copes with up to $t < n/2$ process crashes, which has been shown (in the same paper) to be an upper bound on the number of process crashes that can be tolerated. The algorithms, which implement the read and write operations, are particularly simple. They use of a simple broadcast facility, sequence numbers, and majority quorums. The fact that (a) any quorum contains at least one process that never crashes, and (b) any two majority quorums have a non-empty intersection, are key elements of this construction.

Many constructions of atomic read/write registers on top of message-passing systems have been proposed (e.g., [2,4,8,16–18] to cite a few). They differ in the type and the number of failures they tolerate, the number of messages they need to implement a read or a write operation, the size of control information carried by these implementation messages, and the time complexity of each operation.

Content of the Paper. This paper is on the construction of a (high level) t-tolerant SWMR snapshot object on top of an underlying (low level) asynchronous message-passing system where up to t processes may crash. As $t < n/2$ is an upper bound on the number of process crashes to build an read/write atomic register on top of a crash-prone message-passing system, it follows that $t < n/2$ remains an upper bound when one wants to build a snapshot object.

A simple way to obtain such a construction consists first in using an algorithm (such as one of the previously mentioned ones) to build n SWMR atomic registers on top of the crash-prone asynchronous message-passing system, and then use any algorithm building an SWMR snapshot object (e.g., [1,12]) on top of the read/write shared memory build previously. This construction consists of a simple stacking of existing algorithms: the first layer going from message-passing to n SWMR atomic registers, the second layer going from n SWMR atomic registers to a snapshot object.

While it obeys basic structuring principles, this solution is not satisfactory for the following reason. The stacking-based construction is not genuine. More precisely, building intermediate SWMR atomic registers is a way to build a snapshot object, but is not a problem requirement. Maybe there are simpler and more efficient constructions, which build directly a snapshot object on top of a message-passing system, without requiring this intermediate level. Moreover, being not genuine, the stacking-based construction can be more costly and its engineering more difficult than an ad'hoc construction.

The paper presents a genuine construction of an SWMR snapshot object on top of a message-passing system in which, in any run, any minority of processes may crash. From a number of messages point of view, a write operation requires $O(n)$ messages, while a snapshot operation requires between $O(n)$ and $O(n^2)$ messages (this depends on the concurrency pattern involving the snapshot operation and the number of concurrent write operations). From a time complexity point of view, a write operation requires a round-trip delay, while a snapshot operation requires between one and $(n-1)$ round-trip delays (as before this depends on the concurrency pattern occurring during the snapshot).

Roadmap. The paper is made up of 6 sections. Section 2 presents the basic definitions: system model, one-shot and multi-shot snapshot objects. Section 3 presents a genuine algorithm constructing a one-shot snapshot object. Section 4 proves its correctness. Section 5 shows how to modify the previous algorithm to go from a one-shot to a multi-shot snapshot object. Finally, Sect. 6 concludes the paper. All missing proofs can be found in [7].

2   System Model, and Snapshot Objects

System Model

Processes. The computing model is composed of a set of n sequential processes denoted $p_1, ..., p_n$. Each process is asynchronous which means that it proceeds at its own speed, which can be arbitrary and remains always unknown to the other processes.

A process may halt prematurely (crash failure), but executes correctly its local algorithm until it possibly crashes. The model parameter t denotes the maximal number of processes that may crash in a run. A process that crashes in a run is said to be *faulty*. Otherwise, it is *correct* or *non-faulty*. Let us notice that, as a faulty process behaves correctly until it crashes, no process knows if it is correct or faulty.

Communication. The processes cooperate by sending and receiving messages through bi-directional channels. The communication network is a complete network, which means that any process p_i can directly send a message to any process p_j (including itself). Each channel is reliable (no loss, corruption, nor creation of messages), not necessarily first-in/first-out, and asynchronous (while the transit time of each message is finite, there is no upper bound on message transit times).

A process p_i invokes the operation "send TAG(m) to p_j" to send to p_j the message tagged TAG which carries the value m. It receives a message tagged TAG by invoking the operation "receive TAG()". The macro-operation "broadcast TAG(m)" is a shortcut for "**for each** $j \in \{1, \ldots, n\}$ send TAG(m) to p_j **end for**". (The sending order is arbitrary, which means that, if the sender crashes while executing this macro-operation, an arbitrary – possibly empty – subset of processes will receive the message.)

Let us notice that, due to process and message asynchrony, no process can know if an other process crashed or is only very slow.

Notation. In the following, the previous computation model, restricted by the feasibility predicate $t < n/2$, is denoted $\mathcal{CAMP}_{n,t_{n,t}}[t < n/2]$ ("Crash Asynchronous Message-Passing" model in which any minority of processes may crash).

It is important to notice that, in this model, all processes are a priori "equal". This allows each process to be at the same time a "client" (it invokes high level operations) and a "server" (it locally participates in the implementation of the object that is built).

Message types are denoted with small capital letters, while local variables are denoted with small italics letters, indexed by a process index.

Snapshot Object

Definition. The SWMR snapshot object has been informally presented in the Introduction. It is made up of n components (one per process), and provides the processes with two operations denoted write() and snapshot().

Let $SNAP$ be such an object. When a process p_i invokes write(v), it stores the value v in its component $SNAP[i]$. When a process p_i invokes snapshot(), it obtains the value of all the components $SNAP[1..n]$. A snapshot object is atomic (or linearizable), which means that the operations write() and snapshot() issued by the processes appear as if each of them had been executed instantaneously, at a single point of the time line between its start and its end. Moreover, no two operations appear at the same point of the time line, and the array $reg[1..n]$ returned by a process, when it terminates an invocation of snapshot(), is such that $reg[k] = v$ if the closest preceding write operation issued by p_k is write(v). If there is no such write by p_k, $reg[k] = \perp$ (a default value that, at the application level, no process can write).

One-Shot vs Multi-Shot. In the context of snapshot objects, we distinguish one and multi-shot objects. In both cases, a process can issue as many operations snapshot() as it wants.

- One-shot. No process invokes write(v) more than once.
- Multi-shot. There is no restriction on the number of times a process can invoke write().

In the following we consider first the implementation of a one-shot snapshot object. This construction is then generalized to the case of a multi-shot snapshot object in Sect. 5.

3 Implementing a One-Shot Snapshot Object

Algorithm 1 implements a one-shot snapshot object.

Local Representation of the Snapshot Object. Each process p_i manages a local array $reg_i[1..n]$, which contains its current view of the snapshot object. This array is initialized to $[\bot, \cdots, \bot]$.

Each process p_i manages also a sequence number ssn_i. Initialized to 0, this local variable is used to identify the successive requests generated by the invocations of the operation snapshot() issued by p_i.

Algorithm Implementing the Operation write(v): *Client Side.* This algorithm is described at lines 1–6, executed by the invoking process p_i (client), and lines 15–16, executed by all processes (in their server role).

When p_i invokes write(v), it assigns the value v to its local register $reg_i[i]$ and broadcasts the message WRITE(reg_i) to inform the other processes of its write (lines 1–2). Then, p_i waits for acknowledgments (line 3). Each message WRITE_ACK(reg) carries the current value of $reg_j[1..n]$ of the sender p_j. After p_i received acknowledgments from a majority of processes, it updates its local view of the snapshot object, namely $reg_i[1..n]$, to have it as recent as possible (line 5). This is done, for each local register $reg_i[k]$, by taking the maximum on the value it received and its current value. As we consider here a one-shot snapshot object, a process invokes write() at most once, and consequently, the values in $reg_i[k], reg(1)[k], \cdots, reg(m)[k]$ are all equal to $\bot$ if p_k has not yet invoked write(), or belong to the set $\{\bot, v\}$ if p_k invoked write(v). After the update of $reg_i[1..n]$ is done, p_i returns from the operation.

Algorithm Implementing the Operation write(v): *Server Side.* On the server side, when p_i receives a message WRITE(reg) from a process p_j, it updates its local array $reg_i[1..n]$ to have it as up to date as possible (line 15). It then sends back to p_j the acknowledgment message WRITE_ACK(reg_i) (line 16). As seen above, if p_i knows writes not yet known by p_j, this message allows p_j to known them.

Algorithm Implementing the Operation snapshot(): *Client Side.* As previously, this algorithm is decomposed in two parts. The part described at lines 8–14 is

local variables initialization:
$ssn_i \leftarrow 0$; $reg_i \leftarrow [\bot, \cdots, \bot]$ ($\bot$ is smaller than any value written by a process).
%——

operation write(v) **is**
(1) $reg_i[i] \leftarrow v$;
(2) **broadcast** WRITE(reg_i);
(3) **wait** (WRITE_ACK(reg) received from a majority of processes);
(4) **let** $reg(1), .., reg(m)$ be the arrays received at the previous line;
(5) **for** $k \in \{1, .., n\}$ **do** $reg_i[k] \leftarrow \max(reg_i[k], reg(1)[k], .., reg(m)[k])$ **end for**;
(6) **return**()
end operation.

operation snapshot() **is**
(7) **repeat**
(8) $prev \leftarrow reg_i$;
(9) $ssn_i \leftarrow ssn_i + 1$; **broadcast** SNAPSHOT(reg_i, ssn_i);
(10)   **wait** (SNAPSHOT_ACK(reg, ssn_i) received from a majority of processes);
(11)   **let** $reg(1), .., reg(m)$ be the arrays received at the previous line;
(12)   **for** $k \in \{1, .., n\}$ **do** $reg_i[k] \leftarrow \max(reg_i[k], reg(1)[k], .., reg(m)[k])$ **end for**
(13) **until** $prev = reg_i$ **end repeat**;
(14) **return**(reg_i)
end operation.
%——

when a message WRITE(reg) **is received from** p_j **do**
(15) **for** $k \in \{1, \cdots n\}$ **do** $reg_i[k] \leftarrow \max(reg_i[k], reg[k])$ **end for**;
(16) **send** WRITE_ACK(reg_i) **to** p_j.

when a message SNAPSHOT(reg, ssn) **is received from** p_j **do**
(17) **for** $k \in \{1, .., n\}$ **do** $reg_i[k] \leftarrow \max(reg_i[k], reg[k])$ **end for**;
(18) **send** SNAPSHOT_ACK(reg_i, ssn) **to** p_j.

Fig. 1. One-shot snapshot object in $\mathcal{CAMP}_{n,t}[t < n/2]$ (code for p_i)

executed by the invoking process p_i (client), while lines 17–18 are executed by all processes (in their server role).

The invoking process enters a repeat loop that it will exit when, from its point of view, its local array $reg_i[1..n]$ can no longer be enriched with new values. To this end it uses a local array variable $prev[1..n]$ (whose scope is restricted to the operation snapshot()). After it assigned reg_i to $prev$, p_i broadcasts an inquiry message SNAPSHOT(reg_i, ssn_i), in which the sequence number ssn_i is used to identify the different inquiries broadcast by p_i.

Then, p_i has exactly the same behavior as the one described at lines 3–5 of the write operation. Namely, p_i waits for acknowledgment messages from a majority of processes (those are messages SNAPSHOT_ACK(reg, ssn_i) carrying the appropriate sequence number). Hence, after it has executed lines 10–12, p_i possibly updated its local representation $reg_i[1..n]$ of the snapshot object.

Then, if reg_i has been updated (we have then $reg_i \neq prev$ at line 3), p_i re-enters the repeat loop. If reg_i has not been enriched with new values during the last iteration, p_i returns it as result of it snapshot invocation.

Algorithm Implementing the Operation snapshot(v): *Server Side.* This part (reception of a message SNAPSHOT(reg, ssn) from a process p_j, lines 17–18) is the same as the reception of a message WRITE(reg, ssn). Namely, p_i updates $reg_i[1..n]$ and sends back to p_j an acknowledgment message SNAPSHOT_ACK(reg_i, ssn).

4   Proof of the One-Shot Snapshot Algorithm

4.1   Termination

Lemma 1. *If a correct process p_i invokes* write(), *it terminates. Any invocation of* snapshot() *by a correct process terminate.*

4.2   Definitions and Notations

The following definitions are from [11]. For simplicity, and as they are sufficient for the understanding, we consider here only the failure-free case.

Events. Let op be an operation write() or snapshot(). The execution of an operation op by a process p_i is modeled by two events: an *invocation event*, denoted *invoc*(op), which occurs when p_i invokes the operation, and a *response event*, denoted *resp*(op), which occurs when p_i terminates the operation. The event *invoc*(op) of an operation op occurs when it executes its first statement (line 1 or line 8), and its event *resp*(op) (termination) occurs when it executes its return() statement (line 6 or line 14).

In addition to these events, sending and reception of messages create corresponding communication events [15]. Without loss of generality, it is assumed that no two events occur at the same time.

Histories. A *history* models a run. It is a total order on the events produced by the processes. Given any two events e and f, $e < f$ if e occurs before f in the corresponding history. Let us notice that we always have $e < f$ or $f < e$. A history is denoted $\widehat{H} = \langle E, < \rangle$, where E is the set of events.

A history is *sequential* if (a) its first event is an invocation; (b) each invocation is followed by the matching response event; and (c) each response event – except the last one if the computation is finite – is followed by a an invocation event.

$\widehat{H}|i$ is called a *local history*; it is the sub-sequence of $\widehat{H}$ made up of the events generated by process p_i. Two histories are equivalent if no process can distinguish them, i.e., $\forall\, i, j : \widehat{H}|i = \widehat{H}|j$.

Linearizable Snapshot History. A snapshot-based history $\widehat{H} = \langle E, < \rangle$ is *correct* (or *linearizable*) if there is an equivalent sequential history $\widehat{H_{seq}} = \langle E, <_{seq} \rangle$ in which the sequence of write() or snapshot() operations issued by the processes is such that (a) each operation appears as if it has been executed at a single point of the time line between its invocation and response events, and (b) each snapshot() operation returns an array *reg* such that $reg[i] = v$ if the invocation of write(v) by p_i appears previously in the sequence, and $reg[i] = \perp$ if it does not.

When considering a sequential history it is possible to associate a time instant of the time line with each operation. As, in such a history, all operations are ordered, no two operations are associated with the same time instant.

Given two arrays $reg1$ and $reg2$ returned by two snapshot operations, $reg1 \leq reg2$ is a shortcut for $\forall\, x \in [1..n]\colon (reg1[x] \neq \perp) \Rightarrow (reg2[x] = reg1[x])$, and $reg1 < reg2$ is a shortcut for $(reg1 \leq reg2) \wedge (reg1 \neq reg2)$.

Concurrent Operations. Let op_1 and op_2 be two operations. We say "op_1 precedes op_2" (denoted $\mathsf{op}_1 \to \mathsf{op}_2$) if $resp(\mathsf{op}_1) < invoc(\mathsf{op}_2)$. If $\neg(\mathsf{op}_1 \to \mathsf{op}_2)$ and $\neg(\mathsf{op}_2 \to \mathsf{op}_1)$, we say "$\mathsf{op}_1$ and op_2 are *concurrent*", which is denoted $\mathsf{op}_1 \| \mathsf{op}_2$. It follows that the relation "$\to_{op}$" defined on operations is an irreflexive partial order.

4.3 Basic Lemmas

The next three Lemmas follow directly from the algorithm.

Lemma 2. *Let* $\mathsf{ww} = \mathsf{write}(v)$ *a write operation issued by a process* p_i *and* snap *a snapshot operation returning the array reg.* $(\mathsf{ww} \to \mathsf{snap}) \Rightarrow (reg[i] = v)$.

Lemma 3. *Let* $\mathsf{ww} = \mathsf{write}(v)$ *a write operation issued by a process* p_i *and* snap *a snapshot operation returning the array reg.* $(\mathsf{snap} \to \mathsf{ww}) \Rightarrow (reg[i] = \perp)$.

The following corollary is an immediate consequence of Lemmas 2 and 3.

Corollary 1. *Let* snap *be a snapshot operation returning the array reg, such that* $reg[i] = v$. *There is an operation* write(v) *issued by process* p_i, *and it is such that* write(v) $\to$ snap *or* write(v)$\|$snap.

Lemma 4. *Let* snap_1 *and* snap_2 *be two snapshot operations, returning* $reg1$ *and* $reg2$, *respectively.* $(\mathsf{snap}_1 \to \mathsf{snap}_2) \Rightarrow (reg1 \leq reg2)$.

4.4 A Linearization of the Write and Snapshot Operations

Lemma 5. *Let* snap_1 *and* snap_2 *be two snapshots operations, returning* $reg1$ *and* $reg2$, *respectively. We have* $(reg1 \leq reg2) \vee (reg2 \leq reg1)$.

Lemma 6. *Let* $\mathsf{ww}1 = \mathsf{write}(v1)$ *a write operation issued by a process* p_i, $\mathsf{ww}2 = \mathsf{write}(v2)$ *a write operation issued by a process* p_j, *and* snap *a snapshot operation returning the array reg.* $((\mathsf{ww}1 \to \mathsf{ww}2) \wedge (reg[j] = v2)) \Rightarrow ((reg[i] = v1)$.

Lemma 7. *Given a history $\widehat{H}$ produced by Algorithm 1, there is an equivalent sequential history $\widehat{H'}$ which respects the sequential specification of the one-shot snapshot object.*

Theorem 1. *Algorithm 1 implements a one-shot snapshot object in the system model $\mathcal{CAMP}_{n,t}[t < n/2]$.*

Proof. The proof follows from Lemma 1 (Termination), and Lemma 7 (Linearizability). □

5 Implementing a Multi-shot Snapshot Object

This section extends the previous algorithm from a one-shot snapshot object (at most one write per process) to a multi-shot snapshot object (any number of writes per process).

A Non-blocking Algorithm. It is easy to extend the basic algorithm depicted in Fig. 1, which assumes that each process invokes at most once the write operation, to obtain a multi-shot algorithm in which, despite $t < n/2$ process crashes, at least once process can invoke any number of write operations without being blocked forever. This progress condition is called *non-blocking* (it can be seen as absence of deadlock in the presence of failures).

The extension is as follows. A sequence number is associated with each write or snapshot operation. They are then used to ensure that any snapshot returns an array containing values such that it is possible to build a sequence of all write and snapshot invocations where each snapshot returns the array defined by the most recent write that appear before it in the sequence. This implementation is *non blocking* because (a) it ensures that all write operations terminates, and (b) all snapshot operations which are not concurrent with a write operations terminate. A snapshot operation may not terminate if infinitely often write operations are concurrent with it.

An Always Terminating Algorithm

Underlying Principles. An extension ensuring that any invocation of a write or snapshot operation, issued by a correct process, does terminate, is described in Figs. 2 and 3. To ensure this strong termination property, two mechanisms are added to the basic algorithm.

(1) Every process helps perform all snapshot operations: when a process wants to perform a snapshot operation it broadcasts its query to every process, and, when receiving this query, each process issues a basic snapshot operation (essentially identical to the one-shot snapshot of the previous section). In this way, each process participates to every snapshot operation and in particular every process is aware of all snapshots that are not currently terminated.

---

local variables initialization:
$snw_i \leftarrow 0; sns_i \leftarrow 0; reg_i \leftarrow [\perp, \cdots, \perp];$ **for each** $i, j : repSnap[i, j] = \perp.$

---

operation write(v) **is**
(1) $snw_i \leftarrow snw_i + 1; write\_pending \leftarrow (v, snw_i);$
(2)   wait($write\_pending = \perp$); return()
end operation.

operation snapshot() **is**
(3) $sns_i \leftarrow sns_i + 1;$ Rbroadcast SNAP(p_i, sns_i);
(4)   wait($repSnap[i, sns_i] \neq \perp$); return($repSnap[i, sns_i]$)
end operation.

---

function base_write(wp) **is**
(5) $reg_i[i] \leftarrow wp;$
(6)   broadcast WRITE(reg_i, wp);
(7)   **wait until** (WRITE_ACK(reg, wp) received from a majority of processes);
(8)   **let** R be the set of reg arrays received at the previous line;
(9)   **for** $k \in \{1, \cdots, n\}$ **do** $reg_i[k] \leftarrow \max_{\prec_{sn}} \{r[k] | r \in R \cup reg_i\}$ **end for;**
(10) return()
end function.

function base_snapshot(s, t) **is**
(11) **while** $repSnap[s, t] = \perp$ **do**
(12) $prev \leftarrow reg_i; ssn_i \leftarrow ssn_i + 1;$ broadcast SNAPSHOT(s, t, reg_i, ssn_i);
(13)   **wait** (SNAPSHOT_ACK(s, t, reg, ssn_i) received from a majority of processes);
(14)   **let** R be the set of reg arrays received at the previous line;
(15)   **for** $k \in \{1, \cdots, n\}$ **do** $reg_i[k] \leftarrow \max_{\prec_{sn}} \{r[k] \mid r \in R \cup reg_i\}$ **end for;**
(16)   **if** $prev = reg_i$ **then** Rbroadcast END($source, sn, repSnap[source, sn]$) **end if**
(17) **end while;**
(18) return()
end function.

Fig. 2. Multi-shot snapshot object in $\mathcal{CAMP}_{n,t}[t < n/2]$ (Part 1 of the code for p_i)

(2) To ensure that the snapshot operations are not prevented from terminating by write operations, each process, when there are some snapshot operations currently not terminated, is required to wait for the termination of the oldest snapshot operation among them. In this way, eventually no write operation can be concurrent with a snapshot operation, thereby ensuring their termination.

The corresponding extended algorithm is detailed in Figs. 2 and 3, where (as before) reg_i is the current view of the memory at process p_i. This view is updated when p_i receives a WRITE() or SNAPSHOT() message. The operator $\prec_{sn}$ is on pairs (value, seq. number). It orders them according to their increasing sequence numbers: $((v, a) \prec_{sn} (w, b)) \Leftrightarrow (a < b)$.

Background task: repeat forever
(19)   **if** ($write\_pending \neq \perp$)
          then base_write($write\_pending$); $write\_pending \leftarrow \perp$ **end if**;
(20)   **if** (there are messages SNAP() received and not yet processed);
(21)   **then let** SNAP($source, sn$) **be** the oldest of these messages;
(22)   base_snapshot($source, sn$);
(23)   wait($readSnap[source, sn] \neq \perp$)
(24)   **end if**
end repeat.

when a message WRITE(reg, w) **is received from** p_j **do**
(25)   **for** $k \in \{1, \cdots n\}$ **do** $reg_i[k] \leftarrow \max_{\prec_{sn}}(reg_i[k], reg[k])$ **end for**;
(26)   send WRITE_ACK(reg_i, w) to p_j.

when a message SNAPSHOT(s, t, reg, ssn) **is received from** p_j **do**
(27)   **for** $k \in \{1, \cdots n\}$ **do** $reg_i[k] \leftarrow \max_{\prec_{sn}}(reg_i[k], reg[k])$ **end for**;
(28)   send SNAPSHOT_ACK(s, t, reg_i, ssn) to p_j.

when a message END(s, t, val) **is received from** p_j **do**
(29) $repSnap[s, t] \leftarrow val$.

Fig. 3. Multi-shot snapshot object in $\mathcal{CAMP}_{n,t}[t < n/2]$ (Part 2 of the code for p_i)

Algorithms Implementing the write() *and* snapshot() *Operations.* To perform a write operation, p_i does not immediately start to realize a write operation as in the one-shot algorithm. It records the value to be written into a variable *write_pending* with an appropriate sequence number (line 1). The write operation terminates (line 2) when the write is made in the background task of the algorithm (lines 19–23).

To perform a snapshot operation, a process p_i broadcasts in a reliable way, with the help of the underlying operation Rbroadcast(),[1] the request (message SNAP()) and its associated a sequence number to all processes (including itself) (Line 3). This request is processed in the background task at lines 20 and 22. Function base_snapshot() implements a "basic" snapshot that is essentially the same as for one-shot snapshot (waiting until the process obtains two identical vectors of values for the requested snapshot). Here this basic snapshot is stopped when at least one process has terminated a basic snapshot for the requesting upper layer snapshot. More precisely, the variable *repSnap* is an array such that $repSnap[j, m]$ contains the result of the m-th snapshot initiated by process p_j (and $\perp$ before). This variable is written at line 29 when process p_i is notified

---

[1] The main property of such a broadcast operation is that any message delivered by a (correct or faulty) process is delivered by all correct processes, and at least the messages broadcast by the correct processes are delivered. Hence all correct processes deliver the same set of messages S, and any faulty process delivers a subset of S. Algorithms implementing reliable broadcast in the presence of process crashes are described in many textbooks (e.g. [4,17]).

(by a message END()) that at least one of basic snapshots for the requested upper layer snapshot terminated. Then $repSnap[j, m]$ contains a snapshot value of the m-th snapshot initiated by process $p_j{}^2$.

In its background task (lines 19–23), process p_i performs a write (function base_write) if there a pending write (line 19). It easy to check that the function base_write always terminates. Then, if there are some requests for upper layer snapshots (corresponding to the reception of message SNAP()), process p_i chooses the oldest request and runs a basic snapshot for this request (line 22).

Let us first notice that each process executes *sequentially* the base operations denoted base_write() and base_snapshot(). Let us also notice that a upper layer snapshot terminates as soon as it is not concurrent with processes performing write operations. This follows from the following observation. Let us assume that an upper layer snapshot does not terminate. Then, all corresponding basic snapshots it generates are necessarily stuck in the execution of the underlying basic base_snapshot(). But, if this occurs, no non-crashed process is currently running a base write operation base_write, from which follows that the upper layer snapshot operation terminates.

6   Conclusion

Since a long time, snapshot algorithms suited to asynchronous message-passing reliable systems have been proposed (e.g. in [5,9,14]). These algorithms, which consider process local states and channels states, do not cope with failures, and provides snapshots which cannot always be compared [6,18].

Differently this paper has introduced the notion of a read/write snapshot object built on top of asynchronous message-passing systems in which any minority of processes may crash. A main property of these read/write snapshot lies in their Containment property (they can be totally ordered according to their occurrence order). The paper has considered two types of such snapshot objects: one-shot (in which a process may issue as many snapshot operations as it wants, but is restricted to issue only one write operation), and multi-shot (in which there is no restriction on the number of write operations issued by each process). The paper has also presented two algorithms, one for each type of snapshot object. The two main properties of these algorithms are their fault-tolerance and the total order on the snapshot values they return.

Table 1 compares the cost of the one-shot snapshot algorithm proposed in the paper with the stacking of the read/write snapshot algorithm described in [1], executed on the emulation of SWMR atomic registers in an asynchronous message-passing system described in [3]. This comparison considers the best cases, namely it assumes that each operation is invoked in a concurrency-free context (which is the most frequent case in practice).

---

^{2} Let us notice that it is possible that several processes wrote snapshot values in $repSnap[j, m]$ to help p_j terminate its snapshot invocation. Any of these values is a correct snapshot value.

Table 1. Cost comparison in favorable cases

	Stacking [1] on [3]	Our algorithm
Messages per write	$2n$	$2n$
Messages per snapshot	$8n$	$2n$
Write duration	one round-trip	one round-trip
Snapshot duration	4 round-trips	one round-trip

References

1. Afek, Y., Attiya, H., Dolev, D., Gafni, E., Merritt, M., Shavit, N.: Atomic snapshots of shared memory. J. ACM **40**(4), 873–890 (1993)
2. Attiya, H.: Efficient and robust sharing of memory in message-passing systems. J. Algorithms **34**, 109–127 (2000)
3. Attiya, H., Bar-Noy, A., Dolev, D.: Sharing memory robustly in message passing systems. J. ACM **42**(1), 121–132 (1995)
4. Attiya, H., Welch, J.: Distributed Computing: Fundamentals, Simulations and Advanced Topics, 2nd edn, 414 p. Wiley-Interscience (2004)
5. Chandy, K.M., Lamport, L.: Distributed snapshots: determining global states of distributed systems. ACM Trans. Comput. Syst. **3**(1), 63–75 (1985)
6. Cooper, R., Marzullo, K.: Consistent detection of global predicates. In: Proceedings of Workshop on Parallel and Distributed Debugging. ACM press (1991)
7. Delporte, C., Fauconnier, H., Rajsbaum, S., Raynal, M.: Implementing snapshot objects on top of crash-prone asynchronous message-passing systems, 15 p. Technical report 2037, IRISA, Université de Rennes (F) (2016)
8. Dutta, P., Guerraoui, R., Levy, R., Vukolic, M.: Fast access to distributed atomic memory. SIAM J. Comput. **39**(8), 3752–3783 (2010)
9. Hélary, J.-M., Mostéfaoui, A., Raynal, M.: Communication-induced determination of consistent snapshots. IEEE TPDS **10**(9), 865–877 (1999)
10. Herlihy, M.P.: Wait-free synchronization. ACM Trans. Program. Lang. Syst. (TOPLAS) **13**(1), 124–149 (1991)
11. Herlihy, M.P., Wing, J.M.: Linearizability: a correctness condition for concurrent objects. ACM TOPLAS **12**(3), 463–492 (1990)
12. Imbs, D., Raynal, M.: Help when needed, but no more: efficient read/write partial snapshot. J. Parallel Distrib. Comput. **72**(1), 1–12 (2012)
13. Inoue, M., Masuzawa, T., Chen, W., Tokura, N.: Linear-time snapshot using multi-writer multi-reader registers. In: Tel, G., Vitányi, P. (eds.) WDAG 1994. LNCS, vol. 857, pp. 130–140. Springer, Heidelberg (1994). doi:10.1007/BFb0020429
14. Lai, T.H., Yang, T.H.: On distributed snapshots. Inf. Process. Lett. **25**, 153–158 (1987)
15. Lamport, L.: Time, clocks, and the ordering of events in a distributed system. Commun. ACM **21**(7), 558–565 (1978)
16. Mostéfaoui, A., Raynal, M.: Two-bit messages are sufficient to implement atomic read/write registers in crash-prone systems. In: Proceedings of 35th International ACM Symposium on Principles of Distributed Computing (PODC 2016), pp. 381–390. ACM Press (2016)

17. Raynal, M.: Communication and Agreement Abstractions for Fault-Tolerant Asynchronous Distributed Systems, 251 p. Morgan & Claypool Publishers (2010). ISBN 978-1-60845-293-4
18. Raynal, M.: Distributed Algorithms for Message-Passing Systems, 510 p. Springer (2013). ISBN 978-3-642-38122-5
19. Raynal, M.: Concurrent Programming: Algorithms, Principles and Foundations, 515 p. Springer (2013). ISBN 978-3-642-32026-2
20. Taubenfeld, G.: Synchronization Algorithms and Concurrent Programming, 423 p. Pearson Prentice-Hall (2006). ISBN 0-131-97259-6

Scaling DBSCAN-like Algorithms for Event Detection Systems in Twitter

Joan Capdevila[1,2([⊠])], Gonzalo Pericacho[1],
Jordi Torres[1,2], and Jesús Cerquides[3]

[1] Department of Computer Architecture,
Polytechnical University of Catalonia (UPC), Barcelona, Spain
jc@ac.upc.edu,gonzalo.pericacho@est.fib.upc.edu
[2] Department of Computer Science,
Barcelona Supercomputing Center (BSC-CNS), Barcelona, Spain
jordi.torres@bsc.es
[3] Artificial Intelligence Research Institute (IIIA-CSIC), Bellaterra, Spain
cerquide@iaaa.csic.es

Abstract. The increasing use of mobile social networks has lately transformed news media. Real-world events are nowadays reported in social networks much faster than in traditional channels. As a result, the autonomous detection of events from networks like Twitter has gained lot of interest in both research and media groups. DBSCAN-like algorithms constitute a well-known clustering approach to retrospective event detection. However, scaling such algorithms to geographically large regions and temporarily long periods present two major shortcomings. First, detecting real-world events from the vast amount of tweets cannot be performed anymore in a single machine. Second, the tweeting activity varies a lot within these broad space-time regions limiting the use of global parameters. Against this background, we propose to scale DBSCAN-like event detection techniques by parallelizing and distributing them through a novel density-aware MapReduce scheme. The proposed scheme partitions tweet data as per its spatial and temporal features and tailors local DBSCAN parameters to local tweet densities. We implement the scheme in Apache Spark and evaluate its performance in a dataset composed of geo-located tweets in the Iberian peninsula during the course of several football matches. The results pointed out to the benefits of our proposal against other state-of-the-art techniques in terms of speed-up and detection accuracy.

Keywords: Event detection · Parallel algorithm · Data clustering · DBSCAN · MapReduce · Apache Spark · Twitter

J. Capdevila—Obra Social "la Caixa".

J. Torres—Spanish Ministry of Economy and Competitivity under contract TIN2015-65316 and BSC-CNS Severo Ochoa programs (SEV2015-0493, SEV-2011-00067).

J. Cerquides—The SGR program (2014 SGR 118) of the Catalan Governement and Collectiveware (TIN2015-66863-C2-1-R).

© Springer International Publishing AG 2016
J. Carretero et al. (Eds.): ICA3PP 2016, LNCS 10048, pp. 356–373, 2016.
DOI: 10.1007/978-3-319-49583-5_27

1   Introduction

Event detection seeks to identify and characterize anomalous patterns in data which are typically caused by some real-world phenomena [1]. For example, authors in [2] aimed to detect space-time clusters in a dataset composed of brain cancer cases in Los Alamos, New Mexico during 1973–1991. From the discovered clusters, their goal was to find whether these clusters occurred by chance or due to some real-world cause such as the presence of Los Alamos National Laboratory, a nuclear research and design facility.

Recently, the increasing use of social networks with location services has converted social network users into actual sensors capable of ubiquitously reporting real-world events [3]. These virtual communities enable the simultaneous identification of various types of events ranging from natural disasters [4] to geo-social events [5]. Particularly, Twitter[1] has shown to be more effective and faster than traditional media channels. For example, in reporting Osama Bin Laden death [6] or Mumbai attacks [7].

However, event detection in Twitter poses a set of new challenges [8]. In contrast to classical fields of application, Twitter contains tones of non-event observations such as *memes*, user conversations or *retweets*, making it very hard to uncover newsworthy events [9]. Hence, event detection techniques need to explicitly distinguish between event and non-event tweets in order to uncover these hidden patterns. Furthermore, more than 500 millions tweets are generated worldwide per day[2], entailing a high computational cost to process this huge amount of data in a single machine. Therefore, the parallelization and distribution of such algorithms plays a key role to design and implement practical event detection systems on a national or worldwide scale.

A *bottom-up* approach to retrospectively detect events from spatio-temporal data such as geo-located tweets is based on DBSCAN (Density-Based Spatial Clustering of Applications with Noise) [10]. This clustering algorithm is well-known for its noise resilience capability which enables to handle non-event observations in Twitter. Authors in [11,12] proposed to use the spatio-temporal extension of DBSCAN called ST-DBSCAN [13] to detect specified events (i.e. precipitation and dengue) from text-filtered tweets. Others [14] extended ST-DBSCAN to also consider textual features through the cosine similarity of their term vectors in order to discover various types of unspecified events. Lately, Capdevila et al. [15,16] presented Tweet-SCAN which also considers text features but it instead relies on the Jensen-Shannon distance over probabilistic topic distributions [17] to search among text.

However, the above-mentioned DBSCAN-like techniques were not initially designed to work in geographically large regions and temporarily long periods with lots of observations. On the one hand, the large amount of tweets, n, directly affects the computational cost of DBSCAN which has an average time complexity of $O(n \log n)$. On the other hand, tweets are spread unevenly over large

---

[1] www.twitter.com.

[2] https://blog.twitter.com/2013/new-tweets-per-second-record-and-how.

space-time regions and DBSCAN fails to cluster uneven distributions of tweets, compromising the overall detection accuracy of event detection systems. This uneven distributions are due to the fact that spatial and temporal distributions of tweets are strongly correlated with the activity of the underlying population [18]. Thus, urban areas during peak hours are likely to generate much more tweets than rural areas during off-peak hours.

In this work, we tackle the scaling of DBSCAN-like event detection algorithms, such as Tweet-SCAN [15,16], for large spatio-temporal regions. Given that the length of tweet messages is limited to 140-character by Twitter, we only focus on the scaling of spatio-temporal dimensions, although we note that text disambiguation is essential in event identification and future work should take it into account. As a result of this, we propose a novel density-aware MapReduce scheme implemented in Apache Spark [19] that parallelizes and distributes DBSCAN-like algorithms to scale event detection in Twitter. In particular, we propose an Octree-based method to partition tweets as per its space-time features. Given that these partitions correspond to similarly dense regions, we introduce a MapReduce scheme that computes local DBSCANs for each data partition with its parameters tailored to the local tweet density. Furthermore, our proposal includes a framework to setup these local DBSCAN parameters so that the overall detection performance is optimized. Last, we provide empirical evidence that this scheme scales well to large data sets and is able to detect events in low and high density regions.

The structure of the remaining sections is as follows. In Sect. 2, we introduce the necessary background regarding DBSCAN algorithms and their parallelization through MapReduce. In Sect. 3, we propose the novel density-aware MapReduce scheme to scale event detection on large datasets over large regions. Then, we present in Sect. 4 the empirical results of our proposal. Finally, we list several conclusions from this work in Sect. 5 and point out future work in Sect. 6.

2   Background

DBSCAN-like algorithms constitute a common *bottom-up* approach to the event detection problem [1]. Within this approach, events are defined as groups of points, a.k.a. clusters, whose point density is abnormally high. DBSCAN [10] defines a greedy algorithm through which points are associated to events. Points which are not assigned to any event are considered noise by DBSCAN. Moreover, DBSCAN does not require to specify the number and shape of events. These features make DBSCAN a suitable framework for event detection in contrast to other popular clustering techniques, such as K-Means.

2.1   DBSCAN

DBSCAN (Density-Based Spatial Clustering of Applications with Noise) [10] clusters points that are closely together and marks as noise those that are in low-density regions.

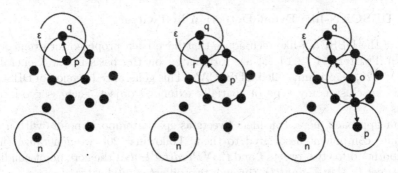

Fig. 1. (left) q is directly density-reachable from p, (middle) q is density-reachable from p and (right) q is density-connected from p

DBSCAN is formalized through the following definitions with respect to its parameters (ϵ and $MinPts$) and a dataset of points DB.

- The ϵ-neighborhood of a point p is the set of points whose distance to p is less or equal than ϵ (see ϵ-circle in Fig. 1).
- A point p is a **core point** if the number of neighbors, in its ϵ-neighborhood, is greater or equal than $MinPts$ (see left Fig. 1 for $MinPts = 4$).
- Given two points p and q, if p is a core point and q belongs to the neighborhood of p, then q is *directly density-reachable* from p (see left Fig. 1).
- q is *density-reachable* from another point p if there is sequence of points $p, r_1, r_2, ..., r_n, q$ such that each point (r_{i+1}) is *directly density-reachable* from the previous r_i (see middle Fig. 1).
- p and q are *density-connected* if there is a point o such that both are *density-reachable* from r (see right Fig. 1).
- A non-empty subset C of DB is a **cluster** if satisfies: (Maximality) For any point $p \in C$ from which q is *density-reachable*, $q \in C$. (Connectivity) For any set of point $p, q \in C$, p is *density-connected* to q.
- A point n is a **noise point** if it does not belong to any cluster (see Fig. 1).
- A point q is a **border point** if it belongs to a cluster but it is not a core point (see left Fig. 1).

The greedy algorithm defined in DBSCAN uncovers clusters of points following on the above definitions. The heuristic starts with an arbitrary point p and if p is determined to be a core point, the algorithm yields a cluster, which at least will contain this point p and its ϵ-neighborhood. The cluster is then expanded to include other neighboring points (core or border) which are also *density-connected* to p. When all density-connected points have been identified, the procedure jumps to the next unvisited point until visiting the whole dataset. Points that after completing this algorithm do not belong to any cluster are set to noise.

2.2   DBSCAN-like Event Detection in Twitter

Most of the DBSCAN-like techniques that have been proposed for event detection in Twitter [11,12,14,15] are formulated on the basis of the Generalized DBCAN [20] algorithm, called GDBSCAN. This generalized version of DBSCAN enables to cluster any type of spatially extended object, such as geo-located tweets.

Our approach, here, considers tweets as spatio-temporal points with a user attribute component associated to them. Following [20], we generalize the ϵ-neighborhood for two tweets t and t', $NPred(t,t')$, and the core point condition for a tweet t, $MinWeight(t)$, through two different predicates.

The predicate for the ϵ-neighborhood of a tweet t w.r.t another tweet t' combines the space-time features through two distinct ϵ_1 ϵ_2 spatio-temporal parameters,

$$NPred(t,t') \equiv dist(t_1,t'_1) \leq \epsilon_1, \; dist(t_2,t'_2) \leq \epsilon_2 \tag{1}$$

where t_1 and t_2 correspond to the spatial and temporal features, respectively. The expression $dist(t_i,t'_i)$ refers to the distances between tweet features, which we propose to be the haversine distance for the spatial dimension and the euclidean, in the time axis.

As for the core point predicate, we impose two conditions. First, the number of neighboring tweets (ϵ_1 ϵ_2-neighborhood) has to be at least $MinPts$, like in DBSCAN. Additionally, users associated to the neighboring tweets must be diverse by at least a μ percentage. These two conditions are expressed as follows,

$$MinWeight(t) \equiv |NPred(t,t')| \geq MinPts, \; UDiv(NPred(t,t')) \geq \mu \tag{2}$$

where $|NPred(t,t')|$ is the cardinality of the predicate in Eq. (1), $UDiv()$ is the percentage of unique users with respect to $MinPts$. This means that a group of tweets will be considered event if it contains at least $MinPts$ tweets and their users are at least unique in a fraction μ with respect to $MinPts$.

These two predicates correspond to those used for Tweet-SCAN [15], except that we here omitted the textual component. Nonetheless, the proposed density-aware scheme could apply to any DBSCAN-like algorithm for event detection that at least considers space-time features.

2.3   MapReduce DBSCAN

As we argued in the Introduction, performing event detection in social networks like Twitter requires to paralellize and distribute existing techniques to scale with current data volumes. Because of this, we propose to scale DBSCAN-like algorithms in a shared-nothing environment through a MapReduce approach [21].

A MapReduce algorithm for DBSCAN, named MR-DBSCAN, was proposed in [22]. This algorithm parallelizes all the critical sub-procedures of DBSCAN, which has been presented in Sect. 2.1. The MR-DBSCAN workflow, shown in Fig. 2, first partitions the full dataset, then performs local DBSCAN clustering

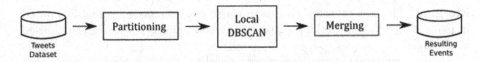

Fig. 2. Simplified MR-DBSCAN workflow

in each partition, and finally merges the local clusters into global ones, which corresponds to events in our case.

An implementation of MR-DBSCAN in Apache Spark was proposed in [23] and was named RDD-DBSCAN. The main difference both algorithms is that RDD-DBSCAN takes advantage of Resilient Distributed Datasets which brings data into memory to speed up computation.

Next, we review each of the MR-DBSCAN stages and highlight the main differences with respect to RDD-DBSCAN.

Partitioning. MR-DBSCAN incorporates a Binary Space Partitioning (BSP) procedure to split data and distribute computation as evenly as possible. Moreover, this approach takes into account the cost of accessing disk when searching for neighboring points within the partition. On the contrary, RDD-DBSCAN simply considers the number of points per partition as the cost function, since points are already loaded into memory and the cost of accessing disk can be ignored.

The BSP partitioning in MR-DBSCAN is performed recursively in each dimension until reaching a maximum cost per partition, $maxCost$, or a minimum partition size, $MinSize$. The former condition enables to balance load among partitions while the latter is set to 2ϵ to ensure the proper functioning of DBSCAN algorithm. Given this latter restriction, the scheme divides the whole region into non-overlapped cells with side length 2ϵ. This enables to reduce the search of candidates splits among all vertical and horizontal lines aligned to cell boundaries. RDD-DBSCAN follows the same approach but it uses instead a maximum number of points per partition, $maxPts$. This variable must be set, at most, to the maximum number of points that can fit into the memory of the machine with the smallest memory available.

The partitioned regions are then enlarged by ϵ in each dimension. In this way, each partition can independently determine its core points by considering points in its ϵ-outer margin. Moreover, the overlap between partitions eases the merging stage to find proper DBSCAN clusters.

Local DBSCAN. A MapReduce job performs this task. First, the mapper emits a partition ID for each point in the dataset based on the partitioning results. Second, the reducer computes the local DBSCAN for each partition as described in Sect. 2.1. RDD-DBSCAN performs this stage entirely in memory given that the partitioning phase has split data so that it fits in memory.

Merging. This is a two-step process in which cluster merging is first computed in parallel for pairs of overlapping partitions and point types are later relabeled accordingly.

Pairs of overlapped partitions are processed parallelly to identify points that are core in both partitions or core and border respectively in each partition. These are the points whose clusters are merged and global identifiers are generated for them.

Relabeling replaces local cluster IDs into global ones and it assigns final point types (core, border, noise) to each point. Since points within the margins might be associated to different types, the relabeling strategy is to keep the more restrictive type, being the list of restrictions Core > Border > Noise.

3   Density-Aware MapReduce Scheme

In the following section, we describe a novel density-aware MapReduce scheme to detect events from tweets. Although the scheme follows the MR-DBSCAN workflow from Fig. 2, individual stages have been modified according to the peculiarities of event detection in Twitter that imposes the DBSCAN-like algorithm introduced in Sect. 2.2.

3.1   Octree-Based Partitioning

Partitioning tweet data as per its spatio-temporal features requires a three dimensional scheme to deal with the geo-location and timestamp metadata of tweets.

Although the cost-based Binary Space Partitioning (BSP) scheme proposed in [22] might be convenient for environments such as Hadoop, the cost of accessing disk becomes irrelevant in Apache Spark given that point search is entirely performed in memory, as we have seen for RDD-DBSCAN [23]. Moreover, both approaches rely on binary splits of data to balance the load among workers. These processes become very costly specially when increasing feature dimensionality (e.g. from 2D to 3D).

Because of this, we propose a naive but effective partitioning scheme based on Octree [24]. Similar to [22,23], our proposal divides the whole space into cubes of side length $2\epsilon_1$ in the spatial and length $2\epsilon_2$ in temporal dimension, which determine the minimum partition size, $MinSize$. Following [23], we consider here a maximum number of points per partition $maxPts$ instead of a cost per partition, given that our scheme is implemented in Apache Spark.

The Octree-based partitioning is exemplified in Fig. 3 and works as follows. The spatio-temporal region containing all tweets is divided in eight equal-sized cubes and each sub-cube is recursively split as long as the $MinSize$ or the $maxPts$ conditions have not yet been achieved. The final leaves of the tree corresponds to the data partitions. As in [22,23], partitions are then enlarged ϵ_1 and ϵ_2 in the space and time dimension, respectively.

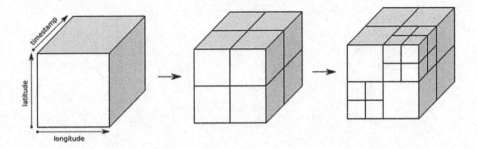

Fig. 3. Example of Octree Partitioning in spatio-temporal dimensions

With this partitioning scheme, we avoid the computation of the best possible split, but we might generate more partitions than necessary. Consequently, the subsequent stages might need to process and merge extra partitions increasing the execution time of these stages. However, we expect that the gain in the partitioning phase pays off the extra time in local DBSCAN and merging phases.

3.2 Density-Aware Local DBSCAN

As we mentioned earlier, one of the main limitations of DBSCAN is that fails to cluster datasets with points unevenly distributed, since DBSCAN parameters ($MinPts$, ϵ) are fixed and cannot be chosen appropriately for each sub-region.

The octree-based partitioning scheme creates spatio-temporal partitions with different density levels. These partitions correspond to different regions in space (e.g. low-density partitions are likely to be rural or deserted areas) and in time (e.g. high-density partitions are prone be at peak hours).

Moreover, the spatio-temporal properties of an event do not vary much from one place to another, or within different time periods; but the number of tweets per event certainly changes as per the user activity. Because of this, we propose to adjust the local $MinPts$ parameter based on the tweet density in each partition in such a way that the denser the partition is, the more tweets are needed to identify such event.

For a fixed set of ϵ_i parameters, we define the optimal $MinPts$ per event as the $MinPts$ value that enables to individually identify each event. We claim that there is a relationship between the optimal $MinPts$ value per event and the local density of tweets in the partition that the event belongs. As we show in Fig. 4, each event, represented by a dot, can be identified individually through an optimal $MinPts$ value that is correlated with the partition tweet density. In what follows, we explicitly assume a linear relationship (slope m, intercept b) between the local density of tweets and the $MinPts$ value.

The fitting of this linear model could be done by performing simple linear regression between the partition tweet density and the individual optimal $MinPts$. However, this approach would not necessarily optimize the overall detection accuracy. Therefore, our proposal estimates these parameters (m and b)

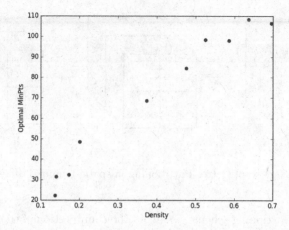

Fig. 4. Relation between the optimal $MinPts$ value per event and its partition density obtained from "La Liga" dataset in Sect. 4.2

through an optimization framework in which detection accuracy is maximized, as we will show in Sect. 4.4.

Introducing the density-aware parameters requires minimal changes on the local DBSCAN stage given that partition densities can be computed in the partitioning phase. Therefore, the local process simply calculates the proper $MinPts$ value through the linear model (m and b) and it performs clustering with that local value through the DBSCAN-like algorithm presented in Sect. 2.2.

3.3   Merging

The merging stage follows a two-step process as MR-DBSCAN [22] and RDD-DBSCAN [23]. Although cluster merging is performed exactly as in these algorithms, we note that the resulting clusters might be different, given that we here merge clusters from partitions with different $MinPts$ value.

On the relabeling step, we must take into account that points in the overlapping margins, which are clustered by different partitions, might be tagged with distinct point types by each partition. In contrast to MR-DBSCAN and RDD-DBSCAN, we must consider here that partitions might have different density levels. Our criteria is that the partition with higher or equal tweet density than the partition that contains the tweet will determine the point type according to the order of significance (Core > Border > Noise).

Relabeling details are shown in Algorithm 1. This algorithm takes as input a tweet or point p together with the density of its partition, and a list of labelings made by each overlapping partitions about this tweet. Note that a tweet belongs to a single partition with density $DensPartBelongs$, but it might be labeled by several partitions. For each tweet, the algorithm iterates over all possible labelings, $Values$. For a given labeling we know the cluster to which the tweet was clustered, $item.p.CluterID$, the density of its partition, $item.DensityPart$,

---

Algorithm 1. Relabel Points

Input : Key: (p,DensPartBelongs), Values: list of
                (p.ClusterID,DensityPart,p.flag)
Output: Key: p, Value:(ClusterID,flag)

1 ClusterID ← NULL;
2 Flag ← Noise;
3 **foreach** *item* ∈ *Values* **do**
4 | **if** *value.DensityPart* ≥ *DensPartBelongs* **then**
5 | | **if** *item.p.flag* == *Border* **then**
6 | | | ClusterID ← item.p.ClusterID;
7 | | | flag ← Border;
8 | | **else if** *item.p.flag* == *Core* **then**
9 | | | ClusterID ← item.p.ClusterID;
10 | | | flag ← Core;
11 | | | break;
12 | |

13 **return** (p,(ClusterID,flag))

---

and the flag that the tweet was associated with it, *item.p.flag*. The algorithm then checks whether the density of the partition in the given labeling is greater or equal to the density of the point's partition. If that is the case, relabeling is done as in MR-DBSCAN. Otherwise, relabeling is performed according to the partition that the tweet belongs.

4 Experimentation

4.1 Infrastructure

We conduct the experiments on a shared-nothing non-dedicated cluster with four physical machines. The cluster is managed by OpenNebula, a cloud computing platform for heterogeneous distributed data center infrastructures, through which we configured four Ubuntu virtual machines with 4 cores, 6 GB of main memory and 60 GB of hard disk space per machine. Machines are connected through a Gigabit Ethernet and Apache Spark Standalone is installed on top of them.

4.2 Datasets

For assessing the performance of the density-aware MapReduce scheme we have chosen two types of datasets: synthetic and real.

Synthetic Datasets. Synthetic datasets are generated in order to test the proposed partitioning scheme under different workloads. In particular, we are interested in measuring the execution time for the Octree-based partitioning and compare against RDD-DBSCAN when increasing the dataset size.

These datasets are created using the Scikit-learn's tool samples generator utility [25]. A Python script generates datasets of points distributed according to a Gaussian mixture model in a three dimensional euclidean space. The script requires as input the number of clusters, the number of observations and the standard deviation of each clusters to the centroid.

Since the experiment will consist in measuring execution time for different sizes of synthetic data, we created five datasets increasing in 100.000 the number of points from one to another, with a starting number of 300.000. Each synthetic data was created with twelve clusters and 1.6 of standard deviation each one.

"La Liga" Dataset. A real Twitter dataset was assembled in order to validate the proposed scheme for the task of event detection. In particular, we have established a long standing connection to the Twitter Streaming API which filtered all geo-located tweets within the bounding box of the Iberian peninsula. The long standing connection was set during four days of the Spanish football league ("La Liga") April 20th, 23rd, 30th and May 8th of 2016.

The aforementioned scenario provides a suitable testbed to measure the detection performance of the proposed event detection scheme. For each day, we have considered as event-related tweets all observations located in the nearby stadium area during the course of the match plus a safety period of 15 min before and after the match. Note that the space-time features for all football games will be very similar, but the number of tweets per event will directly depend on the attendance and the surrounding tweet density. In addition, we have excluded those matches that had less than 5 tweets per event and those that were outliers in terms of the relation of tweet density within the partition versus points per event.

Taking this into account, we ended with 15 events and 91.447 geo-located tweets, which we further split between training and testing following an approximated ratio of 70%/30%. In particular, we considered as training events, those ranging from April 20th to 30th, and testing events, those from May 8th as shown in Table 1. This split also resulted in 65.231 tweets in training and 26.216 tweets in testing.

4.3 Event Detection Metrics

To evaluate the detection accuracy of our proposal, we use extrinsic clustering metrics [26]. Among all extrinsic measures, F-measure is a popular metric for this task, given that mitigates drawbacks from Purity and Inverse Purity.

The F-measure is defined as follows per each event E_i and cluster C_j,

$$F(E_i, C_j) = 2 \cdot \frac{Recall(E_i, C_j) \cdot Precision(E_i, C_j)}{Recall(E_i, C_j) + Precision(E_i, C_j)} \qquad (3)$$

where precision is the proportion of tweets from cluster C_j that are tagged as event E_i. Oppositely, recall is the proportion of tweet from event E_i that are

Table 1. Training and testing football events

Event	Stadium	Event date	Start time	Points
1	Riazor	20 April	19:45	17
2	San Mames	20 April	20:30	16
3	Bernabeu	20 April	21:45	66
4	Mestalla	20 April	20:30	15
5	Rosaleda	20 April	20:30	6
6	Calderon	23 April	18:00	16
7	Camp Nou	23 April	20:15	69
8	Calderon	30 April	18:00	27
9	Benito Villamarín	30 April	20:15	16
10	Anoeta	30 April	15:45	7
11	Los Cármenes	30 April	21:50	7
12	Camp Nou	8 May	16:45	93
13	Ciudad de Valencia	8 May	16:45	9
14	Sánchez Pizjuan	8 May	16:45	24
15	Balaidos	8 May	16:45	15

clustered as C_j. The following expressions formally define precision and recall per each pair of event and cluster.

$$Precision(C_j, E_i) = \frac{|C_j \cap E_i|}{|C_j|} \qquad Recall(C_j, E_i) = \frac{|E_i \cap C_j|}{|E_i|} \qquad (4)$$

Finally, the F-measures from Eq. (3) are combined through a weighted average scheme across all events. For each event, the maximum F-measure with respect to all clusters is considered for averaging.

$$F = \sum_i \frac{|E_i|}{N} max_j F(E_i, C_j) \qquad (5)$$

where N is the total number of tweets.

Purity and Inverse Purity are defined similarly as the weighted average across clusters and events, respectively. While Purity considers the maximum precision w.r.t events, Inverse Purity uses the maximum recall w.r.t. clusters. However, both figures by themselves fail to measure proper clustering. On the one hand, Purity penalizes the noise in a cluster, but it does not reward grouping tweets from the same event together. For example, if we simply make one cluster per observation, we reach trivially a maximum purity value. On the other hand, Inverse Purity rewards grouping tweets together, but it does not penalize mixing items from different events. Here, we can reach maximum Inverse Purity by making a single cluster with all tweets.

, Therefore, we consider the F-measure from Eq. (5) for assessing the event detection performance.

4.4   Evaluation

Execution Times. To validate the goodness of the proposed Octree-based partitioning scheme, we compare its execution time against BSP-based partitioning in different-sized synthetic datasets.

For both schemes, we set algorithm parameters so that all clusters could be discovered at every experiment. Therefore, $\epsilon 1$, $\epsilon 2$ was set to 0.01, $maxPoints$ to 5000 and $MinPts$ to 75. For each experiment, we collected the partitioning time, the clustering and merging time and the total execution time.

Results, Table 2 and Fig. 5, show that the total execution time of the Octree-based approach overcomes the BSP-based approach proposed in RDD-DBSCAN [23]. This improvement is clearly achieved in the partitioning phase due to the fact that Octree partitioning is less expensive than BSP partitioning in computation terms. As expected, the gain in the partitioning phase comes at the expense of an increase at the clustering and merging phase.

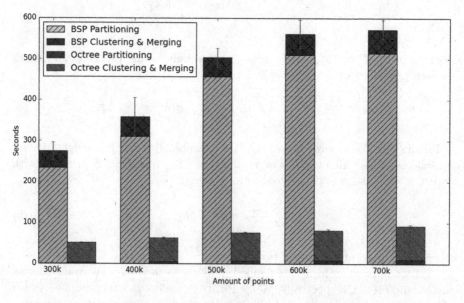

Fig. 5. Execution times for BSP-based and Octree-based MapReduce DBSCAN

Detection Performance. To validate the detection accuracy of the proposed density-aware scheme, we compare the best performing DBSCAN-like model against the density-aware scheme in "La Liga" dataset.

Table 2. Execution times for BSP-based and Octree-based MapReduce DBSCAN

Phase/Data	300k	400k	500k	600k	700k
BSP partitioning	234.28	310.17	456.55	509.46	513.75
Octree partitioning	3.17	5.16	7.13	8.40	10.55
BSP clustering and merging	39.97	48.08	46.45	51.04	58.00
Octree clustering and merging	47.23	57.14	68.87	73.10	81.35
BSP total execution	274.25	358.25	503.00	560.50	571.75
Octree total execution	50.40	62.30	76.00	81.50	91.90

Given that all labeled events shared similar space-time properties (tweets were located nearby stadiums and during the course of football matches), ϵ_1 and ϵ_2 parameters were out of the optimization scope and they were assumed known and constant for all experiments. In particular, we found out that an $\epsilon_1 = 500\,\mathrm{m}$ and $\epsilon_2 = 1\,\mathrm{hr}$ performed reasonably well in this dataset.

Therefore, we aimed to find the best performing configurations of both models by optimizing the *MinPts* parameter for the DBSCAN-like model and the linear parameters (m, b) for the density-aware scheme. The optimizations were performed in "La Liga" training dataset, while the test dataset was used to validate the values found. A greater F-measure value of the density-aware scheme in the training and testing datasets would indicate that our proposal outperforms the basic DBSCAN-like approach.

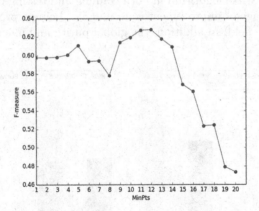

Fig. 6. *MinPts* optimization for DBSCAN-like algorithm

Figure 6 shows the optimization of the *MinPts* parameter for a DBSCAN-like algorithm in terms of F-measure in the training set. As it is depicted, the global maximum is achieved for a *MinPts* of 12 with a overall F-measure value of 0.628.

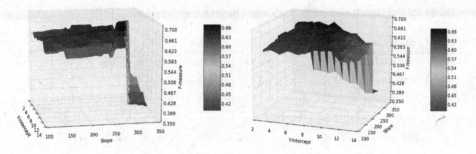

Fig. 7. Linear (m, b) optimization for density-aware scheme

Figure 7 shows the optimization of the linear parameters (m, b) in terms of F-measure for the density-aware scheme. The left figure plots the optimization results in a suitable view to understand the variation of the slope m. The right figure plots the same optimization results in a different angle of view to understand the intercept b. In both axis, a global optimum seems to exist given that extremely high or low slope and intercept values will end up with lower F-measure values. Therefore, the best performing linear model for the density-aware scheme consist of a slope $m = 300$ and a intercept $b = 8$, which results in a F-measure of 0.683.

With this optimal values we now compare the performance of both algorithms in the testing dataset. Results shown in Fig. 8 sustain that the detection performance obtained in the density-aware scheme are higher than the ones of the basic DBSCAN-like algorithm in both training and testing datasets. In both cases, the percentage of improvement is around 5%, being a promising value for future work in the field. In addition, the global purity and inverse purity values

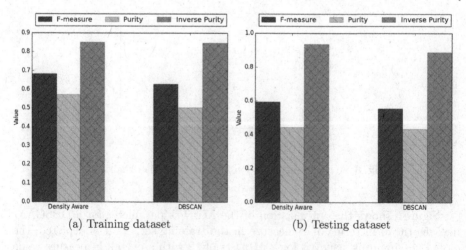

(a) Training dataset   (b) Testing dataset

Fig. 8. F-measure, purity and inverse purity values.

computed for both algorithms and datasets reveal that our proposal is increasing both measures with respect to the traditional algorithm, not prioritising one over the other.

5 Conclusions

In this paper, we identified two major shortcomings when scaling DBSCAN-like algorithms for event detection systems in Twitter. First, the large amount of tweets hampers the use of event detection techniques that run into a single machine. Second, the geographical or temporal scaling of these systems has to explicitly consider that tweeting activity varies in space and time.

To tackle both shortcomings, we proposed a density-aware MapReduce scheme which benefits from local DBSCAN computations to tune its local parameters to the neighboring tweet densities. The rationale for using density-aware parameters is that events in highly dense regions are likely to contain more tweets, while those in low-density regions will contain less.

The assessment of the proposed scheme is performed in a dataset of geo-located tweets in the Iberian peninsula during the course of several football matches. Tweets nearby the stadium during the football game are manually identified as event-related tweets. The evaluation shows that our proposal to incorporate density awareness outperforms classical DBSCAN techniques. Moreover, we also show that the overall execution time improves with respect to RDD-DBSCAN by using a naive but effective Octree-based partitioning scheme.

6 Future Work

The proposed density-aware MapReduce scheme for event detection has been evaluated in a dataset of events which all shared similar spatio-temporal features. Future work should address the evaluation in datasets of heterogeneous events. For example, events that last many hours but are located within a narrow area or events that last few hours but are geographically very spread.

Similarly, we have observed that some clusters detected by our event detection approach did not correspond to real-world events, but to popular places known as landmarks, such as the city centre. In order to avoid detecting these clusters, a textual component could be added in the neighborhood search for selecting tweets which are similar in meaning, as in [14,16]. However, searching for textual objects will cause extra computational cost that might not be disregarded by future research.

As in RDD-DBSCAN, the need to load the complete data set for a given partition into memory still remains open. Future work should focus on this given that the use of disk and memory will bring new ideas to scale up event detection in Apache Spark. For example, we might need to rethink the proposed Octree-based partitioning scheme so that it takes into account the extra-cost to now load data from disk.

References

1. Wong, W., Neill, D.: Tutorial on event detection. In: Special Interest Group on Knowledge Discovery and Data Mining (SIGKDD) (2009)
2. Kulldorff, M., Athas, W., Feurer, E., Miller, B., Key, C.: Am. J. Publ. Health **88**(9), 1377–1380 (1998)
3. Yu, Z.: Tutorial on location-based social networks. In: Proceedings of the 21st International Conference on World wide web (WWW) (2012)
4. Sakaki, T., Okazaki, M., Matsuo, Y.: Earthquake shakes Twitter users: real-time event detection by social sensors. In: Proceedings of the 19th International Conference on World Wide Web (WWW) (2010)
5. Lee, R., Sumiya, K.: Measuring geographical regularities of crowd behaviors for Twitter-based geo-social event detection. In: Proceedings of the 2nd ACM SIGSPATIAL International Workshop on Location Based Social Networks (LBSN) (2010)
6. Newman, N.: Mainstream media and the distribution of news in the age of social discovery. Reuters Institute for the Study of Journalism, University of Oxford (2011)
7. Stelter, B., Cohen, N.: Citizen Journalists Provided Glimpses of Mumbai Attacks. (2008). http://www.nytimes.com/2008/11/30/world/asia/30twitter.html
8. Atefeh, F., Khreich, W.: A survey of techniques for event detection in Twitter. Comput. Intell. **1**, 132–164 (2015)
9. Becker, H., Naaman, M., Gravano, L.: Beyond trending topics: real-world event identification on Twitter. In: Proceedings of the Fifth International Conference on Weblogs and Social Media (2011)
10. Ester, M., Kriegel, H., Sander, J., Xu, X.: A density-based algorithm for discovering clusters in large spatial databases with noise. In: Kdd, vol. 96(34) (1996)
11. Gomide, J., Veloso, A., Meira, W., Almeida, V., Benevenuto, F., Ferraz, F., Teixeira, M.: Dengue surveillance based on a computational model of spatio-temporal locality of Twitter. In: Proceedings of the 3rd International Web Science Conference (2011)
12. Tamura, K., Ichimura, T.: Density-based spatiotemporal clustering algorithm for extracting bursty areas from georeferenced documents. In: IEEE International Conference on Systems, Man, and Cybernetics (SMC) (2013)
13. Birant, D., Kut, A.: ST-DBSCAN: an algorithm for clustering spatial-temporal data. Data and Knowledge Engineering (2007)
14. Singh, S.: Spatial temporal analysis of social media data. Master Thesis at Technische Universität München (2015)
15. Capdevila, J., Cerquides, J., Nin, J., Torres, J.: Tweet-SCAN: an event discovery technique for geo-located tweets. In: Artificial Intelligence Research and Development - Proceedings of the 18th International Conference of the Catalan Association for Artificial Intelligence (2015)
16. Capdevila, J., Cerquides, J., Nin, J., Torres, J.: Tweet-SCAN: An event discovery technique for geo-located tweets. Pattern Recognition Letters. Available online 25 August (2016)
17. Blei, D.: Probabilistic topic models. Commun. ACM. **55**(4), 77–84 (2012)
18. Li, L., Goodchild, M., Xu, B.: Spatial, temporal, and socioeconomic patterns in the use of Twitter and Flickr. Cartography Geogr. Inf. Sci. **40**, 261–277 (2013)
19. Zaharia, M., Chowdhury, M., Franklin, M., Shenker, S., Stoica, I.: Spark: cluster computing with working sets. In: Proceedings of the 2nd USENIX Conference on Hot Topics in Cloud Computing (2010)

20. Sander, J., Ester, M., Kriegel, H., Xu, X.: Density-based clustering in spatial databases: the algorithm GDBSCAN and its applications. Data Mining Knowl. Discov. **2**(2), 169–194 (1998)
21. Dean, J., Ghemawat, S.: MapReduce: simplified data processing on large clusters. Commun. ACM **51**, 107–113 (2008)
22. He, Y., Tan, H., Luo, W., Feng, S., Fan, J.: MR-DBSCAN: a scalable MapReduce-based DBSCAN algorithm for heavily skewed data. Front. Comput. Sci. **8**, 83–99 (2014)
23. Cordova, I., Moh, T.S.: DBSCAN on resilient distributed datasets. In: International Conference on High Performance Computing Simulation (HPCS), pp. 531–540 (2015)
24. Meagher, D.: Octree Encoding: A New Technique for the Representation, Manipulation and Display of Arbitrary 3-D Objects by Computer. Electrical and Systems Engineering Department Rensseiaer Polytechnic Institute Image Processing Laboratory (1980)
25. Pedregosa, F., Varoquaux, G., Gramfort, A., Michel, V., Thirion, B., Grisel, O., Blondel, M., Prettenhofer, P., Weiss, R., Dubourg, V., Vanderplas, J., Passos, A., Cournapeau, D., Brucher, M., Perrot, M., Duchesnay, E.: Scikit-learn: machine learning in Python. J. Mach. Learn. Res. **12**, 2825–2830 (2011)
26. Amigó, E., Gonzalo, J., Artiles, J., Verdejo, F.: A comparison of extrinsic clustering evaluation metrics based on formal constraints. Inf. Retrieval **12**(4), 461–486 (2009)

Towards Parallel CFD Computation
for the ADAPT Framework

Imad Kissami[1,2]([⊠]), Christophe Cérin[1],
Fayssal Benkhaldoun[2], and Gilles Scarella[2]

[1] LIPN, Université de Paris 13, 99,
Avenue Jean-Baptiste Clément, 93430 Villetaneuse, France
[2] LAGA, Université de Paris 13, 99,
Avenue Jean-Baptiste Clément, 93430 Villetaneuse, France
kissami.imad@lipn.univ-paris13.fr

Abstract. In order to run Computational Fluid Dynamics (CFD) codes on large scale infrastructures, parallel computing has to be used because of the computational intensive nature of the problems. In this paper we investigate the ADAPT platform where we couple flow Partial Differential Equations and a Poisson equation. This leads to a linear system which we solve using direct methods. The implementation deals with the MUMPS parallel multi-frontal direct solver and mesh partitioning methods using METIS to improve the performance of the framework. We also investigate, in this paper, how the mesh partitioning methods are able to optimize the mesh cell distribution for the ADAPT solver. The experience gained in this paper facilitates the move to a Service Oriented view of ADAPT as future work.

Keywords: Unstructured mesh · Mesh partitioning · Parallel direct solver · Multi-frontal method · MUMPS · METIS · Multi-physics · Multi-scale and multilevel algorithms

1 Introduction and Context of the Work

In the last recent decades CFD (Computational Fluid Dynamics) used to play an important role in industrial designs, environmental impact assessments and academic studies. The aim of our work is to conduct a parallelization of an unstructured adaptive code for the simulation of 3D streamer propagation in cold plasmas. As a matter of fact, the initial sequential version of the Streamer code needs up to one month for running typical benchmarks.

The generation of streamer discharges is described by coupling electrostatic to the motion of charged particles (electrons, positive and negative ions). The

The funding supports of this work is the EnCoMix AAP SPC project (ANR-11-IDEX-05-02 Ref: SPC/JFG/2013031). The experiments conducted in this work were done on the nodes B500 of the University Paris 13 MAGI Cluster and available at http://cirrus.uspc.fr.

© Springer International Publishing AG 2016
J. Carretero et al. (Eds.): ICA3PP 2016, LNCS 10048, pp. 374–387, 2016.
DOI: 10.1007/978-3-319-49582-5_28

electrostatic is represented by a Poisson equation for the electric potential and the motion of particles is described by a set of convection-diffusion-reaction equations.

We aim at doing a parallelization of both the linear solver issued from the Poisson equation and the evolution equation using domain decomposition and mesh adaptation at 'the same time'. To our knowledge this is the first time that such a challenge is considered. Intuitively speaking, separating the two steps may add delays because we need to synchronize them and to align the execution time on the slowest processor. Considering the two steps simultaneously offers the potential to better overlap different computational steps.

Other authors have tackled the parallelization of either the linear solvers or the evolution equation usually without mesh adaptation. In [1] the authors consider the parallelization of a linear system of electromagnetic equation on non adaptive unstructured mesh. Their time integration method leads to the resolution of a linear system which requires a large memory capacity for a single processor.

In [2] the authors introduce a parallel code which was written in C++ augmented with MPI primitives and the LIS (Linear Iterative Solver) library. Several numerical experiments have been done on a cluster of 2.40 GHz Intel Xeon, with 12 GB RAM, connected with a Gigabit Ethernet switch. The authors note that a classical run of the sequential version of their code might easily exceed one month of calculation. The improvement of the parallel version is due to the parallelization of three parts of the code: the diagonalization of the Schrödinger matrix, advancing one step in the Newton-Raphson iteration, and the Runge-Kutta integrator.

The authors in [3] focused only on the parallelization of a linear solver related to the discretization of self-adjoint elliptic partial differential equations and using multi-grid methods.

It should also be mentioned that authors in [4] have successfully studied similar problems to those presented in this paper. The associated linear systems have been solved using iterative Gmres and CG solvers [5]. One difference is that in our work we consider direct methods based on LU decomposition using the MUMPS solver.

Moreover, the direct solution methods generally involve the use of frontal algorithms in finite element applications. The advent of multi-frontal solvers has greatly increased the efficiency of direct solvers for sparse systems. They make full use of high performance software layers such as invoking level 3 Basic Linear Algebra Subprograms (BLAS) [6,7] library. Thus the memory requirement is greatly reduced and the computing speed greatly enhanced. Multi-frontal solvers have been successfully used both in the context of finite volume, finite element methods and in power system simulations.

The disadvantage of using direct solvers is that the memory size increases much more quickly than the problem size itself. To circumvent this problem, out-of-core multi-frontal solvers have been developed which have the capability of storing objects of the resolution on the disk during factorization.

Another viable alternative is to use direct solvers in a distributed computing environment. MUMPS [8,9] is among the fastest parallel general sparse direct solvers available under public domain.

In order to deal with complex geometries and fluid flows, a large number of mesh cells should be used. Therefore the parallel computing paradigm has to be introduced for coping with this large number of mesh cells. In the parallel computing field, several factors, such as the load balancing, the number of neighboring sub-domains and the halo cells (cells which are at the boundary of sub-domains), affect the performance. A well balanced load has the potential to reduce the amount of waiting processors and the partitioning method can optimize the distribution of the mesh cells across processors, thus it will improve the performance of the parallel application too.

In this paper, we also use METIS [10], an open source mesh partitioning software, and we incorporate it into the streamer code of ADAPT [11], to solve the evolution PDE (Parallel Differential Equation), in order to study the impact of mesh partitioning on the parallel version of ADAPT that we are currently developing.

Moreover we carry out experiments using the parallel multi-frontal direct solver (MUMPS) with matrices extracted from the streamer code of the ADAPT platform. The general strategy is as follows. The linear system of equations is evaluated on different processors corresponding to the local grid assigned to the processor. The right hand side vector is assembled on the host processor and it is injected into the MUMPS solver. At the last step of the MUMPS solver, the solution is assembled centrally on the host processor. This solution is then broadcast to all the processors. We discuss later the pro and cons of such a strategy.

The organization of the paper is the following. In Sect. 2 we introduce the aim of the ADAPT platform and its positioning. In Sect. 3 we discuss about parallel approaches to solve evolution equation coupled with Poisson equation, show the strategy to do a parallelization of our code and do some experiments with METIS. In Sect. 4 we analyze different parts of our code in terms of speedup and efficiency and we provide numerical results that show the efficiency our work. Section 5 concludes the paper.

2   The ADAPT Framework

2.1   Overview

ADAPT [11] is an object oriented platform for running numerical simulations with a dynamic mesh adaptation strategy and coupling between finite element and finite volume methods. ADAPT, as a CFD (Computational Fluid Dynamics) software package, has been developed for realizing numerical simulation on an unstructured and adaptive mesh for large scale CFD applications.

In this paper, in order to tackle the long running time necessary for numerical simulation, we study the MUMPS and METIS toolkits and we integrate them into the ADAPT framework. In fact we perform code coupling between the two main steps of the studied problem. The existing ADAPT implementation is a sequential C++ code for each phenomenon, and the code requires a huge CPU time for executing a 3D simulation. For example, the 3D streamer code may run up to 30 days before returning results, for this reason we decided to do a parallelization of the code. This paper is an important step into this direction.

2.2 Working Environment

To realize all the experiments (sequential and parallel) we worked on the MAGI clusterfootnote http://www.univ-paris13.fr/calcul/wiki which is located at the University of Paris 13, and also on the Ada cluster of Idris[1], one of the national computing facility in France.

3 Parallel Approach

In this paper, we do a parallelization of the evolution equation coupled with the Poisson equation, written as:

$$\begin{cases} \dfrac{\partial u}{\partial t} + F(V, u) = S, \\[2ex] \Delta P = b. \end{cases} \tag{1}$$

given that $F(V, u) = div(u.\overrightarrow{V}) - \Delta u$, $S = 0$, and $V = \overrightarrow{\nabla} P$, the previous system gives :

$$\begin{cases} \dfrac{\partial u}{\partial t} + div(u.\overrightarrow{V}) = \Delta u \\[2ex] \Delta P = b. \end{cases} \tag{2}$$

The first equation is discretized using the finite volume method on an unstructured triangular mesh. The time-integration of the transport equation is performed using an explicit scheme. The discretized form of Poisson equation leads to a linear algebraic system. We obtain the following set of equations:

$$\begin{cases} u_i^{n+1} = u_i^n - \dfrac{\Delta t}{\mu_i} \underbrace{\sum_{j=1}^{m} u_{ij} \overrightarrow{V}_{ij} \overrightarrow{n}_{ij} |\sigma_{ij}|}_{Rez\_conv} + \dfrac{\Delta t}{\mu_i} \underbrace{\sum_{j=1}^{m} \overrightarrow{\nabla} u_{ij} \overrightarrow{n}_{ij} |\sigma_{ij}|}_{Rez\_dissip} \\[3ex] \hphantom{xxxxxxxxxxxxxxxxxxxxxxxxxxxxxxxxxxxxxxx} A.\overrightarrow{P}^n = \overrightarrow{b}^n \end{cases} \tag{3}$$

where m is the number of faces of volume μ_i, $\overrightarrow{n}_{ij}$ is the unit normal vector of the face σ_{ij} (face between volumes μ_i and μ_j) and $|\sigma_{ij}|$ is its length. Other variables denoted by subscript ij represent variables on the face σ_{ij}.

---

[1] http://www.idris.fr.

A is a large sparse matrix, the coefficients of the matrix depend only on the grid topology.

Computation of u_{ij}: In Fig. 1 we took the example when the mesh is split into two sub-domains, and we compute u_{ij} on the face σ_{ij}. For a given face σ_k, suppose T_i and T_j are respectively the cells at the left and right of σ_k. Let's note $\sigma_k = \sigma_{ij}$ and $u_k = u_{ij}$. The Algorithm 1 shows how the u_{ij} is computed on face σ_{ij}.

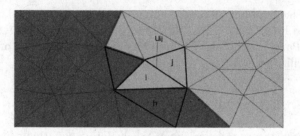

Fig. 1. Computation of u_{ij} in mesh split into two sub-domains

---

Algorithm 1. Compute u_{ij} on face ij

```
 1  F:number of faces;
 2  for k:=1 to F do
 3  │   if dot(V_k.n_k) >= 0 then
 4  │   │   u_k = u_i;
 5  │   end
 6  │   else
 7  │   │   if σk is inner faces then
 8  │   │   │   u_k = u_j;
 9  │   │   end
10  │   │   else if σk is halo faces then
11  │   │   │   u_k = u_h;/* u_h halo value sent by neighbor sub-domain */
12  │   │   end
13  │   end
14  end
```

Computation of $\overrightarrow{\nabla} u_{ij}$: In Fig. 3 we take the same mesh, and we compute $\overrightarrow{\nabla} u_{ij}$ of the face σ_{ij}. The Algorithm 2 shows how the $\overrightarrow{\nabla} u_{ij}$ is computed on volume μ_{ij}. The diamond cell in Fig. 2 is constructed by connection of centers of gravity (i, j) of cells T_i, T_j which shares the face σ_{ij} and its endpoints A, B.

$$\overrightarrow{\nabla} u_{ij} = \frac{1}{2\mu(D_{\sigma_{ij}})}[(u_A - u_B)\overrightarrow{n}_{LR}|\sigma_{LR}| + (u_j - u_i)\overrightarrow{n}_{ij}|\sigma_{ij}|] \qquad (4)$$

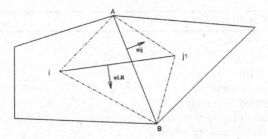

Fig. 2. Diamond cell in 2D

Algorithm 2. Compute value at node (u_{node})

---

1 u_{node}:double;
2 N :number of nodes;
3 $Alpha$:weight coming from the least square method;
4 **for** $n:=1$ **to** N **do**
5   **for** $c:=1$ **to** *inner cells around node n* **do**
6        $u_{node}(n)+ = Alpha * u_j(c)$;
7   **end**
8   **for** $m:=1$ **to** *halo cells around node* **do**
9        $u_{node}(n)+ = Alpha * u_h(m)$;
10   **end**
11 **end**
12 **return** u_{node};

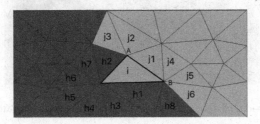

Fig. 3. Computation of ∇u_{ij} in mesh split into two sub-domains

Computation of the Linear System: The system is solved directly by LU decomposition with an implementation for sparse matrices. We use the **Intel MKL library**[2] solvers and **UMFPACK** [12]. Note that in traditional approaches, one splits the mesh to solve both the evolution equation and the linear system in each sub-domain using iterative methods with added communications. In our work we use the same methodology in partitioning the mesh but the linear system is solved with a direct method.

---

[2] https://software.intel.com/en-us/intel-mkl#pid-3374-836.

Algorithm 3. Compute ∇u_{ij} on face ij

---

  1 F:number of faces;

  2 $\vec{\nabla} u$:Vector2d;

  3 **for** $k:=1$ **to** F **do**

  4   A:first node of face;

  5   B:second face node;

  6   i:center of gravity of cell T_i;

  7   j:center of gravity of cell T_j;

  8      $mes = \frac{1}{2\mu(D_{\sigma_{ij}})}$;

  9   **if** *Inner faces* **then**

10          $\vec{\nabla} u(k) =$
             $mes * (u_{node}(A) - u_{node}(B))\vec{n}_{LR}|\sigma_{LR}| + (u_j - u_i)\vec{n}_{ij}|\sigma_{ij}|$;

11   **end**

12   **else if** *Halo faces* **then**

13          $\vec{\nabla} u(k) =$
             $mes * (u_{node}(A) - u_{node}(B))\vec{n}_{LR}|\sigma_{LR}| + (u_h - u_i)\vec{n}_{ih}|\sigma_{ih}|$;

14   **end**

15 **end**

16 **return** $\vec{\nabla} u$;

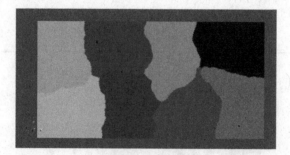

Fig. 4. Decomposition of the computational domain into 8 sub-domains using the METIS method

Parallelization: For the parallelization of CFD simulations, ADAPT employs the domain decomposition method. The 2D unstructured mesh in Fig. 4 was decomposed into eight sub-domains using the METIS algorithm, these partitions have approximately the same size that we may consider as a good property because the workload will be balanced on the homogeneous processors of our platform.

Algorithm 4 provides with a piece of pseudo-code that shows how the parallelization is done in the streamer code according to the coupling of evolution equation with Poisson equation. We can see that most parts of the code are parallel ones (line 19, line 9 to 11 and line 22 to 26) except reading and splitting mesh in the beginning and between lines 14 and 15. Indeed, at this step, we construct matrix A (Eq. 2) that will be used to solve the linear system in line 19. Matrix A is computed one time because it depends only on the mesh.

Our contribution will serve in the future to tackle the 3D version of streamer which includes the same type of equations, same strategy to solve the linear system. The difference is the structure of the grid because we will work with Tetrahedra instead of triangles, which will make the problem much more complicated due to big differences in handling the mesh in the 3D case.

Algorithm 4. Parallel version of ADAPT

---

1 W:double;
2 **if** *rank==0* **then** /* **for the master processor**   */
3 | Read mesh data;
4 | Split mesh with METIS;
5 | Distribute mesh to all processors;
6 **end**
7 W=0;
8 **for** *each rank* **do** /* **for each processor**   */
9 | Initialize conditions and create constants;
10 | Send the information of halos cells to neighbor sub-domains;
11 | Apply boundary conditions;
12 **end**
13 **if** *rank==0* **then**
14 | Construct matrix of linear system;
15 | Split the matrix and send part of each processor;
16 **end**
17 **for** *each iteration* **do**
18 | **for** *all rank* **do** /* **for all processors**   */
19 | | Solve linear system using MUMPS;
20 | **end**
21 | **for** *each rank* **do**
22 | | Send the information of halos cells to neighbor
       | | sub-domains;
23 | | Apply boundary conditions;
24 | | Compute fluxes of convection, diffusion and source term;
25 | | Update solution :
       | | $W^{n+1} = W^n + \Delta t * (rez\_conv + rez\_dissip + rez\_source)$;
26 | | Save results in parallel way using Paraview;
27 | **end**
28 **end**

---

4 Application to Streamer Equations

When non-ionized or low ionized matter is exposed to high intensity electric field, non-equilibrium ionization processors (so-called discharges or streamers) occur.

Because of the reactive radicals they emit, streamers are used for the treatment of contaminated media like exhaust gasses, polluted water or bio-gas.

4.1   The Governing Equation

The streamer consists of a convection-diffusion-reaction for the electron density, an ordinary differential equation for the positive ion density coupled by the Poisson's equation for the electric potential. The model is given by the following equations:

$$\frac{\partial n_e}{\partial t} + div(n_e \overrightarrow{v_e} - De \overrightarrow{\nabla} n_e) = S_e, \tag{5}$$

$$\frac{\partial n_i}{\partial t} = S_e, \tag{6}$$

$$\Delta V = -\frac{e}{\epsilon}(n_i - n_e) \; , \tag{7}$$

$$E = -\overrightarrow{\nabla} V \; , \tag{8}$$

where V is a potential of electric field E, ϵ is the dielectric constant, e the electron charge, n_e and n_i are the number densities of electrons and positive ions, the drift velocity of electrons is $v_e = v_e(E)$ and $D_e = D_e(E, v_e)$ is the diffusion coefficient. The source terms depend on the electron drift velocity and the electron density $S_e = S_e(v_e, n_e)$.

4.2   Numerical Method

The equations of the model are discretized using the finite volume method on an unstructured triangular mesh. The time-integration of the transport equations is performed using an explicit scheme. The discretized form of Poissons equation consists of a linear algebraic system that is solved with a direct method at each time step during the time-integration. We approximate the equation for the electron density (Eq. 3) by the following finite volume method:

$$\frac{\partial n_e}{\partial t} + \frac{1}{\mu(T)} \oint_{\partial T} (n_e \overrightarrow{v_e} - D_e \overrightarrow{\nabla} n_e) \overrightarrow{n} \, \mathrm{d}s = S_e \tag{9}$$

where $\mu(T)$ is the volume of the cell T, $\overrightarrow{n}$ the outward unit normal vector to the faces of the cell T.

The Poisson's equation (Eq. 5) is discretized by a central type approximation which leads to a system of linear equation, as follows:

$$A.\overrightarrow{V}^{n+1} = \overrightarrow{b}^{n+1} \tag{10}$$

A is a matrix of coefficients, $\overrightarrow{V}$ is a vector of unknowns (its dimension is equaled to the total number of cells) and $\overrightarrow{b}$ is a vector of right hand side.

4.3   Parallel Results

Table 1 summarize our results. The speedup in this example shows a good scalability of the present method for solving the convection-diffusion equation coupled with Poisson equation problems using mesh with 529240 cells. For practical applications, the computation time could be reduced from 49h54min (one computing core) down to 5 min (1024 computing cores). This test is made on MAGI cluster at Paris13.

Table 1. Execution time (in s) of different parts of parallel 2D streamer code using mesh with 529240 cells

Compute cores	Total	Convection	Diffusion	Linear solver
1	49 h 54 min 48 s	02 h 51 min 04 s	13 h 06 min 00 s	33 h 57 min 44 s
2	25 h 06 min 27 s	01 h 22 min 57 s	06 h 41 min 02 s	17 h 02 min 27 s
4	12 h 34 min 35 s	00 h 42 min 07 s	03 h 22 min 04 s	08 h 30 min 24 s
8	06 h 27 min 18 s	00 h 22 min 13 s	01 h 46 min 26 s	04 h 18 min 38 s
16	03 h 39 min 45 s	00 h 12 min 37 s	01 h 01 min 40 s	02 h 25 min 26 s
32	01 h 50 min 50 s	00 h 08 min 03 s	00 h 29 min 17 s	01 h 13 min 29 s
64	01 h 01 min 41 s	00 h 03 min 59 s	00 h 17 min 05 s	00 h 40 min 36 s
128	00 h 32 min 44 s	00 h 01 min 52 s	00 h 08 min 22 s	00 h 22 min 29 s
256	00 h 18 min 16 s	00 h 01 min 02 s	00 h 04 min 34 s	00 h 12 min 39 s
512	00 h 10 min 07 s	00 h 00 min 33 s	00 h 02 min 52 s	00 h 06 min 42 s
1024	00 h 05 min 14 s	00 h 00 min 18 s	00 h 01 min 33 s	00 h 03 min 23 s

Scalability Measurement: There are two basic ways to measure the scalability of parallel algorithms:

(a) Strong scaling with a fixed problem size but the number of processing elements are increased.
(b) Weak scaling with problem size and compute elements increasing concurrently.

The speedup is defined as

$$sp = \frac{t_b}{t_N},$$

and the ideal speedup, sp_{ideal}, is naturally equivalent to the number of compute cores. Therefore, the strong scaling efficiency can also be calculated by

$$\frac{s_p}{sp_{ideal}}$$

which shows how far is the measured speedup from the ideal one.

In the this work, the strong scaling measurement is employed and the scaling efficiency is calculated by:

$$\frac{t_b N}{t_N N_b} 100, \ N \geq N_b$$

where t_b is the wall clock time of a base computation, N_b is the number of compute cores used for the base computation, t_N is the wall clock time of a computation with N compute cores.

Figures 5 and 6 illustrate the speedup and the strong scaling efficiency in the computations of our illustrate example with t_b the wall clock times by one compute core. A more detailed injection into the data of this example provides interesting information about the computational efficiency of the individual parts of the parallel simulation. The results of the strong scaling tests, plotted in Fig. 6 depict that the parallel speedup of the different parts increases up to 1024 computational cores, so our parallel strategy shows its efficiency.

4.4   Comparison Between Sequential and Parallel Codes

In Fig. 7 a comparison is made between sequential 2D streamer code and parallel counterpart. We can also observe the propagation of streamer in two cases: more the mesh is fine more the results are accurate (without oscillations). In Table 2, the parallel code takes the same running time (using 64 MPI processors) as the sequential code but the input size is 12 times greater.

To conclude, our strategy although not classical shows to be very efficient, and provides with relevant properties regarding performance.

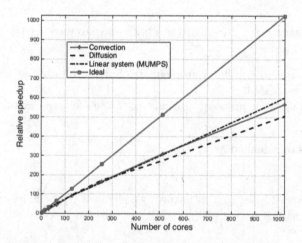

Fig. 5. Speedup of different parts of streamer code using mesh with 529240 cells

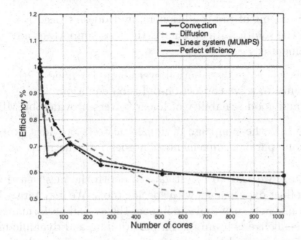

Fig. 6. Efficiency of different parts of streamer code using mesh with 529240 cells

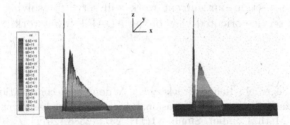

Fig. 7. Plasma discharge in sequential code (left) and parallel one (right)

Table 2. Comparison between sequential and parallel code

	Compute cores	Execution time
Mesh using 43674 elements	1	04 h 30 min
Mesh using 529240 elements	1	150 h 15 min
	64	03 h 59 min

5 Conclusions and Future Work

In this work, we have introduced an effective parallelization of the ADAPT platform for CFD applications. We present the parallelization of the convection-diffusion equation and the linear system. The originality of this work is to solve linear system using a direct method whereas existing studies mainly use iterative methods to solve linear system in this kind of problems. The workflow is realized: (1) using external tools such as METIS for mesh partitioning in order to enable the computational load balance for the global assembly, (2) using MPI to assure communication, (3) using MUMPS solver to solve the system of linear equations. The current approach with MUMPS shows significant advantages in terms of avoiding the problems of pre-conditioners, and doesn't need a lot of iterations to converge to the solution. In summary, the most important advantages of the presented scheme are:

- Efficient memory usage distribution over computer nodes,
- Good scalability to solve convection-diffusion equation,
- Stable, fast and good scalability of linear solvers provided by MUMPS.

We observe that the campaign of numerical tests provides expected results, meaning that our parallel implementation goes into the right direction at the moment.

For the future, we plan to investigate in depth the mesh partitioning problems and to conduct experiments with specific tools. We may target PAMPA [13] and the question is how such tool can impact the overall performance of ADAPT software. The challenge is to mix mesh partitioning and dynamic mesh adaptations. How to manage load balancing in this context? When dealing with three dimensional problems, the question is even more critical. At least, as explained in the discussion section our current work will serve for solving 3D streamer problems and a service oriented view of the ADAPT framework.

References

1. Assous, F., Segré, J., Sonnendrücker, E.: A domain decomposition method for the parallelization of a three-dimensional maxwell solver based on a constrained formulation. Math. Comput. Simul. **81**(11), 2371–2388 (2011)
2. Vecil, F., Mantas, J.M., Cáceres, M.J., Sampedro, C., Godoy, A., Gmiz, F.: A parallel deterministic solver for the Schrodinger-Poisson-Boltzmann system in ultrashort DG-MOSFETS: comparison with Monte-Carlo. Comput. Math. Appl. **67**(9), 1703–1721 (2014)
3. Notay, Y., Napov, A.: A massively parallel solver for discrete poisson-like problems. J. Comput. Phys. **281**, 237–250 (2015)
4. Kumar, P., Markidis, S., Lapenta, G., Meerbergen, K., Roose, D.: High performance solvers for implicit particle in cell simulation. Procedia Comput. Sci. **18**, 2251–2258 (2013)
5. Saad, Y., Schultz, M.H.: GMRES: a generalized minimal residual algorithm for solving nonsymmetric linear systems. SIAM J. Sci. Stat. Comput. **7**(3), 856–869 (1986)
6. Blackford, L.S., Demmel, J., Dongarra, J., Duff, I., Hammarling, S., Henry, G., Heroux, M., Kaufman, L., Lumsdaine, A., Petitet, A., Pozo, R., Remington, K., Whaley, R.C.: An updated set of basic linear algebra subprograms (BLAS). ACM Trans. Math. Softw. **28**, 135–151 (2001)
7. Boisvert, R.F., Dongarra, J.: Preface to the special issue on the basic linear algebra subprograms (BLAS). ACM Trans. Math. Softw. **28**(2), 133–134 (2002)
8. Amestoy, P.R., Duff, I.S., L'Excellent, J.-Y., Koster, J.: MUMPS: a general purpose distributed memory sparse solver. In: Sørevik, T., Manne, F., Gebremedhin, A.H., Moe, R. (eds.) PARA 2000. LNCS, vol. 1947, pp. 121–130. Springer, Heidelberg (2001). doi:10.1007/3-540-70734-4_16
9. Amestoy, P., Guermouche, A., L'Excellent, J.-Y., Pralet, S.: Hybrid scheduling for the parallel solution of linear systems. Parallel Comput. **32**(2), 136–156 (2006)

10. Karypis, G., Kumar, V.: A fast and high quality multilevel scheme for partitioning irregular graphs. SIAM J. Sci. Comput. **20**(1), 359–392 (1998)
11. Benkhaldoun, F., Fort, J., Hassouni, K., Karel, J.: Simulation of planar ionization wave front propagation on an unstructured adaptive grid. J. Comput. Appl. Math. **236**, 4623–4634 (2012)
12. Davis, T.A.: Algorithm 832: UMFPACK V4.3 - an unsymmetric-pattern multi-frontal method. ACM Trans. Math. Softw. **30**(2), 196–199 (2004)
13. Lachat, C., Pellegrini, F., Dobrzynski, C.: PaMPA: parallel mesh partitioning and adaptation. In: 21st International Conference on Domain Decomposition Methods (DD21), Rennes, France, INRIA Rennes-Bretagne-Atlantique, June 2012

Feedback Control Optimization for Performance and Energy Efficiency on CPU-GPU Heterogeneous Systems

Feng-Sheng Lin[1]([✉]), Po-Ting Liu[2], Ming-Hua Li[1], and Pao-Ann Hsiung[2]

[1] Information and Communication Laboratories,
Industrial Technology Research Institute, 31040 Hsinchu, Taiwan
{PatrickCSLin,liminhwa}@itri.org.tw
[2] Department of Computer Science and Information Technology,
National Chung Cheng University, 62102 Chiayi, Taiwan
{lpt101m,pahsiung}@cs.ccu.edu.tw

Abstract. Owing to the rising awareness of environment protection, high performance is not the only aim in system design, energy efficiency has increasingly become an important goal. In accordance with this goal, heterogeneous systems which are more efficient than CPU-based homogeneous systems, and occupying a growing proportion in the Top500 and the Green500 lists. Nevertheless, heterogeneous system design being more complex presents greater challenges in achieving a good tradeoff between performance and energy efficiency for applications running on such systems. To address the performance energy tradeoff issue in CPU-GPU heterogeneous systems, we propose a novel feedback control optimization (FCO) method that alternates between frequency scaling of device and division of kernel workload between CPU and GPU. Given a kernel and a workload division, frequency scaling involves finding near-optimal core frequency of the CPU and of the GPU. Further, an iterative algorithm is proposed for finding a near-optimal workload division that balance workload between CPU and GPU at a frequency that was optimal for the previous workload division. The frequency scaling phase and workload division phase are alternatively performed until the proposed FCO method converges and finds a configuration including core frequency for CPU, core frequency for GPU, and the workload division. Experiments show that compared with the state-of-the-art GreenGPU method, performance can be improved by 7.9%, while energy consumption can be reduced by 4.16%.

Keywords: CPU · GPU · Heterogeneous system · Frequency scaling · Workload division · Performance · Energy efficiency

1 Introduction

With the widespread use of Graphics Processing Units (GPU), there is increasing research on high throughput heterogeneous systems equipped with

© Springer International Publishing AG 2016
J. Carretero et al. (Eds.): ICA3PP 2016, LNCS 10048, pp. 388–404, 2016.
DOI: 10.1007/978-3-319-49583-5_29

CPUs and GPUs. For example, Titan is ranked second in the Top500 [1] list of supercomputers in the world as of June 2014. It has 18,688 nodes, each node contains an AMD Opteron 6274 CPU and a Nvidia K20x general-purpose GPU. Recently, in addition to high performance, energy efficiency is another critical issue in supercomputer designs. Energy efficiency can be defined as the numbers of floating operations per watt of power. Green500 [2] lists the top 500 supercomputers in the order of descending energy efficiency. The top 10 supercomputers in the Green500 list are all equipped with CPUs and NVIDIA K20/K40 series general-purpose GPUs as of June 2014.

Frequency scaling and workload division are both the important issues for performance and energy efficiency on homogeneous multi-core systems, and the complexities of the issues are increased especially on heterogeneous CPU-GPU systems. Here, we conduct two cases studies to motivate our proposal with Intel Xeon E5-2620 CPU and Nvidia Tesla K20c GPU: frequency scaling for CPU and GPU, and workload division between CPU and GPU. We use the applications from Rodinia [3], Nvidia CUDA SDK [4] and the Technical Report [5].

1.1 Case Study on Frequency Scaling

In this case, we manually scale the frequency of CPU and observe the effect on energy efficiency and performance. The energy efficiency can be defined as the number of floating operations per watt of power. The performance here is defined as reciprocal execution time. Figure 1 shows the results, the x-axis represents the CPU frequencies, the y-axis represents the energy efficiency normalized to the maximum efficiency and the performance normalized to the maximum performance in Fig. 1a and b, respectively. In Fig. 1a, we can see that different applications may require different optimal frequency for achieving optimal energy efficiency. For instance, *streamcluster* and *lud* (LU decomposition) have the optimal energy efficiency when the core frequency is set to 1.8 GHz. However, *blackscholes* and *kmeans* have the optimal energy efficiency of the peak core frequency of 2.0 GHz. As for performance in Fig. 1b, we can observe that when the frequency is set to 1.8 GHz, optimal energy efficiency is achieved at the expense of about 10% to 15% performance loss for *streamcluster* and *lud*.

Figure 2 show the results when the former experiment is conducted on GPU, and the results are quite different. We can observe that the applications achieve optimal energy efficiency at different frequencies in Fig. 2a. For example, optimal energy efficiency is achieved for *streamcluster* at 666 MHz, *blackscholes* at 640 MHz, *lud* at 705 MHz, and *kmeans* at 758 MHz. The pattern in achieving energy efficiency is quite different from each other. Moreover, in Fig. 2b, we observe that optimal energy efficiency is achieved at the expense of no more than 7% performance loss.

The above described large varieties in achieving energy efficiency motivate this work to propose a method to scale CPU and GPU frequency that can be applied to most applications. The goal is to suggest frequency setting for CPU and GPU such that optimal or suboptimal energy efficiency can be achieved at negligible performance loss.

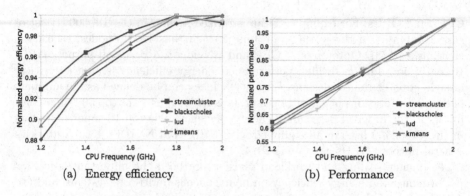

Fig. 1. Effect of scaling CPU cores frequency.

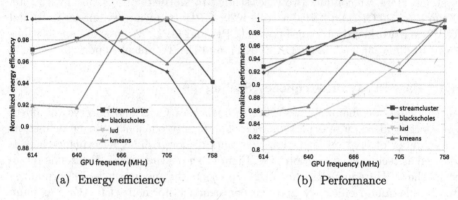

Fig. 2. Effect of scaling GPU cores frequency.

1.2   Case Study on Workload Division

Workload division is a common issue for heterogeneous architectures. We conduct a simple experiment to describe this issue. The workload of an application are divided into two parts, one for a single CPU and the other for a single GPU. For example, if CPU takes 10 % of workload, GPU takes the rest 90%. Thus, CPU and GPU execute the workload in parallel.

The results are shown in Fig. 3. The x-axis is the workload CPU takes. The y-axis is the execution time normalized to the maximum time. As the figure shows, assigning the whole workload for the CPU or for the GPU is not always the best solution. For instance, the best division point of *blackscholes* is 40% for CPU and 60% for GPU; for *streamcluster* is 30% for CPU and 70% for GPU.

In this paper, we propose a two-phase framework. Phase one dynamically divides the workload between CPU and GPU according to execution time and data transfer time. Phase two dynamically scales the frequency according to core utilization. These two phase are executed iteratively to determine the best workload division and frequency for CPU and GPU at runtime.

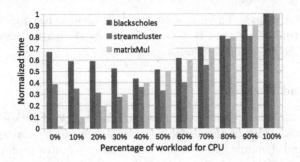

Fig. 3. Execution time with different ratios of workload for CPU and GPU.

The rest of this paper is organized follow. Section 2 introduces the related works and the difference between our work and others. Section 3 first describes assumptions and the related parameters, then introduces the overall framework. Section 4 shows the experiment environment and results. Section 5 concludes this work and shapes the future work.

2 Related Work

In this section, we introduce related work including the research on frequency scaling for energy efficiency, workload division for performance.

2.1 Energy Efficiency

The energy issue on homogeneous architectures has been researched extensively, especially the research on CPUs. Li et al. [6] proposed a scheme that predicts stalls at synchronization barriers, and sets a core into low power mode after it has finished its job faster than the other cores that are still stalled at the barrier. Lim et al. [7] developed an analysis algorithm to for finding the code segments that have concentrated Message Passing Interface (MPI) calls or a MPI call that has spent time beyond a given threshold. The frequency of the CPU is scaled down when the CPU is processing in those segments. Thus, the energy can be reduced with negligible performance loss.

As for GPU architectures, Hong et al. [8] presented an analytical model that controls the activation of GPU cores. It works based on analyzing the memory access patterns and the bandwidth of applications to achieve both the best performance and energy efficiency. Song et al. [9] proposed three models for GPU to predict the power and performance accurately. The power model estimates the power usage based on profiling GPU applications. The performance model reveals the relationship between execution time and GPU performance configurations. The energy model predicts the energy consumption by using performance counter events and the above-mentioned power model and the performance model. The above work focus on CPU-only architectures or

GPU-only architectures. There is a general lack of such research for heterogeneous architectures. Our work targets on frequency scaling for energy efficiency on CPU-GPU heterogeneous systems.

2.2 Workload Division

A lot of research [10–13] have been proposed for workload division on heterogeneous systems. Most of the proposed approaches can be classified into two types: static and dynamic. Static approach usually requires profiling results to construct the database and uses the database to determine the proportion of workload before execution. Luk et al. [10] proposed a technique of compiling for CPU-GPU heterogeneous systems. The technique distributes the data between CPU and GPU based on the profiling database. They focus on determining the data ratio between CPU and GPU to achieve minimum total execution time. This approach requires profiling for all applications and may cause significant overhead. Grewe et al. [13] proposed a static model based on machine learning. This model analyzes the computational characteristics at compile time, and selects the principal characteristics for CPU and GPU to predict partition ratio. Although it does not require profiling, it takes effort to train and maintain the support vector machines (SVM). They also do not consider energy efficiency.

Dynamic approach actives a decision scheme periodically at run time. The decision scheme determines the proportion of workload of next iteration based on the results of previous iteration. Diamos et al. [11] proposed a Harmony runtime system for heterogeneous systems. It dynamically detects the data dependency and assigns the whole kernel function for a suitable device. The suitability is gained from previous run of the kernel. However, Harmony does not consider data decomposition. Ravi et al. [12] proposed a dynamic mapping technique between CPU and GPU. Data are divided into several chunks that are distributed and scheduled to devices. Whenever a device finishes processing a chunk, it requests another one. Therefore, choosing an appropriate chunk size may optimize the performance. The application performance may be affected by heavy communication when a smaller chunk size is chosen. Based on the above research, performance is often a goal and the issue of energy efficiency has not been studied very much.

3   Feedback Control Optimization

In this section, we first describe our assumptions and the related parameters in our work. Then, we introduce the whole framework design of our proposed method, and the two-phase work flow.

3.1   Assumptions and Related Parameters

The target architecture in this work is a single computing node which consists of a single CPU and a single GPU, interconnected with each other through a Peripheral Component Interconnect Express (PCI-E) interface for communication. Both CPU and GPU have hardware counters for measuring the power consumption. The other peripherals include a motherboard, a disk, and memory.

It is assumed in this work target that applications are data-parallel such that not only tasks in an application can be executed in parallel by dividing the data to be processed between CPU and GPU, but the results of the decomposed computations can also be easily merged by simply placing the computation results from different processors in pre-specified locations of memory. For instance, assume A, B and C are three matrices, and the kernel needs to compute $C = A \times B$. Let us divide matrix A row-wise into two sub-matrices, namely A_1 and A_2. Assume that the multiplication of matrices A_1 and B, i.e. $C_1 = A_1 \times B$, is assigned to the CPU, and that of A_2 and B, i.e. $C_2 = A_2 \times B$, is assigned to the GPU. CPU stores the result C_1, and GPU stores the result C_2, into respective memory locations. Then, the partial results can be easily merged by copying the data to the final memory address of matrix C.

The related parameters used in this work are listed in Table 1. For these eleven parameters, x, k and l represent device, kernel and frequency level, respectively. N_x represents the number of available frequency levels of core frequency for device x, where x can be a CPU or a GPU device. For instance, the core frequency of NVIDIA Tesla K20c can be set to 614 MHz, 640 MHz, 666 MHz, 705 MHz, and 758 MHz. Thus N_g is 5 for this device denoted as g. $P_{cur}(k)$ is the percentage of a chunk of kernel k to be assigned to CPU in the current probe iteration, thus $(1 - P_{cur})$ represent the other part on GPU.

Since there are two objectives in this work, namely performance and energy efficiency, a tradeoff factor α is used as a weight, $0 \leq \alpha \leq 1$ such that when $\alpha = 0.5$ the two objectives are given equal importance, when $\alpha > 0.5$, performance is emphasized over energy, and when $\alpha < 0.5$, energy is emphasized over performance. Similarly, $(1 - \alpha)$ is the weight associated with the energy objective. When the difference between the execution time of a kernel k on the CPU at a selected frequency level l, i.e., $T_c(k, CPU, l, CP_{exe})$, and that on the GPU at a selected frequency level l', i.e.,$T_g(k, GPU, l', CP_{exe})$, is less than a given threshold τ, then the process of workload balancing between CPU and GPU is terminated. The threshold τ is called termination threshold.

3.2 Framework Design

The whole framework design is shown in Fig. 4. Initially, the total parallel workload is divided into several chunks of equal size. The initial probe iteration divides the first chunk into two equal portions, one portion is for CPU, and the other is for GPU. Then, the probe iteration goes through the two phases once. We choose the initial chunk division to be equal so that we do not favour CPU or GPU. After the initial probe iteration, further probe iterations are performed, such that each probe iteration consists of two phases as follows:

– Frequency Scaling Phase
  The function of this phase is to profile a given kernel on each type of core at all possible frequencies of each device.

Table 1. The related parameters.

Parameter	Description
N_x	Number of frequency levels of device
$P_{cur}(k)$	Current percentage of chunk assigned to CPU
$P_{next}(k, x)$	Next percentage of chunk assigned to CPU
$CP_{prof}(k, x)$	Percentage of a chunk for profiling
$CP_{exe}(k, x)$	Percentage of a chunk for execution
$u(k, x, l, CP_{prof}(k))$	Core utilization
$t(k, x, l, CP_{prof}(k))$	Profiling time
$T_x(k, x, l, CP_{exe}(k))$	Execution time
$T_{Data}(k, CP_{exe}(k))$	Data transfer time
α	Tradeoff factor
τ	Termination threshold

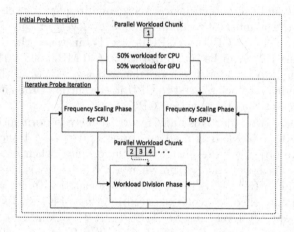

Fig. 4. Framework design.

– Workload Division Phase

The function of this phase is to determine a better data chunk division for the next probe iteration. If the difference between $T_{CPU}(k, CPU, l, P_{cur}(k))$ and $T_{GPU}(k, GPU, l', (1 - P_{cur}(k)))$ is less than the termination threshold τ, the FCO algorithm then terminates and the current frequency and division are used to process the remaining data chunks.

These two phases are executed iteratively until a near optimal solution is found.

Frequency Scaling Phase. The frequency scaling phase is used to determine an optimal frequency for each device (CPU and GPU) such that a given kernel exhibits a tradeoff between the loss in performance and in energy as design by the metric, *LossFactor*.

To make a tradeoff between the loss in performance and in energy, we proposed a metric called $LossFactor(k, x, l, CP_{prof}(k))$ which is as defined in Eq. 1 and is calculated for a given kernel k executed on a given type of device x (CPU or GPU) assigned with a portion $\frac{CP_{prof}(k)}{N_x}\%$ of a chunk and running at a given frequency l. The frequency l at which $LossFactor(k, x, l, CP_{prof}(k))$ is minimal is selected as the optimal frequency for device x. Note that $CP_{prof}(k)$ is fixed in this phase for a given kernel k. In our experiments, $CP_{prof}(k)$ is set to 25%.

$$LossFactor(k, x, l, CP_{prof}(k)) =$$
$$\alpha \times (1 - u(k, x, l, CP_{prof}(k))) + (1 - \alpha) \times (\frac{t(k, x, l, CP_{prof}(k)) - t_{min}}{t_{min}}) \quad (1)$$

Figure 5 shows the detailed flow of the frequency scaling phase. Initially, the device frequency is set to its lowest frequency level. The frequency is then increased to the next higher level and the profiling process is repeated. For each frequency level of each device, the core utilization and the execution time of the kernel are recorded and used to calculate $LossFactor(k, x, l, CP_{prof}(k))$ at that level, as defined in Eq. 1, where l is the frequency level at which profiling was performed, $u(k, x, l, CP_{prof}(k))$ is the core utilization of the kernel k on running on device x at frequency level l. The unused core utilization, i.e., $(1 - u(k, x, l, CP_{prof}(k)))$ is used to represent the amount of energy loss (unused energy). A 100% utilization indicates that the core is fully utilized, and there is no energy loss. If the core utilization is less than 100%, it means that it is possible to throttle down the frequency to improve the utilization. The term $t(k, x, l, CP_{prof}(k))$ is the execution time of profiling $\frac{CP_{prof}(k)}{N_x}$ percentage of a chunk of kernel k on device x at frequency l, it is used as an indicator of performance loss. The lower the execution time is, the better the performance is. Thus, we normalize all execution time based on the minimum execution time t_{min}. As a tradeoff between energy loss and performance loss, a weight α is associated with energy loss and $1 - \alpha$ is associated with the performance loss. When $\alpha = 0.5$, a balanced tradeoff between energy loss and performance loss is assumed.

For the selected workload division, $LossFactor(k, x, l, CP_{prof}(k))$ of the kernel on each device at all possible frequencies are compared and the frequency of a device is selected as that which results in least $LossFactor(k, x, l, CP_{prof}(k))$. A percentage $P_{cur}(k)$ of a chunk for CPU and a percentage $1 - P_{cur}(k)$ of a chunk for GPU are processed by the corresponding device at the selected frequencies. Initially, $P_{cur}(k)$ is set to 50%. It is then optimized in the workload division phase. Note that, the execution time of kernel on GPU includes the data transfer time between CPU and GPU.

Workload Division Phase. The workload division phase is used to determine a workload division for a kernel between CPU and GPU which is better than the

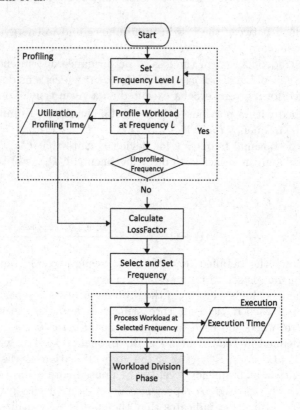

Fig. 5. Frequency scaling of a device.

current one, if any, such that the workload in balanced between the two cores. Figure 6 shows the detailed flow of the workload division phase.

The initial division is 50% of workload for CPU and 50% for GPU. In each probe iteration, we determine a better division such that the computation time is more balanced between CPU and GPU.

Given the current workload division ($P_{cur} : 1 - P_{cur}$) between CPU and GPU for a kernel, we try to find a new division P_{next} such that the workload is more balanced. We first check if the execution time difference between CPU and GPU of the chunk processed under the current division and frequency is less than termination threshold or not. If so, the current division and frequency is the determined solution. In this case, we stop frequency scaling and workload division and use the final division and frequency to process the remaining chunks. If the time difference is larger than the termination threshold, then Eq. 5 is used to calculate the next workload division P_{next}.

Let us discuss how to determine P_{next}, through Eq. 2 to Eq. 6. Equation 2 is basically trying to balance the time for processing workload on the CPU and the GPU. In Eq. 2, $\frac{T_{GPU}}{P_{cur}}$ is the time required to process a unit of workload on the CPU, and $\frac{T_{GPU}}{1-P_{cur}}$ is the time required to process a unit of workload on the GPU.

The term $\frac{T_{CPU}}{P_{cur}} \times P_{next}$ is the estimated time for processing P_{next} percentage of workload on CPU and $\frac{T_{GPU}}{1-P_{cur}} \times (1 - P_{next})$ is that for processing $(1 - P_{next})$ percentage of workload on GPU. Moreover, the time T_{Data}' for transferring $(1 - P_{next})$ percentage of workload (data) between CPU and GPU is also accounted for in Eq. 2.

$$\frac{T_{CPU}}{P_{cur}} \times P_{next} = \frac{T_{GPU}}{1 - P_{cur}} \times (1 - P_{next}) + T_{Data}' \tag{2}$$

The data transfer time T_{Data}' is estimated by linear regression of two profiled data transfer between the two devices as Eq. 3 shows the linear equation used for linear regression, where T_1 and T_2 are the data transfer times for transferring data of size P_1 and P_2, respectively.

$$T_2 - T_{Data}' = m \times (P_2 - (1 - P_{next})) \tag{3}$$

where

- T_{Data}' is the estimated data transfer time for a given data size of $(1 - P_{next})$.
- $m = \frac{T_2 - T_1}{P_2 - P_1}$.

From Eq. 3, we can get Eq. 4.

$$T_{Data}' = T_2 - m \times (P_2 - (1 - P_{next})) \tag{4}$$

By substituting Eq. 4 into Eq. 2, we get Eq. 5, which can be rearranged into Eq. 6.

$$\frac{T_{CPU}}{P_{cur}} \times P_{next} = \frac{T_{GPU}}{1 - P_{cur}} \times (1 - P_{next}) + T_2 - m \times (P_2 - (1 - P_{next})) \tag{5}$$

$$P_{next} = \frac{\frac{T_{GPU}}{1 - P_{cur}} + T_2 - m \times P_2 + m}{\frac{T_{CPU}}{P_{cur}} + \frac{T_{GPU}}{1 - P_{cur}} + m} \tag{6}$$

Using Eq. 6, we can calculate the next workload division P_{next}.

4   Experiments

This section presents the experimental results of the proposed FCO algorithm. We first introduce the experimental setup, including the experiment environment and the benchmarks. Next, we present the experimental results and show the comparison with other methods.

4.1   Experimental Setup

The experimental environment consists of a PC with dual Intel Xeon E5-2620 CPUs. There are six physical cores in a single CPU, twelve logical cores when active hyper-threading technology. The available frequency levels increase at increments of 0.1 GHz from 1.2 GHz to 2.1 GHz. The GPU is Nvidia Tesla K20c

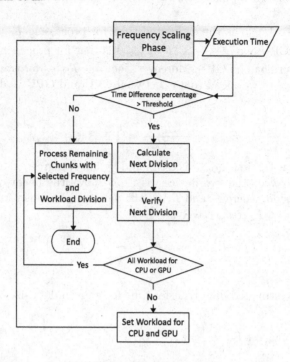

Fig. 6. Workload division flow.

Table 2. Benchmarks

Kernel	Type	Chunk Size	Benchmark Suit	Note
matrixMul	Core-bounded	10000×1600	CUDA Toolkit	Matrix multiplication
lud		4096×4096	Rodinia	LU decomposition
kmeans	Memory-bounded	100000 data points		
Streamcluster		65536 points with 512 dimensions		
Blackscholes	Core-memory-bounded	1000000 options	parsec-cuda	

with 2496 CUDA cores and 4800 MB global memory, the available frequency levels are 614 MHz, 640 MHz, 666 MHz, 705 MHz, 758 MHz. There are 16 GB memory in the PC. We use 64-bit Ubuntu 12.04.3 with 3.8.0-35-generic Linux kernel as the operating system. For the measurement tool, we use performance application programming interface (PAPI) [14] to measure the energy consumption of the CPU and GPU cores.

Table 2 lists the benchmarks used in the experiments. We choose three types of kernel for the experiments, including core-bounded kernel matrix multiplication and LU decomposition, memory-bounded kernel kmeans and streamcluster, and both high core utilization and high memory utilization kernel blackscholes which type is called core-memory-bounded kernel. Matrix multiplication kernel is from the CUDA Toolkit [4]. LU decomposition, kmeans, and streamcluster are from the Rodinia benchmark [3]. Blackscholes is from parsec-cuda [5]. Note that we process 1000 chunks for each kernel.

4.2   Experimental Results

In this section, We first evaluate the effects of scaling frequency on both CPU and GPU. Second, we evaluate the proposed CPU-GPU workload division method. Third, we present the results of the proposed method and compare it with *Static Workload Division* (SWD) method [15] and GreenGPU method [16]. Final, we describe the advantages of the proposed FCO method.

For presenting the experimental results, we use two types of baseline called CPU-baseline and GPU-baseline in our experiment. CPU-baseline is the execution using 128 OpenMP threads running at its peak frequency. GPU-baseline is the execution running at its peak frequency.

Frequency Scaling. Given a kernel and workload division between CPU and GPU, frequency scaling tries to find the optimal frequency for each device (CPU and GPU). Optimal frequency of a device for a kernel workload is defined as the frequency of the device at which the workload allocated to the device is processed by the kernel with the least $LossFasctor$.

Figure 7 shows the result of applying the proposed frequency scaling algorithm to each of five kernels running on the CPU with 128 OpenMP threads. The baseline for comparison is the CPU-baseline. Figure 7a shows the performance loss and Fig. 7b shows the energy reduction when the proposed frequency scaling algorithm is applied to CPU for obtaining better energy efficiency with negligible performance loss of each kernel. We observe that frequency scaling does not incur much performance loss and energy reduction on core-bounded kernels $matrixMul$ and lud and the core-memory-bounded kernel $blackscholes$, because of these kernels are compute-intensive, scaling down the CPU core frequency may impact the execution time significantly. On the other hand, for the memory-bounded kernels $kmeans$ and $streamcluster$, frequency scaling can successfully detect a lower CPU core utilization by these kinds of kernels. Hence, a lower CPU core frequency is selected for these kinds of kernels.

Figure 8 shows the result of applying the proposed frequency scaling algorithm to each of five kernels running on the GPU. The baseline for comparison is GPU-baseline. We observe that the results have a similar trend with that on the CPU. The proposed frequency scaling algorithm does not incur much performance loss and energy reduction on core-bounded and core-memory-bounded kernels.

Workload Division. In this experiment, we focus on workload division only while the frequency of each device is kept constant at its peak frequency. We evaluate the performance and energy reduction of each kernel after workload is balanced between CPU and GPU.

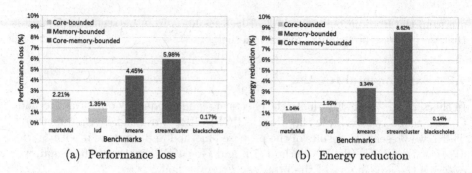

Fig. 7. Performance loss and energy reduction on CPU on frequency scaling. (Baseline: CPU-baseline).

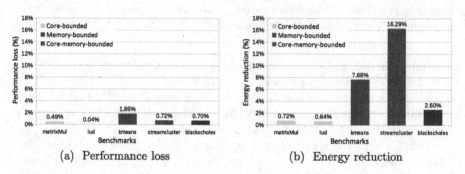

Fig. 8. Performance loss and energy reduction on GPU on frequency scaling. (Baseline: GPU-baseline).

Figure 9 shows the results of this experiment. The proposed workload division algorithm can balance the workload of a kernel between the CPU and the GPU such that idle energy consumption is reduced. Figure 9a shows the speedup of the kernels due to workload division as compared to be balance. The baseline here is the CPU-baseline. Through workload division, both performance and energy reduction can be improved. Not only is the idle time reduced, but most of the workload is also assigned to the device that is good at running the given kernel. Moreover, since the energy efficiency of GPU is much higher than that of CPU, dividing the workload between the CPU and the GPU can thus reduce the total energy consumed. The average speedup of the five kernels is 24.02 and the average energy reduction is 22.58 times, which show the importance of workload division between heterogeneous processors.

Holistic Comparison. The workload for a device which is determined by considering its fraction of computation capability in the system [15] is a static method. The method divides workload base on the multiplication of number of cores and peak frequency in MHz of each device. On the other hand, GreenGPU [16] scales the frequency and divides the workload between CPU

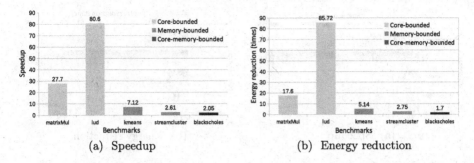

(a) Speedup   (b) Energy reduction

Fig. 9. Speedup and energy reduction on workload division. (Baseline: CPU-baseline)

and GPU incrementally in run-time. The differences between GreenGPU and FCO methods are as follows:

- Frequency scaling algorithm of GreenGPU focuses on scaling only the GPU frequency, but FCO scales the frequency of both the CPU and the GPU.
- GreenGPU adjusts the workload on a device by a fixed increment or decrement of 5 % in each iteration. FCO proposes a model for calculating the workload division between CPU and GPU. The proposed workload division model can find an near-optimal solution more efficiently than GreenGPU.
- GreenGPU ignores the impact of communication time, which may make the division inaccurate.

In this experiment, we enable both the frequency scaling phase and the workload division phase. We also evaluate the speedup and energy reduction for each kernel of the heterogeneous multiprocessor system. Figure 10a and b show the experimental results for the five kernels in terms of the performance speedup and energy reduction, respectively, as compared with the CPU-baseline. Table 3 shows the average improvement of FCO compared with other methods. For speedup in average, FCO is 20.28% higher than SWD, 7.90% higher than GreenGPU, and 2386.27% higher than the CPU-baseline. For energy reduction in average, FCO is 27.39% greater than SWD, 4.16% greater than GreenGPU, and 2318.44% greater than the CPU-baseline. The improvement in energy reduction by applying FCO is not significant. Since SWD allocates most of the workload to GPU and GPU has a much better energy efficiency than CPU, SWD can reduce energy consumption significantly. Similarly, because GreenGPU ignores the overhead in communication time, it may thus allocate more workload to the energy efficient GPU. However, these two methods may impact the performance and incur workload imbalance between CPU and GPU. Hence, the proposed FCO method achieves a much higher speedup than SWD and GreenGPU.

For the next experiment, we compare the probe time of FCO with that of GreenGPU. Probe time is the time to find a solution. Figure 11 shows the results. The proposed FCO method spends only 59.43% of time which GreenGPU spent in average. This is because the proposed workload division algorithm redivides the workload through an analytic model. However, GreenGPU adjusts only 5%

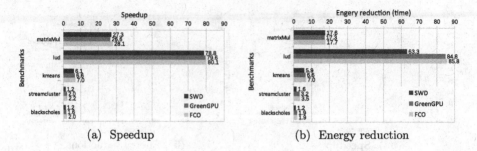

(a) Speedup   (b) Energy reduction

Fig. 10. Speedup and energy reduction due to holistic methods. (Baseline: CPU-Baseline)

Table 3. Average improvement compared with other methods

	Avg. speedup	Avg. energy reduction
vs. SWD	20.28%	27.39%
vs. GreenGPU	7.90%	4.16%
vs. CPU-only	2386.27%	2318.44%

workload in each iteration, thus it may require more iterations to find the work-load balanced solution. This is important for online scheme frameworks such as our proposed method because the overhead of optimization should be as slight as possible.

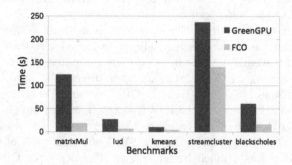

Fig. 11. Time to find solution

5   Conclusions

In this paper, we proposed a feedback control based algorithm for optimizing the performance and energy efficiency of kernel execution in heterogeneous multi-core systems. The experimental results show that the proposed frequency algo-rithm can reduce 11.99% of average energy consumption of memory-bounded applications with negligible performance loss on the GPU. Through workload division, compared with the CPU-baseline of kernel parallelized using 128 OpenMP threads running on the CPU at peak frequency, the average speedup can be improved 2386.27% and the average energy reduction achieves 2318.44%. For the holistic methods, compared with GreenGPU, the proposed FCO method can improve 7.90% times on average speedup and 4.16% times on energy reduction. For the probe time, compared with GreenGPU, the proposed FCO method takes only 39.49% of the time required by GreenGPU. For the future work, we plan to port the proposed method to multi-CPUs and multi-GPUs system. Further, we want to consider more aspects of CPU and GPU (e.g., number of threads) to make the method more complete.

References

1. Top. 500 Supercomputer Sites (2013). http://www.top500.org
2. The Green500 (2013). http://www.green500.org
3. Che, S., Boyer, M., Meng, J., Tarjan, D., Sheaffer, J.W., Lee, S., Skadron, K.: Rodinia: a benchmark suite for heterogeneous computing. In: Proceedings of the IEEE International Symposium on Workload Characterization (IISWC), pp. 44–54. IEEE Press, October 2009
4. NVIDIA CUDA Toolkit 5.5. https://developer.nvidia.com/cuda-toolkit-55-archive
5. Matthew, S., Henry, D., Karthikeyan, S.: Porting CMP benchmarks to GPUs. Department of Computer Sciences, The University of Wisconsin-Madison, Technical report (2011)
6. Li, J., Martinez, J.F., Huang, M.C.: The thrifty barrier: energy-aware synchronization in shared-memory multiprocessors. In: Proceedings of the 10th International Symposium on High Performance Computer Architecture (HPCA), p. 14. IEEE Computer Society, February 2004
7. Lim, M., Freeh, V.W., Lowenthal, D.K.: Adaptive, transparent frequency and voltage scaling of communication phases in MPI programs. In: Proceedings of the ACM/IEEE Conference on Supercomputing (SC). IEEE Press, November 2006
8. Hong, S., Kim, H.: An integrated GPU power and performance model. In: Proceedings of the 37th Annual International Symposium on Computer Architecture (ISCA), pp. 280–289. ACM Press, June 2010
9. Song, S., Su, C., Rountree, B., Cameron, K.W.: A simplified and accurate model of power-performance efficiency on emergent GPU architectures. In: Proceedings of the IEEE 27th International Symposium on Parallel and Distributed Processing (IPDPS), pp. 673–686. IEEE Computer Society, May 2013
10. Luk, C., Hong, S., Kim, H.: Qilin: exploiting parallelism on heterogeneous multiprocessors with adaptive mapping. In: Proceedings of the 42nd Annual IEEE/ACM International Symposium on Microarchitecture (MICRO), pp. 45–55. IEEE Press, December 2009
11. Diamos, G.F., Yalamanchili, S.: Harmony: an execution model and runtime for heterogeneous many core systems. In: Proceedings of the 17th International Symposium on High Performance Distributed Computing (HPDC), pp. 197–200. ACM Press, June 2008
12. Ravi, V.T., Ma, W., Chiu, D., Agrawal, G.: Compiler and runtime support for enabling generalized reduction computations on heterogeneous parallel configurations. In: Proceedings of the 24th ACM International Conference on Supercomputing (ICS), pp. 137–146. ACM Press, June 2010

13. Grewe, D., ÓBoyle, M.F.P.: A static task partitioning approach for heterogeneous systems using OpenCL. In: Knoop, J. (ed.) CC 2011. LNCS, vol. 6601, pp. 286–305. Springer, Heidelberg (2011). doi:10.1007/978-3-642-19861-8_16

14. Weaver, V.M., Johnson, M., Kasichayanula, K., Ralph, J., Luszczek, P., Terpstra, D., Moore, S.: Measuring energy and power with PAPI. In: Proceedings of the 41st International Conference on Parallel Processing Workshops (ICPPW), pp. 262–268. IEEE Press, September 2012

15. Rafique, M.M., Butt, A.R., Nikolopoulos, D.S.: A capabilities-aware framework for using computational accelerators in data-intensive computing. J. Parallel Distrib. Comput. **71**(2), 185–197 (2011)

16. Ma, K., Li, X., Chen, W., Zhang, X., Wang, X.: GreenGPU: a holistic approach to energy efficiency in GPU-CPU heterogeneous architectures. In: Proceedings of the 41st International Conference on Parallel Processing (ICPP), pp. 48–57. IEEE Press, September 2012

The Impact of Panel Factorization on the Gauss-Huard Algorithm for the Solution of Linear Systems on Modern Architectures

Sandra Catalán[1], Pablo Ezzatti[2],
Enrique S. Quintana-Ortí[1], and Alfredo Remón[3]([✉])

[1] Dep. de Ingeniería y Ciencia de la Computación,
Universidad Jaime I, 12.701 Castellón, Spain
{catalans,quintana}@icc.uji.es
[2] Instituto de Computación, Universidad de la República,
11.300 Montevideo, Uruguay
pezzatti@fing.edu.uy
[3] Max Planck Institute for Dynamics of Complex Technical Systems,
30.106 Magdeburg, Germany
remon@mpi-magdeburg.mpg.de

Abstract. The Gauss-Huard algorithm (the GHA) is a specialized version of Gauss-Jordan elimination for the solution of linear systems that, enhanced with column pivoting, exhibits numerical stability and computational cost close to those of the conventional solver based on the LU factorization with row pivoting. Furthermore, the GHA can be formulated as a procedure rich in matrix multiplications, so that high performance can be expected on current architectures with multi-layered memories. Unfortunately, in principle the GHA does not admit the introduction of *look-ahead*, a technique that has been demonstrated to be rather useful to improve the performance of the LU factorization on multi-threaded platforms with high levels of hardware concurrency. In this paper we analyze the effect of this drawback on the implementation of the GHA on systems accelerated with graphics processing units (GPUs), exposing the roles of the CPU-to-GPU and single precision-to-double precision performance ratios, as well as the contribution from the operations in the algorithm's critical path.

Keywords: Linear systems of equations · Gauss-Huard algorithm · LU factorization · Multicore processors · Graphics processing units (GPUs) · Mixed precision · High performance

---

All researchers acknowledge the support from the EHFARS project funded by the German Ministry of Education and Research BMBF.
E.S. Quintana-Ortí was supported by the CICYT project TIN2014-53495-R of the *Ministerio de Economía y Competitividad* and FEDER.

J. Carretero et al. (Eds.): ICA3PP 2016, LNCS 10048, pp. 405–416, 2016.
DOI: 10.1007/978-3-319-49583-5_30

1   Introduction

In 1979, Huard [14] introduced a variant of Gauss-Jordan elimination for the solution of linear systems of equations with the same computational cost as the conventional three-stage procedure based on the LU factorization [9]. This Gauss-Huard algorithm (GHA) received renewed attention in the mid 90s, when (1) a blocked variant was proposed that turned it practical for high performance computing architectures; and (2) column pivoting was added, yielding numerical stability similar to that of a solver based on the LU factorization with row pivoting [6,7,13].

For about 20 years, the blocked version of the GHA with column pivoting remained forgotten, till this algorithm was re-visited for the solution of linear systems on hybrid platforms accelerated with graphics processing units (GPUs) and the Intel Xeon Phi [4,8]. These recent experimental analyses show that, under certain circumstances, the GHA can be a competitive approach to an LU factorization-based solver in GPU-accelerated platforms.

In this paper, we extend our previous study of the GHA, exposing a major hazard which *may explain* why this algorithm was initially abandoned: concretely, the impossibility of overlapping the "panel factorization" stage with the remaining matrix updates during the computation. In particular, as a key contribution of this paper, we reveal that this drawback is especially painful, from the perspective of performance, on modern many-threaded architectures, such as servers equipped with GPU accelerators. Furthermore, the problem exerts important negative impact when aiming to leverage a variant of the GHA that combines mixed precision with iterative refinement (MPIR). In order to strengthen our message, as an additional contribution, we make a side-by-side comparison, along these two axes (acceleration via graphics co-processors and MPIR), with an algorithm based on the LU factorization which, unlike the GHA, can overlap the panel factorization with other computations. Addressing this drawback of the GHA remains an open question.

The rest of the paper is structured as follows. In Sect. 2 we present blocked variants of the GHA with column pivoting and the LU factorization with row pivoting, and discuss the panel factorization bottleneck. In Sects. 3 and 4 we experimentally analyze the effect of this hazard on multicore processors and systems accelerated with GPUs, respectively. In Sect. 5 we outline the impact of this drawback on a solver that leverages mixed precision and iterative refinement. Finally, in Sect. 6 we offer a brief summary and concluding remarks derived from our work.

2   Blocked Algorithms for the Solution of Linear Systems

Linear Systems and GHA. Consider the linear system $Ax = b$, where A is an $n \times n$ general dense matrix, with no particular structure/property, the vector b contains the n independent terms, and x corresponds to the n unknowns. Figure 1 offers an algorithmic description of a blocked variant of the GHA for

$$\begin{array}{|l|}
\hline
\text{Algorithm:} \quad \boxed{\hat{A}, p} := \text{THE GHA \_BLK}(\hat{A}) \\
\hline
\end{array}$$

Fig. 1. Blocked Gauss-Huard algorithm for the solution of $Ax = b$. $P(\cdot)$ denotes a permutation matrix assembled from the pivots contained in its vector argument.

the solution of this linear system using the FLAME notation [10]. Concretely, if $\hat{A} = [A, b]$ on entry, upon completion the last column of $\hat{A}$ is overwritten with the solution x. The algorithm processes n_b columns/rows of $\hat{A}$ per iteration, with n_b often referred to as the (algorithmic) block size. The loop body consists of four operations: block-row elimination (BRE); *panel factorization* (PF), also referred to as block diagonalization, which can be performed via an unblocked variant of the same procedure (see [4] for details); column pivoting (CP); and block-column elimination (BCE).

Linear Systems and LU Factorization. For comparison purposes, Fig. 2 shows a blocked right-looking algorithm for the LU factorization, which is the crucial computation for the solution of a linear systems via this alternative decomposition [9]. (The remaining stages are the application of pivoting and the solution of two triangular linear systems, which contribute little to the computational complexity and computational cost of the complete LU-based solver.) This algorithm also proceeds in steps of n_b columns/rows, with the loop body being composed of four operations: PF, performed via an unblocked version of the same algorithm; row pivoting (RP); triangular solve (TS); and trailing submatrix update (TSU).

Comparison of the Solvers. We first note that both blocked algorithms require $2n^3/3 + O(n^2)$ floating-point operations (flops). Inside their loop bodies, they basically perform similar computations serialized by strict data dependencies. Concretely, consider two operations O_A, O_B, where the first one produces a piece

Algorithm: $[A, p] := \text{LU\_BLK}(A)$

$A \to \left(\begin{array}{c\|c} A_{TL} & A_{TR} \\ \hline A_{BL} & A_{BR} \end{array} \right), p \to (\, p_L \,\|\, p_R \,)$
 where $\quad A_{TL}$ is 0×0 and p_L has 0 elements
 	
 while $m(A_{TL}) < m(A)$ do
 Determine block size n_b
 $\left(\begin{array}{c\|c} A_{TL} & A_{TR} \\ \hline A_{BL} & A_{BR} \end{array} \right) \to \left(\begin{array}{c\|c\|c} A_{00} & A_{01} & A_{02} \\ \hline A_{10} & A_{11} & A_{12} \\ \hline A_{20} & A_{21} & A_{22} \end{array} \right), (\, p_L \,\|\, p_R \,) \to (\, p_0 \,\|\, p_1 \,\|\, p_2 \,)$
 where $\quad A_{11}$ is $n_b \times n_b$ and p_1 has n_b elements
 	
 $\quad$ PF : $\left(\left[\begin{array}{c} A_{11} \\ A_{21} \end{array} \right], \; p_1 \right) := \text{LU\_UNB}\left(\left[\begin{array}{c} A_{11} \\ A_{21} \end{array} \right] \right)$
 	
 $\quad$ RP : $\left[\begin{array}{c\|c} A_{10} & A_{12} \\ \hline A_{20} & A_{22} \end{array} \right] \quad := P(p_1) \left[\begin{array}{c\|c} A_{10} & A_{12} \\ \hline A_{20} & A_{22} \end{array} \right]$
 	
 $\quad$ TS : $A_{12} \qquad\qquad := \text{TRILU}(A_{11})^{-1} A_{12}$
 	
 $\quad$ TSU : $A_{22} \qquad\qquad := A_{22} - A_{21} A_{12}$
 	
 $\left(\begin{array}{c\|c} A_{TL} & A_{TR} \\ \hline A_{BL} & A_{BR} \end{array} \right) \leftarrow \left(\begin{array}{c\|c\|c} A_{00} & A_{01} & A_{02} \\ \hline A_{10} & A_{11} & A_{12} \\ \hline A_{20} & A_{21} & A_{22} \end{array} \right), (\, p_L \,\|\, p_R \,) \leftarrow (\, p_0 \,\|\, p_1 \,\|\, p_2 \,)$
 endwhile

Fig. 2. Blocked algorithm for the LU factorization. $\text{TRILU}(\cdot)$ returns the strictly lower triangular part of its matrix argument setting the diagonal entries of the result to ones.

of data that the second utilizes, and denote this RAW (read-after-write) dependency [11] as $O_A \to O_B$. Then, for the GHA: BRE $\to$ PF $\to$ CP $\to$ BCE; while for the LU factorization: PF $\to$ RP $\to$ TS $\to$ TSU. On the positive side, by appropriately choosing n_b, both algorithms cast a major part of the computations in terms of matrix multiplications (BRE and BCE for the GHA, and TSU for the LU factorization), a BLAS-3 kernel that is known to deliver high performance on current multicore and many-core architectures. Indeed, given the same n_b, the two algorithms, basically, perform the same number of flops in terms of matrix multiplications. On the negative side, PF stands in the critical path for both cases and, since this operation is composed of fine-grain computations, depending on the problem size and number of cores, this may seriously impair the performance of the corresponding algorithm.

Panel Factorization and Look-Ahead. As argued above, PF can easily become a bottleneck on modern parallel architectures. This issue is known, and a solution exist for the LU factorization, that applies *look-ahead* to overlap the factorization of the "next" panel with the updates in the "present" iteration [15]. In particular, Fig. 3 illustrates a variant of the blocked (right-looking) algorithm for the LU factorization that isolates the computations that lie in the critical path of the algorithm. For this purpose, A_{12} and A_{22} are each partitioned into two panels of n_b columns, where the left-hand side partition of A_{22} contains the panel that will be factorized in the next iteration of the algorithm. The "decoupling" of this panel then facilitates that the updates on A_{12}^L, A_{22}^L and the factorization of the latter (critical path operations: $\text{RP}_C, \text{TS}_C, \text{TSU}_C, \text{PF}$) proceed concurrently with the updates on A_{12}^R, A_{22}^R (remainder operations: $\mathsf{RP_R}, \mathsf{TS_R}, \mathsf{TSU_R}$), potentially removing PF from the critical path of the algorithm.

Unfortunately, the application of an analogous *look-ahead* strategy into the GHA does not seem possible, due to the strict dependencies and the organization of the operations in this algorithm.

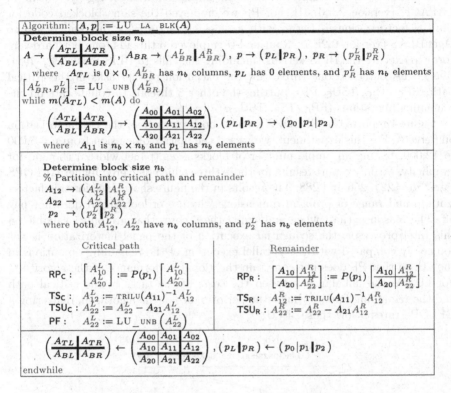

Fig. 3. Blocked algorithm for the LU factorization with separate critical path.

3   LU Factorization on Multicore Processors

The experiment in this section were performed on a system (hereafter ServerA) with an Intel Xeon E5-2603v3 "Haswell" CPU (6 cores at 1.60 GHz) and 32 GB of DDR4 RAM. The (theoretical) peak performance for this server is 76 GFLOPS (billions of flops per second) in IEEE754 double precision (DP) arithmetic or twice that figure in single precision (SP). For this server, we will only employ DP arithmetic.

In order to illustrate the impact of PF, we next compare the performance of the two variants of the LU factorization, with and without look-ahead (see Sect. 2), in ServerA. Hereafter, we refer to these algorithms as LU and LU_LA, respectively. Both routines were linked to the BLIS implementation (version 0.1.8) of the *basic linear algebra subprograms* (BLAS) [18]. Among other functionality, BLIS offers kernels for TS and TSU, delivering competitive performance on many multi-threaded processors, including the Haswell architectures, to other efforts such as Intel MKL, OpenBLAS, and ATLAS [17]. For RP, due to its minor cost, we simply invoked the implementation of legacy routine in LAPACK (version 3.5.0) [1]. For PF we employed the same blocked code for the LU factorization in Fig. 2, with a blocking factor $n'_b < n_b$, and linked to OpenBLAS (version 0.2.15). Routine LU employed 6 threads (one per hardware core) to execute the BLIS kernels (including the calls to BLIS inside PF). Routine LU_LA detached one thread for the execution of the tasks in the critical path (RP_C, TS_C, TSU_C, PF), putting the other 5 threads to collaborate on the remaining operations (RP_R, TS_R, TSU_R).

Figure 4 reports the GFLOPS rates of both versions of the LU factorization on ServerA. For this experiment, we varied the matrix dimension from $n = 5,000$ to 12,000, testing an ample number of blocks sizes (panel widths) though, for simplicity, we only report results for those three which delivered higher GFLOPS rates: $n_b = 224$, 256 and 288. The results in the figure show that, for this factorization, and range of problem dimensions, the use of look-ahead does not pay off. The reason is that, when employing the 6 cores that are only available on this Intel processor, the sequential execution of the panel factorization is not too costly compared with the parallel execution of the remaining operations in the LU, so that PF does not constrain the global performance of the algorithm. For LU_LA, the unbalance between the costs of the tasks in the critical path and the remaining updates hurts the performance of the algorithm, delivering a GFLOPS rates below those of LU.

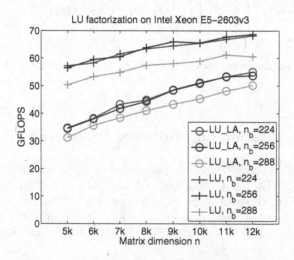

Fig. 4. GFLOPS of the LU factorization with and w/out look-ahead on ServerA.

The basic insight gained from this experiment, which can be applied to the GHA, is that look-ahead is not important when the number of cores in the system is small or moderate. In principle, this observation may be generalized to a scenario where the resources dedicated to the tasks in the critical path are not excessive compared with those in the non-critical updates. However, keep in mind that PF is basically a sequential operation, and no matter how many threads/cores participate in its execution, only low performance can be expected from it.

4   Acceleration of the GHA Using Graphics Co-Processors

The experiments in the remainder of the paper were performed using two Intel-based servers equipped with NVIDIA GPU accelerators. The first system (ServerB) contains an Intel Core i7-4770 CPU (4 cores at 3.40 GHz) plus an NVIDIA K40 (2,880 CUDA cores, 12 GB of GDDR5 RAM). The second system (ServerC) comprises an Intel Core i7-3770 CPU (4 cores at 3.40 GHz) plus an NVIDIA GTX680 (1,536 CUDA cores, 2 GB of GDDR5 RAM). While both GPUs belong to NVIDIA's "Kepler" family, their peak performance, measured in TFLOPS (trillions of flops per second), is quite different: 4.29 SP TFLOPS vs 1.43 DP TFLOPS for the NVIDIA K40; and 3.12 SP TFLOPS vs 0.13 DP TFLOPS for the NVIDIA GTX680. It is worth pointing out the differences in the SP-to-DP ratios: about 24× for the NVIDIA GTX680 and close to 3× for the NVIDIA K40.

We next analyze the actual performance attained with hybrid implementations of the blocked algorithms described in Sect. 2 for the GHA and the LU factorization, including the variants for the latter operation with and without look-ahead: LU and LU_LA, respectively. For simplicity, in the following discussions, we will distinguish between the panel factorization (PF) and the remaining operations of the algorithm, though for LU_LA we will consider that PF includes all operations in the critical path (CP). All three codes adhere to the conventional parallelization strategy on CPU-GPU platforms, off-loading the data-parallel operations to the accelerator, but keeping the execution of control-oriented kernels on the CPU [3,16]. Following this idea, PF is computed on the CPU, while all remaining operations are performed on the GPU. The routines are linked with implementations of the BLAS in libraries specifically tuned for the Intel and NVIDIA architectures (Intel MKL 11.1 and NVIDIA CUBLAS 6.5, respectively). Furthermore, in order to enhance PF, this operation is computed on the CPU via a blocked algorithm analogous to those shown in Sect. 2.

Figure 5 reports the GFLOPS rates of the three algorithms on ServerB, for matrix dimensions ranging from $n = 5,000$ to 15,000; three block sizes $n_b = 64$, 96 and 128; and all codes operating in DP arithmetic. The performance curves show similar trends, with the GFLOPS steadily increasing with the problem size for all three algorithms, and very close rates for the GHA and LU. More important, the introduction of look-ahead in the LU factorization yields a remarkable boost in performance, which for example jumps from about 400 GFLOPS without look-ahead to more than 600 GFLOPS with look-ahead for the largest problem size.

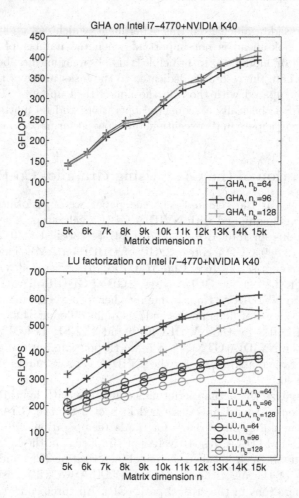

Fig. 5. GFLOPS of the GHA (top) and the LU factorization with and w/out look-ahead (bottom) on ServerB.

A second insight from this experiment is that the optimal block size grows with the problem size. This is natural since, as the cost of the remainder update increases, it is possible to overlap the factorization of a wider panel with it. An optimal solution should therefore vary the block size as the algorithm progresses, decreasing it towards the end of the procedure.

Figure 6 analyzes the distribution of the execution time for the GHA and the LU factorization with look-ahead on both systems, for three large matrix dimensions $n = 10,000$, 12,000 and 15,000; the optimal block size for each dimension; and DP arithmetic. A first aspect to point out are the differences in execution time observed for the two platforms (note the scales in the y-axis), which are explained by the distinct DP performance between the two accelerators: 1.43 and 0.13 DP TFLOPS for the NVIDIA K40 and GTX680, respectively.

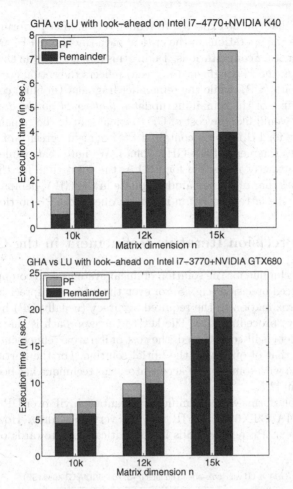

Fig. 6. Distribution of execution time for the GHA and LU_LA (respectively, left and right bar for each problem dimension) on ServerB (top) and ServerC (bottom). (Color figure online)

Let us next focus on the GHA, and remember that, for this blocked algorithm, there is no overlapping between PF and the remainder operations of the procedure. In this scenario, the results in the figure illustrate that the execution time of the GHA on ServerB is negatively affected by the cost of PF, which roughly takes about half of the total time for the three problem sizes. Compared with this, PF occupies a much smaller portion of the total execution time on ServerC. This situation is again explained by the different peak performance of the accelerators, which is about 10× higher for the NVIDIA K40, turning PF into a much more critical task for the system equipped with the faster accelerator.

Let us continue the analysis with the LU factorization with look-ahead. We first remind that this algorithm performs basically the same number of flops as the GHA in operations other than PF, in both cases cast in terms of matrix multiplications that can be expected to render very similar performance. In contrast, for LU_LA the operations in the critical path (including PF) are potentially overlapped with other computations. Taking this into account, in the corresponding bars of Fig. 6, the PF fragment (in green) reflects the actual cost of the tasks in the critical path (CP), while the remainder fragment (in blue) corresponds to the execution time of the remaining updates *that could not be overlapped with CP*. Ideally, we would like the cost of CP to equal that of the remainder update, so that the bars for LU_LA only contain a PF fragment (green), of height equal to the remainder fragment of the GHA (blue). We note that, while the remainder part is not exactly negligible for LU_LA, the total time for this algorithm basically matches that of the remainder update in the GHA, demonstrating that the overhead of the latter algorithm is mostly due to the PF bottleneck.

5   Mixed Precision Iterative Refinement in the GHA

An appealing technique for the solution of linear systems is to compute an initial solution in reduced precision (e.g., SP or even the future half-precision) and then evolve this approximation to the required accuracy (usually DP) by means of a low-cost iterative procedure [12]. The key to this approach is that, in practice, unless the problem is ill-conditioned, the cost of iterative refinement is negligible compared with that of obtaining the initial solution. For the particular case of servers enhanced with some sort of accelerator, this technique has been exploited, among others, in [2,5].

On current platforms with a significant advantage in SP over DP performance (like the NVIDIA GTX680), MPIR may be very rewarding. However, as we will illustrate next, PF again stands in the critical path towards obtaining the

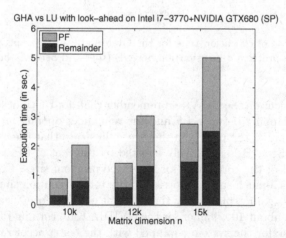

Fig. 7. Distribution of execution time for the GHA and LU_LA (respectively, left and right bar for each problem dimension) on ServerC, using SP arithmetic. (Color figure online)

potential gains that MPIR promises on this type of architectures. In particular, Fig. 7 repeats the last experiment in Sect. 4 to report the distribution of execution time for the GHA and LU_LA, *on* ServerC *only*, for the same three large matrix dimensions $n = 10,000$, $12,000$ and $15,000$; using the optimal block size for each dimension; and *SP arithmetic in this case*.

A crucial observation is that, by operating in SP, both algorithms require execution times, on ServerC, that are close or even outperform those of the corresponding DP versions executed on the system equipped with the much more powerful NVIDIA K40. However, comparing the distribution of the execution time for the GHA on ServerC, using DP (Fig. 6 bottom and Fig. 7), we point out that, in the second case, the PF fragment occupies a much larger fraction of the total time, showing that PF in practice becomes the limiting factor to exploit MPIR in the GHA on this platform. The reason behind this change lies in the much higher SP peak performance of ServerC, which shifts much of the cost of the algorithm towards the factorization of the panel.

6   Concluding Remarks

We have analyzed the solution of dense general systems of linear equations via the GHA and the LU factorization on multicore processors and hybrid platforms equipped with many-core GPU accelerators. Our results show that, on current multicore technology with a small to moderate number of cores, we can expect no significant differences between the two solvers, as the panel factorization does not contribute a significant cost to the algorithm. In contrast, when the matrix multiplications composing these algorithms are off-loaded to a GPU, the acceleration experienced in all parts but the (mostly sequential) panel factorization turn this operation into a performance bottleneck. In the case of the LU factorization, this hazard can be tackled via a technique known as *look-ahead* which, if applied correctly, removes the panel computation from the practical critical path of the algorithm. Unfortunately, the same strategy does not seem to be applicable to the GHA, impairing the ability of the method to solve large linear systems on current GPU-accelerated systems.

The introduction of look-ahead does not come for free, though. When applied directly by modification of the code, it requires a careful adjustment of the panel size, which may need to be varied during the factorization for optimal performance. An application of the same strategy via a runtime eliminates much of the programming burden, potentially introducing a dynamic "recursion" (depth) in the look-ahead, but may still benefit from a fine-grain tuning of the panel dimension.

References

1. Anderson, E., Bai, Z., Bischof, C., Blackford, L.S., Demmel, J., Dongarra, J.J., Du Croz, J., Hammarling, S., Greenbaum, A., McKenney, A., Sorensen, D.: LAPACK users' guide (third ed.). Society for Industrial and Applied Mathematics, Philadelphia, PA, USA (1999)

2. Barrachina, S., Castillo, M., Igual, F.D., Mayo, R., Quintana-Ortí, E.S., Quintana-Ortí, G.: Exploiting the capabilities of modern GPUs for dense matrix computations. Concurrency Comput.: Pract. Exp. **21**, 2457–2477 (2009)
3. Benner, P., Ezzatti, P., Quintana-Ortí, E.S., Remón, A.: Matrix inversion on CPU-GPU platforms with applications in control theory. Concurrency Comput.: Pract. Exp. **25**(8), 1170–1182 (2013)
4. Benner, P., Ezzatti, P., Quintana-Ortí, E.S., Remón, A.: Revisiting the Gauss-Huard algorithm for the solution of linear systems on graphics accelerators. In: Wyrzykowski, R., Deelman, E., Dongarra, J., Karczewski, K., Kitowski, J., Wiatr, K. (eds.) PPAM 2015. LNCS, vol. 9573, pp. 505–514. Springer, Heidelberg (2016). doi:10.1007/978-3-319-32149-3_47
5. Buttari, A., Dongarra, J., Langou, J., Langou, J., Luszczek, P., Kurzak, J.: Mixed precision iterative refinement techniques for the solution of dense linear systems. Int. J. High Perform. Comput. Appl. **21**(4), 457–466 (2007)
6. Dekker, T.J., Hoffmann, W., Potma, K.: Parallel algorithms for solving large linear systems. J. Comput. Appl. Math. **50**(1–3), 221–232 (1994)
7. Dekker, T.J., Hoffmann, W., Potma, K.: Stability of the Gauss-Huard algorithm with partial pivoting. Computing **58**, 225–244 (1997)
8. Dufrechou, E., Ezzatti, P., Quintana-Ortí, E.S., Remón, A.: Solving linear systems on the intel Xeon-Phi accelerator via the Gauss-Huard algorithm. Commun. Comput. Inf. Sci. **565**, 107–117 (2015)
9. Golub, G.H., Van Loan, C.F.: Matrix Computations, 3rd edn. Johns Hopkins University Press, Baltimore (1996)
10. Gunnels, J.A., Gustavson, F.G., Henry, G.M., van de Geijn, R.A.: FLAME: formal linear algebra methods environment. ACM Trans. Math. Softw. **27**(4), 422–455 (2001)
11. Hennessy, J.L., Patterson, D.A.: Computer Architecture: A Quantitative Approach. Morgan Kaufmann Publishers, San Francisco (2011)
12. Higham, N.J.: Accuracy and Stability of Numerical Algorithms, 2nd edn. Society for Industrial and Applied Mathematics, Philadelphia (2002)
13. Hoffmann, W., Potma, K., Pronk, G.: Solving dense linear systems by Gauss-Huard's method on a distributed memory system. Future Gener. Comput. Syst. **10**(2–3), 321–325 (1994)
14. Huard, P.: La méthode simplex sans inverse explicite. EDB Bull, Direction Études Rech. Sér. C Math. Inform. **2**, 79–98 (1979)
15. Strazdins, P.: A comparison of lookahead and algorithmic blocking techniques for parallel matrix factorization. Technical report TR-CS-98-07, Department of Computer Science, The Australian National University (1998)
16. The University of Tennessee at Knoxville. MAGMA: Matrix Algebra on GPU and Multicore Architectures. http://icl.cs.utk.edu/magma/
17. Van Zee, F.G., Smith, T.M., Marker, B., Meng Low, T., van de Geijn, R.A., Igual, F.D., Smelyanskiy, M., Zhang, X., Kistler, M., Austel, V., Gunnels, J., Killough, L.: The BLIS framework: experiments in portability. ACM Trans. Math. Soft. http://www.cs.utexas.edu/users/flame. Accessed 2016
18. Van Zee, F.G., van de Geijn, R.A.: BLIS: a framework for rapidly instantiating BLAS functionality. ACM Trans. Math. Softw. **41**(3), 141–1433 (2015)

Leveraging the Performance of LBM-HPC for Large Sizes on GPUs Using Ghost Cells

Pedro Valero-Lara[1,2]([✉])

[1] The University of Manchester, Manchester, UK
pedro.valero-lara@manchester.ac.uk
[2] Basque Center for Applied Mathematics, Bilbao, Spain

Abstract. Today, we are living a growing demand of larger and more efficient computational resources from the scientific community. On the other hand, the appearance of GPUs for general purpose computing supposed an important advance for covering such demand. These devices offer an impressive computational capacity at low cost and an efficient power consumption. However, the memory available in these devices is (sometimes) not enough, and so it is necessary computationally expensive memory transfers from (to) CPU to (from) GPU, causing a dramatic fall in performance. Recently, the Lattice-Boltzmann Method has positioned as an efficient methodology for fluid simulations. Although this method presents some interesting features particularly amenable to be efficiently exploited on parallel computers, it requires a considerable memory capacity, which can suppose an important drawback, in particular, on GPUs. In the present paper, it is proposed a new GPU-based implementation, which minimizes such requirements with respect to other state-of-the-art implementations. It allows us to execute almost $2\times$ bigger problems without additional memory transfers, achieving faster executions when dealing with large problems.

Keywords: Computational fluid dynamics · Lattice-Boltzmann Method · GPU · CUDA

1 Introduction

The appearance of GPUs has been an important advance, emerging new challenges and opportunities for increasing performance in multiple scientific solvers. Many scientific applications and software packages have already been ported and redesigned to exploit GPUs. These developments have often involved major

P. Valero-Lara—This research has been supported by the Basque Excellence Research Center (BERC 2014–2017) program by the Basque Government, the Spanish Ministry of Economy and Competitiveness MINECO: BCAM Severo Ochoa accreditation SEV-2013-0323. The authors would like to thank the computing facilities of the Extremadura Research Centre for Advanced Technologies (CETA-CIEMAT), and NVIDIA GPU Research Center program for the provided resources.

© Springer International Publishing AG 2016
J. Carretero et al. (Eds.): ICA3PP 2016, LNCS 10048, pp. 417–430, 2016.
DOI: 10.1007/978-3-319-49583-5_31

algorithm changes since some classical solvers may turned out to be inefficient or difficult to tune [1,2]. Fortunately, other solvers are particularly well suited for GPU acceleration and are able to achieve significant performance improvements. The Lattice Boltzmann method (LBM) [3] is one of those examples thanks to its inherently data-parallel nature. Certainly, the computing stages of LBM are amenable to fine grain parallelization in an almost straightforward way. This fundamental advantage of LBM has been consistently confirmed by many previous works [4,5], for a large variety of problems and computing platforms. For instance, Pohl et al. [6] studied several memory access patterns to maximize the temporal locality, optimizing the cache performance over multicore architectures. Also Rinaldi et al. [5] proposed a different ordering of the LBM steps to reduce the number of memory accesses. LBM has been adapted to numerous parallel architectures, such as multicore processors [6], manycore accelerators [5,7,8] and distributed-memory clusters [9–11]. Given the growing popularity of LBM, multiple tools [9,10,12,13] have recently arisen, consolidating this method in academia and industry. In particular, in this work we have considered the LBM-HPC framework [10] as our reference software tool.

Today, we are living a growing demand of higher computational resources from CFD community to be able to simulate and compute more and more complex scenarios. In particular, one of the most important challenges to deal with such scenarios is the excessive memory requirements. Despite LBM is an appropriate method for parallel systems, it requires a high memory capacity for its execution. For instance, to compute bi-dimensional problems using LBM, we need 21 elements (double precision) per mesh (macroscopic) point. These requirements are much bigger for tri-dimensional problems. Our motivation consists of developing a new approach, which minimizes such demand of memory for LBM implementations over CUDA compatible GPUs. We propose the use of *ghost cells* to minimize the memory requirements and to deal with race conditions. This idea forces us to develop a more complex strategy with a different memory mapping and one additional kernel (GPU code). However, this new approach allows us to execute bigger problems over the same platform, avoiding the impressive fall in performance (reducing the memory transfer between CPU and GPU) when other state-of-the-art approaches are considered.

The remainder of this paper is organized as follows. In Sect. 2 we introduce the general numerical and implementation framework for the LBM. After that, we describe the different optimizations and parallel strategies envisaged to achieve high-performance when dealing with large problems. Finally, we discuss the performance results of the proposed techniques in Sect. 3. We conclude in Sect. 4 with a summary of the main contributions of this work.

2   Lattice-Boltzmann Method

2.1   Background

Most of the current methods for simulating the transport equations (heat, mass, and momentum) are based on the use of macroscopic partial differential equations [14]. On the other extreme, we can view the medium from a micro-scopic viewpoint where small particles (molecule, atom) collide with each other (molecular dynamic) [15]. In this scale the inter-particle forces must be identified, which requires to know the location, velocity, and trajectory of every particle. However, there is no definition of viscosity, heat capacity, temperature, pressure, etc. These methods are extremely expensive computationally [15]. However, it is possible to use statistical mechanisms as a translator between the molecular world and the microscopic world, avoiding the management of every individual particle, while obtaining the important macroscopic effects by combining the advantages of both approaches, macroscopic and microscopic, with manageable computer resources. This is the main idea of the Boltzmann equation and the mesoscopic scale [15].

Multiple studies have compared the efficiency of LBM with respect to other "classic" methods based on Navier-Stokes (see [16,17]). They show that LBM can achieve an equivalent numerical accuracy over a large number of applications. In particular, LBM has been used to simulate high Reynolds turbulent flows over Direct Numerical and Large Eddy simulations [18], aeroacoustics problems [19], bio-engineering applications [7], among others. Also, LBM has been efficiently integrated with other methods, such as the Immersed Boundary Method for Fluid-Solid Interaction problems [8,20].

2.2 LBM Formulation

LBM combines some features developed to solve the Boltzmann equation over a finite number of microscopic speeds. LBM presents lattice-symmetry character-istics which allow to respect the conservation of the macroscopic moments [21]. The standard LBM [22] is an explicit solver for incompressible flows. It divides each temporal iteration into two steps, one for propagation-advection (stream-ing) and one for collision (inter-particle interactions), achieving a first order in time and second order in space scheme.

LBM describes the fluid behavior at mesoscopic level. At this level, the fluid is modeled by a distribution function of the microscopic particle (f). Similarly to the Boltzmann equation, LBM solves the particle speed distribution by dis-cretizing the speed space over a discrete finite number of possible speeds. The distribution function evolves according to the following equation:

$$\frac{\partial f}{\partial t} + e\nabla f = \Omega \tag{1}$$

where f is the particle distribution function, e is the discrete space of speeds and Ω is the collision operator. By discretizing the distribution function f in space, in time, and in speed ($e = e_i$) we obtain $f_i(x,t)$, which describes the probability of finding a particle located at x at time t with speed e_i. $e\nabla f$ can be discretized as:

$$e\nabla f = e_i\nabla f_i = \frac{f_i(x + e_i\Delta t, t + \Delta t) - f_i(x, t + \Delta t)}{\Delta t} \tag{2}$$

In this way the particles can move only along the links of a regular *lattice* (Fig. 1) defined by the discrete speeds ($e_0 = c(0,0)$; $e_i = c(\pm 1, 0)$, $c(0, \pm 1)$, $i = 1, \cdots, 4$; $e_i = c(\pm 1, \pm 1)$, $i = 5, \cdots, 8$ with $c = \Delta x / \Delta t$) so that the synchronous particle displacements $\Delta x_i = e_i \Delta t$ never takes the fluid particles away from the *lattice*. In this work, we consider the standard two-dimensional 9-speed *lattice* *D2Q9* [21].

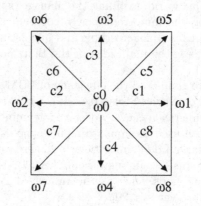

Fig. 1. The standard two-dimensional 9-speed lattice (*D2Q9*) [23].

The operator Ω describes the changes suffered by the collision of the microscopic particles, which affect the distribution function (f). To calculate the collision operator we consider the *BGK* (Bhatnagar-Gross-Krook) formulation [23] which relies upon a unique relaxation time, τ, toward the equilibrium distribution f_i^{eq}:

$$\Omega = -\frac{1}{\tau} \left(f_i \left(x, t \right) - f_i^{eq} \left(x, t \right) \right) \tag{3}$$

The equilibrium function $f^{eq} \left(x, t \right)$ can be obtained by *Taylor* series expansion of the *Maxwell-Boltzmann* equilibrium distribution [22]:

$$f_i^{eq} = \rho \omega_i \left[1 + \frac{e_i \cdot u}{c_s^2} + \frac{\left(e_i \cdot u \right)^2}{2c_s^4} - \frac{u^2}{2c_s^2} \right] \tag{4}$$

where c_s is the speed of sound ($c_s = 1/\sqrt{3}$), u is the vertical or horizontal component (see Algorithm 1) of the macroscopic velocity in the given position, and the weight coefficients ω_i are $\omega_0 = 4/9$, $\omega_i = 1/9$, $i = 1, \ldots, 4$ and $\omega_i = 1/36$, $i = 5, \ldots, 8$ based on the current normalization. Through the use of the collision operator and substituting the term $\frac{\partial f_i}{\partial t}$ with a first order temporal discretization, the discrete Boltzmann equation can be written as:

$$\frac{f_i(x,t+\Delta t) - f_i(x,t)}{\Delta t} + \frac{f_i(x + e_i\Delta t, t + \Delta t) - f_i(x, t + \Delta t)}{\Delta t}$$
$$\doteq -\frac{1}{\tau}\left(f_i\left(x,t\right) - f_i^{eq}\left(x,t\right)\right)$$
(5)

which can be compactly written as:

$$f_i\left(x + e_i\Delta t, t + \Delta t\right) - f_i\left(x,t\right) = -\frac{\Delta t}{\tau}\left(f\left(x,t\right) - f_i^{eq}\left(x,t\right)\right)$$
(6)

The macroscopic velocity u in Eq. 4 must satisfy a Mach number requirement $\mid u \mid /c_s \approx M \ll 1$. This stands as the equivalent of the CFL number[1] for classical Navier Stokes solvers.

As mentioned above, the Eq. 6 is typically advanced in time in two stages, the collision and the streaming stages.

Given $f_i(x,t)$ compute:

$\rho = \sum f_i(x,t)$ and
$\rho u = \sum e_i f_i(x,t)$

Collision stage:

$f_i^*\left(x, t + \Delta t\right) = f_i\left(x,t\right) - \frac{\Delta t}{\tau}\left(f\left(x,t\right) - f_i^{eq}\left(x,t\right)\right)$

Streaming stage:

$f_i\left(x + e_i\Delta t, t + \Delta t\right) = f_i^*\left(x, t + \Delta t\right)$

2.3   LBM Solvers and Implementation

LBM exhibits a high degree of parallelism and is amenable to fine granularity (one thread per lattice node), since the solving of every *lattice* point is totally independent with respect to the others. To compute streaming in parallel, we need two different distribution functions (f_1 and f_2 in Algorithm 1).

In the present work, we have opted to work with the *pull* approach (introduced by [24]), which has been recently considered in [5,8,20]. This is an efficient approach based on a single-loop strategy, in which each *lattice* node can be independently computed by performing one complete time step of LBM. A schematic sketch of this LBM implementation is given in Algorithm 1. Basically, the *pull* approach fuses in a single loop (that iterates over the entire domain), the application of both operations, collision and streaming (see Sect. 2.2) to improve temporal locality. Furthermore it does not need any synchronization among these operations. Also, it eases pressure on memory with respect to other approaches, as the macroscopic level can be completely computed on high levels of memory hierarchy (registers/L1 cache).

Memory management plays a crucial role in LBM implementations. The information of the fluid domain should be stored in memory in such way that

---

[1] Courant Friedrichs Lewy (CFL) number arises in those schemes based on explicit time computer simulations. As a consequence, this number must be less than a certain time to achieve coherent results.

Algorithm 1. LBM *pull.*

1: **for** $ind = 1 \rightarrow Nx \cdot Ny$ **do**
2:     **Streaming**
3:     **for** $i = 1 \rightarrow 9$ **do**
4:         $x_{stream} = x - c_x[i]$
5:         $y_{stream} = y - c_y[i]$
6:         $ind_{stream} = y_{stream} \cdot Nx + x_{stream}$
7:         $f[i] = f_1[i][ind_{stream}]$
8:     **end for**
9:     **for** $i = 1 \rightarrow 9$ **do**
10:         $\rho+ = f[i]$
11:         $u_x+ = c_x[i] \cdot f[i]$
12:         $u_y+ = c_y[i] \cdot f[i]$
13:     **end for**
14:     $u_x = u_x/\rho$
15:     $u_y = u_y/\rho$
16:     *Synchronization point (only) for our approach based on Ghost Cell*
17:     *syncthreads()*
18:     **Collision**
19:     **for** $i = 1 \rightarrow 9$ **do**
20:         $cu = c_x[i] \cdot u_x + c_y[i] \cdot u_y$
21:         $f_{eq} = \omega[i] \cdot \rho \cdot (1 + 3 \cdot cu + cu^2 - 1.5 \cdot (u_x)^2 + u_y)^2$
22:         $f_2[i][ind] = f[i] \cdot (1 - \frac{1}{\tau}) + f_{eq} \cdot \frac{1}{\tau}$
23:     **end for**
24: **end for**

---

reduces the number of memory accesses and keeps the implementation highly efficient by taking advantages of vector units. In this work, we consider a coalescing memory access pattern by using a Structure of Array (SoA) approach. This strategy (*pull-coalescing*) has proven to be very efficient in multicore and GPUs architectures [5, 7, 8, 20]. The discrete distribution function f_i is stored sequentially in the same array (see Fig. 2-top, where Nx and Ny are the number of horizontal and vertical fluid nodes respectively). This way, consecutive threads access adjacent memory locations (coalescing).

Parallelism is abundant in the LBM update and can be exploited in different ways. The recommendable parallelization of LBM over GPUs consists of using a single *kernel* by using a 1D Grid of 1D CUDA block, in which each CUDA-thread performs a complete LBM update on a single *lattice* node [8]. *Lattice* nodes are distributed across GPU cores using a fine-grained distribution (Fig. 2-bottom).

In order to exploit the parallelism found in the LBM, previous studies make use of two different data set [5, 9, 10, 13, 20]. Essentially, it follows an *AB* scheme [8] which holds the data of two successive time steps (A and B) and the simulation alternates between reading from A and writing to B, and vice-versa. In this work, we proposed an alternative to reduce such high memory requirements, adapting the use of *ghost cell* to our target problem (LBM) and platform (GPUs).

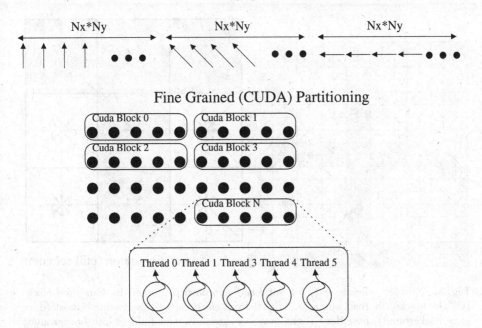

Fig. 2. SoA data layout to store the discrete distribution function f_i in memory (top) and fine-grained distributions of the *lattice* nodes (bottom).

2.4 Ghost Cells

In this subsection, we focus on explaining how we have adapted the use of *ghost cells* to LBM to reduce the memory requirements for GPU-based implementations.

Although, the *ghost cells* strategy is usually used for communication in distributed memory systems [25], we use this strategy to reduce memory requirements and avoid race conditions among the set of CUDA blocks (*fluid blocks*). To minimize the number of *ghost cells* we use the biggest size of CUDA (*fluid block*) blocks possible. The use of *ghost cells* consists of replicating the borders of all immediate neighbors blocks, in our case *fluid blocks*. These *ghost cells* are not updated locally, but provide stencil values when updating the borders of local blocks. Every *ghost cell* is a duplicate of a piece of memory located in neighbors nodes. To clarify, Fig. 3-left illustrates a simple scheme for our interpretation of the *ghost cell* strategy applied to LBM.

In spread operation (Fig. 3-right), some of the lattice-speed into each *ghost cell* are used by adjacent fluid (*lattice*) elements located in neighbors *fluid blocks*. Depending on the position of the fluid units, a different pattern for spread operation is required. For instance, if one fluid element is positioned in one of the corners of fluid block, this takes 5 lattice-speed from 3 different *ghost cells*. Otherwise, if one fluid element is located in other position of the fluid block boundary, it needs to take 3 lattice-speed from one *ghost cell*.

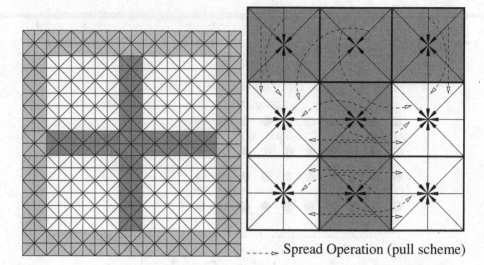
----▷ Spread Operation (pull scheme)

Fig. 3. A simple scheme (left) for our LBM approach composed by four *fluid blocks* (CUDA blocks). Spread operation (right) from *ghost cells* to fluid units. Ghost (dark gray background), boundary (light gray background), and fluid (white background) units.

The information stored in the *ghost cells* are in need of being updated once per time step. The update operation is performed via a second kernel before computing LBM. Basically, this kernel moves some lattice-speed from lattice units to *ghost cells*. This CUDA kernel is composed by as many threads as *ghost cells*. To optimize memory management and minimize divergence, continuous CUDA blocks compute each of the updating cases. To clarify Fig. 4 shows the different data movements applied to each of the cases. In this regard, depending on the location of *ghost cells*, a different number of memory movements are necessary. In particular, if one *ghost cell* is located in one of the *ghost cell* rows or columns (Vertical and Horizontal cases in Fig. 4), this needs to take 6 lattice-speed from 2 different fluid units (3 lattice-speed per fluid unit). However, if one *ghost cell* is positioned in one of the corners (Corner case in Fig. 4), then this *ghost cell* requires 4 lattice-speed from 4 fluid units.

Unlike the standard LBM implementation (*pull* approach) on GPU, the *CUDA* blocks need to be synchronized before computing collision. This is possible via a __syncthreads() call from the kernel side (see Algorithm 1). This synchronization and the use of *ghost cells* among CUDA (*fluid*) blocks guarantees the absence of race conditions.

2.5 Memory Management

It is well known that the memory management has an important influence on performance of parallel computing, in particular on those parallel computers that suffer of a high latency such as Nvidia GPUs or Intel MIC [8]. Furthermore,

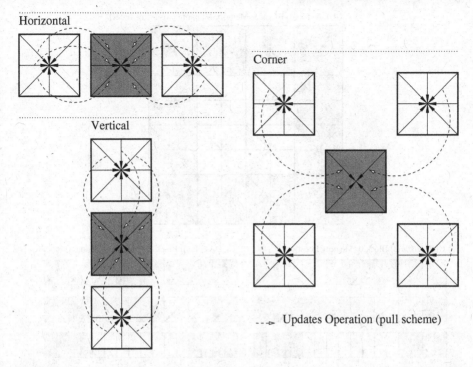

Fig. 4. Update operation from fluid units (white background) to *ghost cells* (gray background), depending on *ghost cells* position.

LBM is a memory-bound algorithm, so that, another important optimization problem is to maximize data locality.

The previous thread-data distribution shown in Fig. 2-bottom does not allow us to exploit coalescence (contiguous threads access to continuous memory locations), when dealing with *ghost cells*, so we proposed a new memory mapping which fits better our particular data structure. Essentially, we follow the same aforementioned strategy (*SoA*), adapting it to our approach based on *ghost cells*. Instead of mapping every lattice-speed in consecutive memory location for the whole fluid domain (Fig. 2), we map the set of lattice-speed of every bidimensional fluid (*CUDA*) block in consecutive memory locations, as graphically illustrated by Fig. 5.

3   Performance Evaluation

To critically evaluate the performance of the proposed LBM solver, next we consider a number of tests executed on one Nvidia Kepler (K20c) GPU with 2496 CUDA cores at 706 Mhz and 5 GB GDDR5 of memory. According to the memory requirements of the GPU kernels, the memory hierarchy of the GPU has been configured as 16 KB shared memory and 48 KB L1, since our codes do not benefit from a higher amount of shared memory on the investigated tests.

CUDA (Fluid) Block & Memory Mapping (wise-row order)

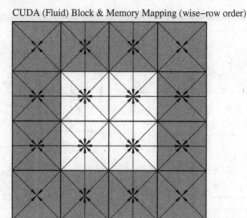

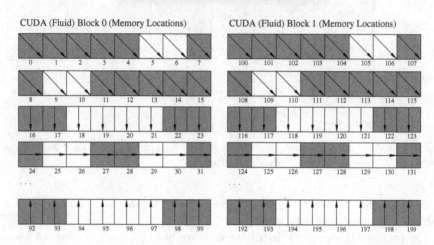

Fig. 5. Memory and CUDA block mapping for the *1 lattice + ghost* approach.

Given the restrictions in terms of number of threads per CUDA (*fluid*) block, we have considered the most appropriate size of fluid block for each of the implementations. For our testbed platform the maximum number of threads per CUDA (*fluid*) block is 2048.

In the following, we analyse the time consumed by both approaches, *2 lattice* (*pull* approach) and *1 lattice + ghost*. Figure 6-left graphically illustrates the execution time for both approaches increasing the size of the problem to be computed. As expected, the *2 lattice* achieves a low execution time against the *1 lattice + ghost* in those problems which can be stored completely in GPU memory (from 9 to 36 millions of fluid nodes) using f_1 and f_2. However, for bigger fluid domains (from 45 millions of nodes), the limit of memory forces us to execute our problem in two-steps when using the *2 lattice* approach. It requires additional memory transfers regarding data dependency of our simulation. In particular, the whole subdomains of both LBM blocks (LBM-Block1/2 in Fig. 6-left) must be transfered from GPU to CPU and vice-versa (CPU/GPU->GPU/CPU-Block1/2 in Fig. 6-left) every time-step. As graphically illustrated by Fig. 6-left, this additional overhead consumes most of the execution time, being the main bottleneck and causing an important fall in performance.

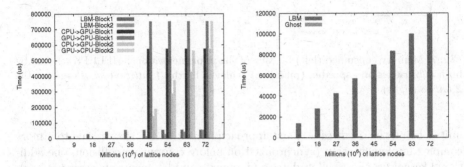

Fig. 6. Time consumed by the *2 lattice* approach (left) and by the *1 lattice+ghost* approach (right).

On the other hand, the *1 lattice + ghost* shows a better performance for large problems (Fig. 6-right). Despite this approach requires 2 kernels, the time consumed by the additional kernel (*Ghost* in Fig. 6-right), which updates the information in *ghost cells*, does not represent an important overhead. Actually, it is less than 2% of the total consumed time.

As previously introduced, one of our main motivations of this work consists of reducing the memory requirements for LBM simulations on GPUs. Figure 7-left illustrates the memory consumed by both approaches. The reduction achieved by our approach (*1 lattice + ghost*) represents almost the half of the memory consumed by the *2 lattice* approach. It allows us to launch bigger simulations obviating additional and computationally expensive memory transfers.

Most of the LBM studies consider the conventional MFLUPS (Millions of Fluid Lattice Updates Per Second ratio) as a metric. As a reference, we also estimate the ideal MFLUPS [26]:

$$MFLUPS_{ideal} = \frac{B \times 10^9}{10^6 \times n \times 6 \times 8} \qquad (7)$$

where $B \times 10^9$ is the memory bandwidth (GB/s), n depends on LBM model ($DxQn$), for our framework $n = 9$, D2Q9. The factor 6 is for the memory accesses, three read and write operations in the spreading step and three read and write operations in the collision step, and the factor 8 is for double precision (8 bytes).

Figure 7-right illustrates the MFLUPS achieved by both approaches and an estimation for the ideal MFLUPS for our platform. The *2 lattice* approach is near ideal performance when dealing with "small" problems (until 36 millions of fluid

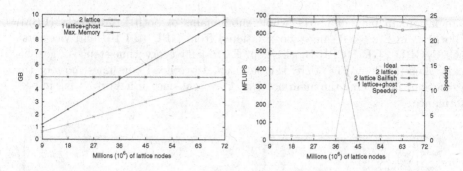

Fig. 7. Memory consumed (left) by each of the implementations. MFLUPS reached by both approaches and speedup (pink line) achieved by the *1 lattice + ghost* against the *2 lattice* (right).

units), being the *1 lattice + ghost* approach almost a 10% slower, due to a more complex implementation (synchronization before computing collision, one additional kernel for ghost cell updates and a more complex memory access pattern). However, when bigger domains are considered (from 45 to 72 millions of fluid units), the *2 lattice* approach turns out to be very inefficient, suffering a dramatic fall in performance. In contract, the performance achieved by *1 lattice + ghost* is kept constant for the rest of tests. Also, as reference, we included the performance achieved by the GPU based implementation provided in the sailfish package [9], which is slower than the other implementations (*2 lattice* and *1 lattice + ghost*).

Additionally Fig. 7-right illustrates the speedup achieved by our new approach against the *2 lattice* implementation. Our approach is slower than the *2 lattice* approach for those problems with a domain equal or smaller than 36 millions of units, however our approach turns out to be faster (speedup near of 25) when dealing with bigger domains.

4   Conclusions

The limitation found in the memory capacity of GPUs and the amount of memory demanded by LBM supposes an important drawback when dealing with large problems. This work presents a new alternative based on *ghost cells*, reducing considerably the memory requirements and keeping a high MFLUPS ratio for large simulations. It was carried out a detailed performance analysis in terms of time, memory requirements, speedup and MFLUPS ratio. Furthermore, the implementation proposed (ghost cell, additional kernel, memory access pattern, synchronizations points, etc.) has been thoroughly detailed.

References

1. Valero-Lara, P., Pinelli, A., Favier, J., Matias, M.P.: Block tridiagonal solvers on heterogeneous architectures. In: Proceedings of the 2012 IEEE 10th International Symposium on Parallel and Distributed Processing with Applications, ISPA 2012, pp. 609–616. IEEE Computer Society, Washington (2012)
2. Valero-Lara, P., Pinelli, A., Prieto-Matias, M.: Fast finite difference poisson solvers on heterogeneous architectures. Comput. Phys. Commun. **185**(4), 1265–1272 (2014)
3. Succi, S.: The Lattice Boltzmann Equation for Fluid Dynamics and Beyond (Numerical Mathematics and Scientific Computation). Numerical Mathematics and Scientific Computation. Oxford University Press, New York (2001)
4. Bernaschi, M., Fatica, M., Melchiona, S., Succi, S., Kaxiras, E.: A flexible high-performance lattice Boltzmann GPU code for the simulations of fluid flows in complex geometries. Concurr. Comput. Pract. Exp. **22**, 1–14 (2010)
5. Rinaldi, P., Dari, E., Vénere, M., Clausse, A.: A lattice-Boltzmann solver for 3D fluid simulation on GPU. Simul. Model. Pract. Theory **25**, 163–171 (2012)
6. Pohl, T., Kowarchik, M., Wilke, J., Iglberger, K., Rüde, U.: Optimization and profiling of the cache performance of parallel lattice Boltzmann codes. Parallel Process. Lett. **13**(4), 549–560 (2003)
7. Bernaschi, M., Fatica, M., Melchionna, S., Succi, S., Kaxiras, E.: A flexible high-performance lattice Boltzmann GPU code for the simulations of fluid flows in complex geometries. Concurr. Comput. Pract. Exp. **22**(1), 1–14 (2010)
8. Valero-Lara, P., Igual, F.D., Prieto-Matías, M., Pinelli, A., Favier, J.: Accelerating fluidsolid simulations (lattice-Boltzmann & immersed-boundary) on heterogeneous architectures. J. Comput. Sci. **10**, 249–261 (2015)
9. Januszewski, M., Kostur, M.: Sailfish: a flexible multi-GPU implementation of the lattice Boltzmann method. Comput. Phys. Commun. **185**(9), 2350–2368 (2014)
10. LBM-HPC. http://www.bcamath.org/en/research/lines/CFDCT/software. Accessed 26 Apr 2016
11. Obrecht, C., Kuznik, F., Tourancheau, B., Roux, J.J.: Scalable lattice Boltzmann solvers for CUDA GPU clusters. Parallel Comput. **39**(6–7), 259–270 (2013)
12. XFlow, N.G.o.C. http://www.xflowcfd.com/. Accessed 26 Apr 2016
13. Palabos, C.C.P. http://www.palabos.org/. Accessed 26 Apr 2016
14. Wendt, J.F., Anderson, J.D.: Computational Fluid Dynamics: An Introduction. Springer, Heidelberg (2008)
15. Mohamad, A.A.: The Lattice Boltzmann Method - Fundamental and Engineering Applications with Computer Codes. Springer, Heidelberg (2011)
16. Axner, L., Hoekstra, A.G., Jeays, A., Lawford, P., Hose, R., Sloot, P.M.: Simulations of time harmonic blood flow in the mesenteric artery: comparing finite element and lattice Boltzmann methods. BioMed. Eng. OnLine (2000)
17. Kollmannsberger, S., Geller, S., Düster, A., Tölke, J., Sorger, C., Krafczyk, M., Rank, E.: Fixed-grid fluidstructure interaction in two dimensions based on a partitioned lattice Boltzmann and p-FEM approach. Int. J. Numer. Meth. Eng. **79**(7), 817–845 (2009)
18. Malaspinas, O., Sagaut, P.: Consistent subgrid scale modelling for lattice Boltzmann methods. J. Fluid Mech. **700**, 514–542 (2012)
19. Marié, S., Ricot, D., Sagaut, P.: Comparison between lattice Boltzmann method and navier-stokes high order schemes for computational aeroacoustics. J. Comput. Phys. **228**(4), 1056–1070 (2009)

20. Valero-Lara, P., Pinelli, A., Prieto-Matias, M.: Accelerating solid-fluid interaction using lattice-Boltzmann and immersed boundary coupled simulations on heterogeneous platforms. Procedia Comput. Sci. **29**, 50–61 (2014). International Conference on Computational Science (2014)
21. He, X., Luo, L.S.: A priori derivation of the lattice Boltzmann equation. Phys. Rev. E **55**, R6333–R6336 (1997)
22. Qian, Y.H., D'Humières, D., Lallemand, P.: Lattice BGK models for Navier-Stokes equation. EPL (Europhys. Lett.) **17**(6), 479 (1992)
23. Bhatnagar, P., Gross, E., Krook, M.: A model for collision processes in gases. i: small amplitude processes in charged and neutral one-component system. Phys. Rev. E **94**, 511–525 (1954)
24. Wellein, G., Zeiser, T., Hager, G., Donath, S.: On the single processor performance of simple lattice Boltzmann kernels. Comput. Fluids **35**(89), 910–919 (2006). Proceedings of the First International Conference for Mesoscopic Methods in Engineering and Science
25. Valero-Lara, P., Jansson, J.: LBM-HPC - an open-source tool for fluid simulations. case study: unified parallel C (UPC-PGAS). In: 2015 IEEE International Conference on Cluster Computing, CLUSTER 2015, Chicago, IL, USA, September 8–11 2015, pp. 318–321 (2015)
26. Shet, A.G., Sorathiya, S.H., Krithivasan, S., Deshpande, A.M., Kaul, B., Sherlekar, S.D., Ansumali, S.: Data structure and movement for lattice-based simulations. Phys. Rev. E **88**, 013314 (2013)

Improving Hash Distributed A* for Shared Memory Architectures Using Abstraction

Victoria Sanz[1,2]([⊠]), Armando De Giusti[1,2], and Marcelo Naiouf[1]

[1] III-LIDI, School of Computer Sciences,
National University of La Plata, La Plata, Argentina
{vsanz,degiusti,mnaiouf}@lidi.info.unlp.edu.ar
[2] CONICET, Ministry of Science,
Technology and Productive Innovation, Buenos Aires, Argentina

Abstract. The A* algorithm is generally used to solve combinatorial optimization problems, but it requires high computing power and a large amount of memory, hence, efficient parallel A* algorithms are needed. In this sense, Hash Distributed A* (HDA*) parallelizes A* by applying a decentralized strategy and a hash-based node distribution scheme. However, this distribution scheme results in frequent node transfers among processors. In this paper, we present Optimized AHDA*, a version of HDA* for shared memory architectures, that uses an abstraction-based node distribution scheme and a technique to group several nodes before transferring them to the corresponding thread. Both methods reduce the amount of node transfers and mitigate communication and contention. We assess the effect of each technique on algorithm performance. Finally, we evaluate the scalability of the proposed algorithm, when it is run on a multicore machine, using the 15-puzzle as a case study.

Keywords: HDA* for shared memory architectures · Abstraction-based node distribution scheme · Hash-based node distribution scheme · Scalability · Combinatorial optimization problems

1 Introduction

A* [1,2] is one of the most widely used search algorithms for solving combinatorial optimization problems.

For that purpose, A* explores the graph that represents the state space of the problem using a cost function $\hat{f}$ to value the nodes, which is defined as follows: $f(\hat{n}) = g(\hat{n}) + h(\hat{n})$, where $g(\hat{n})$ is the known cost of the path from the initial node to the current node n and $h(\hat{n})$ is a heuristic estimate that represents the unknown cost of the path from the current node n to the solution node. In this algorithm, the search tree is generated as the search progresses. During the process, it keeps two data structures: one for the unexplored nodes sorted by $\hat{f}$ (*open list*), and another for the already explored nodes (*closed list*) used to avoid processing the same state multiple times. In each iteration, the most promising

© Springer International Publishing AG 2016
J. Carretero et al. (Eds.): ICA3PP 2016, LNCS 10048, pp. 431–439, 2016.
DOI: 10.1007/978-3-319-49583-5_32

node (according to $\hat{f}$) available on the open list is removed, it is added to the closed list, and legal actions are applied to it to generate successor nodes that will be added to the open list under certain conditions (verification known as *duplicate detection*). The search process continues until the node that represents the solution is removed from the open list.

The major drawback of A* is that it requires high computing power and a large amount of memory. Therefore, over the last years, the development of efficient parallel A* algorithms, for different architectures, has been promoted.

Hash Distributed A* (HDA*) [3] is a parallel A* algorithm in which each processor has its own open/closed lists and performs a quasi-independent search. It uses a standard hash function to assign each state of the problem to a single processor. This hash-based node distribution scheme allows balancing the workload and pruning duplicate nodes (i.e., nodes representing the same state) in an absolute way, as they are always sent to the same processor. This version of HDA* can be run on distributed memory, shared memory, or "hybrid" systems.

Other authors [4] adapted HDA* for multicore machines and noted that the hash-based node distribution scheme results in frequent node transfers among processors. Consequently, they proposed using a special function (an abstraction function) to assign blocks of nodes to processors instead of individual nodes (this version of the algorithm is called AHDA*). In this way, communication is reduced, but there is a trade-off between load balance and communication, which is defined by the block size.

Additionaly, in [5,6] we developed Optimized HDA*, a version of HDA* for multicore machines, which uses a standard hash function to distribute nodes and includes a technique to group several nodes before transferring them to the corresponding thread. This technique reduces the amount of node transfers and mitigates communication and contention.

In this paper, we present Optimized AHDA*, a version of HDA* for shared memory architectures that uses an abstraction-based node distribution scheme and our technique to group several nodes before transferring them to the corresponding thread. We assess the effect of each technique on algorithm performance. Finally, we evaluate the scalability of the proposed algorithm, when it is run on a multicore machine, using the 15-puzzle as a case study.

2   Related Work

The most common and efficient way to parallelize A* is to use a *decentralized strategy* [7]: each process/thread (processor) is equipped with its own local open and closed lists and performs a quasi-independent search. This strategy is suitable both for shared memory and distributed memory architectures. However, communication among the processors is needed due to the following reasons: the workload should be distributed dynamically; duplicate nodes can be generated by different processors and should be pruned in order to prevent processors from performing duplicated work; the termination criterion should be modified because if the search is ended when the first solution is found, there will be no guarantee that such solution is the best one; the costs of the partial solutions found so far should be communicated in order to use them to prune the paths that lead to suboptimal cost solutions.

In this sense, the Hash Distributed A* (HDA*) algorithm [3] parallelizes A* by applying a decentralized strategy and using a standard hash function (the Zobrist function [8]) to assign each state of the problem to a single processor. Thus, when a processor generates a node, it determines who the owner is and transfers the node to that owner. This hash-based node distribution scheme allows balancing the workload and pruning duplicate nodes in an absolute way, as the nodes representing the same state are always sent to the same processor, which performs the duplicate detection procedure. This implementation of HDA* uses the MPI library and asynchronous communication.

On the other hand, the paper [4] presents an implementation of HDA* for multicore machines using the Pthreads library. The authors noted that using a hash-based node distribution scheme may cause the successors of a node to be transferred to different remote threads, instead of assigning some of them to a small subset of remote threads and the rest to the thread that generated them, in order to reduce communication and contention. Consequently, they proposed using a special function (an abstraction function) to assign a set of blocks of the search space (*abstract states*) to each thread, instead of individual states. As a result, they presented AHDA*, a variant of HDA* for multicore machines that uses an abstraction-based node distribution scheme.

The empirical evaluation carried out by these authors on different domains (grid pathfinding, the 15-puzzle problem and STRIPS planning) demonstrates the benefits of using abstraction. However, they only analyzed the speedup as the number of cores increases (they did not assess the speedup as the problem size scales) and, also, the difficulty level of the 15-puzzle instances used is low.

Furthermore, in [5,6] we presented an implementation of HDA* for shared memory architectures, which uses a hash-based node distribution scheme. The algorithm is based on the one proposed in [4], with the following main difference: threads accumulate a customizable quantity of nodes (*LNPT* or Limit of Nodes per Transfer) addressed to another thread before attempting their transfer, i.e. there are no transfers after each node generation as in the original algorithm. This allows reducing contention on the shared data structures used for communication. The experimental work was carried out with the 15-puzzle problem. The benefit of using the LNPT parameter was confirmed. Finally, the scalability of the algorithm was assessed as the number of cores and the problem size increase.

HDA* is currently interesting due to its good scalability. On the other hand, the Sliding Puzzle has recently gained relevance because it is related to real problems such as moving pallets with an automated guided vehicle [9]. Also, there is a need for improving the performance of parallel search algorithms. In this regard, the scalability analysis of AHDA* is an open research line. Moreover, AHDA* may benefit from the techniques presented in our previous research.

3   HDA* Algorithm for Shared Memory Architectures

The HDA* algorithm proposed in [4] is based on the following concepts. Each thread has: its own open and closed lists; an input queue known globally where the rest of the threads will deposit nodes that must be processed by this thread, and which must be protected by a lock to keep its consistency; a local output queue for each peer thread, which does not need to be protected since it will be for thread's own use to prevent it from waiting.

When a thread t_i generates a node that belongs to another thread t_j, it must be communicated by adding it to t_j's input queue at some point. To do this, t_i tries to acquire the lock associated with t_j's input queue. If the lock is obtained, node transfer is done by copying the pointer, and then the lock is released. Otherwise, the pointer is added to the local output queue for t_j.

After t_i carries out a certain number of node expansions from its open list:

1. For each non-empty output queue, it tries to communicate the stored nodes to the respective thread. To do this, t_i tries to acquire the lock associated with the input queue of the corresponding thread. If the lock is obtained, all the pointers to node are transferred. Otherwise, it is not forced to wait.
2. The thread tries to consume the nodes left by other threads on its own input queue. To do this, the thread must acquire the associated lock but it is only forced to wait if its open list is empty.

The allocation of states to threads is done through a *standard hash function*.

3.1   Abstraction-Based Node Distribution Scheme

When a *standard hash function* is used to distribute nodes among threads, there is a high probability that the successors of a node will be assigned to remote threads, considering that this function is effective in balancing the workload [10]. Therefore, this method results in continuous communication of nodes among threads, which causes high contention in the access to input queues.

In order to solve the previous problem, a *special function* that preserves locality and that assigns most of the newly generated successors to the expanding thread and some of them to a small subset of remote threads should be used.

To that end, the state space is divided into disjoint *regions* or *abstract states*. The mapping of states to abstract states is done through an *abstraction function*, which has to be chosen in order to guarantee the following: (a) the successors of any state that do not belong to the same region as their parent state are mapped to a small subset of all of the regions (b) the abstraction function should be computed efficiently. In general, the technique used to generate an abstraction function is domain-dependent and it is based on ignoring some state variables.

The regions are distributed among threads, so each one is in charge of processing the nodes that belong to its assigned regions. When a thread generates a node, it calculates the abstraction function, taking as input the representation of the state, and determines from the resulting value, which characterizes the node's region, the thread that has to compute the node.

To illustrate, the abstraction for the 15-puzzle problem could be based on taking into account only the tiles 1, 2 and 3, hence, each region is composed of all the states that have these tiles at a given position [4]. Then, when a thread expands a node (state) that belongs to a specific region, all the generated nodes (successors) that do not modify the location of the tiles included in the abstraction, will be assigned back to this thread, because they belong to the same region as their parent node.

The amount of tiles included in the abstraction determines the amount of generated regions and the amount of states per region. If few regions are generated, each will contain a lot of states; this approach requires very little communication among threads but augments the load unbalance. Otherwise, if too many regions are generated, each will contain few states; this approach increases communication among threads and improves the load balance.

4   Implementations

4.1   Optimized HDA*

The Optimized HDA* algorithm is similar to the one studied in Sect. 3. It uses the Zobrist function to assign states to threads. The algorithm is summarized below. Implementation details can be found in [5].

Each thread has its own open/closed lists. The node communication strategy is based on the use of input/output queues. With the aim of allowing the pruning of nodes that would lead to suboptimal solutions, threads share a pointer to the best global solution found so far (*best_solution*) and its cost (*best_solution_cost*).

Each thread carries out a series of iterations until it detects the end of the computation. In each iteration, the following stages are performed:

1. Node consumption stage: the thread checks whether its own input queue is not empty. In that case, it tries to acquire the lock associated with the queue. When it obtains the access immediately, it takes all the pointers to nodes that were deposited on the queue, releases the lock, and then for each node whose cost is lower than *best_solution_cost*, it performs the duplicate detection procedure adding the node to the open list as appropriate.
2. Processing stage: the thread expands at most LNPI (Limit of Nodes per Iteration) nodes from its open list. For each extracted node, it verifies if its cost is at least *best_solution_cost*. If so, the thread empties the open list. Otherwise, it checks if the node represents the solution and, in that case, it empties the open list and updates *best_solution* and *best_solution_cost*. When the extracted node is not the solution, it is added to the closed list, it is expanded, and then, for each successor, the Zobrist function is calculated to determine which thread has to process it. When the successor node belongs to this thread, it carries out the duplicate detection and adds the node to its open list as appropriate. Otherwise, the thread stores the node in the local output queue for the destination thread; when the amount of stored nodes is at least the limit LNPT (Limit of Nodes per Transfer), it tries to acquire the

lock associated with the destination thread's input queue and, if it obtains the lock immediately, it transfers the stored nodes[1].
3. Idle stage: the thread goes into this stage when its open list is empty. Firstly, it transfers the nodes stored on each non-empty output queue. Then, it remains waiting until having received work or having detected the end of computation.

4.2 Optimized AHDA*

The algorithm described in Sect. 4.1 was modified in order to allow the user to choose the method that will be used to assign states to threads, between the Zobrist function and the abstraction function mentioned in Sect. 3.1 for the 15-puzzle. In the last case, the user must specify the amount of tiles to be taken into account by the abstraction function.

Each region is identified with a unique ID, which is obtained by concatenating the bits representing the current positions of the tiles involved in the abstraction.

Figure 1 illustrates the method used for generating region IDs, when the abstraction function for the case study takes into account only three tiles. The board represents a region, which is composed of all the states that have the tiles 1, 2 and 3 at (3,3) (3,1) and (1,1) respectively. If the board is imagined as a one-dimensional array, those tiles will be at positions 15, 13 and 5 respectively. Consequently, after concatenating the binary values of these positions, the region ID is obtained, being $(111111010101)_2$ or $(4053)_{10}$.

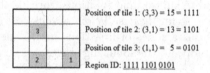

Position of tile 1: (3,3) = 15 = 1111
Position of tile 2: (3,1) = 13 = 1101
Position of tile 3: (1,1) = 5 = 0101
Region ID: 1111 1101 0101

Fig. 1. Method for generating region IDs

In this way, when a node is generated during the search process, the region ID is calculated, and the thread that must process this node is identified.

5   Experimental Results

Experimental tests were carried out on a machine with two Intel Xeon E5620 processors and 32 GB RAM. Each processor has four 2.4 GHZ physical cores.

The tests considered sixteen 15-Puzzle instances presented in [11] (numbered 3, 15, 17, 21, 26, 32, 33, 49, 53, 56, 59, 60, 66, 82, 88, 100) and six of the 10 configurations proposed by [12] (numbered 101–106 in this paper). These configurations present different levels of complexity.

---

[1] In this way, there are no transfers after each node generation as in the original algorithm.

The A* algorithm and the parallel A* algorithms were configured to use a heuristic that is a variation of the *Sum of Manhattan Distances (SMD)* of the tiles [5]. Also, we confirmed in [6] the benefit of using the LNPT parameter and we showed that setting LNPT to 210^2 improves performance for each configuration and number of cores (instead of limiting LNPT to 1 as in the original HDA* algorithm), given that contention caused by communication events is reduced.

In this section, we assess the effect of the following techniques on the performance of HDA* for shared memory architectures: (a) the abstraction-based node distribution scheme presented in Sect. 3.1. (b) the technique to group several nodes before each transfer (LNPT parameter).

With that goal in mind, four versions of HDA* for shared memory machines were generated, which vary in the function used to distribute the load and in the value of the LNPT parameter: (1) Zobrist function and LNPT = 1 (Original HDA*); (2) Abstraction function and LNPT = 1 (Original AHDA*); (3) Zobrist function and LNPT = 210 (Optimized HDA*); (4) Abstraction function and LNPT = 210 (Optimized AHDA*). The amount of tiles considered by the abstraction function for versions (2) and (4) is seven. This value was selected because it represents a good trade-off between load balance and communication.

Figures 2a and b illustrate the speedup obtained by each version of the algorithm, for each initial configuration (sorted by complexity), using 4 and 8 threads/cores, respectively, and the average speedup achieved by each version. The results reveal that, on average, Optimized HDA* improves speedup by 10.2% when using 4 threads/cores, and by 8.63% when using 8 threads/cores, with respect to Original HDA*. Similarly, Original AHDA* improves average speedup by 7.02% when using 4 threads/cores, and by 9.13% when using 8 threads/cores, in relation to Original HDA*. Also, Optimized AHDA* shows an improvement in average speedup of 17.25% and 17.82%, when using 4 and 8 threads/cores respectively, compared to Original HDA*.

Figures 3a and b show the efficiency obtained by each version of the algorithm and for different initial configurations (i.e., as the problem size increases), using 4 and 8 threads/cores, respectively. For each version it is observed that when the problem is scaled, maintaining the number of cores, efficiency generally improves

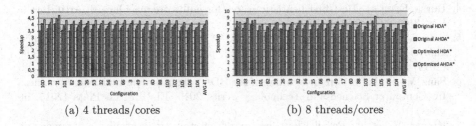

(a) 4 threads/cores   (b) 8 threads/cores

Fig. 2. Speedup obtained by each version of the algorithm

---

[2] This value corresponds to 8KB of data transferred (210 nodes).

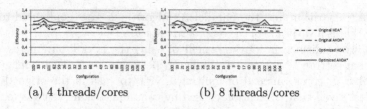

(a) 4 threads/cores   (b) 8 threads/cores

Fig. 3. Efficiency obtained by each version of the algorithm

or remains constant, hence they scale well. To conclude, Optimized AHDA* achieves higher speedup and efficiency.

6   Conclusions and Future Work

In this paper we presented Optimized AHDA*, a version of HDA* for shared memory architectures that uses an abstraction-based node distribution scheme and a technique to group several nodes before transferring them to the corresponding thread. The results revealed that the improvement in average speedup obtained by Optimized AHDA* is about 17% (with respect to the original HDA* algorithm). Also, we showed that Optimized AHDA* scales well.

As for future work, we plan to apply the abstraction-based node distribution scheme to HDA* for distributed memory architectures in order to reduce communication between machines when the algorithm is run on a cluster.

References

1. Hart, P., et al.: A formal basis for the heuristic determination of minimum cost paths. IEEE Trans. Syst. Sci. Cybern. **4**(2), 100–107 (1968)
2. Russel, S., Norvig, P.: Artificial Intelligence: A Modern Approach, 2nd edn. Prentice Hall, New Jersey (2003)
3. Kishimoto, A., et al.: Evaluation of a simple, scalable, parallel best-first search strategy. Artifi. Intell. **195**, 222–248 (2013)
4. Burns, E., et al.: Best-first heuristic search for multicore machines. J. Artif. Intell. Res. **39**(1), 689–743 (2010)
5. Sanz, V., et al.: On the optimization of HDA* for multicore machines. performance analysis. In: Proceedings of PDPTA 2014, pp. 625–631. CSREA Press, Georgia (2014)
6. Sanz, V., et al.: Performance tuning of the HDA* algorithm for multicore machines. In: Computer Science and Technology Series 2015, EDULP, La Plata (2015, in press)
7. Kumar, V., et al.: Parallel best-first search of state-space graphs: a summary of results. In: Proceedings of AAAI 1988, pp. 122–127. AAAI Press, California (1988)
8. Zobrist, A.: A new hashing method with application for game playing. Technical report 88, Computer Sciences Department, University of Wisconsin, Madison (1968)

9. Gue, K., et al.: GridStore: a puzzle-based storage system with decentralized control. IEEE Trans. Autom. Sci. Eng. **11**(2), 429–438 (2014)

10. Zhou, R., et al.: System and method for parallel graph searching utilizing parallel edge partitioning. Patent No. US 2011/0313984 A1, USA (2011)

11. Korf, R.: Depth-first Iterative-Deepening: an optimal admissible tree search. Artif. Intell. **27**(1), 97–109 (1985)

12. Brüngger, A.: Solving hard combinatorial optimization problems in parallel: two cases studies. Ph.D. thesis, ETH Zurich, Diss. ETH No. 12358 (1998)

On a Parallel Algorithm for the Determination of Multiple Optimal Solutions for the LCSS Problem

Bchira Ben Mabrouk[1(✉)], Hamadi Hasni[2], and Zaher Mahjoub[1]

[1] Faculty of Sciences of Tunis, University of Tunis El Manar,
University Campus, Manar II, 2092 Tunis, Tunisia
benmabrouk_bchira@yahoo.fr, zaher.mahjoub@fst.rnu.tn
[2] Higher School of Technology and Computer Science,
Charguia II, 2035 Tunis, Tunisia
hamadi.hasni@ensi.rnu.tn

Abstract. For particular real world combinatorial optimization problems e.g. the longest common subsequence problem (LCSSP) from Bioinformatics, determining multiple optimal solutions (DMOS) is quite useful for experts. However, for large size problems, this may be too time consuming, thus the resort to parallel computing. We address here the parallelization of an algorithm for DMOS for the LCSSP. Considering the dynamic programming algorithm solving it, we derive a generic algorithm for DMOS (A-DMOS). Since the latter is a non perfect DO-loop nest, we adopt a three-step approach. The first consists in transforming the A-DMOS into a perfect nest. The second consists in choosing the granularity and the third carries out a dependency analysis in order to determine the type of each loop i.e. either parallel or serial. The practical performances of our approach are evaluated through experimentations achieved on input benchmarks and random DNA sequences and targeting a parallel multicore machine.

Keywords: Bioinformatics · Combinatorial optimization problem · Dependency analysis · Dynamic programming · Longest common subsequence · Loop nest · Multiple optimal solutions · Multicore machine · Parallelization · Polyhedral algorithm

1 Introduction

A dedicated algorithm for solving an optimization problem (OP), more precisely a combinatorial optimization problem, usually aims at finding a single optimal solution (OS). However, for particular real world OPs e.g. in Bioinformatics, multiple optimal solutions (i.e. solutions with the same objective function value but with different values for the decision variables) may exist and the determination of more than one may be very useful. Indeed, by defining additional criteria depending on the application field, multiple optimal solutions may be classified and discriminated, hence a solution may be preferred to another if it optimizes another objective function (different from that

© Springer International Publishing AG 2016
J. Carretero et al. (Eds.): ICA3PP 2016, LNCS 10048, pp. 440–448, 2016.
DOI: 10.1007/978-3-319-49583-5_33

defining the optimization problem) [1]. It has to be noticed that most traditional optimization techniques generally target only one single optimal solution.

Let us consider a specific combinatorial optimization problem from Bioinformatics, namely the longest common subsequence problem (LCSSP) we address here [2]. For this problem that may be solved by a well known dynamic programming algorithm (DPA) of polynomial complexity [3], an OS is not necessarily significant from the point of view of experts (in Biology, Medicine, Criminology …) [1]. Therefore, having more than one OS increases the possibility of finding a more satisfying one. Remark that for the LCSS, sequential algorithms for determining multiple optimal solutions (DMOS) are known in the literature. We may cite Aho and Ullman [4] who proposed a backtracking method of exponential complexity. Greenberg [5, 6] presented an algorithm also of exponential complexity giving a graph of all prefixes of LCSS for two given sequences of fixed lengths. They have shown that, given a prefix p for the first sequence and a second prefix q for the second, all LCSSs of p and q may be generated in a time proportional to the input size, once the graph was constructed. The problem may be solved as part of the generation of all distinct character chains representing an LCSS or of the generation of all the ways allowing inserting a LCSS in both input chains. Wang et al. [7] used a generic approach based on evolutionary programming for solving multimodal optimization problems, by applying the niching technique in order to determine all optimal solutions. It has to be underlined that, to our knowledge, there is no previous work dealing with the parallelization of algorithms for DMOS of combinatorial optimization problems.

In a previous work [8], we presented a generic sequential approach for DMOS of polynomial complexity. It is mainly based on specific partitions of the iteration space of the DPA which is structured in a DO-loop nest. The experiments we achieved on some large size instances led to notice that the approach may be too time consuming.

Following this work, our aim here is to efficiently parallelize the above approach in order to solve instances of large sizes in a reasonable time. For this purpose we designed a 3-step approach. Starting with the original DPA which is structured in a perfect 2 DO-loop nest, the first step consists in designing a 3 DO-loop nest by adding an outer loop and modifying the nest body in order to determine different OSs. The latter nest being non perfect, we transform it into a perfect one. In the second step, we choose the parallelizing granularity. The third carries out a dependency analysis within the nest in order to determine the type of each loop i.e. serial or parallel.

The remainder of the paper is organized as follows. In Sect. 2, we present the LCSSP and the corresponding DPA. Section 3 is devoted to a brief presentation of our sequential algorithm for DMOS for the LCSSP. In Sect. 4, we describe our parallelization strategy for the sequential algorithm. We then present in Sect. 5 an experimental study that aims at the validation of our contribution. Finally, we recapitulate our study by recalling our main results followed by further perspectives.

2   The LCSS Problem

Experts in Biology, Medicine or Criminology often have to make comparisons between the DNA of two or more living beings. A DNA sample consists of a sequence of molecules that may be either adenine (a), cytosine (c), guanine (g) or thymine (t). If each basic molecule is represented by the initial letter of its name, a DNA sample writes as a character chain whose elements belong to the finite set {a, c, g, t}. Comparing two DNA samples, say X and Y, consists in finding a third sample Z, a subsequence of X and Y, such that the longer Z the more similar X and Y. The determination of such similarity is known as the longest common subsequence problem (LCSSP) [3]. More formally, consider two sequences $X = <x_1, x_2,...,x_m>$ of length m and $Z = <z_1, z_2,..., z_k>$ of length k. Z is a subsequence of X if there exists a strictly increasing sequence of indices $< i_1, i_2,...,i_k >$ in {1...m} such that, for any j = 1,2,...,k, we have $x_{i_j} = z_j$.

Now, given two sequences X and Y, a sequence Z is a common subsequence of X and Y if Z is a subsequence of both X and Y. The LCSSP is an easy COP that may be exactly solved by a dynamic programming algorithm (DPA). Hence, given two sequences X of length m and Y of length n, the DPA may be written as follows [3]:

Sequential DPA

```
DO i = 1, m
   DO j = 1, n
      IF(X[i]=Y[j]) THEN
         C[i,j]=C[i-1,j-1]+1 ; B[i,j]='+'
      ELSE IF (C[i-1,j] ≥ C[i,j-1] ) THEN      nest body
         C[i,j]=C[i-1,j] ; B[i,j]='*'
         ELSE C[i,j]=C[i,j-1] ; B[i,j]='-'
         ENDIF
      ENDIF
   ENDDO
ENDDO
```

Clearly, the DPA has an O(mn) complexity.

3   Multiple Optimal Solutions Determination Approach

3.1   Basic General Idea

Let $E = \{(i, j) \in \mathbf{Z}^2, 1 \leq i \leq m, 1 \leq j \leq n\}$ be the iteration space (IS) of the DPA. Since the corresponding nest body involves the computing of an optimum i.e. uses a logical comparison operator (LCO), this latter may be either large i.e. " $\geq$ " (as done above) or strict i.e. ">". The nest body being executed for each iteration of E i.e. $| E | = mn$ times, our basic idea consists in partitioning E into two subspaces E_1 and E_2 such that the strict (resp. large) LCO is used in E_1 (resp. E_2). Clearly, $2^{| E |} = 2^{mn}$ partitions may be defined i.e. an exponential number in $| E |$. To clarify the fact that two different partitions may induce two different OSs, consider the trivial problem of determining both the value and the position of a minimal element in a given list of, say n, numbers. Assume that the searched element occurs more than once in the list. Obviously, by using ">" (resp. "$\geq$") we obtain the first (resp. last) occurring position. Therefore, randomly using ">" n_1 times and "$\geq$" $n_2 = n - n_1$ times would lead to another occurring position of the searched element.

As to our problem, generating all the $2^{|E|}$ partitions is out of question. Hence, we must limit to a small number of partitions i.e. a polynomial number in $|E|$. Practically, the partition procedure we propose consists in defining a logical condition function in terms of the loop indices of the DPA, and using an IF-THEN-ELSE statement surrounding either totally or partially the nest body. E_1 (resp. E_2) will correspond to the THEN (resp. ELSE) case [7]. The determination of E_1 and E_2 (see below) is based on a specific use of prime numbers.

3.2 Algorithm for Determining Multiple OSs for the LCSS Problem

Our algorithm for determining multiple OSs (A-DMOS) mainly consists in (i) surrounding the DPA 2 DO-loop by an outer loop (k loop) and (ii) modifying the nest body in order to choose either ">" (E_1) or "$\geq$" (E_2).

The designed sequential A-DMOS writes as follows.

Sequential A-DMOS

```
Input : an array Prime involving all prime numbers ≤min(m,n)
DO k=1, n_pr    / n_pr is the number of prime numbers ≤ min(m,n) /
   DO i = 1, m
      DO j = 1, n
         IF (X[i]=Y[j]) THEN C[i,j]= C[i-1,j-1] + 1; B[i,j]='+'
         ELSE IF((i mod Prime[k]=0)AND(j mod Prime[k]=0)) THEN
                  IF (C[i-1,j ]> C[i,j -1]) THEN C[i,j]=C[i-1,j]; B[i,j]='*'/>:E₁/
                  ELSE C[i,j]=C[i,j-1])
                  ENDIF
              ELSE IF (C[i-1,j]≥ C[i,j-1])THEN C[i,j]=C[i-1,j]; B[i,j]='*'/≥:E₂/
                  ELSE C[i,j]=C[i,j-1])
                  ENDIF
              ENDIF
         ENDIF
      ENDDO
   ENDDO
   Save OS_k
ENDDO
```

The complexity of sequential A-DMOS, it is obviously $O(n_{pr} * m * n)$ i.e. polynomial in $E| = m * n$ since $n_{pr} < \min(m, n)$.

4 Parallelization of the A-DMOS for the LCSS Problem

Since A-DMOS has an $O(n_{pr} * m * n)$ complexity i.e. $O(m^2 * n)$ (resp. $O(m * n^2)$) when m < n (resp. n < m), for sequences of large sizes, it is clear that this complexity may, in practice, lead to prohibitive execution times. Hence the interest of the parallelization of A-DMOS. A-DMOS being a 3D polyhedral algorithm (PA) i.e. a DO-loop nest of depth 3, we'll apply the so called polyhedral program automatic parallelization

(PPAP) approach [9]. Notice that A-DMOS is a non perfect nest because of the existence of two bodies: one at depth 3, denoted $H_1(k, i, j)$, and one at depth 1, denoted $H_2(k)$ as detailed below.

```
DO k = 1, n_pr
    DO i = 1, m
        DO j = 1, n
            H₁(k,i,j)     /body1, depth 3/
        ENDDO
    ENDDO
    H₂(k)                 /body2, depth 1/
ENDDO
```

Step1: Transformation of the nest. Several techniques transforming a non perfect nest into a perfect one are known in the literature [10], but we'll use here a specific one better adapted to the structure of our DPA. It consists in adding a third dimension to arrays C and B (see A-DMOS above). This dimension is relative to the first loop counter k i.e. to each determined OS (IS partition). Hence $C(*, *, k)$ and $B(*, *, k)$ will be relative to SO_k. By this way A-DMOS will be a perfect nest. This new version will be denoted PN-A-DMOS.

Step2: Choice of the granularity. In the second step we choose the granularity that may be either coarse (a grain corresponds to the body of loop k), medium (a grain corresponds to the body of loop i) or fine (a grain corresponds to the body of the loop j).

If we choose the coarse granularity (CG), PN-A-DMOS will be reduced to a single loop. An easy semantic analysis permits to see that this loop is obviously parallel i.e. all its n_{pr} iterations may be processed simultaneously since there is no semantic dependency between computing OS_k and computing $OS_{k'}$ for any $k \neq k'$ in $\{1...n_{pr}\}$. Therefore we have a degree of parallelism equal to n_{pr} within the nest. Since the finer the granularity the higher the parallelism degree [11], the fine granularity (FG) would be preferable. We have to mention that we studied in a previous work [2] the parallelization of the original DPA. The dependency analysis according to the polyhedral program automatic parallelization (PPAP) approach [9] led to discover that both loops i and j are serial. A unimodular transformation of the nest led to a new nest where the first loop (denoted i') is serial and the second loop (denoted j') is parallel. If we proceed similarly here we'll easily get a nest, denoted KI'J' where loop k is parallel, loop i' is serial and loop j' is parallel.

It turns out that here we'll choose CG for obvious reasons of practical efficiency. Indeed, since m and n thus n_{pr} may be large, it is more interesting to assign all available processors (of the target parallel machine) to process iterations of the (first) parallel loop k than to distribute them between the two parallel loops k and j. Indeed, the second assignment, contrary to the first, will necessarily induce inter-processors synchronization overhead thus leading to parallel performances worsening [12].

Step3: Dependency analysis. By choosing the CG, this step is trivial as previously mentioned. Therefore parallel A-DMOS (PA-DMOS) may be written as follows:

```
DOPAR k = 1, n_pr          / parallel loop /
  DOSER i = 1, m     / serial loop /
    DOSER j = 1, n   / serial loop /     nest body H(k)
         H₁(k,i,j)
    ENDDOSER
  ENDDOSER
ENDDOSER
```

Remark that if n_{pr} processors are available, each processor will be associated to a specific partition of the iteration space of the nest and compute its own OS. Thus PA-DMOS have a parallel $O(m * n)$ complexity.

If $p < n_{pr}$ processors are available (which is the case in practice because n_{pr} may be large for large m and n), let $n_{pr} = pq + r$ the Euclidean division of n_{pr} by p. We then assign to each of the r first processors the treatment of q + 1 partitions and to each of the p-r remaining processors the treatment of q partitions. We will then have a parallel complexity equal to $O(n_{pr} * m * n/p)$.

5 Experimental Study

In order to validate our contribution and evaluate its practical interest, we achieved a series of experimentations on two input sets of various sizes i.e. Benchmark DNA sequences[1] and Random sequences each of which involves 8 couples. Our algorithms were coded in C under Linux. For the parallel experiments, we used the shared memory OpenMP environment. The parallel implementation is based on shared memory architecture using an API package OpenMP [13]. We specify that we chose 8 values for p (cores) i.e. 2, 4, 6, 8, 10, 16 and 24 in order to fit the target multicore machine (see Table 1) we used for our experiments.

Table 1. Characteristics of the target machine

Model	Dell PowerEdge R810
Number of processors	4
Processor	
Model	Intel Xeon (R) CPU E7-4850
Number of cores	24
Cache L1	32 KB
Cache L2	10×256 KB
Cache L3	24 MB

---

[1] www.ncbi.nlm.nih.gov/genbank/.

Speed-up S_p. We give in Table 2 the values of the absolute speed-up $S_p = T_{seq}/T_p$ [14].

Table 2. Speed-up S_p

Sequences				p							
X	m	Y	N	2	4	6	8	10	12	16	24
Benchmarks											
Ben1_1	203	Ben1_2	191	1.21	1.27	1.24	1.22	1.04	1.03	0.99	0.96
Ben2_1	884	Ben2_2	566	1.32	2.06	2.43	2.75	3.19	3.55	4.60	6.23
Ben3_1	1483	Ben3_2	1443	1.39	2.37	3.07	4.04	4.86	5.75	7.30	9.50
Ben4_1	5986	Ben4_2	3673	1.41	2.67	3.86	4.89	5.99	6.94	8.47	10.88
Ben5_1	10478	Ben5_2	10599	1.72	3.24	4.67	5.98	7.24	8.62	11.17	15.22
Ben6_1	17588	Ben6_2	17092	1.92	3.64	5.36	7.04	8.73	10.33	13.33	17.37
Ben7_1	45603	Ben7_2	36677	1.97	3.70	5.50	7.15	8.57	10.04	12.95	18.68
Ben8_1	67308	Ben8_2	61957	1.99	3.99	5.99	7.99	9.92	11.32	14.53	20.41
Random sequences											
Ran1_1	100	Ran1_2	100	1.24	1.36	1.25	1.14	0.96	0.89	0.83	0.76
Ran2_1	500	Ran2_2	500	1.36	2.27	3.09	3.66	4.15	4.75	4.95	3.76
Ran3_1	1200	Ran3_2	1350	1.44	2.68	3.89	5.01	5.96	6.66	8.51	11.36
Ran4_1	5000	Ran4_2	3250	1.61	3.15	4.58	6.08	7.40	8.34	10.39	14.51
Ran5_1	10550	Ran5_2	10850	1.77	3.46	5.09	6.64	8.36	9.74	12.51	17.86
Ran6_1	20000	Ran6_2	20000	1.93	3.79	5.46	7.22	9.01	10.75	14.12	20.78
Ran7_1	41000	Rand7_2	35600	1.95	3.87	5.72	7.63	9.47	10.97	14.44	21.23
Ran8_1	60000	Ran8_2	60000	1.98	3.94	5.90	7.90	9.83	11.52	14.75	21.36

We remark that for small size sequences, S_p increases slowly and even decreases when p increases. For large size sequences, S_p uniformly increases with p. For fixed p, S_p increases with the lengths of the couples i.e. the product $m * n$ (see Fig. 1).

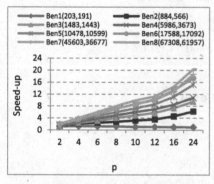

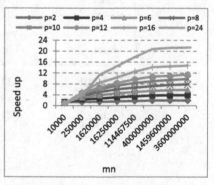

a) Benchmarks : S_p in terms of p   b) Random sequences : S_p in terms of m*n

Fig. 1. Speed-up S_p

6   Conclusion

In this paper, we were interested in an important aspect related to the resolution of a specific real world dynamic programming problem, namely the longest common subsequence problem (LCSSP) a combinatorial optimization problem (COP) arising in Bioinformatics for which the determination of multiple optimal solutions (DMOS) is of high interest for experts. Since large size sequences are generally processed in practice and for which a sequential DMOS algorithm may be too time consuming, we proposed a parallel algorithm to answer experts request in a reasonable time. Our experimental contribution consisted in implementing a parallel version on a target multicore machine on two sequence sets (benchmark and random). Practical experiments could show the interest of our contribution particularly for large size input data. Satisfactory results, in terms of speed-up were obtained.

References

1. Passaro, A., Starita, A.: Particle swarm optimization for multimodal functions: a clustering approach. J. Artif. Evol. Appl. **8**, 1–15 (2008)
2. Mabrouk, B.B., Hasni, H., Mahjoub, Z.: Parallelization of the dynamic programming algorithm for solving the longest common subsequence problem. In: 8th ACS/IEEE International Conference on Computer Systems and Applications (AICCSA 2010), Hammamet, Tunisia, pp. 1–8 (2010)
3. Cormen, T.H., Leiserson, C.E., Rivest, R.L., Stein, C.: Introduction à l'algorithmique. Dunod, Paris (2002)
4. Aho, A.V., Ullman, J.D.: Foundations of Computer Science. Principles of Computer Science Series. W.H. Freeman & Co., C edition, New York (1995)
5. Greenberg, R.I.: Bounds on the number of longest common subsequences. Technical report, Department of Mathematical and Computer Sciences, Loyola University, Chicago, USA (2003)
6. Greenberg, R.I.: Fast and simple computation of all longest common subsequences. Technical report, Department of Mathematical and Computer Sciences, Loyola University, Chicago, USA (2011)
7. Wang, Y., Li, H., Yen, G.G., Song, W.: MOMMOP: multiobjective optimization for locating multiple optimal solutions of multimodal optimization problems. J. IEEE Trans. Cybern. **45**(4), 830–843 (2015)
8. Mabrouk, B.B., Hasni, H., Mahjoub, Z.: On determining multiple optimal solutions for dynamic programming problems-application to the longest common subsequence problem. In: 31st International Conference on Computers and Their Applications (CATA 21016), Las Vegas, NV, USA (2016)
9. Megson, G.M., Chen, X.: Automatic Parallelization for a Class of Regular Computations. World Scientific Publishing Co., River Edge (1997)
10. Ssas, R., Mutka, M: Enabling unimodular transformations. In: ACM/IEEE Conference on Supercomputing, Washington, USA, pp. 753–762 (1996)
11. Grama, A., Karypis, G., Kumar, V., Gupta, A.: Introduction to Parallel Computing. Addison Wesley, Boston (2003)

12. Gengler, M., Ubéda, S., Desprez, F.: Initiation au Parallélisme. Masson, Paris (1996)
13. Quin, M.J.: Parallel programming in C with MPI and OpenMP, International edn. McGraw-Hill Higher Education, Pennsylvania (2003)
14. Cosnard, M., Trystram, D.: Algorithmes et Architectures Parallèles. InterEditions, Paris (1993)

Locality of Computation for Stencil Optimization

Lufeng Yuan, Junhong Liu, Yulong Luo, and Guangming Tan$^{(\boxtimes)}$

State Key Laboratory of Computer Architecture, Institute of Computing Technology,
Chinese Academy of Sciences, Beijing, China
{yuanlufeng,liujunhong,luoyulong,tgm}@ncic.ac.cn

Abstract. Stencil computation is a performance critical kernel that is widely used in scientific and engineering applications. In this paper we develop a redundant computation elimination (RCE) algorithm to exploit temporal locality. We implement the RCE optimization strategy using ROSE compiler infrastructure. The experiments with a benchmark of eleven stencil applications show that temporal locality of RCE averagely improves performance by 15.4% and 10.1% for benchmark without or with SIMD optimization.

Keywords: Optimization · Computation locality · Stencil

1 Introduction

Stencil is significant in scientific and engineering areas. The pattern of data accessing and computing of stencil is always repeated and predictable which has drawn attract from performance tuning and compiler optimization during the last several decades. These work can be classified into memory and computation optimization.

This work focuses on the optimization of Jacobi stencil. A 7-point 3D stencil computation is formulated as:

$$b_{i,j,k} = (a_{i\pm1,j,k} + a_{i,j\pm1,k} + a_{i,j,k\pm1}) * \alpha + a_{i,j,k} * \beta$$

The stencil computation is performed on two 3-dimension $N \times N \times N$ arrays. As shown in Fig. 1, the seven points are multiplied by parameters α and β respectively, before the result are added together. There are 8 floating-point operations for each point (6 adds and 2 multiplies) and 7 load operations for array references.

G.Tan —We would like to express our gratitude to all reviewers constructive comments for helping us polishing this paper. This work is supported by The National Key Research and Development Program of China (2016YFB0201305), National Science and Technology Major Project (2013ZX0102-8001-001-001) and National Natural Science Foundation of China, under grant No. (91430218, 31327901, 61472395, 61272134, 61432018).

© Springer International Publishing AG 2016
J. Carretero et al. (Eds.): ICA3PP 2016, LNCS 10048, pp. 449–456, 2016.
DOI: 10.1007/978-3-319-49583-5_34

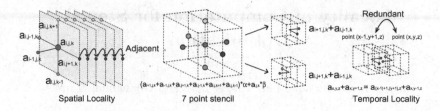

Fig. 1. Compute locality for 7-point stencil.

We propose a new method called *locality of computation* which is used to predict compute behavior of stencil, like locality of reference [5,6,10]. We develop a redundant computation elimination (RCE) to exploit locality of computation during sweeps of stencil computation with SIMD optimization.

The main contributions of this paper include:

- We propose an Redundant Computation Elimination (RCE) algorithm that detects temporal locality in the multi-direction of a loop and provides two redundancy replacements techniques for different situations. In addition, the RCE can cooperate with SIMD and we implement it using ROSE compiler infrastructure.
- We conduct experiments with eleven stencil applications. The result shows that temporal locality of RCE averagely improves performance by 15.4 % and 10.1 % for benchmark without or with SIMD optimization.

2   Redundant Computation Elimination

Based on the behavior of temporal locality, we propose a Redundant Computation Elimination (RCE) algorithm. In addition, we have constructed a source-to-source transformer using ROSE compiler infrastructure [15] to carry out RCE.

As the overview shown in Fig. 2, after compiling source code by ROSE frontend, RCE first rebuilds the abstract syntax tree and converts it to an inclusive representation that contains more legal sub-expressions. Secondly, RCE classifies these legal sub-expressions into multiple sets based their lengths. Thirdly, it performs a DP-based search (dynamic programming) and produces candidates of redundant computation sub-expression pairs. Finally, it performs unit-stride/multiple direction replacement to eliminate redundant computation.

2.1   Search Redundant Computations

For a stencil computation, if the number of child nodes of an **ExprNode** e_i is c_i, then the number of sub-expressions contained in e_i is 2^{c_i}. In a stencil loop that has n_e **ExprNode**, the total number of sub-expression e_{total} is $\sum_{i=1}^{n_e}(2^{c_i})$. To find redundant computation pair among these e_{total} sub-expressions, the search will perform $C_{e_{total}}^2$ comparisons using function $\mathcal{R}()$. The overhead of search is prohibitively expensive, and two strategies are proposed to avoid this problem.

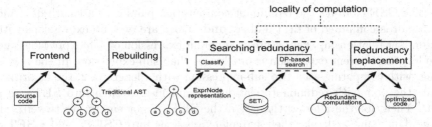

Fig. 2. Overview of RCE

Firstly, there is no need to do comparison between each two sub-expressions, but only between these sub-expressions with the same length, which are probably redundant to each other. Thereby, the sub-expressions are classified into different sets according to their lengths, and comparison function $\mathcal{R}$ is only performed intra-sets.

Secondly, dynamic programming is used to speed up the search algorithm further. Looking at the example,

$$e_1 : (a_{k,j,i} + b_{k,j+1,i})$$
$$e_2 : (a_{k,j+1,i} + b_{k,j+2,i})$$
$$e_3 : (a_{k,j,i} + b_{k,j+1,i}) * c$$
$$e_4 : (a_{k,j+1,i} + b_{k,j+2,i}) * c$$

we find that e_1 and e_2 are redundant computations with offset vector $(0,1,0)$, and their lengths are both 2. The sub-expression e_3 and e_4 are redundant computation with offset vector $(0,1,0)$, and their lengths are both 3. Since e_1 is a sub-expression of e_3 and e_2 is a sub-expression of e_4, the redundant relationship of e_3 and e_4 can be searched based on e_1 and e_2. Algorithm 1 gives the pseudocode of the search algorithm.

Algorithm 1. Search Algorithm

```
 1: Initialization    SET_i ⇐ SET_2
 2: while SET_i ≠ ∅ do
 3:     for all pair in SET_i do
 4:         e_1 ⇐ pair.first
 5:         e_2 ⇐ pair.second
 6:         CSET_1 ⇐ e_1.cset
 7:         CSET_2 ⇐ e_2.cset
 8:         for all c_1 in CSET_2 do
 9:             for all c_2 in CSET_2 do
10:                 if R(c_1 − e_1, c_2 − e_2) ≠ v then
11:                     SET_{i+1} ⇐ pair(c_1, c_2)
12:                 end if
13:             end for
14:         end for
15:     end for
16: end while
17: Output SET_i
```

The $\mathbf{CSET_i}$ stores the redundant computation pairs with a length of i, and each pair is composed of **first** and **second**, which are two sub-expressions with redundant relationship. cset stores the parent expression of sub-expression, and the length of parent expression is one longer than sub-expression. In the beginning, with comparing each two sub-expression with a length of 2, the algorithm finds the pair with redundant relationship and inserts them into $\mathbf{SET_2}$ as a pair. Then, for the i larger than 3, if the $\mathbf{SET_i}$ is not empty, we traverse all redundant pairs and take their parent expressions into $\mathbf{CSET_1}$ and $\mathbf{CSET_2}$. For each sub-expression $\mathbf{c_1}$ in $\mathbf{CSET_1}$ and c_2 in $\mathbf{CSET_2}$, if the return value of $\mathcal{R}(\mathbf{c_1} - \mathbf{e_1}, \mathbf{c_2} - \mathbf{e_2})$ is equal to $\mathbf{v}$, which are the offset vectors of $\mathbf{e_1}$ and $\mathbf{e_2}$, we insert $\mathbf{c_1}$ and $\mathbf{c_2}$ into $\mathbf{CSET_{(i+1)}}$ as the redundant computation pair. If the $\mathbf{CSET_i}$ is empty, the search finishes.

2.2 Eliminate Redundant Computation

After finishing redundant computations search, we get sub-expression pairs with redundant relationship. We refer to the sub-expression that produces computation result as *source*, and the sub-expression that reuses the computation result as *sink*. There is a source sub-expression and sink sub-expression in each pair: the source sub-expression is computed in source iteration, and sink sub-expression is computed in sink iteration.

To eliminate the redundant computation, the positions of source iteration and sink iteration need to be identified first. For a stencil with a problem size of $N = (n_1, n_2..n_d)$, where d denotes dimensionality and n_i denotes the size of the ith dimension, if there exists redundant sub-expression pairs with offset vector $v = (v_1, ..v_d)$, their indices satisfy,

$$source : \forall x_i \in (x_1, ..x_d) \begin{cases} v_i \leq x_i < n_i & v_i > 0 \\ 0 \leq x_i < (n_i + v_i) & v_i \leq 0 \end{cases}$$

$$sink : \forall y_i \in (y_1, ..y_d) \begin{cases} 0 \leq y_i < (n_i - v_i) & v_i > 0 \\ -v_i \leq y_i < n_i & v_i \leq 0 \end{cases}$$

The $x = (x_1, x_2, ..x_d)$ is an index vector of source sub-expression. On the ith dimension, if v_i is positive, the sink sub-expression is executed v_i steps before the source sub-expression and the index x_i varies from v_i to n_i. If v_i is negative or zero, the sink sub-expression is executed v_i steps after the source sub-expression, so the index x_i varies from 0 to $(n_i + v_i)$. The same to $y = (y_1, y_2, ..y_d)$, which is the index vector of sink sub-expression. To eliminate the redundant computation, RCE allocates additional temporary buffers to deliver the computation results from source sub-expression to sink sub-expression. Especially, the temporary buffers are cyclically used and the minimal size of the temporary buffers is determined by redundancy distance rd,

$$rd = \sum_{i=1}^{i \leq d} (v_i' * \prod_{j=0}^{j < i} nn_j), nn_i = (n_i - |v_i|), v_i' = \begin{cases} 0 & v_i < 0 \\ v_i & v_i \geq 0 \end{cases}$$

the v'_i is the number of source iterations before the first sink iterations on i^{th} dimension. If $v_i \geq 0$, v'_i is equal to v_i. If $v_i < 0$, the first sink iteration is at the beginning of ith dimension, and v'_i is equal to 0. The nn_i is the number of source iteration on the ith dimension and it is equal to $(n_i - |v_i|)$. Each v_i contribute lengths $(v'_i * \prod_{j=0}^{j<i} nn_j)$ to temporary buffer, and rd is the sum of these lengths. In the previous example:

$$nn_1 = nn_2 = (8 - 1) = 7$$
$$v'_1 = 1, v'_2 = 0$$
$$rd = 0 * 1 + 1 * (7 * 1) = 8$$

nn_1 and nn_2 are both equal to 7, and v'_1 is equal to 1, v'_0 is equal to 0. rd is equal to 8, which is the number of points between any white point and its sink black points.

On the source iteration, RCE writes the result of source sub-expression into temporary buffer. On the sink iteration, RCE replaces the sink sub-expression using the result in temporary buffer. When there exists multiple sub-expression pairs in program, the pair with longest length is prior to be eliminated. According to the length of redundancy distance rd, two temporary buffer solutions are employed respectively.

3   Experiment

3.1   Methodology

In this section, we perform optimization of compute locality on a stencil benchmark. The benchmark consists of 11 stencil kernels, which are listed in Table 1.

The experiment is conducted on a single node that equipped with Intel(R) Xeon(R) CPU E5-2670 and 32G memory. The frequency of CPU is 2.6 GHZ, and L2 cache size is 256 KB. The operating system is Red Hat Enterprise Linux Server 6.3 (Santiago), and benchmark is complied with ICC 14.01. We use TAU [11] to collect performance information including the number of float point operations and execution time through instrumentation of functions, methods, basic blocks, and statements as well as event-based sampling. We compare four implementations using problem size of 128^3:

- *Original:* The benchmarks are directly compiled by ICC with flag -O0 and executed without any optimization.
- *Original+RCE:* These are the codes optimized by our RCE algorithm and directly compiled by the backend compiler with -O0 flag. This implementation only adopts optimization based on temporal locality.
- *SIMD:* The benchmarks are attached with SIMD pragma and then compiled by icc with -O2 to enable SIMD optimization. This implementation only adopts optimization based on spatial locality.
- *SIMD+RCE:* Compared with previous SIMD implementation, the benchmarks are performed with RCE optimization additionally. This implementation adopts optimization based on spatial locality and temporal locality.

Table 1. R_{ratio} and static operation counts in benchmark of eleven stencils(Original/CSR/ESR+/RCE).

Stencil kernel	R_{ratio}	Load				Arithmetic			
		Original	CSR	ESR+	RCE	Original	CSR	ESR+	RCE
7-point [4]	12.5%	7	5	5	**5**	8	8	8	**7**
13-point [18]	6.7%	13	**9**	11	11	15	15	15	**14**
19-point [13]	4.5%	19	**13**	17	17	22	22	22	**21**
25-point [12]	3.4%	25	**17**	23	23	29	29	29	**28**
27-point [4]	10%	27	**9**	21	21	30	30	27	**27**
himeno [9]	3.1%	31	29	29	**21**	32	32	31	**31**
poisson [17]	10%	19	**14**	17	17	20	20	18	**18**
fdtd	20%	5	3	4	4	5	5	4	**4**
jacobi2d	20%	5	3	5	**3**	5	5	5	**4**
seidel2d [14]	22.2%	9	**3**	6	6	9	9	7	**7**
resid [16]	25%	4	4	4	**2**	4	4	4	**3**

3.2 Result

We first give the R_{ratio} (the ratio of redundant computation to total computation) and the theoretical number of load/computing operations of Original/CSR/ESR+/RCE, listed in Table 1. As the table shows, the CSR only reduces the load operation but ESR+ and RCE reduce arithmetic additionally. Especially, the ESR+ has the capability to eliminate the redundant computation with unit-stride direction offset vector, and RCE can eliminate the redundant computation with multi-direction offset vector, such as **7-point stencil**, **13-point stencil**, **jacobi2d** and **resid**. As a result, the number of computing operations of RCE is smaller than ESR+. Then, in Fig. 3a we compare the number of executing float point operations collected by TAU. In the first bar graph, y-axis denotes flops, and x-axis represents stencil kernels. For all benchmarks, the flops of RCE is smaller than the Original benchmark. The second bar graph shows the number of flops of SIMD and SIMD+RCE, and y-axis is normalized performance to SIMD. The result is similar to the previous bar graph.

The performance of Original benchmark and RCE in Gflops is listed in the first bar graph of Fig. 3b, and is normalized to Original benchmark. The improvement of RCE are 41%, 8.7%, 52.9%, 3.6%,16.7%, 5.4%, 6.7%, 8.8%,2.5%,16%, 7%, and 15.4% on average. The second bar graph shows the performance of SIMD and SIMD+RCE, and the performance is normalized to SIMD implementation which is shown in y-axis. Compared to SIMD, the RCE+SIMD has obvious improvements on most of cases except for **fdtd** and **resid**. The reason is that the offsets vector of **fdtd** and **resid** are $(0, -1, 1)$, $(0, 0, 1)$, and have two very long rd which decreases the performance of cache.

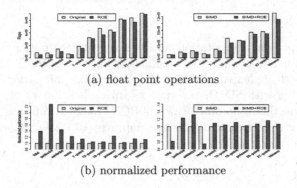

(a) float point operations

(b) normalized performance

Fig. 3. Comparison between Original benchmark, RCE, SIMD, SIMD+RCE

4   Related Work

Locality of reference [5] is a theory describing the behavior of data movement, and is one of the cornerstones of performance optimization. Ding predicts whole-program locality through reuse distance analysis [7]. Gupta employs a quantifiable way to analyze locality using conditional probability [8].

Table 2 summarizes technical features of our RCE and other existing redundancy elimination techniques. CSE [1] is based on available expression analysis (a data flow analysis) to eliminate redundant computing operations. It is useful on a single basic block, but has limitations with respect to loops. CSR [2] can detect reusing opportunities of subscripted variables by performing data dependence analysis over loops and replace these redundant load operations with scalar variables. However, it merely works for load operations, and isn't applicable to computing operations. ESR+ [3] employs value numbering and scalar replacement to perform redundant computation. It combines CSE and CSR together and makes elimination inter-iterations come true. Whereas, ESR+ restricts its elimination to unit-stride dimension, and its scalar replacement also prevents optimization for SIMD. Our RCE overcomes these problems.

Table 2. Comparison of four redundancy elimination techniques. In addition, **CO** is computing operation, **USD** is unit-stride direction replacement and **MD** is multi-directions replacement.

	Method	CO	Inter-interations	
			USD	**MD**
CSE	Value numbering	$\checkmark$	X	X
CSR	Data dependence analysis	X	$\checkmark$	X
ESR+	CSE+CSR	$\checkmark$	$\checkmark$	X
RCE	DP-based search + MDR	$\checkmark$	$\checkmark$	$\checkmark$

5 Conclusion

Stencil is an important computation kernel in scientific computing. In this paper, we design a redundant computation elimination algorithm (RCE) based on compute locality and implement it using ROSE compiler infrastructure. Furthermore, cooperating with SIMD, experiments with a benchmark of eleven stencil applications show that temporal locality of RCE averagely improves performance by 15.4% for original benchmark, while improves 10.1% for benchmark using SIMDization optimization.

References

1. Briggs, P., Cooper, K.D., Simpson, L.T.: Value numbering. Softw.-Practice Exp. **27**(6), 701–724 (1997)
2. Callahan, D., Carr, S., Kennedy, K.: Improving register allocation for subscripted variables. In: ACM Sigplan Notices, vol. 25, pp. 53–65. ACM (1990)
3. Cooper, K., Eckhardt, J., Kennedy, K.: Redundancy elimination revisited. In: Proceedings of the 17th International Conference on Parallel Architectures and Compilation Techniques, pp. 12–21. ACM (2008)
4. Datta, K., Yelick, K.A.: Auto-tuning stencil codes for cache-based multicore platforms. Ph.D. thesis, University of California, Berkeley (2009)
5. Denning, P.J.: The locality principle. Commun. ACM **48**(7), 19–24 (2005)
6. Denning, P.J., Schwartz, S.C.: Properties of the working-set model. Commun. ACM **15**(3), 191–198 (1972)
7. Ding, C., Zhong, Y.: Predicting whole-program locality through reuse distance analysis. In: ACM SIGPLAN Notices, vol. 38, pp. 245–257. ACM (2003)
8. Gupta, S., Xiang, P., Yang, Y., Zhou, H.: Locality principle revisited: a probability-based quantitative approach. J. Parallel Distrib. Comput. **73**(7), 1011–1027 (2013)
9. Himeno, R.: Himeno benchmark (2011)
10. Lam, M., Sethi, R., Ullman, J., Aho, A.: Compilers: Principles, Techniques, and Tools (2006)
11. Malony, A.D., Cuny, J., Tau, S.S.: Tuning and analysis utilities. Technical report, LALP-99-205, Los Alamos National Laboratory Publication (1999)
12. Peng, L., Seymour, R., Nomura, K.-I., Kalia, R.K., Nakano, A., Vashishta, P., Loddoch, A., Netzband, M., Volz, W.R., Wong, C.C.: High-order stencil computations on multicore clusters (2009)
13. Phillips, E.H., Fatica, M.: Implementing the Himeno benchmark with CUDA on GPU clusters. In: 2010 IEEE International Symposium on Parallel & Distributed Processing (IPDPS), pp. 1–10. IEEE (2010)
14. Pouchet, L.-N.: Polybench: The polyhedral benchmark suite, July 2012. http://www.cs.ucla.edu/~pouchet/software/polybench/
15. Quinlan, D., Liao, C., Too, J., Matzke, R., Schordan, M.: Rose compiler infrastructure (2013)
16. Sair, S., Charney, M.: Memory behavior of the spec2000 benchmark suite. IBM TJ Watson Research Center Technical Report (2000)
17. Unat, D., Cai, X., Baden, S.B.: Mint: realizing CUDA performance in 3D stencil methods with annotated C. In: Proceedings of the International Conference on Supercomputing, pp. 214–224. ACM (2011)
18. Zhang, Y., Mueller, F.: Autogeneration and autotuning of 3D stencil codes on homogeneous and heterogeneous GPU clusters. IEEE Trans. Parallel Distrib. Syst. **24**(3), 417–427 (2013)

GPU Computing to Speed-Up the Resolution of Microrheology Models

Gloria Ortega[1]($\boxtimes$), Antonio Puertas[2], Fco Javier de Las Nieves[2],
and Ester Martin-Garzón[1]

[1] Informatics Department, University of Almería,
Agrifood Campus of Int. Excell., ceiA3, 04120 Almería, Spain
{gloriaortega,gmartin}@ual.es
[2] Group of Complex Fluids Physics, Department of Applied Physics,
University of Almería, 04120 Almería, Spain
{apuertas,fjnieves}@ual.es

Abstract. Active microrheology is a technique to obtain rheological properties in soft matter from the microscopic motion of colloidal tracers used as probes and subjected to external forces. This technique extends the measurement of the friction coefficient to the nonlinear-response regime of strongly driven probes. Active microrheology can be described starting from microscopic equations of motion for the whole system including both the host-fluid particles and the tracer. While the main observable is the effective friction coefficient with the bath, tracer position correlation functions describe the tracer motion, and reveal the underlying dynamics of the host bath. On the other hand, pulling the tracer provokes a non-linear non-affine strain field in the host bath, what requires a deep understanding of the dynamics of the system. Different theoretical approaches have been proposed to deal with this problem.

In this work, we present simulations of a tracer dragged by a constant force through a dense bath of hard colloids. The size of the system has been varied, keeping the bath density constant, approaching the hydrodynamic limit. In order to calculate the tracer's position, iterative methods have to be used. These methods are computationally highly demanding, specially when the number of colloidal particles is high. Therefore, it is necessary to use HPC in order to develop and validate this kind of models. The present work shows the results of the considered microrheology method varying the number of colloidal tracers and using GPU computing in order to solve problems of interest.

Keywords: Microrheology model · Friction coefficient · GPU computing · High performance computing

This work has been partially supported by the Spanish Ministry of Science throughout projects TIN15-66680 and FIS-2015-69022-P and CAPAP-H5 network TIN2014-53522, by J. Andalucía through projects P12-TIC-301 and P11-TIC7176, and by the European Regional Development Fund (ERDF).

© Springer International Publishing AG 2016
J. Carretero et al. (Eds.): ICA3PP 2016, LNCS 10048, pp. 457–466, 2016.
DOI: 10.1007/978-3-319-49583-5_35

1   Introduction

Complex fluids are typically suspensions of macromolecules or microparticles in a solvent, where different length and time scales are relevant. These arise from different relaxation modes of the macromolecules, or the different constituents of the system. These different length scales result in a complex mechanical behaviour when the system is strained macroscopically, namely, its rheological behaviour. The stress-strain relation is non-linear; for instance, the viscosity decreases upon increasing the strain rate in shear thinning fluids (such as paints, quicksand or polymer melts), but increases in shear thickening fluids (such as corn starch) [1].

In microrheology, a microscopic stress is applied to the system, typically acting onto a single particle, or tracer, by an external force. Experimentally, this is achieved using magnetic tracers in a non-magnetic sample, and applying an external magnetic field, or in a quasi-transparent system, using opaque tracers that can be trapped by optical tweezers and pulled through the system [10]. This was initially proposed as an alternative technique to conventional (macroscopic) rheology for small, rare or expensive samples. However, it was soon realized that the theoretical analysis of the dynamics of the forced tracer is rather complicated [9], mainly because the strain field around the tracer is non-affine. In the simulations of microrheology, the trajectory of the single tracer is monitored and analysed. The number of trajectories recorded is therefore a major statistical problem, hampered by the slow integration of the equations of motion of the N-body problem.

In this work, we focus on the case of a large tracer in a bath of Brownian quasi-hard spheres. The large size of the tracer implies large finite size effects, which have to be corrected using a theoretical model based on the continuous model of the Navier-Stokes equation. Therefore, a large number of trajectories for different system sizes have to be analysed. This large number of trajectories makes the model computationally expensive and slow. As far as the authors know, there are no parallel software published for the acceleration of the production of every trajectory. Then, we propose to use Graphic Processing Unit (GPU) programming to speed up every trajectory of the model.

Originally GPUs were designed for handling computer graphics, but with the advent of GPU architecture which enables bidirectional communication of information between CPU and GPU, GPUs are now being extensively used for scientific computing, such as the development and validation of models and the acceleration of algebraic procedures [6,7]. Currently, the GPUs are very suitable for highly intensive scientific computations, with relevant reductions of computation times [4]. Moreover, the GPU computing model, based on the computation of thousands of threads which compute same operations, is very appropriated to accelerate the microrheology models where the same computation have to be carried out for thousands of particles.

In Sect. 2 we give an overview of the problem to solve. In Sect. 3 we give a computational analysis and we describe the GPU implementation of the model. In Sect. 4 we analyse the obtained results from the simulations of a tracer dragged by a constant force through a dense bath of hard colloids. Therefore, an execution time analysis for problems with different sizes of the tracer illustrating is carried out. Finally, in Sect. 5 the main conclusions and future research lines are discussed.

2   Description of the Problem

The problem we aim to study is colloidal microrheology, namely, the study of the dynamics of a single Brownian tracer immersed in a bath of Brownian particles, under the application of a constant external force [9]. Because only the trajectory of the tracer particle is studied, although the whole system must be simulated, the statistics of the number of the trajectories poses a major problem. The use of GPU programming is proposed here to shorten the simulation time per trajectory.

In colloidal systems, particles follow Brownian dynamics instead of Newtonian dynamics, typical of molecular or atomic systems. Brownian dynamics is described by the Langevin equation of motion, which for particle j reads,

$$m\frac{d^2 \boldsymbol{r}_j}{dt^2} = \sum_i \boldsymbol{F}_{ij} - \gamma_0 \frac{d\boldsymbol{r}_j}{dt} + \boldsymbol{\eta}_j(t) \ (+\boldsymbol{F}_{\text{ext}}) \tag{1}$$

where the forces considered for the calculation of the particle acceleration are direct interactions, $\boldsymbol{F}_{ij}$, a friction force proportional to the velocity, $\gamma_0 \frac{d\boldsymbol{r}_j}{dt}$ (with γ_0 is the solvent friction coefficient), and the random force, $\boldsymbol{\eta}_j$ [2]. The external force $\boldsymbol{F}_{\text{ext}}$ is applied only to the tracer. The random forces have zero average, $\langle \boldsymbol{\eta}_j(t) \rangle = 0$, and are delta-correlated in time, and linked with the friction forces by the fluctuation-dissipation theorem [2]:

$$\langle \boldsymbol{\eta}_j(t) \cdot \boldsymbol{\eta}_k(t') \rangle = 6\gamma_0 k_{\text{B}} T \, \delta_{jk} \, \delta(t - t') \tag{2}$$

where δ_{ij} is the Kronecker-delta ($\delta_{ij} = 1$ for $i = j$, and zero otherwise) and $\delta(x)$ is the Dirac-delta function, and $k_{\text{B}}T$ is the thermal energy [2].

The simulations are run in a cubic box, with N particles and periodic boundary conditions. All bath particles have the same mass, $m = 1$, and radius, $a = 1$, and the thermal energy is $k_{\text{B}}T = 1$. The tracer has mass $m_t = 1$ and radius a_t, and we focus here in the range of parameters where $a_t > a$. The density of the bath is typically given in colloids by the fraction of the volume occupied by the particles, $\phi = 4/3\pi a^3 n$, where n is the number density; in our system the volume fraction is fixed to $\phi = 0.50$. The solvent friction coefficient of particle i is set to $\gamma_0 = 5a_i\sqrt{mk_{\text{B}}T}/d$. Time is measured in units of the bath Newtonian microscopic time $a\sqrt{m/k_{\text{B}}T}$. The equations of motion are integrated with a time step of $0.0005a\sqrt{m/k_{\text{B}}T}$ using an extension of the velocity Verlet algorithm to include random forces [8], integrating the friction forces analytically.

In the most simple case, particle-particle interactions are hard-sphere like: $V(r) = \infty$ if particles overlap, and $V(r) = 0$ otherwise. For computation purposes, a continuous potential is used (typically an inverse power potential, with a large exponent); in this work, we use $V(r_{ij}) = k_B T(r/d_{ij})^{-36}$, where d_{ij} is the center to center distance $(d_{ij} = (a_i + a_j)$, where a_i is the radius of particle i). Due to the short range of this interaction potential, its cut-off radius is set to $a_i + a_j + a$, what allows the use of typical procedures to speed up the calculation, such as cell or Verlet lists. Despite this, the calculation of the forces is the most time-consuming part of the code.

For microrheology, the system with the (large) tracer particle is equilibrated, and at time $t = 0$ the tracer is pulled with a constant force through the system. The main output of the simulation is the trajectory of the tracer, in addition to other control parameters. The effective friction coefficient measured by the tracer is obtained from the average velocity (calculated as the slope of the displacement vs. time), using the relation $\boldsymbol{F}_{\text{ext}} = \gamma_{\text{eff}} \langle \boldsymbol{v} \rangle$, valid for the stationary regime. The tracer is allowed to travel through the simulation box more than once (obeying the periodic boundary conditions), as we could not identify any different behaviour between the first and consecutive passages.

Due to the finite size of the system, the boundaries affect the measurement of the average tracer velocity. In our case, the periodic boundary conditions in fact simulate the dynamics of a cubic array of tracer particles immersed in a Brownian bath. Theoretical analysis within the (continuous model) Navier-Stokes equation predicts a linear dependence of the inverse friction coefficient with the inverse system size, L, for vanishing forces [3]:

$$\frac{1}{\gamma_{\text{eff}}} - \frac{1}{\gamma_\infty} \propto \frac{1}{L} \tag{3}$$

where γ_∞ is the effective friction coefficient for an infinitely large system. The proportionality constant depends of the details of the bath and the type of array of tracers. Obviously, γ_∞ is the quantity of physical interest, to be compared to theoretical models or experiments.

The procedure to obtain γ_∞ from simulations is thus to run simulations with different system sizes (because the density of the bath must be constant, this must be done changing the number of particles), and extrapolate $1/\gamma_{\text{eff}}$ linearly for $1/L \to 0$. This extrapolation is tricky as small errors in the determination of γ_{eff} for finite L imply large errors in γ_∞ given the long distance between the data and the $1/L = 0$ axis. It is therefore desirable to run simulations with L as large as possible, in a reasonable time, to reduce this error.

As a consequence, the model to compute γ_∞ has large computational requirements and HPC techniques need to be applied to decrease the large time to complete the statistical simulation of the model. In this work, GPU platforms are selected to accelerate the computation of every tracer trajectory since it includes the same operations on the thousands of particles. It perfectly fits on the GPU computational model.

3 Computational Analysis and Parallel Implementation

The goal of the model described in Sect. 2 is the computation of the macroscopic propriety of the colloidal system, γ_{eff}. Therefore, to obtain γ_{eff} the following nested iterative procedures in bottom-up order have to be computed:

- A random tracer trajectory in the $\boldsymbol{F}_{\text{ext}}$ direction, referred to as T_i for a specific number of both particles and its corresponding system size, $L(N)$.
- The recording of $ntraj$ trajectories (T_i) and calculation of their average, T, for a specific value of $L(N)$.
- The computation of T for several values of $L(N)$ to extrapolate γ_{eff} according to Eq. 3.

Therefore, there are three parallelism levels in the model. In this work, our focus is to accelerate the computation of every tracer trajectory, at the bottom level. Then, a time stepping procedure is applied to compute the position of the tracer particle after a differential time interval.

Algorithm 1 shows the pseudocode of the model of bath of Brownian quasi-hard spheres to compute the set of tracer trajectories for a system of N particles. At every time step, two main tasks are completed: (1) identification of the neighbors of N particles (*Neighbors* procedure called in lines 5 and 9 of Algorithm 1); and (2) evaluation of the locations and velocities of the N particles according to the particle-particle interactions among the neighbour particles defined by Eq. 1 (*difus* procedure called in line 7 of Algorithm 1). The complexities of both tasks are $O(N^2)$ and $O(N)$, respectively. So, the first task consumes most of the time. However, it is only computed when a relevant movement of particles is detected in the previous time step.

As above mentioned, to achieve accurate values of γ_{eff}, it is mandatory the study of simulations for large L values, that is, large particle numbers in the system (N). For large values of N, it is worth to accelerate both tasks on GPU platforms.

A key to reduce the computational cost of the model is the definition of a neighbourhood for every particle, which establishes its interaction volume with other particles. Because our system has particles with very different sizes (tracer and bath particles), two particles are considered neighbours when their surface-to-surface distance is smaller than a cut-off distance, set equal to the radius of the bath particles. So, only interactions among neighbour particles are computed and it is necessary the use of an auxiliary structure to store the neighbors of every particle, which is referred to as $Nlist[][]$. Every row, $Nlist[i][]$ with $0 \leq i < N$, stores the information about its neighbourhood, that is, the number of neighbours of the corresponding particle and their indexes. $Nlist$ is stored on the GPU memory by column-major order to improve the coalescence in the device memory accesses. Because $Nlist$ is computed on the GPU, it is not transferred between CPU-GPU.

In Algorithm 1, the process referred to as *Neighbors* is computed on the GPU. Therefore, N threads concurrently compute the list of neighbours for the N particles. Then, every thread i is in charge of: (a) initializing the $NList[i][]$

Algorithm 1. Pseudocode of the model of bath of Brownian quasi-hard spheres.

Require:
    $ntraj$: the number of trajectories,
    $ttraj$: the total time steps of every trajectory,
    N: the number of particles,
    γ_0: friction coefficient,
    $\boldsymbol{F}_{ext}$: external force,
    a_t: the radius of the tracer
    a: the radius of the remaining (bath) particles,
    ϕ: volume fraction,
    mn: the maximum number of neighbors of a particle,
    $Pos[N]$: auxiliary structure to store the position of every particle,
    $Vel[N]$: auxiliary structure to store the velocity of every particle,
    $Init\_Part[N]$: Initial spatial locations of the N particles,
    $NList[N][mn]$: auxiliary structure composed by a list which will store the neighbors of every particle.

Ensure:
    $T[i][t]$: spatial location vector for the tracer at time t in the trajectory i

1:   $threshold = a/2$
2: **for** $i \leftarrow 1$ **to** $ntraj$ **do**
3:      $T[i][0] \leftarrow (0,0,0)$ ▷ Init tracer trajectory at origin of coordinates
4:      $Pos[], Vel[] = Init\_Part[N]$ ▷ Init the location and velocity of N particles
5:      $NList[][] \leftarrow Neighbors(N, Pos[], Vel[], a, mn, NList[][])$ ▷ Computed on GPU
6:      **for** $t \leftarrow 0$ **to** $ttraj$ **do**
7:         $Pos[], T[i][t+1] \leftarrow difus(N, Pos[], Vel[], a, mn, NList[][], T[i][t])$ ▷ on GPU-CPU
8:         **if** a particle has moved $\geq$ that $threshold$ **then**
9:            $NList[][] \leftarrow Neighbors(N, Pos[], ...)$ ▷ Computed on GPU
10: **return** $T[i][t]$ with $0 \leq i \leq ntraj$, $0 \leq t \leq ttraj$ ▷ Return tracer trajectories

---

to empty; (b) calculating the distance of every pair of particles i-j, r_{ij} and the corresponding surface-to-surface distance; and (c) including j in the neighbourhood of i when $ss_{ij} = r_{ij} - d_{ij} < th$ and checking if the number of neighbours is larger than mn.

The process referred to as *difus* (line 7 of Algorithm 1) is computed at the beginning of the trajectory and at every time step it is checked if it must be updated. It consists of: (1) a first stage which provides random movements to the particles on CPU; (2) computing Algorithm 2 to calculate the forces among all the particles according to their locations on the GPU, where N threads compute the interaction forces ($\boldsymbol{F}_{ij}$) among every particle and its neighbours according to the potential defined as $V(r_{ij}) = k_B T(r/d_{ij})^{-36}$ in Sect. 2; (3) next, the position and velocities of particles are updated according to the forces previously computed and the equations of motion, again this updating is computed on GPU and every thread updates the location and velocity of one particle; (4) again,

Algorithm 2. cuForces: kernel to calculate the forces among all the particles on the GPU.

Require:
N, $NList[][]$, $a[]$, $\boldsymbol{Pos}[]$

1: $i \leftarrow blockDim.x \cdot blockIdx.x + threadIdx.x$ ▷ global id of thread
2: **if** $i < N$ **then**
3:     $\boldsymbol{df}_i \leftarrow (0,0,0)$
4:     $neig_i = NList[i][0]$ ▷ $neig_i$ stores the number of neighbors of i
5:     **if** $neig_i > 0$ **then**   ▷ if particle i has neighbours
6:        **for** $j \leftarrow 0$ **to** $neig_i$ **do**
7:           $d_{ij} = a[i] + a[j]$
8:           $\boldsymbol{r}_{ij} = \boldsymbol{Pos}[i] - \boldsymbol{Pos}[j]$ ▷ vector from i particle location to j particle
9:           $r_{ij} = |\boldsymbol{r}_{ij}|$ ▷ distance between i and j particles
10:          $|\boldsymbol{F}_{ij}| = 36\frac{k_{\mathrm{B}}T}{d_{ij}}(\frac{r}{d_{ij}})^{-37}$ ▷ module of the interaction force of i and j
            particles
11:           $\boldsymbol{df}[i] = \boldsymbol{df}[i] + \frac{|\boldsymbol{F}_{ij}|}{d_{ij}}\boldsymbol{r}_{ij}$
12:     **if** $i == 0$ **then**   ▷ the first particle is the tracer particle
13:        $\boldsymbol{df}[i] = \boldsymbol{df}[i] + (|\boldsymbol{F}_{\mathrm{ext}}|, 0, 0)$ ▷ apply $\boldsymbol{F}_{\mathrm{ext}}$ to the tracer at x-edge
14: **return** $\boldsymbol{df}[N]$ ▷ Return the applied forces to every particle by its neighbours

---

Algorithm 2 is executed to compute on the GPU the total force applied over every particle using the new particles locations and update the velocities with these new forces; (5) the center of mass velocity is evaluated on the CPU and (6) the particles velocities are updated in relation to the center of mass on the GPU. This *difus* process consumes most of the computational resources, specially when the cuForces kernel (see Algorithm 2) is called.

Algorithm 2 is devoted to calculating on the GPU the forces among all the particles. Here, it is important to highlight that there is a symmetry relation to compute the interaction forces among the particles, ($\boldsymbol{F}_{ij} = -\boldsymbol{F}_{ji}$) which is considered in sequential versions of the model. However, it is not taken into account in the GPU version. The reason is that the computed forces, $\boldsymbol{F}_{ij}$, related to the pair of particles i, j would have to be communicated between the corresponding pair of threads and it would break the massive parallel execution of threads on the GPU since, in such case, a relevant number of atomic memory writings and synchronization points would be added.

4 Evaluation

Microrheology problems with several sizes have been executed and evaluated on a platform with a GPU. Compute Unified Device Architecture (CUDA) [5] and C have been the used interface and programming language, respectively. The results obtained in terms of performance have shown the advantages of the GPU computing to accelerate this kind of problems when N is large enough.

Table 1. Characteristics of the microrheology problems

N	$ntraj$	$ttraj$
216	5	50
512	5	50
1000	5	50
2197	5	50
4096	5	50

The characteristics of the microrheology problems are shown in Table 1. The computational architectures considered in the experiments are: ($P1$) Bullx R424-E3 Intel Xeon E5 2650 (16 CPU-cores and 8GB RAM) with one Tesla M2070 (Fermi) and ($P2$) Bullx R421-E4 Intel Xeon E5 2620v2 (12 CPU-cores, 64-GB RAM) with a NVIDIA K80 GPU (Kepler GK210). The characteristics of the GPU devices are given in Table 2.

A preliminary study has been carried out, comparing the C sequential code and the C code in combination with the GPU device to accelerate $difus$ and $Neighbors$ on $P1$ and $P2$ platforms. In this study, runtimes for the C sequential ranges from 2001 to 33250 s (1295 to 21953) on $P1$ ($P2$) and runtimes for the GPU accelerated codes range from 704 to 2473 s (535 to 1844) on $P1$ ($P2$), i.e., Fig. 1 shows the runtimes on $P1$ for the C sequential code and the C code in combination with the GPU device.

Figure 2 shows the acceleration factors of the GPU model against the sequential model on platforms $P1$ and $P2$. In this figure, GPU version on $P1$ obtains almost all the best acceleration factors because of the long sequential times on $P1$. Moreover, GPU implementation of the model reduces the runtime by a factor of 13 (12) from the sequential version on $P1$ ($P2$). In other words, we have obtained acceleration factors up to 13× (12×) with respect to the approach without GPU computing. Therefore, the use of GPU computing considerably reduces the runtime and makes feasible the extension of the model.

Table 2. Characteristics of the GPU devices

	M2070	K80
Peak performance (double prec.) (TFlops)	0.51	1.87
Peak performance (simple prec.) (TFlops)	1.03	5.6
Device memory (GB)	5.2	11.2
Clock rate (GHz)	1.2	0.82
Memory bandwidth (GBytes/s)	150	480
Multiprocessors	14	13
CUDA cores	448	4992
Compute capability	2.0	3.7

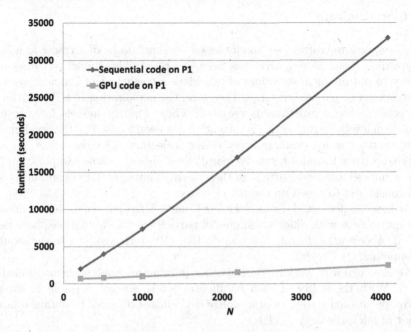

Fig. 1. Runtime in seconds of the microrheology model obtained for every N for both, the sequential version and the GPU approach on $P1$.

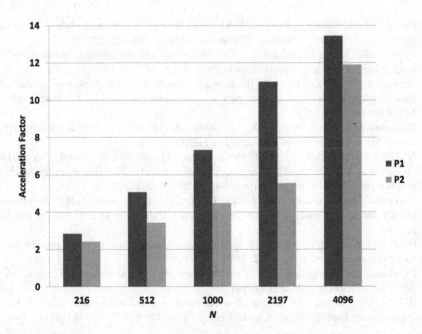

Fig. 2. Acceleration factors of the GPU model against the sequential model on platforms $P1$ and $P2$.

5   Conclusions

In this paper a microrheology model based on simulations of a tracer in a bath of Brownian quasi-hard spheres has been described. This model has shown its validity to obtain accurate values of the friction coefficient of colloidal systems if the number of particles is large. Therefore, the exploitation of HPC platforms to accelerate the simulations is required. These kind of models have several parallelism levels. In this work, our attention has been focused on the acceleration of the routines which evaluate every tracer trajectory. The evaluation of every tracer trajectory includes a massive parallelism since the same computation has to be complete for every particle in the system. Therefore, GPU computing has been considered to speed up the tracer trajectory.

We have implemented the model using C and CUDA interface. Several numerical experiments, with different number of particles in the simulations, have been studied. Acceleration factors range up to 13× (12×) with respect to the sequential approach on $P1$ ($P2$).

We are currently working on the other parallelism levels aforementioned in Sect. 3. With the study of such parallelism levels, we will be able to exploit the computational resources of a multi-GPU cluster in order to obtain a faster output of microrheology models.

References

1. Chen, D.T.N., Wen, Q., Janmey, P.A., Crocker, J.C., Yodh, A.G.: Rheology of soft materials. Ann. Rev. Condens. Matter Phys. **1**(1), 301–322 (2010)
2. Dhont, J.K.G.: An Introduction to Dynamics of Colloids. Studies in Interface Science. Elsevier Science, Amsterdam (1996)
3. Hasimoto, H.: On the periodic fundamental solutions of the Stokes equations and their application to viscous flow past a cubic array of spheres. J. Fluid Mech. **5**, 317–328 (1959)
4. Hennessy, J.L., Patterson, D.A.: Computer Architecture - A Quantitative Approach, 5th edn. Morgan Kaufmann, Burlington (2012)
5. NVIDIA Corporation: CUDA C Programming Guide. PG-02829-001_v7.5 (2015)
6. Ortega, G., Garzón, E.M., Vázquez, F.M., García, I.: The BiConjugate gradient method on GPUs. J. Supercomput. **64**(1), 49–58 (2013)
7. Ortega, G., Vázquez, F.M., García, I., Garzón, E.M.: FastSpMM: an efficient library for sparse matrix matrix product on GPUs. Comput. J. **57**(7), 968–979 (2014)
8. Paul, W., Yoon, D.Y.: Stochastic phase space dynamics with constraints for molecular systems. Phys. Rev. E **52**, 2076–2083 (1995)
9. Puertas, A.M., Voigtmann, T.: Microrheology of colloidal systems. J. Phys.: Condens. Matter **26**(24), 243101 (2014)
10. Wilson, L.G., Poon, W.C.K.: Small-world rheology: an introduction to probe-based active microrheology. Phys. Chem. Chem. Phys. **13**, 10617–10630 (2011)

Applications of Parallel
and Distributed Computing

Methodological Approach to Data-Centric Cloudification of Scientific Iterative Workflows

Silvina Caíno-Lores[1([⊠])], Andrei Lapin[2], Peter Kropf[2], and Jesús Carretero[1]

[1] Department of Computer Science and Engineering,
University Carlos III of Madrid, Leganés, Madrid, Spain
{scaino,jcarrete}@inf.uc3m.es
[2] Computer Science Department, University of Neuchâtel, Neuchâtel, Switzerland
{andrei.lapin,peter.kropf}@unine.ch

Abstract. The computational complexity and the constantly increasing amount of input data for scientific computing models is threatening their scalability. In addition, this is leading towards more data-intensive scientific computing, thus rising the need to combine techniques and infrastructures from the HPC and big data worlds. This paper presents a methodological approach to cloudify generalist iterative scientific workflows, with a focus on improving data locality and preserving performance. To evaluate this methodology, it was applied to an hydrological simulator, EnKF-HGS. The design was implemented using Apache Spark, and assessed in a local cluster and in Amazon Elastic Compute Cloud (EC2) against the original version to evaluate performance and scalability.

Keywords: Cloud computing · Cloudification · Iterative workflows · Map reduce · Apache spark · Hydrology · HydroGeoSphere · Ensemble Kalman filter

1 Introduction

Simulators have become a key tool for scientists working with complex systems and multiphysics models. Nowadays, the computational complexity of these models has increased notably, threatening the scalability of the addressable simulation size, the number of runnable scenarios, and the time required to achieve the results. This is aggravated by the constantly increasing amount of input data originating from geographically distributed sources like sensors, radars or cameras.

In this context, traditional high-performance computing (HPC) techniques are blending with big data analytics and high-throughput computing (HTC)

S. Caíno-Lores—This work has been partially funded under the grant TIN2013-41350-P of the Spanish Ministry of Economics and Competitiveness, the COST Action IC1305 "Network for Sustainable Ultrascale Computing Platforms" (NE SUS), and the FPU Training Program for Academic and Teaching Staff FPU15/00422 by the Spanish Ministry of Education.

© Springer International Publishing AG 2016
J. Carretero et al. (Eds.): ICA3PP 2016, LNCS 10048, pp. 469–482, 2016.
DOI: 10.1007/978-3-319-49583-5_36

paradigms. As an example, there has been a rise of scientific many-task computing (MTC) workflows [7], which are capable to handle the huge data volume and the massive computational requirements of these simulations. We can also see this trend affecting the underlying computing infrastructures, as the number of works trying to mix HPC and big data infrastructures from an architectural and programming modeling perspective are on the rise [16].

Following this trend, big data infrastructures arose as alternatives to traditional HPC infrastructures for some major types of scientific applications, especially those with many loosely-coupled tasks, or heterogeneous tasks with some interdependences [15]. For instance, cloud computing appeared as an affordable possibility to build flexible infrastructures on-demand. This is a popular paradigm that relies of resource sharing and virtualization to provide the end-user with a transparent and scalable system.

Given the benefits of cloud environments, several areas of science and industry are trying to migrate their legacy applications to the cloud, in order to support scalability beyond their private infrastructure. Nevertheless, it is necessary that the cloudification procedure is able to manage resources and data in such way that scientific applications benefit from the underlying infrastructure, without hurting performance and resiliency.

A key aspect in large-scale computing is data locality, defined as the minimization and optimization of information transmissions in order to reduce transfer latencies [20]. In particular, as the scale increases, the degree of data locality in a distributed application has a major impact on its overall scalability, and this is especially critical for data-intensive applications. Hence, we believe that cloudification must pay special attention to inter-node and inter-datacenter data locality.

In this paper, we propose a methodological approach to cloudify generalist iterative workflows, built on legacy simulation kernels, while enforcing data locality. Our interest is in the large family of scientific simulators that make use of iterative procedures to refine and improve their output models. With this methodology, scientists could systematically transform their iterative simulators into cloud-suited applications, taking advantage of the many benefits of the cloud, while minimizing development and operational costs.

To evaluate our proposal, we applied the cloudification methodology to a simulator from the hydrogeology domain [10]. The application was originally built using the message-passing interface (MPI), and it relies on two third-party binaries: GROK and HydroGeoSphere (HGS). We implemented the workflow using Apache Spark,[1] and we tested both applications in a cluster and in Amazon Elastic Compute Cloud (EC2).

The rest of the paper is organized as follows: Sect. 2 discusses works related to cloudification methodologies and strategies, especially for the hydrology domain; Sect. 3 presents the cloudification methodology for generalist iterative simulation workflows; Sect. 4 depicts our case study and the application of the methodology; Sect. 5 provides a performance comparison and scalability assessment of

---

[1] The Apache Spark project is available at http://spark.apache.org/.

the cloudified version of the simulator, against the original MPI implementation; finally, Sect. 6 provides key ideas and insights on future works.

2   Related Work

The migration of data-intensive high-performance simulations to cloud computing infrastructures using high-level paradigms, such as map-reduce, has arisen a strong interest in the scientific and engineering communities. Below, we show some relevant works related to cloudification methodologies, and to the major simulation frameworks in the hydrology area.

2.1   Current Cloudification Methodologies

Cloud computing has been dragging increasing attention in several areas that make use of software applications. How to cloudify these applications and software systems has become a trending topic due to the benefits of cloud-like environments. However, the cloudification problem has been tackled mainly from a business perspective, creating process-oriented migration methodologies, and generalist service-based systems [13]. These works aim to migrate the whole ecosystem of a business, supporting multi-tenancy and virtualization, hence they require major re-engineering efforts. Additionally, these cloudification methodologies do not focus on resource-intensive applications, and their proposed architectures are not suitable for the performance requirements of current simulators.

Following a similar approach as its business-oriented counterparts, Yu et al. [21] propose an application adaptation middleware to allow legacy code migration to the cloud. In this work, a virtualization architecture is implemented by means of a web interface and a Software-as-a-Service market and development platform. Again, this generalist approach is suitable to provide multi-tenancy in desktop applications, but might not suffice for the resource-intensive computations required by HPC simulations.

In order to support the degree of scalability and performance required by modern simulators, one of the key elements to take into consideration in a cloudification procedure is the avoidance of I/O bottlenecks [14]. Given the workflow nature of many state-of-the-art simulators for scientific computing, Srirama et al. [17] proposed a workflow-partitioning strategy to reduce the data communication in the resulting cloud deployment. The aim of this work is similar to ours: migrating scientific workflows to the cloud with a focus on data locality. However, it focuses on task scheduling and the underlying peer-to-peer data-sharing mechanisms required for their efficient communication, while we attempt to provide data locality by design in the resulting applications.

In previous works [4,5], we have introduced a data-centric cloudification methodology for numerical simulations, which aims to assist in the migration of simulators to the clouds via the map-reduce framework, while keeping the manipulation of the original code to a minimum. This paper follows a similar approach, but it applies it to the wide family iterative scientific workflows, present in many scientific areas. These applications, while not pleasingly parallel, still have large sections of parallelizable code that can be distributed, and that need to enforce their data locality properties.

2.2   Cloudification of Hydrological Applications

Having good quality predictions of the behavior of hydrological environmental systems is a key aspect for water management. Such systems are highly heterogeneous regarding their physical characteristics and parameters, hence they rely on complex multi-scale non-linear processes and matrix operations. The inherent computational complexity of these tasks have lead scientists to implement parallel versions of these models in the form of tailored simulators for multi-core environments, as being able to tackle such complex computations fast becomes critical. Some communities have also used grid-like HTC technologies to increase the scale, size and complexity of the addressable problems. Nevertheless, the ever-increasing datasets have shifted the interest towards more data-intensive infrastructures, like compute clouds, looking for flexibility, elasticity, and a satisfactory cost-performance trade-off.

Studies have shown the feasibility of running cloud-based frameworks for multi-scale data analysis, with complexities comparable to the hydrology domain [11, 19]. These works have shown that data and tool integration are easier for end-users in these environments, while performance and storage capability remained comparable to grids. Other works approached the benefits of Cloud Computing from a hybrid perspective, integrating data and computing infrastructures from grids with external cloud providers like Amazon EC2 [6]. This work is particularly relevant, as it shows the feasibility of clouds for a wide range of hydrological problems, covering both computationally intensive HPC simulators, and MTC-like applications with multiple scenarios.

Recent technological and mathematical advances allowed to improve significantly the precision of the simulations by integrating data acquisition techniques with the modeling process [1]. HydroCloud [12] allows to aggregate data from different sources and present it to the user in a single format for further analysis, by using a cloud-based data integration system to store and explore data. A similar research line is followed by our previous work [10]. In it we presented an architecture for a system combining a wireless environmental monitoring module as data source, and a cloud-based computing service to perform environmental simulations. Even though the system was tested in a real-world deployment in the Emmental area in Switzerland, and proven to be operable, the performance of the core simulation procedures have not been assessed nor built for the target infrastructure. In this work, we tackle this issue as a particular case study of our cloudification methodology, with the goal of developing a version of the simulator able to exploit the cloud's capabilities with minimal development.

3   Cloudifying Iterative Workflows

The cloudification methodology we propose aims to (a) guide the migration of an iterative workflow to the cloud, while (b) maintaining a comparable level of performance against a traditional infrastructure. To achieve this, we have built this methodology in a data-centric manner, as data locality plays a major role in the final performance and scalability of cloud-based applications. Inspired in iterative map-reduce schemes, the key to provide locality within our model is that independent simulation steps may rely on different node-local data, with no need for further communication. As cloud-like environments are engineered so that nodes mix computation and storage, this perspective provides a high degree of parallelism that also considers the architecture of the target infrastructure with regard to data management.

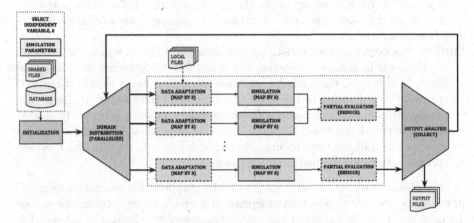

Fig. 1. Overview of the cloudification methodology. Dashed boxes indicate optional stages, which may not be necessary for every iterative workflow.

The proposed methodology is depicted in Fig. 1. It consists of the definition of the following steps:

Key Selection. First, it is necessary to conduct an analysis of the original application in order to find a domain suitable for parallelization. This entails finding an independent variable to act as partitioning key (k, in Fig. 1), which will guide the domain distribution and the following stages.

Domain Partitioning. Once the parallelizable domain is selected, we can model how the input will be distributed across the nodes. This parallelization stage distributes the proper portion of the input, for each value of k. This sets the fraction of the input data or model that will be processed for each instantiation of the guiding independent variable. This stage has critical effects in the final degree of data locality achievable by the simulation, since the proper preparation of the input data and parameters can save subsequent data transfers and communication between the simulations associated with each subdomain.

Simulation. One or more simulation stages wrap the kernels involved in the simulation workflow, in order to simulate each portion of the domain independently and autonomously. This yields the execution of not one, but many smaller simulations. The large number of simulations to be executed factors the inherent complexity of the simulation process, yet it can be massively distributed due to the independent and autonomous nature of each simulation. Considering the previous domain partitioning stage, each simulation will be scheduled in the computing node that holds each domain partition, so no data transfers are required at this point. Therefore, we process the key-specific input in a way that exploits data locality, and minimizes data transfers.

Partial Reduction. Optionally, one or more reduction stages can be defined to filter or join partial outputs before the overall collection and evaluation of results to reduce contention in the synchronization point. This stage can also be used to aggregate node-local data to minimize transfer sizes for the following procedures.

Output Processing. This constitutes an analysis stage, in which the processing methods in charge of creating the input for the following iteration take place. In this step, the output evaluation must be defined to reflect the end criteria, the generation of the following input, and the validity of the results per iteration. In the worst-case scenario, a collection point is typically needed to conduct such analysis. However, in some cases these procedures can be executed in a distributed manner, but this depends heavily in the use case and the selected implementation platform.

The objective of the former steps is to find a parallelizable simulation domain, in which we are able to select an independent variable to act as index for subsequent steps. This shall support the parallelization of the domain in a key-value manner, so that further simulation pipes and optional partial evaluations can take place independently, as seen in massively-parallel data analytics frameworks. Of course, any partition-specific data will only concern the node that is going to process such domain partition, hence we can schedule the computation in the proper node to support data locality. This is particularly interesting if several simulation stages are involved, since they can be scheduled together to benefit from local intermediate files. After these procedures, partial results can be filtered and assessed in parallel as well, again following the initial domain distribution. Finally, these partial results can be analyzed and processed to build the next iteration, but the effects of this synchronization point can be alleviated by previous partial reductions.

4   Case Study: Cloudification of an Hydrological Iterative Workflow

In this section we show how to port EnKF-HGS, a data assimilation workflow, to the cloud using our cloudification methodology. We have chosen EnKF-HGS as case study because it is a real-world application that is in the process of being integrated with other cloud-based components, hence the need for cloudification. Additionally, scalability is key in this scientific field, as the resulting application must be able to cope with larger experiments and new environmental models with increased complexity. This use case is representative of the iterative scientific simulations we tackle with our methodology, both in terms of complexity and resource consumption.

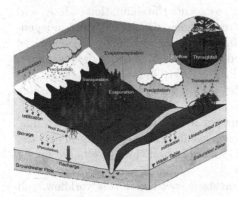

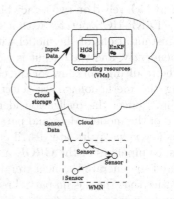

Fig. 2. Typical surface water and groundwater processes in a pre-alpine type of valleys [8].

Fig. 3. Architecture of the real-time environmental monitoring and hydrological modeling system depicted in [10].

4.1   Description of EnKF-HGS

The EnKF-HGS simulator [9] is one of the state-of-the-art simulators in the hydrology domain. This is an MPI implementation of the ensemble Kalman filter (EnKF) technique for data assimilation [3]. Data assimilation is the process of adjusting the simulated model according to environmental field measurements. Therefore, EnKF-HGS provides functionality for dynamic stochastic simulations of the groundwater and surface water profiles composed of the elements depicted in Fig. 2. Moreover, it allows to constantly improve the simulated model by sequentially assimilating fresh field measurements, hence its iterative nature.

EnKF-HGS runs an ensemble of model instantiations – which we call *realizations*– and updates them with data from field measurements. Each simulation in the ensemble of realizations represents a long-running I/O- and compute-intensive process, which comprises the sequential execution of two proprietary simulation kernels: GROK and HydroGeoSphere (HGS) [2,18]. GROK is a pre-processor that prepares the input files for HGS, which is an integrated hydrological modeling simulator. As a Monte Carlo based approach, the EnKF technique needs to perform numerous model simulations in order to achieve the required precision. This amount of computations implies having a dedicated HPC infrastructure, which is not always available to the end-user. Moreover, data acquisition, integration and storage has already been cloudified in this case, following the scheme in Fig. 3. Therefore, porting EnKF-HGS would not just help hydrologists to increase their addressable problem size without a heavy infrastructure investment, but would also ease its integration with this data ecosystem.

4.2   Application of the Methodology

As described, the original application consisted of an MPI implementation of an EnKF, which relied on two legacy binaries to execute the simulation (GROK and HGS). EnKF-HGSoperates with a set of realizations, which constitute independent instantiations of the model with different parameters. They are simulated independently, and the output is gathered afterwards for further processing.

The resulting workflow for the cloudified EnKF-HGS is shown in Fig. 4. Following the methodology, we selected the set of realizations as parallelizable domain. Hence, the realization identifier, r_i, constitutes the key, and the collection of the model's data and parameters per realization, $c_{i,1}, c_{i,2}$, is the value. These key-value pairs are distributed and executed independently across the nodes, as pipelines of the GROK and HGS kernels, and their results are finally gathered to generate the next iteration.

Notice that there is no partial reduction stage specified in this workflow, and the output processing is conducted.

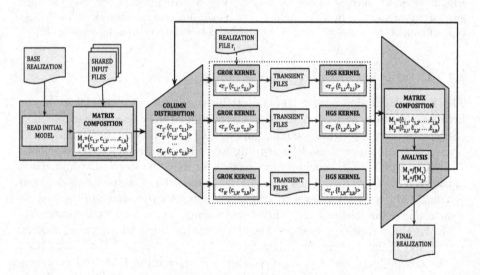

Fig. 4. Final workflow for the cloudified EnKF-HGS.

The resulting application was implemented using the Apache Spark platform. We considered the Spark programming model because it supports functionalities that enable the development of applications that do not fit nicely into the traditional map-reduce paradigm, such as many iterative machine learning algorithms and interactive data analysis tools.

A particularity of the kernel binaries is that they are third-party pre-built black boxes. An effect of this is that they rely on hard-coded input paths for the intermediate files they handle. Nevertheless, in order to improve locality, our methodology approaches the simulation stages as a pipeline, so we can ensure the execution of HGS with the input generated by its corresponding execution of GROK. To achieve this we exploited Apache Spark's partitioning mechanisms to ensure that each full realization is computed in the same node in a pipelined manner.

5 Evaluation

In this section we detail the experimental evaluation that was conducted to demonstrate the suitability of the resulting application to a cloud environment, while preserving its performance. The experiments have been conducted using the experimental setup described below. A thorough discussion is also included to explain the results of the experiments.

5.1 Experimental Setup

We implemented the cloudified application on Apache Spark, on top of the Hadoop Distributed File System (HDFS) and Yet-Another Resource Negotiator (YARN).[2] To configure the environment, we profiled the GROK and HGS binaries to estimate their resource usage. We found that GROK is I/O-intensive, while the HGS kernel is compute-intensive, and it makes full usage of the CPU resources of the machines. Neither of them consume a significant amount of memory in the worker nodes (less than 30 MB for the current model).

The main source for memory usage is the EnKF-HGS workflow running on top of the kernels, due to the large matrices it uses to build and process the realizations. In Spark, these data structures are handled by a specific container acting as the driver of the workflow. For large experiments, this driver process requires up to 7 GB of memory due to its computing needs and the overhead of the platform. We are conducting further optimizations based on the partial reductions present in the methodology, which are currently not included in our implementation.

In order to compare the performance of the resulting application, we ran it on our local cluster against the MPI implementation. We used ten slave nodes, each holding 8 GB of RAM and two Intel Xeon E5405@2.00 GHz processors, with four cores each; and a dedicated node for the driver container with an overall amount of 94 GB of RAM and four Intel Xeon E7-4807@1.87 GHz processors, with six cores each and hyper-threading enabled. These nodes are linked through a 1 GB network. Table 1 shows a summary of the configuration parameters considered in the Spark environment, while Table 2 shows the configuration for its underlying

---

[2] HDFS and YARN belong to the Apache Hadoop project, accessible at http://hadoop.apache.org/.

Table 1. Configuration parameters for the Spark platform.

Spark settings	
Executor memory (MB)	471
Driver memory (MB)	7168
Driver cores	4
Executor overhead (MB)	384
Driver overhead (MB)	717
Serializer	kyro

Table 2. Configuration parameters for the YARN resource manager.

YARN settings		
Core allocation	Min.	1
	Max.	8
Memory allocation (MB)	Min.	256
	Max.	8192
Node CPUs		8
Node memory (MB)		8192

resource manager, YARN. These parameters were selected taking into account the former requirements with respect to the resource consumption of the kernels, and the selected nodes for both infrastructures.

For the execution of the original MPI-based implementation in the local cluster environment, we relied on resource-wise similar eight worker nodes, each holding 8 GB of RAM and two Intel Xeon E5405@2.00 GHz processors, with four cores each, and a Lustre file system[3] for the simulator internal file-based communication.

Additionally, we built two virtual clusters on Amazon EC2 with the instances described in Table 3, one to deploy Spark, and another to run MPI. We relied on compute instances with resources similar to the ones in our cluster. For the Spark deployment, we required a high-availability master node to coordinate the platform, a driver node and ten slaves. The latter roles were fulfilled by spot instances given the inherent fault-tolerant nature of Spark, thus adding the

Table 3. Instance selection for the execution of the cloudified workflow, running on Spark, and the MPI-based application.

Platform	Spark			MPI	
Node role	Master	Driver	Slave	Compute	Storage
Type	t2.small	r3.large	c4.2xlarge	c4.2xlarge	c4.large
Amount	1	1	10	8	3
vCPU	1	2	8	8	4
Memory (GB)	2	15	15	15	7.5
Storage	EBS	SSD	EBS	EBS	EBS
Full price ($/hour)	0.026	0.166	0.419	0.419	0.209
Spot	No	Yes	Yes	No	No
Max. price ($/hour)	-	0.100	0.200	-	-

---

[3] Lustre is an open-source file system available at http://lustre.org/.

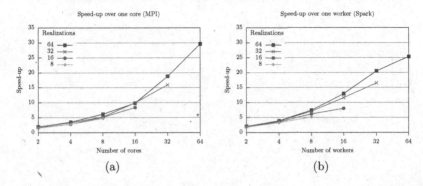

Fig. 5. Speed up results for the original MPI ensemble Kalman filter (a), and its cloudified version (b), running on a local cluster. Results for two and four realizations were not included for visibility reasons, as they are very similar to the results for eight realizations.

benefit of reduced operational costs. In order to run MPI, besides the slaves, it was necessary to include three additional storage nodes running GlusterFS, a cloud-oriented production-ready distributed storage solution.[4] Each storage node was provisioned with an 8 GB general purpose SSD brick, and they were organized in a distributed volume with no data-replication in order to maximize the storage performance. On the compute nodes side, we exploited the FUSE-based Gluster Native Client for highly concurrent access to the file system, there is a need to optimize the concurrent accesses to storage executed by the MPI processes.

5.2   Result Discussion

Figure 5 shows the speed-up of the MPI and Spark implementations, respectively, in our local cluster. For the Spark implementation we executed the simulator from 2 to 64 workers; similarly, the MPI version was executed from 2 to 64 MPI processes, where each process was provided with one CPU core. In both cases, we used a medium-sized hydrological model as input, and we increased the number of realizations from 2 up to 64 to test scaling.

The execution results show that our Spark implementation has a better speed-up than MPI for the majority of experiments. We are currently studying the rationale behind these results, which are related with I/O contention, since the data-transferring mechanism between computations of the HGS model and the MPI EnKF is file-based. In this case, our data-centric approach is particularly beneficial in terms of performance.

However, the MPI implementation shows a noticeably better speed-up for the maximal size of the model with the maximal number of computing workers/processes (64/64). This scalability issue appeared in the Spark implementation due to the specifics of the post-processing logic of the EnKF, which we

---

[4] More information on GlusterFS accessible at https://www.gluster.org/.

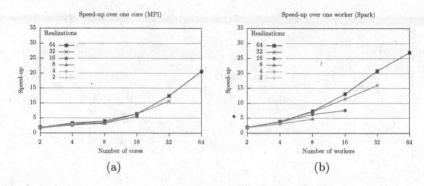

Fig. 6. Speed up results for the original MPI ensemble Kalman filter (a), and its cloudified version (b), running on EC2.

did not tackle in the current work. The post-processing logic includes a set of operations with large-size matrices where complexity of the computation is directly proportional to the number of realizations in the ensemble. This resulted in the reduced performance of the implementation due to the amount of unnecessary data transfers. The MPI implementation performs the post-processing computation in a distributed manner, unlike our Spark implementation, which currently aggregates the output of the realizations in the driver node in order to assemble matrices, and performs the post-processing with no computation distribution. We are working towards designing and implementing the partial reduction stages of the methodology in order to provide a fairer performance comparison in future works.

We conducted identical tests on the virtual clusters to reflect the effects of the infrastructure in the behavior of both versions of EnKF-HGS. Figure 6 shows minimal variations in the speed-up for the cloudified workflow against the local cluster executions, and a significantly decreased speed-up for the original MPI-based implementation. The speed-up degradation of the original implementation increases noticeably with the number of parallel MPI processes, since it equally increases the number of concurrent I/O operations. These results illustrate a tremendous demand to the file system performance, which in our case issued a reduction of the simulator performance.

6   Conclusions

This paper described a data-centric methodological approach to cloudify scientific iterative workflows. The main objective of this methodology is to define the common stages we can find in these kinds of high-performance applications, and model in such way we can maximize parallelism and data locality in the resulting workflow. This would allow scientists to benefit from clouds with minimal development efforts, or to modernize their legacy applications systematically.

To evaluate our methodology, we applied it to an MPI-based hydrological simulator. We implemented this design using Apache Spark, and we tested both applications in a cluster and in Amazon Elastic Compute Cloud (EC2) to assess performance and scalability. As a result, we obtained comparable performance results on small and medium-sized realization sets, on both infrastructures. However, we also encountered a file system-related performance issue due to a file-based communication in the original implementation.

As future work, we will further assess the scalability and efficiency of the cloudified simulator, considering the implementation of relevant aspects of the post-processing stage that are included in the MPI version, but not in the cloudified design. As the speed-up results show that the cloudified application is competitive with MPI in an infrastructure favorable to the latter, we believe that solving this scalability problem would make our solution preferable in the cloud, due to the reduced network bandwidth that would hurt the performance of MPI. Additionally, we will also study the I/O throughput of both implementations, since EnKF-HGS uses files for input, intermediate, and output data, and this could easily induce I/O contention for very large-size models. It is also left for future work to integrate the cloudified application with a memory-centric file system, as it may improve performance in these cases by improving intra-node data locality.

References

1. Bauser, G., Hendricks Franssen, H.J., Fritz, S., Kaiser, H.P., Kuhlmann, U., Kinzelbach, W.: A comparison study of two different control criteria for the real-time management of urban groundwater works. J. Environ. Manage. **105**, 21–29 (2012)
2. Brunner, P., Simmons, C.T.: Hydrogeosphere: a fully integrated, physically based hydrological model. Ground Water **50**(2), 170–176 (2012)
3. Burgers, G., van Leeuwen, P.J., Evensen, G.: Analysis scheme in the ensemble Kalman filter. Mon. Weather Rev. **126**(6), 1719–1724 (1998)
4. Caíno-Lores, S., Fernández, A.G., García-Carballeira, F., Pérez, J.C.: A cloudification methodology for multidimensional analysis: implementation and application to a railway power simulator. Simul. Model. Pract. Theory **55**, 46–62 (2015)
5. Caíno-Lores, S., García, A., García-Carballeira, F., Carretero, J.: A cloudification methodology for numerical simulations. In: Lopes, L., Žilinskas, J., Costan, A., Cascella, R.G., Kecskemeti, G., Jeannot, E., Cannataro, M., Ricci, L., Benkner, S., Petit, S., Scarano, V., Gracia, J., Hunold, S., Scott, S.L., Lankes, S., Lengauer, C., Carretero, J., Breitbart, J., Alexander, M. (eds.) Euro-Par 2014. LNCS, vol. 8806, pp. 375–386. Springer, Heidelberg (2014). doi:10.1007/978-3-319-14313-2_32
6. Chiang, G.T., Dove, M.T., Bovolo, C.I., Ewen, J.: Implementing a grid/cloud escience infrastructure for hydrological sciences. In: Yang, X., Wang, L., Jie, W. (eds.) Guide to e-Science. Computer Communications and Networks, pp. 3–28. Springer, Heidelberg (2011)
7. Duro, F.R., Blas, J.G., Isaila, F., Wozniak, J.M., Carretero, J., Ross, R.: Flexible data-aware scheduling for workflows over an in-memory object store. In: 2016 16th IEEE/ACM International Symposium on Cluster, Cloud and Grid Computing (CCGrid), pp. 321–324. IEEE (2016)
8. Jyrkama, M.I.: A methodology for estimating groundwater recharge. Dissertation Abs. Int. Part B: Sci. Eng. **65**(5), 2524 (2004)

9. Kurtz, W., Hendricks Franssen, H.J., Kaiser, H.P., Vereecken, H.: Joint assimilation of piezometric heads and groundwater temperatures for improved modeling of river-aquifer interactions. Water Resour. Res. **50**(2), 1665–1688 (2014)

10. Lapin, A., Schiller, E., Kropf, P., Schilling, O., Brunner, P., Kapic, A.J., Braun, T., Maffioletti, S.: Real-time environmental monitoring for cloud-based hydrogeological modeling with hydrogeosphere. In: 2014 IEEE International Conference on High Performance Computing and Communications, pp. 959–965 (2014)

11. Lu, S., Li, R.M., Tjhi, W.C., Lee, K.K., Wang, L., Li, X., Ma, D.: A framework for cloud-based large-scale data analytics and visualization: case study on multiscale climate data. In: 2011 IEEE Third International Conference on Cloud Computing Technology and Science (CloudCom), pp. 618–622. IEEE (2011)

12. McGuire, M.P., Roberge, M.C., Lian, J.: Hydrocloud: a cloud-based system for hydrologic data integration and analysis. In: 2014 Fifth International Conference on Computing for Geospatial Research and Application (COM. Geo), pp. 9–16. IEEE (2014)

13. Menychtas, A., Konstanteli, K., Alonso, J., Orue-Echevarria, L., Gorronogoitia, J., Kousiouris, G., Santzaridou, C., Bruneliere, H., Pellens, B., Stuer, P., et al.: Software modernization and cloudification using the artist migration methodology and framework. Scalable Comput. Pract. Exp. **15**(2), 131–152 (2014)

14. Nuthula, V., Challa, N.R.: Cloudifying apps - a study of design and architectural considerations for developing cloudenabled applications with case study. In: 2014 IEEE International Conference on Cloud Computing in Emerging Markets (CCEM), pp. 1–7 (2014)

15. Raicu, I., Foster, I., Zhao, Y.: Many-task computing for grids and supercomputers. In: Workshop on Many-Task Computing on Grids and Supercomputers, MTAGS 2008, pp. 1–11, November 2008

16. Reed, D.A., Dongarra, J.: Exascale computing and big data. Commun. ACM **58**(7), 56–68 (2015)

17. Srirama, S.N., Viil, J.: Migrating scientific workflows to the cloud: through graph-partitioning, scheduling and peer-to-peer data sharing. In: 2014 IEEE International Conference on High Performance Computing and Communications, pp. 1105–1112. IEEE (2014)

18. Therrien, R., McLaren, R., Sudicky, E., Panday, S.: A three-dimensional numerical model describing fully-integrated Subsurface and surface flow and solute transport. Technical report (2010)

19. Yang, C., Goodchild, M., Huang, Q., Nebert, D., Raskin, R., Xu, Y., Bambacus, M., Fay, D.: Spatial cloud computing: how can the geospatial sciences use and help shape cloud computing? Int. J. Digital Earth **4**(4), 305–329 (2011)

20. Yelick, K., Coghlan, S., Draney, B., Canon, R.S., et al.: The Magellan report on cloud computing for science. Technical report, US Department of Energy, Washington DC, USA (2011)

21. Yu, D., Wang, J., Hu, B., Liu, J., Zhang, X., He, K., Zhang, L.J.: A practical architecture of cloudification of legacy applications. In: 2011 IEEE world congress on Services, pp. 17–24. IEEE (2011)

Efficient Parallel Algorithm for Optimal DAG Structure Search on Parallel Computer with Torus Network

Hirokazu Honda[✉], Yoshinori Tamada, and Reiji Suda

Graduate School of Information Science and Technology,
The University of Tokyo, Tokyo 113-8656, Japan
{rosetta,tamada,reiji}@is.s.u-tokyo.ac.jp

Abstract. The optimal directed acyclic graph search problem constitutes searching for a DAG with a minimum score, where the score of a
DAG is defined on its structure. This problem is known to be NP-hard,
and the state-of-the-art algorithm requires exponential time and space.
It is thus not feasible to solve large instances using a single processor.
Some parallel algorithms have therefore been developed to solve larger
instances. A recently proposed parallel algorithm can solve an instance
of 33 vertices, and this is the largest solved size reported thus far. In
the study presented in this paper, we developed a novel parallel algorithm designed specifically to operate on a parallel computer with a torus
network. Our algorithm crucially exploits the torus network structure,
thereby obtaining good scalability. Through computational experiments,
we confirmed that a run of our proposed method using up to 20,736
cores showed a parallelization efficiency of 0.94 as compared to a 1296-
core run. Finally, we successfully computed an optimal DAG structure
for an instance of 36 vertices, which is the largest solved size reported in
the literature.

Keywords: Optimal DAG structure · Optimal bayesian network
structure · Parallel algorithm · Distributed algorithm · Torus network

1 Introduction

In the field of computer science, a directed acyclic graph (DAG) structure frequently appears in, for example, bioinformatics, graph theory, and parallel computing [3,4,6,10,11]. In this study, we adopted a score-based structure search
to construct a DAG structure from observed data [7–9]. The optimal DAG is
defined as one having a minimum score, where a score function is defined on a

R. Suda—This work was supported by JSPS KAKENHI Grant Number 15K20965.
The computational resource of Fujitsu FX10 was awarded by the "Large-scale HPC
Challenge" Project, Information Technology Center, the University of Tokyo. This
research was conducted using the Fujitsu PRIMEHPC FX10 System (Oakleaf-FX)
at the Information Technology Center, the University of Tokyo.

J. Carretero et al. (Eds.): ICA3PP 2016, LNCS 10048, pp. 483–502, 2016.
DOI: 10.1007/978-3-319-49583-5_37

graph structure. The problem of finding a DAG structure with the optimal score is NP-hard [5]. Learning a Bayesian network, which is used for bioinformatics and machine learning [4,6], is an application of this problem. In bioinformatics, a Bayesian network is used as a model for a gene network and applied for new drug development [12]. Inferring larger networks enhances possibility of such gene network researches. Ott et al. [14] developed an algorithm to find the optimal DAG by dynamic programming (DP). Their algorithm requires $O(n \cdot 2^n)$ space and time, where n denotes the number of vertices in the DAG. Although the memory size on a single machine has been increasing in recent years, by using this algorithm, the instance of only approximately 25 vertices can be solved on a single machine. Even if a machine with sufficient memory existed, it would take a day to solve the instance of more than 30 vertices. To meet these time and memory requirements, some parallel algorithms were developed.

Tamada et al. [15] proposed a parallel algorithm. The feature of their algorithm is a reduction in communications between parallel processors achieved by splitting the search spaces. The time and space complexities of their algorithm are $O(n^{\sigma+1}2^n)$, where $\sigma = 1, 2, \ldots > 0$ controls the trade-off between the number of communications and the memory requirement. They succeeded in solving the optimal DAG search problem for 32 vertices. Nikolova et al. developed a more efficient parallel algorithm [13]. They considered a single processor of 2^k processors as a node of a k-dimensional hypercube. They distributed computations to the processors such that the following property is satisfied. When a processor performs a computation, the necessary data for the computation are stored in the processor or its adjacent processors in a k-dimensional hypercube. The time complexity of their algorithm is $O(n^2 \cdot (2^{n-k}+k))$ on 2^k processors. They proved that the maximum storage needed is approximately $\sqrt{2} \cdot 2^{n-k}/\sqrt{n-k}$ elements on 2^k processors, and by this formula, 33 vertices was the limitation in their experimental environment. Their algorithm could linearly scale up to 2048 cores and they stated that it computed the instance of 33 vertices in 1 h and 14 m with 2048 cores.

In this paper, we propose a novel parallel algorithm called TRPOS (Torus Relay for Parallel Optimal Search). As compared to previously developed algorithms, TRPOS is very simple. Although our algorithm is based on Tamada et al.'s parallel algorithm [15], our algorithm does not reduce communications. Our objective was to develop an algorithm that runs efficiently when many cores are used. When executing the program in distributed systems, the important issues are the distribution of the computations and the data, and the manner in which the processors of the systems communicate with each other. In the previous parallel algorithms, a processor communicates directly with others that store necessary data. Nikolova et al.'s algorithm, for example, would communicate efficiently in a distributed system such that the structure of the k-D hypercube can effectively be allocated to processors in the system. A torus interconnect is a popular network hboxtopology for connecting processors in a distributed system. In fact, many supercomputers adopt torus networks, e.g., Fujitsu FX10, IBM Blue Gene/Q, and Cray XK7. We focus on the structure of the network topology, i.e., the torus network in our system, and propose a communication method designed specifically for torus networks. In a torus network system, although processors can communicate with distant processors, it takes more time and data congestion may occur. To avoid congestion, in our algorithm, a processor communicates with only its adjacent processors. The necessary data for a computation are acquired by relaying (Torus Relay). We developed a communication method for a one-dimensional (1D) torus network at first, and then, extended the method to a two-dimensional (2D) torus network.

We applied our algorithm to the optimal Bayesian network search problem. Through computational experiments, we confirmed that a run of our algorithm using up to 20,736 cores shows a parallelization efficiency of 0.94 as compared to a 1296-core run. Note that previous research showed that an algorithm is scalable up to 2048 cores. We also succeeded in computing the instance of 36 vertices in approximately 12 h with 76,800 cores, which is the largest solved size reported in the literature.

2 Preliminaries

2.1 Finding Optimal DAG Structure

In the score-based DAG structure search, a score function is defined on a pair of a vertex and its parents. A score of a vertex is called a local score. A network score is defined as the sum of the local scores of all the vertices in a graph (network). The optimal DAG $\hat{G}$ is defined as the structure, the network score of which is the minimum. In other words, the optimal DAG is defined as

$$\hat{G} \stackrel{\text{def}}{=} \arg \min_{G} \sum_{j=1}^{n} s(X_j, Pa^G(X_j), \boldsymbol{X}),$$

where G is a DAG and $s(X_j, Pa^G(X_j), \boldsymbol{X})$ is a local score function $V \times 2^V \times \mathbb{R}^{N,n} \to \mathbb{R}$ for vertex X_j given the observed input data of an $(m \times |V|)$-matrix $\boldsymbol{X}$, where V is a set of vertices, $Pa^G(X_j)$ represents the set of vertices that are directed parents of the j-th vertex X_j, and m is the number of observed samples.

2.2 Dynamic Programming Algorithm

We present Ott et al.'s algorithm. A DAG structure can be represented by an order of the vertices, that is, a permutation, and the parents of each vertex. The DP algorithm computes these values in DP steps. In detail, the algorithm consists of DP having two layers: one for obtaining the optimal permutation and one for obtaining the optimal parents of each vertex.

Definition 1 (Optimal local score). *We define the function* $F : V \times 2^V \to \mathbb{R}$ *as*

$$F(v, A) \stackrel{\text{def}}{=} \min_{B \subset A} s(v, B, \boldsymbol{X}).$$

A denotes candidate vertices for v's parent. That is, $F(v, A)$ calculates the optimal choice of v's parent from A and returns its local score.

Definition 2 (Optimal network score on a permutation). *Let* π : $\{1, 2, ..., |A|\} \to A$ *be a permutation on* $A \subset V$ *and* Π^A *be a set of all the permutations on* A. *Given a permutation* $\pi \in \Pi^A$, *the optimal network score on* π *is described as*

$$Q^A(\pi) \stackrel{\text{def}}{=} \sum_{v \in A} F(v, \{u \in A : \pi^{-1}(u) < \pi^{-1}(v)\}).$$

A permutation represents the possibility of parent-child relationships between vertices. The vertex u *can be* v*'s parent if* $\pi^{-1}(u) < \pi^{-1}(v)$. *By the definition of* $F(v, A)$, $Q^A(\pi)$ *calculates the optimal parent-child relationships of* π *and returns its network score.*

Definition 3 (Optimal network score). *Let* A *be a set of vertices. We define the function* $M : V \to \mathbb{R}$ *as*

$$M(A) \stackrel{\text{def}}{=} \arg\min_{\pi \in \Pi^A} Q^A(\pi).$$

$M(A)$ *returns the optimal permutation on* A *that derives the minimal score of the network consisting of the vertices in* A. *Thus, solving the optimal DAG structure search problem is equal to computing* $M(V)$, *where* V *represents all the vertices in a DAG.*

Finally, the following theorem provides an algorithm to calculate $F(v, A)$, $M(A)$, and $Q^A(M(A))$ by DP. See [14] for the proof of this theorem.

Theorem 1 (Optimal network search by DP). *The functions* $F(v, A)$, $M(A)$, *and* $Q^A(M(A))$ *can be respectively calculated by the following formulae*

$$F(v, A) = \min\{s(v, A, \boldsymbol{X}), \min_{a \in A} F(v, A \backslash \{a\})\}, \tag{1}$$

$$M(A) = M(A \backslash \{v^*\}) +' \{v^*\}, \tag{2}$$

$$Q^A(M(A)) = F(v^*, A \backslash \{v^*\}) + Q^{A \backslash \{v^*\}}(M(A \backslash \{v^*\})), \tag{3}$$

where

$$v^* = \arg\min_{v \in A}\{F(v, A \backslash \{v\}) + Q^{A \backslash \{v\}}(M(A \backslash \{v\}))\} \tag{4}$$

and $+'$ *is the operation to append a vertex to the end of the permutation. By applying the above equations from* $|A| = 0$ *to* $|A| = |V|$, *we obtain the optimal permutation* π *on* V *and its score* $Q^V(M(V))$ *in* $O(n \cdot 2^n)$ *steps.*

Note that in order to reconstruct the network structure, we need to store the optimal choice of the parents derived in Eq. (1) and the optimal permutation $\pi = M(A)$ in Eq. (3) for all the combinations of $A \subset V$ for the next size of A.

3   Methods

We call a processor in distributed systems a node. As mentioned in Sect. 2, we need to store the intermediate results in each DP step. In order to calculate a new result in a DP step, for example, $F(v, A)$, it is necessary to calculate the initial score $s(v, A, \boldsymbol{X})$, compare it with $F(v, A \backslash \{a\})$'s, and take their minimum. The algorithm needs to collect $F(v, A \backslash \{a\})$'s that were calculated in the previous DP step and stored at (possibly) different nodes. The previous parallel algorithms, including Nikolova et al.'s algorithm, collect all the necessary data for a computation at the same time and then update each $F(v, A)$. However, because it is not necessary to updating a new result at the same time, a node can receive the data and update at any time. In our proposed algorithm, a node relays all the data and updates if the received data include data necessary for a computation. We explain the manner in which each node acquires all the necessary data for a computation by relaying in the following subsections. The feature of our algorithm is that a node communicates with only its adjacent nodes on a torus network. First, we show that the traditional collective communication methods supported by a Message Passing Interface (MPI) are not suitable for this problem. Next, we introduce our parallel algorithm on the simple interconnect network structure, that is, a 1D torus network. Then, we extend our idea to a 2D torus network. Finally, we improve the algorithm with multithread programming. In this section, we refer to the values of the $F(v, A)$, $M(A)$, and $Q^A(M(A))$ functions as *new results* when we focus on a DP step $|A| = a$. In addition, we refer to the results of the previous step, that is, $F(v, A')$'s, $M(A')$'s, and $Q^{A'}(M(A'))$'s for $|A'| = |A| - 1$, as *sub-results*. Thus, the sub-results are the intermediate results required to calculate the new results.

3.1   Proposed Algorithm

An MPI supports some collective communication methods and some distributed systems may ensure that data congestion does not occur when using these communication methods. A node needs to receive all the sub-results required for score calculations and this is realized by *Allgather*. Each node, by using *Allgather*, gathers all the data stored at all the nodes. *Allgather* consumes memory to store all the data simultaneously. Since the memory complexity is exponential in the optimal DAG structure problem, if this operation is used, the memory is exhausted even for a small problem. Therefore, we cannot use MPI collective communication methods to solve the problem efficiently.

Let us consider an algorithm for a 1D torus network, in which the nodes are connected to each other in a circular shape. In this study, we assumed that the system supports *bi-directional* communication and a node simultaneously sends to and receives from its adjacent nodes. Let n be the number of vertices in a DAG and N be the number of nodes. We propose a simple algorithm that does not entail any congestion on the 1D torus network. The idea is that a node communicates with only its adjacent nodes. So that a node receives the required data located in a distant node, each node transfers the entire data in it

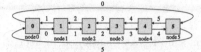

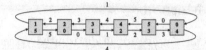

(i) At the first communication step, a node sends its sub-results and receives sub-results from two nodes at distance 1.

(ii) At the second communication step, a node sends sub-results stored in nodes at distance 1 and receives those in nodes at distance 2.

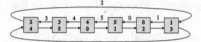

(iii) At the third communication step, a node performs single-directional communication and acquires the final sub-results.

Fig. 1. Example of communications (N = 6). Computational nodes are illustrated as yellow boxes and form the 1D torus network. A number x in a box denotes the sub-results that are stored originally in node x. (Color figure online)

to the adjacent nodes, and this is repeated until all the nodes receive the entire data. At each communication step, a node receives the sub-results sent from its adjacent nodes and simultaneously sends the sub-results that were received at the previous communication step. During the communications, a node also calculates the new results from the received sub-results. If the received sub-results include sub-results required for the new results on the node, the node calculates them while receiving and sending the data. A node obtains sub-results from two nodes at distance 1 at the first communication step, from two nodes at distance 2 at the second step, and so on. When the i-th communication step is complete, a node acquires sub-results from two nodes at distance i from both directions. As an exception, if N is even, a node receives the sub-results originally stored at the farthest node by single-directional communication at the final $\lceil\frac{N-1}{2}\rceil$-th step. Thus, the number of communication steps in a DP step such that all nodes obtain all sub-results is $\lceil\frac{N-1}{2}\rceil$. Figure 1 shows an example of communications where $N = 6$. In the figure, the sub-results stored initially at node x are denoted as x, where node x is a node the rank of which is x, and the ranks are numbered from left to right. Figure 1(i) shows the communication of nodes with their adjacent nodes at the first step. For example, node 2 sends its sub-results to its adjacent nodes, i.e., node 1 and 3, and receives 1 and 3 from them. At the second communication step (ii), having 1 and 3, it sends 3 to node 1 and 1 to node 3 and receives 2 and 4. Finally (iii), it sends only 4 to node 1 and receives 5 from node 3.

In a DP step a, the number of $F(v, A)$'s is $n \cdot \binom{n-1}{a}$ and the number of $Q^A(M(A))$'s is $\binom{n}{a}$, denoted by F_a and Q_a, respectively. In our algorithm, $F(v, A)$ and $Q^A(M(A))$ are numbered as in Tamada et al.'s algorithm (see [15] for details) and are distributed uniformly to a node. Thus, the total number of

$F(v, A)$'s and $Q^A(M(A))$'s that an i-th rank node stores is calculated by the function $Data_N(a, i)$

$$Data_N(a, i) = Ceil_N(F_a, i) + Ceil_N(Q_a, i),$$
$$\text{where } Ceil_N(x, i) = \begin{cases} \frac{x}{N} + 1 & (i < (x \bmod N)) \\ \frac{x}{N} & (\text{otherwise}) \end{cases}.$$

The sub-results stored at the i-th rank node, in a DP step $a + 1$, are $[Ceil_N(F_a, i), Ceil_N(F_a, i+1))$-th $F(v, A)$'s and $[Ceil_N(Q_a, i), Ceil_N(Q_a, i+1))$-th $Q^A(M(A))$'s. Thus, the rank of the node that originally stores the k-th value out of F_a, denoted $rank\_has(k)$, can be calculated as

$$rank\_has(k) = \begin{cases} \frac{k}{(q+1)} & (k < (q+1) \cdot r) \\ r + \frac{k-(q+1)\cdot r}{q} & (\text{otherwise}) \end{cases},$$
$$\text{where } q = \frac{F_a}{N} \text{ and } r = F_a \bmod N.$$

The data that the i-th rank node receives from the right (left) node at the break k-th communication step are originally located at the node, the rank of which is $i+k$ $(i-k)$ (mod N). Therefore, if a node computes a list of nodes that stores the required sub-results in advance, it can determine immediately whether the data received from its adjacent nodes include the sub-results required to compute the new results or not. Hence, by this algorithm, a node have to communicate only with its adjacent nodes and as a result no data congestion occurs.

3.2 Memory Complexity for Communication

As shown in the previous subsection, the algorithm performs bi-directional communications to exchange sub-results. Because of these bi-directional communications, a node needs four communication buffers: two receive and two send buffers. Additionally, two buffers are also needed for sub-results and new results. After a node sends its sub-results, however, it does not need to keep them. Thus, these buffers can be used as communication buffers at the next step. Therefore, the algorithm requires five buffers in total, which we call the first strategy. The size of one buffer is equal to the maximum amount of sub-results that a single node may store, that is, $\max_{a,i} Data_N(a, i)$. Figure 2 shows how to use these five buffers, from buffer 0 to buffer 4. First (i), a buffer, here buffer 0, holds its sub-results. The node sends data in buffer 0 to both the adjacent nodes. Simultaneously, it receives data from both the adjacent nodes. In this example, buffers 2 and 3 are used for this purpose. The new results calculated in this node are stored at buffer 4. At the next communication step (ii), buffers 2 and 3 become send buffers, which store the data received at the first communication step. At this step, the receive buffers are buffers 0 and 1. Then (iii), buffers 0 and 1 become send buffers, and buffers 2 and 3 become receive buffers. At the later communication steps, the functions of the buffers switch between (ii) and (iii).

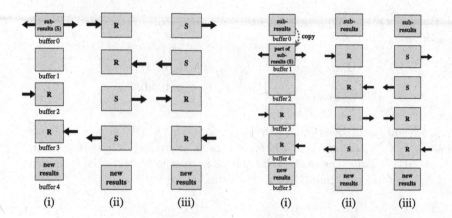

Fig. 2. Use of five buffers (first strategy). The five boxes are buffers, where S is a send buffer and R is a receive buffer.

Fig. 3. Use of six buffers in divided communication (second strategy). The six boxes are buffers, where S is a send buffer and R is a receive buffer.

For solving large problems, the main bottleneck is the memory requirement. The size of the buffers for sub-results and new results cannot be reduced. On the other hand, the communication buffers can be reduced, as a node sends not all the sub-results but the part of them. We call this memory reducing method *divided communication* and a divided part of communication in a DP step a *communication piece*. For example, if we split sub-results into three pieces, the size of a communication buffer is reduced to one third while the number of communication pieces in a DP step increases to three. The more the number of communication pieces increases, the smaller is the communication buffer size. Unlike in the first strategy, however, the fixed buffer for its sub-results is necessary, because a node sends them in the second or later communication pieces. Thus, there are six buffers: two buffers for sub-results and results, and four communication buffers, the size of which depends on the number of communication pieces. We call this the second strategy. Figure 3 shows how these six buffers are used. At the beginning of each communication piece (i), a node copies a part of its sub-results to a send buffer. The transition of buffer usages is the same as in the first strategy (ii, iii). The memory usages of the first and second strategy, denoted by Mem_{fir} and Mem_{sec}, respectively, are

$$Mem_{fir} = 5 \cdot D \quad and \quad Mem_{sec} = 2 \cdot D + 4 \cdot \frac{D}{C},$$

where C is the number of communication pieces and $D = \max_{a,i} Data_N(a, i)$. The size of the communication buffers should be as large as possible and a node should perform the minimum number of communication pieces. The number of communication pieces varies dynamically depending on a. For instance, it can be smaller when a is small or large. This is because the number of communication pieces increases linearly with the amount of sub-results, and the amount of sub-results is a sum of F_a and Q_a, each of which is a convex function of a. The maximum size of Mem_{sec} is the size of the available memory. Therefore, we can calculate the number of communication pieces as

$$C = \left\lceil \frac{4D}{M - 2D} \right\rceil, \tag{5}$$

where M is the size of the available memory. Based on this equation, the algorithm uses a different number of communication pieces for each DP step, where $D = \max_{a,i} Data_N(a, i)$ and a is fixed to the DP step a.

3.3   Disadvantage of Algorithm on 1D Torus Network

The algorithm has a disadvantage on a 1D torus network, the cost of synchronization is high. In the 1D torus network algorithm, a node refers to sub-results in send buffers to calculate new results during a communication step. At the next communication step, a send buffer becomes a receive buffer and then the old sub-results in the send buffer are overwritten by the received new sub-results. Thus, a node must block the next communication until the calculations using the sub-results in the send buffers are completed. Figure 4 shows the situation where such a blocking occurs. When node 2 is calculating the new results from the sub-results in its send buffers (i, ii), its adjacent nodes, here nodes 1 and 3, cannot send to node 2 at the next communication step. Furthermore, since

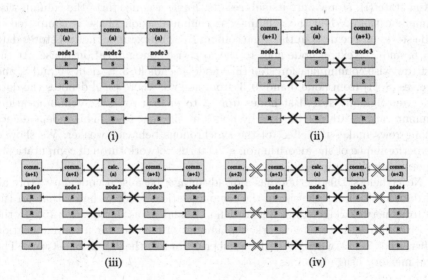

Fig. 4. Situation where blocking occurs. The yellow boxes 0, 1, and so on are computational nodes. The blue boxes below them are their communication buffers. Black crosses represent the first blocking and white crosses the secondary blockings. (Color figure online)

node 1 cannot complete the next communication step because of node 2's block-ing (iii, iv), node 0 cannot perform the communication with node 1 at the next communication step, and the same blocking also occurs between nodes 3 and 4. That is, blockings are propagated. The data of the effect of this blocking on the scalability to the number of processors are shown in Sect. 4. To overcome this disadvantage, we extend the algorithm to a 2D torus network.

3.4 Algorithm on 2D Torus Network

A 2D torus network can be represented by $H \times W$, where H is the number of rows and W is the number of columns. Thus, $N = H \cdot W$. In this paper, the shape of 2D torus network is also denoted by "height" and "width," correspond-ing to the number of rows and columns, respectively. The algorithm extended to a 2D torus network consists of column-wise and row-wise communication phases. Basically, the method is almost the same as the 1D torus network algorithm. It is different point in that, in the column-wise communication phase, a node commu-nicates as Allgather between nodes in the same column without any calculation. Note that, in our implementation, because a node communicates as in the 1D torus network method, it is guaranteed that no data congestion occurs. After a column-wise communication phase, nodes in the same column share the same set of data. Next, a node performs a row-wise communication. During the row-wise communication phase, a node communicates only within the same row and calculates intermediate results as in the 1D torus network algorithm. Figure 5 shows the communication schemes in the 4×4 2D torus network. A node, in the initial state (i), stores only its sub-results. First, a node starts the column-wise communication. When the column-wise communication phase is completed, a node stores all the data in the same column (ii). For example, node 4 stores data $4, 5, 6$, and 7. Next, a node goes to the row-wise communication phase. At the first row-wise communication step (iii), node 4 sends $[0, 3]$ to nodes 0 and 8, and receives $[8, 11]$ from node 0 and $[0, 3]$ from node 8, where $[x, y]$ denotes the data that are originally stored at nodes from x to y. In a row-wise communication, communications are not blocked by nodes in different rows. This independence among rows makes the effect of the synchronous behavior weaker. We showed the performance of the algorithm on a 2D torus network through computational experiments shown in Sect. 4.

Nevertheless, this method has a disadvantage: because a node must store all the data in a column, the size of the communication buffers is larger than for the 1D torus network algorithm. Let us define D and M as in Equation (5). In the algorithm on a 2D torus network, the amount of memory for a communication buffer needs $H \cdot D$, where H is the number of rows of the 2D torus network. The total memory usage becomes

$$Mem_{sec} = 2 \cdot D + 4 \cdot \frac{HD}{C},$$

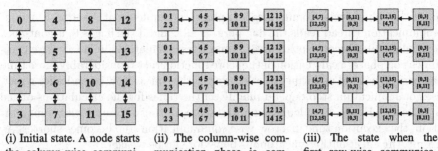

(i) Initial state. A node starts the column-wise communication.

(ii) The column-wise communication phase is complete. Next, a node starts the row-wise communication.

(iii) The state when the first row-wise communication step is complete.

Fig. 5. Communication on a 2D torus network. A box is a computational node, a number x represents the data that node x stores originally, and $[x, y]$ represents the data that are originally stored in node i, where $x \leq i \leq y$. For simplicity, the edges between both end nodes are omitted from the figures.

and then the number of communication pieces is

$$C = \left\lceil \frac{4HD}{M - 2D} \right\rceil.$$

That is, the number of communication pieces is H times than the first strategy. We analyze the relationships between the number of communication pieces and an execution time in Sect. 4.

3.5 Improvement with Multithread Programming

Although we already distribute score calculations to nodes, we further distribute them to CPU cores on a single node. Recent processors have multicores and support multithread programming. If the i-th rank node is able to execute k threads, its j-th thread deals with $Ceil_k(Data_N(a, i), j)$ score calculations. A further improvement in multithread programming can be realized in communications. The communication between nodes can be performed by a single, fixed thread. We call this thread a *communication thread* and all the other threads *non-communication threads*. In a column-wise communication phase, since a node only have to store the received data and does not calculate or update, non-communication threads are idle and wait until the column-wise communication phase is completed. Because initial scores, $s(v, A, X)$, can be computed without sub-results, non-communication threads can calculate them during a column-wise communication phase. Since the time required to complete all the initial score calculations may be longer than a column-wise communication phase, non-communication threads need to determine whether the communication is completed during their calculations. We employ the following simple solution for this problem. We introduce a flag that allows only the communication thread to change its value. The flag is set to 0 before the column-wise communication phase and, if the column-wise communication phase is completed, it is set to 1. A non-communication thread reads the flag periodically, and if the flag is 0, it continues to calculate initial scores; otherwise it completes calculations. In a row-wise communication phase, a calculation of the score function takes considerably more time than comparing and updating. In other words, the times spent by nodes for a row-wise communication step depend mainly on the times for the calculations of the initial scores. Hence, by calculating initial scores during a column-wise communication, the execution time in a row-wise communication step becomes shorter. As a result, the effect of the synchronous behavior can be weaker.

4   Computational Experiments

In the computational experiments, we applied our algorithm to the optimal Bayesian network search problem. We adopted the Bayesian Dirichlet equivalence (BDe) score [8] as a score function. The BDe score calculation time increases linearly with the number of samples in the observed data, denoted by m. The input data for the experiments are generated randomly from the random DAGs. The conditional probabilities of the variables are also assigned at random. The amount of required memory depends not on the number of edges, but vertices. Moreover, because our algorithm is dynamic programming, the number of edges does not affect the execution time.

TRPOS has various parameters, such as the number of nodes (N), the shape of the 2D torus network (H, W), the number of communication pieces, and the problem size (n, m). Moreover, some parameters depend on each other, e.g., the number of columns and the number of communication pieces). Therefore, we need to analyze the relationships between these parameters. First, we confirm that the synchronous behavior has in fact occurred, which is the motivation of the novel 2D communication method. Next, we analyze the relationships between the parameters when no divided communication occurs. Finally, we analyze them when divided communication occurs. In this section, we call our proposed method for a 1D torus network and for a 2D torus network *TRPOS-1D* and *TRPOS-2D*, respectively.

We implemented our algorithm in C programming language (ISO C99). The parallelization was implemented using OpenMP and MPI. We used a Fujitsu FX10 supercomuputer system installed at the Information Technology Center, the University of Tokyo [2]. Fujitsu C/C++ Compiler 1.2.1 is installed and supports OpenMP 3.0 and MPI-2.2. The node consists of a single SPARC 64™ IXfx CPU (16 cores per CPU, 1.848 GHz) and 32 GiB memory [1]. They are connected to each other with a DDR InfiniBand and construct the Tofu 6D torus network; the link throughput is 5.0 GBytes/s. The interconnect provides a 3D torus network as the user view. The number of nodes is 4800 and thus the number of cores is 76,800. Although users are in general allowed to use fewer than 1440 nodes, there are several opportunities in a year when we can use all the nodes as a result of competitive applications. The time limitation for a single job is 24 h. Because the nodes must be used effectively, the system bans the alocation of fewer than 72 nodes when its shape is 2D torus. Thus, we used from 81 nodes to 1440 nodes to conduct experiments on the algorithms and won an opportunity to use all the nodes to attempt to solve an instance of 36 vertices.

4.1 Synchronous Behavior

Before analyzing the results of our experiments, we confirmed that the synchronous behavior in fact occurs as explained in Sect. 3.3. To ensure this, we executed TRPOS-1D in the case where $n = 25$ and $m = 200$. Each node recorded the time when a node completed each communication step (*end time*). In our implementation for this experiment, the time was measured by the *gettimeofday* function in the standard C library. For simplicity, we tested the case where a single-directional communication does not occur, that is, N is odd (here, 19 and 37). Table 1 shows the relative end times in the specified DP step $a = 11$, where all the end times are subtracted from the minimum end time and $N = 19$. Because no first communication is blocked and thus receiving is performed efficiently, the first end time does not depend on the adjacent node. It depends rather on the execution time of the score calculations from the sub-results the node originally has. The first end time ($i = 0$) of node 0 was the latest time among all the first end times (4.04 s). The second communications of the adjacent nodes of node 0, here, nodes 1 and 18, were blocked, and therefore, these second end times became greater (both 4.26 s). The third communications of the nodes at distance 2 from node 0, nodes 2 and 17, were blocked, and therefore these third end times became greater (both 4.29 s). In the later communication steps, similar communication blockings occurred. We clearly observed that synchronous behavior occurred and the delay caused by this was propagated. Note that the first end time of node 13 was also delayed, and we can observe that the propagation of the delay by node 13 occurred.

Table 1. Relative end times (s) of each communication step (i = 0–8) for DP step a = 11 in the case where N = 19, n = 25, and m = 200. To change the measured absolute times to relative times, the minimum time among them (i = 0, node 5) was subtracted from these times. The gray boxes represent the propagation of blocking by nodes 0 and 13.

node	0	1	2	3	4	5	6	7	8	9	10	11	12	13	14	15	16	17	18
i = 0	4.04	3.21	1.83	1.19	0.68	0.00	0.39	0.41	0.86	0.62	0.57	1.98	1.98	3.87	3.55	2.58	2.00	2.07	3.21
1	4.26	4.26	3.43	1.95	1.39	0.87	0.58	1.00	1.00	1.01	2.17	2.17	4.11	4.11	4.12	3.76	2.70	3.23	4.26
2	4.30	4.29	4.29	3.45	1.98	1.43	1.06	1.06	1.06	2.19	2.19	4.14	4.14	4.14	4.14	4.14	3.78	4.29	4.30
3	4.34	4.34	4.31	4.30	3.47	2.01	1.44	1.08	2.21	2.21	4.16	4.16	4.16	4.16	4.17	4.17	4.32	4.32	4.34
4	4.37	4.36	4.35	4.33	4.33	3.48	2.02	2.23	2.23	4.18	4.18	4.18	4.18	4.19	4.19	4.34	4.34	4.36	4.37
5	4.40	4.40	4.38	4.37	4.34	4.34	3.51	2.25	4.20	4.21	4.21	4.21	4.21	4.36	4.36	4.38	4.38	4.39	
6	4.43	4.43	4.41	4.40	4.39	4.36	4.36	4.22	4.22	4.22	4.23	4.23	4.23	4.38	4.38	4.40	4.40	4.41	4.43
7	4.46	4.46	4.45	4.43	4.42	4.41	4.38	4.38	4.24	4.25	4.25	4.25	4.39	4.40	4.41	4.42	4.43	4.45	4.46
8	4.49	4.49	4.48	4.47	4.45	4.44	4.44	4.40	4.40	4.28	4.28	4.40	4.43	4.43	4.45	4.45	4.47	4.47	4.49

Table 2. Maximum and minimum time difference (s) for DP step a

N	19		37		N	19		37		N	19		37	
	min.	max.	min.	max.		min.	max.	min.	max.		min.	max.	min.	max.
$a = 1$	0.0027	0.1035	0.0015	0.1099	9	0.3587	2.4676	0.0887	1.8479	17	0.1344	0.4175	0.0754	0.1843
2	0.0023	0.0028	0.0016	0.0019	10	0.13	3.5564	0.1727	2.6526	18	0.0469	0.1852	0.0363	0.0876
3	0.0027	0.003	0.0014	0.0022	11	0.2137	4.0431	0.209	2.6777	19	0.0318	0.0689	0.0178	0.0402
4	0.0022	0.005	0.0047	0.0071	12	0.2852	3.6019	0.1674	2.4778	20	0.0056	0.0371	0.008	0.0185
5	0.0099	0.0297	0.0017	0.0292	13	0.7306	2.7775	0.0813	1.5643	21	0.0033	0.0085	0.0025	0.0085
6	0.0739	0.17	0.0718	0.1544	14	0.6636	2.1689	0.09	0.8801	22	0.0021	0.0043	0.0021	0.003
7	0.2015	0.5682	0.1086	0.4481	15	0.5604	1.4716	0.1172	0.4936	23	0.0021	0.0029	0.002	0.0027
8	0.373	1.4565	0.1508	1.0898	16	0.3055	0.9018	0.0948	0.3244	24	0.0022	0.0027	0.0016	0.0021
										25	0.0021	0.0027	0.0014	0.002

Next, we analyze the synchronous behavior when the number of processors increases. We call the difference between the minimum and maximum of the end times in a communication step the *time difference*. For instance, in Table 1, the time difference of the last communication step was 0.21 s (= 4.49 − 4.28). By the synchronous behavior, the time difference of the last communication step decreased as compared to that of the first communication step. The maximum (minimum) time difference for a DP step a is the time difference that is the greatest (smallest) among those for communication steps in a DP step a. For instance, in Table 1, the maximum time difference is the first one (4.04 s) and the minimum time difference is the last one (0.21 s). Table 2 shows the maximum and minimum time difference for each DP step a in the case where $N = 19$ and 37. Similar synchronous behavior also occurred in the case of 37 nodes. The maximum time differences for DP step a decreased, because the number of score calculations that a single node peformed decreased. However, these ratios (e.g., $0.74 = 2.65/3.55$ in $a = 10$) were greater than 0.51 (= 19/37). That is, the effect of the synchronous behavior did not scale. Hence, the execution of a DP step does not scale because of communication blockings. This is the main factor that caused the scalability of TRPOS-1D to be not good scalability. We show its scalability in the next subsection.

4.2   No Divided Communication

We compared the execution times of Tamada et al.'s algorithm [15], TRPOS-1D, and TRPOS-2D, in the case where no divided communication occurs. Tamada et al.'s algorithm is also based on Ott et al.'s algorithm [14]. Their algorithm uses point-to-point communications, and therefore, data congestion may occur. Table 3(a) shows the execution times of the algorithms in the case where $n = 28, m = 200$, and N is from 81 to 1296 (i.e., from 1296 to 20,736 cores). Using 81 nodes, Tamada et al.'s method, TRPOS-1D, and TRPOS-2D took 2992.8, 1450.6, and 1169.0 s, respectively. Table 4 and Fig. 6 show a comparison of the scalabilities as compared to the 1296-core run. The relative speedups of 1296 nodes as compared to the 81 nodes run were 2.11, 7.21, and 12.89 respectively, while the ideal relative speedup is 16.0. We can conclude, from these results, that

Table 3. Execution times (s) in the case where $n = 28$ and $m = 200, 1000$

(a) $m = 200$

Tamada et al.'s algo. ($n = 28, m = 200$)				
$N = 81$	162	324	648	1296
2922.8	2498.8	1917.2	1426.6	1387.2

TRPOS-1D ($n = 28, m = 200$)				
$N = 81$	162	324	648	1296
1450.6	760.3	428.6	298.4	201.2

TRPOS-2D ($n = 28, m = 200$)		
$W = 9$	18	36
$H = 9$ 1169.0	591.8	305.5
18 595.6	303.8	161.4
36 308.5	161.5	90.7

(b) $m = 1000$

TRPOS-2D ($n = 28, m = 1000$)		
$W = 9$	18	36
$H = 9$ 4811.1	2413.1	1217.4
18 2414.1	1214.6	619.2
36 1222.3	619.8	319.5

the proposed methods (TRPOS-1D and TRPOS-2D) are much faster and more scalable than Tamada et al.'s algorithm. Furthermore, as compared to TRPOS-1D, TRPOS-2D is faster and more scalable. TRPOS-1D is equal to executing TRPOS-2D in the case where $H = 1$ and $W = N$. Thus, the shape of the nodes affected the execution times and scalabilities. However, if the difference between the height and width was not very large, the execution times were not affected dramatically by its shape (see the execution times of TRPOS-2D, $18 \times 18, 9 \times 36$, and 36×9 in Table 3(a)). Table 3(b) shows the execution times of TRPOS-2D in the case where $n = 28$ and $m = 1000$. In our proposed algorithm, we mainly parallelized the score calculations. If the ratio of the execution times of score calculations to all the execution times is large, the parallelization efficiency increases from the perspective of Amdahl's law. Because of this, the relative speedup of the case where $m = 1000$ was better than that where $m = 200$ (15.06 vs 12.89, Table 4). Hence, although the relative speedup decreased when the number of cores increased in the case where $n = 28$ and $m = 200$, we can expect to obtain a good relative speedup if the problem size is much larger. TRPOS-2D achieved a parallelization efficiency of 0.94 ($= 15.06/16$) as compared to 1296 cores run in the case where $n = 28$ and $m = 1000$ and its scalability was almost linear up to 20,736 cores. These results show that our algorithm maintains good efficiency with many cores. This is a significant improvement as compared to the previous research results, where the scalability was ensured only up to 2048 cores. We can expect that our algorithm is scalable with a still larger number of cores. However, for the reason described above, we could not conduct experiments of the algorithms with more cores.

We show the relationships between the execution times and the problem sizes. As our parallel algorithm is based on a $O(n \cdot 2^n)$ algorithm, the execution times will increase exponentially if the number of nodes is fixed. Table 5 shows the execution times and the relative execution time ratios for $n = 25\text{–}30$ of TRPOS-2D when N is 324 ($= 18 \times 18$). As the problem size increased, the gap between the observed and the ideal times based on the computational complexity became larger. For example, in the case where $m = 200$, the relative execution time ratios as compared to $n = 25$ was 9.50 for $n = 28$, although the ideal is $8.96(= 28 \cdot 2^{28}/(25 \cdot 2^{25}))$. Furthermore, in most problem sizes, the relative execution time ratios of the case where $m = 200$ were smaller than that of the case where $m = 1000$. For example, in the case where $n = 30$, the relative

Table 4. Relative speedups as compared to 81 nodes (1296 cores) run for problem size $n = 28$

	$N = 81$	162	324	648	1296
Tamada et al.'s algo	1.00	1.17	1.52	2.05	2.11
TRPOS-1D	1.00	1.91	3.38	4.86	7.21
TRPOS-2D ($m = 200$)	1.00	1.98	3.85	7.24	12.89
TRPOS-2D ($m = 1000$)	1.00	1.99	3.96	7.77	15.06
ideal speedup	1.00	2.00	4.00	8.00	16.00

Table 5. Execution times (s) in the case where $n = 25$–$30, m = 200, 1000$, and $N = 324 (18 \times 18)$.

n	$m = 200$	$m = 1000$	Ideal
25	31.9(1.00)	116.8(1.00)	1.00
26	66.3(2.08)	241.8(2.07)	2.08
27	146.2(4.58)	581.2(4.98)	4.32
28	303.1(9.50)	1217.4(10.42)	8.96
29	632.2(19.82)	2592.4(22.20)	18.56
30	1365.2(42.80)	5944.7(50.90)	38.40

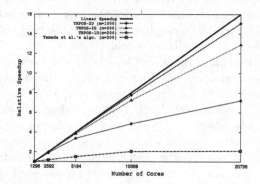

Fig. 6. Relative speedups as compared to the 1296 ($= 9 \times 9 \times 16$) cores run. N is from 81 to 1296 (i.e., from 1296 to 20,736 cores).

execution time ratios were 42.8 for $m = 200$ and 50.9 for $m = 1000$, whereas its ideal ratio is 38.4 ($= 30 \cdot 2^{30}/25 \cdot 2^{25}$). This is because the time to calculate a single score increased, and then, the differences in execution times between nodes increased.

4.3 Divided Communication

As mentioned in Sect. 3, TRPOS-2D must process more communication pieces than TRPOS-1D. Since processing more communication pieces causes a longer execution time, a trade-off exists between the execution time and the number of communication pieces. In order to observe the amount of overhead incurred by the divided communication, we conducted the following two experiments. In Ex. I, the total size of all the communication buffers (M) was limited to between 100 MBytes and 1600 MBytes. Because the divided communication and the synchronous behavior in TRPOS-1D is similar to that in TRPOS-2D, we executed TRPOS-2D in Ex. I. In Ex. II, M was fixed to 100 MBytes, and we executed TRPOS-1D and TRPOS-2D, increasing the number of nodes. By increasing the number of nodes, we can also observe the effects on the scalability. In the case where no divided communication occurs, the execution time and scalability of

TRPOS-2D is better than that of TRPOS-1D. We can determine the trade-off between the inherent scalability and divided communications through Ex. II. In both experiments, we set $n = 26$ and $m = 200$.

Table 6 shows the results of Ex. I. Table 6(a) shows the execution times and the number of communication pieces for DP step a. The number of communication pieces is a convex function of a. The execution times increased when divided communications occurred. However, in our distributed system, the pure time for communications did not increase as a result of divided communication (data are not shown in this paper). In other words, if the size of the data that a node sends is not changed, no communications overhead is incurred as a result of divided communications. To confirm the reason for the increase in execution times, we focused on a specified DP step. Table 6(b) shows the time taken for each communication piece in the case of DP step $a = 10$ in this experiment. When no divided communication occurred (800 and 1600 MBytes), the execution time for $a = 10$ was approximately 21 s. When divided communication occurred, the execution times for $a = 10$ were much more than 21 s, e.g., 47 s. Table 6(c) shows the number of score calculations that nodes in the first row (i.e., nodes $0, 9, \cdots, 72$) performed in each communication piece of DP step $a = 10$, where the size of the communication buffers was 100 MBytes. According to the table, the number of score calculations processed in a communication piece differed among nodes. This is because the required sub-results are received separately for each divide communication piece. The number of calculations that a single node needs to perform for DP step $a = 10$ is 1,049,230 or 1,049,231 ($= F_{10} = 26 \cdot \binom{25}{10}/81$ ($+1$)). Note that, by executing the score calculations in the column-wise phase, the number of score calculations shown in Table 6(c) decreased. Because of the synchronous behavior, the end time of each communication piece was nearly the latest node in the same row. Moreover, the next communication piece is also

Table 6. Results of Ex. I. M is limited to several sizes and N is 81 ($= 9 \times 9$). (a) Execution times (s) and the number of communication pieces for DP step a. (b) Time (s) taken for each communication piece, denoted by i, in a DP step $a = 10$. (c) Number of score calculations that nodes in the first row performed in each communication piece of DP step $a = 10$ when M is 100 MBytes. Gray boxes represent the maximum of score calculations in each communication piece.

(a)

a = 1–8	100 MB	200	400	800	1600
1–8	1	1	1	1	1
9	3	2	1	1	1
10	5	3	2	1	1
11	8	4	2	1	1
12	11	6	3	2	1
13	13	7	4	2	1
14	14	7	4	2	1
15	13	7	4	2	1
16	10	5	3	2	1
17	7	4	2	1	1
18	4	2	1	1	1
19	2	1	1	1	1
20–26	1	1	1	1	1
Exe. time	802.86	555.80	438.37	344.17	256.43

(b)

$i = 1$	100 MB	200	400	800	1600
1	15.8	17.79	23.75	21.05	21.03
2	9.84	11.75	7.21		
3	10.92	5.51			
4	8.12				
5	2.97				
Sum	47.65	35.05	30.96	21.05	21.03

(c)

	$i = 1$	2	3	4	5
node 0	768087	248559	30253	0	0
9	485327	218874	332175	11877	0
18	602167	227841	0	196573	21415
27	629395	260639	158086	0	0
36	383845	478329	186257	0	0
45	608251	188436	0	251481	0
54	468857	419589	134653	0	25008
63	501232	170881	166752	206732	0
72	595917	142363	232512	74560	0

Table 7. Execution times for problem size $n = 26$ when M is 100 MBytes and N is from 81 to 1296 (i.e., from 1296 to 20,736 cores). The sum of the number of communication pieces is shown in the parentheses.

	$9 \times 9(81)$	$9 \times 18(162)$	$18 \times 18(324)$	$18 \times 36(648)$	$36 \times 36(1296)$
TRPOS-1D	407.9[31]	166.0[26]	99.6[26]	72.1[26]	45.9[26]
TRPOS-2D	803.5[105]	301.3[63]	149.1[63]	65.8[42]	35.9[42]

blocked by the latest node in the same column that may process the previous communication piece. Therefore, when the divided communication occurs, the execution time depends on the sum of the maximum calculations in each communication piece. In the case where M is 100 MBytes (show in Table 6(c)), it is 1,855,080 ($= 768,087 + \cdots + 25,008$). On the other hand, if no divided communication occurs (800 and 1600 MBytes), it is at most 1,049,231 ($= F_a$). Hence, the factor that caused the execution time to increase was the deviation in the number of score calculations that a node performs in a communication piece.

Next, we analyze the results of Ex. II. Table 7 shows the execution times and the sum of the number of communication pieces in the entire algorithm in this experiment. Since a node communicates at least once in each DP step, the total number of communication pieces becomes n when no divided communication occurs. TRPOS-1D did not perform divided communication with more than 162 nodes for $n = 26$. In comparison, in TRPOS-2D, the divided communication always occurred. Figure 7 shows the execution times in Ex. II. TRPOS-2D maintained good scalability even if divided communication occurred. The execution time of TRPOS-2D decreased more than the linear scale when the width increased. For example, when N increased from 81 to 162 by doubling the width ($8 \rightarrow 16$), 803.5 s became 301.3 s. This more than linear speedup is because the amount of data stored in a column depends on the width. If the width increased, the data stored in a column decreased, and then, the number of communication pieces decreased. Because of the overhead of the divided communications, TRPOS-2D was slower than TRPOS-1D when the number of cores was small. However, because the inherent scalability of TRPOS-2D was better and the number of communication pieces decreased, the gap between them became smaller as the number of nodes increased, and finally, TRPOS-2D took a shorter time than TRPOS-1D with 1296 nodes.

Finally, we attempted to solve a large size problem. For searching for a much larger size of DAGs, since a huge amount of memory is required, it is necessary to execute the algorithm with more nodes. Therefore, TRPOS-2D would be faster that TRPOS-1D in solving larger problem sizes. We assumed that TRPOS-2D is able to solve the instance for $n = 36$ and $m = 200$ within the limited of 24 h with 76,800 cores. As a result, we succeeded in solving it by using TRPOS-2D in 11 h 38 m with 76,800 ($= 60 \times 80 \times 16$) cores. This is a significant improvement in the size of the problem solved, because the largest size solved previously was 33 [13].

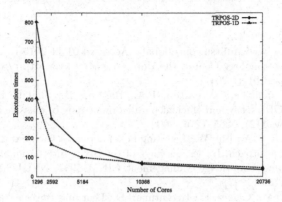

Fig. 7. Execution times (s) in the case where $n = 26$ when M is 100 MBytes. N is from 81 to 1296 (i.e., from 1296 to 20,736 cores).

5   Conclusion

In this paper, we presented a novel parallel algorithm to search for the optimal DAG structure. A torus network is adopted in many distributed systems, and therefore, an algorithm that runs efficiently on them is very important. Our algorithm was developed such that it would be able to run efficiently on torus network distributed systems and we confirmed that its scalability is in fact good and it scales up to 20,736 cores. Our results showed that our algorithm is scalable up to more than ten times as many cores as the existing algorithms. This is important, because the number of cores in distributed systems is increasing and the situation where more than twenty thousand cores are used is becoming common. We also succeeded in solving an instance of 36 vertices without any constraints, which is the largest solved size reported in the literature. Our core idea is that a node communicates with only its adjacent nodes on a distributed system. It enables computational nodes to communicate without any congestion, and as a result, our algorithm runs very efficiently. Since the communication on distributed systems is a major bottleneck of the distributed algorithm, such algorithms developed for distributed systems having a specific topology are becoming increasingly important.

Although we used a 3D torus network system, our algorithm can run on a 2D torus network system. Clearly, we can extend our idea to a 3D torus network. The 3D torus network algorithm further divides the column-wise communication into two dimensions. It enables column-wise communication to be more independent, and therefore the algorithm can be expected to be more efficient and more scalable. Implementation of the 3D torus network algorithm remains further research for the future when a considerably larger distributed system becomes available.

References

1. Fujitsu. http://www.fujitsu.com/global/. Accessed 01 11 2015
2. Information Technology Center, the University of Tokyo. http://www.cc.u-tokyo. ac.jp/. Accessed 01 11 2015
3. Chaiken, R., Jenkins, B., Larson, P.A., Ramsey, B., Shakib, D., Weaver, S., Zhou, J.: SCOPE: easy and efficient parallel processing of massive data sets. Proc. VLDB Endow. 1(2), 1265–1276 (2008)
4. Cheng, J., Bell, D.A., Liu, W.: Learning belief networks from data: an information theory based approach. In: Proceedings of the Sixth International Conference on Information and Knowledge Management CIKM 1997, NY, USA, pp. 325–331. ACM, New York (1997)
5. Chickering, D.M., Geiger, D., Heckerman, D.: Learning Bayesian networks is NP-Hard. Technical report, Citeseer (1994)
6. Friedman, N., Goldszmidt, M.: Learning Bayesian networks with local structure. In: Jordan, M.I. (ed.) Learning in Graphical Models, vol. 89, pp. 421–459. Springer, Netherlands (1998)
7. Friedman, N., Linial, M., Nachman, I., Pe'er, D.: Using Bayesian networks to analyze expression data. J. Comput. Biol. 7(3–4), 601–620 (2000)
8. Heckerman, D., Geiger, D., Chickering, D.M.: Learning Bayesian networks: the combination of knowledge and statistical data. Mach. Learn. 20(3), 197–243 (1995)
9. Imoto, S., Goto, T., Miyano, S.: Estimation of genetic networks and functional structures between genes by using Bayesian networks and nonparametric regression. In: Pacific symposium on Biocomputing, vol. 7, pp. 175–186. World Scientific (2002)
10. Italiano, G.F.: Finding paths and deleting edges in directed acyclic graphs. Inf. Process. Lett. 28(1), 5–11 (1988)
11. Kramer, R., Gupta, R., Soffa, M.L.: The combining DAG: a technique for parallel data flow analysis. IEEE Trans. Parallel Distrib. Syst. 5(8), 805–813 (1994)
12. Lecca, P.: Methods of biological network inference for reverse engineering cancer chemoresistance mechanisms. Drug Discov. Today 19(2), 151–163 (2014). http://www.sciencedirect.com/science/article/pii/S1359644613003930, system Biology
13. Nikolova, O., Zola, J., Aluru, S.: Parallel globally optimal structure learning of Bayesian networks. J. Parallel Distrib. Comput. 73(8), 1039–1048 (2013)
14. Ott, S., Imoto, S., Miyano, S.: Finding optimal models for small gene networks. In: Pacific Symposium on Biocomputing. vol. 9, pp. 557–567. World Scientific (2004)
15. Tamada, Y., Imoto, S., Miyano, S.: Parallel algorithm for learning optimal Bayesian network structure. J. Mach. Learn. Res. 12, 2437–2459 (2011)

Bin Recycling Strategy for an Accuracy-Aware Implementation of Two-Point Angular Correlation Function on GPU

Miguel Cárdenas-Montes[1]([✉]), Juan José Rodríguez-Vázquez[1],
Miguel A. Vega-Rodríguez[2], Ignacio Sevilla Noarbe[1],
and Antonio Gómez-Iglesias[3]

[1] Department of Fundamental Research,
Centro de Investigaciones Energéticas Medioambientales y Tecnológicas,
Madrid, Spain
{miguel.cardenas,jj.rodriguez,ignacio.sevilla}@ciemat.es
[2] Department of Technologies of Computers and Communications,
University of Extremadura, ARCO Research Group, Cáceres, Spain
mavega@unex.es
[3] Texas Advanced Computing Center, The University of Texas at Austin,
Austin, TX, USA
agomez@tacc.utexas.edu

Abstract. Cosmological studies, in particular those relating to the large
scale distribution of galaxies, have to cope with an extraordinary increase
in data volume with the current and upcoming sky surveys. These usually
involve the estimation of N-point correlation functions of galaxy properties. Due to the fact that the correlation functions are based on histogram
construction, they have a high computational cost, which worsens with
the ever growing size of the datasets and the standard sample. At the
same time, correlation functions exhibit a high sensitivity to the accuracy
of the estimation. Therefore, their implementations require maintaining a
high accuracy within a reasonable processing time. GPU computing can
be adopted to overcome the latter problem, but the standard implementation of the histogram construction on GPU lacks the appropriate accuracy for calculating the cosmological correlation functions. In this work,
the *bin recycling strategy* is implemented and evaluated for the estimation of the Two-Point Angular Correlation Function. At the same time
the lack of the appropriate accuracy in the calculation of diverse implementations of histogram construction on GPU is demonstrated. The *bin
recycling strategy* for the Two-Point Angular Correlation Function outperforms other implementations while enabling the processing of a large
number of galaxies. As a consequence of this work, an accuracy-aware
GPU implementation of the Two-Point Angular Correlation Function is
stated and evaluated to assure the correctness of the results.

M. Cárdenas-Montes—The research leading to these results has received funding
by the Spanish Ministry of Economy and Competitiveness (MINECO) for funding
support through the grants FPA2012-30811, FPA2013-47804-C2-1-R, and "Unidad
de Excelencia María de Maeztu": CIEMAT - FÍSICA DE PARTÍCULAS through
the grant MDM-2015-0509.

J. Carretero et al. (Eds.): ICA3PP 2016, LNCS 10048, pp. 503–511, 2016.
DOI: 10.1007/978-3-319-49583-5_38

Keywords: GPU computing · Accuracy · Histogram calculation · Correlation function · Cosmology

1   Introduction

Nowadays many scientific disciplines are generating very large data volumes. In comparison with the previous generation, experiments such as the Dark Energy Survey, or Physics of Accelerated Universe will increase the available data volume in few orders of magnitude. From the point of view of scientific computing in Cosmology, this increment leads to two main barriers: on the one hand, the data have to be analysed within reasonable processing times, and on the other hand, these analyses should be done with the highest precision to produce reliable conclusions.

In Cosmology, the study of the Large-Scale Structure of the Universe can be done through the correlation functions. They encode cosmological information about the mass distribution at different epochs in the history of the Universe, providing constraints to the average matter density and the presence of dark matter and dark energy [1].

One of the most popular tools is the Two-Point Angular Correlation Function (2PACF). Diverse estimators exist for the 2PACF, although the one proposed by [2], (Eq. 1), is the most employed. In any case, all the estimators are based on the construction of histograms, where the number of pairs of galaxies is represented versus the distances between the galaxies.

With the growth of the datasets and the standard sample, and due to the limitations of number representation, an increasing risk of counts loss appears. Two strategies can be implemented to reduce this risk: the reorganization of the kernel flow and the increment of the number of bits in the number representation. It has been demonstrated that the use of larger number representations degrades the processing time [3,4]. On the contrary, the *bin recycling strategy*, which consists of including the sub-histograms accumulation phase in the coincidences calculation part increases the accuracy without degrading the processing time.

In this work, an implementation based on the *bin recycling strategy* is adapted to 2PACF estimation. Previously, it is shown how the standard implementation of histogram construction lacks of the appropriate accuracy to analyse a typical standard sample for large scale structure studies, one million galaxies. The *bin recycling strategy* applied to 2PACF overcomes the lack of accuracy at the same time it does not penalize the performance. To the authors' knowledge, the accuracy and the performance of 2PACF implementations have not been analysed, nor efforts have been done to produce an accuracy-aware implementation.

The rest of the paper is organized as follows: Sect. 2 summarizes the Related Work. The commonalities of the histogram construction on GPU are described in Sect. 3.1. A brief explanation of 2PACF is presented in Sect. 3.2. Weaknesses of floating-point representation are outlined in Sect. 3.3. The Results and the Analysis are shown in Sect. 4. Finally, the Conclusions are presented in Sect. 5.

2   Related Work

Due to the large processing time when analysing large samples, the calculation of the correlation functions in Cosmology has taken advantage of GPU computation. Examples of implementations of correlation functions to GPU computing can be found for 2PACF [5], and shear-shear correlation function [6].

Concerning the floating-point format and its weaknesses, a complete description can be found in [7,8]. In [9], the inexactnesses associated with the use of float representation (operation accuracy and rounding) on GPU, and how the programming affects the final result is presented.

Previous efforts have been performed to improve the accuracy of the construction of histograms on GPU [3]. In this work, the sub-histograms accumulation phase is manipulated to circumvent the limitation of the largest-consecutively-representable integer (see Sect. 3.3). This first attempt evaluates how by moving the accumulation phase—the accumulation of the sub-histograms to create the final histogram—from the global memory of the GPU to the host memory with previous casting to floating-point double precision the accuracy of the final results gets improved.

The *bin recycling strategy* [4] consists of including the sub-histograms accumulation phase on the coincidences calculation phase. By means of this modification, the sub-histograms on shared memory can store the counts in the sub-histograms on global memory—as previously mentioned the accumulation phase has been moved to the host memory—, and then zeroing the bins.

3   Methodology

3.1   Commonalities in the Histogram Construction on GPU

The implementation proposed in [10] is accepted as the most conventional for histogram construction on GPU. Among its positive features, this implementation holds a great flexibility to be adapted to different types of problems, a low complexity which implies that it is easily understandable and adaptable.

The kernel flow of this implementation is as follows. At a given time, each thread is acting on a set of objects. For each pair of objects, the coincidence function is calculated. If the coincidence-value is in the histogram's range, then a count is added in the appropriate bin. For 2PACF, the count-value is the unit, and the coincidence function is the angular-distance between each pair of galaxies. Due to the parallel nature of the GPU architecture, race conditions can be generated. Several threads in a thread block might try to update the number of counts in the same bin. Therefore, an atomic operation for the addition of the count-value is necessary. Concretely the `atomicAdd()` function is required.

In order to increase the degree of parallelism, each thread block has its sub-histogram allocated on shared memory. Threads of different thread blocks act on the number of counts of their own sub-histogram in parallel. If two threads of a thread block update the number of counts of two bins, the atomic function performs the operation in parallel; whereas updates in the same bin are executed sequentially. Once all the coincidences have been calculated and the counts stored in the sub-histograms, they are accumulated in the final histogram on global memory. For this addition, the use of `atomicAdd()` function is also proposed.

Presently, the `atomicAdd()` function is available in 32-bit versions: integer, unsigned integer and floating-point; and 64-bit: unsigned-long-long integer. The absence of an implementation of 64-bit for floating-point representation and the large processing time when using 64-bit integer `atomicAdd()` function have motivated the search of alternative methods for processing large samples.

3.2   The Two-Point Angular Correlation Function

The two-point angular correlation function (2PACF), $\omega(\theta)$, is a computationally intensive function which measures the excess or lack of probability of finding a pair of galaxies separated by a certain angle θ with respect to a random distribution. 2PACF has a computational complexity of $O(N^2)$, where N is the number of galaxies. Although diverse estimators exist for 2PACF, the estimator proposed by [2], (Eq. 1), is the most widely used by cosmologists by virtue of its minimum variance.

$$\omega(\theta) = 1 + \left(\frac{N_{random}}{N_{real}}\right)^2 \cdot \frac{DD(\theta)}{RR(\theta)} - 2 \cdot \frac{N_{random}}{N_{real}} \cdot \frac{DR(\theta)}{RR(\theta)} \tag{1}$$

where

- $DD(\theta)$ is the number of pairs of galaxies for a given angle θ chosen from the observational data catalogue, D, with N_{real} galaxies.
- $RR(\theta)$ is the number of pairs of galaxies for a given angle θ chosen from the random catalogue, R, with N_{random} galaxies.
- $DR(\theta)$ is the number of pairs of galaxies for a given angle θ taking one galaxy from the observational data catalogue D and another from the random catalogue R.

DD, DR and RR are the histograms being constructed in the 2PACF estimation.

3.3   Weaknesses of Floating-Point Representation

By representing figures under the floating-point representation, some limitation on the representation of the figures are assumed. Both simple—32-bit—and double—64-bit—floating-point presentation are limited in the smallest and the largest number representable. Contrary to the integer representation, in floating-point representation not all the integers in the range between the minimum and the maximum number in 32-bit and in 64-bit are representable.

Since in 2PACF the count-value is the unit, the largest-consecutively-representable integer in floating-point representation becomes relevant for the final number of counts accumulated in the most populated bins. In

32-bit floating-point the largest-consecutively-representable integer is 16777216, whereas in 64-bit is 9007199254740992. Considering the kernel flow of the histogram construction on GPU (Sect. 3.1), it is seen that as far as the bins are populated and the number of accumulated counts approaching to the largest-consecutively-representable integer in floating-point, the risk of coincidences loss becomes critical.

This risk implies that once a bin has reached the largest-consecutively-representable integer, the addition of a count in this bin does not produce any increment. Since in most of the cases, the most populated bins can not be predicted, the results are not reliable.

In 2PACF, the kernel goes through all the pairs of galaxies by using a double loop—while-for—. Each thread of a thread block composes the pairs of galaxies executing a for-loop. So that, all the threads of a thread block accumulate the coincidences in their own sub-histogram in shared memory. In our study, a configuration of 64 threads per block is used. If the standard sample size is 10^6 galaxies, then these threads generate 64×10^6 coincidences. This result overflows the largest-consecutively-representable integer in 32-bit floating-point representation.

As was mentioned, the construction of histogram in GPU encompasses two phases: the calculation of the coincidences with the population of the sub-histograms and the accumulation of the sub-histograms in the final histogram.

In the case where each coincidence is signalised with a unit-value and a very large sample size is analysed, the number of coincidences can overflow the largest-consecutively-representable integer. For avoiding this overflow, the *bin recycling strategy* proposes including the accumulation of the sub-histograms in the calculation of the coincidences without waiting the end of this phase [3,4]. The application of the *bin recycling strategy* to 2PACF divides the calculation of the coincidences phase in some parts, accumulating the counts store in an array of sub-histograms on *global memory*, and then resetting to zero the bins of the sub-histograms. Later, the sub-histograms are accumulated in the final histogram on host memory. With the appropriate implementation, this mechanism can avoid reaching the limit of the largest-consecutively-representable integer.

4   Results and Dicussion

All the numerical experiments have been executed in a machine with two Intel Xeon X5570 processors at 2.93 GHz and 8 GB of RAM, and a C2075 NVIDIA GPU card. As an input file one million galaxies coming from the Canada-France-Hawaii Lensing Survey has been used. Nowadays the researchers accept one million galaxies as the usual size of the standard sample in Cosmology.

4.1   Accuracy Analysis

As outlined earlier, an accuracy-aware implementation for 2PACF is the main objective of this work, and as secondary objective the minimization of the impact of the modifications in the processing time. At this point an input file composed of all the galaxies at the same position is used. This allows verifying if the accumulation of counts is correctly executed. For an input file of N galaxies, N^2 counts have to be accumulated during the pair counting. Presently a typical galaxy sample amounts to one million of galaxies. Therefore, our stress test should correctly accumulate 10^{12} counts.

From the previous configuration and with this single-position sample, each thread generates 10^6 counts in zero-th bin. The 64 threads of a thread block generate $64 \cdot 10^6$ counts. This number largely overcomes the largest-consecutively-representable integer. Therefore, the implementation proposed in [10] produces an incorrect result when processing one million galaxies. In this case, it accumulates $2.62144 \cdot 10^{11}$ counts. This figure comes from the product of the active thread blocks 15625 times the largest-consecutively-representable integer, $15625 \times 16777216 = 2.62144 \cdot 10^{11}$. The number of active thread blocks is the result of the division of the input size by the number of threads per block, $\frac{10^6}{64} = 15625$.

On the other hand, the use of the *bin recycling strategy* allows dividing the for-loop in chunks, and therefore the accumulation of counts. After the end of each chunk, the sub-histograms are accumulated and reset to zero. As an example, for the one million object sample the for-loop is divided into four chunks, so that before resetting $64 \times 25 \cdot 10^4 = 16 \cdot 10^6$ counts are accumulated. The numerical experiments demonstrate that the *bin recycling strategy* correctly accumulates 10^{12} counts.

Once it has been demonstrated that the *bin recycling strategy* is able to accurately accumulate very large amount of counts, up to 10^{12}, it can be evaluated the differences in the estimator of 2PACF (Eq. 1) between both implementations. In Fig. 1, the differences between the values of $\omega(\theta)$ obtained with the *bin recycling strategy* minus the implementation proposed in [10] and the percentage of this difference in relation to the value obtained with the *bin recycling strategy* are shown. As observed the differences between both implementations are in the range ± 0.00001 for $\omega(\theta)$ (Fig. 1(a)), and the percentage of these differences in the range $\pm 1.5\%$ (Fig. 1(b)).

4.2   Processing Time Analysis

Regarding the processing time of each implementation, the one recommended by Sanders and Kandrot [10] takes $77099 \pm 17\,\text{ms}$[1] when analysing 2PACF with a sample size of $25 \cdot 10^4$ galaxies. It should be underlined that this sample size is accurately processed since the 64 threads per block generated $64 \times 25 \cdot 10^4 = 16 \cdot 10^6$ counts. On the other hand, the processing time when using the *bin recycling strategy* is $77367 \pm 117\,\text{ms}$. As observed the use of the *bin recycling strategy* introduces a very small additional processing time (an increment around 0.3%).

---

[1] Mean and standard deviation are obtained from 15 executions for all the numerical experiments where processing time comparisons are made.

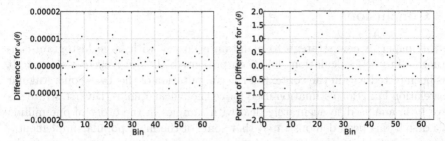

(a) Difference of $\omega(\theta)$ between the *bin re-cycling strategy* and the implementation proposed by Sanders and Kandrot.

(b) Percentage of difference of $\omega(\theta)$ between the *bin recycling strategy* and the implementation proposed by Sanders and Kandrot.

Fig. 1. Difference and percentage of the difference for the estimator $\omega(\theta)$ between the *bin recycling strategy* and the implementation proposed by Sanders and Kandrot.

When processing one million galaxies, the *bin recycling strategy* takes 1224893 ± 1136 ms. In this case the comparison is not possible due to the inability of the previously cited implementation to accurately process this sample size.

As previously mentioned, there are implementations for `atomicAdd()` in 32-bit and 64-bit integer representation. When using 32-bit integer representation and one million single-position sample, the sub-histograms correctly accumulate 64×10^6 counts. Since the final result, 10^{12} counts, exceeds of the largest-representable number, $\approx 2.1 \cdot 10^9$, it fails to correctly accumulate the value of the final histogram. On the other hand, when implementing 64-bit integer representation, this difficulty is overcome and the correct results—both in the sub-histograms and in the final histogram—are obtained, 64×10^6 and 10^{12} counts, respectively.

The comparison between the processing time when implementing 64-bit integer representation and the *bin recycling strategy* shows that the latter one, 1224893 ± 1136 ms, takes clearly shorter than the 64-bit integer representation, 1415185 ± 802 ms (speedup 1.16). In conclusion, the *bin recycling strategy* obtains a better performance than the `atomicAdd()` in 64-bit integer representation.

The absence of the `atomicAdd()` function in 64-bit floating-point representation can be mitigated through using the `atomicCAS()` (atomic Compare And Swap) in double precision floating-point representation. The outline of `atomicCAS()` is as follows: it reads 32-bit or 64-bit word located at some address in global or shared memory, then it computes a comparison with the value stored at the address, and finally it stores the result back to memory at the same address. When implementing this method for executing `atomicAdd()` in double precision, the processing time, 2206617 ± 193 ms, largely increases in comparison with the processing time of the *bin recycling strategy* (1224893 ± 1136) (speedup 1.80). Due to its large processing time, the `atomicCAS()` in 64-bit floating point is discarded as a competitive implementation for 2PACF.

5   Conclusions

In this paper, a new strategy to maintain accuracy with large histogram construction in GPU calculations has been presented: the *bin recycling strategy*. It has been tested within the context of the computation of the Two-Point Angular Correlation Function estimation used for cosmological studies. Diverse strategies have been analysed to accurately deal with samples in the order of one million galaxies. It has been demonstrated that some of the most popular implementations are not able to store the required number of counts per bin to certify the exactness of the results. Among the strategies which validate the requirement of accuracy, the proposed approach shows the best performance when analysing a sample of one million of galaxies.

Acknowledgment. The CFHTLens data is based on observations obtained with MegaPrime/MegaCam, a joint project of CFHT and CEA/DAPNIA, at the Canada-France-Hawaii Telescope (CFHT) which is operated by the National Research Council (NRC) of Canada, the Institut National des Sciences de l'Univers of the Centre National de la Recherche Scientifique (CNRS) of France, and the University of Hawaii. This research used the facilities of the Canadian Astronomy Data Centre operated by the National Research Council of Canada with the support of the Canadian Space Agency. CFHTLenS data processing was made possible thanks to significant computing support from the NSERC Research Tools and Instruments grant program.

References

1. Fu, L., Semboloni, E., Hoekstra, H., Kilbinger, M., van Waerbeke, L., Tereno, I., Mellier, Y., Heymans, C., Coupon, J., Benabed, K., Benjamin, J., Bertin, E., Dore, O., Hudson, M., Ilbert, O., Maoli, R., Marmo, C., McCracken, H., Menard, B.: Very weak lensing in the CFHTLS wide: cosmology from cosmic shear in the linear regime. Astron. Astrophys. **479**(1), 9–25 (2008)
2. Landy, S.D., Szalay, A.S.: Bias and variance of angular correlation functions. Am. J. Phys. **412**, 64–71 (1993)
3. Cárdenas-Montes, M., Rodríguez-Vázquez, J.J., Vega-Rodríguez, M.A., Sevilla-Noarbe, I., Sánchez-Álvaro, E.: Performance and precision of histogram calculation on GPUs: cosmological analysis as a case study. Comput. Phys. Commun. **185**(10), 2558–2565 (2014)
4. Cárdenas-Montes, M., Rodríguez-Vázquez, J.J., Vega-Rodríguez, M.A.: Bin recycling strategy for improving the histogram precision on GPU. Comput. Phys. Commun. **204**, 55–63 (2016)
5. Cárdenas-Montes, M., Vega-Rodríguez, M.Á., Sevilla, I., Ponce, R., Rodríguez-Vázquez, J.J., Sánchez Álvaro, E.: Concurrent CPU-GPU code optimization: the two-point angular correlation function as case study. In: Bielza, C., Salmerón, A., Alonso-Betanzos, A., Hidalgo, J.I., Martínez, L., Troncoso, A., Corchado, E., Corchado, J.M. (eds.) CAEPIA 2013. LNCS (LNAI), vol. 8109, pp. 209–218. Springer, Heidelberg (2013). doi:10.1007/978-3-642-40643-0_22
6. Cárdenas-Montes, M., Vega-Rodríguez, M.A., Bonnett, C., Sevilla-Noarbe, I., Ponce, R., Sánchez-Álvaro, E., Rodríguez-Vázquez, J.J.: GPU-based shear-shear correlation calculation. Comput. Phys. Commun. **185**(1), 11–18 (2014)

7. Goldberg, D.: What every computer scientist should know about floating-point arithmetic. ACM Comput. Surv. **23**, 5–48 (1991)
8. The Institute of Electrical, Electronics Engineers Inc.: IEEE standard for floating-point arithmetic. Technical report, Microprocessor Standards Committee of the IEEE Computer Society, New York, USA, August 2008
9. Whitehead, N., Fit-Florea, A.: Precision and performance: floating point and IEEE 754 compliance of NVIDIA GPUs. Technical report, NVIDIA (2011)
10. Sanders, J., Kandrot, E.: CUDA by Example: An Introduction to General-Purpose GPU Programming, 1st edn. Addison-Wesley Professional, Salt Lake City (2010)

An Efficient Implementation of LZW Compression in the FPGA

Xin Zhou, Yasuaki Ito$^{(\boxtimes)}$, and Koji Nakano

Department of Information Engineering, Hiroshima University,
Kagamiyama 1-4-1, Higashi-Hiroshima 739-8527, Japan
{zhou,yasuaki,nakano}@cs.hiroshima-u.ac.jp

Abstract. The main contribution of this paper is to present a new hardware architecture for accelerating LZW compression using an FPGA. In the proposed architecture, we efficiently use dual-port block RAMs embedded in the FPGA to implement a hash table that is used as a dictionary. Using independent two ports of the block RAM, reading and writing operations for the hash table are performed simultaneously. Additionally, we can read eight values in the hash table in one clock cycle by partitioning the hash table into eight tables. Since the proposed hardware implementation of LZW compression is compactly designed, we have succeeded in implementing 24 identical circuits in an FPGA, where the clock frequency of FPGA is 163.35 MHz. Our implementation of 24 proposed circuits attains a speed up factor of 23.51 times faster than a sequential LZW compression on a single CPU.

Keywords: LZW compression · Hardware algorithm · FPGA · Block RAM

1 Introduction

Data compression is one of the most important tasks in the area of computer engineering. It is always used to improve the efficiency of data transmission and save the storage of data. In this paper, we focus on LZW compression [11]. LZW compression is included in TIFF standard [1], which is widely used in the area of commercial digital printing. The LZW compression algorithm converts an input string of characters into a series of codes using a dictionary that maps strings into codes. Since dictionary tables are created by reading input data one by one, LZW compression is hard to parallelize. The main goal of this paper is to develop an efficient hardware architecture of LZW compression and implement it in an FPGA (Field Programmable Gate Array).

An FPGA is an integrated circuit designed to be configured by a designer after manufacturing. It contains an array of programmable logic blocks, and the reconfigurable interconnects allow the blocks to be inter-wired in different configurations. Since any logic circuits can be embedded in an FPGA, it can be used for general-purpose parallel computing. Recent FPGAs have embedded

© Springer International Publishing AG 2016
J. Carretero et al. (Eds.): ICA3PP 2016, LNCS 10048, pp. 512–520, 2016.
DOI: 10.1007/978-3-319-49583-5_39

block RAMs. A block RAM is an embedded dual-port memory supporting synchronized read and write operations, and can be configured as a 36k-bit or two 18k-bit dual port RAMs [13]. Since FPGA chips maintain relatively low price and its programmable features, it is suitable for a hardware implementation of image processing method to a great extent.

Numerous implementations of variety of LZW compression on FPGAs or VLSIs [3,5,6,8,9], GPUs [2,10], multiprocessor [4] and cluster systems [7] have been proposed to accelerate the computation. However, as far as we know, there is no hardware implementation of the original LZW compression algorithm since it is not easy to implement it.

The main contribution of this paper is to present an efficient hardware architecture for LZW compression algorithm and to implement it in an FPGA. In the proposed architecture, we efficiently use dual-port block RAMs embedded in the FPGA to implement a hash table that is used as the dictionary. According to the experimental results, the throughput of the proposed circuit is 118.73 MB/s when the compression ratio (original image size: compressed image size) is 1.43:1. On the other hand, the throughput is 86.79 MB/s when the compression ratio is 36.72:1. Furthermore, since the proposed circuit of LZW compression uses a few FPGA resources, we have succeeded in implementing 24 identical circuits in an FPGA, where the frequency is 163.35 MHz and each circuit has independent input/output ports that work in parallel. Hence, the implementation of 24 proposed circuits attains a speed up factor that surpasses 23.51 times over a sequential implementation on a CPU.

2 LZW Compression Algorithm

The main purpose of this section is to review LZW compression algorithm. The LZW (Lempei-Ziv-Welch) [11] lossless data compression algorithm converts an input string of characters into a series of codes using a dictionary table that maps strings into codes. If the input is an image, characters may be 8-bit unsigned integers. It reads characters in an input image string one by one and adds an entry in a dictionary table. At the same time, it writes an output series of codes by looking up the dictionary table. Let $X = x_0 x_1 \cdots x_{n-1}$ be an input string of characters and $Y = y_0 y_1 \cdots y_{m-1}$ be an output string of codes. For simplicity, we assume that an input string is a string of 4 characters a, b, c and d. Let C be a dictionary table, which determines a mapping of a code to a string, where codes are non-negative integers. Initially, $C(0) = a$, $C(1) = b$, $C(2) = c$ and $C(3) = d$. By operation AddTable, a new code is assigned to a string.

The LZW compression algorithm finds the longest prefix Ω of the current input that is already added in the dictionary table, and outputs the code of Ω. Let x be the following character of Ω. Since $\Omega \cdot x$ is not in the dictionary table, it is added to the dictionary, where "$\cdot$" denotes the concatenation of string/character. The same procedure is repeated from x. Let $C^{-1}(\Omega)$ denote the index of C where Ω is stored. The LZW compression algorithm is described in Algorithm 1 and Table 1 shows the compression flow of an input string "$cbcbcbcda$". It should have no difficult to confirm that 214630 is output by this algorithm.

Algorithm 1. LZW compression algorithm

```
1: Ω ← x₀;
2: for i ← 1 to n − 1 do
3:    if Ω · xᵢ is in C then
4:       Ω ← Ω · xᵢ;
5:    else
6:       Output(C⁻¹(Ω)); AddTable(Ω · xᵢ); Ω ← xᵢ;
7:    end if
8: end for
9: Output(C⁻¹(Ω));
```

Table 1. LZW compression flow for input string $X = cbcbcbcda$

i	0	1	2	3	4	5	6	7	8	-
x_i	c	b	c	b	c	b	c	d	a	-
Ω	-	c	b	c	cb	c	cb	cbc	d	a
S	-	$cb(4)$	$bc(5)$	-	$cbc(6)$	-	-	$cbcd(7)$	$da(8)$	-
Y	-	2	1	-	4	-	-	6	3	0

Next, let us discuss implementations of dictionary table C. The following operations for a string Ω of characters and the following character x must be supported for LZW compression; determining if $\Omega \cdot x_i$ is in C, returning the value of $C^{-1}(\Omega)$, and performing AddTable($\Omega \cdot x_i$). A straightforward implementation of the dictionary table C, which uses an array such that i-th ($i \geq 0$) element stores $C(i)$. However, since the lengths of strings in C are variable, the straightforward implementation of dictionary C is not efficient. All values of $C(i)$ may be accessed to compute $C^{-1}(\Omega)$. We can use an associative array with keys $C(i)$ and values i, which can be implemented by a balanced binary tree or a hash table. However, these operations take more than $O(|\Omega|)$ time. If the compression ratio is high, Ω may be a long string. Hence, it is not a good idea to use a conventional associative array to implement C.

In this paper, we use a pointer-character table to implement the dictionary table C as shown in Table 2. In this table, a pointer $p(j)$ and a character $c(j)$ are stored for each code j. Also, a back-pointer $q(j, x)$ for every code j and character x is used. Back-pointer table q can be implemented using an associative array which we will discuss later. We can obtain a string $C(j)$ by traversing p until we reach NULL. More specifically, $C(j)$ can be obtained from p and c by the following definition:

$$C(j) = \begin{cases} c(j) & \text{if } p(j) = \text{NULL} \\ C(p(j)) \cdot c(j) & \text{otherwise} \end{cases} \tag{1}$$

We implement operation AddTable($\Omega \cdot x_i$) for dictionary C by performing operation AddTable(j, x_i) for the pointer-character table. If AddTable(j, x_i) is performed, a new entry k with $p(k) = j$ and $c(k) = x_i$ is added to the pointer-character table. In other words, the value k is written in $q(j, x_i)$ of back-pointer table. Using the back-pointer table, we can rewrite LZW compression algorithm in Algorithm 2.

Table 2. A pointer-character table and a back-pointer table

j	0	1	2	3	4	5	6	7	8	9
$p(j)$	NULL	NULL	NULL	NULL	2	1	4	6	3	0
$c(j)$	a	b	c	d	b	c	c	d	a	-
$q(j,a)$	NULL	NULL	NULL	8	NULL	NULL	NULL	NULL	NULL	NULL
$q(j,b)$	NULL	NULL	4	NULL	NULL	NULL	NULL	NULL	NULL	NULL
$q(j,c)$	NULL	5	NULL	NULL	6	NULL	NULL	NULL	NULL	NULL
$q(j,d)$	NULL	NULL	NULL	NULL	NULL	7	NULL	NULL	NULL	NULL
$C(j)$	a	b	c	d	cb	bc	cbc	cbcd	da	-

Algorithm 2. LZW compression algorithm with the back-pointer table

```
1: j ← c⁻¹(x₀);
2: for i ← 1 to n − 1 do
3:    if q(j, xᵢ) ≠ NULL then
4:        j ← q(j, xᵢ);
5:    else
6:        Output(j); AddTable(j, xᵢ); j ← c⁻¹(xᵢ);
7:    end if
8: end for
9: Output(j);
```

We show how Table 2 is created. First, $j \leftarrow c^{-1}(x_0) = 2$ is executed. Next, since $q(j, x_1) = q(2, b)$ is NULL, Output(2) and AddTable(2,b) are executed. The pointer-character table has new entry $p(4) = 2$ and $c(4) = b$. Also, the value 4 is stored in $q(2, b)$, and operation $j \leftarrow c^{-1}(b) = 1$ is executed. In the next iteration of the for-loop, since $q(1, c)$ is NULL, Output(1) and AddTable(1,c) are executed. The pointer-character table has new entry $p(5) = 1$ and $c(5) = c$, and the value 5 is added in $q(1, c)$. Similarly, we can confirm that a series of codes 214630 is output by this algorithm.

3   Our FPGA Architecture for LZW Compression

This section describes our FPGA architecture of the LZW compression algorithm with back-pointer table using block RAMs in Xilinx Virtex-7 FPGA. We use Xilinx Virtex-7 Family FPGA XC7VX485T-2 as the target device [12]. In the following, we use image data in a TIFF image file to be compressed.

First, we show the implementation of the back-pointer table q for TIFF LZW compression. As shown in the above, the back-pointer table needs $2^{20} \times 12$bits = 1.5 MB. Since the size of the internal memory in the FPGA is limited and most entries of the table are not used, we use a hash table to implement the back-pointer table q.

In the proposed FPGA implementation, we use a hash table that is suitable for FPGA implementation. The hash table consists of 1024 buckets B_s

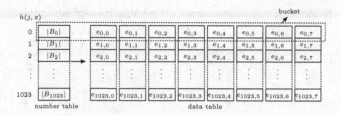

Fig. 1. The arrangement of hash table

$(0 \leq s \leq 1023)$ and each bucket B_s has 8 entries $e_{s,0}, e_{s,1}, \ldots, e_{s,7}$. To implement this hash table, we use two tables, *number table* and *data table*. Let $|B_s|$ denote the number of values stored in bucket B_s. Each element of the number table stores $|B_s|$. Also, the data table stores values of back-pointers. The table is partitioned into 8 tables, each of which stores one of the 8 entries. Each entry stores 12-bit pointer j, 8-bit character x and 12-bit back-pointer $q(j, x)$. Figure 1 illustrates the structure of the hash table.

Let $h(j, x)$ be a hash function returning a 10-bit number, where pointer j is 12 bits and character x is 8 bits. To specify a 10-bit number, we use a hash function $h(j, x) = ((j << 4) \oplus (j >> 6)) \oplus (x << 1) \wedge \text{0x3FF}$. Using this hash function, we select a bucket in address $h(j, x)$ and store the value of back-pointer in one of the eight entries in the bucket. However, the bucket may be full, that is, eight values are already stored in the bucket. If this is the case, called *conflict*, the current value of each address $(h(j, x) + i) \wedge \text{0x3FF}$ is read for $i = 1, 2, \ldots$ until a bucket that has unused entries is found. We can easily find whether the bucket B_s is full or not by referring $|B_s|$ in the number table. Regarding the size of the hash table, since the total size of the hash table is 8192 and at most 3837 elements are added, conflict may occur, but it is clear that the hash table can store all data.

In the LZW compression, it is necessary to find whether a value of back-pointer is already stored or not. Since the data table is partitioned into 8 tables, we read 8 values at the same time. Therefore, given an address of bucket from the hash function, we can find whether a value that includes the back-pointer is stored or not without checking eight entries in the bucket one by one.

On the other hand, the number table consists of 1024 entries with 4 bits that represent the number of used entries in each bucket. Using the number table, we can simply determine an element whether it is already stored or not. Recall that we need to initialize all entries in the hash table whenever compression for each code segment is finished, that is, ClearCode is output. Since each entry represents the number of used entries in each bucket, we set each entry to zero without clearing the data tables.

In the proposed architecture, we perform LZW compression algorithm described in Algorithm 2. The main part of the architecture is the hash table as described in the above. There are three operations for the hash table, (i) *initialize operation*, (ii) *find operation*, and (iii) *add operation*. We show the details of these operations, as follows.

Initialize Operation: As shown in the above, we clear only the number table to initialize the hash table. However, the next characters cannot be input during the initialization. Therefore, in the proposed architecture, we use two number tables and switch them in turn whenever ClearCode is output. Since the number table has 1024 entries, the initialize operation can be performed while another code segment is processed.

Find Operation: This operation corresponds to "$q(j, x_i) \neq$ NULL", "$j \leftarrow q(j, x_i)$", and "Output(j)" in Algorithm 2. In the operation, first, we obtain the address of the hash table by computing $h(j, x)$. After that, we find whether a back-pointer $q(j, x)$ is stored in $B_{h(j,x)}$. As shown in the above, we can simultaneously read eight values in a bucket and the number of values in a bucket is read from the number table to read valid data. Since each entry in the hash table has the values of j and x, we can find it by comparing j and x read from the hash table with input values j and x. Therefore, we can check at most 8 entries in $B_{h(j,x)}$ at the same time. After comparing, if $q(j, x)$ is found, output it. Otherwise, we check whether $B_{h(j,x)}$ is full or not. If $|B_{h(j,x)}| < 8$, that is, $B_{h(j,x)}$ is not full, we can find $q(j, x)$ does not exist in the hash table and output NULL. If not, we perform the above operation for bucket $B_{(h(j,x)+i)\wedge \text{0x3FF}}$ for $i = 1, 2, \ldots$ until we find whether $q(j, x)$ is stored or not.

Add Operation: It is performed as operation AddTable in Algorithm 2. Indeed, it is performed after the find operation as described in Algorithm 2. The entry to be stored locates in the bucket which was referred last in the find operation. Therefore, according to the result of the find operation, we add j, x and $q(j, x)$ to the hash table and increment the corresponding number of stored values in the number table.

In order to implement the hash table, we use block RAMs configured as dual-port mode [13]. Each of the number table consists of one 18k-bit block RAMs. Also, two 18k-bit block RAMs are assigned to one of the 8 tables in the data table. Since we use two tables for the number table, eighteen 18k-bit block RAMs are used in total. For the number table, its dual-port is used as reading port and writing port. They are used to perform the find and add operations, respectively. On the other hand, for the data table, we also use the dual-port as reading port and writing port for each. To reduce the clock cycles, we always suppose that for input string of characters $x_0, x_1, \ldots, x_{n-1}$, the condition $q(j, x_i) =$ NULL is satisfied. Using this, we can continuously input characters unless the condition $q(j, x_i) =$ NULL is not satisfied. When the condition is not satisfied, we need to wait to input the next character.

4 Experimental Results

This section shows the implementation results of the proposed architecture for LZW compression algorithm in the FPGA. We have implemented the proposed circuit for LZW compression algorithm and evaluated it in VC707 board [14] equipped with the Xilinx Virtex-7 FPGA XC7VX485T-2. The experimental

Table 3. Implementation results of the proposed hardware algorithm

Number of circuits	1	24	Available
Slice registers	104 (0.02%)	3120 (0.51%)	607200
Slice LUTs	346 (0.11%)	7782 (2.56%)	303600
18K-bit block RAMs	18 (0.87%)	432 (20.97%)	2060
Clock frequency [MHz]	179.99	163.35	—

"Crafts"   "Flowers"   "Graph"

Fig. 2. Three gray scale images with 4096 × 3072 pixels used for experiments

Table 4. Computing time for three images

Images	Compression ratio	CPU [ms]	FPGA [ms]	Speed-up
"Crafts"	1.43:1	109.10	101.07	1.08:1
"Flowers"	1.72:1	93.60	107.93	0.87:1
"Graph"	36.72:1	46.79	138.26	0.34:1

results of the implementation is shown in Table 3. We also use Intel Core i7-4790 (3.6 GHz) to evaluate the running time of the sequential LZW compression. In the experiment, we have used three gray scale images with 4096 × 3072 pixels as shown in Fig. 2, which are converted from JIS X 9204-2004 standard color image data. The image "Graph" has high compression ratio since it has large areas with similar intensity levels. The image "Crafts" has low compression ratio since it has small details.

Table 4 shows the time of compression on CPU and FPGA and the compression ratio (original image size: compressed image size). In our implementation on the FPGA, to save the usage of block RAMs of FPGA, As shown in Table 4, for only one proposed circuit of LZW compression, the results show that implementation on FPGA is not faster than the implementation on the CPU. However, since the proposed circuit uses very few FPGA resources, we have succeeded in implementing 24 identical LZW compression circuits in an FPGA, where the frequency is 163.35 MHz. Simply calculated, for image "Crafts", our implementation with 24 circuits runs up to 23.51 times faster than sequential LZW compression on a single CPU.

For gray scale image "Graph" which has high compression ratio with 4096 × 3072 pixels, the proposed circuit of LZW compression compresses 4096 × 3072 × 1Byte original data in 138.26 ms, that is, the throughput of the proposed circuit is 86.79 MB/s. On the other hand, for gray scale image "Crafts" which has low compression ratio, the throughput is 118.73 MB/s.

5   Conclusions

We have presented a hardware architecture for LZW compression algorithm of compressing images. In the proposed architecture, we efficiently use dual-port block RAMs embedded in the FPGA to implement a hash table that is used as the dictionary. It was implemented in a Virtex-7 family FPGA XC7VX485T-2. The experimental results show that our module provides a throughput up to 118.73 MB/s. Since the proposed circuit uses a few resources of the FPGA, we have succeeded in implementing 24 identical LZW compression circuits in an FPGA. The implementation of 24 LZW compression circuits attains a speed up factor of 23.51 over the sequential implementation on the CPU.

References

1. Adobe Developers Association: TIFF Revision, 6, June 1992. http://partners. adobe.com/public/developer/en/tiff/TIFF6.pdf
2. Funasaka, S., Nakano, K., Ito, Y.: Fast LZW compression using a GPU. In: Proceedings of International Symposium on Computing and Networking, pp. 303–308 (2015)
3. Helion Technology: LZRW3 Data Compression Core for Xilinx FPGA, October 2008
4. Klein, S.T., Wiseman, Y.: Parallel lempel Ziv coding. Discrete Appl. Math. **146**(2), 180–191 (2005)
5. Lin, M.: A hardware architecture for the LZW compression and decompression algorithms based on parallel dictionaries. J. VLSI Sig. Process. Syst. Sig. Image Video Technol. **26**(3), 369–381 (2000)
6. Lin, M., Lee, J., Jan, G.E.: A lossless data compression and decompression algorithm and its hardware architecture. IEEE Trans. Very Large Scale Integr. (VLSI) Syst. **14**(9), 925–936 (2006)
7. Mishra, M.K., Mishra, T.K., Pani, A.K.: Parallel Lempel-Ziv-Welch (PLZW) technique for data compression. Int. J. Comput. Sci. Inf. Technol. **3**(3), 4038–4040 (2012)
8. Navqi, S., Naqvi, R., Riaz, R.A., Siddiqui, F.: Optimized RTL design and implementation of LZW algorithm for high bandwidth applications. Electr. Rev. **4**, 279–285 (2011)
9. Prakash, S., Purohit, M., Raizada, A.: A novel approach of speedy-highly secured data transmission using cascading of PDLZW and arithmetic coding with cryptography. Int. J. Comput. Appl. **57**(19), 1–7 (2012)
10. Shyni, K., Kumar, K.V.M.: Lossless LZW data compression algorithm on CUDA. IOSR J. Comput. Eng. **13**, 122–127 (2013)

11. Welch, T.A.: A technique for high-performance data compression. IEEE Comput. **17**(6), 8–19 (1984)
12. Xilinx Inc.: 7 Series FPGAs Configuration User Guide (2013)
13. Xilinx Inc.: 7 Series FPGAs Memory Resources User Guide, November (2014)
14. Xilinx Inc.: VC707 Evaluation Board for the Virtex-7 FPGA User Guide (2014)

Shared Memory Tile-Based vs Hybrid Memory GOP-Based Parallel Algorithms for HEVC Encoder

Héctor Migallón[✉], Otoniel López-Granado, Vicente Galiano,
Pablo Piñol, and Manuel P. Malumbres

Department of Physics and Computer Architecture, Miguel Hernández University,
Avda. de la Universidad s/n, 03202 Elche, Alicante, Spain
{hmigallon,otoniel,vgaliano,pablop,mels}@umh.es

Abstract. After the emergence of the new High Efficiency Video Coding standard, several strategies have been followed in order to take advantage of the parallel features available in it. Many of the parallelization approaches in the literature have been performed in the decoder side, aiming at achieving real-time decoding. However, the most complex part of the HEVC codec is the encoding side. In this paper, we perform a comparative analysis of two parallelization proposals. One of them is based on tiles, employing shared memory architectures and the other one is based on Groups Of Pictures, employing distributed shared memory architectures. The results show that good speed-ups are obtained for the tile-based proposal, especially for high resolution video sequences, but the scalability decreases for low resolution video sequences. The GOP-based proposal outperforms the tile-based proposal when the number of processes increases. This benefit grows up when low resolution video sequences are compressed.

Keywords: HEVC · Video coding · Parallel encoding · Shared memory · Distributed shared memory

1 Introduction

The emergence of the new High Efficiency Video Coding (HEVC) standard [1], developed by the Joint Collaborative Team on Video Coding (JCT-VC), makes possible to deal with nowadays and future multimedia market trends, like 4K- and 8K-definition video content. The HEVC standard improves coding efficiency in comparison with the H.264/AVC [2] High profile, yielding the same video quality at half the bit rate [3]. However, this increase in the compression efficiency is bound to an increase in the computational complexity. Several works about

This research was supported by the Spanish Ministry of Economy and Competitiveness (MINECO) and the European commission (FEDER funds) under Grant TIN2015-66972-C5-4-R.

complexity analysis and parallelization strategies for the HEVC standard can be found in the literature [4,5]. Many of the parallelization research efforts have been conducted on the HEVC decoding side, like the developments in [6,7]. Nevertheless, the HEVC encoder's complexity is several orders of magnitude greater than the HEVC decoder's complexity. A number of works can also be found in the literature about parallelization on the HEVC encoder side. In [8] the authors propose a fine-grain parallel optimization in the motion estimation module of the HEVC encoder. The work presented in [9] focuses in the intra prediction module, removing data dependencies between sub-blocks. Some recent works focus on changes in the scanning order. For example, in [10], the authors propose a frame scanning order based on a diamond search, obtaining a good scheme for massive parallel processing. In [11], the authors propose to change the HEVC deblocking filter processing order. In [12], the authors present a coarse grain parallelization of the HEVC encoder based on Groups of Pictures (GOPs). In [13], the authors compare slices and tiles encoding performance in HEVC. In [14], a parallelization of the HEVC encoder at slice level is evaluated. In [15], two parallel versions of the HEVC encoder using slices and tiles are analyzed.

In this work, we present a comparison of two parallelization proposals of the HEVC encoder. The first one is performed at a tile level, especially suitable for shared memory architectures, whereas the other one is performed at a GOP level, over hybrid memory architectures. The aim of this paper is to determine which parallelization approach obtains a better performance and scalability as the number of processes increases.

2   Shared Memory Tile-Based Parallel Algorithm

Tiles are rectangular divisions of a video frame which can be independently encoded and decoded. This is a new feature included in the HEVC standard which is not present in previous standards. The shape of tiles and the absence of a data header for each tile, make them more efficient than slice partitioning, regarding compression performance [13]. In our tile-based parallel algorithm, each frame is split in as many tiles as the number of parallel processes to use, and each process handles one different tile. When all the processes have finished their work, synchronization is carried out, in order to properly write the encoded bit stream and to proceed with the next frame. A tile consists of an integer number of Coding Tree Units (CTUs), and, for a specific frame resolution, we can obtain multiple and heterogeneous tile partition layouts. For example, the partition of a frame into 8 tiles can be done by dividing the frame into 1 column by 8 rows (1×8), 2 columns by 4 rows (2×4), 4 columns by 2 rows (4×2), and 8 columns by 1 row (8×1). In addition, the width of each tile column and the height of each tile row can be set up independently, so we can have a plethora of symmetric and asymmetric layouts. In our work, for each layout, we have used the column widths and the row heights which produce the most homogeneous tile shapes. In the example shown in Fig. 1, a Full HD (1920×1080 pixels) frame is divided into 10 tiles using a layout of 5 columns (with a width of 6 CTUs each), and 2 rows (with a height of 8 and 9 CTUs, respectively). As every tile has an integer number of CTUs, in many layouts a tile partition where every node processes the same number of CTUs is not possible. Moreover, a perfect load balanced layout (in which each process encodes the same number of CTUs) does not always guarantee an optimal processing work balance because the computing resources needed to encode every single CTU are not exactly the same. Different layouts also produce different bit streams with different R/D performances. Note that, in the last steps of a tile encoding, every process needs information from the rest of the frame. Because of the amount of data to be shared between processes, this proposal is especially suitable for shared memory architectures and prevents distributed memory platforms from obtaining good parallel efficiencies.

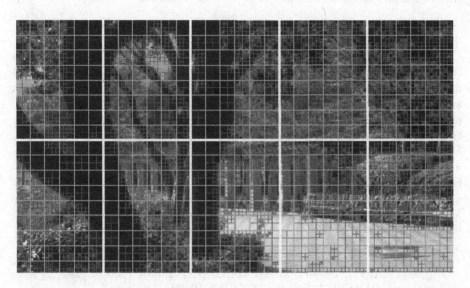

Fig. 1. Layout of a Full HD frame (1920 × 1080) from ParkScene sequence with 10 tiles (5 columns with a width of 6 CTUs; 2 rows with a height of 8 and 9 CTUs each)

3   Hybrid Memory GOP-Based Parallel Algorithm

In this section, we depict a parallel algorithm for the HEVC encoder at a GOP level. This algorithm, named DMG-AI (Distributed Memory GOP - All Intra), is fully described in [12], and it has been tested on a hybrid memory framework, managed by the Message Passing Interface (MPI) [16]. In the algorithm, there is a coordinator process which performs the data load balancing by distributing GOPs among the coding processes. It assigns the video data to the rest of processes, and also collects both statistical data and encoded data, in order to write the final bit stream output. In the beginning of the coding procedure, the coordinator process receives an MPI message from the rest of processes (coding processes), requesting a new GOP to encode. Note that, in All Intra mode, a GOP consists of one single video frame. After receiving the requests, the coordinator process assigns one different GOP of the video sequence to each one of the requesting processes. When one of the coding processes finishes its work, it sends the encoded data to the coordinator process. Then the coordinator process assigns a new GOP to the coding process. This procedure is repeated until all the GOPs of the video sequence have been encoded. In this algorithm, when one coding process becomes idle, it is immediately assigned a new GOP to encode, so there is no need to wait until the rest of processes have finished their work. This fact yields good speed-up values. The coordinator process is mapped onto a processor which also runs one coding process, because its computational load is negligible. The final bit stream is exactly the same as the one produced by the sequential algorithm, so there is no R/D degradation.

4   Numerical Experiments

In this section, we present the evaluation of the parallel algorithms introduced in Sects. 2 and 3, regarding parallel performance and R/D performance (PSNR and bit rate). For the tests, the HEVC reference software HM v16.3 [17] has been modified to implement both algorithms. For the tile-based parallel algorithm, the OpenMP API v3.1 [18] has been used, and for the GOP-based parallel algorithm, MPI v2.2 has been used, regardless of whether a strictly distributed memory, a strictly shared memory, or a hybrid memory layout is used to run the GOP-based tests. The parallel platform used is a HP Proliant SL390 G7 (a distributed memory multiprocessor with 24 nodes). Each node is equipped with two Intel Xeon X5660. Each X5660 includes six processing cores at 2.8 GHz. QDR Infiniband has been used as the communications network. The video sequences used in the experimental tests are the following:

- *Traffic* (TRAFFI), *PeopleOnStreet* (PEOPON): 2560 × 1600 pixels
- *ParkScene* (PARKSC), *Tennis* (TENNIS): 1920 × 1080 pixels
- *FourPeople* (FOURPE), *Kristen&Sara* (KRI&SA): 1280 × 720 pixels
- *PartyScene* (PARTSC), *BasketballDrill* (BASKDR): 832 × 480 pixels

Tile-Based Parallel Algorithm. First of all, we analyze the performance of the tile-based parallel algorithm in order to see how the tile partitioning affects both the speed-up and the coding efficiency. We have evaluated this proposal for 2, 4, 6, 8, 9, and 10 processes. In Fig. 2, we present the encoding speed-up evolution for *Traffic* and *People* sequences in AI mode. A speed-up of up to 9.3x is obtained when 10 processes are used. Note that, for a certain number of parallel processes, different speed-ups are obtained depending on the tile partitioning layouts. This is mainly due to the fact that some tile partition layouts produce an unbalanced processing load. For example, for a video resolution of 2560 × 1600 (and a CTU size of 64 × 64), a frame consists of 40 × 25 CTUs. If we divide the frame using the 10 × 1 layout, then each one of the 10 processes will have to encode the same number of CTUs ($4 \times 25 = 100$ CTUs). This represents a perfectly balanced load. But if we divide the frame using the 1×10 layout, then 5 processes will have to encode $40 \times 2 = 80$ CTUs. The other 5 processes will have to encode $40 \times 3 = 120$ CTUs, so they will have to deal with 50% more CTUs. In general, tile partitioning layouts based on columns of CTUs or on square tiles obtain better parallel performance.

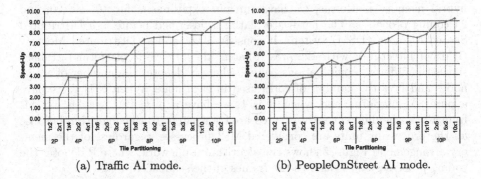

(a) Traffic AI mode.   (b) PeopleOnStreet AI mode.

Fig. 2. Speed-Up evolution for 4K video sequences with different number of processes and tile partitioning for $QP = 37$

In Fig. 3 we show the average speed-up value for each video resolution with the best tile partitioning layout. As can be seen, for 4K, Full HD, and HD Ready video resolutions we obtain a good speed-up scalability up to 10 cores. However, for lower resolutions the speed-up scalability drops from 8 cores and beyond. Besides, in general, the average speed-up for a given number of processes decreases as the video resolution does.

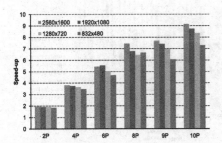

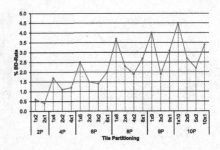

Fig. 3. Average speed-up evolution using the best tile partitioning layout.

Fig. 4. % BD-Rate evolution for Tennis (1920×1080) video sequence.

Regarding R/D performance, in Fig. 4 we show the % of BD-rate increase for each tile partitioning layout, using Bjontegaard method [19]. This value measures the bit rate overhead compared with the sequential version using one tile per frame. As can be seen, the overhead increases as the number of processes does. This is an expected behavior because tiles are known to reduce compression efficiency. Square-like tile partitioning layouts perform better than the others, providing lower overhead values. In these tiles, more redundancies between neighboring CTUs of the same tile exist, which can be exploited.

GOP-Based Parallel Algorithm. To evaluate the DMG-AI algorithm on hybrid memory platforms, we have run our experiments for 10, 16, 20, and 24 coding processes. The hardware platform described before is a Distributed Shared Memory (DSM) system. It consists of 24 nodes (Distributed Memory (DM) architecture), with 12 cores (Shared Memory (SM) platforms). Table 1 shows the different combinations tested, where N denotes the number of active nodes and R is the number of cores used in each node. When N is 1, we have a pure SM platform, and when R is 1, we have a pure DM system. In this framework, the different setups tested are transparent to the algorithm because all the processing units are considered MPI processes, regardless of the memory arrangement. Figure 5 shows the algorithm framework, where P denotes the coding processes and I denotes the frames of the sequence.

Table 1. DSM parallel structures.

Number of MPI processes	Number of nodes × Number of cores (N,R)
10	(10, 1), (5, 2), (2, 5), (1, 10)
16	(16, 1), (8, 2), (2, 8), (1, 16)
20	(20, 1), (5, 4), (4, 5), (2, 10)
24	(8, 3), (6, 4), (4, 6), (3, 8)

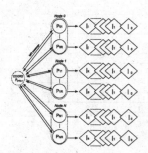

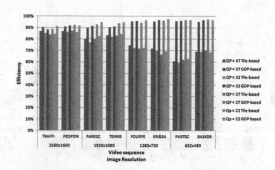

Fig. 5. DMG-AI: parallel distribution.

Fig. 6. Tile based vs. GOP based parallel efficiencies.

Tile-Based vs. GOP-Based Parallel Algorithms. Figure 6 presents the parallel efficiency for 10 processes and for both algorithms. For the tile-based proposal, the efficiency values for the different tile layouts are averaged, and for the

GOP-based approach, the results for the different framework setups are averaged. The GOP-based efficiency values are always better than the ones obtained by the tile-based proposal, being scarce for high resolution sequences, but becoming significant as the resolution decreases. Most times, the best efficiency values are obtained when a low value for the Quantization Parameter (QP) is used. A low QP value is used when we want to improve the reconstructed video quality (and a larger bit stream is generated). In this situation, the workload increases and the parallel efficiency improves. In the hybrid memory platform, disk access is a bottleneck. Regarding R/D performance, the GOP-based approach always outperforms the tile-based proposal because, as stated before, it produces exactly the same bit stream than the sequential version and, therefore, there is no R/D performance degradation.

5 Conclusions

In this paper we have compared two parallelization proposals for the HEVC encoder using the All Intra coding mode. The first one is based on tiles and it is especially suitable for shared memory platforms. It obtains good speed-up values, although for low resolution sequences, the parallel scalability decreases. Moreover, the R/D performance decreases as the number of tiles increases. The other approach, which is based on GOPs, is suitable for both shared and distributed memory architectures. It yields good parallel performance, obtaining efficiency values of up to 97%. Besides, it outperforms the tile based proposal, especially when low resolution video sequences are encoded by a high number of processes. The GOP-based approach has been tested using up to 24 processes, showing good scalability, without varying R/D performance. We have observed that the disk access is a bottleneck and, in future work, this can be avoided with the use of a parallel disk access system.

References

1. Bross, B., Han, W., Ohm, J., Sullivan, G., Wang, Y.-K., Wiegand, T.: High Efficiency Video Coding (HEVC) Text Specification Draft 10, Document JCTVC-L1003 of JCT-VC, Geneva, January 2013
2. ITU-T, ISO/IEC JTC 1, Advanced Video Coding for Generic Audiovisual Services, ITU-T Rec. H.264 and ISO/IEC 14496–10 (AVC) version 16 (2012)
3. Ohm, J., Sullivan, G., Schwarz, H., Tan, T.K., Wiegand, T.: Comparison of the coding efficiency of video coding standards - including high efficiency video coding (HEVC). IEEE Trans. Circuits Syst. Video Technol. 22(12), 1669–1684 (2012)
4. Bossen, F., Bross, B., Suhring, K., Flynn, D.: HEVC complexity and implementation analysis. IEEE Trans. Circuits Syst. Video Technol. 22(12), 1685–1696 (2012)
5. Chi, C.C., Alvarez-Mesa, M., Juurlink, B., Clare, G., Henry, F., Pateux, S., Schierl, T.: Parallel scalability and efficiency of HEVC parallelization approaches. IEEE Trans. Circuits Syst. Video Technol. 22(12), 1827–1838 (2012)
6. Chi, C., Alvarez-Mesa, M., Lucas, J., Juurlink, B., Schierl, T.: Parallel HEVC decoding on multi- and many-core architectures. J. Sig. Process. Syst. 71(3), 247–260 (2013)

7. Bross, B., Alvarez-Mesa, M., George, V., Chi, C.C., Mayer, T., Juurlink, B., Schierl, T.: HEVC real-time decoding. In: Proceedings of SPIE, vol. 8856, pp. 88 561R–88 561R–11 (2013)
8. Yu, Q., Zhao, L., Ma, S.: Parallel AMVP candidate list construction for HEVC. In: VCIP 2012, pp. 1–6 (2012)
9. Jiang, J., Guo, B., Mo, W., Fan, K.: Block-based parallel intra prediction scheme for HEVC. J. Multimedia 7(4), 289–294 (2012)
10. Luczak, A., Karwowski, D., Maćkowiak, S., Grajek, T.: Diamond scanning order of image blocks for massively parallel HEVC compression. In: Bolc, L., Tadeusiewicz, R., Chmielewski, L.J., Wojciechowski, K. (eds.) ICCVG 2012. LNCS, vol. 7594, pp. 172–179. Springer, Heidelberg (2012). doi:10.1007/978-3-642-33564-8_21
11. Yan, C., Zhang, Y., Dai, F., Li, L.: Efficient parallel framework for HEVC deblocking filter on many-core platform. In: Data Compression Conference (DCC), p. 530, March 2013
12. Migallón, H., Galiano, V., Piñol, P., López-Granado, O., Malumbres, M.P.: Distributed memory parallel approaches for HEVC encoder. J. Supercomputing, 1–12 (2016)
13. Misra, K., Segall, A., Horowitz, M., Xu, S., Fuldseth, A., Zhou, M.: An overview of tiles in HEVC. IEEE J. Sel. Topics Sig. Process. 7(6), 969–977 (2013)
14. Piñol, P., Migallón, H., López-Granado, O., Malumbres, M.P.: Slice-based parallel approach for HEVC encoder. J. Supercomputing 71(5), 1882–1892 (2015)
15. Migallón, H., Piñol, P., López-Granado, O., Malumbres, M.P.: Subpicture parallel approaches of HEVC video encoder. In: 2014 International Conference on Computational and Mathematical Methods in Science and Engineering, vol. 1, pp. 927–938 (2014)
16. MPI Forum, MPI: A Message-Passing Interface Standard. Version 2.2, 4th September 2009. http://www.mpi-forum.org. Accessed Dec 2009
17. HEVC Reference Software. http://hevc.hhi.fraunhofer.de/svn/svnHEVCSoftware/tags/HM-16.3/
18. OpenMP Architecture Review Board, OpenMP Application Program Interface, version 3.1 (2011). http://www.openmp.org
19. Bjontegaard, G.: Improvements of the BD-PSNR model. Video Coding Experts Group (VCEG), Berlin (Germany), Technical report VCEG-M33, July 2008

GPU-Based Heterogeneous Coding Architecture for HEVC

Gabriel Cebrián-Márquez[1](✉), Héctor Migallón[2], José Luis Martínez[1], Otoniel López-Granado[2], Pablo Piñol[2], and Pedro Cuenca[1]

[1] Albacete Research Institute of Informatics (I3A),
University of Castilla-La Mancha (UCLM),
Plz. de la Universidad 2, 02071 Albacete, Spain
{Gabriel.Cebrian,JoseLuis.Martinez,Pedro.Cuenca}@uclm.es
[2] Department of Physics and Computer Architecture,
Miguel Hernández University, 03202 Elche, Spain
{hmigallon,otoniel,pablop}@umh.es

Abstract. The High Efficiency Video Coding (HEVC) standard has nearly doubled the compression efficiency of prior standards. Nonetheless, this increase in coding efficiency involves a notably higher computing complexity that should be overcome in order to achieve real-time encoding. For this reason, this paper focuses on applying parallel processing techniques to the HEVC encoder with the aim of reducing significantly its computational cost without affecting the compression performance. Firstly, we propose a coarse-grained slice-based parallelization technique that is executed in a multi-core CPU, and then, with finer level of parallelism, a GPU-based motion estimation algorithm. Both techniques define a heterogeneous parallel coding architecture for HEVC. Results show that speed-ups of up to 4.06× can be obtained on a quad-core platform with low impact in coding performance.

Keywords: H.265 · HEVC · Heterogeneous · Parallel encoding · GPU

1 Introduction

The High Efficiency Video Coding (HEVC) [7] standard was established in early 2013 by the Joint Collaborative Team on Video Coding (JCT-VC). With the aim of improving the coding efficiency of state-of-art coding standards, HEVC introduced several new coding tools, outperforming its predecessor H.264/Advanced Video Coding (AVC) [8] by up to 50% in terms of compression performance [10]. Among others, these tools include a highly flexible quadtree partitioning scheme, which divides the picture into square blocks named coding tree units (CTU).

This work was jointly supported by the Spanish Ministry of Economy and Competitiveness (MINECO) and the European Commission (FEDER funds) under projects TIN2015-66972-C5-2-R and TIN2015-66972-C5-4-R, and by the Spanish Ministry of Education, Culture and Sports under the grant FPU13/04601.

© Springer International Publishing AG 2016
J. Carretero et al. (Eds.): ICA3PP 2016, LNCS 10048, pp. 529–536, 2016.
DOI: 10.1007/978-3-319-49583-5_41

While these new coding tools allow to achieve good coding efficiency results, they imply a considerable increase in encoding time. For this reason, HEVC places special emphasis on a hardware friendly design and parallel-processing architectures. In fact, the standard defines two parallel algorithms: Tiles and Wavefront Parallel Processing (WPP). Additionally, HEVC has also maintained the concept of slices from previous standards, which can also be used for parallelization purposes. Basically, all of these three parallelization techniques rely on creating picture partitions that break some dependencies for prediction.

At this point, this paper proposes a heterogeneous coding architecture composed by a multi-core CPU and a GPU. The proposed algorithm makes use of slices to allow the distribution of the encoding process over different processing units. Concurrently, a GPU-based motion estimation (ME) algorithm is carried out entirely in the device. As a result, the execution time can be notably reduced, achieving speed-ups of up to 4.06× on a quad-core CPU using 4 threads with low impact on coding efficiency.

The remainder of this paper is organized as follows. Section 2 includes a technical background of HEVC, while Sect. 3 identifies the related work in the topic. Section 4 introduces our proposed heterogeneous coding architecture, showing some results in Sect. 5. Finally, Sect. 6 concludes the paper.

2   Technical Background

As mentioned in the introduction of this paper, one of the main objectives of the HEVC standard is to achieve considerably higher coding efficiency compared to previous standards. One of the most important novelties introduced by HEVC is the new picture partitioning, which is now performed following a quadtree structure as shown in Fig. 1. Each picture is partitioned into 64 × 64 pixel square regions called CTUs, which can be recursively divided into 4 smaller sub-regions called coding units (CU), whose size range from 64 × 64 to 8 × 8. These structures can be partitioned, in turn, into prediction units (PU), with up to eight different partitioning schemes, and transform units (TU), whose size range from 32 × 32 to 4 × 4 and are organized in a tree structure named residual quadtree (RQT).

The huge amount of possibilities introduced by the standard allows the encoder to perform a very flexible coding. However, it also involves a notable

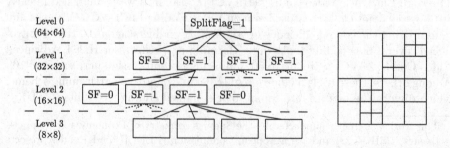

Fig. 1. Example of CTU quadtree structure defined in HEVC

increase in its computational complexity. With the aim of reducing this complexity, HEVC defines some parallelization techniques such as Tiles and WPP. On the one hand, the standard defines Tiles as rectangular shape partitions where dependencies are broken across tile boundaries, making it possible to process them independently. However, the in-loop filters can still cross these boundaries in order to improve the overall coding efficiency. On the other hand, WPP allows the creation of rows as picture partitions that can be processed in parallel. In this case, unlike Tiles, entropy coding is allowed to cross partitions in order to minimize coding losses. However, this is achieved by introducing a delay of two CTUs between consecutive rows in order to preserve some dependencies.

A slice, in turn, is a partition of a frame which can be independently decoded with regard to other slices in the same frame. The size and shape of a slice can be arbitrary, although it is required that the CTUs contained in it are consecutive in coding order. While their main aim is to improve the error resilience of the standard by avoiding the propagation of errors across slices, they have also been used as a way of parallelism. As a counterpart, however, each slice introduces a header that might cause some overhead in terms of coding efficiency.

3   Related Work

Several state-of-art works address the complexity analysis and parallelization strategies of the HEVC standard [2,5]. As for other parallelization techniques, authors in [6] present a variation of WPP called Overlapped Wavefront (OWF) in which the decoding of consecutive pictures is overlapped. With regard to the encoder, authors in [11] propose a fine-grained parallel optimization of the ME module of the encoder, allowing to perform the motion vector prediction of all PUs available in a CU at the same time. Alternatively, other works focus on altering the scanning order, e.g. a diamond-based CU scanning order is proposed in [9] with the aim of obtaining a good scheme for massively parallel platforms.

Other works make use of GPU devices in the encoding process. Authors in [13] propose a scheme similar to the one in this paper based on GPU plus multi-core CPU platforms, but the major shortcoming of this paper lies in the fact that the encoder used in the tests does not include all coding tools, and thus results are not comparable. In [12], authors propose a GPU-based ME algorithm that differs in some aspects from the one in this paper. In particular, the pattern used in this paper is a diamond search, which might not obtain the best candidate in some cases. However, fractional ME is also performed in the device, which leads to higher speed-up values, but the absence of motion vector predictors (MVP) has some negative effects on the resulting coding efficiency.

4   Proposed Heterogeneous Coding Architecture

As seen before, parallelism is possible in both the encoder and the decoder making use of the algorithms defined in the standard. However, these algorithms are not adequate for some parallel architectures such as those based on GPUs.

This implies that it is necessary to develop efficient algorithms for these heterogeneous platforms. This section will show the details of the proposed coding algorithm designed for GPU-based heterogeneous architectures. First, a coarse-grained slice-based parallelization technique will be shown, followed by a GPU-based motion estimation algorithm. After that, it will be described how both techniques can cooperate at two different levels.

4.1 Slice-Based Parallel Coding

As mentioned in Sect. 2, a slice is a partition which can be independently decoded with regard to the other slices in the same frame. Similarly, slices can also be encoded in an isolated way, making it possible to exploit their inherent parallelism in such a way that every slice is encoded by a different thread.

Our proposed approach is to divide each frame into as many slices as available processing units. For example, if a hardware platform is composed of a quad-core CPU, each frame could be divided into four different slices. It has to be noted, though, that in order to maximize the parallel efficiency of the algorithm, each partition is assigned the same number of CTUs.

In those coding configurations in which inter prediction takes place, it is required to establish a synchronization mechanism at the end of each frame. This is caused by the fact that the decoded picture buffer (DPB) has to be updated with the reconstructed version of the frames after their encoding. In order to avoid costly memory transfers, a shared memory scheme has been utilized.

4.2 GPU-Based Inter Prediction Algorithm

Whereas the slice-based algorithm is able to achieve coarse-grained parallelism of the encoding process, it is still possible to further exploit the proposed heterogeneous architecture. In particular, one of the most computationally expensive operations of the encoder is the ME algorithm. This operation consists in estimating the motion vectors (MV) that describe the transformation from the current frame to the reference frames with the lowest rate-distortion cost. It is performed by subtracting the corresponding partitions from the reference pictures, involving a large number of repetitive operations. Considering the nature of this algorithm, it should be noted the convenience of a GPU architecture.

In order to avoid delays caused by data transfers and kernel executions, this algorithm is performed asynchronously. This is shown in Fig. 2. As can be seen, the original frames are copied to the device as soon as a group of pictures (GOP) starts being processed. In order to be referenced, these are replaced with their reconstructed versions once they are encoded. With regard to the assignation of workload to the device, the host queues the motion estimation of the following CTU to the one that is currently being processed. This is possible thanks to a double buffer that holds the motion information of the current CTU, while it allocates the space necessary for next one. Exceptionally, for the first CTU in a frame, the host might need to wait for the device to finish.

Similarly to the regular ME algorithm, the device calculates the MVs for all the possible PUs in which a CTU is divided and their associated costs.

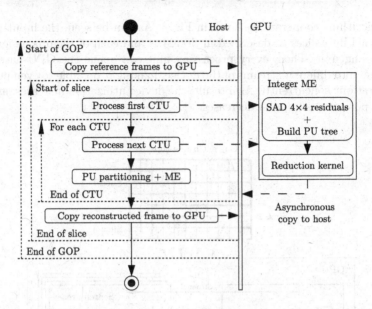

Fig. 2. GPU-based inter prediction algorithm diagram

This is performed in two steps, and thus it is divided in two different GPU kernels. The first kernel executes the operations required to calculate the sum of absolute differences (SAD) residuals across a search area in the reference frame, while the second one determines the best MV in terms of SAD cost.

The first kernel relies on the fact that every PU size established by the standard is divisible by four, and thus it is possible to calculate the residual information of a PU from the composition of its 4×4 SAD partitions. Following this approach, the previously mentioned kernel distributes a device thread to each sample (i.e. possible MV) in the reference search area. Each thread is responsible for calculating all the 4×4 SAD blocks in a CTU. Once these blocks are calculated, every thread puts them together to obtain the PUs into which a CTU might be divided. At this point, the device has at its disposal the prediction costs for each position in the search area and every PU. Therefore, the second kernel consists of a reduction algorithm that selects the best MV in terms of SAD. The set of MVs and their corresponding costs is sent back to the host.

With this information, the encoder is able to skip the first step of the ME module, which corresponds to the integer ME. Instead of performing the search, the host only needs to obtain the MV that the device asynchronously calculated and copied beforehand, thus reducing the computational complexity of the ME.

4.3 Joint Heterogeneous Architecture

While the proposed slice-based algorithm performs a coarse-grained parallelization of the encoding, the GPU-based ME algorithm is able to speed up one of the most computationally expensive modules of the encoder. The way in which both algorithms cooperate is shown in Fig. 3. As can be seen, the input frames are divided into slices as described in Sect. 4.1, and each of them is assigned to a processing unit. Then, every processing unit can queue the GPU-based ME algorithm into different streams of the device, making it possible to even perform the operations concurrently. As a result, the device utilization increases, and the relative power consumption decreases.

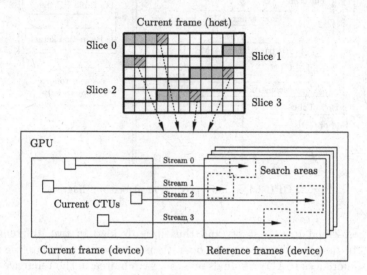

Fig. 3. Combination of the slice-based algorithm and the GPU-based proposal (4 threads)

With regard to the scalability of the algorithm, it is only restricted by the hardware platform in use. On the one hand, the slice-based algorithm is as scalable as the number of available processing units. On the other hand, while the GPU-based algorithm has been designed in an efficient way, the device could limit the amount of parallelism if it cannot process as many CTUs as required.

5   Performance Evaluation

The experiments have been executed on the HEVC Test Model (HM-16.3) [1] reference software, following the guidelines and coding conditions provided by the JCT-VC in [4]. In this regard, Low Delay B has been the selected configuration, and the QP values are 22, 27, 32 and 37. The encodings have been carried out using the Main profile and 8-bit depth. Sequences of classes C and D have been used, which include the 832×480 (C) and 416×240 (D) resolutions.

The hardware platform used in the experiments is composed of an Intel® Core™ i7-2600 CPU running at 3.40 GHz and an NVIDIA® GeForce® GTX 560 Ti GPU running 384 CUDA cores at the frequency of 1.6 GHz. The encoder has been compiled with GCC 5.3.1 and NVIDIA CUDA 7.5, and executed on Ubuntu 16.04 (Linux 4.4.0-22). Turbo Boost and Hyper-Threading have been disabled to achieve the reproducibility of the results.

With regard to the parametrization of the encoder, the sample adaptive offset (SAO) filter has been disabled, as well as the *LFCrossSliceBoundary* flag. This can be justified by the fact that slices should be completely independent for parallel processing, but these filters introduce some dependencies. In the case of the proposed algorithm, the encoder is executed using 4 threads.

The results will be provided in terms of speed-up and Bjøntegaard delta rate (BD-rate). The latter represents the percentage of bit rate variation between two sequences with the same objective quality [3]. Therefore, a negative value implies that the proposal improves the coding efficiency of the baseline encoder.

Table 1. Results of the proposed algorithm using four threads

Class	Video sequence	BD-rate (%)	Encoding speed-up
C	BasketballDrill	2.12	3.91
	BQMall	2.94	3.60
	PartyScene	1.85	3.79
	RaceHorses	2.51	4.06
D	BasketballPass	4.80	3.54
	BQSquare	5.51	3.41
	BlowingBubbles	4.32	3.43
	RaceHorses	4.39	3.72
	Mean values	3.55	3.68

Table 1 shows the results of the proposed GPU-based heterogeneous coding architecture compared to the baseline encoder with just one slice per frame. As can be seen, the obtained BD-rate is directly related to the resolution of the input sequence. Smaller resolutions involve smaller slices, and thus more broken dependencies and more overhead. In terms of speed-up, the results show that the achieved parallel efficiency is considerably high, obtaining values that are greater than the maximum theoretical of $4\times$. The cases in which this is not true can be justified by the fact that not all the slices take the same amount of time to be encoded, even if they contain the same number of CTUs.

6   Conclusions

The HEVC standard has opened the door to a great number of new applications and video formats such as UHD with the aim of fulfilling the demands of the market. However, the improved coding efficiency of HEVC has also led to a notable increment in the computational complexity of the encoder. In order to achieve real-time encoding, it has become a requirement to develop fast and efficient coding algorithms. Accordingly, this paper proposes a GPU-based heterogeneous architecture for HEVC which combines a coarse-grained parallelization technique and a GPU-based ME algorithm. While the former is able to achieve coarse-grained parallelism by removing existing dependencies, the latter speeds up the most computationally expensive module of the encoder.

An experimental evaluation of the algorithm has shown that the encoding can be speeded up by 3.68× on average with four threads, showing efficient utilization of resources of the GPU-based heterogeneous platform. As a consequence, there is a low impact in coding efficiency of 3.55% in BD-rate.

References

1. HEVC Test Model (HM) Reference Software. https://hevc.hhi.fraunhofer.de/
2. Álvarez-Mesa, M., Chi, C.C., Juurlink, B., George, V., Schierl, T.: Parallel video decoding in the emerging HEVC standard. In: IEEE International Conference on Acoustics, Speech and Signal Processing (ICASSP), pp. 1545–1548, March 2012
3. Bjøntegaard, G.: Calculation of average PSNR differences between RD-curves. Technical report VCEG-M33, ITU-T Video Coding Experts Group (VCEG) (2001)
4. Bossen, F.: Common test conditions and software reference configurations. Technical report JCTVC-L1100, January 2013
5. Bossen, F., Bross, B., Shring, K., Flynn, D.: HEVC complexity and implementation analysis. IEEE Trans. Circuits Syst. Video Technol. **22**(12), 1685–1696 (2012)
6. Chi, C.C., Álvarez-Mesa, M., Lucas, J., Juurlink, B., Schierl, T.: Parallel HEVC decoding on multi- and many-core architectures. J. Sign. Process. Syst. **71**(3), 247–260 (2013)
7. ISO/IEC, and ITU-T: High Efficiency Video Coding (HEVC). ITU-T Recommendation H.265 and ISO/IEC 23008–2 (version 3), April 2015
8. ISO/IEC, and ITU-T: Advanced video coding for generic audiovisual services. ITU-T Recommendation H.264 and ISO/IEC 14496–10 (version 10), February 2016
9. Łuczak, A., Karwowski, D., Maćkowiak, S., Grajek, T.: Diamond scanning order of image blocks for massively parallel HEVC compression. In: Bolc, L., Tadeusiewicz, R., Chmielewski, L.J., Wojciechowski, K. (eds.) ICCVG 2012. LNCS, vol. 7594, pp. 172–179. Springer, Heidelberg (2012). doi:10.1007/978-3-642-33564-8_21
10. Ohm, J.R., Sullivan, G.J., Schwarz, H., Tan, T.K., Wiegand, T.: Comparison of the coding efficiency of video coding standards - including high efficiency video coding (HEVC). IEEE Trans. Circuits Syst. Video Technol. **22**(12), 1669–1684 (2012)
11. Qin, Y., Zhao, L., Ma, S.: Parallel AMVP candidate list construction for HEVC. In: IEEE Visual Communications and Image Processing (VCIP), pp. 1–6, November 2012
12. Radicke, S., Hahn, J.U., Grecos, C., Wang, Q.: A highly-parallel approach on motion estimation for high efficiency video coding (HEVC). In: IEEE International Conference on Consumer Electronics (ICCE), pp. 187–188, January 2014
13. Wang, X., Song, L., Chen, M., Yang, J.: Paralleling variable block size motion estimation of HEVC on CPU plus GPU platform. In: IEEE International Conference on Multimedia and Expo Workshops (ICMEW), pp. 1–5, July 2013

Optimizing GPU Code for CPU Execution Using OpenCL and Vectorization: A Case Study on Image Coding

Pedro M.M. Pereira[1,2], Patricio Domingues[1,2], Nuno M.M. Rodrigues[1,2], Gabriel Falcao[2,3], and Sergio M.M. de Faria[1,2(✉)]

[1] School of Management and Technology, Polytechnic Institute of Leiria, Leiria, Portugal
pedrommpereira@gmail.com,
{patricio.domingues,nuno.rodrigues,sergio.faria}@ipleiria.pt
[2] Instituto de Telecomunicações, Lisbon, Portugal
[3] Department of Electrical and Computer Engineering, University of Coimbra, Coimbra, Portugal
gff@deec.uc.pt

Abstract. Although OpenCL aims to achieve portability at the code level, different hardware platforms requires different approaches in order to extract the best performance for OpenCL-based code. In this work, we use an image encoder originally tuned for OpenCL on GPU (OpenCL-GPU), and optimize it for multi-CPU based platforms. We produce two OpenCL-based versions: (i) a regular one (OpenCL-CPU) and (ii) a CPU vector-based one (OpenCL-CPU-Vect). The use of CPU vectorization exploits the OpenCL support, making it much simpler than directly coding with SIMD instructions such as SSE and AVX. Globally, while the OpenCL-GPU version is the fastest when run on a high end GPU requiring around 580 s to encode the Lenna image, its performance drops roughly 65 % when run unchanged on a multicore CPU machine. For the CPU tuned versions, OpenCL-CPU encodes the Lenna image in 805 s, while the vectorization-based approach executes the same operation in 672 s. Results show that meaningful performance gains can be achieved by tailoring the OpenCL code to the CPU, and that the use of CPU vectorization instructions through OpenCL is both rather simple and performance rewarding.

Keywords: OpenCL · Multicore · Manycore · Image encoding · SIMD

1 Introduction

High performance computing has been a rather difficult and selective discipline, mostly due to hardware and software limitations. The advent of multicore CPUs

S.M.M. de Faria—Financial support provided in the scope of R&D Unit 50008, financed by FCT/MEC through national funds and co-funded by FEDER - PT2020 partnership agreement.

© Springer International Publishing AG 2016
J. Carretero et al. (Eds.): ICA3PP 2016, LNCS 10048, pp. 537–545, 2016.
DOI: 10.1007/978-3-319-49583-5_42

and manycore GPUs has boosted the case for high performance, allowing for low cost high performance computing. The emergence of the OpenCL (Open Computing Language) standard [12] and its main focus on code portability regardless of the underlying platform – CPU, GPU and other accelerators – is seen as a major asset for software development. However, while OpenCL achieves code portability, the same cannot be said of performance portability. Indeed, the range of supported platforms is too different to allow for write once, performance everywhere code [11].

We assess and tune the performance of the Multimedia Multiscale Parser (MMP) OpenCL-based software. MMP is a computationally demanding image encoder/decoder algorithm. In lossy mode and set for high quality compression, the sequential version of MMP can take half an hour on an Intel i7 CPU to encode the 512×512 pixels 8-bit gray Lenna image. Our code base is an OpenCL version of MMP previously optimized for GPUs [2]. We first assess the performance of the OpenCL code base on multicore CPU platforms, measuring the performance port penalty. We then optimize the OpenCL code base for multicore CPU platforms, producing the OpenCL-CPU version. Finally, we further optimize the OpenCL-CPU version, applying vector-based instructions, resorting solely to OpenCL for this purpose.

One of the main motivations for this work is to evaluate a GPU-optimized OpenCL code vs. a CPU-optimized OpenCL code, avoiding the trap from comparing a non-CPU optimized version of a code vs. a GPU-tailored one [8]. Another motivation is to assess the support of OpenCL for CPU-vectorization, which facilitates the use of SIMD instructions. We believe that the main contributions of this work are: (i) assessing the performance port penalty of OpenCL when running an untouched GPU-optimized code on a multicore CPU; (ii) assessing the gain achieved through optimization for multicore CPU and; (iii) evaluation of the performance gain of using CPU-based vectorization instructions through OpenCL. Although this study relies solely on the MMP application, the fact that the MMP algorithm is a computational demanding image encoder/decoder, with sequential dependencies among individual input blocks, insures some representativeness as an application for parallelization. The remainder of this paper is outlined as follows. Section 2 reviews related work. Section 3 summarizes the MMP algorithm. Section 4 presents the main optimizations. Section 5 presents performance results. Finally, Sect. 6 concludes the paper.

2   Related Work

The main goal of the OpenCL standard is to provide a portable abstraction over parallel heterogeneous hardware [12]. The hardware can be CPU, manycore GPU, FPGA or any other so called accelerator device that has parallel computing capabilities. Shen et al. argue that while OpenCL aims to be platform neutral, it is strongly biased towards the manycore models of GPUs [11]. Joo Lee et al. [7] thoroughly analyze the performance of OpenCL for CPUs. Their main conclusions are: (i) API overhead is non negligible, (ii) memory allocation flags do not change performance and the (iii) programming model can affect the compiler-supported vectorization.

The existence of vectorization support through Single Instruction Multiple Data (SIMD) reinforces the CPU attractiveness for high performance computing [4]. Mitra et al. report performance gains ranging from 1.34 to 5.54× on the SSE-based Neon benchmark of the OpenCV library, at the cost of laborious hand-tuning optimizations [9]. One of the main advantage of OpenCL for CPU platforms is the abstraction layer it provides regarding to SIMD instructions. For instance, the Intel OpenCL compiler provides for implicit vectorization, automatically applying SSE/AVX instructions to OpenCL kernels [3,5]. On top of the implicit use of vectorization by the OpenCL compiler, the OpenCL framework allows for the explicit use of vectorization, through vector-oriented datatype, such as, for instance, *int4*. This way, the programmer can explicitly requests vectorization, without having to go to the lower details of vectorization instructions. This is one of the performance path that we explore in this work.

3   The Multimedia Multiscale Parser

The Multidimensional Multiscale Parser (MMP) is a pattern-matching-based compression algorithm. It suited to compress multimedia images, where it lossy compression mode can achieve good compression ratio and maintain good image quality [10]. While compressing, MMP dynamically builds a dictionary of patterns that it uses for approximating the content of the input image. Specifically, the input content is split in blocks, each having 16×16 pixels. The whole grid of blocks laid over the image is processed sequentially, one block at the time, from left to right and top to bottom. For every input block, MMP assesses the patterns that exist in its dictionary to find the one that is the closest to the original one, yielding the lowest overall distortion. For this purpose, MMP computes the Lagrangian cost J between the input block and all blocks existing in the dictionary. The Lagrangian cost is given by the equation $J = D + \lambda.R$, where D measures the distortion between the original block and the candidate block, R represents the number of bits needed to encode the approximation and λ is a numerical configuration parameter. The λ parameter steers the algorithm towards more compression quality (low λ) or lower bit rate (high λ). MMP also explores patterns that are not yet in the dictionary, computing their Lagrangian cost J. This is done with the goal of finding new patterns more suited for the input being processed, i.e., yield lowest Lagrangian cost. For these possible patterns to be, MMP uses a multiscale approach, which enables the approximation of image blocks with different sizes. Specifically, while the input image is processed in basic blocks of 16×16 pixels, for each individual block, all possible subscale blocks (8×4, 16×2, 1×1, etc.) are tested to find the best possible matches. When the search is exhausted, MMP selects the best block or set of sub-blocks. The exhaustive search for the best fitted block or set of sub-blocks is the main cause for the high computational complexity of MMP. Having found a set of new blocks/sub-blocks, MMP proceeds to update the dictionary of patterns.

First, MMP searches through the dictionary looking for blocks that might be identical or approximate (within a given radius) to the newly proposed blocks. If no close block to the new ones are found, MMP adds the new block/sub-blocks to the dictionary. The computing processes – block and sub-blocks search and dictionary update – is repeated for every single block of the input image. Since the dictionary might be updated after an input block is encoded, the encoding operation of input block i can only start after processing of input block $i - 1$ has finished. This effectively constitutes a synchronization point for every input block, voiding the possibilities for parallel processing of multiple input blocks.

The OpenCL version of MMP. The OpenCL-based version of MMP (MMP-OpenCL) aims to exploit the parallelism provided by the algorithm, partitioning every input block into sub-blocks (scales). For this purpose, the MMP OpenCL version resorts to three kernels: (1) *optimize_block*; (2) *j_reducter* and (3) *update_dict*. The *optimize_block* kernel computes the distortion and the Lagrangian cost for every scale of the current input block combined with the whole set of same-scale blocks of the dictionary. The *j_reducter* kernel performs a reduction operation over the results computed by *optimize_block*. The kernel returns, for each scale, the block or set of sub-blocks that yield the lowest Lagrangian cost. Finally, when the selected block/sub-blocks does not exist in the dictionary, the *update_dict* analyzes whether it should be inserted, and if so, inserts it in the dictionary. The execution flow for MMP-OpenCL unrolls as follows: the kernel *optimize_block* and the kernel *j_reducter* are called in sequence. The number of calls for both kernels depends on (i) the input block, and therefore, on the input image and (ii) on the value set for the parameter λ. The kernel *update_dic* is run once per input block, just before the encoding operation for the block is completed. The first version of MMP-OpenCL targeted GPU (henceforth, MMP-OpenCL-GPU), with the main optimizations linked to the underlying hardware. A particular focus was to balance the workload among the GPU workers, so that all workers performed, roughly, the same amount of work. Another important focus was to organize data and threads in order to achieve aligned and coalesced memory accesses, as this has a major impact on performance [1,6].

4   Optimizing MMP for OpenCL-CPU

The OpenCL platform can directly be mapped to GPUs since they have hundreds of PE cores. However, CPUs have a much lower number of cores, although each core is more powerful than a GPU core. This way, mapping fine-grained OpenCL work to CPU is inefficient and a coarser approach needs to be followed [11]. For instance, fine-grained parallelization on a multicore CPU restricts cache utilization, since one work-item only processes a small proportion of the data. Another mismatch is due to the different memory hierarchy of CPUs and GPUs. In particular, the GPU memory hierarchy is explicitly exposed to the application, which can select a faster but smaller local memory or a larger but slower global memory. In contrast, the CPU memory hierarchy is not accessible to applications.

Thus, under OpenCL on CPUs, all objects declared for local memory are mapped to the global memory.

Memory Mapping. When mapping OpenCL on CPUs, the host and device share the same memory space. Since OpenCL requires explicit data transfers but does not impose restrictions on memory access patterns, it is up to the compiler and to the device driver to select whether or not to actually replicate the data or just read it from already allocated space. To overcome this irregularity, we applied the so called *zero copy* technique. This way, by changing the data transfer functions to *clEnqueueMapBuffer* and *clEnqueueUnmapMemObject*, we get an OpenCL memory pointer to the same mapped region. By mapping a region, we inform that the host now has the right to read and write. Conversely, when the region is unmapped, the device kernel regains the access control to the memory.

Memory Access. GPU code with explicit memory coalescing suffers performance degradation on CPUs. A GPU optimal code will have a column-major access pattern to enable more effective transactions of global memory loads and stores in opposition to the required row-major order necessary to preserve the cache locality within each CPU thread. On the CPU, the OpenCL-GPU coalesced memory optimization was causing heavy cache misses. We removed the coalesced memory optimization, and returned to a simpler access pattern, more suited to CPUs.

Optimizing Access to Metadata. GPU devices have special purpose registers to hold workers' local and global IDs. These special registers speed up access to these metadata. CPUs lack these registers and thus repeated calls such as *get_global_id(0)*, for instance inside a loop, are costly. To avoid this overhead, we changed the code to prefetch the local ID, local size and the number of work groups from explicitly private-defined variables.

Fostering Loop Unrolling. The GPU optimized version of the code resorted to a 9-version *optimize_block* kernel linked to prediction modes. Prediction modes of MMP try to leverage the probability that neighbor pixels are similar. Note that only frontier pixels from previously encoded blocks can be used for prediction. The prediction modes are similar to the intraframe prediction feature of the H.264 coding standard.

The number of prediction modes that can actually be used with a given block depends on the dimension of the block/sub-block and on the location in the image of the block. For instance, for any of the blocks of the top row of the input image, prediction mode 0 cannot be used, since it requires the pixels from the upper block which does not exist. On the GPU code, the *optimize_block* kernel resorts to shared memory. The amount of shared memory is directly proportional to the number of prediction modes that the kernel has to handle. As the amount of shared memory limits the number of threads that can be simultaneously running – more shared memory reduces the number of simultaneous threads and vice-versa –, the GPU code had 9 different *optimize_block* kernels, each one tailored for the best shared memory/number of threads ratio. On the OpenCL CPU code, we no longer use shared memory, since there is only one thread per block.

However, the MMP-OpenCL-CPU code has 8 loops whose number of iterations is dependent on the number of active prediction modes. Thus, in order to promote a more fine-grained loop unrolling and ease the task of the compiler, we created 9 kernels, which only differed on constant values set for the loops.

Explicit Vectorization. Besides the implicit optimization attempted by compilers, the OpenCL developer can explicitly promote the use of vectorization by declaring variables as vector datatypes such as *int4* and *float8* in the kernel code. The compiler attempts to employ vector-based instructions making use of the explicit knowledge conveyed by the variables declared as vector datatypes. For OpenCL-MMP-CPU, work item vectorization was fairly simple. The kernel *update_dict* was vectorized by using the *int4* datatype and by padding the aligned data. The vectorization of the kernels *optimize_block* and *j_reducter* required padding the data in an adaptive manner since the MMP block being processed can have one of possible sizes. This was dealt with a switch-case adapted to whether the data could fit in 2, 4 or 8 bytes.

Vectorization of Data Reduction. SIMD vectorization was further used to optimize data reduction that forms the core of the *j_reducter*. Specifically, after having completed the usual iterative sum to obtain a vector with 8 elements, the 8-element vector is further reduced to a scalar by performing a vector addition on its high and low parts, that is, adding *vector.hi* + *vector.lo* into an *int4* vector. The procedure is repeated for the *int4* vector, yielding an *int2* vector, and then again for the *int2* vector. This way, the reduction sum on an 8-element vector is performed through vectorization.

5 Main Experimental Results

Experimental Setup. The tests reported in this study were performed on two machines: (i) a multiprocessor server with two Intel Xeon SixCore E5-2620 V2 2.1 GHz CPUs and (ii) a laptop with an Intel core i7-2670QM 2.20 GHz CPU. Each CPU of the server has 6 physical cores, for a total of 12 physical cores for the whole server. The laptop has a single CPU with 4 physical cores. As each physical core hosts two virtual cores, the server has a total of 24 virtual cores and the laptop has 8 virtual cores.

For the GPU-based tests, the server was fitted with an NVIDIA Titan Black Edition GPU. The laptop has a built-in NVIDIA 570M GPU. Note that the GTX 570M is a mobile budget oriented GPU, while the Titan Black Edition is a high-end GPU. The 570M has 336 cores and an announced performance of 0.772 TFLOPS for single-precision FP. The Titan Black Edition has 2880 cores and can deliver a top performance of 5.121 TFLOPS on 32-bit single-precision FP computation. The OS of both machines was Ubuntu 14.04/64 bit with the 3.13.0-36 generic Linux kernel. The development stack was CUDA 6.5 (GPUs) and Intel OpenCL SDK 1.1/Runtime 15.1 × 65 5.0.0.57 (CPUs). The C compiler was GCC 4.8.2.

Table 1. Execution times (seconds) for the various MMP versions

	Laptop	Server 4M	Server 2M
Sequential	1708.924	1964.599	2063.880
OpenCL-GPU on GPU	583.006 (2.93x)	496.002 (3.45x)	506.688 (3.37x)
OpenCL-GPU on CPU	976.386 (1.75x)	1029.942 (1.66x)	1035.793 (1.65x)
OpenCL-CPU on CPU	815.928 (2.09x)	967.754 (1.77x)	1023.300 (1.67x)
OpenCL-CPU on CPU (SIMD)	671.736 (2.54x)	901.732 (1.90x)	958.546 (1.78x)

Main Results. To assess the performance of OpenCL on CPUs and on GPUs, all versions were run 15 times. The test consisted on encoding the 8-bit gray level 512×512 pixel *Lenna* image with MMP. The parameter λ was set to 10, a value that promotes quality, requiring significant computing power. The dictionary was allowed to grow up to $50,000$ elements, a large value that does not hinder the quality of the compression. Table 1 shows the execution times, in seconds, for the various version of MMP and, within parentheses, the speedup relatively to the corresponding sequential (non-multithreaded) version. The *server 4M* and *server 2M* columns correspond to the server machine with different hardware RAM memory modules: *server 4M* refers to the server fitted with four 8 GiB DDR3/1600 MHz modules, while *server 2M* identifies the use of two 16 GiB DDR3/1333 MHz modules.

Surprisingly, for executions that solely use the CPU, the laptop performs roughly 15 % faster than the server. This is due to the faster system memory of the laptop. The importance of the memory system is further highlighted by the execution time differences between the two memory configurations of server: *Server 4M* is roughly 5 % faster than *Server 2M*. This can be explained by the fact that (i) the RAM modules of the 4M configuration are clocked at a higher frequency than the ones of the 2M configuration (1600 MHz vs. 1333 MHz) and that (ii) having four memory modules better suits a four memory channel CPU such as the Xeon SixCore E5-2620 V2, especially on a multiprocessor setting.

Overall, the GPU optimized version of OpenCL yields the fastest execution times, achieving a speedup over the sequential version of $2.93\times$ for the laptop plus GPU and $3.45\times$ for Server 4M plus GPU. These results highlight the importance of the GPU, with the more powerful Titan GPU yielding faster results than the 570M. When the SIMD-based optimization is considered, the performance gain over the GPU-optimized version run on CPU is 1.454 for the laptop and 1.081 for the fastest server configuration. For the laptop, the SIMD optimization adds a 20 % speedup over the non-SIMD OpenCL-CPU version, and around 1.07 for the server. Globally, the SIMD-enabled OpenCL version achieves a 2.54 speedup over the sequential version vs. 2.93 for the OpenCL-GPU version ran on the laptop GPU. This means that substantial speedup can still be achieved with OpenCL when no GPU is available. Additionally, enabling explicit usage of SIMD instructions in OpenCL can provide some performance improvement.

6 Conclusion

This paper studies the performance implications of several optimizations of an OpenCL-based code. Specifically, an originally optimized for GPU OpenCL version of the MMP encoder/decode is adapted to multicore CPUs and further optimized through SIMD vectorization instructions. The results show that although the GPU-based version yields the fastest performance when ran on GPUs, this version suffers a significant performance drop when executed on non-GPU environment. This confirms the need to adapt OpenCL codes accordingly to their hardware execution environments. Indeed, by optimizing the OpenCL code for CPU, a 2.54 performance improvement was achieved over the sequential version, closer to the 2.93 speedup yielded by the GPU-based version. Part of the overall performance improvement of the CPU-oriented versions is due to the use of SIMD-based optimizations. This is interesting as the OpenCL framework makes for an easy and almost transparent use of SIMD-based instructions. This way, the developer can access some performance benefits of CPU-based vectorization with minimal effort. This makes for an interesting case for considering CPU-oriented optimization for OpenCL codes.

References

1. Che, S., Sheaffer, J.W., Skadron, K.: Dymaxion: optimizing memory access patterns for heterogeneous systems. In: ICHPCNSA, p. 13. ACM (2011)
2. Domingues, P., Silva, J., Ribeiro, T., Rodrigues, N.M.M., Carvalho, M.B., Faria, S.M.M.: Optimizing memory usage and accesses on CUDA-based recurrent pattern matching image compression. In: Murgante, B., Misra, S., Rocha, A.M.A.C., Torre, C., Rocha, J.G., Falcão, M.I., Taniar, D., Apduhan, B.O., Gervasi, O. (eds.) ICCSA 2014. LNCS, vol. 8583, pp. 560–575. Springer, Heidelberg (2014). doi:10.1007/978-3-319-09147-1_41
3. Dong, H., Ghosh, D., Zafar, F., Zhou, S.: Cross-platform OpenCL code and performance portability investigated with a climate and weather physics model. In: 41st International Conference on ICPPW, pp. 126–134. IEEE (2012)
4. Hwu, W.M.: What is ahead for parallel computing. J. Parallel Distrib. Comput. **74**(7), 2574–2581 (2014)
5. Intel: Writing Optimal OpenCL Code with Intel OpenCL SDK (2011)
6. Jang, B., Schaa, D., Mistry, P., Kaeli, D.: Exploiting memory access patterns to improve memory performance in data-parallel architectures. IEEE Trans. Parallel Distrib. Syst. **22**(1), 105–118 (2011)
7. Lee, J.H., Patel, K., Nigania, N., Kim, H., Kim, H.: OpenCL performance evaluation on modern multi core CPUs. In: IEEE 27th International Symposium on IPDPS, pp. 1177–1185. IEEE (2013)
8. Lee, V.W., Kim, C., Chhugani, J., Deisher, M., Kim, D., Nguyen, A.D., Satish, N., Smelyanskiy, M., Chennupaty, S., Hammarlund, P., Singhal, R., Dubey, P.: Debunking the 100X GPU vs. CPU myth. SIGARCH Comput. Archit. News **38**, 451–460 (2010)
9. Mitra, G., Johnston, B., Rendell, A.P., McCreath, E., Zhou, J.: Use of SIMD vector operations to accelerate application code performance on low-powered ARM and Intel platforms. In: IEEE 27th International Symposium on IPDPS, pp. 1107–1116. IEEE (2013)

10. Rodrigues, N.M., da Silva, E.A., de Carvalho, M.B., de Faria, S.M., da Silva, V.M.M.: On dictionary adaptation for recurrent pattern image coding. IEEE Trans. Image Proces. **17**(9), 1640–1653 (2008)
11. Shen, J., Fang, J., Sips, H., Varbanescu, A.L.: Performance traps in OpenCL for CPUs. In: PDP2013, pp. 38–45. IEEE (2013)
12. Stone, J.E., Gohara, D., Shi, G.: OpenCL: a parallel programming standard for heterogeneous computing systems. Comput. Sci. Eng. **12**(3), 66–73 (2010)

Improving the Performance of Cardiac Simulations in a Multi-GPU Architecture Using a Coalesced Data and Kernel Scheme

Raphael Pereira Cordeiro[1], Rafael Sachetto Oliveira[2],
Rodrigo Weber dos Santos[1], and Marcelo Lobosco[1(✉)]

[1] Programa em Modelagem Computacional, UFJF, Juiz de Fora, Brazil
raphael.cordeiro@engenharia.ufjf.br,
{rodrigo.weber,marcelo.lobosco}@ufjf.edu.br
[2] Departamento de Ciência da Computação, UFSJ, São João del Rei, Brazil
sachetto@ufsj.edu.br

Abstract. In this paper we evaluate a new coalesced data and kernel scheme used to reduce the execution costs of cardiac simulations that run on multi-GPU environments. The new scheme was tested for an important part of the simulator, the solution of the systems of Ordinary Differential Equations (ODEs). The results have shown that the proposed scheme is very effective. The execution time to solve the systems of ODEs on the multi-GPU environment was reduced by half, when compared to a scheme that does not implemented the proposed data and kernel coalescing. As a result, the total execution time of cardiac simulations was 25 % faster.

Keywords: High performance computing · Parallel computing · Multi-GPU · Cardiac electrophysiology · Computational modeling

1 Introduction

The phenomenon of electric propagation in the heart comprises a set of complex non-linear biophysical processes. Computer models [8] have become valuable tools for the study and comprehension of such complex phenomena, as they allow different information acquired from different physical scales and experiments to be combined to generate a better picture of the whole system functionality. Not surprisingly, the high complexity of the biophysical processes translates into complex mathematical and computational models. The modern cardiac models are described by non–linear systems of partial differential equations (PDE) coupled to a non–linear set of ordinary differential equations (ODE) resulting in a problem with millions of variables and hundreds of parameters.

M. Lobosco—The authors would like to thank UFJF, UFSJ, FINEP, FAPEMIG, CAPES, and CNPq.

J. Carretero et al. (Eds.): ICA3PP 2016, LNCS 10048, pp. 546–553, 2016.
DOI: 10.1007/978-3-319-49583-5_43

The bidomain model [14] is considered to be the most complete description of the electrical activity in cardiac tissue. Under suitable assumptions the bidomain equations (a non-linear system of PDEs) may be reduced to a simpler model, called monodomain, which is less computationally demanding. Unfortunately, large scale simulations, such as those resulting from the discretization of an entire heart, are still a computational challenge. In spite of the difficulties and the complexity associated with the implementation and use of these models, the benefits and applications justify their use. Computer models have been used during the tests of new drugs, development of new medical devices, new techniques of non–invasive diagnosis for several cardiac disease, cardiac arrhythmia, reentry, fibrillation or defibrillation and have been the research topic of many studies [5,6,9,13].

However, the demand of fine discretization for the solution of the PDEs and nonuniform, heterogeneous tissue electric conductivity have prevented, in the past, the study of the aforementioned phenomena on cardiac tissues that include microscopic structures. In our previous work [3], we presented a solution for this problem based on multi-GPU platforms (clusters equipped with graphics processing units) that allows fast simulations of microscopic tissue models. The solution was based on merging two different high performance techniques that we have previously investigated for cardiac modeling: Cluster computing based on message passing communications (MPI) [11,12,15]; and GPGPU (General-purpose computing on graphics processing units) [1,10].

In this paper we extend the Multi-GPU solver for simulations of microscopic tissue models, presented in [3] by coalescing the data and GPU kernels executions in the multi-GPU environment. This new scheme was tested only for the solution of the systems ODEs. The results have shown that the proposed scheme is very effective. The execution time to solve the systems of ODEs on the multi-GPU environment was reduced by half, when compared to a scheme that does not implemented the proposed data and kernel coalescing.

2   The Heterogeneous Monodomain Model

In this work, we use the detailed Microscopic Model presented first in [3]. These model can be described mathematically by a reaction-diffusion type partial differential equation (PDE) called monodomain model, given by

$$\beta C_m \frac{\partial V(x,y,t)}{\partial t} + \beta I_{ion}(V(x,y,t), \boldsymbol{\eta}(x,y,t)) = \nabla \cdot (\boldsymbol{\sigma}(x,y)\nabla V(x,y,t)) + I_{stim}(x,y,t)$$

$$\frac{\partial \boldsymbol{\eta}(x,y,t)}{\partial t} = \boldsymbol{f}(V(x,y,t), \boldsymbol{\eta}(x,y,t)), \quad (1)$$

where V is the variable of interest and represents the transmembrane potential, i.e. the difference between intracellular to extracellular potential; $\boldsymbol{\eta}$ is a vector of state variables that also influence the generation and propagation of the electric wave, and usually includes the intracellular concentration of different ions (K^+, Na^+, Ca^{2+}) and the permeability of different membrane ion channels; β is the surface-volume ratio of heart cells; C_m is the membrane capacitance, I_{ion} the total ionic current, which is a function of V and η, I_{stim} is the current due to an external stimulus and σ is the monodomain conductivity tensor. We assume that no–flux boundary conditions ($\mathbf{n} \cdot \sigma \nabla V = 0$ on $\partial \Omega$) are imposed.

In this work, the Bondarenko et al. model [4] (BDK) that describes the electrical activity of left ventricular cells of mice was considered to simulate the kinetics of η in Eq. 1. In order to numerically solve Eq. 1, the reaction and diffusion part can be split by employing the Godunov operator splitting [14]. Each time step involves the solution of two different problems: a nonlinear system of ODEs For the discretization of the nonlinear system of ODEs we used the simple explicit Euler method with a time step $\Delta t = 0.0001$ ms. To solve the PDE we used the Finite Volume Method (FVM). The detailed equations and formulation of these method can be found in [3].

3   Multi-GPU Implementation

Large scale simulations, such as those resulting from fine spatial discretization of a tissue, are computationally expensive. For example, if we use the typical discretization of the detailed Microscopic Model ($8\,\mu$m) with a 1 cm $\times$ 1 cm tissue, and the BDK, which has 41 differential variables, is used as cardiac cell model, a total of $1250 \times 1250 \times 41 = 64,062,500$ unknowns must be computed at each time step. In addition, to simulate 100 ms of cardiac electrical activity 64 millions of unknowns of the nonlinear systems of ODEs must be computed one million times (with $\Delta t_o = 0.0001$ ms) and the PDE with 1.5 million of unknowns must be computed ten thousand times. To deal with this high computational cost, two distinct tools for parallel computing were used together: MPI and GPGPU.

3.1   Parallel Implementation

The MPI library was used to implement a parallel solver suitable to be used in a cluster of CPUs. These parallel implementation uses the PETSc [2] and MPI [7]. It uses a parallel conjugate gradient preconditioned with ILU(0) (with block Jacobi in parallel) to solve the linear system associated to the the PDE of the monodomain model. More details about this implementation can be found in [3].

To solve the non-linear systems of ODEs, the explicit Euler method was used. No dependency exists between the solutions of the different systems of ODEs of each finite volume $Vol_{i,j}$. Therefore, it is quite simple to implement a parallel version of the code: each MPI process is responsible for computing a fraction Np of the total number of volumes of the simulation, where Np is the number of processes involved in the computation.

3.2   Multi-GPU Implementation with Non Coalesced Kernel

The multi-GPU with non coalesced kernel implementation was first described in [3]. In this implementation, the linear system associated to the PDE of the monodomain model is solved as in the cluster implementation. Therefore, the multi-GPU code also solves the PDE with the parallel conjugate gradient preconditioned with ILU(0) available in PETSc. However, the solution of the systems of ODEs is accelerated by using multiple GPUs. Two kernels have been developed to solve each of the systems of ODEs related to BDK model. The first kernel is responsible for setting the initial conditions of the systems of ODEs, whereas the second one integrates the systems of ODEs at each time step.

Both kernel implementations were optimized in many different ways. The state variables of M cardiac cells were stored in an array called SV, whose size is equal to $M \times Neq$, where Neq is the number of ODEs of the ionic model (in this work, Neq is equal to 41). The SV array was organized in such way that the first M entries correspond to the first state variable, followed by M entries of the next state variable, and so on. Moreover, for all ionic models, the first M entries of the SV array correspond to the transmembrane potential V. During the solution of PDE, after the integration of the ODEs systems, the transmembrane potential of each node should be passed to the PETSc solver. Due to the memory organization chosen for the SV array, this is straightforward task since the M first entries of the array correspond to the transmembrane potential V of each node. This organization allows us to avoid extra memory transactions between CPU and GPU, improving performance. Another implementation choice that impact performance positively was the way the SV array has been allocated. The SV array was allocated in global GPU memory using the *cudaMallocPitch* routine from the CUDA API. This routine may pad the allocation in order to ensure that corresponding memory addresses of any given row will continue to meet the alignment requirements for the coalescing operations performed by the hardware. In short, a strict coalescing requires that thread j out of n threads has to access data $u[j]$ if $u[0]$ is accessed by thread 0, i.e. each thread should perform data access by stride n. Therefore, in the first kernel, to set the initial conditions, each thread sets the values of all its state variables. The kernel that solves the system of ODEs operates similarly, i.e. each thread computes and updates its state variables writing to the right position in memory that corresponds to their variables.

For the parallelization, the domain was divided in N_p nonoverlapping subdomains, where N_p is the number of MPI processes or processing cores. The parallel solution of the PDE is implemented via PETSc, with each processing core p responsible for updating the variables associated to subdomain T_p. In our computational environment each machine or node has more CPU cores (8) than GPUs (2). Therefore, for the solution of the ODEs each GPU device will be responsible for processing more than one task, with the tasks being assigned to the GPUs in a round-robin fashion. Figure 1 show the domain decomposition for a problem with $Np = 16$ and two machines (each with 8 cores and 2 GPU devices). Four tasks would be assigned to each GPU device. For instance, at Node 0, GPU 0 would process tasks T_1, T_3, T_5 and T_7, and GPU 1 the tasks T_2, T_4, T_6 and T_8.

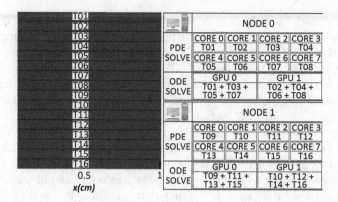

Fig. 1. Linear parallel decomposition of tissue. Example for the case of two nodes

3.3   Multi-GPU Implementation with Coalesced Kernel

The main problem regarding the original multi-GPU solver is that several processes can access the same GPU at the same time. With this strategy, each process using a GPU allocates a separate storage and scheduling resources on the GPU, causing an overhead in the GPU memory management. Moreover, when processes share the GPU their scheduling resources must be swapped on and off the GPU also causing an unnecessary overhead.

To deal with the overheads of the original code, we separated the processes in groups, where only one process communicates and execute kernels in the GPU (kernel coalescing). In order to do this we used the routine *MPI_Comm_split*, which creates new groups of communication based on a user defined splitting strategy. We created as many groups as we have GPUs and, the zeroth process of each group is the only one that can communicate with the GPU, updating the state vector in the GPU, and the others processor's vector in the CPU and executing the computing kernels. Similarly, each GPU communicate with only one group. Doing so, the GPUs still have the same amount of ODEs to solve, but will do it only once, because the data is coalesced. The difference between the two implementations can be seen in the pseudo-codes 1 and 2.

Algorithm 1. Original Code Implementation

```
    main
2:    ... initialize all the preliminary computation ...
      ... define subdomain to which each process is responsible ...
4:    ... define stimulus and send it to GPU ...
      while t ≤ final_time do
6:       ... update state vector in GPU ...
         ... solve ODEs in GPU ...
8:       ... update array in CPU ...
         ... solve PDEs in CPU ...
10:   end-while
    end-main
```

Algorithm 2. Group Code Implementation

---

main
2: ... initialize all the preliminary computation ...
    ... define subdomain to which each process is responsible ...
4: ... split processes into groups ...
    ... define stimulus ...
6: if $local\_rank = 0$ do
    ... gather stimulus from group's processes and send stimulus to GPU ...
8: end-if
    while $t \leq final\_time$ do
10:    if $local\_rank = 0$ do
       ... gather arrays from group and update state vector in GPU ...
12:    ... solve ODEs in GPU ...
       ... scatter the result between the processes in CPU ...
14:    end-if
    ... solve PDEs in CPU ...
16: end-while
    end-main

As in [3], for the solution of the ODEs both sequential and parallel (CUDA) codes used single precision. For the solution of the PDE we have used double precision. We have shown in [10] that the use of single precision in CUDA does not affect the numerical precision of the solver.

4 Performance Evaluation

This section evaluates the performance of the coalesced kernel (CK) scheme presented in this work, comparing it with the previous non coalesced kernel (NCK) scheme. The experiments were executed on 2 nodes of a cluster. Each machine has two Intel $E5620$ quad-core processors, with 12 GB of main memory, two Tesla C1060 GPUs, each one with 240 CUDA cores and 4 GB of global memory. Linux 2.6.32, CUDA driver version 6.0, OpenMPI version 1.6.2, nvcc release 6.0 and gcc version 4.4.7 were used to run and compile all codes. All versions were executed at least 5 times, and all standard deviations were below 1.6 %. The average execution time, in seconds, is then used to calculate the speedup, defined as the sequential execution time divided by the parallel execution time.

The simulations were performed using the microscopic model with spatial discretization of 8 μm, in cardiac tissue of 0.5 cm × 0.5 cm size that was stimulated in the center and was executed for 10 ms; the other values used in the simulation are $\sigma_m = 0.0$, $\sigma_c = 0.4\,\mu S/\mu m$, $G_p = 0.5\,\mu S$, $G_i = 0.33\,\mu S$, $G_c = 0.062\,\mu S$, $\beta = 0.14\,cm^{-1}$, $C_m = 1.0\,\mu F/cm^2$, $\Delta t_p = 0.01\,ms$, $\Delta t_o = 0.0001\,ms$.

The coalesced kernel (CK) scheme and the non coalesced kernel (NCK) one were evaluated using 11 distinct hardware configurations: 1 node with 1 GPU and 1; 2; 4 and 8 CPUs; 1 node with 2 GPUs and 2; 4 and 8 CPUs; 2 nodes with 2 GPUs and 8 and 16 CPUs; 2 nodes with 4 GPUs and 4; 8 and 16 CPUs. For each scheme, we collected the time to compute the ODE, the PDE and the total execution time. The communication time between CPUs and GPUs was less than 0.2 %, and for this reason it was ignored.

Figure 2 presents the performance gains obtained by the use of the CK scheme, compared with the use of the NCK scheme. The gains are higher when

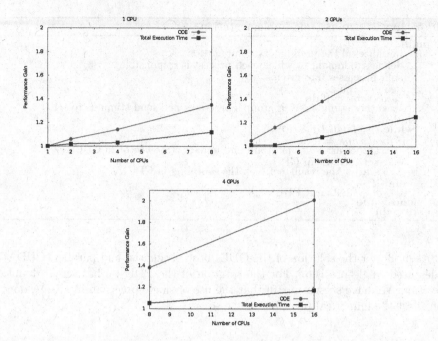

Fig. 2. Comparison between CK and NCK schemes. The configurations are grouped by the number of GPUs: 1 GPU (top left), 2 GPUs (top right) and 4 GPUs (bottom)

more CPUs are used, which confirms that the CK scheme was effective in its purpose of improving performance through the use of the coalesced scheme. Gains up to 2-fold were obtained in the ODE time in the configurations that used 16 CPUs and 2 GPUs, which speeds up the total computation time by a factor of 25%. Both schemes were executed in almost the same time in the configuration that uses one GPU and one CPU. This is the expected behavior, since in this configuration there is only one kernel to be launched to the GPU, so the schemes are equivalents in this configuration. The time to solve the PDE was almost the same in both schemes, which was also expected because only the CPU is used for this task. The differences in execution time are explained by the time employed to solve the ODEs: the CK scheme keeps this time constant, regardless of the number of CPUs used in the computation, while in the NCK scheme the time to solve the ODE increases with the number of CPUs. Finally, using the CK scheme the ODE execution time scales linearly with the number of GPUs.

5   Conclusion

This paper extended the multi-GPU solver for simulations of microscopic tissue models [3] by presenting a new scheme that coalesces the data and GPU kernels executions in the multi-GPU environment. This new strategy was very effective in its purpose of reducing the kernel execution overhead, improving the performance to solve the ODEs up to 2-fold and the total execution time up to 1.25 in comparison with the technique used in our previous work. It was also observed that the new coalescing scheme was responsible for scaling linearly the time to solve the ODEs with the number of GPUs.

References

1. Amorim, R.M., dos Santos, R.W.: Solving the cardiac bidomain equations using graphics processing units. J. Comput. Sci. **4**(5), 370–376 (2012)
2. Balay, S., Buschelman, K., Eijkhout, V., Gropp, W.D., Kaushik, D., Knepley, M.G., McInnes, L.C., Smith, B.F., Zhang, H.: PETSc users manual. Technical report (2004)
3. Barros, B.G., Oliveira, R.S., Meira Jr., W., Lobosco, M., Santos, R.W.: Simulations of complex and microscopic models of cardiac electrophysiology powered by multi-platforms. Comput. Math. Methods Med. **2012**, 1–13 (2012). Article ID 824569
4. Bondarenko, V.E., Szigeti, G.P., Bett, G.C., Kim, S.J., Rasmusson, R.L.: Computer model of action potential of mouse ventricular myocytes. Am. J. Physiol. - Heart Circulatory Physiol. **287**, H1378–H1403 (2004)
5. Campos, F.O., Wiener, T., Prassl, A.J., Weber dos Santos, R., Sanchez-Quintana, D., Ahammer, H., Plank, G., Hofer, E.: Electroanatomical characterization of atrial microfibrosis in a histologically detailed computer model. IEEE Trans. Biomed. Eng. **60**(8), 2339–2349 (2013)
6. Dos Santos, R.W., Kosch, O., Steinhoff, U., Bauer, S., Trahms, L., Koch, H.: MCG to ECG source differences: measurements and a two-dimensional computer model study. J. Electrocardiol. **37**, 123–127 (2004)
7. Groop, W., Lusk, E.: User's guide for mpich, a portable implementation of MPI. Technical report, Argonne National Laboratory (1994)
8. Hodgkin, A., Huxley, A.: A quantitative description of membrane current and its application to conduction and excitation in nerve. J. Physiol. **117**, 500–544 (1952)
9. Panfilov, A., Müller, S., Zykov, V., Keener, J.: Elimination of spiral waves in cardiac tissue by multiple electrical shocks. Phys. Rev. E **61**(4), 4644 (2000)
10. Rocha, B.M., Campos, F.O., Amorim, R.M., Plank, G., Santos, R.W.D., Liebmann, M., Haase, G.: Accelerating cardiac excitation spread simulations using graphics processing units. Concurrency Comput. Pract. Experience **23**(7), 708–720 (2011)
11. dos Santos, R.W., Plank, G., Bauer, S., Vigmond, E.J.: Parallel multigrid pre-conditioner for the cardiac bidomain model. IEEE Trans. Biomed. Eng. **51**(11), 1960–1968 (2004)
12. dos Santos, R.W., Plank, G., Bauer, S., Vigmond, E.J.: Preconditioning techniques for the bidomain equations. In: Barth, T.J., et al. (eds.) Domain Decomposition Methods in Science and Engineering. Lecture Notes in Computational Science and Engineering, vol. 40, pp. 571–580. Springer, Heidelberg (2004)
13. Weber do Santos, R., Campos, F.O., Ciuffo, L.N., Nygren, A., Giles, W., Koch, H.: ATX-II effects on the apparent location of m cells in a computational human left ventricular wedge. J. Cardiovasc. Electrophysiol. **17**, S86–S95 (2006)
14. Sundnes, J., Terje Lines, G., Tveito, A.: An operator splitting method for solving the bidomain equations coupled to a volume conductor model for the torso. Math. Biosci. **194**(2), 233–248 (2005)
15. Xavier, C., Oliveira, R., Vieira, V.F., dos Santos, R.W., Meira, W.: Multi-level parallelism for the cardiac bidomain equations. Int. J. Parallel Prog. **37**, 572–592 (2009)

Service Dependability and Security in Distributed and Parallel Systems

Dynamic Verifiable Search Over Encrypted Data in Untrusted Clouds

Xiaohong Nie[1], Qin Liu[1]([✉]), Xuhui Liu[1], Tao Peng[2], and Yapin Lin[1]

[1] College of Computer Science and Electronic Engineering, Hunan University,
Changsha 410082, People's Republic of China
gracelq628@hnu.edu.cn
[2] School of Information Science and Engineering, Central South University,
Changsha 410083, People's Republic of China

Abstract. The scalable and elastic storage capabilities of cloud computing motivate enterprises and individuals to outsource their data and query services to cloud platforms. Since the cloud service provider (CSP) is outside the trusted domain of cloud users, existing research suggests encrypting data before outsourcing and employing searchable symmetric encryption (SSE) to facilitate keyword-based search on the ciphertexts. To make SSE be more applicable in cloud computing, Kurosawa et al. proposed a dynamic verifiable SSE (DVSSE) scheme, which employed inverted indexes and the RSA accumulator to enable the user to search and update files in a verifiable way. However, their scheme works only under the assumption of an *honest but curious* CSP. In this paper, we propose a secure DVSSE scheme, $DVSSE_S$, for the untrusted cloud environments. Specifically, $DVSSE_S$ is constructed in two different ways. The basic $DVSSE_S$, called $DVSSE_S$-1, is constructed based on the Merkle hash tree (MHT) and BLS signatures, which can be easily extended from DVSSE. Since $DVSSE_S$-1 incurs a heavy cost during the update phase, the advanced $DVSSE_S$, called $DVSSE_S$-2, utilizes random permutations to improve the performance. Extensive experiments on real data set demonstrate the efficiency and effectiveness of our proposed scheme.

Keywords: Cloud computing · Searchable symmetric encryption · Dynamic · Verifiability

1 Introduction

Cloud computing as a new computing paradigm enables ubiquitous and on-demand access to a shared pool of configurable computing resources through

Q. Liu—This work was supported in part by NSFC grants 61632009, 61402161,61472131,61272546; the Hunan Provincial Natural Science Foundation of China (Grant No. 2015JJ3046); the CERNET Innovation Project (Grant No. NGII20150407, NGII20150408); and the Science and Technology Key Projects of Hunan Province (2015 TP1004).

J. Carretero et al. (Eds.): ICA3PP 2016, LNCS 10048, pp. 557–571, 2016.
DOI: 10.1007/978-3-319-49583-5_44

networks [1,2]. Due to the scalable and elastic storage capabilities of cloud computing, there is an increasing number of enterprises and individuals becoming cloud users that outsource their data and query services to cloud platforms [3]. Since the cloud service provider (CSP) that operates the cloud platform is outside the trusted domain of the cloud users, existing research suggests encrypting data before outsourcing and employing searchable symmetric encryption (SSE) [4,5] to facilitate keyword-based search on the ciphertexts.

In a typical cloud application of SSE, a user first builds a searchable index $\mathcal{I}$ from the universal keyword set $\mathcal{W}$ and a collection of files $\mathcal{D}$. Then, she encrypts $\mathcal{I}$ to generate $\widetilde{\mathcal{I}}$ and applies the symmetric key encryption (SKE) to generate a collection of ciphertexts $\mathcal{C}$. Once uploading $\widetilde{\mathcal{I}}$ and $\mathcal{C}$ to the cloud, the user is able to efficiently retrieve the encrypted files containing keyword w by an encrypted search token TK_w. On receiving the search request, the CSP will evaluate TK_w on $\widetilde{\mathcal{I}}$ and return all the matched files to the user, who will perform decryption locally to recover file contents. Since $\mathcal{I}$, $\mathcal{D}$, and TK_w are encrypted under the user's private key, the CSP cannot know what keywords the user is searching for and what files are returned in the search phase.

The notion of SSE was introduced by Song et al. [4], where both the user query as well as the data were encrypted under a symmetric key. The main drawback of their approach is that the server has to scan the whole file collection while conducting searches, and thus the search cost grows linearly with the number of files in the collection. Curtmola et al. [6] provided a rigorous security definition and constructed two schemes, SSE-1 and SSE-2, based on an encrypted inverted index. Compared with SSE-1, SSE-2 is more secure and has been proven to be secure against adaptive chosen keyword attacks (CKA2). SSE-1 is secure against chosen-keyword attacks (CKA1), but yields an optimal search time $O(r)$, where r is the number of files that contain a keyword.

However, both SSE-1 and SSE-2 do not have properties of dynamic and verifiability. Recently, Kamara et al. [7] constructed a dynamic SSE scheme based on an extended inverted index, where the user can add and delete files in an efficient way. Their scheme is proven to be CKA2-secure. Subsequently, Kamara et al. [8] extended their scheme to a parallel search setting. However, their above dynamic SSE schemes are not verifiable. Kurosawa et al. [9] constructed a UC-secure verifiable SSE scheme, in which the user can detect any cheating behavior of the malicious servers. While UC-security is a stronger notion of security than CKA2-security, their construction requires a linear search time.

The above SSE schemes are either *static* or *unverifiable*, that is, the user cannot simultaneously update (add, delete, modify) the file collection and verify the integrity of the file collection as well as the search results. To enable SSE to be more applicable to cloud environments, Kurosawa et al. [10] proposed a dynamic verifiable SSE (DVSSE) scheme, which employed inverted indexes and the RSA accumulator [11,12] to enable the user to search and update files in a verifiable way. However, in their scheme, the CSP is assumed be to *honest but curious*. That is, the CSP will always correctly execute a given protocol. In reality, the CSP may violate the pre-defined protocol in order to get profit.

In such a circumstance, the user may suffer security risks and economic losses if she fails to detect the cheating behaviors of the CSP.

In this paper, we propose a secure DVSSE scheme, $DVSSE_S$, for the untrusted cloud environments. Specifically, $DVSSE_S$ is constructed in two different ways. The basic $DVSSE_S$, called $DVSSE_S$-1, utilizes the Merkle hash tree (MHT) [13] and BLS signatures [14] to examine whether the CSP obeys a given protocol or not. Although $DVSSE_S$-1 can be simply derived from the original DVSSE, it will incur a heavy workload on the user in the update phase. To improve the performance of $DVSSE_S$-1, the advanced $DVSSE_S$, called $DVSSE_S$-2, is constructed based on random permutations. By hiding critical information from the CSP, the probability of detecting the cheating behaviors will be largely increased. The main contributions of this paper are as follows:

- To the best of our knowledge, it is the first attempt to devise a secure DVSSE scheme in an untrusted cloud environment.
- The proposed scheme allows the user to efficiently detect any cheating behaviors of the malicious CSP.
- Extensive experiments have been performed on real data sets to validate the effectiveness and efficiency of our proposed scheme.

Paper organization. We provide the preliminaries in Sect. 2 before formulating the problem in Sect. 3. We construct $DVSSE_S$-1 and $DVSSE_S$-2 in Sects. 4 and 5, respectively. Finally, we evaluate the proposed scheme in Sect. 6 and conclude this paper in Sect. 7.

2 Preliminaries

2.1 System Model

The system consists of two types of entities: the CSP and the cloud user (user for short). The CSP maintains the cloud platform, which locates on a large number of interconnected cloud servers with abundant hardware resources, to provide data storage and query services. The user outsources her encrypted data to the cloud, and later she will perform updates on ciphertexts and retrieve data of interest in a verifiable way.

A file collection $\mathcal{D}$ contains n files $\{D_1, \ldots, D_n\}$, where each file D_j, associated with identifier j, is described by a set of keywords for $j \in [1, n]$. Let $\mathcal{W} = \{w_1, \ldots, w_m\}$ denote the universal specific keywords extracted from $\mathcal{D}$. The user then builds a searchable index $\mathcal{I} = \{\mathcal{I}_{w_i}\}$ for each keyword $w_i \in \mathcal{W}$.

Let $\mathcal{C}$ and $\widetilde{\mathcal{I}}$ denote the encrypted version of $\mathcal{D}$ and $\mathcal{I}$ encrypted under the user's private key SK, respectively. Next, she calculates the accumulated values $\mathbf{A}$ for local storage before outsourcing $\{\mathcal{C}, \widetilde{\mathcal{I}}\}$ to the cloud. To retrieve files containing keyword w, the user will generate a search token TK_w based on SK and send TK_w to the CSP, which will evaluate TK_w on $\widetilde{\mathcal{I}}$ to find the matched ciphertexts $\mathcal{C}_w$. Then, the CSP will calculate proofs Π, and return $RSL = \{\mathcal{C}_w, \Pi\}$ to the user. Once verified the integrity of file collection and search results by Π and $\mathbf{A}$, the user will recover file contents with SK. For quick reference, the most relevant notations used in this paper are shown in Table 1.

Table 1. Summary of notations

Notation	Description
$\mathcal{D}$	A collection of n files $\{D_1, \ldots, D_n\}$
$\mathcal{W}$	A dictionary of m distinct keywords $\{w_1, \ldots, w_m\}$
$\mathcal{I}, \widetilde{\mathcal{I}}$	The index and its encrypted version
TK_{w_k}	The search token generated for keyword w_k
TK_*	The update token
$\mathcal{C}_{w_k}$	The ciphertexts of files containing keyword w_k
$\varPhi$	The BLS signatures on MHT

2.2 Adversary Model

The users are assumed to be fully trusted. The communication channels are assumed to be secured under existing security protocols such as SSL and SSH. The CSP is the potential attacker, which is assumed to be *malicious*. That is, the CSP may violate the pre-defined protocol in order to obtain the information about the stored data and the received message.

Existing SSE schemes resort to the weakened security guarantee for efficiency concerns. That is, they will reveal the *access pattern* and *search pattern* but nothing else during the search process. As defined in [6], access pattern refers to the outcome of search results, i.e., which files have been returned; The search pattern refers to whether two searches were performed for the same keyword.

As existing SSE schemes, our $DVSSE_S$ scheme will reveal the access pattern and search pattern to the CSP during search phase. Our $DVSSE_S$ scheme mainly aims to preserve user privacy from the following aspects:

- **File privacy.** The file contents are kept secret from the CSP.
- **Keyword privacy.** The keyword contents are kept secret from the CSP.

2.3 RSA Accumulator

The RSA accumulator [12] is an efficient data authentication mechanism that provides a constant-size digest for an arbitrarily large set of inputs, and a constant-size witness for any element in the set such that it can be used to verify the (non-)membership of the element in this set.

Let κ be security parameter, and let $p = 2p' + 1$ and $q = 2q' + 1$ be two large primes, where p', q' are primes such that $|pq| > 3\kappa$. Let $\mathbf{N} = pq$ and let $\mathbb{G}$ be cyclic group of size $(p-1)(q-1)/4$, where g is a generator of $\mathbb{G}$. For a set of elements $E = \{y_1, \ldots, y_n\}$ with $y_i \in \{0,1\}^\kappa$, the RSA accumulator works as follows:

- For each y_i, we choose a random prime x_i, denoted as $\mathcal{P}(y_i)$, such that $f(x_i) = y_i$. The accumulated value for E can be calculated as $Acc(E) = g^{\prod_{i=1}^{n} \mathcal{P}(y_i)}$ mod $\mathbf{N}$.

- For any subset $E' \subseteq E$, a witness $\pi = g^{\prod_{y_i \in E - E'} P(y_i)} \bmod \mathbf{N}$ can be produced.
- The subset test can be carried out by checking $Acc(E) = \pi^{\prod_{y_i \in E'} P(y_i)} \bmod \mathbf{N}$.

3 Problem Formulation

Given a file collection $\mathcal{D} = \{D_1, \ldots, D_n\}$ and the universal keywords $\mathcal{W} = \{w_1, \ldots, w_m\}$, the DVSSE scheme is constructed as follows:

In the store phase, user Alice encrypts each file D_i with SKE under her private key SK and outputs a set of ciphertexts $\mathcal{C} = \{(1, C_1), \ldots, (n, C_n)\}$. For each keyword $w_i \in \mathcal{W}$, Alice utilizes her private key SK to generate a label of fixed length, $label(w_i)$, and an n-bit padding, $pd(w_i)$.

Alice then builds the searchable indexes $\mathcal{I} = \{\mathcal{I}_{w_i} | w_i \in \mathcal{W}\}$, where $\mathcal{I}_{w_i}$ is an n-bit string that will be set as follows:

$$\mathcal{I}_{w_i}[j] = \begin{cases} 1, & \text{if } w_i \text{ is contained in } D_j \\ 0, & \text{otherwise} \end{cases} \tag{1}$$

where $\mathcal{I}_{w_i}[j]$ is the j-th bit of $\mathcal{I}_{w_i}$.

Next, Alice outputs the encrypted index $\widetilde{\mathcal{I}}_{w_i}$ by performing $pd_{w_i} \bigoplus \mathcal{I}_{w_i}$ for $w_i \in \mathcal{W}$. Finally, Alice will upload $\widetilde{\mathcal{I}} = \{(label(w_i), \widetilde{\mathcal{I}}_{w_i}) | w_i \in \mathcal{W}\}$ and $\mathcal{C}$ to the cloud and keep the accumulated values $\mathbf{A} = (\mathbf{A}_C, \mathbf{A}_I)$ locally as follows:

$$\mathbf{A}_C = F(\prod_{i=1}^{n} f(i, C_i)),$$
$$\mathbf{A}_I = F(\prod_{i=1}^{m} \prod_{j=1}^{n} f(label(w_i), j, \widetilde{\mathcal{I}}_{w_i}[j])),$$

where f and F are functions related to the RSA accumulator, the details of which can be found in Sect. 4.

In the search phase, Alice generates a search token $TK_{w_k} = \{label(w_k), pd(w_k)\}$ with her private key SK to retrieve files containing keyword w_k. Once receiving TK_{w_k}, the CSP will locate $\widetilde{\mathcal{I}}_{w_k}$ with $label(w_k)$, and then recover $\mathcal{I}_{w_k}$ by performing $\widetilde{\mathcal{I}}_{w_k} \bigoplus pd(w_k)$. Let C_{w_k} denote the set of ciphertexts to be returned. The CSP will add (i, C_i) to $\mathcal{C}_{w_k}$ if $\mathcal{I}_{w_k}[i] = 1$. Then, it calculates the proofs $\Pi = (\pi_C, \pi_I)$ as follows:

$$\pi_C = \prod_{i \notin \mathcal{C}_{w_k}} f(i, C_i).$$
$$\pi_I = \prod_{i=1, i \neq k}^{m} \prod_{j=1}^{m} f(label(w_i), j, \widetilde{\mathcal{I}}_{w_i}[j])$$

To verify the integrity of the file collection, Alice first constructs $x_i = f(i, C_i)$ from the returned ciphertexts $\mathcal{C}_{w_k}$ and tests whether the following equation holds:

$$\mathbf{A}_C = F(\pi_C \cdot \prod_{i \in \mathcal{C}_{w_k}} x_i)$$

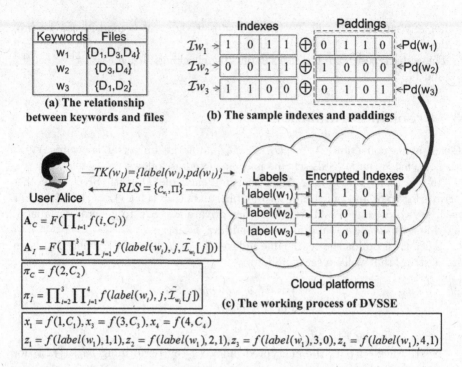

Fig. 1. The working process of DVSSE. User Alice generates a search token, TK_{w_1}, to the CSP, which will return ciphertexts $\mathcal{C}_{w_1} = \{(1, C_1), (3, C_3), (4, C_4)\}$ and proofs $\Pi = (\pi_C, \pi_I)$.

If so, Alice verifies the integrity of the search results by first constructing $z_j = f(label(w_k), j, \widetilde{\mathcal{I}}_{w_k}[j])$. Then, she tests whether the following equation holds:

$$\mathbf{A}_I = F(\pi_I \cdot \textstyle\prod_{j=1}^{n} z_j)$$

In order to explain the problem more clearly, we use the example as shown in Fig. 1 to illustrate the working process of DVSSE. From Fig. 1, we know that DVSSE works well while the CSP is honest. However, Alice cannot detect the CSP's cheating behaviors if it disobeys the protocol. To illustrate, suppose that the CSP only returns C_1, C_3 and discards C_4 for TK_{w_1}. The CSP first generates a fake index $\mathcal{I}'_{w_1} = [1010]$ and encrypts it by performing $[1010] \bigoplus [0110] = [1100]$. It is worth noticing that, the CSP is able to generate encrypted index for w_1 at will given the search token TK_{w_1}. Therefore, it convinces Alice to accept the search results by forging π'_C, π'_I as follows:

$$\pi'_C = \pi_C \cdot f(4, C_4)$$
$$\pi'_I = \pi_I \cdot z_4 / f(label(w_1), 4, 0)$$

The main reason for the CSP to successfully deceive the user is that *too much information is exposed to the CSP in the calculation of the proofs*. Therefore, we first construct DVSSE$_S$-1, which allows the user to compute proofs in advance. These proofs will be stored in a MHT structure and signed by the user with BLS signatures. Although DVSSE$_S$-1 can be easily extended from the original DVSSE, it will incur a heavy cost on the user during update. To improve its performance, we construct DVSSE$_S$-2, which hides file identifiers from the CSP by using random permutations. Given a set of shuffled file identifiers, the CSP cannot know which identifier should be used to forge a fake proof.

4 Basic DVSSE

4.1 Construction of DVSSE$_S$-1

Suppose that the security of the whole system is ensured under parameter κ. Let $SKE = (Gen, Enc, Dec)$ be a symmetric-key encryption(SKE) scheme [15]. The key generation algorithm Gen takes a security parameter κ as its inputs to generate a secret key k_e. The encryption algorithm Enc takes a key k_e and a file D_i as its inputs and returns a ciphertext C_i. The decryption algorithm Dec takes a key k_e and a ciphertext C_i as its inputs, and returns D_i if k_e is the key under Gen. Let $H : \{0,1\}^* \rightarrow \{0,1\}^\kappa$ be a collision-free hash function, and let $PRF_K : \{0,1\}^\kappa \times \{0,1\}^*$ be a pseudorandom function (PRF), where K is a key. DVSSE$_S$-1 is constructed as shown in Fig. 2:

(Initial phase)
1. $Gen(1^\kappa) \rightarrow (PK, SK)$: The user randomly chooses two κ-bit strings k_1, k_2, as the keys of PRFs. Then, she generates a random signing key pair (spk, ssk), runs

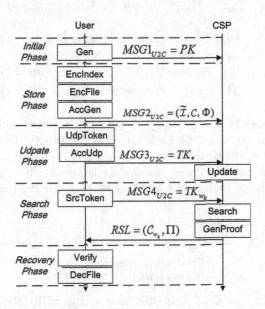

Fig. 2. The working process of DVSSE$_S$.

$SKE.Gen(1^\kappa)$ to generate k_e, and generates $(\mathbf{N} = pq, g)$ as shown in Sect. 2.3. Let $\mathcal{P}(y)$ be a random prime x such that $f(x) = y$. She chooses a random permutation σ on $\{1, \ldots, m\}$ and sets the public key PK and private key SK as:

$$PK = (\mathbf{N}, g, f, spk),$$
$$SK = (p, q, k_1, k_2, k_e, ssk, \sigma).$$

(Store phase)

2. $EncIndex(SK, \mathcal{I}) \rightarrow \widetilde{\mathcal{I}}$: The user first constructs $\mathcal{I} = \{\mathcal{I}_{w_i} | w_i \in \mathcal{W}\}$ with Eq. 1. For each keyword $w_i \in \mathcal{W}$, she then computes:

$$
\begin{aligned}
label(w_i) &= [PRF_{k_1}(w_i)]_{1,\ldots,128}, \\
pd(w_i) &= [PRF_{k_2}(w_i)]_{1,\ldots,n}, \\
\widetilde{\mathcal{I}}_{w_i} &= pd(w_i) \oplus \mathcal{I}_{w_i},
\end{aligned}
\tag{2}
$$

where $[S]_{1,\ldots,n}$ denotes the 1-th to n-th bits of string S. She then sets $\widetilde{\mathcal{I}} = \{(label(w_{\sigma(i)}), \widetilde{\mathcal{I}}_{w_{\sigma(i)}}) | i \in [1, m]\}$.

3. $EncFile(\mathcal{D}, SK) \rightarrow \mathcal{C}$: For each file $D_i \in \mathcal{D}$, the user runs $SKE.Enc(k_e, D_i)$ to generate the ciphertext C_i. The ciphertext collection $\mathcal{C} = \{(1, C_1), \ldots, (n, C_n)\}$.

4. $AccGen(PK, SK, \mathcal{I}, \mathcal{C}) \rightarrow (\mathbf{A}, \Phi)$: Given ciphertext collection $\mathcal{C}$, the user computes $\mathbf{A} = (\mathbf{A}_C, \mathbf{A}_I, v)$, where $\mathbf{A}$ will be stored locally and ϕ will be uploaded to the cloud:

$$
\begin{aligned}
\mathbf{A}_C &= g^{\prod_{i=1}^{n} \mathcal{P}(H(i, H(C_i)))} \quad \text{mod } \mathbf{N}, \\
\mathbf{A}_I &= g^{\prod_{i=1}^{m} \prod_{j=1}^{n} \mathcal{P}(H(label(w_i), j, \widetilde{\mathcal{I}}_{w_i}[j]))} \quad \text{mod } \mathbf{N}.
\end{aligned}
\tag{3}
$$

For each keyword $w_l \in \mathcal{W}$, she calculates proofs $\Pi_l = (\pi_{C_l}, \pi_{I_l})$ as follows:

$$
\begin{aligned}
\pi_{C_l} &= g^{\prod_{\mathcal{I}_{w_l}[i]=0} \mathcal{P}(H(i, H(C_i)))} \quad \text{mod } \mathbf{N}, \\
\pi_{I_l} &= g^{\prod_{i=1, i\neq l}^{m} \prod_{j=1}^{n} \mathcal{P}(H(label(w_i), j, \widetilde{\mathcal{I}}_{w_i}[j]))} \quad \text{mod } \mathbf{N}.
\end{aligned}
\tag{4}
$$

Given a sequence of proofs $\{\Pi_{\sigma(1)}, \ldots, \Pi_{\sigma(m)}\}$, the user constructs a MHT by setting the leaf nodes as the hash values of the proofs. To reflect updates, a version number v will be introduced to the MHT, where v is initialized to 0 and will be incremented by 1 once an update happens. Then, she employs the BLS signature scheme to sign the MHT as that in [16] and generates a set of signatures ϕ.

(Search phase)

5. $SrcToken(w_k, SK) \rightarrow TK_{w_k}$: To retrieve files containing keyword w_k, the user calculates $label(w_k) = [PRF_{k_1}(w_k)]_{[1,\ldots,128]}$ and $pd(w_k) = [PRF_{k_2}(w_k)]_{[1,\ldots,n]}$. Then, she sends $TK_{w_k} = (label(w_k), pd(w_k))$ to the CSP.

6. $Search(TK_{w_k}, \widetilde{\mathcal{I}}) \rightarrow \mathcal{C}_{w_k}$: The CSP locates $\widetilde{\mathcal{I}}_{w_k}$ with $label(w_k)$, and then computes $\widetilde{\mathcal{I}}_{w_k} \oplus pd(w_k)$ to recover $\mathcal{I}_{w_k}$. Then, it sets $\mathcal{C}_{w_k} = \{(i, C_i) | \mathcal{I}_{w_k}[i] = 1\}$.

7. $GenProof(TK_{w_k}, PK, \mathcal{C}) \rightarrow \Pi$: Given the search token TK_{w_k}, the CSP runs the *Search* algorithm to obtain the matched ciphertexts $\mathcal{C}_{w_k}$. Then, it sets $\Pi = \{\pi_C, \pi_I, \Omega\}$ as follows:

$$\pi_C = g^{\prod_{i \notin \mathcal{C}_{w_k}} \mathcal{P}(H(i,H(C_i)))} \bmod \mathbf{N},$$
$$\pi_I = g^{\prod_{i=1, i \neq k}^{m} \prod_{j=1}^{n} \mathcal{P}(H(label(w_i), j, \widetilde{\mathcal{I}}_{w_i}[j]))} \bmod \mathbf{N}. \tag{5}$$

Here, Ω is the auxiliary information for verification, which are the node siblings on the path from the leaves $H(\pi_C)$ and $H(\pi_I)$ to the root of the MHT.

8. $Verify(PK, SK, \mathcal{C}_{w_k}, \Phi, \Pi, \mathbf{A}) \rightarrow \{0,1\}$: The client first computes $x_i = \mathcal{P}(H(i, H(C_i)))$ for each $(i, C_i) \in \mathcal{C}_{w_k}$ and checks if the following equation holds:

$$\mathbf{A}_C = (\pi_C)^{\prod_{i \in \mathcal{C}_{w_k}} x_i} \bmod \mathbf{N}. \tag{6}$$

Next, the user reconstructs $\mathcal{I}_{w_k}$ from $\mathcal{C}_{w_k}$ and computes $\widetilde{\mathcal{I}}_{w_k} = \mathcal{I}_{w_k} \oplus pd(w_k)$. Then, she computes $z_j = \mathcal{P}(H(label(w_k), j, \widetilde{\mathcal{I}}_{w_k}[j]))$ for $j \in [1, n]$ and checks if the following equation holds:

$$\mathbf{A}_I = (\pi_I)^{\prod_{j=1}^{n} z_j} \bmod \mathbf{N}. \tag{7}$$

Finally, she reconstructs the MHT based on the version number v and auxiliary information Ω and verifies the correctness of signatures. If all the checks succeed, this algorithm outputs 1, otherwise it outputs 0.

9. $DecFile(\mathcal{C}_{w_k}, SK) \rightarrow \{D_i\}_{i \in \mathcal{C}_{w_k}}$: If the output of the *Verify* algorithm is 1, the user runs $SKE.Dec(k_e, C_i)$ to recover D_i from $C_i \in \mathcal{C}_{w_k}$.

(Update phase)
10. $UpdToken(SK, op) \rightarrow TK_*$: If $op = Modify(D_i, D_i')$, the user runs $SKE.Enc(k_e, D_i')$ to generate the ciphertext (i, C_i') and sends $TK_* = (i, C_i')$ to the CSP. If $op = Delete(i)$, the user sends $TK_* = (i, \mathbf{delete})$ to the CSP. If $op = Add(n+1, D_{n+1})$, the user first runs $SKE.Enc(k_e, D_{n+1})$ to generate the ciphertext $(n+1, C_{n+1})$. Then, she constructs an m-bit string V, where the i-th bit, denoted as $V[i]$, is set as follows:

$$V[i] = \begin{cases} 1, & if\ w_i\ is\ contained\ in\ D_{n+1} \\ 0, & otherwise \end{cases} \tag{8}$$

Next, the user computes $a_i = [PRF_{k_2}(w_i)]_{n+1} \oplus V[i]$ for $i \in [1, m]$, where $[S]_{n+1}$ denotes the $(n+1)$-th bit of string S. She sends $TK_* = \{(n+1, C_{n+1}), (a_{\sigma(1)}, \ldots, a_{\sigma(m)})\}$ to the CSP.

11. $Update(TK_*, \widetilde{\mathcal{I}}, \mathcal{C}) \rightarrow (\mathcal{C}', \widetilde{\mathcal{I}}')$: If $TK_* = (i, C_i')$, the CSP will modify C_i to C_i' and set $\widetilde{\mathcal{I}}' = \widetilde{\mathcal{I}}$. If $TK_* = (i, \mathbf{delete})$, the CSP will modify C_i to $\mathbf{delete}$ and set $\widetilde{\mathcal{I}}' = \widetilde{\mathcal{I}}$. If $TK_* = \{(n+1, C_{n+1}), (a_{\sigma(1)}, \ldots, a_{\sigma(m)})\}$, the CSP will add $(n+1, C_{n+1})$ to $\mathcal{C}$ and add $a_{\sigma(i)}$ as the last element of $\widetilde{\mathcal{I}}_{w_{\sigma(i)}}$.

12. $AccUpd(PK, SK, TK_*, \Phi, \mathbf{A}) \rightarrow (\Phi', \mathbf{A}')$: If $TK_* = (i, C_i')$, the user computes $x_i = \mathcal{P}(H(i, H(C_i)))$ and $x_i' = \mathcal{P}(H(i, H(C_i')))$ and updates $\mathbf{A}_C$ to $\mathbf{A}_C'$ by setting:

$$\mathbf{A}_C' = \mathbf{A}_C^{x_i'/x_i} \mod \mathbf{N}. \tag{9}$$

If $TK_* = (i, \mathbf{delete})$, the user sets $\mathbf{A}_C' = \mathbf{A}_C$ and $\Phi' = \Phi$. If $TK_* = \{(n + 1, C_{n+1}), (a_{\sigma(1)}, \ldots, a_{\sigma(m)})\}$, the user computes $z_i = \mathcal{P}(H(label(w_i), n + 1, a_i)$ for $i \in [1, m]$, and updates $\mathbf{A}_I$ to $\mathbf{A}_I'$ by setting:

$$\mathbf{A}_I' = \mathbf{A}_I^{\prod_{i=1}^m z_i} \mod \mathbf{N}. \tag{10}$$

The construction of our update phase is the same as that of the DVSSE scheme, except that the user needs to update the version number and run Eq. 4 to re-calculate $\{\Pi_1, \ldots, \Pi_m\}$ while modifying and adding a file. Furthermore, a new MHT tree will be re-constructed and signed with the BLS signature scheme.

4.2 Security Sketch

Our security goal is to preserve keyword privacy and file privacy against the malicious CSP. First, we will show that DVSSE$_S$-1 leaks no extra information compared with the DVSSE scheme, which has been proven to have UC-security in [10]. In the store phase, the message from the user to the CSP is $MSG1_{U2C} = \{\mathcal{C}, \widetilde{\mathcal{I}}, \Phi\}$, where $\mathcal{C}$ and $\widetilde{\mathcal{I}}$ are generated in the same way as the DVSSE scheme, and Φ contains information about proofs, which can be calculated by the CSP in the search phase of the DVSSE scheme. In the update phase, the message from the user to the CSP is $MSG2_{U2C} = \{TK_*, \Phi'\}$, where the update token TK_* is generated in the same way as the DVSSE scheme, and Φ' contains only the information about the updated proofs. In the search phase, the message from the user to the CSP is $MSG3_{U2C} = \{TK_w\}$, the construction of which is the same as the DVSSE scheme. Therefore, in above stages, DVSSE$_S$-1 leaks no more information, and is as secure as the DVSSE scheme.

Then, we will show that our scheme works well while the CSP disobeys the protocol. In DVSSE$_S$-1, the proofs are pre-calculated by the user, the integrity of which will be ensured by the MHT and BLS signatures. Due to the security of the BLS signature scheme, the CSP cannot convince the user to accept the fake proofs without the user's signing key ssk. Furthermore, the version number is incorporated into MHT to record the updates. Therefore, the user can verify whether the CSP performed updates or not by checking the version number.

5 Advanced DVSSE

5.1 Construction of DVSSE$_S$-2

DVSSE$_S$-2 applies random permutations to shuffle file identifiers, so that the relationship between the file and its identifer is hidden from the CSP. Therefore, in the Gen algorithm, the user chooses a random permutation ρ_i for each keyword

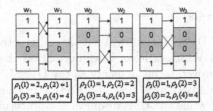

Fig. 3. The shuffle process of $DVSSE_S$-2.

$w_i \in \mathcal{W}$. Since the MHT and BLS signatures will not be used in $DVSSE_S$-2, the user will not generate signing key pairs (spk, ssk) in the *Gen* algorithm.

The main differences between two constructions lie in algorithms *AccGen*, *GenProof*, *Verify*, and *AccUpd*.

- $AccGen(PK, SK, \mathcal{I}, \mathcal{C}) \to (\mathbf{A})$: The user calculates $\mathbf{A} = (\mathbf{A}_C, \mathbf{A}_I)$ as follows:

$$\mathbf{A}_C = g^{\prod_{i=1}^{n} \mathcal{P}(H(i, H(C_i)))} \mod \mathbf{N},$$
$$\mathbf{A}_I = g^{\prod_{i=1}^{m} \prod_{j=1}^{n} \mathcal{P}(H(label(w_i), \rho_i(j), \widetilde{\mathcal{I}}_{w_i}[j]))} \mod \mathbf{N}. \tag{11}$$

where $\rho_i(j)$ is the shuffled identifier of file D_j for keyword w_i. The random permutation has the property: if $\mathcal{I}_{w_i}[j] = b$ then $\mathcal{I}_{w_i}[\rho_i(j)] = b$, where $b \in \{0,1\}$. In other words, ρ_i first classifies file identifiers into two types: T_1 (the identifiers of files containing keyword w_i) and T_2 (the identifiers of files excluding keyword w_i), and then shuffles them respectively. Given the relationship between keywords and files as shown in Fig. 1-(a), the sample shuffled process is shown in Fig. 3.

- $GenProof(TK_{w_k}, PK, \mathcal{C}, \widetilde{\mathcal{I}}) \to \Pi$: The CSP first obtains the search results $\mathcal{C}_{w_k}$ by running the *Search* algorithm, and then it computes the proofs $\Pi = (\pi_C, \pi_I)$ by setting:

$$\pi_C = g^{\prod_{i \notin \mathcal{C}_{w_k}} \mathcal{P}(H(i, H(C_i)))} \mod \mathbf{N},$$
$$\pi_I = g^{\prod_{i \neq k}^{m} \prod_{j=1}^{n} \mathcal{P}(H(label(w_i), j, \widetilde{\mathcal{I}}_{w_i}[j]))} \mod \mathbf{N}. \tag{12}$$

- $Verify(PK, SK, \mathcal{C}_{w_k}, \Pi, \mathbf{A}) \to \{0,1\}$: Given the search results $\mathcal{C}_{w_k}$, the user first computes $x_i = \mathcal{P}(H(i, H(C_i)))$ for each $(i, C_i) \in \mathcal{C}_{w_k}$, and checks if Eq. 6 holds. Next, the user reconstructs $\mathcal{I}_{w_k}$ from $\mathcal{C}_{w_k}$ and computes $\widetilde{\mathcal{I}}_{w_k} = \mathcal{I}_{w_k} \bigoplus pd(w_k)$. Then, she computes $z_j = \mathcal{P}(H(label(w_k), \rho_i(j), \widetilde{\mathcal{I}}_{w_k}[j]))$ for $j \in [1, n]$ and checks whether Eq. 7 holds. If all the checks succeed, this algorithm outputs 1, otherwise it outputs 0.

- $AccUpd(PK, SK, TK_*, \mathbf{A}) \to \mathbf{A}'$: If $TK_* = (i, C_i')$, the user computes $x_i = \mathcal{P}(H(i, H(C_i)))$ and $x_i' = \mathcal{P}(H(i, H(C_i')))$ and updates $\mathbf{A}_C$ to $\mathbf{A}_C'$ running Eq. 9. If $TK_* = (i, \mathbf{delete})$, the user sets $\mathbf{A}_C' = \mathbf{A}_C$. If $TK_* = \{(n + 1, C_{n+1}), (a_{\sigma(1)}, \ldots, a_{\sigma(m)})\}$, the user computes $z_i = \mathcal{P}(H(label(w_i), n + 1, a_i))$ for $i \in [1, m]$, and updates $\mathbf{A}_I$ to $\mathbf{A}_I'$ by running Eq. 10.

5.2   Security Analysis

In the construction of DVSSE$_S$-2, Φ will not be constructed and transferred to the CSP. Therefore, DVSSE$_S$-2 leaks less information than DVSSE$_S$-1. Since DVSSE$_S$-1 has been proven to be as secure as the DVSSE scheme, the security of DVSSE$_S$-2 can be derived from that of DVSSE$_S$-1. Then, we will show that DVSSE$_S$-2 works well while the CSP disobeys the protocol. In DVSSE$_S$-2, the relationship between file identifier and file contents is concealed by the random permutation. To forge a proof, the CSP should guess the shuffled identifier. Taking the application as shown in Fig. 1 as an example, to convinces the user to accept the incomplete search results $\mathcal{C}_{w_1} = \{(1, C_1), (3, C_3)\}$, the CSP needs to generate $\pi'_I = \pi_I^{(\mathcal{P}(H(label(w_1)),\rho_1(4),0))/(\mathcal{P}(H(label(w_1)),\rho_1(4),1))}$. Since the random permutations are kept secret by the user, it is hard for the CSP to construct π'_I. If keyword w_i appears in X files, the probability of succeeding in guessing the identifier is $1/X$. Therefore, the user is able to detect the cheating behaviors of the malicious CSP with a high probability.

6   Evaluation

6.1   Parameter Setting

Experiments are conducted on a local machine, running the Microsoft Windows 7 Ultimate operating system, with an Inter Core i3 CPU running at 2.3 GHz and 4 GB memory. The programs are implemented in Java, compiled using Eclipse 4.3.2. The cryptographic algorithms are implemented with JPBC library [17].

To validate the effectiveness and efficiency of DVSSE$_S$-1 and DVSSE$_S$-2 in practice, we conduct a performance evaluation on a real data set, the Internet Request For Comments dataset (RFC) [18]. This data set has 6,870 plaintext files with a total size about 349 MB. The average size of each file is 52 KB. We use Hermetic Word Frequency Counter [19] to extract keywords from each RFC file, and choose [1, 5] keywords for each file after ranking them with frequency of occurrence. In the experiments, we select $n = 1,000$ files from the data set, where the number of distinct keywords is $m = 884$, and each keyword appears in 1~44 files. We execute each experiment multiple times to obtain the average execution time [20].

6.2   Experiment Results

We compared the performance of our scheme with DVSSE [10] in terms of the execution time. For algorithms *EncFile* and *DecFile* three schemes utilize SKE to encrypt files and decrypt ciphertexts, and thus incur the same execution time. Specifically, given n = 1, 000 files, it costs about 890 ms to encrypt the file collection and about 1400 ms to recover the files.

Figure 4 shows the execution time for algorithms *EncIndex* and *AccGen* in the store phase and the execution time for the *GenProof* algorithm in the search phase. Since our indexes and files are encrypted in the same way as the DVSSE

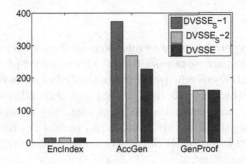

Fig. 4. The execution time in the store and search phases.

scheme, three schemes incur the same execution time, which costs about 14.37s. The *SrcToken* and *Search* algorithms are very efficient, which costs about 1.35 ms and 290 ms, respectively. For the AccGen algorithm, the execution time for DVSSE, DVSSE$_S$-1 and DVSSE$_S$-2 is about 226.7 s, 373.7 s, and 268.5 s, respectively. In the *AccGen* algorithm, DVSSE$_S$-1 needs to build and sign a MHT for generating Φ, and thus it incurs the most execution time; DVSSE$_S$-2 spends more time than DVSSE for the calculation of shuffle function $\{\rho_1, \ldots, \rho_m\}$. For the *GenProof* algorithm, the DVSSE$_S$-1 scheme incurs the maximum cost due to the construction of auxiliary information Ω.

Figure 5 shows the execution time for the *AccUpd* algorithm in the update phase and the execution time for the Verify algorithm in the recovery phase. In the update phase, the cost for deleting a file is close to zero. Furthermore, the *UpdToken* and Update algorithms are very efficient, which costs less than 10 ms for adding/modifying a file. For the *AccUpdate*, the DVSSE$_S$-1 needs the most time for reconstructing and re-signed the updated MHT. For the Verify algorithm, the DVSSE$_S$-1 needs the most time for reconstructing the hash tree.

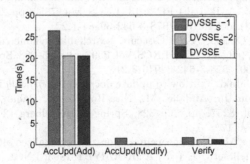

Fig. 5. The execution time in the update and recovery phases.

7   Conclusion

In a cloud computing environment, a malicious CSP may delete some encrypted files to save memory space or tamper the search results for profit. In this paper, we propose a secure DVSSE scheme for the untrusted cloud environment. Experiment results show that the proposed $DVSSE_S$ scheme allows the user to perform search, update, and verification in an efficient way. However, our $DVSSE_S$ scheme supports only single-keyword search. As part of our future work, we will try to design a multi-keyword $DVSSE_S$ scheme to achieve conjunctive keyword searches in cloud computing.

References

1. Liu, Q., Tan, C.C., Wu, J., Wang, G.: Towards differential query services in cost-efficient clouds. IEEE Trans. Parallel Distrib. Syst. **25**(6), 1648–1658 (2014)
2. Xiao, M., Wu, J., Huang, L., Wang, Y., Liu, C.: Multi-task assignment for crowd-sensing in mobile social networks. In: Proceedings of IEEE INFOCOM, pp. 2227–2235 (2015)
3. Liu, Q., Wang, G., Wu, J.: Time-based proxy re-encryption scheme for secure data sharing in a cloud environment. Inf. Sci. **258**, 355–370 (2014)
4. Song, D.X., Wagner, D., Perrig, A.: Practical techniques for searches on encrypted data. In: Proceedings of IEEE S&P, pp. 44–55 (2000)
5. Golle, P., Staddon, J., Waters, B.: Secure conjunctive keyword search over encrypted data. In: Manulis, M., Sadeghi, A.-R., Schneider, S. (eds.) ACNS 2016. LNCS, vol. 9696, pp. 31–45. Springer, Heidelberg (2004). doi:10.1007/978-3-540-24852-1_3
6. Curtmola, R., Garay, J., Kamara, S., Ostrovsky, R.: Searchable symmetric encryption: improved definitions and efficient constructions. In: Proceedings of ACM CCS, pp. 79–88 (2006)
7. Kamara, S., Papamanthou, C., Roeder, T.: Dynamic searchable symmetric encryption. In: Proceedings of ACM CCS, pp. 965–976 (2012)
8. Kamara, S., Papamanthou, C.: Parallel and dynamic searchable symmetric encryption. In: Sadeghi, A.-R. (ed.) FC 2013. LNCS, vol. 7859, pp. 258–274. Springer, Heidelberg (2013). doi:10.1007/978-3-642-39884-1_22
9. Kurosawa, K., Ohtaki, Y.: UC-secure searchable symmetric encryption. In: Keromytis, A.D. (ed.) FC 2012. LNCS, vol. 7397, pp. 285–298. Springer, Heidelberg (2012). doi:10.1007/978-3-642-32946-3_21
10. Kurosawa, K., Ohtaki, Y.: How to update documents *verifiably* in searchable symmetric encryption. In: Abdalla, M., Nita-Rotaru, C., Dahab, R. (eds.) CANS 2013. LNCS, vol. 8257, pp. 309–328. Springer, Heidelberg (2013). doi:10.1007/978-3-319-02937-5_17
11. Benaloh, J., Mare, M.: One-way accumulators: a decentralized alternative to digital signatures. In: Helleseth, T. (ed.) EUROCRYPT 1993. LNCS, vol. 765, pp. 274–285. Springer, Heidelberg (1994). doi:10.1007/3-540-48285-7_24
12. Camenisch, J., Lysyanskaya, A.: Dynamic accumulators and application to efficient revocation of anonymous credentials. In: Yung, M. (ed.) CRYPTO 2002. LNCS, vol. 2442, pp. 61–76. Springer, Heidelberg (2002). doi:10.1007/3-540-45708-9_5
13. Merkle, R.C.: Protocols for public key cryptosystems In: Proceedings of IEEE S&P, p. 122 (1980)

14. Boneh, D., Lynn, B., Shacham, H.: Short signatures from the weil pairing. In: Boyd, C. (ed.) ASIACRYPT 2001. LNCS, vol. 2248, pp. 514–532. Springer, Heidelberg (2001). doi:10.1007/3-540-45682-1_30
15. Bellare, M., Desai, A., Jokipii, E., Rogaway, P.: A concrete security treatment of symmetric encryption. In: Proceedings of IEEE FCS, pp. 394–403 (1997)
16. Wang, Q., Wang, C., Li, J., Ren, K., Lou, W.: Enabling public verifiability and data dynamics for storage security in cloud computing. In: Backes, M., Ning, P. (eds.) ESORICS 2009. LNCS, vol. 5789, pp. 355–370. Springer, Heidelberg (2009). doi:10.1007/978-3-642-04444-1_22
17. De Caro, A., Iovino, V.: jpbc: Java pairing based cryptography. In: Proceedings of IEEE ISCC (2011)
18. RFC, Request for comments database. http://www.ietf.org/rfc.html
19. HERMETIC, Hermetic word frequency counter. http://www.hermetic.ch/wfc/wfc.htm
20. Xie, K., Wang, L., Wang, X., Xie, G., Zhang, G., Xie, D., Wen, J.: Sequential and adaptive sampling for matrix completion in network monitoring systems. In: Proceedings of IEEE INFOCOM, pp. 2443–2451 (2015)

Reducing TCB of Linux Kernel Using User-Space Device Driver

Weizhong Qiang[✉], Kang Zhang, and Hai Jin

Services Computing Technology and System Lab, Cluster and Grid Computing Lab,
Big Data Technology and System Lab School of Computer Science and Technology,
Huazhong University of Science and Technology, 430074 Wuhan, China
wzqiang@hust.edu.cn

Abstract. The Linux kernel has enormous code size, which makes it a
prime target exploited by attackers to steal the privacy of the system, or
even to crash the system. Especially, the untrusted Linux device drivers,
which take the largest code size of kernel, bring great threats to the
kernel. However, current research that tries to isolate the Linux device
drivers, either has a large attack surface due to the complex features
exposed to applications, or leaves the device drivers in the TCB (*Trusted
Computing Base*). We move the device drivers into user-space to reduce
the TCB of kernel, and alter the OS features as libraries to decrease kernel's attack surface. This paper presents an architecture based on proxy
driver and library OSes to separate untrusted and unmodified device
drivers from kernels enhanced with a narrower system call interface. We
discuss the implementation of a prototype, and also the case study about
an unmodified Ethernet card driver supported by the prototype. The
evaluation of the case study shows an acceptable performance overhead.
We manage to narrow the attack surface by reducing 81.6% of the system
calls, and reduce the TCB by decreasing the code base (inside TCB) of
the Ethernet card driver into 900 LoC.

Keywords: Secure kernel · Trusted computing base · Library operating
system · User-space device driver

1 Introduction

The monolithic Linux kernel has sheer code size, which makes it a prime target
for attackers to exploit the system. The Linux kernel version 3.14.12, for example,
has 12,000K LoC, and has 291 kernel vulnerabilities reported from 2011 to 2013
[1]. From the exploit category analyzed by Tsai *et al.* [2], 40.5 % of the kernel
vulnerabilities is from the system calls, which shows that the complexity of
system calls introduces a large number of attack surface due to the complex

W. Qiang—This work is supported by National Natural Science Foundation of China
under grant No. 61370106, and National Basic Research Program of China (973
Program) under grant No. 2014CB340600.

© Springer International Publishing AG 2016
J. Carretero et al. (Eds.): ICA3PP 2016, LNCS 10048, pp. 572–585, 2016.
DOI: 10.1007/978-3-319-49583-5_45

features exposed to the user space. Besides, the method of running the device drivers as loadable kernel modules at the same level as Linux kernel gives more opportunities for attackers to crash the kernel. Any vulnerability in the device drivers [3,4] can be exploited to damage the entire system.

There are some past attempts about reducing the attack surface of the kernel [2,5,6]. An automated approach is proposed in the KRAZOR [7] system to measure and reduce the kernel's attack surface in runtime. Systems like [6] take advantage of the LibOS (*Library Operating System*) to reduce the attack surface. Unfortunately, these attempts either cannot decrease the number of kernel vulnerabilities, or do not include the consideration about how to protect the kernel from the untrusted device drivers. For instance, the proposed system in [2] still has a large number of kernel vulnerabilities caused by untrusted device drivers, and the TCB of the kernel has not been reduced in KRAZOR [7].

There are also some efforts about reducing the TCB of the kernel, including the method about excluding untrusted kernels, and the method about isolating untrusted device drivers. Numerous virtualization-based security systems [8–10] are proposed to reduce the TCB by completely excluding untrusted kernels. These systems focus on the security of applications by including alternative minimized kernels, rather than the security of the original kernels themselves. On the other hand, some systems have been proposed to isolate device drivers for kernels [11,12]. However, the isolation could be breached [13], and then the compromised device driver [4] could be exploited to crash the rest of the kernel. Silas et al. [13] solve the problem by completely separating the untrusted device drivers into the user space. However, this work [13] is not able to provide a narrowed attack surface.

Our work is proposed to provide both of the two features, reducing the attack surface and the TCB of the kernel. We propose an architecture, which reduces the TCB of the kernel by moving device drivers from kernel-space into the user-space, and reduces the attack surface by narrowing the system call interface. In general, we introduce the Z-LibOS, which is a user-space library operating system, to provide narrowed system call interface. We also use UML (*User Linux Mode*) [14] in user-space to provide kernel runtime support for unmodified device drivers, and add a stub driver into the UML which is responsible for handling the kernel function that is not supported by UML. We also add a component into the kernel, called proxy driver, to allocate the kernel resources, such as DMA (*Direct Memory Access*) memory, for the device drivers in user-space. Finally, we construct a communication channel between the stub driver and proxy driver to deliver necessary information, such as the request of kernel function. The contributions of this paper are summarized as follows:

- We present an architecture, called RAT (*Reducing Attack surface and TCB*), which can both reduce the TCB of the kernel, and limit the attack surface of the kernel.
- We illustrate how the privileged and untrusted device drivers are moved into user-space to provide minimized TCB, and how the LibOS is utilized to provide a narrower system call interface. Unlike previous LibOS systems, we can support unmodified device drivers in user-space.

– We implement a prototype, and take an Ethernet card driver as a case study on this prototype. We evaluate the performance, and the experimental results indicate that the proposed system incurs acceptable performance overhead.

The rest of this paper is organized as follows. Section 2 provides the problem definition of our work. Section 3 presents the architecture design. The detailed implementation and its support to an Ethernet card driver will be discussed in Sect. 4. Section 5 gives the evaluation of the prototype. Section 6 discusses the related work. The conclusion is given in Sect. 7.

2   Problem Definition

2.1   Threat Model and Assumptions

We make the standard assumptions seen in related work [8–10] that aims at reducing TCB. All user-space components, including UML, stub driver, Z-LibOS, device drivers, and other applications, are excluded from the TCB of the kernel. Therefore, the attackers could insert malicious code into these components without affecting the kernel. We assume that the proxy driver is ideally designed to be a secure and trusted component, and is part of the TCB. The attackers could obtain all device drivers' resources allocated by the proxy driver, and use them to exploit attacks, such as DMA attack. The attacks against the user-space drivers are out of scope, which means the drivers could be breached, and the data processed by them could be stolen. The applications themselves are supposed to protect the confidential data by using cryptographic approach.

2.2   Goals

The design of RAT is based on the following goals:

1. **Supporting the transparency for applications and device drivers:** It is not required to modify the existing device drivers and applications, when RAT is deployed. The transparency of applications and device drivers improves the practicality of the implementation of RAT.
2. **Providing narrow system call interface:** The attack surface from applications to the kernel is made up of system calls. By limiting the system call interface provided by the kernel, the attack surface could be reduced to a great extent.
3. **Minimizing code base of proxy driver:** The proxy driver completes the privileged operations requested by the device drivers in user-space. As part of the TCB, the proxy driver should have small amount of LoC to facilitate formal verification.
4. **Isolating user-space device drivers:** Running device drivers in user-space cannot completely prevent the drivers from crashing the kernel. For example, the device driver can still use the DMA resources, allocated by the proxy driver, to launch DMA attack.

3   Architecture

The overall architecture of the system is illustrated in Fig. 1, with unmodified components represented in grey. All components, including applications and UML [14], are supposed to be linked to the Z-LibOS which is a library providing the OS functions. The Z-LibOS provides a narrower system call interface to applications by implementing a subset of Linux system calls. Therefore, the attack surface of kernel is reduced. The device drivers are supposed to run in userspace. By adding a stub driver into the UML for each type of device, a kernel-like runtime environment in user-space can be supplied for drivers. By adding the proxy driver into the kernel, the bridge between the kernel and user-space device drivers can be supplied. The proxy driver is generic and with minimum function.

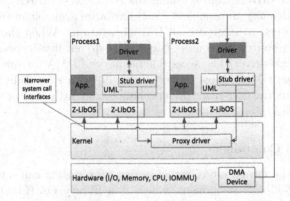

Fig. 1. Overview of the RAT architecture

3.1   Architecture Overview

We use UML as the kernel-like runtime in user-space, which enables multiple virtual Linux kernel-based operating systems to run as an application within a normal Linux system (known as the host). We implement the Z-LibOS to scoop out the system call implementation of the kernel and refactor it as a library. Applications only need to be linked to Z-LibOS, while not being required to be modified and compiled to get the support of Z-LibOS.

A component called *stub driver* is implemented for each type of drives, and amended into UML kernel, in order to resolve driver-specific symbols that cannot been understood by original UML kernel directly. For example, a PCI-based device driver uses the `PCI_register_driver()` function to register a PCI device driver. However, the UML kernel has no knowledge about this external symbol of this device driver. Therefore, the stub driver specific for PCI-based device is needed for resolving these unknown functions.

In order to move the whole device driver code out of kernel, a component called *proxy driver* is implemented as kernel module to allow user-space device drivers to use kernel functions. The proxy driver is the bridge of communication between the kernel and user-space device drivers, e.g., allocating kernel resources to the device drivers. For instance, when a system interrupt occurs, the kernel will issue a request to proxy driver, then the proxy driver will make upcalls to the related device driver (actually to the stub driver firstly). When a network device driver needs to notify the kernel to process the incoming packets, the related stub driver will issue downcalls to the proxy driver.

RAT runs each device driver as a user-space process, which is a UML process. By putting the device drivers into user-space, the threat to the kernel caused by the vulnerabilities in device drivers is supposed to be mitigated. However, some threats still exist, e.g., the compromised device driver can launch DMA attack. Some isolation mechanisms should be provided to prevent the compromised user-space drivers from crashing the rest of system. RAT uses IOMMU (*Input-output Memory Management Unit*) hardware available in Intel and AMD CPUs and chipsets, to interpose all DMA operations. When the proxy driver allocates DMA resources for a user-space device driver, it will specify a IOMMU page table for this driver. The accessible memory of DMA for this device driver is limited by the IOMMU page table, which will check the validity of the DMA access. Therefore, the user-space drivers cannot arbitrarily read or write physical memory via DMA.

3.2   Z-LibOS Component

Comparing to the native Linux kernel, a narrower system call interface is provided by the Z-LibOS component, which is a library OS (LibOS) for multi-process applications, including the UML process.

The library OS [2] refactors the function of the kernel into an application library, by providing the counterpart OS function in user-space and reducing the system call interface with an approach restricting system calls. In the approach that restricts system calls [2], only a subset of system calls are accessible to the LibOS to construct the user-space OS function. Traditionally, when applications call system functions provided by `glibc`, the corresponding code in `glibc` will issue system calls to enter into the kernel. In the library OS, the `glibc` is modified to turn the system calls into function calls to the library OS. Moreover, the original system calls are restricted to reduce the interface between user-space and kernel, by utilizing the `seccomp` mechanism [15], which is available after the Linux 2.6.12. The `seccomp` allows a process to create an immutable BPF *Berkeley Packet Filter*) program that specifies any allowed system calls.

Although the above mentioned library OS can reduce the attack surface of the kernel by narrowing the system call interface, it cannot directly support unmodified device drivers which run in the runtime provided by UML. There are three main reasons why the library OS is unable to support the UML directly. First, some indispensable system calls for UML, such as `ptrace`, `sigalstack`, are not supported in the library OS. Second, the library OS will handle some signals incorrectly. For example, it will terminate the process when handling the `SIGSTOP` signal, rather than stop the process. Finally, the library OS implements a user-space file system, which prevents the UML from accessing the host file systems. Z-LibOS is designed to address the three problems in order to support the UML. Once the UML can be executed on the Z-LibOS, the unmodified device drivers can be inserted into the UML.

3.3   Stub Driver Component

Introducing a stub driver in UML for each device driver can provide the support of unmodified device drivers, which enables us to achieve the first goal of our work, i.e., supporting the transparency for the device drivers.

The functions of stub driver include: resolving unknown external symbols of device drivers, and transmitting data and control information between device drivers and the kernel. The control information, such as registration request of device drivers, is important for registering device drivers, and allocating kernel resource for devices. For example, if a PCI-based device driver calls the `pci_register_driver()` function to register itself to the kernel, this function call will jump to the stub driver. Then, the stub driver will send `REGISTER` command to the proxy driver which will accomplish the registration task for the device driver.

A communication channel is needed between the stub driver and the proxy driver, for the transmission of data and control information. We consider the shared memory to implement the communication channel, because the communication through shared memory is efficient. Comparing to other communication techniques, such as RPC (*Remote Procedure Call*), the shared memory approach could provide better performance.

3.4   Proxy Driver Component

The proxy driver is the back-end driver for the stub driver. Each proxy driver is corresponding to one stub driver, which is then responsible for one type of device driver. The most important design goal of the proxy driver is to minimize its code size. Otherwise, there is no significance of the reduction of TCB. What's worse is that the number of kernel vulnerabilities could be increased due to the adoption of proxy driver. To minimize the code base, the proxy driver only includes two functions: delivering the request of function calls from stub driver to the kernel, and transmitting data between the kernel and stub drivers.

The proxy driver firstly registers itself to the kernel, which allows the kernel to call back to the proxy driver when some event occurs. For example, when a network packet arrives, the kernel will call the proxy driver's `ndo_xmit_frame()` function. The proxy driver contains the necessary interfaces representing a device driver. For instance, an Ethernet card proxy driver contains the `probe()` function, and network callback functions include `ndo_open()`, `ndo_xmit_frame()`, etc.

The definition of these interfaces is the same as the definition of the original interfaces between native device drivers and the kernel. However, unlike the original interfaces which directly contain the function to drive the devices, these interfaces only contain the function of transmitting data from/to, delivering interrupts to the stub drivers.

4   Implementation

We implement a prototype based on the Linux 3.14 kernel, and the Intel processor with VT-d extensions. Our implementation also includes a proxy driver and stub driver specifically to support the Ethernet card driver.

We implement the Z-LibOS by adapting the LibOS architecture from Graphene [2] system, and extending it to execute UML. In detail, we add 7 system calls to the original Graphene implementation for running UML, and manage to execute the e1000 Gigabit Ethernet card driver by implementing a proxy driver with around 900 lines of code.

4.1   LibOS Extension

Z-LibOS shares the same architecture as the Graphene [2]. However, as mentioned in Sect. 3.2, the implementation of existing LibOSes cannot directly support unmodified device drivers which run in the runtime provided by UML. Therefore, Z-LibOS has to implement some necessary extensions to Graphene system in order to support the UML processes.

The Z-LibOS firstly extends necessary system calls into the Graphene. The Graphene uses 50 system calls to replace 131 system calls in Linux 3.14. Seven system calls is added to Graphene in order to support the UML. Z-LibOS also improve the existing system calls of Graphene. Table 1 summarizes the system call extension of Z-LibOS.

Table 1. System call extension (The letter Y/N means whether there is relative support for the corresponding system call; "Using the host" means using the corresponding system call in the host OS)

System call	Graphene	Z-LibOS
ptrace	N	Using the host
Sigaltstack	N	Using the host
Statfs	N	Using the host
io_setup	N	Using the host
io_getevents	N	Using the host
modify_ldt	N	Using the host
Madvise	N	Using the host
Kill	Y	Extending the SIGSTOP sigal
Getrlimit	Y	Extending RLIMIT_CORE function
Setitimer	Y	Extending ITIMER_REAL

For example, the RLIMIT_CORE function of getrlimit system call, which Graphene does not implement, is added to return the core limit of kernel to the UML. For another example, in Graphene system, the SIGSTOP signal is handled by killing the process, which obviously violates the definition of the function of SIGSTOP. Therefore, we extend the kill system call to send the signal to the appropriate process, and modify the signal handler of Graphene to actually stop the process.

Another consideration of Z-LibOS is to allow the UML to access some important file systems, which are disallowed in the Graphene system. For example, the UML needs to read the /proc/mounts which records the information of the file systems mounted on /dev/shm, to get the physical path of tmpfs. Therefore, we allow UML to access the necessary file systems, including proc, dev, tmpfs, by constructing a local copy of the information for those file systems, and guiding UML to access them.

4.2   Proxy Driver and Stub Driver

We have elaborated the function of proxy driver and stub driver in Sect. 3. In this section, we focus on the communication of proxy driver and stub driver, including the shared communication channel, and data transmission. We also discuss the implementation of the handling of the device interrupt.

Shared Communication Channel. As discussed in Sect. 3, the stub driver and proxy driver need to communicate with each other to transmit data, and deliver control information. We construct a shared channel between these two drivers by mapping kernel-space memory into user-space. The shared memory mechanism provides an efficient access between components in kernel-space and user-space. The shared communication channel holds three kinds of information, control information, interrupt information, and data that needs to be transmitted.

Interrupt Handling. In our implementation, the device interrupts are handled in user-space, as shown in Fig. 2. When the device receives a data packet, it will generate an interrupt, which triggers the interrupt handler of the corresponding proxy driver. Then, the proxy driver sends this interrupt to the stub driver by writing it to the shared memory. The stub driver will receive the interrupt from the proxy driver by reading the shared memory, and the it will then trigger the interrupt handler of the device drivers. When the handing of interrupt is done by

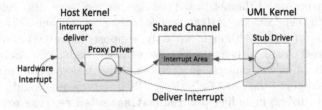

Fig. 2. Interrupt handling

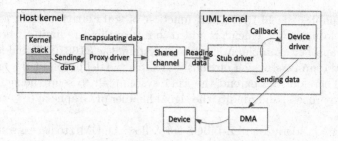

Fig. 3. Sending data packets

the device driver, the stub driver will unmark the interrupt by sending a UNMARK command to the proxy driver.

Data Transmission. The next implementation detail is the transmitting of data packets between the kernel and user-space device drivers. Figure 3 depicts the flow of sending data packets. When the kernel needs to send data packets, it calls the transmission function of the proxy driver. For example, the transmission function of a network device driver is xmit_frame(). Then, the proxy driver encapsulates the data into a message, which includes the length and the data, and finally writes the message into the shared memory.

The stub driver will check the shared memory to obtain the packets from the kernel, and then it invokes the transmission function of device driver to send the data packets. In order to make the stub driver be able to invoke the transmission function, when the device driver registers itself to the UML kernel, the UML will export the driver structure (which contains the address of transmission function) of the device driver to the stub driver. Finally, the device driver can send data packets to the DMA, which delivers the data to the device.

Receiving the data packet is similar to the process of sending data. Once a packet arrives, the device will generate an interrupt, which will then be delivered to the user-space device drivers as analyzed in "Interrupt Handling". Then, the device drivers will handle the interrupt, and read the packet from the DMA memory. Finally, the stub driver transmits the received packets to the proxy driver.

4.3   Network Driver Case Study

We implement an Ethernet card proxy driver and its related stub driver, which support the e1000 device driver, a Gigabit Ethernet card driver based on PCI. Although we only support the e1000 device driver, other Ethernet card drivers, such as e1000e, ixgb, can also be supported with a few changes in the implementation. For example, in order to support the e1000e, three PCI interfaces could be added into the stub driver, including pci_request_selected_regions_exclusive(), pcie_capability_read_word(), pcie_capability_write_word().

To support the e1000 driver with the proposed architecture, we firstly insert it into the UML with `insmod`. Then, we need to implement the corresponding stub driver, (1) to handle some of the symbols of the device driver's implementation that are unknown to UML kernel, (2) to define a user-space PCI structure for the device driver to support the PCI-like environment in user-space. Finally, we need to implement the corresponding proxy driver, (1) to define an Ethernet card driver structure for registering the proxy driver into the kernel, (2) to contain handlers to handle the requests from the related stub driver. It is worth mentioned that the handlers could check the requests for the purpose of preventing malicious attacks from the driver to the kernel, because the device driver is now with lower privilege than the kernel.

5 Evaluation

To evaluate the prototype, the operation overhead of Z-LibOS is measured by executing LMBench [16] benchmark, and then the performance of device driver is tested by running the Netperf [17] benchmark. We also present the security analysis for the prototype. We run the test on a laptop, which has a Intel Core i5-3337U CPU with double cores at 1.80 GHz, 1 GB system memory, and an ethernet card with Realtek PCIe GBE family controller. This machine runs Ubuntu 12.04 LTS with Linux kernel version 3.14. In order to test the case study, we also choose to run the e1000 with version 7.3.21-k8-NAPI.

5.1 Low-Level Operation Overhead of Z-LibOS

Z-LibOS implements part of the kernel function in user-space. Thus, the performance of operations like `read`, `write` will be affected by the adoption of Z-LibOS architecture. To measure the performance of these operations, we use the LMBench to evaluate the overhead. The LMBench is executed on three different environments: on the native Linux kernel, on the RAT, and on the Graphene. The results are summarized in Table 2, and each measurement is a mean value counted by 1,000 times running.

Since the Z-LibOS is developed based on the Graphene system, we compare the overhead difference between RAT and Graphene. While RAT has the same performance as the Graphene when testing `syscall` and `read`, it has some performance penalty when testing `write` and `open/close` operations. The penalty is caused by the fact that the UML needs to access some specified host file systems. For example, the UML process needs to write information to the files in `/root/.uml/`. The signal-related tests also show some penalty because the RAT extends the signal handler of Graphene for transmitting and handling the signal `SIGSTOP`. For example, when a process exits, it will send some signals to its parent. Thus, the `fork+exit` introduces some penalty due to the signal handling.

Table 2. LMBench comparison among native, RAT and Graphene. Execution time is microseconds, and lower is better

Test	Linux (us)	RAT (us)	Graphene (us)
Syscall	0.06	0.06	0.06
Read	0.12	0.13	0.13
Write	0.16	0.23	0.17
Open/close	1.47	2.09	1.51
Select tcp	17.66	18.81	18.24
sig_install	0.14	0.14	0.13
Siguser1	1.02	1.04	0.13
fork+exit	360	350	323
fork+exec	936	980	1000
fork+sh	2087	2380	2362

Table 3. Network performance for use-space e1000 Ethernet card driver. The overhead with minus prefix means better performance

Test	Throughput		
	Linux-e1000	RAT-e1000	Penalty(%)
TCP_STREAM	16999 Mbits/s	13763 Mbits/s	24 %
UDP_STREAM TX	27711 Mbits/s	23965 Mbits/s	13 %
UDP_STREAM RX	18601 Mbits/s	16582 Mbits/s	12 %
UDP_RR	7053 Tx/s	7717 Tx/s	−9 %

5.2   Device Driver Performance

To understand the performance overhead imposed by moving the e1000 Ethernet card driver into the user-space, we consider Netperf benchmark to test the TCP streaming, UDP streaming, and UDP request-response performance. Every measurement is the mean value obtained by running the corresponding test 1000 times.

Table 3 summarizes the experiment results. We use TCP_STREAM benchmark to measure TCP receiving throughput by running it with 87380 bytes of receiving buffers and 16834 bytes of sending buffers. Comparing to the situation that device driver runs on native Linux, this test shows 24% performance penalty on RAT. The two UDP_STREAM are used to measure throughput for transmitting and receiving 64 bytes UDP packets. The results incur about 12%–13% performance penalty. These three results indicate that the performance penalty imposed by network driver running in RAT is negligible.

The driver latency is measured by the UDP_RR benchmark. It has better performance than the native Linux, which benefits from the fact that the data packet transmission could occur in user-space. For example, when the user-space device driver receives a network packet, it will tell the kernel to receive the packet by giving the address of packet to the kernel. Then, the kernel will directly transmit the packets to applications. This data transmission occurs in user-space without entering into the kernel.

5.3 Security Analysis

We reduce 81.6% of the system calls by using 57 system calls (the native Linux has 310 system calls) to support the UML which is required to support user-space device drivers. In the case study of Ethernet driver, we reduce the code base (inside kernel) of the Ethernet card driver (original 15K LoC) into 900 LoC. Since the device drivers are moved into the user-space, the exploit of untrusted drivers has very limited chance to crash the kernel. Alternatively, it can only impact the user-space UML processes that holds these untrusted drivers.

The PCI resources allocated by the proxy driver in the kernel will be used by the device driver in user-space to manage the device, such as getting the device state. The stub driver will remap the memory address of the allocated PCI resources into the user-space, and then return the user-space address to the device driver. When a malicious device driver read/write the PCI address space which does not belong to itself, the UML process that holds this driver will be terminated by the kernel.

Since the device drivers receive and send data packets in user-space, attackers can more easily steal sensitive data by compromising the driver process. We need to mention that the focus of our work is to protect the kernel, rather than the applications themselves. We assume that applications can use some secure techniques, such as cryptographic methods, to protect the sensitive data.

6 Related Work

The core contribution of our work includes an architecture reducing the TCB and attack surface of the Linux kernel by moving the device drivers into the user-space and narrowing the system call interface.

6.1 Re-organization of Kernels

Several alternative operating systems provide small code base of the TCB for the kernel, including microkernels [18,19], Nested kernel [20]. The TCB of these systems are composed of the privileged small kernels, firmware, and hardware. A microkernel is the near-minimum amount of software that can provide the mechanisms needed to implement an operating system. Device drivers in this kernel architecture are usually simple, and not able to support sufficient function for devices. However, the Linux device drivers are typically more complex. Our work aims at moving the complex Linux device drivers out of the kernel's TCB, while keeping sufficient function for devices.

6.2   Kernels' TCB Reduction Based on Virtualization

Virtualization plays an important role in protecting computing system, because its core runs at the most privileged level, and has small code size. Flicker [8] and TrustVisor [9] are the typical systems to reduce TCB based on hardware virtualization, which exclude the untrusted kernel out of the TCB. Nevertheless, their fundamental limitation is that applications need be explicitly modified and compiled to get the support of the reduced TCB. Wimpy kernel [10] takes advantage of the small hypervisor to provide on-demand isolated I/O for the sensitive applications. Although these virtualization-based security systems exclude untrusted kernels from the TCB, they focus on the security of applications, rather than the security of the original kernel themselves.

6.3   Device Driver Isolation

Buggy or malicious device drivers [3,4] can always crash the monolithic kernel. This kind of threat is firstly recognized in Nooks [21], where page table permissions are used to mitigate the effect of buggy or malicious device drivers' code on the rest of the kernel. However, not all vulnerabilities in the drivers can be prevented by Nooks. Alternatively, user-space device driver is a valid method to separate buggy device drivers and conveniently debug the drivers. SUD [13], a system that runs the Linux device drivers as user-space processes, is able to protect the kernel from all possible bugs in device drivers. However, SUD still has a very large attack surface because its system call interface has not been reduced. RAT can reduce attack surface by narrowing the system call interface.

7   Conclusion

Reducing the attack surface and TCB of kernel is needed to make the kernel more secure. This paper presents an architecture based on the user-space driver and narrowed system call interface to reduce the TCB and the attack surface of Linux kernel. It also presents a detailed implementation of the prototype, and discusses a concrete case study of Ethernet card driver. The evaluation shows that the desired reduction and efficiency goals for the trusted base of the Linux kernel can be achieved.

References

1. Linux Kernel Security Vulnerabilities. http://www.cvedetails.com
2. Tsai, C.C., Arora, K.S., Bandi, N., Jain, B., Jannen, W., John, J., Kalodner, H.A., Kulkarni, V., Oliveria, D., Porter, D.E.: Cooperation and security isolation of library OSes for multi-process applications. In: Proceedings of the 9th European Conference on Computer System, pp. 474–495. ACM (2014)
3. Linux kernel i915 driver memory corruption vulnerability. http://cve.mitre.org
4. Butti, L., Tinnes, J.: Discovering and exploiting 802.11 wireless driver vulnerabilities. J. Comput. Virol. 4, 25–37 (2008)

5. Kurmus, A., Tartler, R., Dorneanu, D., Heinloth, B., Rothberg, V.: Attack surface metrics and automated compile-time OS kernel tailoring. In: Proceedings of the 20th Network and Distributed System Security Symposium, pp. 1–18 (2013)
6. Porter, D.E., Boyd-Wickizer, S., Howell, J., Olinsky, R., Hunt, G.C.: Rethinking the library OS from the top down. In: Proceedings of the 6th International Conference on Architectural Support for Programming Languages and Operating System, pp. 291–304. ACM (2011)
7. Kurmus, A., Dechard, S., Kapitza, R.: Quantifiable run-time kernel attack surface reduction. In: Dietrich, S. (ed.) DIMVA 2016. LNCS, vol. 8550, pp. 212–234. Springer, Heidelberg (2014)
8. McCune, J.M., Parno, B.J., Perrig, A., Reiter, M.K., Isozaki, H.: Flicker: an execution infrastructure for TCB minimization. In: Proceedings of the 3rd ACM SIGOPS/EuroSys European Conference on Computer Systems, pp. 315–328. ACM (2008)
9. McCune, J.M., Li, Y., Qu, N., Zhou, Z., Datta, A., Gligor, V., Perrig, A.: Trustvisor: efficient TCB reduction and attestation. In: Proceedings of the 2010 IEEE Symposium on Security and Privacy, SP 2010, pp. 315–328. ACM (2010)
10. Zhou, Z., Yu, M., Gligor, V.D.: Dancing with giants: wimpy kernels for on-demand isolated I/O. In: Proceedings of the 2014 IEEE Symposium on Security and Privacy, SP 2014, pp. 38–46. IEEE (2014)
11. Herder, J.N., Bos, H., Gras, B., Homburg, P., Tanenbaum, A.S.: Fast byte-granularity software fault isolation. In: Proceedings of the 2009 IEEE Dependable Systems and Networks Conference, pp. 45–58. IEEE (2009)
12. Chubb, P.: Linux kernel infrastructure for user-level device drivers. In: Proceedings of the Workshop on Object Systems and Software Architectures (2004)
13. Boyd-Wickizer, S., Zeldovich, N.: Tolerating malicious device drivers in Linux. In: Proceedings of the 2010 USENIX Annual Technical Conference, USENIX Association, pp. 11–20 (2010)
14. Dike, J.: User mode Linux. In: Proceedings of the 5th Annual Linux Showcase and Conference, pp. 3–14. ACM (2001)
15. SECure COMPuting with Filters. https://www.kernel.org/doc/Documentation/p-rctl/seccomp_filter.txt
16. MvVoy, L., Staelin, C.: lmbench: portable tools for performance analysis. In: Proceedings of the 1996 USENIX Annual Technical Conference, USENIX Association, pp. 279–294 (1996)
17. Jones, R.: Netperf: A network performance benchmark. version 2.45. http://www.netperf.org
18. Bershad, B.N., Savage, S., Pardyak, P., Sirer, E.G., Fiuzynski, M.E., Becker, D., Chambers, C., Eggers, S.: Extensibility safety and performance in the spin operating system. In: Proceedings of the 15th ACM Symposium on Operating Systems Principles, pp. 267–283. ACM (1995)
19. Liedtke, J.: On micro-kernel construction. In: Proceedings of the 15th ACM Symposium on Operating Systems Principles, SOSP 1995, pp. 237–250. ACM (1995)
20. Dautenhahn, N., Kasampalis, T., Dietz, W., Criswell, J., Adve, V.: Nested kernel: an operating system architecture for intra-kernel privilege separation. In: Proceedings of the Twentieth International Conference on Architectural Support for Programming Languages and Operating Systems, pp. 191–206. ACM (2015)
21. Swift, M.M., Bershad Brian, N., Levy, H.N.: Improving the reliability of commodity operating systems. In: Proccedings of the 19th ACM Symposium on Operating systems Principles, pp. 207–222. ACM (2003)

OBC Based Optimization of Re-encryption for Cryptographic Cloud Storage

Huidong Qiao[1,2(✉)], Jiangchun Ren[1], Zhiying Wang[1], Haihe Ba[1],
Huaizhe Zhou[1], and Tie Hong[1]

[1] College of Computer, National University of Defense Technology,
Changsha 410073, China
{qiaohuidong13, jcren, zywang, haiheba,
huaizhezhou, tiehong}@nudt.edu.cn
[2] College of Computer and Communication, Hunan Institute of Engineering,
Xiangtan 411100, China

Abstract. In a cryptographic cloud storage system, it's still very inefficient to revoke a user's access right to a large file. This is because the ciphertext of the file, which is stored in the cloud, has to be decrypted and encrypted again under a new key (re-encryption), in order to prevent the revoked user from accessing the file with the previous key. For improving the performance of re-encryption operation, we propose orderly block chaining (OBC) encryption mode. In the decryption of a ciphertext produced by OBC, all blocks of ciphertext must be set in the correct position. Without the information about correct permutation order, it is infeasible for a user to decrypt any one of the blocks, even if he holds the encryption key. Thus, the file, which is encrypted by OBC, can be re-encrypted by just re-permuting the sequence of ciphertext blocks in another order. Experimental results show that OBC based optimization can sharply cut down the cost of re-encryption, while keeping the security of the data.

Keywords: Re-encryption · Encryption mode · Cryptographic cloud storage

1 Introduction

Instead of building and maintaining a private storage infrastructure, outsourcing the data to a public cloud offers an immediate and dynamic storage service for customers in a flexible mode with the fewer cost. But generally speaking, a public cloud storage service provider usually cannot be thought as a fully trusted party, but only a semi-trusted party. So security problems, such as data confidentiality and data integrity, have hindered the users to switch to the public could.

To solve the problem, Kamara and Lauter [1] proposed a secure cloud storage architecture which builds a cryptographic access control system on top of a public

The work is funded in part by the National Natural Science Foundation of China (No. 61303191). And it is also supported by a grant from the National High Technology Research and Development Program of China (863 Program) (No. 2015AA016010).

J. Carretero et al. (Eds.): ICA3PP 2016, LNCS 10048, pp. 586–595, 2016.
DOI: 10.1007/978-3-319-49583-5_46

cloud infrastructure. In their scheme, the data owner (DO) picks a random key k to encrypt the file F using symmetric cipher to produce $E_k(F)$. Then ciphertext-policy attribute-based encryption (CP-ABE) [2] scheme is suggested to be used, for encrypting the key k and producing $E'_T(k)$ under the T which is an access structure according to the access control policy that the DO defined. Finally, the ciphertext $E'_T(k)$ together with the $E_k(F)$ are uploaded to the cloud. If the attributes of a data user (DU) match the policy defined in T, after downloading the ciphertexts, he can retrieve the file key k from $E'_T(k)$, then recover the file F from $E_k(F)$ with k.

CP-ABE offers an efficient access control tool to DO. However, performance of this cryptographic cloud storage could be poor, if the access control policy changed dynamically, especially for the revocation. Most researches of the revocation in a CP-ABE system is to achieve the revocation of the DU's private key, or the revocation of the DU's attribute. These schemes usually produce a ciphertext $E'_{T'}(k)$ to replace original $E'_T(k)$. The revoked DU will not be able to decrypt $E'_{T'}(k)$, then the $E_k(F)$ without k. This is shown in the case (a) of Fig. 1. But considering the case (b) of Fig. 1, if a DU store the file key k in local machine before revocation (caching the whole file in the local is usually uneconomic for the DU), he can directly recover the file F from $E_k(F)$ using the key k. Hence, a secure revocation should be performed in this way: (1) DO produces the ciphertext $E_{k'}(F)$ by re-encrypting F with a new key k', then produces $E'_{T'}(k')$ with the new policy T'; (2) DO uploads $E_{k'}(F)$ and $E'_{T'}(k')$ to replace $E_k(F)$ and $E'_T(k)$. Obviously, the operation cost of this revocation will be expensive, especially the re-encryption of the file F when it is a large file. This is the problem we try to solve in our research. And the main contribution of this paper are: (1) orderly block chaining (OBC) encryption mode, whose special property can be applied in re-encryption, (2) optimization of re-encryption based on OBC, which can sharply cut down the expensive cost of re-encryption of large file.

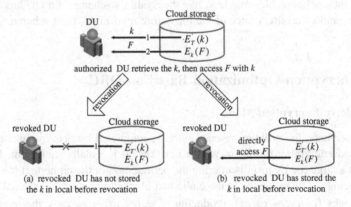

Fig. 1. Revocation in cryptographic cloud storage

2 Related Works

By far, most dynamic access control schemes (for example, the schemes in [3, 4]) focus on the key revocation. However, as mentioned above, the re-encryption of the file is necessary in revocation, and the re-encryption of a large file is the most costly operation of the revocation. To improve performance, Backes et al. [5] adopted a simple scheme named lazy revocation. The re-encryption in lazy revocation will be postponed until the file is modified for the first time after a revocation. But for most systems, the DU's access right to the file need to be immediately revoked when the DO make the revocation. To achieve the immediate revocation, Vimercati et al. [6] proposed an over-encryption scheme. However, their system does not improve the performance of re-encryption. It only moves the computation cost of DO to the cloud service provider (CSP). If there are a lot of files owned by a lot of users in the cloud, the CSP may undertake an expensive cost to fulfill the user's frequent requests.

Similar to the over-encryption, the proxy re-encryption (PRE) allows a proxy to translate the ciphertext, which is encrypted with the original key, into a ciphertext which is encrypted with another key. Meanwhile, the proxy cannot obtain any information about the plaintext. But most of the PRE schemes are proposed in the asymmetric encryption setting, so they are not suitable for large file re-encryption. To realize proxy re-encryption in the symmetric setting, Syalim et al. [7] proposed a symmetric PRE cipher. The scheme firstly transforms the plaintext into a pseudo message sequence using the All-or-nothing transform (AONT) [8], then utilizes characteristics of AONT to implement efficient proxy re-encryption. The security of their scheme is mainly based on the characteristics of AONT. If a user has already stored the key of AONT before revocation, the scheme will be not that secure, because their proxy re-encryption scheme employs a weak encryption (that is pointed out in [7]) to reduce the computation cost. For purely improving the performance of re-encryption operation, Cheng et al. [9] suggested another idea based on the AONT. They used an enriched Rabin's information dispersal algorithm (IDA) [10] and a variant of the AONT in their scheme. Nevertheless, like the Syalim's scheme, if a DU has stored the AONT key and an arbitrary slice of the file before revocation, their scheme will be not that secure.

3 Re-encryption Optimization Based on OBC

3.1 Orderly Encryption Mode

For block ciphers, the ordinary re-encryption is completed by decrypting file with the old key and encrypting file again with a new key. It is usually inefficient. If we can re-encrypt a large file by just disordering the permutation of the ciphertext blocks of file and producing a new sequence of the ciphertext blocks (e.g. with the original sequence C of 5 blocks $(c_0, c_1, c_2, c_3, c_4)$, producing $C' = (c_1, c_4, c_3, c_0, c_2)$), the re-encryption performance will be highly improved. But to the best of our knowledge, for most encryption modes of block cipher, this re-permutation of ciphertext blocks cannot be a secure re-encryption. For example, re-permutation can be proved not secure for the Cipher Block Chaining (CBC) mode. Let the n blocks of message be denoted $M = m_1, m_2, \ldots, m_n$. CBC mode outputs the ciphertext $C = c_0, c_1, c_2, \ldots, c_n$, where $c_0 = IV$ and $c_i = E(c_{i-1} \oplus m_i, K)$, for $i = 1, 2, \ldots, n$. IV is a random initialization vector and K is the encryption key. In decryption, one computes $m_i = c_{i-1} \oplus D(c_i, K)$. Let the blocks of C be disordered in a random permutation order to form a new sequence C'. A revoked DU, who obtains C' and holds the encryption key K and IV, will have additional difficulties to decrypt C'. It is for the reason that, to decrypt the block c_i, one has to pick out the adjacent blocks c_i and c_{i-1}. But in fact, given a block c_i, a revoked DU can try every block of C' one by one (denoted as c_j) to compute $m_i = c_j \oplus D(c_i, K)$, until the result m_i "makes sense" or it matches a known block of M. In the worst case, n-1 times computation of the block decryption will be performed. So the computation cost of this procedure is $O(n)$, and the whole blocks of C' can be decrypted in polynomial time. Thus, re-permutation is not a secure re-encryption for CBC encryption mode.

To make the re-permutation to be a secure re-encryption, we need a new encryption mode, whose output ciphertext blocks is strongly chained in order. And without the correct permutation of all blocks, even if one has the encryption key, he will not be able to retrieve any information from the ciphertext blocks.

Definition. Suppose that a block cipher encryption mode transforms blocks of a message $M = m_1, m_2, \ldots, m_n$ into a sequence of ciphertext blocks $C = c_1, c_2, \ldots, c_s$ with the encryption key, for some s, $s \geq n$. We say that the encryption mode is *orderly*, if

- Both the encryption mode and its inverse are efficiently computable (that is, computable in polynomial time).
- Holding the encryption key, one must put every block of ciphertext into the correct position (the original block position in sequence C) in decryption, or he cannot recover any one of the blocks of M.

Suppose that the blocks of C is disordered to produce a new sequence C' by random re-permutation, and a revoked DU does not record any information about the permutation order of C. If s is large enough, C' will be secure against the revoked DU. It is because he must put every block into the correct position before recovering any block of M, and there're $s!$ potential permutations to test. Actually, when s is 256, the search space will be larger than 2^{1683}. Hence, the re-permutation is an ideal re-encryption for the files encrypted by *orderly* encryption mode. But to our best knowledge, most encryption mode of block ciphers is *not orderly*. For example, CBC is *not orderly*, because a revoked DU, who knows nothing about the permutation information, can always recover any block of M in polynomial time. And obviously, ECB is *not orderly*. So we propose a new encryption mode—OBC encryption mode.

3.2 Orderly Block Chaining (OBC) Encryption Mode

Firstly, we design a block encryption operation—*BEncrypt* as the base of OBC encryption mode. Let the input blocks to be $b_1, b_2, \ldots, b_n$. *BEncrypt* outputs $c_1, c_2, \ldots, c_n$ by computing $c_i = E(b_i, b_{i-1} \oplus c_{i-1})$, for $i = 1$ to n, $b_0 = IV$ and $c_0 = K$. IV is a random initialization vector and K is the encryption key of the *BEncrypt*. The encryption function E can be any cipher such as DES, AES, or etc. For E, the first parameter b_i is the plaintext, and $b_{i-1} \oplus c_{i-1}$ is the encryption key. In decryption of *BEncrypt*, one computes $b_i = D(c_i, b_{i-1} \oplus c_{i-1})$, where D is the decryption of E. On the base of *BEncrypt*, we propose OBC as follows:

- Use *BEncrypt* to encrypt the plaintext blocks $m_1, m_2, \ldots, m_n$ one by one from m_1 to m_n with K and IV to generate n blocks $t_1, t_2, \ldots, t_n$, and
- Use *BEncrypt* to encrypt the blocks $t_1, t_2, \ldots, t_n$ one by one from t_n to t_1 with K and IV to generate n blocks ciphertext $c_1, c_2, \ldots, c_n$.

The procedure of OBC can be described as Fig. 2.

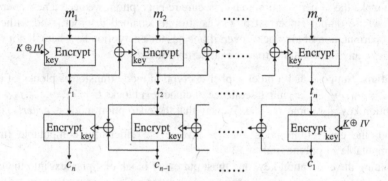

Fig. 2. Orderly block chaining (OBC) encryption mode

The inverse of OBC is:
- Decrypt the ciphertext blocks $c_1, c_2, \ldots, c_n$ one by one from c_1 to c_n with K and IV to generate n blocks $t_n, t_{n-1}, \ldots, t_1$, and
- Decrypt the blocks $t_1, t_2, \ldots, t_n$ one by one from t_1 to t_n with K and IV to generate n blocks plaintext $m_1, m_2, \ldots, m_n$.

Theorem 1. OBC is an *orderly* encryption mode.

Proof. Obviously, the OBC and its inverse are both computable in polynomial time. For proving that OBC is orderly, we need to discuss *BEncrypt* firstly. The inverse of *BEncrypt* is $b_i = D(c_i, b_{i-1} \oplus c_{i-1})$, for $1 \le i \le n$ and $b_0 = IV, c_0 = K$. Thus, holding the ciphertext $c_1, c_2, \ldots, c_n$, the K and the IV, to recover a block b_i, one needs to compute

$$b_i = D(c_i, D(c_{i-1}, \ldots, D(c_2, D(c_1, K \oplus IV) \oplus c_1) \ldots \oplus c_{i-2}) \oplus c_{i-1})$$

It means that one must follow the correct permutation order of $c_1, c_2, \ldots, c_i$ to compute the decryption. Since OBC utilizes 2 rounds of the *BEncrypt*, to recover a plaintext block m_i encrypted by OBC, one need to compute

$$m_i = D(t_i, D(t_{i-1}, \ldots, D(t_2, D(t_1, K \oplus IV) \oplus t_1) \ldots \oplus t_{i-2}) \oplus t_{i-1})$$

So he has to recover the blocks $t_1, t_2, \ldots, t_i$ before decrypting m_i. And for recovering t_1, the computation is

$$t_1 = D(c_n, D(c_{n-1}, \ldots, D(c_2, D(c_1, K \oplus IV) \oplus c_1) \ldots \oplus c_{n-2}) \oplus c_{n-1})$$

As a result, for decrypting any block m_i, one should set *all* ciphertext blocks $c_1, c_2, \ldots, c_n$ in precise order from c_1 to c_n, or he will not be able to finish the decryption. Hence, OBC is an *orderly* encryption mode.

3.3   OBC Based Efficient Re-encryption

If a file is encrypted by the OBC, an efficient re-encryption can be achieved by simply re-permuting the ciphertext blocks of the file in another random permutation order. Suppose that the input blocks sequence is denoted as $B = b_1, b_2, \ldots, b_n$. Our re-encryption operation will transform the B into $B' = b'_1, b'_2, \ldots, b'_n$, where $b'_{pk_i} = b_i$, for $i = 1$ to n. The sequence of the integers $pk_1, pk_2, \ldots, pk_n$ is the permutation key, where $1 \leq pk_i \leq n$ for $1 \leq i \leq n$, and $pk_i \neq pk_j$ for $i \neq j$.

To keep the security of the random re-permuting, we utilize permutation key generation (*PkeyGen*) algorithm to generate the uniform random permutation as the permutation key. Suppose that we have a random-number generator *RANDOM*. A call to *RANDOM(a, b)* returns an integer between a and b, inclusive, with each such integer being equally likely. *PkeyGen* is described in Algorithm 1.

Algorithm 1. Permutation Key Generation Algorithm *PkeyGen*

Input: numbers of *PK* elements n
Output: permutation key *PK*
1   construct an integer array $pk_1, pk_2, \ldots, pk_n$
2   set $pk_1, pk_2, \ldots, pk_n$ with the number from 1 to n
3   for i=1 to n do
4   swap $pk_i \leftrightarrow pk_{RANDOM(i,n)}$
5   end for
6   return $pk_1, pk_2, \ldots, pk_n$

PkeyGen will be equally likely to produce every permutation of the numbers 1 through n (proof can be found in [12]).

4   Security Analysis

In our scheme, the file uploaded to a public cloud is encrypted by OBC, and the re-encryption is performed by the re-permutation. So the file is computational secure against unauthorized DUs or outside attackers. And if the CSP is not authorized, CSP also will not be able to retrieve the keys and the files. We focus on the security discussion about the potential attackers that come from the revoked DUs. A revoked DU may store the encryption keys and the previous permutation key in local before the revocation. After a re-encryption, the permutation order will be changed in random, but the encryption keys remain the same. Based on the orderly property of OBC, the revoked DU cannot decrypt any ciphertext, if the number of ciphertext blocks is large enough. In general, the ciphertext of a file that is divided into 256 blocks for permutation will be safe enough to perform re-encryption, if the revoked DU does not record the permutation information.

However, the collusion between the CSP and the revoked DU may disclose the re-encrypted file. In fact, if at the base of relaxing restriction, this collusion is always practical in various revocation schemes. It is because even the DO perform the ordinary re-encryption all by himself (download file, decrypt file, encrypt file with a new key and upload file), the CSP may still keep the previous copy of the file, and the revoked DU may store the previous keys. Then, collusion can take place anytime, if CSP and the revoked DU combine their knowledge together. Samanthula et al. [11] proposed a scheme to solve the problem by distributing the file between two clouds. Their scheme operates under the assumption that the probability of collusion between two CSPs is negligible. Under this assumption, we can also distribute a file between different CSPs to resist the collusion between one CSP and the revoked DU.

Hash caching attack (HCA) is another noteworthy threat to our system. HCA is performed by the revoked DU. For economic consideration, usually, a DU is not willing to store the whole file in the local. But a DU may compute the hash values of the blocks and cache them in local (that is, the DU recorded the permutation information before revocation). The revoked DU can perform HCA by computing hash values of the blocks of new ciphertext, and comparing them with those cached in local, to find out the original permutation of the ciphertext blocks. Then, a revoked DU could still decrypt the blocks in the correct permutation order. To simply resist HCA, we can make the cost of HCA is equal to or higher than the cost of caching the whole file. For example, assuming that MD5 algorithm is the hash function, when setting the length of the permutation blocks as 128 bits, the cost of HCA will be more expensive than directly caching the whole file in local (because of the equal cost in storage and the extra cost in hash computation). But in this case, the ciphertext need to be divided into more blocks for permutation. Our re-encryption operation mainly includes *PKeyGen* and re-permutation. Computation cost of re-permutation depends on the file size, that of *PKeyGen* depends on the number of permutation blocks. Then for the same file, the performance of re-encryption will degrade with the increase of the number of permutation blocks.

Fortunately, the cost, that a revoked DU would accept to perform HCA, is always limited. We can decrease the number of permutation blocks to a relatively small number. Suppose that the maximal storage cost of HCA which the revoked DU would accept is L bits (taking MD5 as the hash function). To achieve secure re-encryption, we can divide the ciphertext of a file into more than $(256 + n)$ blocks for re-encryption, where $n = L/128$. It makes sure that at least 256 blocks' hash value will not be recorded by the revoked DU. Then his success probability to restore the correct permutation is less than $1/256!$. In this way, the number of blocks can be kept in an appropriate range, and high performance can be achieved in the re-encryption.

5 Performance Evaluation

In performance evaluation, we compare our scheme with the plain re-encryption scheme (PREN). PREN represent the simplest method of re-encryption without any performance optimization. PREN re-encrypts the file by directly decrypting the ciphertext with the previous key and then encrypting plaintext with a new key. In the experiments of PREN, CBC mode is applied to encrypt or decrypt the files. The blocks encryption computation of CBC and OBC is performed with AES-128. We use RC4 algorithm to implement *RANDOM* operation of *PKeyGen*. Because our most concern is the optimization of computation performance, instead of cloud storage server, only PC is employed to measure the computation efficiency of our scheme and PREN. We conducted the experiments on the same machine which has a Intel® Core™ i7-320M CPU running at 2.9 GHz with 8 GB RAM. The experimental programs are run on Windows 7 x64 system. All the programs are implemented in single thread for measuring absolute time consumption of the two schemes. Experimental programs are C programs based on the OpenSSL toolkit (OpenSSL 1.0.2d 9 Jul 2015). The primitive ciphers of PREN and our scheme (such as AES, RC4 and etc.) are implemented with the functions of OpenSSL.

In the experiments, a file whose size is 512 MB is employed, and the number of permutation blocks which the file is divided, varies from 2^8 to 2^{20}. The experimental

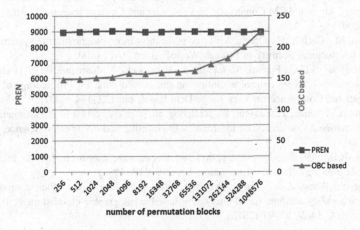

Fig. 3. Measured performance of re-encryption

result shows that the running time of our re-encryption increases from 148 ms to 224 ms with the number of blocks increasing from 2^8 to 2^{20}. Certainly, the performance of PREN does not vary with the number of permutation blocks, and the average time consumption of PREN is 9010 ms. Comparing to the PREN, our scheme makes an efficient performance optimization in computation efficiency of the re-encryption. The experimental results are shown in Fig. 3.

6 Conclusions

In this paper, we present the definition of the orderly encryption mode. The file, which is encrypted by orderly encryption mode, can be re-encrypted by simply re-permuting the blocks of ciphertext in random order. And we propose OBC encryption mode which satisfy the definition of orderly encryption mode. Based on OBC encryption mode, the re-encryption optimization can be efficiently implemented in cryptographic cloud storage system. We analyzed the security and performance of the OBC based re-encryption. The experimental results proved that the new method offers an efficient improvement in re-encryption for the dynamic access control of cryptographic cloud storage.

References

1. Kamara, S., Lauter, K.: Cryptographic cloud storage. In: 14th Financial Cryptograpy and Data Security International Conference, pp. 136–149 (2010)
2. Bethencourt, J., Sahai, A., Waters, B.: Ciphertext-policy attribute-based encryption. In: 2007 IEEE Symposium on Security and Privacy, pp. 321–334 (2007)
3. Castiglione, A., De Santis, A., Masucci, B., Palmieri, F., Castiglione, A., Huang, X.: Cryptographic hierarchical access control for dynamic structures. IEEE Trans. Inf. Forensic Secur. 11(10), 2349–2364 (2016)
4. Ostrovsky, R., Sahai, A., Waters, B.: Attribute-based encryption with non-monotonic access structures. In: 14th ACM Conference on Computer and Communications Security, pp. 195–203 (2007)
5. Backes, M., Cachin, C., Oprea, A.: Lazy revocation in cryptographic file systems. In: 3rd IEEE International Security in Storage Workshop, pp. 1–11 (2005)
6. Di Vimercati, S.D.C., Foresti, S., Jajodia, S., Paraboschi, S., Samarati, P.: Over-encryption: management of access control evolution on outsourced data. In: Proceedings of the 33rd International Conference on Very Large Data Bases, pp. 123–134 (2007)
7. Syalim, A., Nishide, T., Sakurai, K.: Realizing proxy re-encryption in the symmetric world. In: International Conference on Informatics Engineering and Information Science, pp. 259–274 (2011)
8. Rivest, R.L.: All-or-nothing encryption and the package transform. In: 4th International Workshop on Fast Software Encryption, pp. 210–218 (1997)
9. Cheng, Y., Wang, Z.-Y., Ma, J., Wu, J.-J., Mei, S.-Z., Ren, J.-C.: Efficient revocation in ciphertext-policy attribute-based encryption based cryptographic cloud storage. J. Zhejiang Univ. Sci. C 14(2), 85–97 (2013)

10. Rabin, M.O.: Efficient dispersal of information for security, load balancing, and fault tolerance. J. ACM **36**(2), 335–348 (1989)
11. Samanthula, B.K., Howser, G., Elmehdwi, Y., Madria, S.: An efficient and secure data sharing framework using homomorphic encryption in the cloud. In: 1st International Workshop on Cloud Intelligence (2012)
12. Cormen, T.H., Leiserson, C.E., Rivest, R.L., Stein, C.: Introduction to Algorithms: Third edition (2009)

Performance Modeling and Evaluation

Modeling Performance of Hadoop Applications: A Journey from Queueing Networks to Stochastic Well Formed Nets

Danilo Ardagna[1]([✉]), Simona Bernardi[2], Eugenio Gianniti[1],
Soroush Karimian Aliabadi[3], Diego Perez-Palacin[1], and José Ignacio Requeno[4]

[1] Dip. di Elettronica, Informazione e Bioingegneria,
Politecnico di Milano, Milan, Italy
{danilo.ardagna,eugenio.gianniti,diego.perez}@polimi.it
[2] Centro Universitario de la Defensa, Academia General Militar,
Zaragoza, Spain
simonab@unizar.es
[3] Department of Computer Engineering, Sharif University of Technology,
Tehran, Iran
skarimian@ce.sharif.ir
[4] Dpto. de Informática e Ingeniería de Sistemas, Universidad de Zaragoza,
Zaragoza, Spain
nrequeno@unizar.es

Abstract. Nowadays, many enterprises commit to the extraction of *actionable knowledge* from huge datasets as part of their core business activities. Applications belong to very different domains such as fraud detection or one-to-one marketing, and encompass business analytics and support to decision making in both private and public sectors. In these scenarios, a central place is held by the MapReduce framework and in particular its open source implementation, *Apache Hadoop*. In such environments, new challenges arise in the area of jobs performance prediction, with the needs to provide Service Level Agreement guarantees to the end-user and to avoid waste of computational resources. In this paper we provide performance analysis models to estimate MapReduce job execution times in Hadoop clusters governed by the YARN Capacity Scheduler. We propose models of increasing complexity and accuracy, ranging from queueing networks to stochastic well formed nets, able to estimate job performance under a number of scenarios of interest, including also unreliable resources. The accuracy of our models is evaluated by considering the TPC-DS industry benchmark running experiments on Amazon EC2 and the CINECA Italian supercomputing center. The results have shown that the average accuracy we can achieve is in the range 9–14%.

Keywords: MapReduce · Performance models

1 Introduction

The implementation of Big Data applications is steadily growing today [17]. According to recent analyses, the Big Data market reached $16.9 billion in 2015

© Springer International Publishing AG 2016
J. Carretero et al. (Eds.): ICA3PP 2016, LNCS 10048, pp. 599–613, 2016.
DOI: 10.1007/978-3-319-49583-5_47

with a compound annual growth rate of 39.4%, about seven times the one of the overall ICT market [2].

From the technological perspective, MapReduce is capable of analyzing very efficiently large amounts of unstructured data, i.e., it is a viable solution to support both the variety and volume requirements of Big Data analyses [22]. MapReduce has been adopted in multiple application domains, e.g., machine learning, graph processing, and data mining [34], and its open source implementation, Hadoop 2.x, recently introduced a wide set of performance enhancements (e.g., SSD support, caching, and I/O barriers mitigation). IDC estimates that Hadoop touched half of the world data last year [20] supporting both traditional batch and interactive data analysis applications [32].

In this context, one of the main challenges [25,33] is that the execution time of a MapReduce job is generally unknown in advance. Because of this, predicting the execution time of Hadoop jobs is usually done empirically through experimentation, requiring a costly setup [15]. An alternative is to develop models for predicting performance. Models may be used to support design-time decisions during the initial development and deployment of Big Data applications. For example, design-time models can help to determine the appropriate size of a cluster or to predict the budget required to run Hadoop in public Clouds (a trending scenario, since by 2020 nearly 40% of Big Data analyses will be supported by public Clouds [2]). Models can also be kept alive at run-time and lead the dynamic adjustment of the system configuration [6,30], for instance to cope with workload fluctuations or to reduce energy costs.

Unfortunately, modeling the performance of such systems is very challenging. Indeed, production Hadoop environments are nowadays very large massively parallel systems where map and reduce tasks coordinate exhibiting precedence constraints and strict synchronization barriers. Moreover, with Hadoop 2.x, resources are dynamically allocated between the map and reduce stages. Additionally, in our context, the stakeholders interested in the performance evaluation of Hadoop processes are its users rather than its developers. Therefore, the complexity and novelty of these systems together with the lack of full knowledge of their development details make unclear the concepts that should be included in a performance model in order to be both accurate and manageable by performance evaluation tools.

Our focus in this paper is to provide design-time performance analysis models to estimate MapReduce jobs execution time in Hadoop clusters governed by the YARN Capacity Scheduler. This work combines real experimentation and model-based evaluation exploring different properties of the MapReduce process. This exploration is used to unveil the characteristics of the YARN Capacity Scheduler that have the highest influence in its performance and therefore should be represented in the models used for a model-based performance evaluation. We propose queueing network (QN) models and stochastic well formed nets (SWNs) of incremental complexity and accuracy able to estimate MapReduce job execution times for multiple users and under unreliable resources. In particular, we analyze a Cloud-based scenario where the cluster, to save execution costs, includes also spot virtual machines (VMs) [14]. The utilization of spot VMs offers large discounts in VM prices, with the drawback of a non-guaranteed availability level. We combine the performance and availability dynamics of Cloud resources in a single *performability* model that allows us to evaluate how failures caused by a sudden increase in the price of spot resources by the Cloud provider, which entails a deallocation of VMs, degrade the system performance.

We evaluate the accuracy of our models on real systems by performing experiments based on the TPC-DS industry benchmark for business intelligence data warehouse applications. Amazon EC2 and the CINECA Italian supercomputing center have been considered as target deployments.

QN and SWN model simulation results and experiments performed on real systems have shown that the accuracy we can achieve is within 30% of the actual measurements in the worst case. With respect to previous literature works, to the best of our knowledge ours is one of the first contribution able to study the performance of Hadoop-2.x-based clusters, where the dynamic allocation of resources between map and reduce stages makes the performance analysis much more challenging.

This paper is organized as follows. Section 2 presents our novel proposals for Hadoop modeling, via both QNs and SWNs. Next, Sect. 3 reports some experimental results to validate and study the properties of our models. In Sect. 4 we compare our work with other proposals available in the literature and finally draw the conclusions in Sect. 5.

2   Modeling Hadoop 2.x Applications Performance

In this paper we provide performance models of incremental complexity and accuracy, ranging from QNs to SWNs, able to estimate Hadoop 2.x jobs performance under a number of scenarios of interest.

Modeling the performance of Hadoop 2.x clusters is challenging since, differently from the previous release where resources, i.e., CPU *slots*, were statically split for mappers and reducers, in the latest Hadoop containers are assigned dynamically among ready tasks, leading to a better cluster utilization. Modeling the dynamic assignment of the available resources is the main contribution of this paper. In particular, we focus on clusters governed by the Capacity Scheduler, which allows for partitioning the cluster among multiple customers through queues, each queue being regulated by a FIFO policy. In the following we assume that queues are partitioned and hence we can focus on single class systems (actually, the Capacity scheduler provides for queues to borrow resources when some others are empty, however this scenario is left as part of our future work).

The parallel execution of multiple tasks within higher level jobs is usually modeled in the QN literature with the concept of fork/join: jobs are spawned at a fork node in multiple tasks, which are then submitted to queueing stations modeling the available servers. After all the tasks have been served, they synchronize at a join node. Unfortunately, there is no known closed-form solution for fork-join networks with more than two queues, unless a special structure exists [24].

Hence, the performance metrics of such networks must be computed by considering the Markov Chain underlying the QN, which represents the possible states of the system [24]. However, such approaches are not fit for Hadoop systems, since the state space grows exponentially with the number of tasks [13,27], in the order of thousands in realistic MapReduce jobs. For this reason, a number of approximation methods have been proposed. In particular, [29] proposed a good approximation technique that, however, is based on service time exponential distribution, which is not the case for Hadoop deployments. Our initial experiments showed that mapper and reducer times follow general distributions, which can be approximated by phase type or in some cases Erlang. Under exponential time hypothesis, the relative error observed in our simulations was around 50–60%. Some other approaches, e.g., [24], are based on an approximate mean value analysis technique and use an iterative hierarchical approach. Along the same lines, [34] combines a precedence graph and a QN to capture the intra-job synchronization constraints, thus being able to estimate the synchronization delays introduced by the communication among mappers and reducers. Unfortunately, even if the approach is rather accurate (around 15% accuracy on real systems), the authors assume that CPU slots are statically assigned to mappers and reducers, hence the proposed method cannot be adopted to estimate performance under the Hadoop 2.x dynamic resource assignment policy.

For this reason, we developed simulation models based on the concept of finite capacity region (FCR) available in modern QN simulators [10]. Unfortunately, QN models capture the behavior of Hadoop 2.x with some approximations. In Subsect. 2.2 we rely on SWNs and provide a model capturing the behavior of real Hadoop 2.x systems. Moreover, we investigate an advanced Cloud-based scenario where some resources are provided by unreliable spot instances and we evaluate the performance of jobs in case of failure.

2.1   Queueing Network Model

This section discusses a proposal of QN model for MapReduce applications running upon YARN Capacity Scheduler.

The performance model is depicted in Fig. 1. It is a closed QN model where the number of concurrent users is given by H and they start off in the delay center, characterized by the average think time Z. When a user submits her job, this is forked into as many map task requests as stated in the job profile, which then enter the FCR. FCRs model situations where several service centers access resources belonging to a single limited pool, competing to use them. Hence, the FCR enforces an upper bound on the total number of requests served at the same time within itself, allowing tasks to enter according to a FIFO policy, but also supporting prioritization of different classes. The FCR includes two multi-service queues that model the map and reduce execution stages. The FCR and multi-service queues capacities are equal to the total number of cores available in the cluster. In this way, we can model the dynamic assignment of YARN containers to map and reduce tasks whenever they are ready. Map tasks are executed by the first multi-service queue and synchronize after completion by joining back to

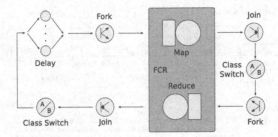

Fig. 1. Queueing network model

a single job request; the reduce phase is modeled analogously. Note that the map join is external to the FCR in order to model that when map tasks complete they release container cores, which can be assigned to tasks ready in the FCR FIFO queue. Moreover, the reduce fork is also external to the FCR to model correctly applications characterized by a number of reducers larger than the total cluster capacity.

YARN Capacity Scheduler implements a FIFO scheduling policy within the same queue and containers are allocated to the next job only after all reduce tasks have obtained their resources. The class switches present in the QN are meant to enforce that reduce tasks waiting for resources obtain them with priority. Despite this, the model in Fig. 1 is still an approximation: notwithstanding the higher priority associated to reducers, subsequent users' mappers can still occupy part of the servers available in the FCR when the preceding job has an overall number of map tasks that is not multiple of the cluster capacity. In such a case, the last map wave leaves room for serving further requests, hence the following user can overtake part of the capacity and the reduce stage of the first user will not start processing at full capacity until those mappers complete.

As a final consideration, note that the discussed model is rather general and can be easily extended to consider also Tez or Spark applications, where a Tez directed acyclic graph node or Spark stage is associated to a corresponding multi-server queue.

2.2 Stochastic Well Formed Net Models

The stochastic well formed net (SWN) in Fig. 2 is able to capture completely the behavior of the Capacity Scheduler policy. Jobs execution is modeled by a closed workload, where the $nU1$ users compete to access the cluster and cycle between demanding to execute the MapReduce scenario (subnet in the dotted rectangle), and spending an external delay period between the end of one response and the next request (mean firing time of the *think* transition). The basic color class *User* consists of a single subclass *User1* and the job identities are captured by assigning a token of different color to each job $u_1, \ldots, u_{nU1}$.

To enforce the FIFO scheduling each job is assigned an ID i. The initial marking $M3$ of the place $IDs1$ is set to the first index of the color class ID, and

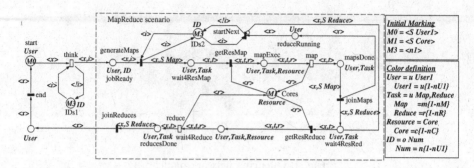

Fig. 2. Basic SWN model

once transition *think* sends a job to the ready state it increases this index by one. The transition *generateMaps* will start the job that has the index equal to the one it is getting from place *IDs2*. In other words, the job that has its turn will start the Map phase. Whenever a job gets resources for all of its reduce tasks (place *wait4ResRed* drains), the job with the next index will be started thanks to the transition *startNext*, which updates the *IDs2* place with the next index.

When a job x is ready to be processed and it has its turn—i.e., the place *jobReady* is marked with a token $\langle x, i \rangle$ and the *IDs2* place is marked with the same index i—nM map tasks are generated (firing of *generateMaps* transition). Such tasks, associated to job x, are represented by nM pairs $\langle x, t \rangle$, where the color t belongs to the subclass *Map* of the basic color class *Task*. Each task $\langle x, t \rangle$ needs to acquire a resource r to be executed (firing of *getResMap* transition) and map tasks can be concurrently executed according to resource availability. The set of resources is defined by the basic color class *Resource*, which consists of a unique partition *Core* including nC resources. The timed transition *map* models the duration of the map task execution and its firing time is an Erlang-distributed random variable. The map stage is finished when all the map tasks $\langle x, t \rangle$ associated to job x have been executed: the firing of the *joinMaps* transition models the beginning of the next processing step, where nR reduce tasks are generated. The reducing step is similar to the mapping step, the only difference is that the reduce tasks, associated to job x, are represented by nR pairs $\langle x, t \rangle$ where the color t belongs to the subclass *Reduce* of the basic color class *Task*. Finally, observe that the map tasks $\langle y, t \rangle$, associated to a job y, are generated when all the reduce tasks $\langle x, t \rangle$, associated to the previous job x, are not waiting for resource availability. This condition is modeled by the inhibitor arc inscription from place *wait4ResRed* to transition *startNext*.

The models considered so far can capture the behavior of MapReduce systems running on an enterprise infrastructure or public Clouds based on standard resources. Cloud providers (see, e.g., Amazon EC2) offer another type of resource loaning, *spot*, in which customers bid for the instance price. The VM instances are billed the spot price, which is set by the infrastructure provider and fluctuates periodically depending on current energy costs, which vary throughout

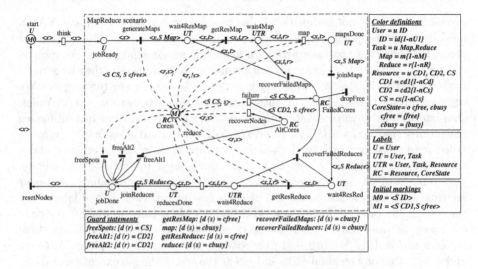

Fig. 3. SWN model with spot resources

the day, and also on the overall supply and demand of virtual resources. Spot instances are usually available at a competitive price. However, if the provider raises the spot price above user's bid while she is using spot instances, these can be arbitrarily terminated without notice. Hence, on one side spot resources are an opportunity for lowering the execution cost of MapReduce applications, but on the other side they introduce availability threats.

The model introduced in Fig. 3 allows for exploring different configurations and to evaluate MapReduce jobs performance degradation in case of spot instances termination. In particular, we assume that once spot VMs fail, a monitoring component replaces them with the same number of on-demand resources. Since we are interested in the performance degradation of the job currently in execution, we can drop the FIFO mechanism from the model of Fig. 2, i.e., the places *IDs1*, *IDs2*, and *reduceRunning*; the transition *startNext*; and the color class *ID*. The model in Fig. 3 introduces also a new color class *CoreState*, which consists of two singleton subclasses *cfree* and *cbusy*, to record the state of a node. To enable this, the color domain of the place *Cores* is set to the Cartesian product *Resource × CoreState*. This change enables the place *Cores* to track the occupied cores as well as the free cores. Transitions *getResMap* and *getResReduce* are modified to change the core status from "free" to "busy" whenever they own a core, and vice versa for transitions *map* and *reduce*. The color class *Resource* is enriched with two new subclasses *CoreSpot (CS)* and *CoreDemand2 (CD2)*, which model spot instances and the on-demand nodes triggered to replace spot resources. The color definition *Core* is renamed to *CoreDemand1 (CD1)* to model the on-demand nodes that are initially started together with spot resources. The places *FailedCores* and *AltCores* are added to identify the failed nodes and the alternative nodes waiting for recovery. The timed transition *failure* takes all the spot instances from the available nodes with a rate proportional to the failure probability. When spot instances fail due to a low bid, it takes at most a YARN heartbeat for the monitoring component to figure out the loss. After this short delay, the replacing process starts with acquiring on-demand nodes. As soon as the new on-demand VMs are ready with running NodeManagers, they have to be registered with the ResourceManager in order to be used by the running job. We summed up all these delays and introduced the timed transition *recoverNodes*, characterized by an appropriate rate. Moreover, we included three instantaneous transitions (*recoverFailedMaps*, *recoverFailedReduces*, and *dropFree*) to move a failed map or reduce task to the waiting list and to drop the failed spot nodes that were not occupied by any task. Since our goal is to evaluate the average performance of the job when a failure happens (note that a failure can occur anytime between the start and end of the job execution and in the latter case the job might complete before new on-demand VMs become available), we have to create the same environment for every successive run of the job. Then, three transitions *freeAlt1*, *freeAlt2*, and *freeSpots* are added to free the places *AltCores* and *Cores* from any residual *CD2* and *CS* at the end of the job execution and one outgoing arc is connected to the transition *generateMaps* to put back the spot cores in the place storing available nodes. As a result, spot failures can happen again while the simulator is running the next iteration. In this way we ensure that every job submission is subject to failure and obtain relevant statistical results.

3   Experimental Analysis and Validation

The models presented in the previous sections have been validated by performing an experimental campaign on Amazon EC2 and CINECA, the Italian super-computing center. The target version was Hadoop 2.6.0. The Amazon cluster included 30 m4.xlarge instances with a total of 120 vCPUs configured to support 240 containers overall. On PICO[1], the Big Data cluster available at CINECA, we used several configurations ranging from 40 to 120 cores and set up the scheduler to provide one container per core.

The dataset used for testing has been generated using the TPC-DS benchmark[2] data generator, creating at a scale factor ranging from 250 GB to 1 TB several files directly used as external tables by Hive. We chose the TPC-DS benchmark as it is the industry standard for benchmarking data warehouses. We used the GreatSPN [7] and JMT [10] tools with 10% accuracy and 95% confidence interval for the performance analysis of the SWN and QN models, respectively. Next, we performed experiments on five Hive queries, dubbed R1–5 and shown in Fig. 4. The profiling phase has been conducted on a dedicated cluster, extracting average task durations from at least twenty runs of each query. The numbers of map and reduce tasks varied, respectively, in the ranges $(4, 1560)$ and $(1, 1009)$. Parsing Hadoop logs it is also possible to obtain lists of task execution times, which are needed for the replayer in JMT service centers. These

---

[1] http://www.hpc.cineca.it/hardware/pico.

[2] http://www.tpc.org/tpcds/.

```
select avg(ws_quantity),
       avg(ws_ext_sales_price),
       avg(ws_ext_wholesale_cost),
       sum(ws_ext_wholesale_cost)
from web_sales
where (web_sales.ws_sales_price
      between 100.00 and 150.00) or (
      web_sales.ws_net_profit
between 100 and 200)
group by ws_web_page_sk
limit 100;
```

(a) R1

```
select avg(ss_quantity), avg(
       ss_net_profit)
from store_sales
where ss_quantity > 10 and
      ss_net_profit > 0
group by ss_store_sk
having avg(ss_quantity) > 20
limit 100;
```

(b) R3

```
select inv_item_sk,inv_warehouse_sk
from inventory where
     inv_quantity_on_hand > 10
group by inv_item_sk,inv_warehouse_sk
having sum(inv_quantity_on_hand)>20
limit 100;
```

(c) R2

```
select cs_item_sk, avg(cs_quantity)
       as aq
from catalog_sales
where cs_quantity > 2
group by cs_item_sk;
```

(d) R4

```
select inv_warehouse_sk, sum(
       inv_quantity_on_hand)
from inventory
group by inv_warehouse_sk
having sum(inv_quantity_on_hand) > 5
limit 100;
```

(e) R5

Fig. 4. Interactive queries

logs are also used to choose a proper distribution with right parameters for the *map* transition in the SWN models. As discussed earlier in Sect. 2, the execution time of map tasks fits better with more general distributions, like Erlang (in particular we used Erlang-2 for R1, Erlang-4 for R2 and R3 and Erlang-5 for R4 and R5). The shape and rate parameters are set according to each query profile. The other timed transitions appearing in the SWN models are considered to be exponentially distributed.

3.1 QN and SWN Models Validation

To start off with, we show results for the validation of the QN and SWN models discussed in Sect. 2. We feed the models with parameters evaluated via the experimental setup and compare the measured response times with the simulated ones. Specifically, we consider as a quality index the accuracy on response time prediction, defined as $\vartheta = (\tau - T)/T$, where τ is the simulated response time, whilst T is the average measured one.

Among these experiments, we considered both single user scenarios, repeatedly running the same query on a dedicated cluster with $Z = 10\,\mathrm{s}$, and multiple user scenarios.

Table 1 shows the results of the QN and SWN models validation. For all the experiments we report the number of concurrent users, the overall cores available in the cluster, the dataset scale factor, and the total number of map and reduce tasks, plus the above mentioned metric. In the worst case, the relative error

Table 1. QN and SWN models accuracy

Query	Users	Cores	Scale [GB]	n^M	n^R	T [ms]	τ_{QN} [ms]	ϑ_{QN} [%]	τ_{SWN} [ms]	ϑ_{SWN} [%]
R1	1	240	250	500	1	55410	50753.34	−8.40	50629.58	−8.63
R2	1	240	250	65	5	36881	27495.31	−25.45	37976.82	2.97
R3	1	240	250	750	1	76806	77260.03	0.60	83317.27	8.48
R4	1	240	250	524	384	92197	78573.96	−14.72	89426.51	−3.01
R1	1	60	500	287	300	378127	411940.93	8.94	330149.74	−12.69
R3	1	100	500	757	793	401827	524759.36	30.59	507758.68	26.36
R3	1	120	750	1148	1009	661214	759230.77	14.82	698276.75	5.61
R4	1	60	750	868	910	808490	844700.85	4.48	806366.51	−0.26
R3	1	80	1000	1560	1009	1019973	1053829.78	−1.00	1020294.84	0.03
R5	1	80	1000	64	68	39206	36598.32	−6.65	38796.47	−1.04
R1	3	20	250	144	151	1002160	1038951.05	3.67	909217.89	−9.27
R1	5	20	250	144	151	1736949	1215490.20	−30.02	1428894.40	−17.74
R2	3	20	250	4	4	95403	112050.45	17.45	99219.94	4.00
R2	5	20	250	4	4	145646	97619.46	−32.97	88683.10	3.09
R1	5	40	250	144	151	636694	660241.29	3.70	613577.53	−3.63
R2	3	40	250	4	4	86023	105785.41	22.97	119712.30	−17.81
R2	5	40	250	4	4	90674	103173.38	13.78	117582.82	29.68

can reach up to 32.97%, which is in line with the expected accuracy in the performance prediction field [23]. Moreover, the SWN model achieves a higher accuracy, with the average relative error decreasing from the 14.13% of QNs down to 9.08%.

3.2 Spot Failure Analysis

To evaluate the SWN model of Fig. 3 we considered query R1 running on the 1 TB dataset with 15 VMs, 4 cores each. Without failures, the execution time of R1 is 556680 ms, where around 57% of the time is spent in the map stage. The baseline simulation time is $\tau_0 = 533438$ ms, yielding a −4.18% relative error. We define the performance degradation as $\eta(t) = (\tau(t) - \tau_0)/\tau_0$, where $\tau(t)$ is the simulated response time obtained via the SWN model in Fig. 3 when the recovery time is t. To measure the recovery time of our system on Amazon EC2, we switched off one of the VMs, started a new VM after 30 s and evaluated the time instant when the first task is assigned for execution to the new instance. In ten experiments, the mean recovery time was equal to 331715 ms, where the time to start the new instance was around 180 s.

In the first analysis we consider a conservative scenario where the failure is injected into the system in an early stage of query execution and we fixed the mean time to failure to 50 s. We considered a cluster with 7 spot VMs out of 15 and we varied the recovery time between 120 and 480 s. In this way we estimate system performance degradation in a range where the VMs startup is either faster (e.g., in container-based systems where the startup time is negligible and the recovery time is due only to YARN NodeManagers startup) or slower than

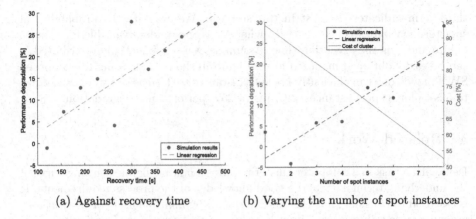

(a) Against recovery time   (b) Varying the number of spot instances

Fig. 5. Performance degradation and cost reduction

on Amazon EC2. The simulation reported in Fig. 5a shows, as expected, that the more the recovery process stalls, the more performance degrades, and it can reach up to 25% if the recovery process takes 8 min.

Note that, in some cases we obtained negative values for $\eta(t)$ because simulation data is subject to inaccuracies. This is why we rely on linear regression to estimate the performance degradation trend. In this and the next analysis we obtained a p-value equal to 0.001 for the full model F-test, meaning that the regression line is a good fit except for white noise.

In the second experiment, the mean recovery time is fixed to 331715 ms, the average we measured in our experiments, and the number of spot instances is increased from 1 to 7 out of the total of 15 VMs. The result is shown in Fig. 5b, which reports the curve for the cost reduction due to using spot instances as well as the performance degradation. Cost reduction is computed as $C_r = C(s;p)/C(0;0)$, where $C(s;p)$ is the cluster cost when s spot instances are used, with a failure probability p. $C(0;0)$ is the case where no spot instance is used. $C(s;p)$ can be computed as:

$$C(s;p) = \delta(R - s) + ps\delta + (1 - p)s\sigma \tag{1}$$

where R is defined to be the total number of VMs, while δ and σ are hourly prices for on-demand and spot instances, respectively. δ and σ are set to \$0.285 and \$0.0313, respectively. The latter is the average spot price from the Amazon website in the last two weeks at the time of writing.

It should be noted that, according to the experiments, the job execution time is less than an hour: according to the Amazon pricing policy [1], in case spot instances are abruptly terminated users are not charged for partial hour usage. The first term on the right hand side of Eq. 1 is the cost of the initial on-demand instances, while the second term is the price the user should pay to acquire the same number of on-demand instances as the lost spot ones in case of failure. Finally, with probability $(1 - p)$ spot instances do not fail and the third term indicates the cost in this scenario. We evaluate the probability of spot termination as $p = \mathbb{P}(X < T)$, where X is the random variable for time to failure and T is the execution time. Assuming X is exponentially distributed, p can be easily obtained in closed form. Figure 5b shows that, using the proposed SWN model, one can efficiently use spot instances to decrease cluster costs, down to 52.5% for 8 spot instances with just a 25% performance degradation.

4   Related Work

Deploying a task in a computer cluster requires a non-negligible learning curve of the underlying technology and a good knowledge of the process requirements. It is essential to consider that clusters are shared by multiple users or institutions, are vulnerable to hardware failures and have a monetary cost. The minimization of the starvation between user jobs, the impact of the execution errors and the optimization of operational costs are important issues.

Modeling and simulating the configuration of a high-performance distributed computer framework allows for predicting the behavior of the tasks before execution. They enable the detection of potential problems such as bottlenecks, the tolerance to hardware malfunctioning as well as a finer estimation of the resources usage, the running time and throughput (i.e., time and resources are two of the main parameters for guaranteeing a fair scheduling among user jobs and inferring the billing). Initial works for studying generic Cloud systems have been already proposed. For example, Bruneo et al. [11] introduce a Stochastic Reward Petri net model representing an Infrastructure as a Service Cloud where the load conditions can change dynamically, although it has not been validated with real data, yet. More concretely, analytical models such as [4,16,21,26,35] use mathematical equations for representing a MapReduce system and quantifying the throughput of a particular resource (i.e., network, hardware disk, or CPU). In this paper, we propose two general purpose modeling abstractions for describing the MapReduce environment such as SWNs and QNs. Regression techniques for estimating the response time of future jobs based on past experiences are exploratory approaches not considered in this paper.

Several works describe the adoption of Petri nets (PNs) for MapReduce modeling. For instance, Castiglione et al. [12] describe a Big Data architecture based on Hadoop by means of stochastic PNs and apply Mean Field Analysis to obtain average metrics and estimate its performance. Another approach, presented by Barbierato et al. [8], exploits Generalized Stochastic Petri Nets alongside other formalisms such as process algebras or Markov chains to develop multi-formalism models and capture HQL queries. Adopting the presented tool, the authors investigate how performance depends on some configuration parameters. In literature colored PNs have also been adopted to assess the feasibility of a distributed file system project [3]. The authors design a deployment of HDFS exploiting spare resources in a cluster of workstations available for teaching in their university, so as to provide a sufficiently available distributed file system. PNs are used to assess system availability in a number of configurations of interest. More recently,

Ruiz et al. [31] formalize the MapReduce paradigm using Prioritized Timed Colored Petri Nets to obtain complete and unambiguous models of the system behavior. They evaluate the correctness of the system and carry out a trade-off analysis of the number of resources versus processing time and resource cost with CPN Tools [18]. Further works with PNs and MapReduce are oriented to measuring performance under failures [19] or studying the fault tolerance mechanism [28].

On the other side, QNs have also been introduced for modeling Cloud systems. Bardhan and Menascé [9] apply QN models for predicting the completion time of the map phase of MapReduce jobs within simple configurations of Hadoop. Alipour et al. [5] develop a Cloud provider independent model with QNs that represents entities involved in the Hadoop MapReduce phases, and customize it for a specific Cloud deployment. Finally, in Yu and Li [36], an analytical queueing mode has been developed to investigate the utilizations and mean waiting times of mappers and reducers, respectively.

Previous works are able to model Hadoop 1.0 clusters with static resource allocation at different levels of detail. Our SWN or QN models are able to capture the dynamic assignment of YARN resource containers and allow for estimating performance in new Hadoop 2.x clusters.

5 Conclusions

In this paper we proposed SWN and QN models for the performance prediction of MapReduce applications running on clusters governed by the Capacity Scheduler. Our preliminary results have shown how our simulation models are effective in capturing the dynamic resource assignment implemented in Hadoop 2.x and can achieve 9% accuracy, thus making them suitable for capacity planning decisions at design-time. In our future work we plan to extend our models to cope with multiple classes in shared clusters governed also by the Fair Scheduler and with job preemptions. Finally, we will embed the models into a design space exploration tool for Cloud resources cost minimization.

Acknowledgments. This work has received funding from the European Union Horizon 2020 research and innovation program under grant agreement No. 644869 (DICE). Experimental data are available as open data at https://zenodo.org/record/58847#. V5i0wmXA45Q.

References

1. Amazon EC2 pricing. http://aws.amazon.com/ec2/pricing/
2. The digital universe in 2020. http://idcdocserv.com/1414
3. Aguilera-Mendoza, L., Llorente-Quesada, M.T.: Modeling and simulation of Hadoop distributed file system in a cluster of workstations. In: Cuzzocrea, A., Maabout, S. (eds.) MEDI 2013. LNCS, vol. 8216, pp. 1–12. Springer, Heidelberg (2013). doi:10.1007/978-3-642-41366-7_1

4. Ahmed, S.T., Loguinov, D.: On the performance of MapReduce: a stochastic approach. In: IEEE International Conference on Big Data, pp. 49–54. IEEE (2014)
5. Alipour, H., Liu, Y., Gorton, I.: Model driven performance simulation of cloud provisioned Hadoop MapReduce applications. In: Proceedings of the 8th International Workshop on Modeling in Software Engineering, MiSE 2016 (2016)
6. Ardagna, D., Ghezzi, C., Mirandola, R.: Rethinking the use of models in software architecture. In: Becker, S., Plasil, F., Reussner, R. (eds.) QoSA 2008. LNCS, vol. 5281, pp. 1–27. Springer, Heidelberg (2008). doi:10.1007/978-3-540-87879-7_1
7. Baarir, S., Beccuti, M., Cerotti, D., De Pierro, M., Donatelli, S., Franceschinis, G.: The GreatSPN tool: recent enhancements. ACM SIGMETRICS PER **36**(4), 4–9 (2009)
8. Barbierato, E., Gribaudo, M., Iacono, M.: Modeling apache hive based applications in big data architectures. In: VALUETOOLS 2013 Proceedings (2013)
9. Bardhan, S., Menascé, D.: Queuing network models to predict the completion time of the map phase of MapReduce jobs. In: Proceedings of the Computer Measurement Group International Conference (2012)
10. Bertoli, M., Casale, G., Serazzi, G.: JMT: performance engineering tools for system modeling. SIGMETRICS Perform. Eval. Rev. **36**(4), 10–15 (2009)
11. Bruneo, D., Longo, F., Ghosh, R., Scarpa, M., Puliafito, A., Trivedi, K.S.: Analytical modeling of reactive autonomic management techniques in IAAS clouds. In: IEEE CLOUD 2015 Proceedings (2015)
12. Castiglione, A., Gribaudo, M., Iacono, M., Palmieri, F.: Exploiting mean field analysis to model performances of big data architectures. Future Gener. Comput. Syst. **37**, 203–211 (2014)
13. Chu, W.W., Sit, C.M., Leung, K.K.: Task response time for real-time distributed systems with resource contentions. IEEE Trans. Softw. Eng. **17**(10), 1076–1092 (1991)
14. Dubois, D.J., Casale, G.: OptiSpot: minimizing application deployment cost using spot cloud resources. Clust. Comput. **19**, 1–17 (2016)
15. Gibilisco, G.P., Li, M., Zhang, L., Ardagna, D.: Stage aware performance modeling of DAG based in memory analytic platforms. In: Cloud (2016)
16. Herodotou, H.: Hadoop performance models (2011)
17. Jagadish, H.V., Gehrke, J., Labrinidis, A., Papakonstantinou, Y., Patel, J.M., Ramakrishnan, R., Shahabi, C.: Big data and its technical challenges. Commun. ACM **57**(7), 86–94 (2014)
18. Jensen, K., Kristensen, L.M., Wells, L.: Coloured Petri nets and CPN tools for modelling and validation of concurrent systems. Int. J. Softw. Tools Technol. Transf. **9**(3–4), 213–254 (2007)
19. Jin, H., Qiao, K., Sun, X.H., Li, Y.: Performance under failures of MapReduce applications. In: CCGrid 2011 Proceedings (2011)
20. Kambatla, K., Kollias, G., Kumar, V., Grama, A.: Trends in big data analytics. J. Parallel Distrib. Comput. **74**(7), 2561–2573 (2014)
21. Krevat, E., Shiran, T., Anderson, E., Tucek, J., Wylie, J.J., Ganger, G.R.: Applying performance models to understand data-intensive computing efficiency. Technical report, DTIC Document (2010)
22. Laney, D.: 3D data management: controlling data volume, velocity, and variety. Technical report, META Group (2012)
23. Lazowska, E.D., Zahorjan, J., Graham, G.S., Sevcik, K.C.: Quantitative System Performance. Prentice-Hall, Upper Saddle River (1984)

24. Liang, D.R., Tripathi, S.K.: On performance prediction of parallel computations with precedent constraints. IEEE Trans. Parallel Distrib. Syst. **11**(5), 491–508 (2000)

25. Lin, M., Zhang, L., Wierman, A., Tan, J.: Joint optimization of overlapping phases in MapReduce. SIGMETRICS Perform. Eval. Rev. **41**(3), 16–18 (2013)

26. Lin, X., Meng, Z., Xu, C., Wang, M.: A practical performance model for Hadoop MapReduce. In: 2012 IEEE International Conference on Cluster Computing Workshops (CLUSTER WORKSHOPS), pp. 231–239. IEEE (2012)

27. Mak, V.W., Lundstrom, S.F.: Predicting performance of parallel computations. IEEE Trans. Parallel Distrib. Syst. **1**(3), 257–270 (1990)

28. Marynowski, J.E., Santin, A.O., Pimentel, A.R.: Method for testing the fault tolerance of MapReduce frameworks. Comput. Netw. **86**, 1–13 (2015)

29. Nelson, R.D., Tantawi, A.N.: Approximate analysis of fork/join synchronization in parallel queues. IEEE Trans. Comput. **37**(6), 739–743 (1988)

30. Polo, J., Becerra, Y., Carrera, D., Steinder, M., Whalley, I., Torres, J., Ayguadé, E.: Deadline-based MapReduce workload management. IEEE Trans. Netw. Serv. Manag. **10**(2), 231–244 (2013)

31. Ruiz, M.C., Calleja, J., Cazorla, D.: Petri nets formalization of Map/Reduce paradigm to optimise the performance-cost tradeoff. In: 2015 IEEE Trustcom/BigDataSE/ISPA, vol. 3, pp. 92–99. IEEE (2015)

32. Shanklin, C.: Benchmarking Apache Hive 13 for Enterprise Hadoop. https://hadoop.apache.org/docs/r2.4.1/hadoop-yarn/hadoop-yarn-site/CapacityScheduler.html

33. Verma, A., Cherkasova, L., Campbell, R.H.: ARIA: automatic resource inference and allocation for MapReduce environments. In: ICAC 2011 Proceedings (2011)

34. Vianna, E., Comarela, G., Pontes, T., Almeida, J.M., Almeida, V.A.F., Wilkinson, K., Kuno, H.A., Dayal, U.: Analytical performance models for MapReduce workloads. Int. J. Parallel Program. **41**(4), 495–525 (2013)

35. Yang, X., Sun, J.: An analytical performance model of MapReduce. In: CCIS 2011 (2011)

36. Yu, X., Li, W.: Performance modelling and analysis of MapReduce/Hadoop workloads. In: LANMAN 2015 Proceedings (2015)

D-SPACE4Cloud: A Design Tool
for Big Data Applications

Michele Ciavotta, Eugenio Gianniti[(✉)], and Danilo Ardagna

Dip. di Elettronica, Informazione e Bioingegneria, Politecnico di Milano, Milan, Italy
{michele.ciavotta,eugenio.gianniti,danilo.ardagna}@polimi.it

Abstract. The last years have seen a steep rise in data generation world-wide, with the development and widespread adoption of several software projects targeting the Big Data paradigm. Many companies currently engage in Big Data analytics as part of their core business activities, nonetheless there are no tools or techniques to support the design of the underlying infrastructure configuration backing such systems. In particular, the focus in this paper is set on Cloud deployed clusters, which represent a cost-effective alternative to on premises installations. We propose a novel tool implementing a battery of optimization and prediction techniques integrated so as to efficiently assess several alternative resource configurations, in order to determine the minimum cost cluster deployment satisfying Quality of Service constraints. Further, the experimental campaign conducted on real systems shows the validity and relevance of the proposed method.

Keywords: MapReduce · Optimization · Queueing networks

1 Introduction

Nowadays, the Big Data adoption has moved from experimental projects to mission-critical enterprise-wide deployments, providing new insights, competitive advantage, and business innovation [20]. IDC estimates that the Big Data market grew from \$3.2 billion in 2010 to \$16.9 billion in 2015 with a compound annual growth rate of 39.4%, about seven times the one of the overall ICT market [5]. From the technological perspective, the MapReduce programming model is one of the most widely used solutions to support Big Data applications [25]. Its open source implementation, Apache Hadoop, is able to manage large datasets over either commodity clusters or high performance distributed topologies [40]. MapReduce has attracted the interest of both industry and academia, as it overtakes the scalability level that can be achieved by traditional data warehouse and business intelligence technologies [25].

E. Gianniti—This work has received funding from the European Union Horizon 2020 research and innovation program under grant agreement No. 644869 (DICE). Experimental data are available as open data at https://zenodo.org/record/58847#. V5i0wmXA45Q.

© Springer International Publishing AG 2016
J. Carretero et al. (Eds.): ICA3PP 2016, LNCS 10048, pp. 614–629, 2016.
DOI: 10.1007/978-3-319-49583-5_48

However, the adoption of Hadoop and other Big Data technologies is complex. The deployment and setup of an implementation is time-consuming, expensive, and resource-intensive. Companies need an *easy button* to accelerate the deployment of Big Data analytics [18]. The pay-per-use approach and the almost infinite capacity of Cloud infrastructures can be used efficiently in supporting data intensive computations. Many Cloud providers already include in their offering MapReduce based platforms, among which Microsoft HDInsight [8] or Amazon Elastic MapReduce [2]. IDC estimates that, by 2020, nearly 40% of Big Data analyses will be supported by public Clouds [5], while Hadoop touched half of the world data last year [22].

In the very beginning, MapReduce jobs were meant to run on dedicated clusters to support batch analyses via a FIFO scheduler [32,33]. Nevertheless, MapReduce applications have evolved and, nowadays, they entail also interactive queries, submitted by different users and performed on shared clusters, possibly with some guarantees on their execution time [42,43]. In such systems, capacity allocation becomes one of the most important aspects. Determining the optimal number of nodes in a cluster shared among multiple users performing heterogeneous tasks is an important and difficult problem [37]. In this context, one of the main challenges [37,43] is that the execution time of a MapReduce job is generally unknown in advance.

Our focus in this paper is to provide a software tool able to support system administrators and operators in the capacity planning process of shared Hadoop 2.x Cloud clusters supporting both batch and interactive applications with deadline guarantees. Having such information available at design-time enables operators to make more informed decisions about the technology to use and to fully exploit the potential offered by the Cloud infrastructure. We formulate the capacity planning problem by means of a mathematical model, with the aim of minimizing the cost of Cloud resources. The problem considers multiple VM types as candidates to support the execution of Hadoop applications from multiple user classes. Through a search space exploration, our approach optimizes the configuration of a shared cluster in terms of VM type and instances number considering specific Cloud provider pricing models (namely, reserved and spot instances [1]).

Our work is one of the first contributions facing the problem of optimal sizing of Hadoop 2.x Cloud systems adopting the Capacity Scheduler [6]. We demonstrate the effectiveness of our approach by considering Hive queries [4] and the TPC-DS industry benchmark for business intelligence and data warehouses [9] as reference application. Amazon EC2 and the CINECA Italian supercomputing center have been considered as target deployments.

This paper is organized as follows. Section 2 presents in detail the problem addressed in the paper. In Sect. 3 we focus on the formulation of the optimization problem and on the design-time exploration algorithm to solve it implemented by our D-SPACE4Cloud tool. In Sect. 4 we evaluate the effectiveness of our optimization method. Finally, in Sect. 5 we compare our work with other proposals available in the literature and draw the conclusions in Sect. 6.

2   Problem Statement

In this section we aim at introducing some important details of the problem addressed in this work. We envision the following scenario, wherein a company needs to set up a cluster to carry out efficiently a set of interactive Big Data queries. A Hadoop 2.x cluster featuring the YARN Capacity Scheduler and running on a public Cloud IaaS is considered a fitting technological solution for the requirements of the company.

In particular, the cluster must support the parallel execution of Big Data applications in the form of Hadoop jobs or Hive/Pig queries. Different classes $\mathcal{C} = \{i \mid i = 1, \ldots, n\}$ gather applications that show a similar behavior. The cluster composition and size, in terms of type and number of VMs, must be decided in such a way that, for every application class i, H_i jobs are guaranteed to execute concurrently and complete before a prearranged deadline D_i.

Moreover, YARN is configured in a way that all available cores can be dynamically assigned to either Map or Reduce tasks. Finally, in order to limit the risk of data corruption and according to the practices suggested by major Cloud vendors [2,8], the datasets reside on an external storage infrastructure [3,7] accessible at quasi-constant time.

As, in general, IaaS providers feature a limited, but possibly large, catalog of VM configurations $\mathcal{V} = \{j \mid j = 1, \ldots, m\}$ that differ in capacity (CPU speed, number of cores, available memory, etc.) and cost, making the right design-time decision poses a challenge that can lead to important savings throughout the cluster life-cycle. We denote with τ_i the VM type j used to support jobs of class i and with ν_i the number of VMs of such a kind allocated to class i. In this scenario, we consider a pricing model derived from *Amazon EC2* [1]. The provider offers: (1) *reserved* VMs, for which it adopts a one-time payment policy that grants access to a certain number of them for the contract duration; and (2) *spot* VMs, for which customers bid and compete for unused datacenter capacity, yielding very competitive hourly fees. In order to obtain the most cost-effective configuration, we rely on reserved VMs for the bulk of computational needs and complement them with spot VMs. In the following, R_i is the number of reserved VMs assigned to class i, whilst s_i is the number of spot VMs. Let σ_{τ_i} be the unit cost for spot VMs of type τ_i, whilst π_{τ_i} is the effective hourly cost for one reserved VM, i.e., it is the unit upfront payment normalized over the contract duration. Overall, the cluster hourly renting out costs can be calculated as follows:

$$\text{cost} = \sum_{i \in \mathcal{C}} (\sigma_{\tau_i} s_i + \pi_{\tau_i} R_i) \tag{1}$$

Let $\nu_i = R_i + s_i$: as the reliability of spot VMs depends on market fluctuations, to keep a high Quality of Service (QoS) the number of spot VMs is bounded not to be greater than a fraction η_i of ν_i for each class i.

Reducing the operating costs of the cluster by using efficiently the leased virtual resources is in the interest of the company. This translates into a Resource

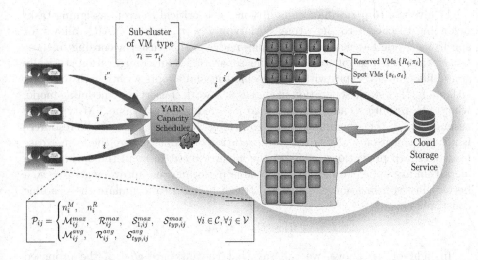

$$P_{ij} = \begin{cases} n_i^M, & n_i^R \\ \mathcal{M}_{ij}^{max}, & \mathcal{R}_{ij}^{max}, \quad \mathcal{S}_{1,ij}^{max}, \quad \mathcal{S}_{typ,ij}^{max}, \quad \forall i \in \mathcal{C}, \forall j \in \mathcal{V} \\ \mathcal{M}_{ij}^{avg}, & \mathcal{R}_{ij}^{avg}, \quad \mathcal{S}_{typ,ij}^{avg} \end{cases}$$

Fig. 1. Reference system

Provisioning problem where the renting out costs must be minimized subject to the fulfillment of QoS requirements, namely H_i per-class concurrency level given certain deadlines D_i. In the following we assume that the system supports H_i users for each class and that users work interactively with the system and run another job after a think time exponentially distributed with mean Z_i, i.e., the system is represented as a closed model [24]. In order to rigorously model and solve this problem, it is crucial to predict with fair confidence the execution times of each application class under different conditions: level of concurrency, cluster size, and composition. Following the approach presented in [37], it is possible to derive from Hadoop logs a *job profile*, i.e., a concise behavior characterization for each class. Following the notation brought forth in [27,37], given a certain VM of type j, the job profile P_{ij} for application class i aggregates the following information: (1) n_i^M and n_i^R, respectively the total number of Map and Reduce tasks per job; (2) $\mathcal{M}_{ij}^{max}$, $\mathcal{R}_{ij}^{max}$, $\mathcal{S}_{1,ij}^{max}$, and $\mathcal{S}_{typ,ij}^{max}$, the maximum duration of a single Map, Reduce, and Shuffle task (notice that the first Shuffle wave of a given job is distinguished from all the subsequent ones); (3) $\mathcal{M}_{ij}^{avg}$, $\mathcal{R}_{ij}^{avg}$, and $\mathcal{S}_{typ,ij}^{avg}$, i.e., the average duration of Map, Reduce, and Shuffle tasks, respectively. Given the amount and type of resources allocated, the concurrency level, and the job profile, the estimated execution time can generically be expressed as in (2):

$$T_i = \mathcal{T}\left(P_{i,\tau_i}, \nu_i; H_i, Z_i\right), \quad \forall i \in \mathcal{C}. \tag{2}$$

What is worthwhile to note is that the previous formula represents a general relation describing either closed form results based on bounds, as those presented in [27], or the average execution times derived via simulation, the approach adopted in this paper. Since the execution of jobs on a suboptimal VM type might give rise to performance disruptions, it is critical to avoid assigning tasks belonging to class i to the wrong VM type $j \neq \tau_i$. Indeed, YARN allows for specifying Node Labels and partitioning nodes in the cluster according to these labels, then it is possible to enforce this separation. Our configuration statically splits different VM types with this mechanism and adopts within each partition either a further static separation in classes or a work conserving scheduling mode, where idle resources can be assigned to jobs requiring the same VM type. The assumption on the scheduling policy governing the exploitation of idle resources is not critical: it only affects the interpretation of results, where the former case leads to sharp predictions, while in the latter the outcomes of the optimization algorithm are upper bounds, with possible performance improvements due to a better cluster utilization. Equations (2) can be used to formulate the deadline constraints as:

$$T_i \leq D_i, \quad \forall i \in \mathcal{C}. \tag{3}$$

In light of the above, we can say that the ultimate goal of the proposed approach is to determine the optimal VM type selection τ_i and number and pricing models of VMs $\nu_i = R_i + s_i$ for each class i such that the sum of costs is minimized, while the deadlines and concurrency levels are met.

Table 1. Model parameters

Parameter	Definition
$\mathcal{C}$	Set of application classes
$\mathcal{V}$	Set of VM types
H_i	Number of concurrent users for class i
Z_i	Class i think time [ms]
D_i	Deadline associated to applications of class i [ms]
η_i	Maximum percentage of spot VMs allowed to class i
σ_j	Unit hourly cost for spot VMs of type j [€/h]
π_j	Effective hourly price for reserved VMs of type j [€/h]
$\mathcal{P}_{ij}$	Job profile of class i with respect to VM type j

The reader is referred to Fig. 1 for a graphical overview of the main elements of the considered resource provisioning problem. Furthermore, in Table 1 a complete list of the parameters used in the models presented in the next sections is reported, whilst Table 2 summarizes the decision variables.

3   Problem Formulation and Solution

In the following we present the optimization model and techniques exploited by the D-SPACE4Cloud tool in order to determine the optimal VM mix given

Table 2. Decision variables

Variable	Definition
ν_i	Number of VMs assigned for the execution of applications from class i
R_i	Number of reserved VMs booked for the execution of applications from class i
s_i	Number of spot VMs assigned for the execution of applications from class i
x_{ij}	Binary variable equal to 1 if class i is hosted on VM type j

the profiles characterizing the applications under study and the possible Cloud providers to host the virtual cluster. Further, we describe the heuristic algorithm adopted to efficiently tackle the resource provisioning problem by exploiting the presented models.

3.1 Optimization Model

Basic building blocks for this tool are the models of the system under study. First of all, we need a quick, although rough, method to estimate completion times and operational costs: to this end, we exploit a mathematical programming formulation based on jobs execution time bounds (see [27]). In this way, it is possible to swiftly explore several possible configurations and point out the most cost-effective among the feasible ones. Afterwards, the required resource configuration can be fine-tuned using more accurate, even if more time consuming and computationally demanding, queueing network (QN) simulations, reaching a precise prediction of the expected response time.

According to the previous considerations, the first step in the optimization procedure consists in determining the most cost-effective resource type, based on their price and the expected performance. This will be done by exploiting a set of logical variables x_{ij}: we will enforce that only $x_{i,\tau_i} = 1$, thus determining the optimal VM type τ_i for application class i. We address this issue proposing the following mathematical programming formulation:

$$\min_{\mathbf{x},\boldsymbol{\nu},\mathbf{s},\mathbf{R}} \quad \sum_{i\in\mathcal{C}} (\sigma_{\tau_i}s_i + \pi_{\tau_i}R_i) \tag{P1a}$$

subject to:

$$\sum_{j\in\mathcal{V}} x_{ij} = 1, \quad \forall i \in \mathcal{C} \tag{P1b}$$

$$\mathcal{P}_{i,\tau_i} = \sum_{j\in\mathcal{V}} \mathcal{P}_{ij}x_{ij}, \quad \forall i \in \mathcal{C} \tag{P1c}$$

$$\sigma_{\tau_i} = \sum_{j\in\mathcal{V}} \sigma_j x_{ij}, \quad \forall i \in \mathcal{C} \tag{P1d}$$

$$\pi_{\tau_i} = \sum_{j \in \mathcal{V}} \pi_j x_{ij}, \quad \forall i \in \mathcal{C} \tag{P1e}$$

$$x_{ij} \in \{0, 1\}, \quad \forall i \in \mathcal{C}, \forall j \in \mathcal{V} \tag{P1f}$$

$$(\boldsymbol{\nu}, \mathbf{s}, \mathbf{R}) \in \arg \min \sum_{i \in \mathcal{C}} (\sigma_{\tau_i} s_i + \pi_{\tau_i} R_i) \tag{P1g}$$

subject to:

$$s_i \leq \frac{\eta_i}{1 - \eta_i} R_i, \quad \forall i \in \mathcal{C} \tag{P1h}$$

$$\nu_i = R_i + s_i, \quad \forall i \in \mathcal{C} \tag{P1i}$$

$$\mathcal{T}(\mathcal{P}_{i,\tau_i}, \nu_i; H_i, Z_i) \leq D_i, \quad \forall i \in \mathcal{C} \tag{P1j}$$

$$\nu_i \in \mathbb{N}, \quad \forall i \in \mathcal{C} \tag{P1k}$$

$$R_i \in \mathbb{N}, \quad \forall i \in \mathcal{C} \tag{P1l}$$

$$s_i \in \mathbb{N}, \quad \forall i \in \mathcal{C} \tag{P1m}$$

Problem (P1) is a bilevel resource allocation problem where the outer objective function (P1a) considers running costs. The first set of constraints, (P1b), associates each class i with only one VM type j, hence the following constraints, ranging from (P1c) to (P1e), pick the values for the inner problem parameters.

The inner objective function (P1g) has the same expression as (P1a), but in this case the prices σ_{τ_i} and π_{τ_i} are fixed, as they have been chosen at the upper level. The following constraints, (P1h), enforce that spot instances do not exceed a fraction η_i of the total assigned VMs and constraints (P1i) add all the VMs available for class i, irrespective of the pricing model. Further, constraints (P1j) mandate to respect the deadlines D_i. In the end, all the remaining decision variables are taken from the natural numbers set, according to their interpretation.

The presented formulation of Problem (P1) is particularly difficult to tackle, as it is a mixed integer nonlinear programming (MINLP) problem depending on $\mathcal{T}$. According to the literature about complexity theory [17], integer programming problems belong to the NP-hard class, hence the same applies to (P1). However, since there is no constraint linking variables belonging to different application classes, we can split this general formulation into several smaller and independent problems, one per class i. As it will be discussed in the following section, we evaluated the average job completion time $\mathcal{T}$ by considering bounds and relying on QN models simulation.

3.2   Solution Technique

The aim of this section is to provide a brief description of the optimization approach embedded in D-SPACE4Cloud. The tool implements an optimization mechanism that efficiently explores the space of possible configurations.

Figure 2 depicts the main elements of the D-SPACE4Cloud architecture that come into play in the optimization scenario. The tool takes as input a description of the considered problem, consisting in a set of applications, a set of suitable VMs for each application along with the respective job profiles for each machine, and QoS constraints expressed in terms of deadlines D_i for each considered application. Specifically, all these parameters are collected in a JSON file provided as input to the tool. The *Initial Solution Builder* generates a starting solution for the problem using a MINLP formulation where the time expression T appearing in constraint (P1j) is a convex function: then the inner level of (P1) is a convex nonlinear problem and we exploit the Karush-Kuhn-Tucker conditions to speed up the solution process. For more details the reader is referred to [27]. It must be highlighted, at this point, that the quality of the returned solution can still be improved: this because the MINLP relies on an approximate representation of the Application-Cluster liaison. For this reason, a QN model is exploited to get a more accurate execution time assessment. This model allows to estimate MapReduce jobs execution time with an average error around 14% with respect to real systems. The increased accuracy leaves room for further cost reduction; however, since QNs simulation is time consuming, the space of possible cluster configurations has to be explored in the most efficient way, avoiding to evaluate unpromising configurations.

In the light of such considerations, a heuristic approach has been adopted and a component called *Parallel Local Search Optimizer* has been devised. Internally, it implements a parallel hill climbing (HC) technique to optimize the number of replicas of the assigned resource for each application; the goal is to find the minimum number of resources to fulfill the QoS requirements. This procedure is applied independently, and in parallel, on all application classes and terminates when a further reduction in the number of replicas would lead to an infeasible solution. As soon as all the classes reach convergence, it is possible to retrieve from the D-SPACE4Cloud tool a JSON file listing the results of the overall optimization procedure.

For the sake of clarity, HC is a local-search-based procedure that operates on the current solution performing a change, a so-called *move*, in the structure of the solution in such a way that the newly generated solution could possibly show an improved objective value. If the move is successful it is applied again on the new solution and the process is repeated until no further improvement is possible. The HC algorithm stops when a local optimum is found; however, if the objective to optimize is convex, HC is able to find the global optimum. This is the case of the considered cost function (1), which is linear in the number of VMs in the cluster, since VM prices are fixed at the first level. Hence, every feasible instance of the inner problem can be heuristically solved to optimality through HC. The initial solution S, obtained from the MINLP solution, is evaluated using the QN model and each one of its parts is optimized separately and in parallel. If the partial solution S_i is infeasible the size of its personal cluster is increased by one unit until it becomes feasible. Otherwise, the procedure attempts to decrease the cost function by reducing the cluster size. One-VM moves might seem problematic, but, given the quite accurate initial solution, the tool only needs to explore a small neighborhood of possible configurations. Finally, it is

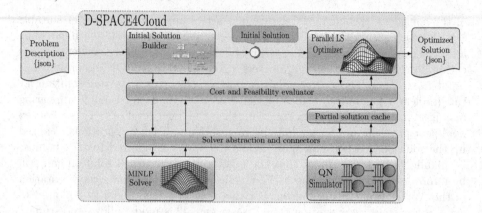

Fig. 2. D-SPACE4Cloud architecture

worth pointing out that every time the total number of machines in a cluster is incremented or decremented the best mix of pricing models (i.e., R_i, s_i) is computed so as to minimize the configuration cost.

4   Experimental Analysis

In this section we show the results of several experiments performed to validate the proposed approach. All these experiments have been performed on two Ubuntu 14.04 VMs hosted on an Intel Xeon E5530 2.40 GHz equipped server. The first VM ran D-SPACE4Cloud and the MINLP solver which was used to generate an initial solution for the optimization problem presented in Sect. 3.1 (see [27] for further details). The second one, instead, ran JMT 0.9.3 [13], a QN simulator.

4.1   Experimental Setup and Design of Experiments

In order to obtain job profiles, we devised a set of five SQL queries denoted with R1–5 (see [16]). We then generated synthetic data compliant with the specifications of the industry standard benchmark TPC-DS [9] and executed the queries on Apache Hive [4]. Notice that we generated data at several scale factors ranging from 250 GB to 1 TB. Since profiles collect statistical information about jobs, we repeated the profiling runs at least twenty times per query. Properly parsing the logs allows to extract all the parameters composing every query profile, for example average and maximum task execution times, number of tasks, etc. Profiling has been performed on Amazon EC2, by considering m4.xlarge instances, and on PICO[1], the Big Data cluster offered by CINECA, the Italian supercomputing center. The cluster rented on EC2 was composed of 30 computational

---

[1] http://www.hpc.cineca.it/hardware/pico.

nodes, for a total of 120 vCPUs hosting 240 containers, whilst on PICO we used up to 120 cores configured to host one container per core. In the first case every container had 2 GB RAM and in the second 6 GB. Along with profiles, we also collected lists of task execution times to feed into the replayer in JMT service centers. In the end, we determined query profiles for different VM types.

4.2 Queueing Network Validation

This section shows results validating the accuracy of the underlying QN model. Table 3 reports the average percentage error ϑ obtained by comparing the queries execution time extracted from logs, T, with the ones evaluated from QN simulation, denoted with τ: $\vartheta = \frac{\tau - T}{T}$. Among these experiments, we considered both single user scenarios, repeatedly running the same query on a dedicated cluster with $Z_i = 10$ s, and multiple users scenarios. In the worst case, the relative error can reach up to 32.97%, which is perfectly in line with the expected accuracy in the performance prediction field [24], while the average relative error is 14.13% overall.

Table 3. Queueing network model validation

Query	H_i	#Cores	Dataset [GB]	#Maps	#Reducers	T [ms]	τ [ms]	ϑ [%]
R1	1	240	250	500	1	55410	50753.34	−8.40
R2	1	240	250	65	5	36881	27495.31	−25.45
R3	1	240	250	750	1	76806	77260.03	0.60
R4	1	240	250	524	384	92197	78573.96	−14.72
R1	1	60	500	287	300	378127	411940.93	8.94
R3	1	100	500	757	793	401827	524759.36	30.59
R3	1	120	750	1148	1009	661214	759230.77	14.82
R4	1	60	750	868	910	808490	844700.85	4.48
R3	1	80	1000	1560	1009	1019973	1053829.78	−1.00
R5	1	80	1000	64	68	39206	36598.32	−6.65
R1	3	20	250	144	151	1002160	1038951.05	3.67
R1	5	20	250	144	151	1736949	1215490.20	−30.02
R2	3	20	250	4	4	95403	112050.45	17.45
R2	5	20	250	4	4	145646	97619.46	−32.97
R1	5	40	250	144	151	636694	660241.29	3.70
R2	3	40	250	4	4	86023	105785.41	22.97
R2	5	40	250	4	4	90674	103173.38	13.78

4.3 Scenario-Based Experiments

The optimization approach described in Sect. 3 needs to be validated, ensuring that it is capable of catching realistic behaviors we expect of the system under analysis. We test this property with a set of assessment runs where we fix all the problem parameters but one and verify that the solutions follow an intuitive evolution.

The main axes governing performance in Hadoop clusters hosted on public Clouds are the level of concurrency and the deadlines. In the first case, increasing H_i and fixing all the remaining parameters, we expect a need for more VMs to support the rising workload, thus leading to an increase of renting out costs. On the other hand, if at fixed parameters we tighten the deadlines D_i, again we should observe increased costs: the system will require a higher parallelism to shrink response times, hence more computational nodes to support it.

For the sake of clarity, we performed single-class experiments: considering only one class per experiment allows for an easier interpretation of the results. Figure 3 reports the solutions obtained with the 250 GB dataset profiles. The average running time for these experiments is about two hours. All the mentioned figures show the cost in € /h plotted against decreasing deadlines in ms for both the real VM types considered: CINECA is the 20-core node available on PICO, whilst m4.xlarge is the 4-core instance rented on Amazon AWS. In Figs. 3a and b the expected cost increase due to tightening deadlines is apparent for two representative queries, R1 and R3, considering 10 concurrent users. Further, in both cases it is cheaper to provision a Cloud cluster consisting of the smaller Amazon-offered instances, independently of the deadlines. It is then interesting to observe that R1 shows a different behavior if the required concurrency level increases. Figure 3c shows that, as the deadlines become tighter and tighter, it is possible to identify a region where executing the workload on larger VMs becomes more economic.

5   Related Work

Capacity planning and architecture design space exploration are important problems analyzed in the literature [10,14]. High level models and tools to support software architects (see, e.g., Palladio Component Model and PerOptirex design environment [12,23], or stochastic process algebra [36] and the PEPA Eclipse plugin [30]) have been proposed for identifying the best configuration given a set of QoS requirements; unfortunately they neither support Cloud-specific abstractions nor do directly address the problem of deriving an optimized configuration for Cloud and Big Data clusters. On the other side, capacity management and cluster sizing for Big Data applications has received also a widespread interest by both academia and industry. The starting point is the consideration that Hadoop often requires an intense tuning phase in order to exhibit its full potential. For this reason, *Starfish*, a self-tuning system for analytics on Hadoop, has been proposed [19]. The resource provisioning problem, instead, has been faced by Tian and Chen [35]. The goal is the minimization of the execution cost for a

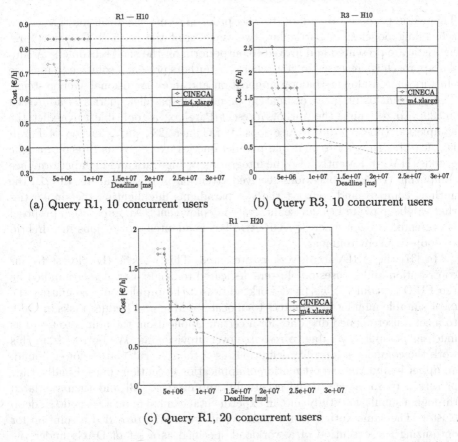

(a) Query R1, 10 concurrent users   (b) Query R3, 10 concurrent users

(c) Query R1, 20 concurrent users

Fig. 3. Cluster costs with varying deadlines

single application. They present a cost model that depends on the dataset size and on some characteristics of the considered application.

Verma et al. [38] proposed a framework for the profiling and duration prediction of applications running on heterogeneous resources. An approach to this problem based on closed QNs is presented in [11]. This work is noteworthy as it explicitly considers contention and parallelism on compute nodes to evaluate the execution time of a MapReduce application. However, the weak spot of this approach is that it contemplates the Map phase alone. Vianna et al. [39] worked on a similar solution; however the validation phase has been carried out considering a cluster dedicated to the execution of a single application at a time. Both Map and Reduce phases are considered in [34]. In this work the Map phase is modeled as an M/G/1 queue, whereas for the Reduce phase a multi-server queue have been used.

Castiglione et al. [15] introduce a novel modeling approach based on mean field analysis and provide fast approximate methods to predict the performance of Big Data systems. Deadlines for MapReduce jobs are considered in [31].

The work proposes to adapt to the problem some classical multiprocessor scheduling policies; in particular, two versions of the Earliest Deadline First heuristic are presented and proved to outperform off-the-shelf schedulers. A similar approach is presented in [41], where the authors present a solution to manage clusters shared among Hadoop application and more traditional Web systems. The problem of progress estimation of multiple parallel queries is addressed in [29]. To this aim, the authors present Parallax, a tool able to predict the completion time of MapReduce jobs. ParaTimer [28], an extension of Parallax, features support to multiple parallel queries expressed as directed acyclic graphs (DAGs). Recently, also the integration of Big Data and high performance computing (HPC) applications received attention in the literature. In [21], the authors compare and contrast the two paradigms, highlighting the similarities that can be exploited to devise integrated deployments. An integration proposal is presented in [26], where RADICAL-Pilot is adopted to run jobs in a hybrid Hadoop-HPC environment.

In [37] the ARIA framework is presented. This work is the closest to our contribution and focuses on clusters dedicated to single user classes handled by the FIFO scheduler. The framework addresses the problem of calculating the most suitable number of resources to allocate to Map and Reduce tasks in order to meet a user-defined due date for a certain application; the aim is to avoid as much as possible costs due to resource over-provisioning. We borrow from this work the compact job profile definition, used there to calculate a lower bound, an upper bound, and an estimation of application execution times. Finally, they present a performance model eventually improved in [43] and then validated through a simulation study and an experimental campaign on a 66-node Hadoop cluster. The same authors, in a more recent work [42], provided a solution for optimizing the execution of a workload specified as a set of DAGs under the constraints of a global deadline or budget. All the above mentioned works are based on Hadoop 1.0, where CPU slots are statically allocated to Map and Reduce tasks and the basic FIFO scheduler is considered. To the best of our knowledge, ours is one of the first contribution coping with Hadoop 2.x shared clusters based on the Capacity scheduler, hence relaxing Hadoop 1.0 limitations.

6   Conclusions

In this paper we have proposed a novel approach to provisioning Cloud clusters to support data intensive applications over Hadoop YARN managed clusters. We have developed a mathematical programming formulation of the underlying optimization problem. In order to achieve a favorable trade-off between prediction accuracy and running times, we have adopted a heuristic approach that exploits the fast solvers available for mathematical programming problems for the initial exploration of the solution space and then relies on the precise, but slower, QN simulation. Moreover, our experimental validation shows how our tool is a valuable contribution towards identifying the best VM type, since we have highlighted situations where sticking to small instances and scaling out proves to be less economic than switching to better equipped VMs that allow for a smaller number of replicas: the decreased replication factor compensates the increased unit price in a not obvious way.

Moving from the presented results, an interesting research direction for our future work lies in the characterization of complex workflows expressed as DAGs, e.g., Tez or Spark jobs. Another relevant aspect to investigate is the usage of more sophisticated techniques for the heuristic exploration of the solution space, in order to attain further speedup and, possibly, extend our method to the runtime cluster management scenario.

References

1. Amazon EC2 pricing. http://aws.amazon.com/ec2/pricing/
2. Amazon Elastic MapReduce. https://aws.amazon.com/elasticmapreduce/
3. Amazon Simple Storage Service. https://aws.amazon.com/s3/
4. Apache Hive. https://hive.apache.org
5. The digital universe in 2020. http://idcdocserv.com/1414
6. Hadoop MapReduce next generation — Capacity Scheduler. http://hortonworks.com/blog/benchmarking-apache-hive-13-enterprise-hadoop/
7. Microsoft Azure Storage. http://azure.microsoft.com/en-us/services/storage/
8. Microsoft HDInsight. http://azure.microsoft.com/en-us/services/hdinsight/
9. TPC-DS benchmark. http://www.tpc.org/tpcds/
10. Aleti, A., Buhnova, B., Grunske, L., Koziolek, A., Meedeniya, I.: Software architecture optimization methods: a systematic literature review. IEEE Trans. Softw. Eng. **PP**(99), 1 (2013)
11. Bardhan, S., Menascé, D.A.: Queuing network models to predict the completion time of the map phase of MapReduce jobs. In: International CMG Conference (2012)
12. Becker, S., Koziolek, H., Reussner, R.: The Palladio component model for model-driven performance prediction. J. Syst. Softw. **82**(1), 3–22 (2009)
13. Bertoli, M., Casale, G., Serazzi, G.: JMT: performance engineering tools for system modeling. SIGMETRICS Perform. Eval. Rev. **36**(4), 10–15 (2009)
14. Brosig, F., Meier, P., Becker, S., Koziolek, A., Koziolek, H., Kounev, S.: Quantitative evaluation of model-driven performance analysis and simulation of component-based architectures. IEEE Trans. Softw. Eng. **41**(2), 157–175 (2015)
15. Castiglione, A., Gribaudo, M., Iacono, M., Palmieri, F.: Exploiting mean field analysis to model performances of big data architectures. Future Gener. Comput. Syst. **37**, 203–211 (2014)
16. Ciavotta, M., Gianniti, E., Ardagna, D.: D-SPACE4Cloud: a design tool for big data applications. Technical report (2016). arXiv:1605.07083
17. Garey, M.R., Johnson, D.S.: Computers and Intractability: A Guide to the Theory of NP-Completeness. W. H. Freeman & Co., New York (1990)
18. Greene, M.A., Sreekanti, K.: Big data in the enterprise: we need an "easy button" for Hadoop (2016)
19. Herodotou, H., Lim, H., Luo, G., Borisov, N., Dong, L., Cetin, F.B., Babu, S.: Starfish: a self-tuning system for big data analytics. In: CIDR (2011)
20. Jagadish, H.V., Gehrke, J., Labrinidis, A., Papakonstantinou, Y., Patel, J.M., Ramakrishnan, R., Shahabi, C.: Big data and its technical challenges. Commun. ACM **57**(7), 86–94 (2014)

21. Jha, S., Qiu, J., Luckow, A., Mantha, P., Fox, G.C.: A tale of two data-intensive paradigms: applications, abstractions, and architectures (2016). http://arxiv.org/abs/1403.1528
22. Kambatla, K., Kollias, G., Kumar, V., Grama, A.: Trends in big data analytics. J. Parallel Distrib. Comput. **74**(7), 2561–2573 (2014)
23. Koziolek, A., Koziolek, H., Reussner, R.: PerOpteryx: automated application of tactics in multi-objective software architecture optimization. In: QoSA 2011 Proceedings, QoSA-ISARCS 2011, pp. 33–42. ACM, New York (2011)
24. Lazowska, E.D., Zahorjan, J., Graham, G.S., Sevcik, K.C.: Quantitative System Performance. Prentice-Hall, Englewood Cliffs (1984)
25. Lee, K.H., Lee, Y.J., Choi, H., Chung, Y.D., Moon, B.: Parallel data processing with MapReduce: a survey. SIGMOD Rec. **40**(4), 11–20 (2012)
26. Luckow, A., Paraskevakos, I., Chantzialexiou, G., Jha, S.: Hadoop on HPC: integrating Hadoop and pilot-based dynamic resource management. In: 2016 IEEE International Parallel and Distributed Processing Symposium Workshops (IPDPSW), pp. 1607–1616 (2016)
27. Malekimajd, M., Ardagna, D., Ciavotta, M., Rizzi, A.M., Passacantando, M.: Optimal map reduce job capacity allocation in cloud systems. SIGMETRICS Perform. Eval. Rev. **42**(4), 51–61 (2015)
28. Morton, K., Friesen, A., Balazinska, M., Grossman, D.: Estimating the progress of MapReduce pipelines. In: ICDE (2010)
29. Morton, K., Balazinska, M., Grossman, D.: ParaTimer: a progress indicator for MapReduce DAGs. In: SIGMOD (2010)
30. OMG: PEPA: performance evaluation process algebra (2015). http://www.dcs.ed.ac.uk/pepa/tools/
31. Phan, L.T.X., Zhang, Z., Zheng, Q., Loo, B.T., Lee, I.: An empirical analysis of scheduling techniques for real-time cloud-based data processing. In: SOCA (2011)
32. Polo, J., Carrera, D., Becerra, Y., Torres, J., Ayguadé, E., Steinder, M., Whalley, I.: Performance-driven task co-scheduling for MapReduce environments. In: NOMS (2010)
33. Rao, B.T., Reddy, L.S.S.: Survey on improved scheduling in Hadoop MapReduce in Cloud environments (2012)
34. Tan, J., Wang, Y., Yu, W., Zhang, L.: Non-work-conserving effects in MapReduce: diffusion limit and criticality. In: SIGMETRICS (2014)
35. Tian, F., Chen, K.: Towards optimal resource provisioning for running MapReduce programs in public clouds. In: CLOUD (2011)
36. Tribastone, M., Gilmore, S., Hillston, J.: Scalable differential analysis of process algebra models. IEEE Trans. Softw. Eng. **38**(1), 205–219 (2012)
37. Verma, A., Cherkasova, L., Campbell, R.H.: ARIA: automatic resource inference and allocation for MapReduce environments. In: Proceedings of the Eighth International Conference on Autonomic Computing, June 2011
38. Verma, A., Cherkasova, L., Campbell, R.H.: Profiling and evaluating hardware choices for MapReduce environments: an application-aware approach. Perform. Eval. **79**, 328–344 (2014)
39. Vianna, E., Comarela, G., Pontes, T., Almeida, J.M., Almeida, V.A.F., Wilkinson, K., Kuno, H.A., Dayal, U.: Analytical performance models for MapReduce workloads. Int. J. Parallel Program. **41**(4), 495–525 (2013)
40. Yan, F., Cherkasova, L., Zhang, Z., Smirni, E.: Optimizing power and performance trade-offs of MapReduce job processing with heterogeneous multi-core processors. In: CLOUD (2014)

41. Zhang, W., Rajasekaran, S., Duan, S., Wood, T., Zhu, M.: Minimizing interference and maximizing progress for Hadoop virtual machines. SIGMETRICS Perform. Eval. Rev. **42**(4), 62–71 (2015)
42. Zhang, Z., Cherkasova, L., Loo, B.T.: Exploiting cloud heterogeneity to optimize performance and cost of MapReduce processing. SIGMETRICS Perform. Eval. Rev. **42**(4), 38–50 (2015)
43. Zhang, Z., Cherkasova, L., Verma, A., Loo, B.T.: Automated profiling and resource management of pig programs for meeting service level objectives. In: ICAC (2012)

Porting Matlab Applications to High-Performance C++ Codes: CPU/GPU-Accelerated Spherical Deconvolution of Diffusion MRI Data

Javier Garcia Blas[1(✉)], Manuel F. Dolz[1], J. Daniel Garcia[1], Jesus Carretero[1], Alessandro Daducci[2], Yasser Aleman[3,4], and Erick Jorge Canales-Rodriguez[4,5]

[1] Dpto. de Informática, Universidad Carlos III de Madrid, Leganés, Spain
{fjblas,mdolz,jdgarcia,jcarrete}@inf.uc3m.es
[2] Signal Processing Lab, École Polytechnique Fédérale de Lausanne,
Lausanne, Switzerland
alessandro.daducci@epfl.ch
[3] Instituto de Investigación Sanitaria Gregorio Marañón, Madrid, Spain
yaleman@hggm.es
[4] Centro de Investigación Biomédica en Red de Salud Mental (CIBERSAM),
Oviedo, Spain
ecanales@fidmag.com
[5] FIDMAG Germanes Hospitalàries, Barcelona, Spain

Abstract. In many scientific research fields, Matlab has been established as *de facto* tool for application design. This approach offers multiple advantages such as rapid deployment prototyping and the use of high performance linear algebra, among others. However, the applications developed are highly dependent of the Matlab runtime, limiting the deployment in heterogeneous platforms. In this paper we present the migration of a Matlab-implemented application to the C++ programming language, allowing the parallelization in GPUs. In particular, we have chosen RUMBA-SD, a spherical deconvolution algorithm, which estimates the intravoxel white-matter fiber orientations from diffusion MRI data. We describe the methodology used along with the tools and libraries leveraged during the translation task of such application. To demonstrate the benefits of the migration process, we perform a series of experiments using different high performance computing heterogeneous platforms and linear algebra libraries. This work aims to be a guide for future developments that are implemented out of Matlab. The results show that the C++ version attains, on average, a speedup of 8× over the Matlab one.

Keywords: Matlab · Magnetic resonance imaging · Linear algebra

J.G. Blas—This work was supported by the EU project ICT 644235 "REPHRASE: REfactoring Parallel Heterogeneous Resource-Aware Applications" and project TIN2013-41350-P "Scalable Data Management Techniques for High-End Computing Systems" from the *Ministerio de Economía y Competitividad*, Spain. We gratefully acknowledge the support of NVIDIA Corporation with the donation of the Tesla K40 GPU used for this research.

© Springer International Publishing AG 2016
J. Carretero et al. (Eds.): ICA3PP 2016, LNCS 10048, pp. 630–643, 2016.
DOI: 10.1007/978-3-319-49583-5_49

1   Introduction

In recent years, diffusion magnetic resonance imaging (MRI) has played an important role in the investigation of morphological features of brain tissues. When the diffusion is constrained by the presence of obstacles, this technique yields information about the confining geometry. It provides a new dimension of MRI contrast based on water mobility, because of the different cellular environment experienced by water molecules. The study of this phenomenon has made possible a deeper knowledge of the microanatomy of the living brain and others complex tissues, due to its noninvasive nature. From the set of methods and algorithms proposed to date for analyzing this type of medical imaging, we will focus on the collection of MATLAB routines, namely HARDI-Tools[1], dedicated to the intravoxel reconstruction from High Angular Resolution Diffusion Imaging (HARDI) data.

In this sense, the use of the MATLAB language has become over the years *de facto* standard for designing and prototyping a wide range of applications in both science and engineering areas. Because of its easy programming model, the scientific and technical communities have chosen to use this high-level language for developing application prototypes, which require the computation of linear algebra problems. By contrast, many of these prototypes have moved to a production stage without being properly adapted and optimized to handle large workloads. Therefore, today it is possible to find numerous examples of MATLAB-implemented applications running on high-performance production platforms but not fully exploiting the benefits of such parallel hardware.

The aim of this work is to introduce the technologies and tools for an adequate migration of MATLAB-based applications to high performance-oriented and compiled programming languages, such as C or C++. In particular, this paper focuses on the use case of the spherical deconvolution method, referred as RUMBA-SD (Robust and Unbiased Model-Based Spherical Deconvolution [5]). RUMBA-SD is among the most advanced methods to date for detecting crossing fibers in white matter[2]. Specifically, our contributions with this paper are as follows:

- We introduce the implementation of RUMBA-SD, included in HARDI-Tools.
- We describe the steps taken and the tools used for the migration of the MATLAB-based application to the C++ language.
- We present the parallel C++ version of RUMBA-SD that relies on the Armadillo library [24] and takes advantage of current multi-core architectures.
- We perform an exhaustive evaluation that demonstrates the benefits of the migration and analyze best combinations of parallel heterogeneous platforms and linear algebra libraries for running the application studied.

---

[1] HARDI-Tools have been implemented by researchers from the Foundation for Research and Teaching FIDMAG (Barcelona, Spain), the Center for Neurosciences of Cuba (Havana, Cuba) and the Medical Imaging Laboratory of the Hospital Gregorio Marañón (Madrid, Spain). http://neuroimagen.es/webs/hardi_tools/.

[2] See: http://hardi.epfl.ch/static/events/2013_ISBI/.

The rest of the paper is structured as follows. Section 2 revisits a few related works that intersect with the contributions presented in this paper. Section 3 describes the two C++ linear algebra libraries used during the migration task. Section 4 focuses on the RUMBA-SD reconstruction method and Sect. 5 details the methodology used for parallelizing it. Finally, Sect. 6 presents the experimental evaluation using different parallel architectures and linear algebra libraries, and Sect. 7 closes the paper with a few concluding remarks and future works.

2   Related Work

According to the state-of-the-art, there exist different approaches developed to address MATLAB portability-related issues. We classify these related works in three categories: (i) source-to-source compilers for automatically migrating MATLAB codes to HPC-compiled languages, e.g., C/C++ or Fortran; (ii) HPC libraries and parallel programming models for the MATLAB language; and (iii) high-level HPC libraries to easily translate the MATLAB application into a compiled language.

As for the first approach, we highlight some well-known source-to-source compilers and related solutions in the area. Being MATLAB a programming environment, its framework comes along with the "out-of-the-box" transcompiler MCC [25], capable of transforming MATLAB codes into C/C++ or Fortran languages and compiling them into a single MEX executable. Nevertheless, there can also be found free alternatives. The Falcon [9] compiler translates MATLAB applications to Fotran 90 codes; other compilers such as Conlab [10] and Otter [22] are designed to generate source code for both distributed and shared memory platforms. However, transforming a MATLAB application does not only mean translating instruction by instruction to an HPC environment, but also to highly tune it. For example, the Falcon compiler replaces the code when it finds matches for optimized syntactic and routine patterns. Another alternative is the Kapf preprocessor [15] that addresses its efforts on automatically detect portions of source code that match BLAS operations and replace them with the corresponding routine call.

Focusing on the second alternative, i.e., when the translation by a transcompiler does not generate enough performance improvements, enhancements can be applied directly to the MATLAB code. For example, one can link the MATLAB application against proprietary BLAS libraries optimized for general-purpose architectures (e.g. AMD ACML [3], Intel MKL [18], and IBM ESSL [13]) or specific (cuBLAS [19] for NVidia GPUs). Complementary third-party implementations of BLAS can also be found, e.g., GotoBLAS [17], Atlas [32] or GSL [11]. Other frameworks, such as the OpenMP extensions and the Parallel toolbox [26,27], allow users, within the MATLAB application, to fully exploit shared- and distributed-memory architectures equipped with accelerators.

Finally, even if it is possible to manually translate the MATLAB code, high-level programming tools and libraries for parallel computing can be used to ease the porting task. Thanks to the high-level API offered by some of these libraries, similar to that from MATLAB, migrating its code to C/C++ becomes much simpler. For instance, the C++ libraries Eigen [12] and VienaCL [23] provide a single and simple interface for BLAS routines in addition to the OpenMP, OpenCL and CUDA programming models. Other libraries, like Armadillo [24], aim at achieving a good balance between speed and usability. Among the main advantages stands out its high level of abstraction, being very similar to the MATLAB syntax. Armadillo is very useful for developing algorithms directly in C++ in order to rapidly port the application to a production stage. Alternatively, the library ArrayFire [16] supports interfaces for C, C++, Java, Fortran and R and is integrated with CUDA-based codes.

In this paper we adopt the last approach to migrate the use case implemented in MATLAB using the Armadillo and ArrayFire libraries. While this approach is the most costly in terms of time and complexity, we believe it offers a great deal compared to other approaches and room for performance improvement with respect to the original MATLAB version.

3 Linear Algebra in C++ Environments

In order to gain insights into modern C++ implementations of linear algebra libraries, in this section we briefly describe, as background, the two main dense linear algebra libraries leveraged during the migration task: Armadillo [24] and ArrayFire [16]. These can be considered part of the current state-of-the-art of high-level API linear algebra libraries pursuing compatibility among platforms and robustness.

In particular, Armadillo is a linear algebra library offering a high level syntax (API) to ease the development effort of algorithms in C++. Basically, its power resides in the fact that the major part of the linear algebra procedures offered are simplified as basic arithmetic operations overloaded using C++ features. Indeed, the library can be considered as a mere interface to other well-known production linear algebra libraries, such as OpenBlas, Intel MKL or ATLAS. Thus, depending on how Armadillo is built and linked against, it will directly interact, at its bottom, with one of such libraries. Being aware that these libraries already highly-tuned for current parallel architectures, the use of Armadillo for this development turns the application migrated as an already tuned one. As an example of the Armadillo operations, Listing 1.1 displays the matrix-matrix multiplication using its high-level API.

On the other hand, ArrayFire is an open source library for linear algebra programming proving, as well, high-level interfaces for the C, C++, Java, R and Fortran languages. It has been designed for using a large range of systems, from a single GPU systems to large multi-GPU supercomputers. Similar to the example shown for the matrix-matrix multiplication in Armadillo, Listing 1.2 represents the same example using the interface of ArrayFire. The main differences between these solutions are that in ArrayFire, matrices A and B are allocated in the GPU memory (Lines 9–10) and the matrix multiplication is carried out in the GPU (Line 11).

Listing 1.1. Matrix-matrix multiplication implemented in Armadillo.

```
1   #include <iostream>
2   #include <armadillo>
3
4   using namespace std;
5   using namespace arma;
6
7   int main() {
8     mat A, B, C;
9     A = randu<mat>(5000,5000);
10    B = randu<mat>(5000,5000);
11    C = A * B;
12    return 0;
13  }
```

Listing 1.2. Matrix-matrix multiplication implemented in ArrayFire.

```
1   #include <iostream>
2   #include <arrayfire>
3
4   using namespace std;
5   using namespace af;
6
7   int main() {
8     array A, B, C;
9     af_randn(&A,5000,5000,fp32);
10    af_randn(&B,5000,5000,fp32);
11    C = matmul(A, B);
12    return 0;
13  }
```

4 Fiber ODF Reconstruction with RUMBA-SD

The water diffusion process in biological tissues is not equal in all directions due to the presence of obstacles and barriers that limit the natural molecular movement. This phenomenon is typically characterized by means of the diffusion tensor imaging (DTI) technique, which can be used to infer the main orientation of the neural tracts at each voxel (i.e., three dimensional pixel). This second-order tensor is defined as a 3×3 symmetrical positive definite matrix (see Eq. 1):

$$D = \begin{pmatrix} D_{xx} & D_{xy} & D_{xz} \\ D_{yx} & D_{yy} & D_{yz} \\ D_{zx} & D_{zy} & D_{zz} \end{pmatrix} \tag{1}$$

The diffusion tensor can be represented as an ellipsoid, where the orientations and length of its three main axes are defined by the eigenvectors and eigenvalues of the diffusion tensor matrix, as depicted in Fig. 1.

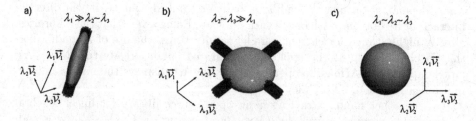

Fig. 1. The microstructural organization of the neural tracts inside a voxel can be revealed from diffusion MRI by the diffusion tensor ellipsoid

The diffusion tensor turns out to be a suitable model in voxels containing a single set of parallel fibers (see Fig. 1(a)). In this case the principal axis of the ellipsoid matches the orientation of the fiber group. Similarly, the diffusion tensor is effective to characterize the diffusion in brain regions where this process occurs without interacting with tissues and, therefore, has a spherical geometry (see Fig. 1(c)). However, in regions of the brain where several fibers intersect, this model does not permit inferring the orientations of the fiber bundles (see Fig. 1(b)). In fact, different fiber crossings may lead to similar diffusion tensors (e.g., see Fig. 2).

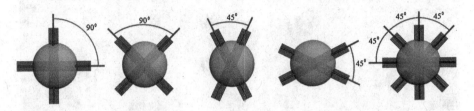

Fig. 2. Different crosses can generate the same fiber diffusion ellipsoid

Such limitation of the DTI model has driven recent developments of numerous sampling protocols, diffusion models and reconstruction techniques. Among these, the RUMBA-SD technique is based on the assumption that each voxel is composed of a large number of diffusion tensors and that each of them corresponds to a compartment containing a single set of parallel fibers with a predefined orientation. The aim of the method is to estimate the volume fraction of each of these compartments in order to obtain, for each voxel, the fiber orientation distribution function (ODF). Figure 3 shows the fiber ODFs estimated by RUMBA-SD at each voxel in a region of interest from real diffusion MRI data. The orientations in which the fiber ODF achieves its maximum values coincide with the fibers orientations. Notice that each local fiber ODF is colored using the RGB orientation code: $[x, y, z] - [r, b, g]$. In this case, the red color stands for the left-right orientation, blue (b) represents the top-bottom orientation and green (g) indicates the antero-posterior orientation.

5 Parallel HARDI (pHARDI)

Within the set of techniques included in HARDI-Tools, in this paper we have focused on the parallelization of the RUMBA-SD method (the source code presented in this work is available at the project Web site[3]), namely pHARDI. However, because of the modular design of the proposed solution, including new methods in the future will not require considerable efforts.

As shown in Fig. 4, pHARDI has a layer-based design, which allows the use of multiple linear algebra accelerators in a wide range of devices, such as multi-core devices GPU (both CUDA and OpenCL) or even co-processors, like Intel Xeon Phi. In the case the platform that does not incorporate any accelerator, our

---

[3] See: https://bitbucket.org/fjblas/phardi.

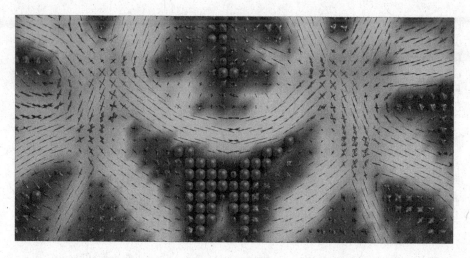

Fig. 3. Visualization of the fiber ODFs estimated by RUMBA-SD at each voxel in a brain region from real diffusion MRI data. The background image is the generalized fractional anisotropy map derived from the fiber ODF. (Color figure online)

solution can also run on multi-core processors using highly-tuned linear algebra libraries. We use Armadillo on top of the linear algebra accelerators for providing a common interface. Additionally, we take advantage of Armadilllo for reflecting most of the MATLAB language (e.g. *remap*, *reshape*, etc.).

With the aim of supporting GPU devices, we have developed two different versions: one that is totally based on the Armadillo library and a second leveraging the ArrayFire library. To develop the second approach, only fragments of code that are computationally more expensive, namely kernels, have been implemented using ArrayFire routines. It is important to remark that both solutions use a *column-major* logical layout of the matrices and volumes handled, in both CPU and GPU. Therefore, no additional changes in the memory access pattern are required in the code for running both versions.

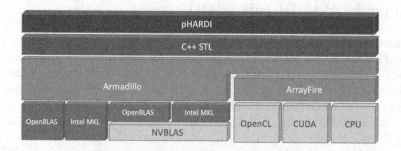

Fig. 4. Layered software architecture of pHARDI

We note that the only drawback of using Armadillo is the lack of parallelization of element-wise operations (as shown in Sect. 6). In order to cope with this, we have parallelized these operations using OpenMP. However this approach limits the portability to accelerated solutions like NVBLAS. In contrast, ArrayFire supports automatic element-wise operations, which facilitates the development and increases performance.

Regarding data management, we have chosen the ITK library [14], which facilitates the management for reading and writing data in different formats related to the medical imaging area, such as DICOM and Nifti. Another advantage of using ITK is the support for automatic file compression. This fact, significantly reduces the storage space required by the applications.

pHARDI supports two data access patterns for processing the input data. The first pattern separately processes each slice from the input data volumes ($x \times y \times z$), resulting in a total of z slices, each one of $x \times y \times t$ voxels, being t the number of orientations. The second layout processes all pixels from the volumes in a single matrix. This matrix has a dimension of $n \times m$ elements, where n corresponds with the amount of evaluated orientations (e.g. 100) and m with the amount of voxels on each volume (e.g. 125 megapixels).

Listing 1.3. pHARDI computation kernel: intravox fiber reconstructor in RUMBA-SD.

```
1   for (size_t i = 0; i < Niter; ++i) {
2       Ratio = mBessel_ratio<T>(n_order,Reblurred_S);
3
4       #pragma omp parallel for simd
5       for (size_t k = 0; k < SR.n_cols; ++k )
6           for (size_t j = 0; j < SR.n_rows; ++j)
7               SR(j,k) = Signal(j,k) * Ratio(j,k);
8       KTSR = KernelT * SR;
9       KTRB = KernelT * Reblurred;
10
11      #pragma omp parallel for simd
12      for (size_t k = 0; k < fODF.n_cols; ++k)
13          for (size_t j = 0; j < fODF.n_rows; ++j)
14              fODF(j,k) = fODF(j,k) * KTSR(j,k) / (KTRB(j,k) + std::
                    numeric_limits<double>::epsilon());
15
16      Reblurred = Kernel * fODF;
17
18      #pragma omp parallel for simd
19      for (size_t k = 0; k < Signal.n_cols; ++k)
20          for (size_t j = 0; j < Signal.n_rows; ++j)
21              SUM(j,k) = (pow(Signal(j,k),2) + pow(Reblurred(j,k),2))/2 - (
                    sigma2(j,k) * (Signal(j,k) * Reblurred(j,k)) / sigma2(j,
                    k)) * Ratio(j,k);
22
23      sigma2_i = (1.0/N) * sum( SUM , 0) / n_order;
24
25      #pragma omp parallel for
26      for (size_t k = 0; k < sigma2_i.n_elem; ++k)
27          sigma2_i(k) = std::min<T>(std::pow<T>(1.0/10.0,2),std::max<T>(
                    sigma2_i(k), std::pow<T>(1.0/50.0,2)));
28
29      sigma2 = repmat(sigma2_i, N, 1);
30  }
```

Listing 1.3 shows the most time consuming part of RUMBA-SD. This code is executed a determined number of iterations ($Niter$). Each iteration is composed by three matrix multiplications and multiple element-wise multiplications. As far as we know, Armadillo lacks of a parallel implementation of element-wise multiplication calls, so these calls have been parallelized by OpenMP, while preserving the data access primitives of Armadillo. As explained before, Armadillo stores matrices in a row-major way. Loops are also parallelized by applying the *simd* OpenMP pragma, with the aims of vectorizing the content of each loop.

6   Experimental Evaluation

In this section we detail the experimental evaluation carried out that demonstrates the benefits of the migrated application. The experiments have been conducted using different multi-core processors and accelerators and several highly-tuned linear algebra libraries on the bottom of Armadillo and ArrayFire. In the following we describe in detail the target platform, software and configurations used during the experimentation phase.

- *Platform.* The evaluation has been carried out on a machine consisting of two multi-core Intel Xeon E5-2630 v3 processor with a total of 8 physical cores running at 2.40 GHz, hyperthreading activated, equipped with 128 GB of RAM, and executing Linux Ubuntu 14.04×64 OS. This machine is also equipped with a NVidia Tesla K40 and a GTX 680 under CUDA version 7.5. The compilers used are GCC 5.1 and Intel 15.1. After that, the source code has been compiled using both -O3 and -DNDEBUG flags.
- *pHARDI configuration.* The experimental results using the pHARDI framework have been obtained using different linear algebra libraries, concretely OpenBLAS, Atlas, NVBLAS, Intel MKL, and ArrayFire. In the case of Atlas, we compiled the application using the auto-tuned optimal parameters. It is important to remark that all the experiments have been performed using single and double precision floating point numbers. To guarantee integrity of the results, we performed five consecutive executions and computed the average execution times.
- *Input data.* For each of the linear algebra libraries tested within pHARDI, we run the application using a real diffusion MRI dataset acquired from healthy subject. Specifically, whole-brain HARDI data were acquired in a 3T Philips Achieva scanner (Sant Pau Hospital, Barcelona) with a 8-channel head coil along 100 different gradient directions on the sphere in q-space with constant $b = 2000\,\mathrm{s/mm}^2$. Additionally, $1b = 0$ volume was acquired with in-plane resolution of $2.0 \times 2.0\,\mathrm{mm}^2$ and slice thickness of 2 mm. The acquisition was carried out without undersampling in the k-space (i.e., $R = 1$). The final dimension of this dataset is $128 \times 128 \times 60 \times 101$ voxels.

For the experimental evaluation, we have used two different data layouts for processing the input data. In both cases, the reconstruction process is obtained after 300 iterations of the RUMBA-SD algorithm.

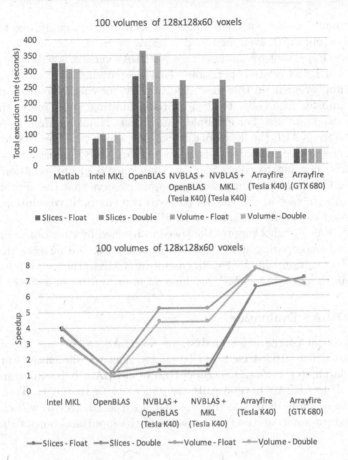

Fig. 5. Overall execution time of pHARDI on different linear algebra accelerators.

6.1   Accelerators Evaluation

Figure 5 (left) plots the execution time (left) and the respective speedups achieved, including I/O time (right). As can be seen, the versions that attained the highest performance are the ones using the ArrayFire implementation. Obviously, the main advantage of this version is due to the high computational capacity of the GPUs. In this case, both BLAS3 and element-wise operations are offloaded to the GPU. However, we observe that there are not remarkable differences between the two GPU models analyzed. In the future, we intend to carry out a more detailed analysis on this aspect. An additional observation is that the version linked against the Intel MKL library delivers the best performance for the CPU-based cases. Although the MATLAB version of the applications uses underneath the same Intel MKL library for executing linear algebra kernels, our C++-ported implementation makes it more efficient thanks to the use of parallelized element-wise multiplication and optimized I/O operations via the ITK library. Finally, we do not contemplate Atlas in Fig. 5, mainly due to the bad performance obtained, even for tuned versions.

It is also important to highlight that NVBLAS version is only able to offload to the GPU BLAS3-related operations. This shortcoming substantially limits the room for improvement in this case. Additionally, for each offloaded operation a memory transfer from host to device arises, limiting, even more, the performance of this approach. For example, this process is not required in ArrayFire, and thanks to its API, the developer can specify which variables should be maintained in the device memory. This feature is especially important for iterative applications, needing to compute more than once a given operation over the same data. Given the experimental results, we observe that the approach based on NVBLAS (in case of the volume pattern) is a competitive solution, where it is not needed to modify the initial Armadillo code.

Finally, Fig. 5 (right) reports the speedup reached by each of the linear algebra solutions, comparing with MATLAB as reference. We observe that reduce the overall execution time by 8×. In case of Intel MKL, the major improvement comes from the use of OpenMP, reaching an improvement of 4× over MATLAB.

6.2   NVBLAS Evaluation

Figure 6 plots a comparative analysis of NVBLAS, where the tile dimension varies from 256 to 16384 elements (threads). The tile dimension corresponds with the parameter *cublasXtSetBlockDim* of cuBLAS. It is important to note that not all the BLAS Level-3 calls are offloaded to the GPU. That decision is based on a simple heuristic that estimates if the BLAS call will execute for long enough to amortize the PCI transfers of the input and output data to the GPU [20].

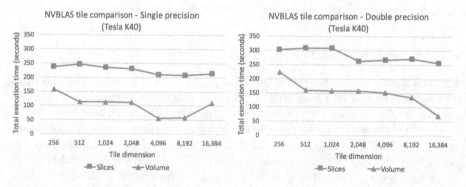

Fig. 6. Evaluation of different tile dimensions in NVBLAS, for single and double precision

Figure 7 compares two GPUs (GTX 680 and Tesla K40) in terms of the tile dimension. We observe that there is not a significant different in terms of performance. However, the selection of an adequate tile dimension is a key factor.

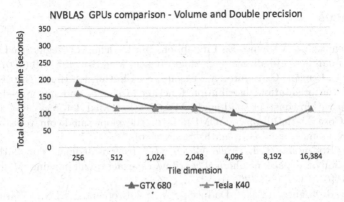

Fig. 7. Evaluation of different GPUs, varying the tile dimension at double precision and the volume access pattern.

7   Conclusions

This paper has presented a case study where an application, initially implemented in the MATLAB language, has been ported to C++ language. The benefits are numerous, particularly due to its robustness, flexibility, and portability. Concretely, the medical use case ported is now compliant with a wide range of parallel hardware, such as multi-core processors, accelerators and co-processors, and multiple highly-tuned linear algebra libraries. We believe that this new application can tremendously aid researches in the area o studying the diffusion MRI of the human brain to get responses, as the experiments require now much less time to complete.

Although the porting task can be cumbersome, we observed that using modern C++ libraries, such as Armadillo or ArrayFire, for performing linear algebra operations, greatly alleviates the burden of the developer carrying out the task.

In general, we observed that the execution time of the migrated application is 8× faster, on average, than the original MATLAB version. The performed experiments demonstrate that the pair Armadillo and NVBLAS provide multiple advantages: a similar source code, automatic parallelization on BLAS level 3, and a good performance. As a remark, one of the main issues we observed for the ArrayFire library is the limited support for developing applications using multiple GPUs. As future work, we plan to develop additional libraries that enable the use of multi-GPUs in ArrayFire. An additional future research line is to automatically detect parallel patterns in the application, and parallelize them accordingly, so as to take advantage of all the devices available on a platform. The approach introduced in this work can be extended to also implement other important intravoxel reconstruction methods, including model-free techniques like q-ball imaging [30] and its extensions [1,2,4,29], diffusion orientation transforms [7,21], diffusion spectrum imaging [6,31], as well as approaches based on parametric diffusion models and other spherical deconvolution algorithms [28] (e.g., for more details see the evaluation study by [8]).

References

1. Descoteaux, M., Angelino, E., Fitzgibbons, S., Deriche, R.: Regularized, fast, and robust analytical Q-ball imaging. Magn. Reson. Med. **58**, 497–510 (2007)
2. Aganj, I., Lenglet, C., Sapiro, G., Yacoub, E., Ugurbil, K., Harel, N.: Reconstruction of the orientation distribution function in single- and multiple-shell q-ball imaging within constant solid angle. Magn. Reson. Med. **64**, 554–566 (2010)
3. AMD Core Math Library (ACML): http://developer.amd.com/tools-and-sdks/cpu-development/amd-core-math-library-acml/
4. Canales-Rodríguez, E.J., Melie-García, L., Iturria-Medina, Y.: Mathematical description of q-space in spherical coordinates: exact q-ball imaging. Magn. Reson. Med. **61**(6), 1350–1367 (2009)
5. Canales-Rodríguez, E.J., Daducci, A., Sotiropoulos, S.N., Caruyer, E., Aja-Fernández, S., Radua, J., Mendizabal, J.M.Y., Iturria-Medina, Y., Melie-García, L., Alemán-Gómez, Y., et al.: Spherical deconvolution of multichannel diffusion MRI data with non-Gaussian noise models and spatial regularization. PloS ONE **10**(10), e0138910 (2015)
6. Canales-Rodríguez, E.J., Iturria-Medina, Y., Alemán-Gómez, Y., Melie-García, L.: Deconvolution in diffusion spectrum imaging. NeuroImage **50**(1), 136–149 (2010)
7. Canales-Rodríguez, E.J., Lin, C.P., Iturria-Medina, Y., Yeh, C.H., Cho, K.H., Melie-García, L.: Diffusion orientation transform revisited. NeuroImage **49**(2), 1326–1339 (2010)
8. Daducci, A., Canales-Rodriguez, E.J., Descoteaux, M., Garyfallidis, E., Gur, Y., Lin, Y.C., Mani, M., Merlet, S., Paquette, M., Ramirez-Manzanares, A., Reisert, M., Rodrigues, P.R., Sepehrband, F., Caruyer, E., Choupan, J., Deriche, R., Jacob, M., Menegaz, G., Prckovska, V., Rivera, M., Wiaux, Y., Thiran, J.P.: Quantitative comparison of reconstruction methods for intra-voxel fiber recovery from diffusion MRI. IEEE Trans. Med. Imaging **33**, 384–399 (2014)
9. De Rose, L., Padua, D.: Techniques for the translation of MATLAB programs into Fortran 90. ACM Trans. Program. Lang. Syst. **21**(2), 286–323 (1999). doi:10.1145/316686.316693
10. Drakenberg, P., Jacobson, P., Kgstrm, B.: A CONLAB compiler for a distributed memory multicomputer. In: PPSC, pp. 814–821 (1993). http://dblp.uni-trier.de/db/conf/ppsc/ppsc1993-2.html#DrakenbergJK93
11. Gough, B.: GNU Scientific Library Reference Manual, 3rd edn. Network Theory Ltd., Cambridge (2009)
12. Guennebaud, G., Jacob, B., et al.: Eigen v3 (2010). http://eigen.tuxfamily.org
13. IBM: Engineering Scientific Subroutine Library
14. Johnson, H.J., McCormick, M.M., Ibanez, L.: The ITK Software Guide Book 1: Introduction and Development Guidelines, vol. 1. Kitware, Inc., Clifton Park (2015)
15. Kuck and Associates, Inc.: KAP for IBM Fortran and C. http://www.kai.com/product/ibminf.html. Accessed 5 May 2016
16. Malcolm, J., Yalamanchili, P., McClanahan, C., Venugopalakrishnan, V., Patel, K., Melonakos, J.: ArrayFire: a GPU acceleration platform. In: SPIE Defense, Security, and Sensing, p. 84030A. International Society for Optics and Photonics (2012)
17. Markoff, J.: Writing the fastest code, by hand, for fun: a human computer keeps speeding up chips. New York Times **53**, 28 (2005)
18. Intel Math Kernel Library (MKL). http://software.intel.com/en-us/intel-mkl/
19. nVidia: cuBLAS Library User Guide (2012). https://developer.nvidia.com/cubla. accedido el 18 de Mayo de 2016

20. NVidia: CUDA Toolkit documentation: NVBLAS (2016). http://docs.nvidia.com/cuda/nvblas
21. Ozarslan, E., Shepherd, T.M., Vemuri, B.C., Blackband, S.J., Mareci, T.H.: Resolution of complex tissue microarchitecture using the diffusion orientation transform (DOT). Neuroimage **31**(3), 1086–1103 (2006)
22. Quinn, M.J., Malishevsky, A., Seelam, N.: Otter: bridging the gap between MATLAB and ScaLAPACK. In: Proceedings of the Seventh International Symposium on High Performance Distributed Computing 1998, pp. 114–121. IEEE (1998)
23. Rupp, K., Rudolf, F., Weinbub, J.: ViennaCL - a high level linear algebra library for GPUs and multi-core CPUs. In: International Workshop on GPUs and Scientific Applications, pp. 51–56 (2010)
24. Sanderson, C.: Armadillo: an open source C++ linear algebra library for fast prototyping and computationally intensive experiments (2010)
25. The Mathworks, Inc.: C/C++ Compiler Suite. http://www.mathworks.com. Accessed 5 May 2016
26. The Mathworks, Inc.: Multicore-Capable Code Generation Using OpenMP (2016). http://es.mathworks.com/products/matlab-coder/features.html#multicore-capablecodegenerationusingopenmp. accedido el 18 de Mayo de
27. The Mathworks, Inc.: Parallel Computing Toolbox (2016). http://es.mathworks.com/products/parallel-computing/. accedido el 18 de Mayo de
28. Tournier, J.D., Yeh, C.H., Calamante, F., Cho, K.H., Connelly, A., Lin, C.P.: Resolving crossing fibres using constrained spherical deconvolution: validation using diffusion-weighted imaging phantom data. NeuroImage **42**, 617–625 (2008)
29. Tristan-Vega, A., Aja-Fernandez, S., Westin, C.F.: On the blurring of the funk-radon transform in Q-ball imaging. Med. Image Comput. Comput. Assist. Interv. **12**(Pt. 2), 415–422 (2009)
30. Tuch, D.S.: Q-ball imaging. Magn. Reson. Med. **52**, 1358–1372 (2004)
31. Wedeen, V.J., Hagmann, P., Tseng, W.Y., Reese, T.G., Weisskoff, R.M.: Mapping complex tissue architecture with diffusion spectrum magnetic resonance imaging. Magn. Reson. Med. **54**(6), 11377–11386 (2005)
32. Whaley, R.C., Dongarra, J.J.: Automatically tuned linear algebra software. In: International Conference on Supercomputing (ICS) (1998)

On Stochastic Performance and Cost-Aware Optimal Capacity Planning of Unreliable Infrastructure-as-a-Service Cloud

Weiling Li[1], Lei Wu[2], Yunni Xia[1(✉)], Yuandou Wang[1], Kunyin Guo[1], Xin Luo[1], Mingwei Lin[4], and Wanbo Zheng[3]

[1] College of Computer Science, Chongqing University, Chongqing, China
xiayunni@hotmail.com
[2] College of Mathematical Sciences, University of Electronic Science and Technology of China, Chengdu, China
[3] College of Optoelectronic Engineering, Chongqing University, Chongqing, China
[4] Faculty of Software, Fujian Normal University, Fuzhou, China

Abstract. Performance evaluation of cloud data-centers has drawn considerable attention from academy and industry. In this study, we present an analytical approach to the performance analysis of Infrastructure-as-a-Service cloud data-centers with unreliable task executions and resubmissions of unsuccessful tasks. Several performance metrics are considered and analyzed under variable load intensities, failure frequencies, multiplexing abilities, and service intensities. We also conduct a case study based on a real-world cloud data-center and employ a confidence interval check to validate the correctness of the proposed model. For the performance optimization and optimal capacity planning purposes, we are also interested in knowing the minimized expected response time subject to the constraint of request rejection rate, hardware cost in terms of the cost of physical machines and the request buffer. We show that the optimization problem can be numerically solved through a simulated-annealing-based algorithm.

Keywords: IaaS cloud · Performance · Optimal capacity planning · Simulated annealing

1 Introduction

Cloud data-centers are key enablers for the scalability of the cloud platform. Cloud computing relies on data-centers to deliver expected services. The widespread adoption of the cloud computing paradigm mandates the exponential

This work is in part supported by NSFC under Grant Nos. 61472051, 61170183, 61272093, 61572523, and 61202347; Young Scientist Foundation of Chongqing No. cstc2013kjrc-qnrc0079; Fundamental Research Funds for the Central Universities under project Nos. 106112014CDJZR185503 and CDJZR12180012; Science foundation of Chongqing No. cstc2014jcyjA40010; China Postdoctoral Science Foundation No. 2015M570770; Chongqing Postdoctoral Science special Foundation no. Xm2015078.

© Springer International Publishing AG 2016
J. Carretero et al. (Eds.): ICA3PP 2016, LNCS 10048, pp. 644–657, 2016.
DOI: 10.1007/978-3-319-49583-5_50

growth in the data-centers' computational, network, and storage resources. Managing the computational resources to deliver specified performance [1] is among the key challenges.

Expected request response time which decides system responsiveness and request rejection rate which determines users' satisfaction are usually considered as the most important performance metrics to evaluate a service system. As will be discussed later in this paper, cloud data-centers are usually subject to errors/faults, and error/failure-handling activities could have strong impact on final performance. Due to the difficulties with building monolithic models capable of capturing related factors, measurement-based approaches are frequently used [2–4]. However, these approaches are intractable due to exhaustive experimentations. Therefore, their value is limited. Comprehensive analytical performance models are more preferable in this situation. Although some other analytical models [5–8] are proposed, those works are limited mainly because they assume the system failure-free to simplify the performance/QoS calculation.

This paper focuses on analytical performance analysis of IaaS cloud data-centers with request rejection and resubmission. For this purpose, a stochastic model is proposed and product-form expressions of multiple performance metrics are derived. We validate the model by experiment based on a actual IaaS cloud and the results indicate our model is trustable. For the optimal capacity planning and cost saving purposes, which are conflicting with each other, we are also interested in knowing the best system responsiveness that can be achieved. We employ a simulated-annealing-based algorithm to solve this problem.

2   System Model

IaaS cloud is a form of cloud computing that provides virtualized computing resources over the Internet. The cloud management unit of an IaaS data-center maintains a request buffer for consecutively-arrived requests, which can be usually described by an arrival rate, λ. The capacity of such buffer, denoted by c, can be specified before using (e.g., the capacity limit can be specified through the $FRAME\_SIZE$ property in OpenStack). Requests arrived either leave by rate θ or are resubmitted by rate $1-\theta$ when the capacity limit is reached. For the performance evaluation purpose, we are interested in knowing request response time, i.e., the expected interval time between request arrival and the corresponding VM ready for execution (e.g., the time of $INSTANCE\_SPAWNED$ defined in OpenStack).

As shown by Fig. 1, VM instantiation requires multiple steps and interferences with various services and components. Averaged speed (or process rate) of the cloud management unit to spawn a VM, denoted by μ, can be obtained by the reciprocal of averaged instantiation times, e.g., intervals between $INSTANCE\_BUILDING$ times and $INSTANCE\_SPAWNED$ times in OpenStack. With the help of VM multiplexing [9] mechanism supported by today's multi-core/multi-threading technologies, multiple VMs can be instantiated on a same PM. The maximum number of VMs that can be instantiated

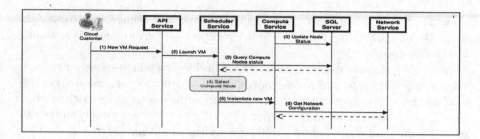

Fig. 1. Sequence chart of VM instantiation on OpenStack

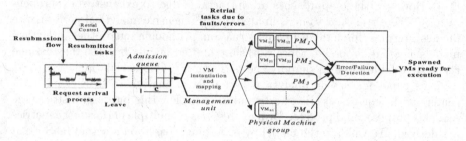

Fig. 2. The cloud provisioning control-flow of an IaaS data-center with task errors/faults

on a PM, denoted by m, is usually bounded. Note that high multiplexing level is not always welcomed because VM interference may cause performance and reliability degradation.

Moreover, Fig. 1 suggests potential of unsuccessful VM instantiation because interactions with local or remote services and components are often error/failure-prone.

Errors/failures can strongly impact cloud performance due to the overhead needed to conduct compensation/transactional-rollback activities and re-instantiate the faulty request. Based on the above discussions, an abstract control-flow model of VM instantiation on unreliable IaaS cloud data-center is illustrated in Fig. 2. It abstracts away implementation details of IaaS cloud paradigm while preserving the control-flow contents useful for performance analysis in a context of queueing-networks. Its objective is to derive the quantitative effects of varying request arrival rates, VM instantiation rates, resource scale, and error intensity on cloud performance. The system under study is consequently mapped into an instance of queuing network problems solved in the following section.

3 Stochastic Analysis

Let $N(t) = n$ mean that the number of tasks waiting or being instantiated is n at time t, $M(t) = m$ mean that the number of requests being resubmitted m, and $X(t) = (N(t), M(t))$ denote the system state at time t, the resulting state space is therefore $E \in \{0, 1, \ldots, k\} \times \{0, 1, \ldots, \infty\}$. Since the inter-arrival time, VM instantiation time, and resubmission processing time are all exponentially distributed, $X(t)$ is a Markovian process on state space E.

Based on the state transition chart, the corresponding transition-rate matrix, Q, can be derived as:

$$Q = \begin{bmatrix} A_0 & C & & & & \\ B_1 & A_1 & C & & & \\ & B_2 & A_2 & C & & \\ & & \ddots & \ddots & \ddots & \\ & & & B_{k-1} & A_{k-1} & \widetilde{C} \\ & & & & \widetilde{B_k} & \widetilde{A_k} \end{bmatrix} \tag{1}$$

It is easy to see that $X(t)$ is irreducible and non-periodical. Let $\pi_{k,j}(t)$ denote the probability that the Markovian process is at state (k, j) and $\pi_{k,j} = \lim_{t \to \infty} \pi_{k,j}(t)$, we have that $\pi_{k,j}$ can be calculated as below if the stationary distribution exists:

$$\pi_{k,j} = \pi_{k,j-1} \prod_{l=g+1}^{j} \rho_l \tag{2}$$

where

$$\rho_l = \frac{e \times f \times \mu + (1 - \theta)\lambda}{l \times \theta \times \mu' + e \times (1 - f)\mu} \tag{3}$$

It is easy to see that ρ_l decreases with l. Consequently, there exists $u \in N^+$ such that $\rho_u < 1$ and

$$\sum_{j=g+1}^{\infty} \left\{ \prod_{l=g+1}^{j} \left(\frac{e \times f \times \mu + (1 - \theta)\lambda}{l \times \theta \times \mu' + e \times (1 - f)\mu} \right) \right\}$$

$$= \sum_{j=g+1}^{\infty} \left\{ \prod_{l=g+1}^{j} \rho_l \right\} < \sum_{j=g+1}^{u} (\rho_{g+1})^{j-g} + \sum_{j=u+1}^{\infty} \left(\prod_{l=g+1}^{j} \rho_l \right)$$

$$< \sum_{j=g+1}^{u} (\rho_{g+1})^{j-g} + (\rho_{g+1})^{u-g} \sum_{j=u+1}^{\infty} \left(\prod_{l=u+1}^{j} \rho_l \right) \tag{4}$$

$$< \sum_{j=g+1}^{u} (\rho_{g+1})^{j-g} + (\rho_{g+1})^{u-g} \sum_{j=u+1}^{\infty} (\rho_l)^{j-u}$$

$$= \sum_{j=g+1}^{u} (\rho_{g+1})^{j-g} + (\rho_{g+1})^{u-g} \frac{\rho_u}{1 - \rho_u} < \infty$$

The above derivation leads to

$$\sum_{j=g+1}^{\infty} \left\{ \prod_{l=g+1}^{j} \left(\frac{e \times f \times \mu + (1 - \theta)\lambda}{l \times \theta \times \mu' + e \times (1 - f)\mu} \right) \right\} < \infty \tag{5}$$

and therefore the stationary distribution exists according to the limit theorems of birth-death processes.

Since the stationary distribution exists, we have the steady-state probabilities of each state as:

$$\pi Q = 0, \sum_{i=0}^{k-1} \sum_{j=0}^{g} \pi_{i,j} + \sum_{j=0}^{\infty} \pi_{k,j} = 1 \tag{6}$$

Since the stationary distribution exists, we also have:

$$\begin{aligned}
\pi_{k-1,g}\lambda + (1-\theta)\pi_{k,g-1}\lambda + e(1-f)\mu \\
= \pi_{k,g}(e \times \mu + \lambda(1-\theta) + \theta \times g \times \mu') \\
-\pi_{k,g+1}(g+1) \times \theta \times \mu'
\end{aligned} \tag{7}$$

From (2) we have:

$$\pi_{k,g+1} = \pi_{k,g} \frac{\lambda(1-\theta) + e \times f\mu}{(g+1)\theta \times \mu' + e \times (1-f)\mu} \tag{8}$$

Combining the above equation with (7), we have:

$$\pi_{k,g-1}\lambda(1-\theta) = \pi_{k,g}(e \times (1-f)\mu + g \times \theta \times \mu') \tag{9}$$

which suggests that $A_k = \widetilde{A_k}$ and $B_k = \widetilde{B_k}$.

According to (6) and (9), we have:

$$\begin{aligned}
T_0 \frac{1}{W} A_0 + T_1 \frac{1}{W} B_1 = 0 \\
T_i \frac{1}{W} C + T_{i+1} \frac{1}{W} A_{i+1} + T_{i+2} \frac{1}{W} A_{i+2} = 0, 0 \le i \le k-2 \\
T_{k-1} \frac{1}{W} C + T_k \frac{1}{W} A_k = 0
\end{aligned} \tag{10}$$

where T_0 is a basic solution of $T_0(V_k A_k + V_{k-1}C) = 0$ and $\pi_{i,j}$ is subject to:

$$\begin{aligned}
(\pi_{0,0}, \ldots, \pi_{0,g}) = T_0 \frac{1}{W} \\
(\pi_{i,0}, \ldots, \pi_{i,g}) = (\pi_{0,0}, \ldots, \pi_{0,g})V_i, 0 < i \le k \\
\pi_{k,j} = T_0 \frac{1}{W} V_k \omega_1 \prod_{l=g+1}^{j} \frac{e \times f \times \mu + (1-\theta)\lambda}{l \times \theta \times \mu' + e \times (1-f)\mu}
\end{aligned} \tag{11}$$

where ω_1 is a column vector with its dimension being $g+1$ and is equal to $(0,..,0,1)^T$.

and, V_k is subject to:

$$\begin{aligned}
V_0 &= I \\
V_1 &= -A_0(B_1)^{-1} \\
V_2 &= -(V_0 C + V_1 A_1)(B_2)^{-1} \\
V_i &= -(V_{i-2}C + V_{i-1}A_{i-1})(B_i)^{-1}, 2 < i \le k
\end{aligned} \tag{12}$$

W is calculated as:

$$W = T_0(\sum_{i=0}^{k} V_i)\omega + T_0 V_k \omega_1 \sum_{j=g+1}^{\infty} (\prod_{l=g+1}^{j} \frac{e \times f \times \mu + (1-\theta)\lambda}{l \times \theta \times \mu' + e \times (1-f)\mu})) \qquad (13)$$

From (10), we have:

$$T_1 \frac{1}{W} = -T_0 \frac{1}{W} A_0 (B_1)^{-1} = T_0 \frac{1}{W} V_1 \qquad (14)$$

and similarly:

$$T_2 \frac{1}{W} = -T_0 \frac{1}{W} (V_1 A_1 + C)(B_2)^{-1} = T_0 \frac{1}{W} V_2 \qquad (15)$$

Consequently, we can finally have:

$$T_i = -T_0 V_i \qquad (16)$$

and the product form solution of T_i can be obtained by using this equation.

Combining (16) with (2), we can obtain the solutions of steady-state probabilities of all states, $\pi_{i,j}$. Note that a similar derivation skill can be found in [10].

4   Performance Results

We consider the following as the performance metrics: (1) Expected request response time, T; and (2) Request rejection rate, R.

As suggested by Fig. 2, T denotes the expected interval between request arrival and the moment of the corresponding VM being instantiated and ready for execution. Response time is a frequently used measure of efficiency and responsiveness of computer systems. Lower response time also allows for a higher system reliability since in an unreliable system failures/errors are more likely to happen when a longer response time is needed.

To analyze T, we first have to calculate the probability that a cloud task enters the resubmission state, P_r:

$$P_r = (1-\theta)(\sum_{j=0}^{\infty} \pi_{k,j}) + f(1 - \sum_{j=0}^{\infty} \pi_{k,j}) \qquad (17)$$

The expected number of retrials of a cloud task, N_r, can be obtained as:

$$N_r = \frac{1}{1-P_r} - 1 \qquad (18)$$

The expected time for a task to wait before it is resubmitted to the arrival task flow, T_r, can therefore be calculated as:

$$T_r = \frac{\lambda'/\mu' + \frac{P_0(\lambda'/(g \times \mu'))(\lambda'/\mu')^g}{g!(1 - \lambda'/(g \times \mu'))}}{\lambda'} \qquad (19)$$

where P_0 denotes the probability that no task being resubmitted:

$$P_0 = \frac{1}{\sum_{l=0}^{g-1} \frac{(\lambda'/\mu')^l}{l!} + \frac{(\lambda'/\mu')^g}{g!}} \left(\frac{1}{1 - \lambda'/g \times \mu'} \right) \tag{20}$$

and λ' is the rate of resubmission flow into the arrival task flow:

$$\lambda' = (\lambda + \lambda')[(\sum_{j=0}^{\infty} \pi_{k,j})(1 - \theta) + (1 - \sum_{j=0}^{\infty} \pi_{k,j})f] \tag{21}$$

where λ' can be calculated as:

$$\lambda' = \lambda \frac{\sum_{j=0}^{\infty} \pi_{k,j}(1 - \theta) + f - \sum_{j=0}^{\infty} \pi_{k,j} \times f}{1 - \sum_{j=0}^{\infty} \pi_{k,j}(1 - \theta) - f + \sum_{j=0}^{\infty} \pi_{k,j} \times f} \tag{22}$$

The expected total time for a task to spend before its final successful trial on condition that it is not rejected, T_b, can therefore be obtained as:

$$T_b = N_r(T_r \sum_{j=0}^{\infty} \pi_{k,j} + (T_r + T_v)(1 - \sum_{j=0}^{\infty} \pi_{k,j})) \tag{23}$$

where T_v is calculated as:

$$T_v = \frac{1}{\mu} + \sum_{j=0}^{g} \pi_{0,j} \frac{\rho(\rho \times e)^e}{\lambda''(1 - \rho)^2 \times (e)!} \tag{24}$$

$\rho = \frac{\lambda''}{e \times \mu}$ and

$$\lambda'' = (\lambda + \lambda')(1 - \sum_{j=0}^{\infty} \pi_{k,j}) \tag{25}$$

Finally, we have T as:
$$T = T_b + T_v \tag{26}$$

Request rejection rate, R, can be expressed as the ratio of the number of rejected tasks, due to the capacity constraint or PM failures/errors, to the total number of requests submitted to the IaaS data-center. For user satisfaction, a low rejection rate is always preferable.

$$R = \theta \sum_{j=0}^{\infty} \pi_{k,j} \tag{27}$$

5   Case Study and Model Validation

For the model validation purpose, we conduct a case study on a real-world cloud data-center, the **Course-Management and Assignment-Submission**

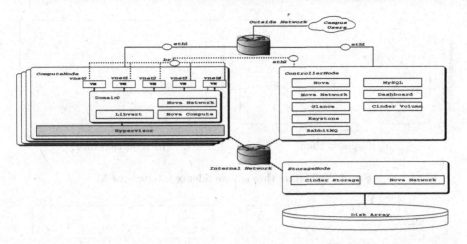

Fig. 3. The architectural view of the Course-Management and Assignment-Submission cloud

cloud for undergraduate students of ChongQing University (CQU). Its protocol and architectural views are illustrated in Fig. 3.

The cloud system is based on a symmetric server group of 6 Sugon I450 servers (4-CPU Intel Xeon 5506/128G RAM/15TB RAID but only 3-CPU/8G RAM/4TB RAID is assigned as cloud users' space). Each PM can therefore concurrently support no more than 32 VMs. The capacity of the waiting buffer for requests c is 16. The faulty rate f is 0.13–0.79%. The occurrence rate of impatient wait is 11.3% when the waiting buffer is fully occupied, meaning that $\theta = 0.113$

As shown in Table 1, the logfile covers time-stamps of each request's arrival and departure time in consecutive periods of 60 minutes from 09:00 to 22:00, Feb. 26, 2016.

For the model validation purpose, we derive 90% confidence intervals from the experimental performance data. By using a normal distribution as the fitting function, we derive the confidence interval of T as:

$$intv(T) = [\bar{ct} - z_{1-a/2}\frac{sdv}{\sqrt{\hat{s}}}, \bar{ct} + z_{1-a/2}\frac{sdv}{\sqrt{\hat{s}}}] \tag{28}$$

where $\bar{ct}$ stands for the mean of experimental request response time, sdv its standard deviation, $\hat{s}$ the sample size, z the z-distribution, and α the confidence level (Fig. 4).

Finally, the confidence interval of R is also based on a Bernoulli distribution as the fitting function:

$$intv(R) = [\bar{r} - z_{1-a/2}\sqrt{\frac{\bar{r} - \bar{r}^2}{\hat{s}}}, \bar{r} + z_{1-a/2}\sqrt{\frac{\bar{r} - \bar{r}^2}{\hat{s}}}] \tag{29}$$

where $\bar{r}$ stands for the experimental rejection rate.

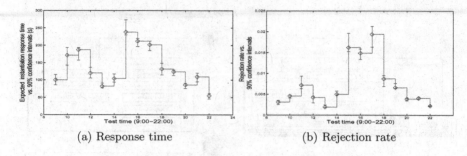

(a) Response time   (b) Rejection rate

Fig. 4. Validation through confidence interval check

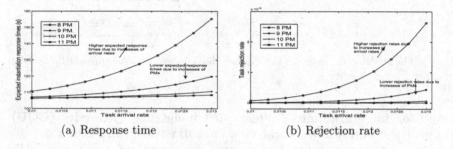

(a) Response time   (b) Rejection rate

Fig. 5. Analytical performance results vs. arrival rate at different number of PMs

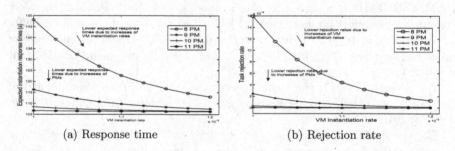

(a) Response time   (b) Rejection rate

Fig. 6. Analytical performance results vs. VM instantiation rate at different number of PMs

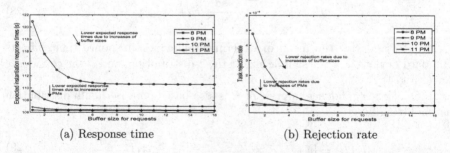

(a) Response time   (b) Rejection rate

Fig. 7. Analytical performance results vs. request buffer size at different number of PMs

Table 1. Theoretical results and confidence intervals

Test time	T	CI	$R(10^{-3})$	$CI(10^{-3})$
09:00	100.1 s	[85.8–115.7 s]	3.12	[2.52–3.53]
10:00	171.6 s	[143.0–193.7 s]	4.59	[4.06–4.82]
11:00	187.2 s	[157.3–195.2 s]	7.18	[6.35–9.35]
12:00	119.6 s	[105.3–136.5 s]	4.24	[2.94–4.52]
13:00	81.9 s	[76.7–91.0 s]	1.94	[1.76–2.41]
14:00	104.0 s	[93.6–117.0 s]	5.06	[4.82–5.76]
15:00	237.9 s	[230.1–273.0 s]	16.24	[15.29–19.65]
16:00	211.9 s	[196.3–219.7 s]	14.88	[13.41–15.88]
17:00	201.5 s	[184.6–211.9 s]	19.41	[16.35–21.29]
18:00	131.3 s	[114.4–148.2 s]	8.71	[6.88—9.47]
19:00	123.5 s	[113.1–128.7 s]	6.59	[6.41–7.59]
20:00	85.8 s	[75.4–91.0 s]	3.88	[3.47–4.06]
21:00	109.2 s	[94.9–119.6 s]	4.06	[3.76–4.35]
22:00	54.6 s	[45.5–61.1 s]	2.23	[2.12–2.29]

Table 1 and Fig. 5 imply the correctness of the proposed theoretical model.

Figure 6 illustrates performance changes with variations in request arrival rates when $m = 2, c = 8, \mu = 0.00125, \mu' = 0.01, g = 4, f = 0.08, \theta = 0.1$. Increasing arrival rate leads to higher expected response time and rejection rate. IaaS cloud maintains a small number of PMs. It can be seen that clouds with more PMs are more resistant to performance loss when arrival rate increases.

Figure 7(a) illustrates performance changes with variations in VM instantiation rates when $m = 2, c = 8, \mu' = 0.01, g = 4, f = 0.08, \theta = 0.1, \lambda = 0.01$. Increasing VM instantiation rate leads to lower expected response time and rejection rate. It can also be seen that clouds with fewer PMs are more sensitive to performance improvements when VM instantiation rate increases.

Figure 7(b) illustrates performance changes with variations in buffer sizes. The growth of such size leads to lower expected response time and rejection rate. Such performance improvements are strong when the size is small. It is also seen that clouds with more PMs always have higher performance.

6 Cost-Aware Optimal Capacity Planning

As shown in previous sections, the proposed model is capable of giving validated performance results when input parameters are known. We are also interested in deciding optimal system capacity with highest performance and under cost constraints, which are conflicting with each other.

This problem can be formulated as:

$$Min \quad T(n, c, m, g)$$
$$s.t. \quad R(n, c, m, g) < RJ$$
$$n \times cpm < CPM$$
$$cbf(c) < CBUF \tag{30}$$
$$cm(m) \times n < CM$$
$$GLO < g < GUP$$

where n, k, m, g, as previous defined, serve as decision variables, cpm denotes the cost of one single PM, $cbf : N^+ \rightarrow Real$ is a function to identify the cost of the request buffer, $cm : N^+ \rightarrow Real$ is a function to identify the cost of maintaining a certain level of multiplexing. Request arrival rate, VM instantiation rate, abandonment rate of impatient request, faulty rate and resubmission rate are given and serve as input constants in the optimization.

The proposed optimization problems are examples of non-linear, integer (or discrete) programming problems. As n, c, m, g are allowed to be integer, the overall problem is a nonlinear, integer programming problem. In general, it can be shown that all integer programming problems belong to the class of NP-hard problems.

We employ the simulated annealing approach to solve the proposed optimization problem. Given a current state i with energy E_i, a next state $(i+1)$ with energy E_{i+1} is produced through perturbation. If the energy difference between the two consecutive states is smaller than or equal to zero then the state $i+1$ is accepted as the current state. If it is greater than zero, then the state $i+1$ is accepted with probability $exp((E_i - E_{i+1})/k_B T)$, where k_B is the Boltzmann

Table 2. Optimal solutions of the cost-aware expected-response-time minimization problem

Input condition	Constraints	Optimal solution	Minimized T
$\lambda = 0.0118$, $\mu = 0.01$, $\mu' = 0.01$, $f = 0.2, \theta = 0.24$	$RJ = 0.007, CPM = 1.2$, $CBUF = 3, CM = 1.4$, $GLO = 3, GUP = 4$	$c = 15, n = 1$, $m = 7, g = 4$	$T = 128.5959\,\text{s}$
$\lambda = 0.0222$, $\mu = 0.0085$, $\mu' = 0.01$, $f = 0.2, \theta = 0.24$	$RJ = 0.007, CPM = 4.8$, $CBUF = 3, CM = 5.6$, $GLO = 2, GUP = 4$	$c = 16, n = 3$, $m = 15, g = 4$	$T = 185.6574\,\text{s}$
$\lambda = 0.01$, $\mu = 0.0043$, $\mu' = 0.02$, $f = 0.08, \theta = 0.17$	$RJ = 0.001, CPM = 4.8$, $CBUF = 12, CM = 5.6$, $GLO = 5, GUP = 8$	$c = 1, n = 2$, $m = 13, g = 8$	$T = 50.5507\,\text{s}$

Algorithm optimize_T: Algorithm for solving the cost-aware performance optimization problem.

Input: (1) Expected response time calculation model; (2) Rejection rate computation model; (3) $n^{(init)}$, $c^{(init)}$, $m^{(init)}$, $g^{(init)}$: initial guesses for the number of PMs, the size of request buffer, the maximum number of concurrent VMs that a PM can support, the maximum number of resubmitted tasks that the cloud management unit can concurrently support; (4) the cost models of PMs, request buffer, and multiplexing level; (5) upper and lower bounds of g; (6) TP_{low} the lower bound of temperature; (7) n_f: maximum number of iterations per temperature; (8) a: temperature scale factor.

Output: Optimal numbers of n, c, m, g that minimize T.

1. declare TP: temperature;
2. declare i: number of iterations;
3. declare TV: vector of T;
4. declare r: random number;
5. declare d: number of past solutions that need to be checked;
6. $n \leftarrow n^{(init)}$, $c \leftarrow c^{(init)}$, $m \leftarrow m^{(init)}$, $g \leftarrow g^{(init)}$;
7. $T \leftarrow T(n, c, m, g)$;
8. $TP \leftarrow T$;
9. while $TP > TPlow$, $GLO < g < GUP$, $cbf(c) < CBUF$, $n*cpm < CPM$, $R(n, c, m, g) < RJ$, $cm(m) < CM$
10. $i \leftarrow 1$;
11.   while $i <= n_I$
12.   . $(n', c', m', g') \leftarrow$ generate_neighbor(n, c, m, g);
13. $T' \leftarrow T(n', c', m' g')$;
14. $r \leftarrow$ rand( );
15.   if $T' < T$ or $e^{(T-T')/TP} > r$
16. $n \leftarrow n'$, $c \leftarrow c'$, $m \leftarrow m'$, $g \leftarrow g'$;
17. $T \leftarrow T'$;
18. $i \leftarrow i + 1$;
19. $TV \leftarrow$ store_last_T(TV, T);
20.   if check_termination_criteria(TV, d)
21.   break;
22. $TP \leftarrow TP*a$;
23. print n, c, m, g, T;

Fig. 8. The simulated-annealing-based algorithm

constant and TP the temperature. This rule of accepting the new state is called Metropolis criterion and the algorithm is known as the Metropolis algorithm.

The process of finding the optimal solution for combinatorial optimization problems has an interesting analogy with the physical annealing process. Solutions in a combinatorial optimization problem are equivalent to the states of the solid while the cost of a solution is equivalent to the energy of a state. Given the current solution i with cost $f(i)$, a next solution $(i+1)$ with cost $f(i+1)$ is generated using a generation mechanism from the neighborhood of the current solution. The probability of accepting the next solution is 1 if $f(i+1) \leq f(i)$, otherwise, the next solution is accepted with probability $exp((f(i) - f(i+1)/TP))$. TP is the temperature or the control parameter. Thus, simulated annealing can be viewed as an iteration of Metropolis algorithm evaluated at decreasing values of the temperature. Although simulated annealing does not guarantee 100% optimality of the solution, it can be proved that asymptotically it converges to the global optimal solution.

For example, we assume the cost function of cbf and cm are as follows:

$$cbf(c) = \begin{cases} 1 & if \ 0 < c \leq 8 \\ 1.5 & elseif \ 9 < c \leq 32 \\ 2.2 & elseif \ 33 < c \leq 64 \end{cases} \tag{31}$$

$$cm(c) = \begin{cases} 1 & if \ 0 < c \leq 8 \\ 1.6 & elseif \ 9 < c \leq 16 \\ 4.3 & elseif \ 17 < c \leq 32 \end{cases} \tag{32}$$

Based on the above cost functions, we employ the algorithm shown in Fig. 8 to derive optimal solutions for different parameter settings given in Table 2.

7   Conclusions and Further Studies

A comprehensive performance-determination model is proposed in this work. for failure/error-prone IaaS cloud data-centers with request rejection and resubmission. We consider expected request response time and request rejection as the performance metrics and study the impact of varying system conditions (error intensity, VM instantiation rate, multiplexing ability, request load, etc.) on cloud performance. For the model validation purpose, we conduct a confidence interval check based on performance test results of a real-world cloud application. For the optimal capacity planning purpose, we formulate the proposed performance model into a optimization problem. Aiming at minimizing expected response time with constraints of request rejection rate and system capacity cost (in terms of the cost of physical machines and the request buffer). We show that the optimization problem can be solved through a simulated-annealing-based algorithm.

References

1. Rao, J., Wei, Y.D., Gong, J.Y., Xu, C.Z.: QoS guarantees and service differentiation for dynamic cloud applications. J. IEEE Trans. Netw. Serv. Manag. **10**, 43–55 (2013)
2. Ostermann, S., Iosup, R., Yigitbasi, N., Fahringer, T.: A performance analysis of EC2 cloud computing services for scientific computing. In: Proceedings of International Conference on Cloud Computing, pp. 931–945 (2009)

3. Yigitbasi, N., Iosup, A., Epema, D., Ostermann, S.: C-meter: a framework for performance analysis of computing clouds. In: Proceedings of International Symposium on Cluster Computing and the Grid, pp. 472–477 (2009)
4. Deelman, E., Singh, G., Livny, M., Berriman, J.B., Good, J.: The cost of doing science on the cloud: the Montage example. In: Proceedings of International Conference High Performance Computing, Networking, Storage and Analysis, pp. 1–12 (2008)
5. Xia, Y.N., Zhou, M.C., Luo, X., Pang, S.C., Zhu, Q.S., Li, J.: Stochastic modeling and performance analysis of migration-enabled and error-prone clouds. IEEE Trans. Ind. Inf. 11, 495–504 (2015)
6. Xiong, K., Perros, H.: Service performance and analysis in cloud computing. In: Proceedings of World Conference on Services-I, pp. 693–700 (2009)
7. Dai, Y.S., Yang, B., Dongarra, J., Zhang, G.: Cloud service reliability: modeling and analysis. In: Proceedings of IEEE Pacific Rim International Symposium on Dependable Computing, pp. 784–789 (2009)
8. Yang, B., Tan, F., Dai, Y.S., Guo, S.C.: Performance evaluation of cloud service considering fault recovery. In: Proceedings of International Conference on Cloud Computing, pp. 571–576 (2009)
9. Meng, X.: Efficient resource provisioning in compute clouds via VM multiplexing. In: Proceedings of International Conference Autonomic Computing (ICAC 2010), pp. 11–20 (2010)
10. Zhu, R., Zhu, Y.: Performance analysis of call centers based on M/M/s/k+G queue with retrial, feedback and impatience. In: Proceedings of International Conference on Grey Systems and Intelligent Services, pp. 1779–1784 (2009)

A Distributed Formal Model for the Analysis and Verification of Arbitration Protocols on MPSoCs Architecture

Imen Ben Hafaiedh[1,2], Maroua Ben Slimane[1,3(✉)], and Riadh Robbana[1,4]

[1] FST, Laboratoire LIP2, Université de Tunis El Manar, 2092 Tunis, Tunisie
ben.hafaiedh.imen@gmail.com, benslimanemaroua@gmail.com,
riadh.robbana@gmail.com
[2] ISI, Université de Tunis El Manar, 2092 Tunis, Tunisie
[3] EPT, Université de Carthage, 2078 La Marsa, Tunisie
[4] INSAT, Université de Carthage, 1080 Tunis, Tunisie

Abstract. In digital system design, control access protocols are used to allocate shared resources. Whenever a resource, such as a bus is shared, an arbiter is required to assign the access to the resource at a particular time. In SoC (System on Chip) architectures, the design, analysis and implementation of such arbiter, are becoming increasingly important due to their significant impact on the performance and efficiency of such systems. In this paper, we provide a high-level abstract and formal model of MPSoCs architecture. The proposed model provides a way to easily implement, analyze and compare different arbitration protocols. It also allows to study relevant properties such as fairness, mutual exclusion and deadlock freedom at a high level of abstraction. The studied protocols as well as the MPSoC architecture have been modeled in a distributed manner which makes the generation of a distributed implementation more relevant.

1 Introduction

As we are approaching the era of a billion transistors on a single chip, more processors (devices) can be placed on a System on Chip (SoC). Most of these processors communicate to access a required shared resource such as a buffer, channel or a bus. Thus when the SoC bus, for example, is connected with more devices, contentions occur while multiple processors request the bus at the same time. This makes on-chip bus based communication a major challenge for the system designer in the current SoC technology. The communication architectures must be able to adapt themselves according to the requirements of the processors. Hence, bus arbiters are proposed. The efficiency of SoCs depends considerably on the protocol used by these arbiters for bus allocation and how these protocols could be balanced and time efficient. Thus, the choice of the arbitration protocol plays an essential role in deciding the performance of bus based systems [1,2].

Multiple bus systems performance could be guaranteed by adopting effective bus arbitration protocols (policies) which could ensure several requirements such as deadlock freedom, fairness, simplicity and time efficiency [3,4].

© Springer International Publishing AG 2016
J. Carretero et al. (Eds.): ICA3PP 2016, LNCS 10048, pp. 658–674, 2016.
DOI: 10.1007/978-3-319-49583-5_51

Analyzing properties of these different protocols at a high-level system description could be considerably helpful to compare their performance without having to go into very low-level implementation details. Indeed, existing hardware description tools are in general too detailed to provide an easy way to formally analyze, compare or study specific properties of arbitration protocols [5]. Moreover, as such descriptions are overly complex because of hardware related details, their simulation is often relatively slow. We claim that arbitration protocols as well as Multiple-bus multiprocessors architecture could be naturally specified at a high abstract level by expressive high-level features such as *Connectors* and *Glues* specifying rich interaction models between the different devices. Such features are provided by several component-based frameworks like those described in [6,7].

In [7], such rich interaction models allow the description of different distributed and complex systems based on high-level expressive notions like multi-party interactions and global *priorities*. The use of these notions leads to much more concise specifications which are more adequate to provide a comprehension of the global behavior of the different protocols and for the verification of their global properties.

This paper attempts to define an abstract formal model allowing to decide at a high-level about the appropriate arbitration protocol to implement. This choice is in general related to a set of requirements and properties (fairness, time efficiency...). Thus if such properties could be studied at a high-level, one can decide about the protocol to use without having to go into low level implementation details. To reach this purpose, we first propose an abstract formal model of multiple bus MPSoC architecture using a component based framework namely BIP (Behavior-Interaction-Priority) [7,8]. This framework offers an expressive interaction model based on a rich notion of glues called *connectors* [9,10] and an interesting notion of priority between interactions [11,12]. Based on our abstract model and on BIP notions, in particular on priorities, we second propose how one can describe a set of well-known arbitration protocols namely fixed, equal and rotating priority protocols.

The second contribution of this paper is the distributed aspect of the proposed model. In fact, our model is designed in a distributed manner, which means that a set of local arbiters, associated each to a device, control the access to the different buses. Such a model makes a distributed implementation easily generated. Thus a set of experimental results are then easily obtained to allow efficiency analysis.

Paper Organization: Sect. 2, reviews the related work. In Sect. 3, we give an overview about the component-based (BIP) framework adopted to design the proposed high-level model. In Sect. 4, we describe our proposed abstract formal model for multiple bus MPSoC architecture. Then, in Sect. 5 we explain how this model can be parameterized to define several well-known arbitration protocols. Section 6 depicts some experimental results obtained from our automatically derived implementation. In Sect. 7, we sum up and discuss possible perspectives.

2   Related Work

The design of hardware systems in particular MPSoCs, is in general based upon hardware description level using languages such as VHDL [5]. These existing languages offer different description levels including architectural, register-transfer, gate and switch levels. This makes the description of MPSoCs with such tools very complex as it contains many hardware related details which may not be directly relevant to the aspects under study. And thus simulation tools handle these models often slowly. Indeed, in the context of arbitration protocols, many existing researches [1,2] have proposed analysis and performance study but at hardware level. Moreover, the different obtained results are mainly based only on simulations and test sequences generated by these hardware tools [4,13] and not on formal validation. However, if one is only interested in high-level functional design of hardware systems, in particular the correctness of the distributed algorithms used in hardware, then hardware description languages may not be the most appropriate choice for such a study.

In [14,15], similar abstract high-level approaches have been proposed. In [14], their model uses LOTOS [16] and it was limited to a single bus architecture with one centralized arbiter to manage conflicts. In our model however, we propose a multiple bus architecture and we focus on a distributed model of the different arbitration protocols. A distributed model means that arbitration protocols, in our case, are ensured by a set of local arbiters associated each to a device of the SoC and not by one single centralized controller. Our distributed model makes the generation of a distributed low-level implementation comes naturally.

Similarly in [15], only single bus architecture is studied. However, in the present work, we propose a high-level analysis approach for systems with *multiple bus* architecture, which makes the arbitration protocols completely different with more interesting issues to take into account. Indeed, in multiple bus protocols there are two types of conflicts to manage. First, a conflict between processors to get a bus access and second, a conflict between buses, which is not studied in [15]. Moreover, with a multiple bus architecture parallel executions of processors are now possible and so more complex configurations and combinations appear and have to be taken into account.

3   BIP Framework

In this section, we present a high-level modeling formalism for the description of a multiple bus network architecture. We choose to specify our model using the BIP (Behavior-Interaction-Priority) component framework [7] as it is a framework with formal semantics that relies on rich interaction models between components [9]. These interaction models are based on multi-party *interactions* for synchronizing *components* and in particular *priorities* for scheduling between interactions [17]. Moreover, this framework provides different tools for property verification and distributed code generation.

Definition 1 (Atomic component). *An atomic component K is a Labeled Transition System (LTS) defined by a tuple (Q, V, P, δ, q_0) where Q is a set of states, V is a finite set of variables, P is a set of communication ports, a transition relation $\delta \subseteq Q \times P \times Q$ and $q_o \in Q$ is the initial state.*

As usually, $q_1 \xrightarrow{a} q_2$ denotes $(q_1, a, q_2) \in \delta$

In practice, each variable may be associated to a port and modified through interactions involving this port. We also associate a *guard* and an *update function* to each transition. A guard is a predicate on variables that must be true to allow the execution of the transition. An update function is a local computation triggered by the transition that modifies the variables. Atomic components in BIP interact using *interactions*.

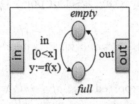

Fig. 1. Example of atomic component.

Figure 1 shows an atomic reactive component with two ports *in*,*out*, variables *x*,*y* and control states *empty*,*full*. At control state *empty*, the transition labeled *in* is possible if $0 < x$. When an interaction through *in* takes place, the variable *x* is eventually modified and a new value for *y* is computed. From control state *full*, the transition labeled *out* can occur. The omission of guard and function for this transition means that the associated guard is *true* and the internal computation micro-step is empty.

Definition 2 (Interaction). *Given a set of n atomic components $K_i = (Q_i, V_i, P_i, \delta_i, q_{0_i})$ for $i \in [1, n]$, in order to build their composition, we require their sets of ports to be pairwise disjoint, i.e. for any two $i \neq j$ from $[1, n]$, $P_i \cap P_j = \emptyset$. The composed system is defined on $P = \bigcup_{i=1}^{n} P_i$ and the set of its ports is defined by a set of interactions. Where an interaction a is defined by a non empty subset of P representing a joint transition of the set of transitions labeled by these ports. Note that each interaction defines itself a port of the composition which is useful for defining systems hierarchically (Definition 3).*

Composition of components allows to build a system as a set of components that interact by respecting constraints of an interaction model. In BIP interactions are structured by *connectors*. A *connector* is a macro notation for representing sets of related interactions in a compact manner. To specify the interactions of a connector, two types of synchronizations are defined:

- strong synchronization or *rendez-vous*, when the only interaction of a connector is the maximal one, i.e., it contains all the ports of the connector.
- weak synchronization or *broadcast*, when interactions are all those containing any port initiating the broadcast.

To characterize these two types of synchronizations, a connector may associate to the set of ports it connects two types:

- A *trigger* port of a connector is a complete port which can initiate an interaction without synchronizing with other ports of the connector. It is represented graphically by a triangle.
- A *synchron* port of a connector which is an incomplete port, hence needs synchronization with other ports, and is denoted by a circle.

Let γ be a connector connecting a set of ports $\{p_i\}_{i=1}^n$, then γ is defined as follows:

Definition 3 (Connector). *A connector γ is defined as a tuple $(p_\gamma[x], \mathcal{P}_\gamma, \delta_\gamma)$ where:*

- $p_\gamma[x]$ *is a port called the* exported *port of γ with x as associated variable,*
- $\mathcal{P}_\gamma = \{p_i[x_i]\}_{i=1}^n$ *is the set of connected ports called the* support set *of γ. These ports are typed by the information whether they are trigger or synchron. x_i is a variables associated to p_i.*
- $\delta_\gamma = (G, U, D)$ *where,*
  - G *is a guard of γ, an arbitrary predicate $G(\{x_i\}_{i\in[1,n]})$,*
  - U *is an upward update function of γ of the form, $x := F^u(\{x_i\}_{i\in[1,n]})$,*
  - D *is a downward update function of γ of the form, $\cup_{p_i}\{x_i := F_{x_i}^d(x)\}$.*

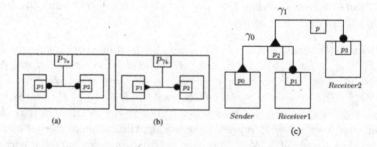

Fig. 2. Example of connectors.

Example of connectors is depicted in Fig. 2. In (a), the connector a relates the ports p_1 and p_2, which it defines as synchron, to an exported port p_{γ_a}. In this connector, if we suppose that there is no variables, then the only feasible interaction is $p_1 p_2$ which is also the interaction represented by the exported port p_{γ_a}. In (b), the interaction between p_1 and p_2 is asymmetric as p_1 is a trigger and can occur alone, even if p_2 is not possible. Nevertheless, the occurrence of p_2 requires the occurrence of p_1. Thus, if no variables are defined, the interactions defined by (b) are p_1 and p_1p_2. Thus p_{γ_b} represents both interactions. Connectors sometimes need to be structured, having types associated to groups of ports. This is necessary to represent some interactions, which otherwise cannot be represented by a flat connector (see Fig. 2(a) and (b)). Structured connectors (see Fig. 2(c)) are created by the combined mechanism of exporting port from a connector and instantiating connectors, where a port of the connector is an exported port of another instantiated connector. In (c), The connector γ_0 relates the port p_0 (trigger) of the *Sender* component with the port p_1 (synchron) of the *Receiver*$_1$ component, and exports the port p_2. It represents a set of interactions involving respectively the port sets. γ_1 is a structured connector joining the port p_2 (trigger) of connector γ_0 with the port p_3 (synchron) of the *Receiver*$_2$ component and exports the port p. It represents the set of interactions involving respectively the port sets $\{\{p_0\}, \{p_0p_1\}, \{p_0p_3\}, \{p_0p_1p_3\}\}$.

The intuition behind the notion of exported port is that a connector allows to relate a set of inner ports (of connected components) to a new port (the exported port) which allows to provide a notion of encapsulation by defining the interface of the obtained composite component.

The composition of BIP components with a connector γ defines an LTS (Definition 4).

Definition 4 (Composition of components). *The composition of n components K_i by a connector γ is denoted by $K = \gamma(K_1, \dots, K_n)$ and it defines an LTS (Q, P, δ) such that $Q = \prod_{i=1}^{n} Q_i$ and δ is the least set of transitions satisfying the following rule:*

$$\frac{a = \{p_i\}_{i \in [1,n]}, \ \forall i \in [1,n]. \ q_i^1 \xrightarrow{p_i} q_i^2 \ \wedge \ \forall i \notin [1,n]. \ q_i^1 = q_i^2}{(q_1^1, \dots, q_n^1) \xrightarrow{a} (q_1^2, \dots, q_n^2)}$$

The purpose of this work is to provide a formal high level model of multiple bus architecture. We propose a way to easily model, study and compare different arbitration protocols using the different features offered by BIP, in particular priority (Definition 5) which is an important issue when dealing with arbitration protocols as it provides a way to solve conflicts between devices sharing common resources (buses).

Definition 5 (Priority in BIP). *A priority order denoted by $<$ is a strict partial order on the set of interactions γ. We denote that an interaction a has lower priority than b by $a < b$. A system $S = (Q, P, \delta)$ controlled by a priority order $<$ defines an LTS $(Q, P, \delta_<)$ where $\delta_<$ is defined by the following rule:*

$$\frac{q^1 \xrightarrow{a} q^2 \ \wedge \ \nexists b \in \gamma. \ (a < b \wedge \ q^1 \xrightarrow{b})}{q^1 \xrightarrow{a}_< q^2}$$

Figure 3 depicts an example of composition of BIP components with priorities. Two interactions between the set of components are defined. In this example to simplify notation we suppose that transitions are labeled by interactions, and not by the exported port of the corresponding connector.

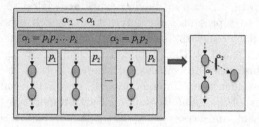

Fig. 3. Semantics of composite component with priorities.

In the semantics of the composition and with respect to priorities, stating that $\alpha_2 < \alpha_1$, only the transition corresponding to the interaction with higher priority appears.

Note that previous defined priorities are called static. BIP allows to define another type of priorities called dynamic priorities [12,18]. In this case each priority rule is guarded by a constraint on variables. Then, the priority rule is applied only if the guard is provided.

4   A Distributed Formal Model of Multiple-Bus MPSoCs Architecture

Our purpose is first to provide a formal model for a multiple-bus architecture. Then, based on this model, different arbitration protocols could be easily modeled and analyzed. Using the notions of BIP framework already described in Sect. 3, we propose to model a multiple-bus architecture by defining the set of processors as a set of BIP atomic components. Comparing to the model presented in [15], we are here interested in multiple-bus and not a single one, thus, we use also a set of BIP atomic components to model the set of shared buses. In the case of a centralized setting, a single centralized arbiter is modeled by a unique component and the arbitration protocol is carried out by the behavior of this unique arbiter. In this paper, as we are intending a distributed implementation of the bus allocation arbiter, no unique component is modeling the arbiter, but a set of *local* arbiters, each one associated to a component whether it is a processor or a bus. The set of local arbiters of the processors is, as the processors, modeled by a set of BIP components $\{P_1, P_2, \ldots, P_N\}$. The set of local arbiters associated to buses are also modeled by a set of BIP components $\{B_1, B_2, \ldots, B_M\}$ (see Fig. 4). In our model, we do not explicitly model the different buses and processors as they are passive devices controlled each by a local arbiter. Thus, we only give the description of the different arbiters.

Arbitration protocols are then achieved by the interaction between the different arbiters.

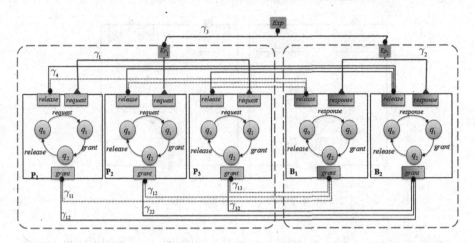

Fig. 4. A distributed model for multiple-bus architecture.

Our model contains N local arbiters associated each to a processor and M local arbiters associated each to a bus. For the sake of readability, we limit the figure describing our model to 3 processor arbiters namely $\{P_1, P_2, P_3\}$ and 2 bus arbiters namely B_1 and B_2 (see Fig. 4). Note that, such a model can be easily extended to N and M arbiters. This is ensured by the fact that all components have the same behavior, thus technically we can easily instantiate as much BIP components as needed.

In this work, we focus on three well-known arbitration protocols namely: Fixed priority, Equal priority and Rotating priority protocols [13]. Figure 4, describes the overall structure of our model which is the same for the description of the different protocols. In other words, components, their behaviors and the structure of connectors are the same for all protocols. In this model, protocol policies are ensured by the notion of priority offered by BIP (Definition 5). Based on this concept, BIP gives the possibility to define priorities between interactions, even though these interactions did not involve any common component. This notion is very powerful in particular in the context of distributed systems.

Indeed, the difference between the models of the different protocols is only some minor changes on priority rules defined between interactions. In other words, components of our model, their behaviors and the structure of connectors are the same for the different protocols. Each protocol is coded using a different set of priority rules defined between the set of possible interactions of our model. (see Definition 5). For this reason, we explain first the model, depicted in Fig. 4. Then we describe how it can easily model the set of equal, fixed and rotating priority protocols. We start by the description of the behavior of the different BIP components, and the description of the structure of connectors, then we detail the different priority rules ensuring the arbitration strategy.

Figure 5 describes the behavior and the set of ports of BIP components modeling the processor arbiter P_i and the bus arbiter B_j. Both components have 3

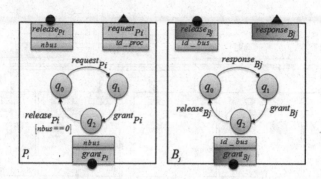

Fig. 5. Processor and bus arbiters.

states namely q_0, q_1 and q_2, where q_0 is the initial state. The different transitions of the arbiters are labeled by one of their ports. These ports define how arbiters interact with the rest of components. The set of variables associated to these ports can be read and updated through connectors. The behavior of the processor arbiter can be described as follows:

- Initially in state q_0, P_i can make a request by firing the transition labeled by the port $request_{P_i}$. As this port is a trigger port, P_i can fire this transition with no need to synchronize with any other components.
- In q_1, when P_i gets a bus access the transition labeled by $grant_{P_i}$ is fired. If it is the case, P_i goes to state q_2.
- In state q_2, P_i has already a bus access. It can stay in this state as much as it needs the bus. Once it decides to release it, the transition labeled by $release_{P_i}$ is then fired.

Figure 5 describes also the BIP component B_j of a bus arbiter. This arbiter is quite a passive arbiter, as the protocol policy is ensured by priority rules defined between interactions.

In our model, the set of BIP components $\{P_1, P_2, P_3, B_1, B_2\}$ interact using a set of BIP connectors namely $\{\gamma_1, \gamma_2, \gamma_3, \gamma_4, \{\gamma_{ij}\}_{i \in [1,3]}^{j \in [1,2]}\}$. γ_1, γ_2 and γ_3 define one *structured* connector:

- γ_1: a broadcast connector which connects 3 ports $\{request_{P_i}, \{i = 1, 2, 3\}\}$, one of each processor arbiter. It describes the request procedure by the set of its feasible interactions.
- γ_2: a broadcast connector is connecting bus arbiters through ports $response_{B_1}$ and $response_{B_2}$.
- γ_3: a rendez-vous connector which connects $\gamma 1$ and $\gamma 2$ through its exported ports Ep_1 and Ep_2 respectively.

This structured connector allows to detect any bus request of processors and also to detect bus liberation.

If there is an available bus for a given processor and if the protocol policy is respected as it will be described later, the transition labeled by ports $grant_{P_i}$

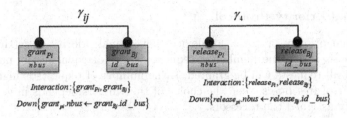

Fig. 6. Grant connector γ_{ij} and release connector γ_4.

and $grant_{B_i}$ is fired and the interaction $G_i = \{grant_{P_i}, grant_{B_j}\}$ can take place. This interaction is achieved through the rendez-vous connector γ_{ij}.

– γ_{ij}: a rendez-vous connector defining the unique interaction $G_{ij} = \{grant_{P_i}, grant_{B_j}\}$ assigning the bus B_j to the processor P_i (see Fig. 6).

Later, when a processor P_i decides to release a bus B_j, then the transition $release_{P_i}$ is fired and the interaction $\{release_{P_i}, release_{B_j}\}$ took place. This interaction is performed through γ_4 connector.

– γ_4: a Rendez-vous connector defining the unique interaction $G_i = \{release_{P_i}, release_{B_j}\}$ (see Fig. 6).

Based on this model of the multiple bus multiprocessor architecture, we now can describe different arbitration protocols by the means of interactions between the already described components. Indeed, each allocation strategy will be ensured as a different interaction model in our architecture. In the next Section, we propose to model these strategies as a simple set of priorities between interactions.

5   Arbitration Protocol Design

Based on the previously described model, protocol policies can be now ensured based on the notion of priority offered by BIP (Definition 5). Based on this concept, BIP gives the possibility to define priorities between interactions, even though these interactions did not involve any common component. This notion is very powerful in particular in the context of distributed systems. Protocol policies are defined as a set of priority rules between interactions. These priority rules are defined in particular on the set of interactions assigning buses to processors which corresponds to the interactions defined by the set of grant connectors $\{\gamma_{ij}\}_{i\in\{1,3\}}^{j\in\{1,2\}}$ (see Fig. 4). Thus if one wants to give priority to the processor P_1 over the rest of processors when accessing to the bus B_1, one has simply to give the highest priority to the interaction G_{11} over the set of interactions $\{G_{i1}\}_{i\in\{2,3\}}$.

5.1 Equal-Priority Protocol

In the equal priority protocol, all devices have equal priority of getting a bus upon request. When the number of requests is less or equal to the number of free buses, all requests will be granted. If the number of requests is higher than the number of free buses, then the choice of the winners depends in general on the priority assigned to processors.

However, when no priority is defined between processors, which is the case of the equal priority protocol, then conflict between requests to the buses will be solved at the level of the BIP engine using the FIFO rule. Thus in our high-level model, we do not assign any priority to processors, moreover we do not even ensure any strategy to manage conflict because at low BIP level (BIP engine) when no priority is specified requests will be treated in a FIFO order. So to model and analyze the equal-priority protocol one needs only to take the model already described in Sect. 4.

5.2 Fixed-Priority Protocol

In the fixed priority protocol, each processor is assigned a fixed and unique priority [3]. When more than M processors are requesting a bus at the same time, the set of M processors with the highest priority will get a bus. This priority between processors is defined in our model as a priority between interactions. In particular between the interactions of assigning buses to processors namely G_{ij} which assign the bus j to the processor i. Thus, we define a set of priority rules between the interactions $\{G_{ij}\}_{i\in\{1,3\}}^{j\in\{1,2\}}$.

For example if we have as a priority between processors; $P_3 < P_2 < P_1$, then in our model we define the following priority rules:

$$G_{31} < G_{21} < G_{11} \text{ and } G_{32} < G_{22} < G_{12}$$

5.3 Rotating-Priority Protocol

In the rotating priority protocol, each device is given a different priority in each arbitration cycle [3]. Which means that, if a device has the highest priority in a first cycle, it will have the lowest priority in the next one, if it gets a bus. Priorities in this protocol are not static as they are updated after every bus allocation. To model this protocol, we first propose to build upon the already described model. The idea is simply to add a new port $update_{P_i}$ for each processor arbiter and a local variable $P_i.pr$ storing the value of the priority of the corresponding processor (See Fig. 7). The new defined port $update_{P_i}$ is connected to $grant$ port of each bus arbiter which allows to update the priority once a bus allocation is performed. The transition labeled by the port $update_{P_i}$ is then possible in all processor states to update the values of priority variables $\{P_i.pr\}_{i\in\{1,3\}}$ after each bus access (See Fig. 7). Second, we use conditions on priority rules defined as guards on variables. Which means that a priority rule takes sense only when its condition is valid. Thus, if we can make such a condition changing its validity

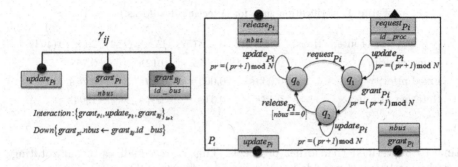

Fig. 7. Processor behavior and update connector for rotating priority protocol.

dynamically, we can define some kind of *dynamic* priorities. Based on this principle, to model the rotating priority protocol, we define a set of priority rules and their conditions based on the following expression:

$$(G_{ij} < G_{kj})_{i,k \in \{1,3\}}^{j \in \{1,2\}} \; If(P_k.pr > P_i.pr)\{i \neq k\}$$

If the condition of each priority rule can be updated and thus its validity keeps changing, the corresponding priority rule will not be always applied. This is performed by the update transition added at the level of the different processors allowing to update the variables $\{P_i.pr\}_{i \in \{1,3\}}$ after each bus access (See Fig. 7).

In this Section we have described different arbitration protocols for MPSoCs architecture based on almost the same BIP model. The different protocols policies are coded using priority rules offered by BIP by making minor changes at the level of these rules. We now provide high-level analysis and experimental results obtained from the automatically generated code.

6   Implementation and Experimental Results

We propose to use the set of tools offered by BIP to verify and analyze the different proposed models. In particular, we use RT-DFinder tool [19,20] to verify the property of deadlock freedom of the already described arbitration protocols.

RT-DFinder is a compositional verification tool for deadlock detection where verification is applied only to high level models for checking safety properties such as invariants and deadlock-freedom. Based on this tool, we have proven the deadlock freedom of the already described BIP models of the different arbitration protocols at a high abstract level with no need to code generation. This is very interesting in the case of studying new protocols or new variants of protocols. Indeed, one can decide about deadlock freedom of any protocol at a high-level and thus can modify and adjust the protocol easily.

Table 1 shows the execution time for analyzing and detecting Deadlocks of our models for different arbitration protocols by increasing the number of processors and buses. Numerical results show that the rotating priority model needs more

Table 1. Verification time for detecting deadlocks (second)

N × M (Nbr of interactions)	3 × 2 (16)	6 × 4 (52)	15 × 5 (154)	20 × 10 (404)
Equal priority	0.033 s	0.061 s	0.12 s	0.75 s
Fixed priority	0.039 s	0.063 s	0.19 s	0.78 s
Rotating priority	0.13 s	0.31 s	22.7 s	1904 s

time to be verified than other protocols. This is expected, as in our rotating priority model, we have added a new port named update. Thus, more interactions are involved which leads to increase the time needed by RT-Dfinder to compute interactions. In addition, we have used *dynamic* priorities [12]. This means that priority rules are not static and depend on predefined guards. So, more time is needed by RT-Dfinder to compute unequal constraints for interactions.

Table 2. Analyzing/detecting deadlocks for equal priority protocol

N × M (Nbr of interactions)	25 × 15 (754)	30 × 20 (1204)	75 × 25 (3754)	100 × 50 (10004)
Time (second)	2.7	3.8	120.1	814.9

Extending our model to any number of processors and buses could be easily performed as the different BIP components (processors and buses) have the same behavior. For instance, we measure, in Table 2, the verification time for the equal priority model for systems with more important number of components. Extending easily the model to an important number of processors and buses provides a way to study how protocols may react in the context of more complex architectures and thus with more conflicts to manage. Notice that increases the number of components increases consequently the number of conflicts interactions and so requires more important time of exploration to detect deadlocks and more memory resources. We now give some experimental results allowing to study fairness property of the different protocols. Indeed, fairness is a key property when it comes to allocation protocols [21]. Ensuring fairness by a protocol means that all processors will get eventually a bus if they ask for it.

The fairness property is formally described using temporal logic as follows:

$$For\ each\ processor\ P_i\ (i \in \{1,2,3\}): G\ (Request_{P_i} \rightarrow F\ Grant_{P_i})$$

Table 3 presents the results related to the fairness of the different protocols. It gives the number of times a processor gets the access to the bus computed for an architecture of 6 processors and 4 buses and by increasing the total requests to a bus ($k \times 10^2$). In the case of the Fixed priority protocols, we suppose that priorities are defined as follows: $P_6 < P_5 < P_4 < P_3 < P_2 < P_1$.

Table 3. Number of grants per processor, $k \times 10^2$ is the total number of requests to buses

k	Equal-priority						Fixed-priority						Rotating-priority					
	P_1	P_2	P_3	P_4	P_5	P_6	P_1	P_2	P_3	P_4	P_5	P_6	P_1	P_2	P_3	P_4	P_5	P_6
1	17	18	16	18	16	15	34	26	25	13	0	0	17	17	16	17	16	17
10	169	168	162	169	177	155	321	270	245	162	0	0	167	167	165	167	166	168
100	1686	1650	1639	1664	1716	1645	3221	2843	2329	1605	0	0	1668	1665	1666	1667	1665	1669

As expected, the fixed priority protocol does not ensure fairness. Processors with lower priorities (in this case P_5 and P_6) never get a bus access, if the rest of processors with higher priorities ask for a bus. For this reason, the total of grants of different processors is equal to the number of requests minus two, that is the two requests of the two processors with the lower priorities whose never get a bus access. Notice that, in our experiments as well as in our model, processors ask for a bus access continuously. For other request profiles, the results may be different. E.g. the fixed priority protocol is likely to be appropriate if the request frequency is inversely proportional to the priority (the higher the priority, the lower the request rate).

The equal and the rotating priority protocols indeed ensure fairness as all processors get an access to a bus in almost the same proportion. The equal priority protocol is not always expected to ensure fairness as it depends on the implementation of the required arbitration mechanism. If it implements fair choice then fairness is guaranteed by the protocol. Notice that, in the results presented in Table 3, our equal priority model is fair. This is expected as, in the absence of specified priorities, the mechanism implemented in BIP engine treats requests in a FIFO order. This means that any processor that has made a request will eventually get a bus access.

We propose also to check the mutual exclusion on bus access for an architecture of 3 processors and 2 buses. For this purpose, we assume that it is impossible to get access to the same bus by more than one processor at the same time.

Thus, the access of the different processors P_i ($i \in \{1, 2, 3\}$) to the bus B_j ($j \in \{1, 2\}$) has to be mutually exclusive. Then, our model must guarantee the following set of properties for each bus:

Property 1: $G \neg [(grant_{P_1} grant_{B_1} \wedge grant_{P_2} grant_{B_1} \wedge grant_{P_3} grant_{B_1}) \vee$
$(grant_{P_1} grant_{B_1} \wedge grant_{P_2} grant_{B_1}) \vee (grant_{P_1} grant_{B_1} \wedge grant_{P_3} grant_{B_1}) \vee$
$(grant_{P_2} grant_{B_1} \wedge grant_{P_3} grant_{B_1})]$
Property 2: $G \neg [(grant_{P_1} grant_{B_2} \wedge grant_{P_2} grant_{B_2} \wedge grant_{P_3} grant_{B_2}) \vee$
$(grant_{P_1} grant_{B_2} \wedge grant_{P_2} grant_{B_2}) \vee (grant_{P_1} grant_{B_2} \wedge grant_{P_3} grant_{B_2}) \vee$
$(grant_{P_2} grant_{B_2} \wedge grant_{P_3} grant_{B_2})]$

As our model represents a multiple-bus architecture, then, the previous defined properties are insufficient to ensure its correctness. In addition, it is necessary to guarantee that the scenario when a processor is granted by more than one bus simultaneously can never occur. The access of P_i ($i \in \{1, 2, 3\}$) to the bus B_1 and B_2 are mutually exclusive. Thus, our model has also to satisfy the following properties:

$$Property\ 3\text{: } G\ \neg(grant_{P_1} grant_{B_1} \land grant_{P_1} grant_{B_2})$$
$$Property\ 4\text{: } G\ \neg(grant_{P_2} grant_{B_1} \land grant_{P_2} grant_{B_2})$$
$$Property\ 5\text{: } G\ \neg(grant_{P_3} grant_{B_1} \land grant_{P_3} grant_{B_2})$$

Notice that, with respect to the structure of our model depicted in Fig. 4 the *grant* port of each bus component $\{B_j\}_{j \in \{1,2\}}$ is connected to three different rendez-vous connectors $\{\gamma_{1j}, \gamma_{2j}, \gamma_{3j}\}_{j \in \{1,2\}}$. According to BIP semantics [17], it is impossible to fire two synchronization involving common ports. This guarantees that a bus can be granted only for one processor at a time. In addition, it guarantees that buses B_1 and B_2 cannot give the access to the same processor at the same time. Consequently, our model guarantees structurally the set of the different mutual exclusion properties.

The use of BIP is also highly motivated by the fact that BIP tools [22] offer an automatically generated distributed code. Thus, once a model is proven to be deadlock free or a set of relevant properties have been analyzed (such as fairness), further performance analysis could be provided based on the generated code [23].

We are also working on a distributed formal model for the round-robin arbiter for Networks-on-Chip (NoCs) architecture [24,25] based on the real-time version of BIP which integrates temporal aspect [26].

7   Conclusion

We have proposed a high-level formal and abstract model for multiple-bus multiprocessors architecture. The proposed model provides also a way for describing different arbitration protocols in a distributed and abstract manner, which allows to easily analyze and verify their different properties without having to implement them in a concrete system. Indeed, in this paper we have proposed models for three well-known protocols namely, *equal priority*, *fixed priority* and *rotating priority*. We have also performed several property verification of the studied protocols and derived a distributed implementation of the proposed models. Then experimental results have been provided using the different tools offered by the BIP framework. Different new protocols could be also easily described using the same principle, in particular if it is based on the same multiple bus architecture. As a future work, we are considering to model new SoC communication architectures as crossbar architecture [27] and thus to study and verify its corresponding arbitration protocols as Round-Robin Protocol [24] and Time Division Multiple Access (TDMA) [28].

References

1. John, L.K., Liu, Y.: Performance model for a prioritized multiple-bus multiprocessor system. IEEE Trans. Comput. **45**(5), 580–588 (1996)

2. Yang, Q., Raja, R.: Design and analysis of multiple-bus arbiters with different priority schemes. In: Parallel Architectures (Postconference PARBASE-1990), pp. 276–295 (1990)
3. El-Guibaly, F.: Design and analysis of arbitration protocols. IEEE Trans. Comput. **38**, 161–171 (1989)
4. Doifode, N., Padole, D., Bajaj, P.R.: Design and performance analysis of efficient bus arbitration schemes for on-chip shared bus multi-processor SoC. Int. J. Comput. Sci. Netw. Secur. (IJCSNS) **8**(9), 250–255 (2008)
5. Chu, P.P.: RTL Hardware Design Using VHDL: Coding for Efficiency, Portability, and Scalability. Wiley-IEEE Press, Hoboken (2006)
6. Fassino, J.-P., Stefani, J.-B., Lawall, J.L., Muller, G.: Think: a software framework for component-based operating system kernels. In: 16th IEEE Real Time Systems Symposium (2002)
7. Basu, A., Bozga, M., Sifakis, J.: Modeling heterogeneous real-time components in BIP. In: SEFM. IEEE Computer Society, pp. 3–12 (2006)
8. Graf, S., Quinton, S.: Contracts for BIP: hierarchical interaction models for compositional verification. In: Derrick, J., Vain, J. (eds.) FORTE 2007. LNCS, vol. 4574, pp. 1–18. Springer, Heidelberg (2007). doi:10.1007/978-3-540-73196-2_1
9. Bliudze, S., Sifakis, J.: The algebra of connectors - structuring interaction in BIP. IEEE Trans. Comput. **57**(10), 1315–1330 (2008)
10. Bozga, M., Jaber, M., Sifakis, J.: Source-to-source architecture transformation for performance optimization in BIP. In: Proceedings of SIES 2009, pp. 152–160 (2009)
11. Ben-Hafaiedh, I., Graf, S., Mazouz, N.: Distributed implementation of systems with multiparty interactions and priorities. In: Barthe, G., Pardo, A., Schneider, G. (eds.) SEFM 2011. LNCS, vol. 7041, pp. 38–57. Springer, Heidelberg (2011). doi:10.1007/978-3-642-24690-6_5
12. Basu, A., Bidinger, P., Bozga, M., Sifakis, J.: Distributed semantics and implementation for systems with interaction and priority. In: Suzuki, K., Higashino, T., Yasumoto, K., El-Fakih, K. (eds.) FORTE 2008. LNCS, vol. 5048, pp. 116–133. Springer, Heidelberg (2008). doi:10.1007/978-3-540-68855-6_8
13. Chung, C.-M., Chiang, D.A., Yang, Q.: A comparative analysis of different arbitration protocols for multiprocessors. J. Comput. Sci. Technol. **11**(3), 313–325 (1996)
14. Chehaibar, G., Garavel, H., Mounier, L., Tawbi, N., Zulian, F.: Specification and verification of the powerscale[tm] bus arbitration protocol: an industrial experiment with LOTOS. In: Gotzhein, R., Bredereke, J. (eds.) Formal Description Techniques IX: Theory, Application and Tools. IFIP AICT, pp. 435–450. Springer, Berlin (1996). doi:10.1007/978-0-387-35079-0_28
15. Ben-Hafaiedh, I., Susanne, G., Jaber, M.: Model-based design and distributed implementation of bus arbiter for multiprocessors. In: IEEE ICECS, pp. 65–68 (2011)
16. Bolognesi, T., Brinksma, E.: Introduction to the ISO specification language LOTOS. Comput. Netw. **14**, 25–59 (1987)
17. Bliudze, S., Sifakis, J.: Algebraic semantics of hierarchical connectors in the BIP framework. Technical report, Verimag, February 2007
18. Bonakdarpour, B., Bozga, M., Quilbeuf, J.: Model-based implementation of distributed systems with priorities. Des. Autom. Embed. Syst. **17**(2), 251–276 (2013)
19. Astefanoaei, L., Rayana, S.-B., Bensalem, S., Bozga, M., Combaz, J.: Compositional verification for timed systems based on automatic invariant generation. Log. Methods Comput. Sci. (LMCS) **11** (2015)

20. Bensalem, S., Bozga, M., Sifakis, J., Nguyen, T.-H.: Compositional verification for component-based systems and application. In: Cha, S.S., Choi, J.-Y., Kim, M., Lee, I., Viswanathan, M. (eds.) ATVA 2008. LNCS, vol. 5311, pp. 64–79. Springer, Heidelberg (2008). doi:10.1007/978-3-540-88387-6_7
21. Taub, D.: Arbitration and control acquisition in the proposed ieee 896 futurebus. IEEE Micro **4**, 28–41 (1984)
22. Bonakdarpour, B., Bozga, M., Jaber, M., Quilbeuf, J., Sifakis, J.: A framework for automated distributed implementation of component-based models. Distrib. Comput. **25**, 383–409 (2012)
23. Bliudze, S., Cimatti, A., Jaber, M., Mover, S., Roveri, M., Saab, W., Wang, Q.: Formal verification of infinite-state BIP models. In: Finkbeiner, B., Pu, G., Zhang, L. (eds.) ATVA 2015. LNCS, vol. 9364, pp. 326–343. Springer, Heidelberg (2015). doi:10.1007/978-3-319-24953-7_25
24. Shin, E.S., Mooney, V.J., Riley, G.F.: Round robin arbiter design and generation. In: International Symposium on System Synthesis (2002)
25. Jou, J., Lee, Y.: An optimal round-robin arbiter design for NoC. J. Inf. Sci. Eng. **26**(6), 2047–2058 (2010)
26. Abdellatif, T., Combaz, J., Sifakis, J.: Rigorous implementation of real-time systems - from theory to application. Math. Struct. Comput. Sci. **23**, 882–914 (2013)
27. Murali, S., Benini, L., De Micheli, G.: An application-specific design methodology for on-chip crossbar generation. Comput.-Aided Des. Integr. Circ. Syst. **26**(7), 1283–1296 (2007)
28. Lahiri, K., Raghunathan, A., Lakshminarayana, G.: LOTTERYBUS: a new high performance communication architecture for system-on-chip designs. In: Design Automation Conference, pp. 15–20 (2001)

Synthetic Traffic Model of the Graph500 Communications

Pablo Fuentes[1(✉)], Enrique Vallejo[1], José Luis Bosque[1], Ramón Beivide[1],
Andreea Anghel[2], Germán Rodríguez[3], Mitch Gusat[2], and Cyriel Minkenberg[3]

[1] University of Cantabria, Santander, Spain
{fuentesp,vallejoe,bosquejl,beividej}@unican.es
[2] IBM Zurich Research Laboratory, Rüschlikon, Switzerland
{aan,mig}@zurich.ibm.com
[3] Rockley Photonics, Pasadena, USA
german.rodriguez.herrera@gmail.com,
cyriel.minkenberg@rockleyphotonics.com

Abstract. As BigData applications have gained momentum over the
last years, the Graph500 benchmark has appeared in an attempt to steer
the design of HPC systems to maximize the performance under memory-
constricted application workloads. A realistic simulation of such benchmarks for architectural research is challenging due to size and detail
limitations, and synthetic traffic workloads constitute one of the least
resource-consuming methods to evaluate the performance. In this work,
we propose a synthetic traffic model that emulates the behavior of the
Graph500 communications. Our model is empirically obtained through
a characterization of several executions of the benchmark with different
input parameters. We verify the validity of our model against a characterization of the execution of the benchmark with different parameters. Our
model is well-suited for implementation in an architectural simulator.

1 Introduction

BigData applications have become ubiquitous and gather the interest of system
architects and designers. The Graph500 benchmark [1] appeared in 2010 with
the aim of influencing the design of new systems, so they better adjust to the
memory- and IO-bounded requirements of data intensive applications. Based on
the execution of a BFS within a graph, it is currently one of the most known

C. Minkenberg—The authors would like to thank the European HiPEAC Network
of Excellence for partially funding this work through a Collaboration Grant, as well
as Cristóbal Camarero for his help. This work has been supported by the Spanish
Ministry of Education, FPU grant FPU13/00337, the Spanish Science and Technol-
ogy Commission (CICYT) under contract TIN2013-46957-C2-2-P, and by the Mont-
Blanc project. The Mont-Blanc project has received funding from the European
Union's Horizon 2020 research and innovation programme under grant agreement
No. 671697.

© Springer International Publishing AG 2016
J. Carretero et al. (Eds.): ICA3PP 2016, LNCS 10048, pp. 675–683, 2016.
DOI: 10.1007/978-3-319-49583-5_52

BigData-focused benchmarks [3]. Therefore, it is strongly useful for the evaluation and design of parallel computers, specially their memory and network subsystems.

Network simulators constitute a useful tool for network architects in the design and evaluation of new systems. Synthetic traffic models have smaller computational and memory requirements than full system and trace-driven simulation alternatives while retaining the core characteristics of the workload they represent. However, synthetic traffic models have traditionally consisted of permutations to determine the destination or set of destinations for the messages from a given node, which isn't a fitting scheme for the behavior of BigData applications.

The objective of this work is to establish a network traffic model of the Graph500 benchmark workload. Our model replicates the staged structure of the benchmark with large batches of uniformly distributed messages ending in a collective allreduce operation. Total amount of messages per stage is defined as a function of message aggregation and the number of explored edges, obtained empirically from a characterization of several benchmark executions with different input parameters. A similar procedure can be followed to adapt our model to emulate a BFS execution upon graphs of a different nature. This model can be handily integrated in a network simulator to forecast the network impact on system performance upon the Graph500 benchmark workload. It achieves good scalability both in size of the simulated network and maximum graph size explored in the benchmark, without requiring intensive computation.

2   Analysis of the Benchmark Communications

In [10] Suzumura *et al.* offer a thorough description of the different implementations of the Graph500 benchmark, and works from Anghel *et al.* [2] and Fuentes *et al.* [6] provide a more thorough characterization of the communications in the *simple* implementation of the benchmark.

Communications along the benchmark execution are structured into multiple batches of point-to-point messages succeeded by a point-to-point notification to all other processes which signals the end of a tree level. These batches are separated by a phase of synchronization through an all-reduce comprising a reduction and a broadcast, and correspond to the levels of the tree obtained from the BFS execution. The amount of messages is close to evenly distributed across each stage but varies significantly between tree levels, with two big levels typically representing $\sim 80\%$ of the total. The impact of the point-to-point messages which signal the end of a tree level is negligible. The likewise sporadic all-reduce is only important because it synchronizes the generation of new messages. Therefore, from a network usage perspective the major communications are the point-to-point exchanges during each tree level. These communications are highly homogeneous spatially due to the even distribution of the graph across processes. Graph500 exploits message aggregation to reduce network traffic, with every message grouping multiple queries up to a value named *coalescing size*.

Graphs in the benchmark are generated through a Kronecker matrix product similar to the Recursive MATrix (R-MAT) scale-free graph generation algorithm [4]. Graphs generated by R-MAT emulate the behavior of small-world phenomena, where a small fraction of the nodes (or *vertices*) have a significantly large number of direct connections (or *edges*) with other nodes, and a large proportion of the vertices have a low number of edges (or *vertex degree*). Previous works such as [4,8] characterize the distribution of the vertex degree in such graphs as power-law or lognormal. Groër *et al.* [7] provide a more accurate model as a series expansion from normal distributions, and Seshadhri *et al.* [9] simplify it as a combination of a lognormal and an exponential tail distribution.

In our model we consider a lognormal distribution of the vertex degree to make it simpler to implement yet sufficiently accurate. This distribution is used to select the degree of the root vertex, and can be readily replaced by the series expansion of Groër *et al.* [7] or the formula of Seshadhri *et al.* [9] should a more precise distribution be needed.

3   Graph500 Network Traffic Model

Our model consists of a traffic generator structured in multiple stages: for each stage, a given number of messages is dispatched from every process. Once a process has sent all its messages, it sends one message to every other process (representing the end-of-phase notification) and it enters into a collective all-reduce operation. This operation consists of a reduce operation (where all the process send to the same destination) and a broadcast (in which the destination spreads the result from the data gathering). Within each stage, the traffic consists of point-to-point messages uniformly distributed temporally and spatially.

Message generation rate depends fundamentally on the node capabilities of the system, and we introduce it as an input parameter to the model that is constant across any execution. Message destination is randomly selected among all the other processes in the application. Each process sends in every level a fixed amount of messages defined through a set of equations before entering the all-reduce operation. These equations have been obtained through a statistical analysis of the average from a set of executions of the benchmark for different input parameters.

This analysis has been conducted by establishing a linear combination that fits the observed values through a model fitting tool based on the function described by Chambers and Hastie in [5]. The coefficients of said linear combinations have then been generalized to follow the variations with the input parameters. The measurements are oblivious to the infrastructure employed, so they can be extrapolated to any other system. In each stage the amount of messages delivered per process is expressed as a function of the number of edges explored per tree level and the amount of message aggregation that is being performed, represented by a *coalescing size* parameter that is by default constant in the benchmark implementation. Table 1 presents a summary of the abbreviations employed in the model equations, with a brief description of each parameter. The

Table 1. List of abbreviations employed in the equations.

Abbr.	Parameter	Description
m_{proc}	Messages per process	Number of messages sent from each process
c_s	Coalescing size	Amount of explored edges aggregated per message
p	Number of processes	Number of processes employed in the benchmark execution
E_l	Edges per tree level	Total number of edges explored within each stage of the BFS
d_r	Degree of the root	Number of edges connected to the root vertex
s	Scale	Base 2 log of the number of vertices in the graph
f_e	Edgefactor	Half of the average vertex degree
l	Tree level	Stage of the tree in the BFS execution, starting at 0

number of messages sent in the point-to-point communications is determined by Eq. 1, considering the *coalescing size* as a parameter of the model.

$$m_{proc} = \frac{1}{c_s} \cdot \frac{E_l}{p} \cdot \frac{p-1}{p} \tag{1}$$

3.1   Relation Between Number of Edges Per Tree Level and Root Vertex Degree

The total number of explored edges across the whole BFS execution is almost constant for a pair of given *scale* and *edgefactor* parameter values, but its distribution between tree levels varies heavily. Simply averaging multiple executions with the same input parameters masks the actual behavior, as occurs in the histogram in Fig. 1a which does not seem to follow any clear distribution. This histogram corresponds to the number of new edges traversed in a graph during the third tree level, obtained by running a BFS for every possible root in the graph.

Our approach is to determine the number of explored edges per tree level as a function of the degree of the root vertex, which heavily influences the distribution. Figures 1(b–d) display the average distribution of the number of explored edges during the third tree level for the same graph in Fig. 1a, with three different ranges of root degree: roots with only one neighbour (Fig. 1b), roots with 10 to 20 neighbors (Fig. 1c) and roots with a high root degree of 10,000 neighbors or more (Fig. 1d). It can be observed that for each range of the root degree there is only one predominant peak, as opposed to the histogram for all roots in the graph shown in Fig. 1a where there were multiple peaks of similar impact.

This heavy dependence on the root degree occurs because roots with low vertex degree will originate a low amount of communications at first tree levels,

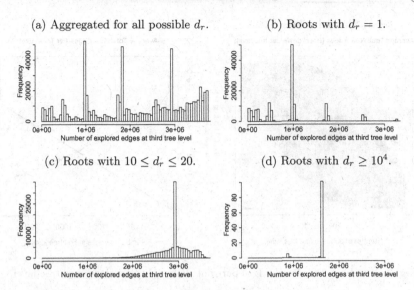

Fig. 1. Histogram of the number of explored edges in the third tree level, with different root degree d_r. Graph with scale $s = 17$ and edgefactor $f_e = 16$.

shifting the biggest part of the graph traversal to higher levels, whereas roots with high degree will rapidly explore the majority of the graph and present low (or non-existent) communication at higher levels.

Our model characterizes the mean amount of visited edges per tree level as a function of the root degree and the graph parameters (*scale* and *edgefactor*). This method has the benefit of adjusting reasonably to the observed behavior while remaining low-demanding computer-wise. The first tree level is trivially determined as the root degree. The selection of the root degree will be performed randomly following a lognormal distribution, as discussed in Sect. 2.

Figure 2 depicts the average number of edges upon the root degree, broken down per tree level. X-axis is displayed in logarithmic scale. Results correspond to the same data used for the histograms in Fig. 1. The three blocks circled in red correspond with the average number of explored edges in the third tree level whose distribution was presented in Figs. 1(b–d). Some values in Fig. 2 are interpolated, as not all the vertex degrees are present in a graph. Note that Y-axis in Fig. 2b is also in logarithmic scale. The aggregated amount of edges remains almost constant, since the size of the graph is independent of the vertex selected as root (and consequently the amount of edges to traverse during the BFS will be similar). However, the distribution of those edges among the tree levels varies significantly, further confirming our motivation to relate the communications to the vertex degree at the tree root. In the following subsection we will present an equation linking the number of edges per tree level to the root degree.

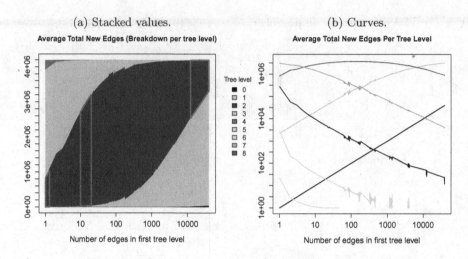

(a) Stacked values.   (b) Curves.

Fig. 2. Number of explored edges per root degree, broken down per tree level.

3.2 Number of Explored Edges per Tree Level

Our model approximates the evolution of the average number of explored edges per vertex for each tree level (as shown in Fig. 2b) through a polynomial of degree 2 as the one described in Eq. 2 (in the next page), where d_r is the root degree, and the A, B and C factors depend on the *scale*, *edgefactor* and tree level. The first tree level is an exception to this, with the number of explored edges being defined directly as the degree of the root vertex (and originating messages only at one process, the one hosting the root). We consider a notation for the tree level l that spans from $l = 0$.

We have approximated A, B and C in each tree level to fit the observed values for several combinations of *scales* $s = 16, 17, 18, 19, 20, 23, 25$ and *edgefactors* $f_e = 16, 20, 32, 45, 64$. For each explored combination, we have run a BFS for every vertex in the graph, and measured the average number of explored edges per level for each root vertex degree. Then we have obtained an expression that fits the evolution of each of the parameters in Eq. 2 with the *scale* and *edgefactor* parameters as well as the tree level, presented in Eqs. 3–5. Additionally, we know that the maximum number of edges that can be traversed is twice the number of edges in the graph, because each edge is traversed in both ways. We limit the total number of edges traversed across all tree levels below that limit; when none the processes can send any more messages, the execution of the model is ended.

$$\ln\left(\bar{E}_l\right) \approx A \cdot \ln^2\left(d_r\right) + B \cdot \ln\left(d_r\right) + C, \qquad l \geq 1 \tag{2}$$

$$A = -0.133 + 0.0046 \cdot s + e^{l+0.01257 \cdot f_e - 0.1829 \cdot s - 3.6554} \tag{3}$$

$$B = 2 - l \cdot (0.91 + 0.002 \cdot f_e - 0.012 \cdot s) \tag{4}$$

$$C = e^{1+(1+0.004 \cdot f_e) \cdot e^{-\left(0.0011 \cdot s^2 - 0.0451 \cdot s + 2.09\right)} \cdot l \cdot (4.5 + 0.078 \cdot s - l)} \tag{5}$$

4   Model Validation

To validate our model, we have employed measured values from a set of Graph500 executions with parameters different than those employed to obtain the model. Since the impact of message aggregation is clearly defined by Eq. 1, we focus the validation in a crosscheck between the prediction from our model and the values obtained through the measurement of an actual run of the benchmark. Figure 3 displays the average number of explored edges $\bar{E}_l$ for all possible root vertices in a graph of *scale* $s = 22$ and *edgefactor* $f_e = 16$. Points correspond to the measured values, whereas lines are the fittings obtained through our model. The fitting curves approximate clearly the observed behavior, following the same trends as the measurements for every stage of the execution. The model reproduces the staged behavior and replicates the dependence on the root degree, observing a similar proportion between the impact of each stage in the total amount of explored edges. From the third level $l = 2$ we observe that the model result is truncated for large root degrees when the maximum number of edges given by the *scale* and *edgefactor* are explored.

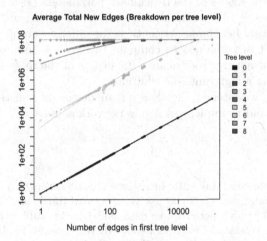

Fig. 3. Validation of the model. Points correspond to measured average values from a real execution, lines correspond to the fittings from the model.

The dynamic range of the observed values is very large due to its logarithmic nature; this implies that any deviation in the prediction will incur in a very large absolute error. Still, the relative error of our model for this second tree level is lower than 18% in more than 90% of the cases. For the third tree level, which amounts the largest amount of communications for most root degrees, the model is still able to reproduce the same behavior with an average relative error of 12.5%. The total number of explored edges across the graph presents a relative error below 12%, which is corrected when the maximum value is reached and the edges in the last levels are truncated. A similar analysis has been conducted upon graphs of *scale* $s = 18$ and *edgefactor* $f_e = 40$, with analogous results.

5   Conclusions

Current evaluations of BigData workloads consist mostly of full-system simulations of the real applications, or rely on the use of traces. Both options limit severely the size and detail of the network that can be investigated via simulation - which confers observability otherwise unattainable. Here we have introduced a novel computationally non-intensive synthetic traffic model of the most scalable implementation of the Graph500 benchmark. We have analyzed the distribution of the benchmark communications in stages and its relation with the number of explored edges per tree level. Furthermore, we have identified a strong connection to the degree of the vertex selected as root of the tree.

We have modeled the benchmark behavior as a set of stages of point-to-point messages separated by all-reduce collective operations. The number of messages is defined as a linear model of the benchmark parameters (*scale*, *edgefactor*) for each stage within the BFS computation (*tree level*). Using an empirical characterization of actual benchmark executions for different graph parameters, we have defined a set of equations to compute the average number of edges per tree level for any given tree root degree; the degree of the root vertex is decided randomly following a lognormal distribution.

As next steps, we intend to expand our model using a distribution for the characterization, and to implement it in a network simulator.

References

1. Graph500 benchmark, May 2016. http://www.graph500.org/
2. Anghel, A., Rodriguez, G., Prisacari, B.: The importance and characteristics of communication in high performance data analytics. In: 2014 IEEE International Symposium on Workload Characterization (IISWC), pp. 80–81. IEEE (2014)
3. Beamer, S., Asanovic, K., Patterson, D.: Locality exists in graph processing: workload characterization on an Ivy bridge server. In: 2015 IEEE International Symposium on Workload Characterization (IISWC), pp. 56–65, October 2015
4. Chakrabarti, D., Zhan, Y., Faloutsos, C.: R-mat: a recursive model for graph mining. In: Proceedings of 2004 SIAM International Conference on Data Mining, pp. 442–446 (2004)
5. Chambers, J., Hastie, T.: Statistical Models in S. Wadsworth & Brooks/Cole, Pacific Grove (1992)
6. Fuentes, P., Bosque, J.L., Beivide, R., Valero, M., Minkenberg, C.: Characterizing the communication demands of the Graph500 benchmark on a commodity cluster. In: Proceedings of 2014 IEEE/ACM International Symposium on Big Data Computing, pp. 83–89 (2014)
7. Groër, C., Sullivan, B.D., Poole, S.: A mathematical analysis of the r-mat random graph generator. Networks **58**(3), 159–170 (2011)

8. Kim, M., Leskovec, J.: Multiplicative attribute graph model of real-world networks. In: Kumar, R., Sivakumar, D. (eds.) WAW 2010. LNCS, vol. 6516, pp. 62–73. Springer, Heidelberg (2010). doi:10.1007/978-3-642-18009-5_7

9. Seshadhri, C., Pinar, A., Kolda, T.G.: An in-depth study of Stochastic Kronecker graphs. In: 2011 IEEE 11th International Conference on Data Mining (ICDM), pp. 587–596. IEEE (2011)

10. Suzumura, T., Ueno, K., Sato, H., Fujisawa, K., Matsuoka, S.: Performance characteristics of Graph500 on large-scale distributed environment. In: 2011 IEEE International Symposium on Workload characterization (IISWC), pp. 149–158. IEEE (2011)

Author Index